1999
First Grou
Bus
Handbook

British Bus Publishing

Body codes used in the Bus Handbook series:

Type:
A   Articulated vehicle
B   Bus, either single-deck or double-deck
BC   Express - high-back seating in a bus body
C   Coach
M   Minibus with design capacity of 16 seats or less
N   Low-floor bus (*Niederflur*), either single-deck or double-deck
O   Open-top bus (CO = convertible - PO = Partial open-top)

Seating capacity is then shown. For double-decks the upper deck quantity is followed by the lower deck.

Door position:-
C   Centre entrance/exit
D   Dual doorway.
F   Front entrance/exit
R   Rear entrance/exit (no distinction between doored and open)
T   Three or more access points

Equipment:-
L   Lift for wheelchair   TV   Training Vehicle.
M   Mail compartment   RV   Used as tow bus or Engineers vehicle.
T   Toilet   w   Vehicle is withdrawn from service.

e.g. - B32/28F is a double-deck bus with thirty-two seats upstairs, twenty-eight down and a front entrance/exit.
       N43D is a low-floor bus with two doorways.

Re-registrations:-
Where a vehicle has gained new index marks the details are listed at the end of each fleet showing the current mark, followed in sequence by those previously carried starting with the original mark.

Other books in the series:
The Scottish Bus Handbook
The Ireland & Islands Bus Handbook
The North East Bus Handbook
The Yorkshire Bus Handbook
The Lancashire, Cumbria and Manchester Bus Handbook
The Merseyside and Cheshire Bus Handbook
The North and West Midlands Bus Handbook
The East Midlands Bus Handbook
The South Midlands Bus Handbook
The North and West Wales Bus Handbook
The South Wales Bus Handbook
The Chilterns and West Anglia Bus Handbook
The East Anglia Bus Handbook
The South East Bus Handbook
The South West Bus Handbook
The South Central Bus Handbook

Annual books are produced for the major groups:
The 1999 Stagecoach Bus Handbook
The 1999 FirstBus Bus Handbook
The 1999 Arriva Bus Handbook
Editions for earlier years are available. Please contact the publisher.

Associated series:
The Hong Kong Bus Handbook
The Leyland Lynx Handbook
The Model Bus Handbook
The Postbus Handbook
The Toy & Model Bus Handbook - Volume 1 - Early Diecasts
The Fire Brigade Handbook (fleet list of each local authority fire brigade)
The Fire Brigade Handbook - Special Appliances Volume 1
The Fire Brigade Handbook - Special Appliances Volume 2
The Police Range Rover Handbook

Contents

1999 FirstGroup Bus Handbook

The 1999 FirstGroup Bus Handbook is a special edition of the Bus Handbook series which contains the various fleets of FirstGroup plc. The Bus Handbook series is published by British Bus Publishing, an independent publisher of quality books for the industry and bus enthusiasts. Further information on these may be obtained from the address below.

Although this book has been produced with the encouragement of, and in co-operation with, FirstGroup plc management, it is not an official FirstGroup fleet list and the vehicles included are subject to variation, particularly as the vehicle investment programme continues. Some vehicles listed are no longer in regular use on services but are retained for special purposes. Also, out of use vehicles awaiting disposal are not all listed. The services operated and the allocation of vehicles to subsidiary companies are subject to variation at any time, although accurate at the time of going to print. The contents are correct to May 1999

To keep the fleet information up to date we recommend the Ian Allan publication, Buses, published monthly, or for more detailed information, the PSV Circle monthly news sheets.

Principal Editors: David Donati and Bill Potter

Acknowledgments:
We are grateful to Cliff Beeton, Terry Catton, Keith Grimes, Mark Jameson, Ken Jubb, Tony Wilson, the PSV Circle and the management and officials of FirstGroup and their operating companies, for their kind assistance and co-operation in the compilation of this book.

The cover picture was supplied by FirstGroup, while that on page 1 by Tony Wilson.

ISBN 1 897990 86 3
Published by British Bus Publishing Ltd
The Vyne, 16 St Margaret's Drive, Wellington,
Telford, TF1 3PH
© British Bus Publishing Ltd, May 1999
E-mail A2GWP@AOL.COM
internet:- http://www.britishbuspublishing.co.uk

FIRSTGROUP

FirstGroup plc leads the way in advanced high standard bus and rail systems. It also holds a major interest in Bristol International Airport and in September 1998 commenced its first overseas bus operation in Hong Kong. Ranking as the UK's largest operator of bus services, the Group was formed in 1995 as a result of the merger of Badgerline Group plc and GRT Bus Group PLC. The geographical coverage of the company runs from Aberdeen in the north to Cornwall in the south and from Pembrokeshire to Norfolk with an operational fleet of some 9800 vehicles.

To reflect the diversification of its interests, December 1997 saw FirstGroup replace the former FirstBus name. Consequently all bus and rail operations have been re-branded with 'First' prefix and familiar 'f'. FirstGroup is a Scottish registered company and has its Corporate Headquarters at Weymouth Street, London, where the Chairman, Trevor Smallwood OBE, and the Finance Director, Tony Osbaldiston, are based. Operational Headquarters are at Aberdeen where the Deputy Chairman and Chief Executive, Moir Lockhead OBE is based.

GRT Bus Group plc came into being on 23rd January 1989 following a management and employee buy-out of Grampian Transport. However, the origins of the Group can be traced back to 1898 when the assets of the Aberdeen city tram services were transferred to the town council. Following deregulation of the bus industry in 1986, Grampian Regional Transport was incorporated as a subsidiary of Grampian Regional Council. In December 1987 Grampian Transport acquired the business of Mairs, a company primarily involved in private hire coach work.

Further expansion followed in July 1989 with the acquisition of Kirkpatrick of Deeside, a company founded in the 1950s by Tom Kirkpatrick, which provided an addition to the coaching activities. Coach services were introduced later in 1989 with vehicles from Mairs fleet liveried for Scottish Citylink with daily duties taking the vehicles to Birmingham, Middlesborough and Glasgow.

In June 1990 it was announced that GRT's bid for Midland Bluebird had placed it as the preferred bidder. This was just one of the operators within the Scottish Transport Group being sold by the Government. The deal was completed in September and doubled the number of vehicles.

The Group underwent further expansion with the acquisition of Northampton Transport from Northampton Borough Council in October 1993 and 93.6 per cent of Leicester CityBus from Leicester City Council. The balance of the ordinary share capital was retained by Trent Motor Traction Company Limited. Both Northampton Transport and Leicester CityBus were incorporated under the 1985 Act and have been in the passenger transport business since the turn of the century.

In 1994 the directors believed that there remained considerable opportunities to acquire both publicly and privately owned bus operators and took the decision to float GRT Bus Group plc on the stock exchange. The placing also provided an opportunity for the existing shareholders to realise part of their investment, though the directors and employees continued to hold a significant proportion of the equity. The successful flotation raised £17 million of new money and dealings commenced in GRT's shares on 5th May 1994.

The first major acquisition following the flotation was Norwich based Eastern Counties with a fleet of 375 buses. The acquisition of SMT, which operates public services in Edinburgh and the Lothians was completed in October 1994. At the time of the acquisition SMT had a fleet of approximately 370 buses. Following quickly on from the acquisition of SMT was the announcement of an offer for Reiver Ventures Limited, trading as Lowland Omnibuses Limited which operate bus services in the Borders region.

Reiver Ventures Limited was formed to effect the management and employee buy-out of Lowland Omnibuses Limited as part of the privatisation of the bus operating subsidiaries of the Scottish Transport Group. The acquisition by GRT of Lowland, which operated 160 buses, was completed in November 1994.

At the time of the merger GRT comprised the operations of Grampian Transport, Northampton Transport, Leicester CityBus which are primarily city based while Midland Bluebird, Lowland, Eastern Counties and SMT provide town, inter-urban and rural services. The Grampian Regional Transport name finally disappeared in March 1998 with the change of name to First Aberdeen.

On the other hand, Badgerline started operations in April 1985 when the country operations of Bristol Omnibus Company Limited, then trading as Bristol Country Bus, were re-launched and re-branded as Badgerline. A striking new livery of yellow and green, (also white on minibuses), was introduced, together with the then familiar Badger motif.

Badgerline Limited was formed as a separate company later that year within National Bus Company and commenced as a separate entity from Bristol Omnibus from 1st January 1986. The company opened its Head Office at the aptly named Badger House in Oldmixon Crescent, Weston-super-Mare. It inherited depots at Bath, Bristol, Weston-super-Mare and Wells and most noted for the use of the Badger as a motif displayed to the rear of each vehicle.

Under the Government's privatisation programme for the industry, Badgerline became the second bus company to be privatised when on 23rd September 1986, it was acquired from National Bus Company under a management and employee buy-out. Eighty staff participated in the buy-out by purchasing shares in the company. At that time Badgerline operated 400 buses, employed 950 staff and had a turnover of £15 million.

From those early beginnings, the Group grew into one of the larger bus groups in the UK bus and coach industry, principally by the acquisition of other bus companies.

In preparation for this expansion, the holding company, then known as Badgerline Holdings Limited, was separated from the original Badgerline operations and moved to a new Group Head Office at Badger Manor, Edingworth, near Weston-super-Mare in 1987.

The first expansion of Badgerline took place in 1987 when 39 per cent interest in Western National was acquired from NBC with the balance held by Plympton Coachlines and financial institutions. The holding rose to 67 per cent in 1988, and the balance was acquired in 1989. Western National was one of four parts formed from the original Western National Omnibus Company in 1983 and was responsible for the operations in south Devon and Cornwall, including a share in the Plymouth joint services. The later arrangements were suspended with the introduction of deregulation in 1986. Local operators Grenville of Camborne and Robert's Coaches were added to the company in 1988.

In 1988, the group acquired Midland Red West Holdings Limited, the holding company of Midland Red West and City Line in Bristol. Midland Red West was the first of the Midland Red companies to be sold as part of the NBC disposals, secured by a management/employee bid in December 1986. Included with the company were all coaches that ran under the Midland Red Coaches name, an operation which has since been closed.

The principal operating area was Hereford and Worcester, though a base in Birmingham allowed the company to operate into the West Midlands metropolitan county, where a considerable fleet now operates on commercial and tendered services. Midland Red West took the rump of the Bristol Omnibus Company in 1987 in a joint bid with its management. These operations concentrated on City services in Bristol and the fleet-name City Line was adopted. With the merger of Badgerline and Midland Red West Holdings in 1988, both city and country services in Bristol were once again brought under the same management.

In early 1990 the group extended its geographical reach with the acquisition of South Wales Transport and the associated fleets of Brewers and United Welsh Coaches. SWT was privatised through a management buy-out in 1987 since when it took over the local operations of Brewers of Maesteg. Some two years later a reorganisation of the Port Talbot operations moved vehicles and crews from SWT to the Brewers subsidiary. Brewers also commenced a number of routes previously operated by the now defunct National Welsh company in the Bridgend area. The reorganisation also transferred United Welsh Coaches to Brewers while still retaining their trading identity. SWT now concentrates on the Swansea area and southwest Wales where much of the local operation is based on minibuses and Darts and from April 1998 will again become one unit.

The next operator to join the group in April 1990, was Eastern National, which operated in Essex and parts of Hertfordshire. Eastern National was purchased by its management on Christmas Eve 1986. Expansion into London was achieved following successful tendering under the London Regional Transport tendering arrangements.

To meet this expansion two depots were opened in northeast London, at Walthamstow and at Ponders End. Some three months into Badgerline ownership Eastern National was split into two companies. Thamesway was set up to cover the London area operations and the southern part of Essex while Eastern National retained operations in north Essex and parts of Hertfordshire. A livery of crimson and yellow was applied to the vehicles transferred to Thamesway. These two operations now for part of Essex Buses Ltd., which continues with the two operators licenses.

June 1990, and Wessex of Bristol joined the fold with a fleet of 33 coaches used mainly on National Express contracts. Wessex also has its heritage as part of the original Bristol fleet and this operation helped expand the Badgerline role within the National Express service network. Subsequently, Wessex has developed into local bus operations in Bristol, branded as Sky Blue it used Leyland Nationals previously with other group companies though these have been replaced with Volvo B6s.

In November 1993 Badgerline Group was floated on the London Stock Exchange. The reasons for this move was given as a desire to make further acquisitions and to reduce the high level of gearing resulting from the earlier acquisitions. Some £36 million of new capital was raised which would allow the Group to finance future investment and acquisitions. At this time the group fleet consisted of 2,359 vehicles; 395(17%) double-deck, 831(35%) single-deck buses and coaches, 1006(43%) midibuses and 127(five per cent) minibuses.

On 22nd February 1994 it was announced that Badgerline proposed the acquisition of the PMT group, the supplier of bus services in the north Staffordshire and south Cheshire region. The PMT group was formed in 1986, again to enable the management to acquire the company from the former National Bus Company. PMT had grown since then with the acquisition of parts of the Crosville business operating on the Wirral and Chester, and later acquisition of Pennine Blue in Ashton-under-Lyne, Greater Manchester. Included in the deal were the now dormant Crosville Ltd., S Turner & Sons Ltd., Paramount Leisure Ltd., plus the repair and maintenance company PMT Engineering Limited, though the Crosville name is continued for the Wirral area and Pennine used for the vehicles based in eastern part of Greater Manchester.

The hand-over of PMT was completed on 10th March and less than two weeks later it was announced that Badgerline had offered to acquire the whole of Rider Holdings Limited, through a new subsidiary, Badgerline Yorkshire. The fleets involved were Yorkshire Rider, Rider York and Quickstep, though the Yorkshire Rider fleet has subsequently been split into four autonomous operations, each with its own identity.

Since the formation of what is now FirstGroup, there have been a number of significant acquisitions. People's Provincial, based at Fareham in Hampshire, joined the Group in October 1995, the company then operated 150 vehicles with 300 people. Services were operated around Gosport, Fareham and Portsmouth and gave the Group exposure to the strong south coast market for the first time. In April 1996, Portsmouth Transit which operated 150 vehicles under the Red Admiral and Blue Admiral fleet names was also acquired. This company was based in Portsmouth and operated services in a similar area to People's Provincial. The two operations were combined under the Provincial name with a new red and ivory livery, and provided customers with the benefit of a co-ordinated network in the area.

In January 1996, the Group acquired a 20 per cent interest in Mainline Partnership Ltd., the company that operates around Sheffield, Rotherham and Doncaster under the Mainline name.

Greater Manchester Buses North (GMBN) was acquired in April 1996. This operation then consisted approximately 950 vehicles in north Manchester, Salford, Wigan, Bolton, Bury, Rochdale and Oldham. Over 2,000 people were employed by the operation, which has recently been re-branded as First Manchester.

June 1996 saw the acquisition of SB Holdings Ltd., which runs bus services in the Glasgow area with 1,250 buses and 3,500 employees. The business included Strathclyde's Buses fleet, Kelvin and GCT.

In October 1996 Strathclyde launched a Quality Partnership with Glasgow City Council and Strathclyde Passenger Transport Authority which involved a £21 million investment in 200 high specification buses over two years, together with measures to make bus travel easier and safer. Bus priority, traffic management schemes and real time information will be provided by the City Council and the PTA. In November 1996, the Strathclyde companies received a new red livery and subsequently the entire Glasgow operation will be branded First Glasgow. During 1997 FifeFirst branded bus services were introduced to compete with Stagecoach's Fife company following Stagecoach's registration of services in Glasgow. Vehicles for this unit were supplied from the Lowland fleet with the first journey, on service 56 from Edinburgh to Ballingry running on 9th June.

FirstGroup are involved with three rail franchises. The Group acquired a 24.5 per cent holding in Great Western Holdings in February 1996 with the company subsequently acquiring the remainder of the shares in March 1998. Great Western Trains (GWT) run services between London Paddington and South Wales, the west of England and Cotswolds with high speed trains. After the initial involvement in GWT the Management team Great Western Holdings successfully won the North Western Trains franchise which is also now operated by FirstGroup. Awarded in December 1996, the Great Eastern Railway 7-year franchise began in January 1997 for which a green and dark blue livery has been adopted.

Also during 1997 FirstGroup purchased the London-based operation of CentreWest which included the former London Transport operations to the west of London and the adjoining Berkshire operation, The Bee Line. On the south coast, the operations of Southampton Citybus were acquired in spring.

Planned purchase of around 520 vehicles in 1997 included 257 Dennis Darts with Plaxton Pointer bodywork and 207 Mercedes-Benz Vario O814 minibuses with the then new Plaxton Beaver 2 body style. Some vehicles from

Optare were also included with ten 'Excel' integral single-deck buses for Leicester and six MetroRider minibuses for PMT. FirstGroup placed an £80 million order for 914 new vehicles. This comprised £50 million for 584 vehicles in 1997-98 and an initial order worth £30 million in 1998-99.

In December 1997 a further order was announced for buses to be delivered between April 1998 and October 1999. Most interesting are 40 Volvo articulated buses the first type B10LE are now delivered to First Manchester and have Wright Fusion. Later deliveries will be of type B7 and feature Wright new body styling. Wright will also supply the bodywork for the full-length single-deck vehicles which comprise 140 Volvo chassis and 170 Scania. A further 125 Volvo Olympians will be bodied by Alexander (100) and at Plaxton's Wigan factory (25), and there will be 100 Dennis Darts. Concluding the order will be 105 Mercedes-Benz Vario minibuses, all with Plaxton Pointer 2 bodywork. These orders exclude those needed for CentreWest which, subject to tenders, are expected to be 30 low floor double-deck buses and 76 midibuses. The level of investment is likely to be maintained and will lead to lower engineering costs and enhanced reliability.

In an initiative to tempt travellers on to public transport, the new buses offer an enhanced product and feature a whole range of passenger benefits such as low floor access, double-glazing and climate control, extra legroom and high quality seating, low emission and lower noise levels complying with Euro II standards and new interior bus design creating a welcoming environment.

In December 1997, together with the name change, the Group introduced a UK-wide corporate livery to identify their new high-specification buses. Throughout the country, except London, all FirstGroup's high quality vehicles look the same, making the premium product easily identifiable to passengers. The livery of these new vehicles in a base colour of light grey with magenta and dark blue livery lines. Branded First, local branding is applied behind the entrance door and below the driver's cab window. Other vehicle liveries were adapted to carry the new First branding on the existing colours.

FirstGroup aims to be at the forefront of the industry in its commitment to the environment. In January 1996, the company launched the UK's first purpose-built Compressed Natural Gas (CNG) bus and this is currently in service with City Line in Bristol in a special livery of silver and grey and a further batch of six CNG buses entered service in Northampton during 1997.

As part of its environmental initiative, the company introduced low sulphur diesel to most fleets in January 1996 ahead of EU legislation and from the same date, the majority of new vehicles have been fitted with engines that meet Euro 2 specification.

FirstGroup operates the only two sections of Guided Busways in the UK and was recently successful in it's bid to run a third in Edinburgh. The first, near Ipswich, is on Eastern Counties 'Superoute 66' at Kesgrove and was launched in January 1995. The combined effect of modern vehicles, a more frequent service, bus priority measures and real time passenger information has seen a 40 per cent increase in passengers since the introduction. The service reached a milestone in August 1996 when the millionth passenger was carried.

The introduction of a guideway and service improvements in Scott Hall Road, Leeds, in October 1995 has resulted in a passenger growth of 50 per cent. A second phase of 400 meters of guideway in a central reservation opened in November 1996 and a third phase completed in Spring 1997. The services using the guideway are operated by First Leeds with modern Scania single-deck buses branded Superbus.

In Edinburgh FirstGroup were recently successful in winning the City Of Edinburgh Rapid Transit project (CERT) which is anticipated to open late 2001. A guided busway system, the CERT scheme will be one of the best in Europe and involves 9km of guided busway, Park & Ride at Ingliston and Hermiston (total 1245 spaces), interchange with guided bus at Edinburgh Park Railway Station and on-street halts in the city centre. During peak hours there will be a dedicated service to and from the airport every 10 minutes, park and ride will operate every 10 minutes, local feeder services every 5 minutes. The system will be operated by FirstGroup using high quality articulated and single deck vehicles – offering low floor easy access for customers, double glazing, low emission engines and spacious and comfortable interiors.

FirstGroup has made major investments in new depot facilities with Camborne (Western National) opening in 1994; James Street, York (First York) in June 1995; Cherry Row, Leeds (First Leeds) in April 1996 and a new depot for First Huddersfield, at Old Fieldhouse Lane opened in December 1996 and a new depot at Bradford in 1997. A new depot replacing two separate sites in Livingston was commissioned in 1998 for First Midland Bluebird. New depots in Bath and Bristol (the latter replacing two First City Line sites) are due to open in the summer of 1999 for First Bristol. Meanwhile a single replacement for the Hoeford and Hilsea depots of First Hampshire is being sought.

In addition to its bus and rail activities, FirstGroup owns other businesses including Badger Retail in Bristol and Weston-super-Mare. In December 1997 the Group acquired a 51% shareholding in Bristol International Airport. In the last year passenger volumes increased by 11%, making Bristol one of the UK's fastest growing regional airports. Construction of the new terminal building is well underway and is on schedule for opening in March 2000. As mentioned above, the Group commenced it's first international bus operation in September 1998 running bus services in Hong Kong for a five-year period in partnership with New World Development Company Limited. The operation has been named New World First and took over 105 routes and 700 buses, which were formerly operated by China Motor Bus. A promise of substantial numbers of new vehicles was made with the proposals and these are in the process of being delivered.

Deliveries of over 200 new buses have already been made, these include Dennis Darts and Tridents, future deliveries will include 10.3m and 11.3m Tridents and Volvo Super Olympians.

The theme for 1998 was TwinTrack in which the group proposed to the government that it was prepared to invest up to fifty million pounds in Aberdeen, Leeds and Manchester and was looking to the government to match this with funding for the local authorities. This was considered by the company to be a pilot scheme which, if successful would be replicated throughout the country. Delivery of new buses to the three cities would number 35, 270 and 160 respectively. FirstGroup has the best portfolio of bus operations in the country with 75% of their operations in urban areas. Through their Quality Partnership initiatives, where they now have more schemes than any other operator, they are in a prime position to develop their core bus business and to help government achieve the aspirations expressed in its Transport White Paper.

FirstGroup welcomes the setting up of the Integrated Transport Commission and are working closely at local level to help develop new five-year transport plans as outlined in the White Paper. They were particularly pleased to become the major private sector partner in the new East Leeds Quality Bus Initiative, which is the largest public/private Quality Partnership announced to date. The scheme will cost in the region of £10m, of which FirstGroup's investment will be £3.75m, towards the provision of infrastructure for guided busways. This is the first time that the Group has made a contribution to public infrastructure and is part of their innovative 'TwinTrack' proposals to assist local authorities in the funding of new projects aimed at improving the reliability of bus operations.

In April, reorganisation within the company saw First Cymru replace Brewers and SWT; Wessex join First Bristol and later in the year changes to CentreWest's Bee Line and London Buslines. As a result, the fleet lists are now presented from the north, starting with Aberdeen, and progressing in geographical order concluding with Western National. This is followed by the NWFB overseas fleet.

Two English fleets purchased during the past year have been the Sheffield-based Mainline operation and the southwest GAG company that operated as North Devon and Southern National. While Mainline is now one of the larger FirstGroup fleets, North Devon (also known as Red Bus) is being incorporated into Western National while the Southern National vehicles are part of First Bristol.

Seven hundred and eighty vehicles are on order for the remainder of 1999 and early 2001 and these will increase the numbers in FirstGroup Corporate livery. The single-deck order will comprise 105 Volvo with Wright Renown bodies; 75 Scania L94 with Wright Axcess Floline bodies; 60 Mercedes-Benz Citaro integrals and a further 20 articulated buses from Volvo/Wright. Alexander will body 100 low floor double-deck Volvo products while Plaxton will supply the bodies for 130 Dennis Tridents. There will be 10 Plaxton-bodied coaches and thirty Optare Solo mini buses. The Midibus order calls for 60 Volvo B6 with Wright bodywork and 190 Dennis Darts to be bodied by Alexander (100) Marshall (80) and Plaxton (10).

FIRST ABERDEEN

Aberdeen - Mairs Coaches - Kirkpatrick of Deeside

First Aberdeen Ltd; Kirkpatrick of Deeside Ltd
395 King Street, Aberdeen, AB24 5RP
G E Mair Hire Services Ltd, St Peter Street, Aberdeen AB2 3HU

001	K1GRT	Mercedes-Benz 0405G	Alexander Cityranger	AB60T	1992	
019	HRS262V	Leyland Atlantean AN68A/1R	Alexander AL	O45/29D	1980	
020	HRS271V	Leyland Atlantean AN68A/1R	Alexander AL	O45/29D	1980	
021	HRS278V	Leyland Atlantean AN68A/1R	Alexander AL	O45/29D	1980	
022	URS318X	Leyland Atlantean AN68C/1R	Alexander AL	O45/29D	1982	
023	YSO231T	Leyland Atlantean AN68A/1R	Alexander AL	O45/29D	1978	
031	LSK570	MCW MetroRider MF154/26	MCW	C29F	1989	Mair, Dyce, 1992
040	ESK955	Volvo B58-56	Duple Dominant II	C51F	1979	Kirkpatrick, Banchory, 1991
041	ESK956	Volvo B10M-61	Plaxton Paramount 3200 III	C53F	1988	Alexander's, Aberdeen, 1989
044	ESK957	Volvo B10M-61	Plaxton Paramount 3200 III	C57F	1988	Alexander's, Aberdeen, 1989
045	K67HSA	Toyota Coaster HDB30R	Caetano Optimo II	C18F	1993	
047	LSK476	Dennis Javelin 8.5SDL1903	Plaxton Paramount 3200 III	C35F	1988	
052	PSU623	Leyland Tiger TRCLXC/3RH	Plaxton Paramount 3200 E	C53F	1986	
087	TSU651	Volvo B10M-60	Jonckheere Deauville P599	C51FT	1989	
092	J11GRT	Volvo B10M-60	Jonckheere Deauville P599	C49FT	1992	
093	K3GRT	Volvo B10M-60	Jonckheere Deauville P599	C49FT	1993	
094	K4GRT	Volvo B10M-60	Jonckheere Deauville P599	C47FT	1993	
095	R3FAL	Scania K124IB4	Irizar Century 12.35	C49FT	1998	
096	P2GRT	Scania K113CRB	Irizar Century 12.35	C51FT	1997	
097	P4GRT	Scania K113CRB	Irizar Century 12.35	C51FT	1997	

101-110

Leyland Olympian ONLXB/1R*   Alexander RH   B47/26D*   1984   *101-3 are B47/24D
*101-3/8 are ONLXB/1R(6LXCT)

| 101 | A101FSA | 103 | A103FSA | 105 | A105FSA | 107 | A107FSA | 109 | A109FSA |
| 102 | A102FSA | 104 | A104FSA | 106 | A106FSA | 108 | A108FSA | 110 | A110FSA |

112-121

Leyland Olympian ONLXB/1RV*   Alexander RH   B47/26D*   1985   *121 is B47/24D
*113/7/8/20/1 are ONLXB/1RV(6LXCT)

| 112 | B112MSO | 114 | B114MSO | 116 | B116MSO | 118 | B118MSO | 120 | B120MSO |
| 113 | B113MSO | 115 | B115MSO | 117 | B117MSO | 119 | B119MSO | 121 | B121MSO |

| 122 | E122DRS | Leyland Olympian ONCL10/2RZ | Alexander RH | BC47/33F | 1988 |
| 123 | E123DRS | Leyland Olympian ONCL10/2RZ | Alexander RH | BC47/33F | 1988 |

Five open-top buses are used for tourist excursions in Aberdeen, the 'Granite City' which is renowned for the dominance of its architecture by this material. The newest of the open-tops, all of which are Atlanteans that retain their dual-door layout, is 22, URS318X.
Murdoch Currie

13

First Aberdeen, albeit in its original guise as Aberdeen City Council, celebrated its centenary in 1998. In the summer of that year sixteen Dennis Dart SLFs were delivered. These were the first low floor buses for the city and introduced the willow leaf pastel livery which is only being applied to the latest vehicles that meet the group's high quality interior specification. *Billy Nichol*

124-131
Leyland Olympian ONCL10/2RZ Alexander RH   B49/29D   1988

124	E124DRS	126	E126DRS	128	E128DRS	130	E130DRS	131	E131DRS
125	E125DRS	127	E127DRS	129	E129DRS				

201-206
Dennis Dart 9.8SDL3054 Alexander Dash   B40F   1995-96

201	N201VSA	203	N203VSA	204	N204VSA	205	N205VSA	206	N206VSA
202	N202VSA						

207-222
Dennis Dart SLF Plaxton Pointer 2   N37F   1998

207	R207MSA	211	R211MSA	214	R214MSA	217	R217MSA	220	R220MSA
208	R208MSA	212	R212MSA	215	R215MSA	218	R218MSA	221	R221MSA
209	R209MSA	213	R213MSA	216	R216MSA	219	R219MSA	222	R222MSA
210	R210MSA							

268-300
Leyland Atlantean AN68A/1R Alexander AL   B45/29D   1980   *268/9/92/6 are O45/29D

268	HRS268V	292	LRS292W	296	LRS296W	299	LRS299W	300	LRS300W
269	HRS269V	295	LRS295W					

301-315
Leyland Atlantean AN68C/1R Alexander AL   B45/29D   1981

301	NRS301W	307	NRS307W	311	NRS311W	313	NRS313W	315	NRS315W
305	NRS305W	310	NRS310W	312	NRS312W	314	NRS314W	

Opposite, top:- **First Aberdeen still operate a number of Leyland Atlanteans which carry a smart cream and green livery on their Alexander bodywork. The operation provides the city services while rural routes into the city are generally provided by Stagecoach. Pictured on Union Street is 333, XSS333Y.** *Billy Nicol*
Opposite, bottom:- **While operating as Grampian, the Aberdeen fleet received many Mercedes-Benz buses based on the O405 underframe. These were bodied by Wright and Optare, while a single articulated example was bodied by Alexander. Pictured on** *Gold Service* **12 is 541, P541BSS which formed part of the 1997 delivery from Optare.** *Murdoch Currie*

316-330 — Leyland Atlantean AN68C/1R — Alexander AL — B45/29D — 1982

316	URS316X	320	URS320X	323	URS323X	326	URS326X	329	URS329X
317	URS317X	321	URS321X	324	URS324X	327	URS327X	330	URS330X
319	URS319X	322	URS322X	325	URS325X	328	URS328X		

331-345 — Leyland Atlantean AN68D/1R — Alexander AL — B45/29D — 1983

331	XSS331Y	334	XSS334Y	337	XSS337Y	340	XSS340Y	344	XSS344Y
332	XSS332Y	335	XSS335Y	338	XSS338Y	341	XSS341Y	345	XSS345Y
333	XSS333Y	336	XSS336Y	339	XSS339Y	343	XSS343Y		

401-409 — Mercedes-Benz 709D — Alexander Sprint — B23F — 1993

401	K401HRS	403	K403HRS	405	K405HRS	407	K407HRS	409	K409HRS
402	K402HRS	404	K404HRS	406	K406HRS	408	K408HRS		

432	2GRT	MCW MetroRider MF150/10	MCW	BC23F	1987
433	TRS333	MCW MetroRider MF150/10	MCW	BC23F	1987

501-514 — Mercedes-Benz O405 — Wright Endurance — B49F — 1993

501	L501KSA	504	L504KSA	507	L507KSA	510	L510KSA	513	L513KSA
502	L502KSA	505	L505KSA	508	L508KSA	511	L511KSA	514	L514KSA
503	L503KSA	506	L506KSA	509	L509KSA	512	L512KSA		

515-524 — Mercedes-Benz O405 — Optare Prisma — B49F — 1995

515	M1GRT	517	M517RSS	519	M519RSS	521	M521RSS	523	M523RSS
516	M516RSS	518	M518RSS	520	M520RSS	522	M522RSS	524	M524RSS

525-549 — Mercedes-Benz O405 — Optare Prisma — B47F* — 1995-97 — *525 is B49F

525	N525VSA	530	N530VSA	535	N535VSA	540	P540BSS	545	P545BSS
526	N526VSA	531	N531VSA	536	N536VSA	541	P541BSS	546	P546BSS
527	N527VSA	532	N532VSA	537	N537VSA	542	P542BSS	547	P547BSS
528	N528VSA	533	N533VSA	538	N538VSA	543	P543BSS	548	P548BSS
529	N529VSA	534	N534VSA	539	N539VSA	544	P544BSS	549	P549BSS

550-561 — Scania L94UB — Wright Axcess Floline — N40F — 1998

550	S550JSE	553	S553JSE	556	S556JSE	558	S558JSE	560	S560JSE
551	S551JSE	554	S554JSE	557	S557JSE	559	S559JSE	561	S561JSE
552	S552JSE	555	S555JSE						

Mairs Coaches is one of two coaching units linked to the First Aberdeen bus operation. The fleet provides some vehicles for Scottish Citylink as well as buses on contract work. Pictured in Edinburgh is 705, PSU628, a Jonckheere Jubilee-bodied Volvo coach.
Phillip Stephenson

562-567

		Scania L94UB	Wright Axcess Floline	N40F	1999

562	T562	564	T564	565	T565	566	T566	567	T567
563	T563								

Mairs Coaches

704	PSU629	Volvo B10M-61	Van Hool Alizée	C53F	1984	
705	PSU628	Volvo B10M-61	Jonckheere Jubilee P599	C51FT	1987	Buddens, Woodfalls, 1990
706	FSU333	Volvo B10M-60	Jonckheere Deauville P599	C51FT	1989	Marbill, Beith, 1993
708	F634JSO	Mercedes-Benz 609D	Made-to-Measure	C19F	1989	
710	LSK571	Mercedes-Benz 609D	Made-to-Measure	C24F	1993	
713	H36USO	Mercedes-Benz 709D	Reeve Burgess Beaver	B23F	1991	
714	P20GRT	Scania L94IB	Irizar Intercentury	C51FT	1997	
715	PSU968	Mercedes-Benz 609D	Scott	C22F	1990	
717	H37USO	Mercedes-Benz 709D	Reeve Burgess Beaver	B23F	1991	
718	LSK573	Mercedes-Benz 609D	Scott	C24F	1988	
719	LSK475	Renault-Dodge S56	Alexander AM	BC23F	1988	Northampton, 1994
720	LSK572	Renault-Dodge S56	Alexander AM	BC23F	1987	Northampton, 1994
722	WSU460	Volvo B10M-61	Van Hool Alizée	C53F	1985	Selwyn, Runcorn, 1994
724	NRS302W	Leyland Atlantean AN68C/1R	Alexander AL	B45/29D	1981	
727	HRS280V	Leyland Atlantean AN68A/1R	Alexander AL	B45/29D	1980	
728	PSU609	Volvo B10M-62	Plaxton Premiere 320	C49FT	1994	Hylton Castle, E Boldon, 1998
729	FSU335	Volvo B10M-62	Plaxton Premiere 320	C49FT	1994	Travellers, Hounslow, 1998
730	R5FAL	Scania K124IB4	Irizar Century 12.35	C49FT	1998	
731	J11AFC	Volvo B10M-60	Jonckheere Deauville P599	C49FT	1992	
732	737ABD	Volvo B10M-61	Jonckheere Deauville P599	C51FT	1988	
733	PSU627	Volvo B10M-61	Jonckheere Deauville P599	C51FT	1989	River Valley, S' Valence, 1991
734	WSU447	Volvo B10M-60	Jonckheere Deauville P599	C51FT	1990	Redwing, Camberwell, 1994
735	GSU390	Volvo B10M-61	Duple 340	C57F	1988	Yorkshire Rider, 1996
740	LSK530	Dennis Javelin 8.5SDL1903	Plaxton Paramount 3200 III	C35F	1988	Dewar, Falkirk, 1992
741	XWL539	DAF MB230LB615	Plaxton Paramount 3500 III	C49FT	1992	SMT, 1995
742	JSV426	DAF SB3000DKV601	Van Hool Alizée	C49FT	1992	SMT, 1995

Kirkpatrick

902	H34USO	Mercedes-Benz 709D	Reeve Burgess Beaver	B23F	1991	
903	E108JNH	Renault-Dodge S56	Alexander AM	BC23F	1987	Northampton, 1994
905	781GRT	Leyland Tiger TRCLXC/2RH	Plaxton Paramount 3200 E	C49F	1986	
906	LSK529	Dennis Javelin 8.5SDL1903	Plaxton Paramount 3200 III	C35F	1988	Dewar, Falkirk, 1992
907	H39USO	Mercedes-Benz 709D	Reeve Burgess Beaver	B23F	1991	
908	H35USO	Mercedes-Benz 709D	Reeve Burgess Beaver	B23F	1991	
909	LSK546	Mercedes-Benz 307D	Devon Conversions	M12	1986	Rigblast, Dyce, 1993
911	LSU917	Leyland Tiger TRCTL11/2R	Plaxton Supreme V Express	C53F	1982	Leicester Citybus, 1995
915	PSU624	Leyland Tiger TRCLXC/3RH	Plaxton Paramount 3200 E	C53F	1986	Grampian, 1996

Recent coaches for the Aberdeen fleets are five Irizar-bodied Scanias. Three are allocated to the main fleet while two, including 714, P20GRT, pictured in Glasgow in Scottish Citybus livery, are allocated to the Mairs Coaches operation.
Murdoch Currie

Special Event vehicles:

PA171	CWG273	Leyland Tiger PS1	Alexander	C38F	1980	preservation, 1996
25	CRG325C	Daimler CVG6	Alexander B	B37/29R	1965	
56	SRS56K	AEC Swift 2MP2R	Alexander W	B43D	1972	preservation, 1988
61	HSO61N	Leyland Leopard PSU4C/4R	Alexander AY	C45F	1975	
79	RG1173	Albion PMA28	Walker	B31R	1930	shed, Streatham, 1988

Previous Registrations:

2GRT	D32XSS	LSK475	E110JNH	PSU624	D53VSO
737ABD	F950RNV	LSK529	F739WMS	PSU627	F913YNV
781GRT	D55VSO	LSK530	F369MUT	PSU628	D95BNV
ESK955	HSE696V	LSK546	D951VSS	PSU629	B229LSO, 737ABD
ESK956	F101HSO	LSK570	F632JSA	PSU631	B497CBD
ESK957	F104HSO	LSK571	D424UHC	PSU968	D318VVV
FSU333	G845GNV	LSK572	E106JNH	RG1173	RG1173, TSK716
GSU390	E407RWR	LSK573	F327WCS	TRS333	D330VVV
JSU390	?	LSU917	YJF17Y	TSU651	F87CBD
JSV426	J812KHD	PSU609	F408DUG	WSU460	B122DMA, SEL392
K950HSA	K983XND	PSU623	D52VSO	XWL539	J795KHD

Allocations

Aberdeen (King Street)

Mercedes-Benz Mini	401	402	403	404	405	406	407	408
	409	434	435	436	437	438	439	708
	709	710	713	715	716	718		
MetroRider	31	432	433					
Renault-Dodge	440	441	442					
Toyota-Optimo	45							
Javelin	739	740						
DAF Coach	741	742						
Tiger Coach	49	52	915					
Volvo B10M	41	44	87	92	93	94	702	704
	705	706	722	731	732	733	734	917
Scania	96	97	714					
Dart	201	202	203	204	205	206	207	208
	209	210	211	212				
Mercedes-Benz O405	501	502	503	504	505	506	507	508
	509	510	511	512	513	514	515	516
	517	518	519	520	521	522	523	524
	525	526	527	528	529	530	531	532
	533	534	535	536	537	538	539	540
	541	542	543	544	545	546	547	548
	549							
Mercedes-Benz O405G	1							
Atlantean	19	20	21	22	23	268	269	275
	279	281	292	293	295	296	297	299
	300	301	302	303	304	305	307	309
	310	311	312	313	314	315	316	317
	318	319	320	321	322	323	324	325
	326	327	328	329	330	331	332	333
	334	335	336	337	338	339	340	341
	343	344	345	723	727			
Olympian	101	102	103	104	105	106	107	108
	109	110	111	112	113	114	115	116
	117	118	119	120	121	122	123	124
	125	126	127	128	129	130	131	

Banchory (Dee Street)

Mercedes-Benz mini	904	907	909	916
Tiger	905	911		
Renault-Dodge	910			

EDINBURGH

Edinburgh - Lowland - Midland - SMT - Fife - Kings of Dunblane

Lowland Omnibuses Ltd, 14-16 Eskbank Road, Dalkeith, Midlothian, EH22 1HH
Midland Bluebird Ltd, Carmuirs House, 300 Stirling Road, Larbert, Stirlingshire, FK5 3NJ

37	MDS862V	Leyland National 2 NL116AL11/1R	East Lancs Greenway (1994)	B49F	1980	Glasgow (Kelvin), 1998
51	K473EDT	Mercedes-Benz O405	Alexander Cityranger	B51F	1992	Mercedes-Benz , 1993

52-57		Mercedes-Benz O405	Wright Endurance	B51F	1993	
52	L552GMS	**54**	L554GMS	**55** L555GMS	**56** L556GMS	**57** L557GMS
53	L553GMS					

58	L140MAK	Mercedes-Benz O405	Wright Endurance	B51F	1994	Mercedes-Benz, 1995

61-70		Mercedes-Benz O405	Optare Prisma	B49F	1995	SMT, 1996
61	N61CSC	**63** N63CSC	**65** N65CSC	**67** N67CSC	**69** N69CSC
62	N62CSC	**64** N64CSC	**66** N66CSC	**68** N68CSC	**70** N70CSC

71	P171DMS	Mercedes-Benz O405	Optare Prisma	B49F	1997	
72	P172DMS	Mercedes-Benz O405	Optare Prisma	B49F	1997	
73	P173DMS	Mercedes-Benz O405	Optare Prisma	BC49F	1997	
74	P174DMS	Mercedes-Benz O405	Optare Prisma	BC49F	1997	
75	P875YKS	Mercedes-Benz O405	Optare Prisma	B49F	1997	
76	P876YKS	Mercedes-Benz O405	Optare Prisma	B49F	1997	
77	P877YKS	Mercedes-Benz O405	Optare Prisma	B49F	1997	
78	P878YKS	Mercedes-Benz O405	Optare Prisma	B49F	1997	
79	P879YKS	Mercedes-Benz O405	Optare Prisma	BC49F	1997	
101	FSU381	Leyland Tiger TRBTL11/2R	Alexander AT	BC49F	1983	
102	FSU382	Leyland Tiger TRBTL11/2R	Alexander AT	BC49F	1983	
103	FSU383	Leyland Tiger TRBTL11/2R	Alexander AT	BC49F	1983	
104	ALS104Y	Leyland Tiger TRBTL11/2R	Alexander AT	BC49F	1983	Glasgow (Kelvin), 1998
105	FSU380	Leyland Tiger TRBTL11/2R	Alexander AT	BC49F	1983	
108	FSU308	Leyland Tiger TRBTL11/2R	Duple Dominant II Express	C47F	1983	Kelvin Scottish, 1986
112	B262BYS	Leyland Tiger TRBLXB/2RH	Alexander TS	B53F	1985	Glasgow (Kelvin), 1999

Midland Bluebird and Lowland use a single numbering scheme though the two operations, both provide buses for SMT, formerly Eastern Scottish, services. Pictured in SMT livery is Mercedes-Benz 78, P878YKS, a Lowland bus currently based at Dalkeith.
Richard Walter

19

Four Leyland Tiger buses new to the Shearings bus operation joined First Lowland from Northampton during 1998. Pictured at Musselburgh with SMT names is 188, G56RND. This batch of buses carry Alexander N-type bodies that were only assembled at the factory in Belfast. *Richard Walter*

114	FSU334	Leyland Tiger TRBTL11/2R	Alexander TE	C46F	1983	
116	SSU816	Leyland Tiger TRBTL11/2RP	Alexander TC	C47F	1983	
117	BSV807	Leyland Tiger TRBTL11/2RP	Alexander TC	C47DL	1983	Kelvin Scottish, 1988
118	7881UA	Leyland Tiger TRBTL11/2RP	Alexander TC	C42DL	1983	
119	A119GLS	Leyland Tiger TRBTL11/2RP	Alexander TE	BC47F	1983	Glasgow (Kelvin), 1999
122	B242BYS	Leyland Tiger TRBLXB/2RH	Alexander TS	B53F	1985	Glasgow (Kelvin), 1999
129	SSU859	Leyland Tiger TRCTL11/3RH	Duple Laser	C46FT	1984	
130	693AFU	Leyland Tiger TRCTL11/3RH	Duple Laser	C51FT	1984	
136	SSU897	Leyland Tiger TRCLXC/2RH	Plaxton Paramount 3200 E	C49F	1984	Clydeside Scottish, 1985
138	OVT798	Leyland Tiger TRCLXC/2RH	Plaxton Paramount 3200 E	C49F	1984	Western Scottish, 1986

141-145		Leyland Tiger TRCTL11/3RH	Duple 340		C49FT	1987	
141	SSU841	142	SSU857	143	KSU834	144	FSV634	145	156ASV

150	WSU487	Leyland Tiger TRCTL11/3R	Plaxton Paramount 3200 E	C53F	1983	Grampian, 1991
151	WSU489	Leyland Tiger TRCTL11/3R	Plaxton Paramount 3200 E	C53F	1983	Grampian, 1991
152	GSU338	Leyland Tiger TRCTL11/3R	Plaxton Paramount 3200 E	C57F	1983	Grampian, 1991
153	GSU339	Leyland Tiger TRCTL11/3R	Plaxton Paramount 3200 E	C57F	1983	Grampian, 1991
154	PSU625	Leyland Tiger TRCLXC/2RH	Plaxton Paramount 3200 E	C53F	1986	Grampian, 1991
155	PSU622	Leyland Tiger TRCLXC/2RH	Plaxton Paramount 3200 E	C53F	1986	Grampian, 1991
156	WSU479	Leyland Tiger TRCTL11/3RH	Plaxton Paramount 3200 E	C48FT	1984	Grampian, 1993
157	YJF16Y	Leyland Tiger TRCTL11/2R	Plaxton Supreme V Express	C53F	1982	Leicester Citybus, 1995
158	101ASV	Leyland Tiger TRCTL11/3R	Plaxton Supreme IV	C57F	1982	Kings of Dunblane, 1995
159	FNM868Y	Leyland Tiger TRCTL11/3R	Plaxton Supreme V	C53F	1983	Kings of Dunblane, 1995
160	D591MVR	Leyland Tiger TRCTL11/3RZ	Plaxton Paramount 3200 III	C53F	1987	Kings of Dunblane, 1995
161	D599MVR	Leyland Tiger TRCTL11/3RZ	Plaxton Paramount 3200 III	C53F	1987	Kings of Dunblane, 1995
162	E60MMT	Leyland Tiger TRCTL11/3RZ	Duple 340	C55F	1987	Kings of Dunblane, 1995
163	HSU247	Leyland Tiger TRCL10/3ARZA	Duple 340	C55F	1989	Kings of Dunblane, 1995
164	SSU821	Leyland Tiger TRCL10/3ARZA	Plaxton Paramount 3500 III	C53F	1991	Kings of Dunblane, 1995

171-180

			Leyland Tiger TRBTL11/2R		Alexander TS		B53F*		1983	Glasgow (Kelvin), 1999

*176/7 are B60F

171	OUS11Y	173	OUS13Y	175	OUS15Y	177	OUS17Y	179	OUS19Y
172	OUS12Y	174	OUS14Y	176	OUS16Y	178	OUS18Y	180	OUS20Y

No.	Reg	Chassis	Body	Type	Year	History
186	F50ENF	Leyland Tiger TRBL10/3ARZA	Alexander N	B55F	1989	Leicester, 1998
187	F37ENF	Leyland Tiger TRBL10/3ARZA	Alexander N	B55F	1989	Northampton, 1998
188	G56RND	Leyland Tiger TRBL10/3ARZA	Alexander N	B55F	1989	Northampton, 1999
189	G55RND	Leyland Tiger TRBL10/3ARZA	Alexander N	B55F	1989	Northampton, 1999
190	F622XWY	Leyland Tiger TRCTL11/3ARZA	Plaxton Paramount 3200 III	C53F	1988	Yorkshire Rider, 1997
191	F621XWY	Leyland Tiger TRCTL11/3ARZA	Plaxton Paramount 3200 IIIE	C53F	1988	Yorkshire Rider, 1997
192	WSU480	Leyland Tiger TRCTL11/3RH	Duple Caribbean 2	C51F	1985	Leicester, 1998
193	F616XWY	Leyland Tiger TRCTL11/3ARZA	Plaxton Paramount 3200 IIIE	C53F	1988	Yorkshire Rider(C), 1998
194	A669KUM	Leyland Tiger TRBTL11/2R	Duple Dominant	BC47F	1983	Yorkshire Rider(C), 1998
195	A659KUM	Leyland Tiger TRBTL11/2R	Duple Dominant	BC47F	1983	Yorkshire Rider(C), 1998
196	A661KUM	Leyland Tiger TRBTL11/2R	Duple Dominant	BC47F	1983	Yorkshire Rider(C), 1998
197	F38ENF	Leyland Tiger TRBL10/3ARZA	Alexander N	B55F	1989	Leicester, 1999
198	G54RND	Leyland Tiger TRBL10/3ARZA	Alexander N	B55F	1989	Leicester, 1999
199	G53RND	Leyland Tiger TRBL10/3ARZA	Alexander N	B55F	1989	Leicester, 1999

201-213

			Dennis Dart SLF		Plaxton Pointer		N35F		1996-97	

201	P201NSC	204	P204NSC	207	P207NSC	210	P210NSC	212	P212NSC
202	P202NSC	205	P205NSC	208	P208NSC	211	P211NSC	213	P213NSC
203	P203NSC	206	P206NSC	209	P209NSC				

214-218

			Dennis Dart SLF		Plaxton Pointer 2		N38F*		1997	*216-8 are N39F

214	P214NSC	215	P215NSC	216	P216YSH	217	P217YSH	218	P218YSH

219-229

			Dennis Dart SLF		Plaxton Pointer 2		N37F		1997	

219	R219GFS	221	R221GFS	224	R224GFS	226	R226GFS	228	R228GFS
220	R220GFS	223	R223GFS	225	R225GFS	227	R227GFS	229	R229GFS

230-234

			Dennis Dart SLF		Plaxton Pointer 2		N37F		1998	

230	R430PSH	231	R431PSH	232	R432PSH	233	R433PSH	234	R434PSH

237	P828YUM	Dennis Dart SLF	Plaxton Pointer 2	N39F	1997	Yorkshire Rider (York), 1998
238	P832YUM	Dennis Dart SLF	Plaxton Pointer 2	N39F	1997	Yorkshire Rider (York), 1998
239	P835YUM	Dennis Dart SLF	Plaxton Pointer 2	N39F	1997	Yorkshire Rider (York), 1998

240-251

			Dennis Dart SLF		Plaxton Pointer 2		N38F		1998-99	

240	S240CSF	243	S243CSF	246	S246CSF	248	S248CSF	250	S250CSF
241	S241CSF	244	S244CSF	247	S247CSF	249	S249CSF	251	S251CSF
242	S242CSF	245	S245CSF						

252-263

			Dennis Dart SLF		Plaxton Pointer 2		N35F		1998	Yorkshire Rider (C), 1999

252	R342HYG	255	R335HYG	258	R341HYG	260	R330HYG	262	R332HYG
253	R343HYG	256	R326HYG	259	R329HYG	261	R331HYG	263	R464JFS
254	R324HYG	257	R327HYG						

301	J301ASH	Leyland Tiger TR2R56V16Z4	Alexander Q	BC49F	1991	
302	J302ASH	Leyland Tiger TR2R56V16Z4	Alexander Q	BC49F	1991	
303	J303ASH	Leyland Tiger TR2R56V16Z4	Alexander Q	BC49F	1991	
304	J304ASH	Leyland Tiger TR2R56V16Z4	Alexander Q	BC49F	1991	
311	PSF311Y	Leyland Tiger TRBTL11/2R	Alexander AT	C49F	1982	SMT, 1996
312	PSU322	Leyland Tiger TRBTL11/2R	Alexander AT	C49F	1982	SMT, 1996
313	PSF313Y	Leyland Tiger TRBTL11/2R	Alexander AT	C49F	1982	Eastern Scottish, 1985
314	PSF314Y	Leyland Tiger TRBTL11/2R	Alexander AT	C49F	1982	Eastern Scottish, 1985
315	PSF315Y	Leyland Tiger TRBTL11/2R	Alexander AT	C49F	1982	Eastern Scottish, 1985
316	PSF316Y	Leyland Tiger TRBTL11/2R	Alexander AT	C49F	1982	Eastern Scottish, 1985

320-327

			Leyland Tiger TRBTL11/2RP		Alexander TE		C49F		1983	Eastern Scottish, 1985

320-21 SMT, 1996

320	A328BSC	322	A322BSC	324	A324BSC	326	A326BSC	327	A327BSC
321	A329BSC	323	A323BSC	325	A325BSC				

328	D328DKS	Leyland Tiger TRBTL11/2RH	Alexander TE	C49F	1987	
329	D329DKS	Leyland Tiger TRBTL11/2RH	Alexander TE	C49F	1987	
330	D330DKS	Leyland Tiger TRBTL11/2RH	Alexander TE	C49F	1987	
331	A20SMT	Leyland Tiger TRCTL11/2R	Plaxton Paramount 3200 E	C49F	1984	SMT, 1996
332	WSV135	Leyland Tiger TRCTL11/2RH	Plaxton Paramount 3200 E	C49F	1984	SMT, 1996
333	WSV140	Leyland Tiger TRCTL11/2R	Plaxton Paramount 3200 E	C49F	1984	SMT, 1996
335	A13SMT	Leyland Tiger TRCTL11/2RH	Plaxton Paramount 3200 II	C49F	1985	SMT, 1996
336	WSV136	Leyland Tiger TRCTL11/2RH	Plaxton Paramount 3200 II	C49F	1985	SMT, 1996
337	WSV137	Leyland Tiger TRCTL11/2RH	Plaxton Paramount 3200 II	C49F	1985	SMT, 1996
338	WSV138	Leyland Tiger TRCTL11/2RH	Plaxton Paramount 3200 II	C49F	1985	SMT, 1996
339	A9SMT	Leyland Tiger TRCTL11/2RH	Plaxton Paramount 3200 II	C49F	1985	SMT, 1996
340	A10SMT	Leyland Tiger TRCTL11/2RH	Plaxton Paramount 3200 II	C49F	1985	SMT, 1996
341	A14SMT	Leyland Tiger TRCTL11/2RH	Plaxton Paramount 3200 II	C49F	1985	SMT, 1996
342	A12SMT	Leyland Tiger TRCTL11/2R	Plaxton Paramount 3200 II E	C53F	1985	Ian Glass, Haddington, 1991
345	A15SMT	Leyland Tiger TRCTL11/3RH	Duple 340	C53F	1987	SMT, 1996
346	A16SMT	Leyland Tiger TRCTL11/3RH	Duple 340	C53F	1987	SMT, 1996
347	A17SMT	Leyland Tiger TRCTL11/3RH	Duple 340	C53F	1987	SMT, 1996
348	A18SMT	Leyland Tiger TRCTL11/3RH	Duple 340	C53F	1987	SMT, 1996
349	D349ESC	Leyland Tiger TRBTL11/2RP	Alexander TE	C49F	1987	SMT, 1996
350	D350ESC	Leyland Tiger TRBTL11/2RP	Alexander TE	C49F	1987	SMT, 1996
351	D351ESC	Leyland Tiger TRBTL11/2RP	Alexander TE	C49F	1987	SMT, 1996

352-370		Leyland Tiger TRBLXB/2RH	Alexander TS	B53F	1984	Glasgow (Kelvin), 1998
352	A22VDS	**359** A29VDS	**364** A34VDS	**366** A36VDS	**370** A40VDS	
353	A23VDS	**362** A32VDS	**365** A35VDS	**367** A37VDS		

370	PSU320	Leyland Royal Tiger B50	Roe Doyen	C44FT	1984	Eastern Scottish, 1989
376	D276FAS	Leyland Tiger TRCTL11/3RH	Alexander TE	C53F	1987	Highland Scottish, 1987
388	KSU388	Leyland Tiger TRCTL11/3RH	Duple 340	C46FT	1987	Kelvin Scottish, 1989
389	BSS76	Leyland Tiger TRCTL11/3R	Jonckheere Jubilee	C51FT	1984	Ian Glass, Haddington, 1991
390	KSU390	Leyland Tiger TRCTL11/2R	Plaxton Paramount 3200 E	C49F	1983	Eastern Scottish, 1985
391	KSU391	Leyland Tiger TRCLXC/2RH	Plaxton Paramount 3200 E	C49F	1984	Western Scottish, 1986
392	KSU392	Leyland Tiger TRCTL11/2RH	Plaxton Paramount 3200 II	C49F	1985	Eastern Scottish, 1987
393	KSU393	Leyland Tiger TRCTL11/2RH	Plaxton Paramount 3200 II	C49F	1985	Eastern Scottish, 1985
394	KSU394	Leyland Tiger TRCTL11/3RH	Plaxton Paramount 3200 III	C48FTL	1987	
395	NBD107Y	Leyland Tiger TRCTL11/3R	Plaxton Paramount 3200 E	C49F	1983	Glasgow (Kelvin), 1998
396	B287KPF	Leyland Tiger TRCTL11/3RH	Plaxton Paramount 3200 II E	C50FT	1985	Glasgow (Kelvin), 1998
397	PSU321	Leyland Tiger TRCTL11/3R	Plaxton Paramount 3200	C49FT	1983	Glasgow (Kelvin), 1998
400	RMS400W	Leyland Leopard PSU3G/4R	Alexander AT	BC49F	1981	
403	TMS403X	Leyland Leopard PSU3G/4R	Alexander AYS	BC49F	1982	
414	ULS714X	Leyland Leopard PSU3G/4R	Alexander AT	BC49F	1982	
416	ULS716X	Leyland Leopard PSU3G/4R	Alexander AT	BC49F	1982	
417	ULS717X	Leyland Leopard PSU3G/4R	Alexander AT	BC49F	1982	
419	WFS154W	Leyland Leopard PSU3F/4R	Alexander AYS	B53F	1980	Alexander (Fife), 1982
421	XMS421Y	Leyland Leopard PSU3G/4R	Alexander AYS	BC49F	1982	
451	GSO80V	Leyland Leopard PSU3E/4R	Alexander AYS	B53F	1980	Fife Scottish, 1988
457	CSF155W	Leyland Leopard PSU3F/4R	Alexander AYS	B53F	1981	Fife Scottish, 1988

Three interesting single-deck buses are shown here. On the colour page are Dennis Dart 219, R219GFS, seen in corporate livery, 302, J302ASH, one of four Lowland Tigers with Alexander Q-type bodywork which were initially used on Border services but pictured at Longnidry and 504, P504XSH, one of the early Scania L113 buses with Wright bodywork and fore-runner for many now being delivered to group fleets.
Tony Wilson

Bannockburn depot provides vehicles for services that operate in the city of Stirling where 515, R445ALS, from the 1998 intake is seen with the route-branding used on corporate liveried vehicles. While the group delivery of full-length buses featured both Volvo and Scania products, those supplied to Midland/Lowland comprised only the latter. *Paul Wigan*

467	HSU247	Leyland Leopard PSU5D/4R(TL11) Plaxton Supreme IV	C53F	1981	Ex Grampian, 1991
468	HSU273	Leyland Leopard PSU5D/4R(TL11) Plaxton Supreme IV	C53F	1981	Grampian, 1991
469	UTU23V	Leyland Tiger TRCTL11/2R Sp Duple Dominant II	C53F	1980	Glasgow (Kelvin), 1998
474	LMS374W	Leyland Leopard PSU3F/4R Alexander AYS	B53F	1980	
476	LMS376W	Leyland Leopard PSU3F/4R Alexander AYS	B53F	1980	
486	LMS386W	Leyland Leopard PSU3F/4R Alexander AYS	B53F	1980	
497	FSU302	Leyland Leopard PSU3G/4R Duple Dominant II Express	C49F	1981	
498	RMS398W	Leyland Leopard PSU3G/4R Alexander AT	BC49F	1981	
501	M151PKS	Scania N113CRL Wright Pathfinder	BC49F	1995	
502	M152PKS	Scania N113CRL Wright Pathfinder	BC49F	1995	
503	P503XSH	Scania L113CRL Wright Axcess-ultralow	NC47F	1996	
504	P504XSH	Scania L113CRL Wright Axcess-ultralow	NC47F	1996	
505	P505XSH	Scania L113CRL Wright Axcess-ultralow	NC47F	1996	
506	P506XSH	Scania L113CRL Wright Axcess-ultralow	NC47F	1996	

507-512

Scania L113CRL   Wright Axcess-ultralow   N48F   1995   Yorkshire Rider, 1997

507	N407ENW	509	N409ENW	510	N410ENW	511	N411ENW	512	N406MWY
508	N408ENW								

513-526

Scania L113CRL   Wright Axcess-ultralow   N40F   1998

513	R443ALS	516	R446ALS	519	R449ALS	522	R522BMS	525	S525UMS
514	R544ALS	517	R447ALS	520	S520UMS	523	S523UMS	526	S526UMS
515	R445ALS	518	R448ALS	521	R521BMS	524	R524BMS		

551-566

Scania N113CRB   Wright Endurance   N49F   1994

551	L551HMS	555	L555HMS	558	L558JLS	561	L561JLS	564	L564JLS
552	L552HMS	556	L556HMS	559	L559JLS	562	L562JLS	565	L565JLS
553	L553HMS	557	L557JLS	560	L60HMS	563	L563JLS	566	L566JLS
554	L554HMS								

Pictured in Edinburgh is First Midland Bluebird's 696, F679XMS which, despite its Scottish index mark, has only recently arrived in the country from the English CentreWest operation. New to London Buses, this Alexander-bodied batch were registered by the bodybuilder as part of the build requirement. *Paul Wigan*

567-574

Scania N113CRL — Wright Pathfinder — N49F — 1995

567	M567RMS	569	M569RMS	571	M571RMS	573	N573VMS	574	N574VMS
568	M568RMS	570	M570RMS	572	N572VMS				

575-581

Scania L113CRL — Wright Axcess-ultralow — N47F — 1996

575	P575DMS	577	P577DMS	579	P579DMS	580	P580DMS	581	P581DMS
576	P576DMS	578	P578DMS						

582-586

Scania L113CRL — Wright Axcess-ultralow — N40F — 1998

582	R582YMS	583	R583YMS	584	R584YMS	585	R585YMS	586	R586YMS

587-592

Scania L113CRL — Wright Axcess-ultralow — N40F — 1998

587	R587BMS	589	R589BMS	590	R590BMS	591	R591BMS	592	R592BMS
588	R588BMS							

602	C698ECV	Mercedes-Benz L608D	Reeve Burgess	B19F	1985	Essex Buses, 1998
603	C678ECV	Mercedes-Benz L608D	Reeve Burgess	B20F	1985	Essex Buses, 1998
604	C812SDY	Mercedes-Benz L608D	Alexander AM	B20F	1986	Bluebird, 1992
607	D226UHC	Mercedes-Benz L608D	Alexander AM	B20F	1986	Bluebird, 1992
612	D534KGL	Mercedes-Benz L608D	Robin Hood	B20F	1986	Essex Buses, 1998
614	C695ECV	Mercedes-Benz L608D	Reeve Burgess	B20F	1986	Essex Buses, 1998
615	F610XMS	Mercedes-Benz 811D	Alexander AM	B28F	1988	CentreWest, 1998
616	F626XMS	Mercedes-Benz 811D	Alexander AM	B28F	1988	CentreWest, 1998
617	F623XMS	Mercedes-Benz 811D	Alexander AM	B28F	1988	CentreWest, 1998
625	H925PMS	Mercedes-Benz 709D	Reeve Burgess Beaver	B25F	1990	
626	H926PMS	Mercedes-Benz 709D	Reeve Burgess Beaver	B25F	1990	

632-641

Mercedes-Benz 709D   Alexander AM   B25F*   1991   *637-641 are BC23F

632	H972RSG	634	H974RSG	636	H976RSG	638	J775WLS	640	J778WLS
633	H973RSG	635	H975RSG	637	J774WLS	639	J776WLS	641	J779WLS

642   J310XLS   Mercedes-Benz 711D   Reeve Burgess Beaver   BC25F   1992   Kings of Dunblane, 1995

651-659

Mercedes-Benz 709D   Alexander Sprint   B25F   1993

651	K651DLS	653	K653DLS	655	K655DLS	657	K657DLS	659	K659DLS
652	K652DLS	654	K654DLS	656	K656DLS	658	K658DLS		

674	KEX532	Mercedes-Benz 609D	Mellor	B16F	1989	Aberdeenshire CC, 1998
675	K175YVC	Mercedes-Benz 811D	Wright NimBus	B33F	1993	Lothian Transit, 1996

686-690

Mercedes-Benz 711D   Alexander Sprint   B25F   1995

686	N686WLS	687	N687WLS	688	N688WLS	689	N689WLS	690	N690WLS

691-697

Mercedes-Benz 811D   Alexander AM   B28F   1988-89   CentreWest, 1998

691	F612XMS	693	F675XMS	695	F950BMS	696	F679XMS	697	F671XMS
692	F656XMS	694	F688XMS						

705-727

Leyland Atlantean AN68A/1R   Alexander AL   B45/29D*   1977-78   Grampian, 1991-93   *715/19/20 are B45/31F

705	ORS205R	709	ORS209R	715	ORS215R	719	XSA219S	720	XSA220S
708	ORS208R								

735	YSO235T	Leyland Atlantean AN68A/1R	Alexander AL	B45/34F	1978	SMT, 1996
744	DSA244T	Leyland Atlantean AN68A/1R	Alexander AL	B45/29D	1979	Grampian, 1996
748	DSA248T	Leyland Atlantean AN68A/1R	Alexander AL	B45/34F	1979	SMT, 1996
749	DSA249T	Leyland Atlantean AN68A/1R	Alexander AL	B45/34F	1979	Midland Bluebird, 1996
750	DSA250T	Leyland Atlantean AN68A/1R	Alexander AL	B45/29D	1979	Grampian, 1996
758	CWG720V	Leyland Atlantean AN68A/1R	Alexander AL	B45/29F	1980	Glasgow, 1998
759	WAG373X	Leyland Atlantean AN68C/1R	Roe	B43/31F	1981	Glasgow, 1998
760	NRS308W	Leyland Atlantean AN68C/1R	Alexander AL	B45/29D	1981	Aberdeen, 1998
761	HRS261V	Leyland Atlantean AN68A/1R	Alexander AL	B45/34F	1980	Grampian, 1996
765	HRS265V	Leyland Atlantean AN68A/1R	Alexander AL	O45/34F	1980	Grampian, 1997
774	HRS274V	Leyland Atlantean AN68A/1R	Alexander AL	O45/34F	1980	Grampian, 1998
776	HRS276V	Leyland Atlantean AN68A/1R	Alexander AL	B45/29D	1980	
787	HSO287V	Leyland Atlantean AN68A/1R	Alexander AL	B45/29D	1980	Aberdeen, 1998
788	HRS288V	Leyland Atlantean AN68A/1R	Alexander AL	B45/34F	1980	Grampian, 1997

800-807

MCW Metrobus DR132/6   Alexander RL   B45/33F   1985   800-4 Kelvin Central, 1990

800	B100PKS	802	B102PKS	804	B104PKS	806	B106PKS	807	B88PKS
801	B101PKS	803	B103PKS	805	B105PKS				

808-813

MCW Metrobus DR102/52   Alexander RL   B45/33F*   1986   *812/3 are BC45/33F

808	D108ELS	810	D110ELS	811	D111ELS	812	143ASV	813	110ASV
809	D109ELS								

814	HSU301	MCW Metrobus DR132/9	Alexander RL	BC45/33F	1986	
815	D115ELS	MCW Metrobus DR132/9	Alexander RL	BC45/33F	1986	
816	D116ELS	MCW Metrobus DR132/9	Alexander RL	BC45/33F	1986	

817-821

MCW Metrobus DR132/10   Alexander RL   BC47/33F   1987

817	365UMY	818	VXU444	819	WLT724	820	TSV612	821	E209JKS

830	ULS630X	MCW Metrobus DR102/28	Alexander RL	B45/33F	1982	
831	ULS631X	MCW Metrobus DR102/28	Alexander RL	B45/33F	1982	Kelvin Central, 1989
833	ULS633X	MCW Metrobus DR102/28	Alexander RL	B45/33F	1982	Kelvin Central, 1989
840	ULS640X	MCW Metrobus DR104/10	Alexander RL	B45/33F	1982	KCB Network, 1996
843	ULS643X	MCW Metrobus DR104/10	Alexander RL	B45/33F	1982	
859	BLS437Y	MCW Metrobus DR102/33	Alexander RL	B45/33F	1983	
868	BLS446Y	MCW Metrobus DR102/33	Alexander RL	B45/33F	1983	
870	A470GMS	MCW Metrobus DR102/39	Alexander RL	B45/33F	1984	
877	A477GMS	MCW Metrobus DR102/39	Alexander RL	B45/33F	1984	
881	B581MLS	MCW Metrobus DR102/39	Alexander RL	B45/33F	1984	
882	B582MLS	MCW Metrobus DR102/39	Alexander RL	B45/33F	1984	

Almost thirty front-engined Volvo B55s are still operated in the Lowland fleet. Pictured at Galashiels - where four are based - is 1084, HSF84X, which carries an Alexander R-type body. The Volvo B55 was the continuation of the Ailsa model which was built with Volvo units until Volvo acquired the plant and commenced assembly of buses under its own name. *Paul Wigan*

883	B583MLS	MCW Metrobus DR132/2	Alexander RL	B45/33F	1984	
884	B584MLS	MCW Metrobus DR132/2	Alexander RL	B45/33F	1984	Kelvin Central, 1990
885	B585MLS	MCW Metrobus DR102/40	Alexander RL	B45/33F	1984	
887	B587MLS	MCW Metrobus DR132/3	Alexander RL	B45/33F	1984	Kelvin Central, 1990
888	B588MLS	MCW Metrobus DR132/3	Alexander RL	B45/33F	1984	
893	B93PKS	MCW Metrobus DR102/47	Alexander RL	B45/33F	1984	Kelvin Central, 1990
894	B94PKS	MCW Metrobus DR102/47	Alexander RL	B45/33F	1984	
895	B95PKS	MCW Metrobus DR102/47	Alexander RL	B45/33F	1984	
896	B96PKS	MCW Metrobus DR102/47	Alexander RL	B45/33F	1984	
898	B98PKS	MCW Metrobus DR132/6	Alexander RL	B45/33F	1985	
899	B99PKS	MCW Metrobus DR132/6	Alexander RL	B45/33F	1985	

901-913

| | | Leyland Olympian ONLXB/1R | Eastern Coach Works | B45/32F* | 1982 | SMT, 1996 |
| | | | | | | *901/3 are BC45/32F |

| 901 | ULS101X | 905 | ULS105X | 907 | ULS107X | 909 | ULS109X | 912 | ULS112X |
| 903 | ULS103X | 906w | ULS106X | 908 | ULS108X | 911 | ULS111X | 913 | ULS113X |

916-943

| | | Leyland Olympian ONLXB/1R | Alexander RL | B45/32F | 1983-84 | SMT, 1996 |

916	ALS116Y	923	ALS123Y	928	ALS128Y	935	ALS135Y	940	A140BSC
917	ALS117Y	924	ALS124Y	929	ALS129Y	936	A136BSC	941	A141BSC
918	ALS118Y	925	ALS125Y	932	ALS132Y	937	A137BSC	942	A142BSC
919	ALS119Y	926	ALS126Y	933	ALS133Y	938	A138BSC	943	A143BSC
922	ALS122Y	927	ALS127Y	934	ALS134Y	939	A139BSC		

The first Alexander-bodied Olympians for SMT were supplied in 1983 and featured the then new RL-type bodywork. From this initial batch, 937,A137BSC, is seen turning into Princes Street, Edinburgh carrying SMT names and Livingston garage codes. *Paul Wigan*

945-950

945-950		Leyland Olympian ONLXB/1R	East Lancashire		B47/32F	1984		Lowland, 1997	
945	A81RRP	947	A77RRP	948	A78RRP	949	A79RRP	950	A80RRP
946	A82RRP								

951	D901CSH	Leyland Olympian ONTL11/1RH	Alexander RL	BC43/27F	1987	
952	D902CSH	Leyland Olympian ONTL11/1RH	Alexander RL	BC43/27F	1987	
959	B159KSC	Leyland Olympian ONTL11/1RH	Alexander RL	B45/32F	1985	Eastern Scottish, 1985
960	B160KSC	Leyland Olympian ONTL11/1RH	Alexander RL	B45/32F	1985	Eastern Scottish, 1986
961	B161KSC	Leyland Olympian ONTL11/1R	Alexander RL	B45/32F	1985	SMT, 1996
962	B162KSC	Leyland Olympian ONTL11/1R	Alexander RL	B45/32F	1985	SMT, 1996

1049-1058

1049-1058		Volvo B55-10 MkIII		Alexander RV	B44/37F	1984		SMT, 1996	
1049	B149GSC	1051	B151GSC	1053	B153GSC	1055	B155GSC	1057	B157GSC
1050	B150GSC	1052	B152GSC	1054	B154GSC	1056	B156GSC	1058	B158GSC

1076-1095

1076-1095		Volvo B55-10 MkIII		Alexander RV	B44/35F	1981		SMT, 1996	
1076	HSF76X	1081	HSF81X	1085	HSF85X	1088	HSF88X	1093	HSF93X
1077	HSF77X	1082	HSF82X	1086	HSF86X	1091	HSF91X	1094	HSF94X
1078	HSF78X	1083	HSF83X	1087	HSF87X	1092	HSF92X	1095	HSF95X
1080	HSF80X	1084	HSF84X						

1101-1107

1101-1107		Volvo Citybus B10M-50		Northern Counties	H45/31F	1991		Manchester, 1998	
1101	H701GVM	1102	H702GVM	1104	H704GVM	1106	H706GVM	1107	H707GVM

1169-1173

1169-1173		Volvo Citybus B10M-50		Alexander RV	B44/37F	1985		SMT, 1996	
1169	B169KSC	1170	B170KSC	1171	B171KSC	1172	B172KSC	1173	B173KSC

There have been significant developments between the Alexander-bodied Olympian shown on the previous page and 1336, S936AKS, shown above. The chassis is now made by Volvo rather than Leyland, while Alexander is now part of the Mayflower group which also owns chassis manufacturer, Dennis. The Royale body design is shown in FirstGroup corporate willow-leaf livery. Olympian production for the home market has now ceased. *Richard Walter*

1187	E187HSF	Volvo Citybus B10M-50		Alexander RV		BC45/35F	1987		SMT, 1996	
1188	E188HSF	Volvo Citybus B10M-50		Alexander RV		BC45/35F	1987		SMT, 1996	
1189	E189HSF	Volvo Citybus B10M-50		Alexander RV		BC45/35F	1987		SMT, 1996	
1190	E190HSF	Volvo Citybus B10M-50		Alexander RV		BC45/35F	1987		SMT, 1996	

1201-1212   Volvo B10B-58   Alexander Strider   B51F   1993   SMT, 1996

1201	L201KFS	**1204**	L204KSX	**1207**	L207KSX	**1209**	L209KSX	**1211**	L211KSX
1202	L202KFS	**1205**	L205KSX	**1208**	L208KSX	**1210**	L210KSX	**1212**	L212KSX
1203	L203KSX	**1206**	L206KSX						

1213	L213KSX	Volvo B10B-58	Wright Endurance	B51F	1993	SMT, 1996

1301-1323   Volvo Olympian   Alexander Royale RV   B42/29F   1998

1301	R301LKS	**1306**	R306LKS	**1311**	R311LKS	**1316**	R416RMS	**1320**	R420YMS
1302	R302LKS	**1307**	R307LKS	**1312**	R312LKS	**1317**	R417YMS	**1321**	R421YMS
1303	R303LKS	**1308**	R308LKS	**1313**	R313LKS	**1318**	R418YMS	**1322**	R422YMS
1304	R304LKS	**1309**	R309LKS	**1314**	R314LKS	**1319**	R419YMS	**1323**	R423YMS
1305	R305LKS	**1310**	R310LKS	**1315**	R315LKS				

1324-1338   Volvo Olympian   Alexander Royale RV   B42/29F   1998-89

1324	S924AKS	**1327**	S927AKS	**1330**	S930AKS	**1333**	S933AKS	**1336**	S936AKS
1325	S925AKS	**1328**	S928AKS	**1331**	S931AKS	**1334**	S934AKS	**1337**	S937AKS
1326	S926AKS	**1329**	S929AKS	**1332**	S932AKS	**1335**	S935AKS	**1338**	S938AKS

1400	HDZ5480	Renault S75	Wright NimBus	B28F	1990	CentreWest, 1998
1401	HDZ5446	Renault S75	Wright NimBus	B28F	1990	CentreWest, 1998

After running a large number of Renault S75 minibuses, SMT chose the Optare MetroRider for deliveries in 1992, and further examples have been taken into stock since. Numerically the first, 1503, J503WSX, is seen leaving the Safeway store in Hawick in Autumn sunshine. *Paul Wigan*

1471-1502   Renault S75   Reeve Burgess Beaver   B31F   1991   SMT, 1994-96

1471	H471OSC	1477	H477OSC	1484	H484OSC	1491	H491OSC	1497	H497OSC
1472	H472OSC	1478	H478OSC	1485	H485OSC	1492	H492OSC	1498	H498OSC
1473	H473OSC	1479	H479OSC	1486	H486OSC	1493	H493OSC	1499	H499OSC
1474	H474OSC	1481	H481OSC	1487	H487OSC	1494	H494OSC	1501	H501OSC
1475	H475OSC	1482	H482OSC	1489	H489OSC	1495	H495OSC	1502	H502OSC
1476	H476OSC	1483	H483OSC	1490	H490OSC	1496	H496OSC		

1503-1527   Optare MetroRider   Optare   B31F*   1992-94   SMT, 1995-96; 1523 is B25FL

1503	J503WSX	1508	J508WSX	1513	K513BSX	1518	L518KSX	1523	L523KSX
1504	J504WSX	1509	J509WSX	1514	K514BSX	1519	L519KSX	1524	L524KSX
1505	J505WSX	1510	J510WSX	1515	K515BSX	1520	L520KSX	1525	L525KSX
1506	J506WSX	1511	J511WSX	1516	K516BSX	1521	L521KSX	1526	L526KSX
1507	J507WSX	1512	J512WSX	1517	K517BSX	1522	L522KSX	1527	L527KSX

1528	M284SMS	Optare MetroRider	Optare	BC25F	1995	Owned by Central RC

1530-1537   Optare MetroRider   Optare   BC32F*   1994   *1530-2 are B32F

1530	L720JKS	1532	L722JKS	1534	L724JKS	1536	L726JKS	1537	L727JKS
1531	L721JKS	1533	L723JKS	1535	L725JKS				

Opposite, top:- **Volvo Olympian 1306 was one of six Royales to enter service at Livingston depot in 1998. Vehicles at this former SMT garage still carry the SMT name, though now part of the Midland Bluebird operation and with new facilities opened to replace two separate sites.** *Murdoch Currie*
Opposite, bottom:- **In 1997 FirstGroup commenced services in Fife following the introduction of suburban express services into Glasgow operated by Stagecoach. The Fife First livery is that used in Glasgow as illustrated by Scania 510, N410ENW, which was transferred from Yorkshire Rider for the scheme. The vehicle was pictured in Dumbarton, though this vehicle is based at the eastern end of the service in Edinburgh.** *Tony Wilson*

1538-1542		Optare MetroRider MR15		Optare		B22F	1997	
1538	P538YSH	1539	P539YSH	1540	P540YSH	1541	P541YSH	1542	P542YHS

1602	SSX602V	Seddon Pennine 7	Alexander AYS	B60F	1979		Eastern Scottish, 1985
1607	SSX607V	Seddon Pennine 7	Alexander AYS	B60F	1979		Eastern Scottish, 1985
1665	DSD965V	Seddon Pennine 7	Alexander AT	C49F	1979		SBG Engineering, 1990
1670	NFS984T	Seddon Pennine 7	Plaxton Supreme IV Express	C49F	1979		Lothian Transit, 1994
1676	LSC936T	Seddon Pennine 7	Alexander AYS	BC49F	1982		SMT, 1996
1683	JFS983X	Seddon Pennine 7	Alexander AYS	B49F	1982		Midland Bluebird, 1997
1686	JFS986X	Seddon Pennine 7	Alexander AYS	B53F	1982		Eastern Scottish, 1985
1715	G715OSH	Leyland Swift LBM6T/1RS	Reeve Burgess Harrier	C29F	1989		
1739	M399OMS	Omni	Omni Citizen	B16FL	1994		SMT, 1996
1749	H649USH	Ford Transit VE6	Deansgate	M15	1991		Grieve, Hawick, 1994

1974-1986		Leyland Lion LDTL11/2R		Alexander RH		BC49/37F*	1986-87	SMT, 1996
						*1980/4-6 are BC45/35F; 1976/7 are BC45/37F		
1974	C174VSF	1977	C177VSF	1980	C180VSF	1983	C183VSF	1985	D185ESC
1975	C175VSF	1978	C178VSF	1981	C181VSF	1984	D184ESC	1986	D186ESC
1976	C176VSF	1979	C179VSF	1982	C182VSF				

2101-2105		Scania K113CRB		Plaxton Paramount 3500 III		C49FT*	1990	*Seating varies
2101	PSU316	2102	LAT662	2103	PSU317	2104	PSU314	2105	PSU315

2106	M106PKS	Scania K113CRB	Van Hool Alizée	C49FT	1995		
2107	N107VKS	Scania K113CRB	Van Hool Alizée	C49FT	1996		
2110	K535RJX	DAF MB230TL615	Van Hool Alizée HE	C57F	1983		On seasonal loan
2202	692FFC	Volvo B10M-61	Jonckheere Jubilee P599	C51FT	1989		Laing, Thornton Heath, 1991
2203	TSU682	Volvo B10M-61	Jonckheere Jubilee P599	C46FT	1989		Grampian, 1992
2204	ESK958	Volvo B10M-61	Plaxton Paramount 3200 III	C48FT	1989		Grampian, 1992
2205	FSU315	Volvo B10M-60	Plaxton Paramount 3200 III	C46FT	1989		Wallace Arnold, 1993
2206	PSU631	Volvo B10M-61	Jonckheere Deauville P50	C53F	1985		Aberdeen (Mairs), 1999
2207	144ASV	Volvo B10M-60	Jonckheere Deauville P599	C51FT	1989		Redwing, Camberwell, 1994
2208	K924RGE	Volvo B10M-60	Jonckheere Deauville P599	C51FT	1993		Park's, 1995
2304	VXI8734	DAF MB200DKFL600	Duple Caribbean 2	C51F	1986		Ian Glass, Haddington, 1991
2307	ESX257	DAF MB200DKTL600	Van Hool Alizée	C46FT	1982		Ian Glass, Haddington, 1991
2309	KSU389	DAF SB2300DHS585	Smit Euroliner	C53F	1985		Ian Glass, Haddington, 1991
2310	FFS10X	DAF MB200DKTL600	Plaxton Supreme VI	C57F	1982		Shanks, Galashiels, 1992
2311	L521EHD	DAF MB230TL615	Van Hool Alizée HE	C51FT	1994		On seasonal loan
2408	J8SMT	Dennis Javelin 12SDA1929	Plaxton Paramount 3200 III	C53F	1992		SMT, 1996
2409	L109OSX	Dennis Javelin 12SDA2131	Plaxton Premiére 320	C53F	1994		SMT, 1996

The Leyland Lion was introduced by Leyland to compete with the Volvo Citybus double-deck variant of the B10M. The numbers built were small, finding niche markets with the Scottish Bus Group and Nottingham City Transport. The SMT batch now numbers thirteen and were initially used, with high-back seating, on commuter services into Edinburgh. Pictured in the home of Scotland's new Parliament is 1976, C176VSF. *Paul Wigan*

2410	L110OSX	Dennis Javelin 12SDA2131	Plaxton Premiére 320	C53F	1994	SMT, 1996
2419	A19SMT	Dennis Javelin 12SDA1907	Duple 320	C53FT	1988	SMT, 1996
2427	KBZ3627	Dennis Javelin 12SDA1907	Duple 320	C53F	1988	Ian Glass, Haddington, 1991
2428	KBZ3628	Dennis Javelin 8.5SDL1903	Duple 320	C35F	1988	Ian Glass, Haddington, 1991
2429	KBZ3629	Dennis Javelin 12SDA1907	Duple 320	C53F	1989	Ian Glass, Haddington, 1991
2501	R81GNW	EOS E180Z	EOS 90	C44FT	1998	On seasonal loan
2502	R82GNW	EOS E180Z	EOS 90	C44FT	1998	On seasonal loan
2505	T105AUA	EOS E180Z	EOS 90	C44FT	1999	On seasonal loan
2506	T106AUA	EOS E180Z	EOS 90	C44FT	1999	On seasonal loan
2509	N49FWU	EOS E180Z	EOS 90	C44FT	1996	On seasonal loan

Special Event vehicles:

9487	487GFR	AEC Reliance 2U3RA	Harrington Grenadier	C34F	1964	Owned by Prestige Tours
1723	AWG623	AEC Regal	Alexander	C31F	1947	Ex preservation, 1986

Ancilliary vehicles:

602	C698ECV	Mercedes-Benz L608D	Reeve Burgess	B20F	1985	Bluebird, 1992
606	C821SDY	Mercedes-Benz L608D	Alexander AM	B20F	1986	Bluebird, 1992
691	D232UHC	Mercedes-Benz L608D	Alexander AM	BC20F	1986	Grampian, 1997
1463	E467JSG	Renault-Dodge S56	Alexander AM	BC25F	1987	SMT, 1996
(1603)	SSX603V	Seddon Pennine 7	Alexander AYS	TV	1979	Eastern Scottish, 1985
(1689)	JSF929T	Seddon Pennine 7	Alexander AT	TV	1979	Eastern Scottish, 1985
(1698)	SSC108P	Seddon Pennine 7	Alexander AT	TV	1979	Eastern Scottish, 1985
9904	DMS348C	Leyland Leopard PSU3/3R	Alexander AY	RV	1965	
9920	G601OSH	Ford Transit VE6	Dormobile	M16	1989	Lowland, 1997
9920	D420ASF	Renault-Dodge S56	Alexander AM	B16FL	1986	SMT, 1996
9921	XMS244R	Leyland Leopard PSU3C/3R	Alexander AY	RV	1977	Midland Scottish, 1991
9927	D227UHC	Mercedes-Benz L608D	Alexander AM	BC20F	1986	Grampian, 1997
9931	C695ECV	Mercedes-Benz L608D	Reeve Burgess	B20F	1985	Bluebird, 1992
9932	D753DSH	Renault-Dodge S56	Alexander AM	B21F	1986	SMT, 1996
9933	D402ASF	Renault-Dodge S56	Alexander AM	B21F	1986	SMT, 1995
9934	C107HGL	Mercedes-Benz L608D	Reeve Burgess	B20F	1986	Essex Buses, 1998
9935	H488OSC	Renault S75	Reeve Burgess Beaver	B31F	1991	SMT, 1994
9967	RSX84J	Daimler Fleetline CRG6LXB	Alexander AD	O44/31F	1971	Alexander Fife, 1986
9984	JSF927T	Seddon Pennine 7	Alexander AT	TV	1979	Eastern Scottish, 1985
9985	JSF930T	Seddon Pennine 7	Alexander AT	TV	1979	Eastern Scottish, 1985
9993	DDB157C	Leyland Leopard PSU3/3R	Alexander Y	RV	1965	SMT, 1996
9995	CSG29C	Bristol Lodekka FLF6G	Eastern Coach Works	RV	1965	SMT, 1996

Previous registrations

101ASV	BLS107Y	FSU315	F412DUG	PSU316	G101RSH
110ASV	D113ELS	FSU334	BMS514Y	PSU317	H103TSH
143ASV	D112ELS	FSU355	D517RCK	PSU320	A562BSX
144ASV	G170RBD	FSU380	ALS105Y	PSU321	VTY131Y, WLT388
156ASV	D145HMS, 692FFC, D625GSG	FSU381	ALS101Y	PSU322	PSF322Y
365UMY	E617NLS	FSU382	ALS102Y	PSU622	D51VSO
487GFR	From new	FSU383	ALS103Y	PSU625	D54VSO
692FFC	F914YNV	GSU338	ERF72Y, 4327PL, FEH778Y	PSU631	B497CBD
693AFU	A130ESG	GSU339	ERF73Y, 8636PL, FEH780Y	RSX84J	RXA51J, PSU314
7881UA	A118GLS	HSU247	LPN355W	SSU816	A116GLS
A9SMT	B339RLS	HSU273	LPN357W, 411DCD, OUF51W	SSU821	A121ESG
A10SMT	B340RLS	HSU301	D114ELS	SSU841	D141HMS
A12SMT	B267KPF	KBZ3627	E888MSX	SSU857	D142HMS
A13SMT	B335RLS, GCS245, WSV144	KBZ3628	E900MSX	SSU859	-
A14SMT	B341RLS	KBZ3629	F777UFS	SSU897	A168UGB
A15SMT	D345ESC	KEX532	F364DVR	TSU682	F912YNV
A16SMT	D346ESC	KSU388	D320RNS	TSV612	E620NLS
A17SMT	D347ESC	KSU389	B88KSF	UTU23V	UTU23V, SCK869
A18SMT	D348ESC	KSU390	TFS317Y	VXI8734	C700USC
A19SMT	F250OFP	KSU391	A185UGB	VXU444	E618NLS, FSU309, E771PSG
A20SMT	A331BSC	KSU392	B342RLS	WLT724	E619NLS
A119GLS	A119GLS, WLT770, A9KGB	KSU393	B343RLS	WSU479	A75JFA
B287KPF	B287KPF, BXZ521	KSU394	D501CSH	WSU480	B569LSC
BSS76	A678DSF	KSU834	D143HMS	WSU487	A21GBC
BSV807	A117GLS, WLT415, A253WYS	LAT662	G102RSH	WSU489	A22GBC
ESK958	F104SSE	NBD107Y	NBD107Y, WLT596	WSV135	A332BSC
ESX257	WFR612Y	NFS984T	LSC950T, PSU322	WSV137	B337RLS
FFS10X	VTT14X, LAT662	OVT798	A184UGB	WSV138	B338RLS
FSV634	D144HMS	PSU314	H104TSH	WSV140	A330BSC
FSU308	BLS108Y	PSU315	H105TSH		

Allocations

Balfron (Dunmore Street) - Midland Bluebird

Mercedes-Benz	637	639					
Leopard	468	498					
Mercedes-Benz O405	51	52	58				
Tiger coach	103	104	105	150	151	154	159
Metrobus	831	859	870	885	893	894	

Bannockburn (Cowie Road, Stirling) - Midland Bluebird

Mercedes-Benz	625	626	632	633	634	636	638	651
	652	653	655	656	688	689	690	
MetroRider	1523	1528						
Dart	201	202	249	250				
Leopard	403	414	416	417	419	451	474	
Tiger	101	102	116	117	143	152	153	158
	172	179	194	195	196	359	362	
Mercedes-Benz O405	53	54	55	56	57	79		
Scania L	513	514	515	516	517	518	523	524
	525	526						
Metrobus	801	803	807	815	816	818	820	830
	840	843	881	884	896	898		

Dalkeith (Eskbank Road) - Lowland - SMT

Renault-Dodge	1424	1471	1476					
Transit	1749							
MetroRider	1504	1505	1506	1507	1508	1509	1514	1518
	1519	1520	1521	1522				
Dart	206	207	208	209	210	211	212	213
	214	215						
Tiger bus	187	189						
EOS coach	2509							
Scania coach	2101	2102	2103	2110				
Volvo B10M coach	2205	2206						
DAF coach	2307	2309	2311					
Javelin coach	2428	2429						
Tiger coach	337	389	394					
Mercedes-Benz O405	75	76	77	78				
Volvo B55	1058	1076	1077	1078	1080	1081	1082	1083
	1085	1086	1087	1088	1091	1092		
Volvo Citybus	1101	1102	1104	1106	1107	1169	1170	1173
Olympian	1305	1307	1308	1309	1310	1311	1312	1313
	1314	1315	1317	1318	1319	1321	1323	

Dunfermline ( ) - Fife First

Dart	216	217	218
Scania bus	511	512	

Edinburgh (Westfield Avenue) - Midland Bluebird - Fife First

Renault-Dodge	1400	1489	1491	1492	1493	1494	1496	1499
	1502							
Dart	225	226	227	228	229	230	231	232
	233	234	235	236	237	238	239	245
	248							
Scania bus	503	504	505	506	507	508	509	510
	575	576	577	578				
Tiger	171	178	186	192	197	198	199	345
	346	347						
Scania	2104	2105	2106	2107				
DAF	2110							
Volvo	2208							
Olympian	905	907	908	922	923	927	945	946
	947	948	949	950				

For many years the Alexander Y-type and its variants have been mostly associated with Scottish bus operation. Once the Leyland Leopard became only available semi-automatic or automatic transmission the Scottish Bus Group ordered a large number of the type based on Seddon chassis. The remaining few now reside with Lowland, though most are withdrawn. Pictured a few months ago, 1677, LSC937T, illustrates the type. *Murdoch Currie*

Galashiels (Duke Street) - Lowland

MetroRider	1510	1535	1536				
DAF coach	2304						
Leopard	468						
Tiger	324	325	328	364	366	388	393
EOS coach	2501	2502					
Scania bus	501	502					
Mercedes-Benz O405	71	72	73	74			
Volvo B55	1084	1093	1094	1095			
Volvo Citybus	1189	1190					

Hawick (Dovecote Street) - Lowland

Renault-Dodge	1421	1430			
Mercedes-Benz	653				
MetroRider	1503	1532	1533	1537	1538
Tiger coach	329	392			
Scania coach	2106				
Javelin	2419				

Jedburgh ( ) - Lowland

Tiger coach	322	323	396	469
Javelin	2408			

Kelso (Roxburgh Street) - Lowland

Outstation:- Berwick

MetroRider	1539	1540	1541					
Mercedes-Benz	640	641	675					
Tiger coach	173	174	175	176	177	315	316	330
	331	338	390					
Javelin coach	2409	2410						
Seddon	1607	1631	1632	1633	1634	1639	1665	

Larbert (Stirling Road) - Midland Bluebird - Kings of Dunblane

Mercedes-Benz	616	617	642	654	657	659	686	687
Leopard	400	457	462	486				
Tiger coach	108	114	118	130	144	157	160	161
	162	163	164	180	190	191	193	353
	365	370						
Volvo	2202	2203	2207					
Dart	240	241	242	281				
Scania bus	519	551	552	553	554	555	556	558
	562	563	564	565	566	579	580	581
	587	588	589	590	591			
Atlantean	705	708	709	719	720	748	750	760
	774	776	787	788				
Metrobus	800	802	804	805	806	808	809	810
	811	813	814	817	819	821	833	868
	882	883	887	888	895	899		
Olympian	1301	1322						

Linlithgow (High Street) - Midland Bluebird - SMT (to close during 1999)

Mercedes-Benz	635	658						
Renault-Dodge	1436	1475						
National	34	37						
Tiger	136	138	155	156				
Volvo	2204							
Scania bus	557	559	560	561	567	568	569	570
	571	572	573	574				
Metrobus	812							

Livingston (Deans) - Midland Bluebird - SMT

MetroRider	1511	1512	1513	1515	1516	1517	1524	1525
	1526	1527						
Tiger	142	145	332	333	335	340	341	
Volvo B10B	1201	1202	1203	1204	1205	1206	1207	1208
	1209	1210	1211	1212	1213			
Dart	203	204	205	243	246	247	251	280
Mercedes-Benz O405	61	62	63	64	65	66	67	68
	69	70						
Atlantean	735	758	759	761				
Lion	1974	1976	1977	1978	1979	1980	1981	1982
	1983	1985	1986					
Olympian	901	911	912	913	917	924	925	926
	931	932	933	934	935	936	938	939
	940	941	961	962	1302	1303	1304	1306
	1316	1320	1324	1325	1326	1327	1328	

Musselburgh (The Mall) - Lowland - SMT

Omni	1739						
Mercedes-Benz	674						
Tiger coach	314	342					
Dart	219	220	221	223	224		
Tiger	188	311	312	313	320	321	327
Scania	520	521	522	582	583	584	585	586
Volvo B55	1057						
Olympian	916	937	951	952	959	960	1329	1330
	1331	1332	1333	1334	1335	1336	1337	1338

North Berwick (Tantallon Road) - Lowland - SMT

MetroRider	1530						
Tiger	301	302	303	349	350	351	395
Javelin	2427						
Volvo B55	1049	1056					
Volvo Citybus	1188						

Peebles - Lowland

Renault-Dodge	1472						
MetroRider	1534	1542					
Seddon	1670						
Swift	1715						
DAF coach	2310						
Tiger	119	304	326	336	367	376	391	397
Olympian	919	928	929	942	943		

Unallocated

Renault-Dodge	1401	1422	1425	1426	1473	1474	1475	1477
	1478	1479	1481	1482	1483	1484	1485	1486
	1487	1490	1495	1497	1498	1501		
Seddon	1602	1676	1683	1686			
Leopard	130	421	467				
Tiger	112	339	348	352			
Royal Tiger	370						
Atlantean	715	744	749				
Lion	1984						
Volvo B55	1055						
Volvo Citybus	1187						
Olympian	903	909	918				

FIRST GLASGOW

Glasgow - Ayrshire - Kelvin

First Glasgow (No1) Ltd, 197 Victoria Road, Larkfield, Glasgow, G42 7AD
First Glasgow (No2) Ltd, 197 Victoria Road, Larkfield, Glasgow, G42 7AD

A2-39		Volvo-Ailsa B55-10 MkIII		Alexander RV		B44/35F		1981	
2	TGG378W	9	TGG385W	16	CSU224X	23	CSU231X	32	CSU240X
5	TGG381W	10	TGG386W	17	CSU225X	27	CSU235X	38	CSU246X
8	TGG384W	11	CSU219X	20	CSU228X	30	CSU238X	39	CSU247X

A41-80		Volvo-Ailsa B55-10 MkIII		Alexander RV		B44/35F		1982	
41	KGG101Y	47	KGG107Y	55	KGG115Y	65	KGG125Y	75	KGG135Y
42	KGG102Y	48	KGG108Y	56	KGG116Y	67	KGG127Y	76	KGG136Y
43	KGG103Y	49	KGG109Y	58	KGG118Y	68	KGG128Y	77	KGG137Y
44	KGG104Y	50	KGG110Y	59	KGG119Y	70	KGG130Y	78	KGG138Y
45	KGG105Y	51	KGG111Y	60	KGG141Y	71	KGG131Y	79	KGG139Y
46	KGG106Y	52	KGG112Y	62	KGG122Y	74	KGG134Y	80	KGG140Y

A83-116		Volvo-Ailsa B55-10 MkIII		Alexander RV		B44/35F		1983	
83	OGG179Y	90	OGG186Y	99	A562SGA	106	A732PSU	111	A737PSU
85	OGG181Y	92	OGG188Y	100	A563SGA	107	A733PSU	113	A739PSU
86	OGG182Y	93	OGG189Y	101	A564SGA	108	A734PSU	114	A741PSU
87	OGG183Y	94	OGG190Y	103	A566SGA	109	A735PSU	115	A742PSU
88	OGG184Y	95	OGG191Y	105	A568SGA	110	A736PSU	116	A743PSU
89	OGG185Y								

A117	A483UYS	Volvo-Ailsa B55-10 MkIII	Marshall	B44/35F	1984
A118	A484UYS	Volvo-Ailsa B55-10 MkIII	Marshall	B44/35F	1984

A119-133		Volvo-Ailsa B55-10 MkIII		Alexander RV		B44/35F		1984	
119	B999YUS	123	B24YYS	126	B27YYS	129	B30YYS	132	B33YYS
120	B21YYS	124	B25YYS	127	B28YYS	130	B31YYS	133	B34YYS
122	B23YYS	125	B26YYS	128	B29YYS				

First Glasgow introduced coaches during 1997 to compete with Stagecoach Express on limited stop services into Scotland's largest city. Pictured about to leave for the 'new' town of Cumbernauld is CV8, P769XHS.
Brian Ridgway

AH2-6 Volvo Citybus B10M-50 Alexander RV B47/25F* 1984 *6 is B47/27FL

2	A600TNS	3	A601TNS	4	A603TNS	5	A602TNS	6	A604TNS

AH7-76 Volvo Citybus B10M-50 Alexander RV B47/37F 1989

7	F89JYS	21	F793LSU	35	G283OGE	50	G298OGE	64	G692PNS
8	F90JYS	22	F794LSU	36	G284OGE	51	G299OGE	65	G693PNS
9	F91JYS	23	F795LSU	37	G285OGE	52	G300OGE	66	G694PNS
10	F92JYS	24	G409OGD	38	G286OGE	53	G301OGE	67	G695PNS
11	F93JYS	25	G410OGD	39	G287OGE	54	G302OGE	68	G696PNS
12	F94JYS	26	G411OGD	40	G288OGE	55	G303OGE	69	G697PNS
13	F95JYS	27	G412OGD	42	G290OGE	56	G304OGE	70	G698PNS
14	F96JYS	28	G413OGD	43	G291OGE	57	G685PNS	71	G699PNS
15	F97JYS	29	G414OGD	44	G292OGE	58	G686PNS	72	G700PNS
16	F98JYS	30	G415OGD	45	G293OGE	59	G687PNS	73	G701PNS
17	F99JYS	31	G416OGD	46	G294OGE	60	G688PNS	74	G702PNS
18	F790LSU	32	G280OGE	47	G295OGE	61	G689PNS	75	G703PNS
19	F791LSU	33	G281OGE	48	G296OGE	62	G690PNS	76	G704PNS
20	F792LSU	34	G282OGE	49	G297OGE	63	G691PNS		

AH77-101 Volvo Citybus B10M-50 Alexander RV B47/37F 1990

77	G521RDS	82	G526RDS	87	G531RDS	92	G536RDS	97	G541RDS
78	G522RDS	83	G527RDS	88	G532RDS	93	G537RDS	98	G542RDS
79	G523RDS	84	G528RDS	89	G533RDS	94	G538RDS	99	G543RDS
80	G524RDS	85	G529RDS	90	G534RDS	95	G539RDS	100	G544RDS
81	G525RDS	86	G530RDS	91	G535RDS	96	G540RDS	101	G545RDS

CD91-95 Dennis Dorchester SDA806 Alexander TC C47F 1984

91	A206UYS	92	A202UYS	93	A203UYS	94	A204UYS	95	A205UYS

CD286-290 Dennis Dorchester SDA806 Alexander TE C49F 1984

286	A106UYS	287	A107UYS	288	A108UYS	289	A109UYS	290	A110UYS

CM274-281 MCW Metrobus DR102/52 Alexander RL BC45/33F 1986

274	D674MHS	275	D675MHS	277	D677MHS	279	D679MHS	281	D681MHS

CO40	B697BPU	Leyland Olympian ONTL11/2RSp	Eastern Coach Works	C45/28F	1985	Northumbria, 1995
CO41	A102FPL	Leyland Olympian ONTL11/2R	Eastern Coach Works	C45/28F	1985	Northumbria, 1995
CO57	C215UPD	Leyland Olympian ONTL11/2RSp	Eastern Coach Works	C45/24F	1986	Northumbria, 1993

CO209-CO216 Leyland Olympian ONLXB/1RH Alexander RL BC47/27F 1986

209	C809KHS	212	C802KHS	214	C804KHS	215	C805KHS	216	C806KHS
211	C801KHS	213	C803KHS						

CO244-CO249 Leyland Olympian YN2RV18Z4 Alexander Royale RL BC47/28F 1994

244	WLT741	246	WLT357	247	WLT677	248	WLT910	249	WLT678
245	WLT770								

CS1	P25RFS	Scania L94IB	Irizar Intercentury	C55F	1997	
CS2	P26RFS	Scania L94IB	Irizar Intercentury	C55F	1997	
CT30	WLT760	Leyland Tiger TRCTL11/3RH	Duple 320	C53F	1986	Munro, Uddingston, 1994
CT66	B200DGG	Leyland Tiger TRCLXC/2RH	Alexander TE	C49F	1985	
CT99	CSU932	Leyland Tiger TRCTL11/3RH	Duple 320	C53F	1986	Luton & District, 1992
CT203	FGG603X	Leyland Tiger TRBTL11/2R	Alexander AT	C49F	1982	Kelvin Scottish, 1989

CV4-10 Volvo B10M-62 Plaxton Première 320 C55F 1997

4	P765XHS	6	P767XHS	8	P769XHS	9	P770XHS	10	P771XHS
5	P766XHS	7	P768XHS						

CV11	KCB758	Volvo B10M-61	Duple 340	C57F	1988	Grampian (Mairs), 1997

CV12-16 Volvo B10M-62 Plaxton Première 320 C53F 1997

12	R342GHS	13	R343GHS	14	R344GHS	15	R345GHS	16	R346GHS

DM135-150

MCW Metrobus DR102/33   Alexander RL   B45/33F   1983

135	BLS426Y	139	BLS430Y	143	BLS436Y	145	BLS439Y	149	BLS444Y
136	BLS427Y	140	BLS431Y	144	BLS438Y	146	BLS440Y	150	BLS445Y
137	BLS428Y								

DM156-167

MCW Metrobus DR102/39*   Alexander RL   B45/33F   1984   * DM162 is DR102/40
DM164-7 are DR102/47

156	A475GMS	160	B580MLS	164	B89PKS	166	B91PKS	167	B92PKS
159	B579MLS	162	B586MLS	165w	B90PKS				

DM168	G390OGD	MCW Metrobus DR102/72	MCW	B46/31F	1989	
GM63	H844UUA	Optare MetroRider	Optare	B29F	1991	Optare demonstrator, 1991

LO1	C807KHS	Leyland Olympian ONLXB/1RH	Alexander RL	BC47/27F	1986	Kelvin Central, 1993
LO2	C808KHS	Leyland Olympian ONLXB/1RH	Alexander RL	BC47/27F	1986	Kelvin Central, 1993
LO3	C810KHS	Leyland Olympian ONLXB/1RH	Alexander RL	BC47/27F	1986	Kelvin Central, 1993
LO4	C113BTS	Leyland Olympian ONLXB/1RV	Alexander RL	B47/32F	1986	Kelvin Central, 1993
LO5	C114BTS	Leyland Olympian ONLXB/1RV	Alexander RL	B47/32F	1986	Kelvin Central, 1993
LO6	C115BTS	Leyland Olympian ONLXB/1RV	Alexander RL	B47/32F	1986	Kelvin Central, 1993
LO12	CGG835X	Leyland Olympian ONTL11/1R	Eastern Coach Works	B46/31F	1982	
LO14	CGG837X	Leyland Olympian ONTL11/1R	Eastern Coach Works	B46/31F	1982	

LO22-45

Leyland Olympian ONTL11/1R   Eastern Coach Works   B47/31F   1983

22	KGG142Y	26	KGG146Y	34	KGG154Y	42	A371TGB	44	A373TGB
23	KGG143Y	31	KGG151Y	35	KGG155Y	43	A372TGB	45	A374TGB
25	KGG145Y	32	KGG152Y	41	KGG161Y				

LO48	J137FYS	Leyland Olympian ON2R50G13Z4	Leyland	B47/31F	1991	
LO49	J138FYS	Leyland Olympian ON2R50G13Z4	Leyland	B47/31F	1991	

LO50-101

Leyland Olympian ON2R50C13V3   Alexander RL   B47/31F   1993

50	K350SDS	61	L161UNS	72	L172UNS	82	L182UNS	92	L192UNS
51	L551USU	62	L162UNS	73	L173UNS	83	L183UNS	93	L193UNS
52	L552USU	63	L163UNS	74	L174UNS	84	L184UNS	94	L194UNS
53	L553USU	64	L164UNS	75	L175UNS	85	L185UNS	95	L195UNS
54	L554USU	65	L165UNS	76	L176UNS	86	L186UNS	96	L196UNS
55	L155UNS	66	L166UNS	77	L177UNS	87	L187UNS	97	L197UNS
56	L156UNS	67	L167UNS	78	L178UNS	88	L188UNS	98	L198UNS
57	L157UNS	68	L168UNS	79	L179UNS	89	L189UNS	99	L199UNS
58	L158UNS	69	L169UNS	80	L180UNS	90	L190UNS	100	L202UNS
59	L159UNS	70	L170UNS	81	L181UNS	91	L191UNS	101	L201UNS
60	L160UNS	71	L171UNS						

LO102	C448BKM	Leyland Olympian ONTL11/2RSp	Eastern Coach Works	C45/28F	1985	Northumbria, 1995
LO103	C212UPD	Leyland Olympian ONTL11/2RSp	Eastern Coach Works	C45/28F	1985	Northumbria, 1995
LO104	C213UPD	Leyland Olympian ONTL11/2RSp	Eastern Coach Works	C45/28F	1985	Northumbria, 1995
LO105	C211UPD	Leyland Olympian ONTL11/2RSp	Eastern Coach Works	C45/28F	1985	Northumbria, 1995
LO115	ALS120Y	Leyland Olympian ONLXB/1R	Alexander RL	B45/32F	1983	
LO117	ALS130Y	Leyland Olympian ONLXB/1R	Alexander RL	B45/32F	1983	
LO118	ALS131Y	Leyland Olympian ONLXB/1R	Alexander RL	B45/32F	1983	
LO119	C112BTS	Leyland Olympian ONLXB/1RV	Alexander RL	B47/32F	1986	Strathtay, 1989
LO123	A981FLS	Leyland Olympian ONLXB/1R	Alexander RL	B45/32F	1983	Fife Scottish, 1989
LO124	A982FLS	Leyland Olympian ONLXB/1R	Alexander RL	B45/32F	1983	Fife Scottish, 1989
LO125	A983FLS	Leyland Olympian ONLXB/1R	Alexander RL	B45/32F	1983	Fife Scottish, 1989
LO126	A984FLS	Leyland Olympian ONLXB/1R	Alexander RL	B45/32F	1983	Fife Scottish, 1989

MA133-161

Mercedes-Benz 811D   Alexander AM   B28F   1988   CentreWest, 1997
*133/45/61 are B26F; 160 is BC28F

133	F611XMS	137	F627XMS	143	F691XMS	149	F661XMS	156	F690XMS
134	F613XMS	139	F632XMS	144	F692XMS	151	F663XMS	159	F693XMS
135	F618XMS	140	F658XMS	145	F639XMS	154	F676XMS	160	F702XMS
136	F622XMS	142	F659XMS	148	F660XMS	155	F687XMS	161	F947BMS

Following the withdrawal of First Glasgow's last MetroRiders in 1998, minibus services are now operated by various Mercedes-Benz models. During 1998, eight Vario O814 models were transferred from Essex Buses' Eastern National operation with a further six from Yorkshire Rider. Pictured shortly after being repainted in Glasgow's colours is MA208, P708PWC. *Billy Nicol*

MA162-168

Mercedes-Benz 709D — Plaxton Beaver — B23F — 1994-95 — Yorkshire Rider, 1998

162	M201VWU	164	M254VWU	166	M256VWU	167	M260VWU	168	M261VWU
163	M208VWU	165	M255VWU						

MA201-208

Mercedes-Benz Vario O814 — Plaxton Beaver 2 — B27F — 1997 — Essex Buses, 1998

201	P701PWC	203	P703PWC	205	P705PWC	207	P707PWC	208	P708PWC
202	P702PWC	204	P704PWC	206	P706PWC				

MA209	R401HYG	Mercedes-Benz Vario O814	Plaxton Beaver 2	B27F	1998	Yorkshire Rider, 1998
MA210	R402HYG	Mercedes-Benz Vario O814	Plaxton Beaver 2	B27F	1998	Yorkshire Rider, 1998
MA211	R403HYG	Mercedes-Benz Vario O814	Plaxton Beaver 2	B27F	1998	Yorkshire Rider, 1998
MA212	R404HYG	Mercedes-Benz Vario O814	Plaxton Beaver 2	B27F	1998	Yorkshire Rider, 1998
MA213	S271LGA	Mercedes-Benz Vario O814	Plaxton Beaver 2	B27F	1998	Yorkshire Rider, 1998
MA214	S272LGA	Mercedes-Benz Vario O814	Plaxton Beaver 2	B27F	1998	Yorkshire Rider, 1998

MB46-70

MCW Metrobus DR102/072 — MCW — B46/31F* — 1989 — *62-6 are BC43/29F

46	G384OGD	51	G389OGD	57	G395OGD	62	G400OGD	67	G405OGD
47	G385OGD	53	G391OGD	58	G396OGD	63	G401OGD	68	G406OGD
48	G386OGD	54	G392OGD	59	G397OGD	64	G402OGD	69	G407OGD
49	G387OGD	55	G393OGD	60	G398OGD	65	G403OGD	70	G408OGD
50	G388OGD	56	G394OGD	61	G399OGD	66	G404OGD		

MD1-8

Dennis Dart SLF — East Lancashire Spryte — N37F — 1997

1	P852VUS	3	P854VUS	5	P856VUS	7	P858VUS	8	P859VUS
2	P853VUS	4	P855VUS	6	P857VUS				

MD9	P860VUS	Dennis Dart	Plaxton Pointer	B40F	1997
MD10	P861VUS	Dennis Dart	Plaxton Pointer	B40F	1997

MD13-18

Dennis Dart 9.8SDL3017 — Alexander Dash — B41F — 1992 — Ex Stagecoach Scotland, 1992

13	J513FPS	15	J515FPS	16	J516FPS	17	J517FPS	18	J518FPS
14	J514FPS								

MD19-28

Dennis Dart SLF — Plaxton Pointer — N40F — 1997

19	P626WSU	21	P628WSU	23	P630WSU	25	P632WSU	27	P634WSU
20	P627WSU	22	P629WSU	24	P631WSU	26	P633WSU	28	P635WSU

MD29-43

Dennis Dart SLF — UVG Urbanstar — N39F — 1997 — 29 UVG demonstrator, 1997

29	P2UVG	32	P750XUS	35	P753XUS	38	P757XUS	41	P760XUS
30	P748XUS	33	P751XUS	36	P754XUS	39	P758XUS	42	P761XUS
31	P749XUS	34	P752XUS	37	P756XUS	40	P759XUS	43	P762XUS

MD44-56

Dennis Dart SLF — Plaxton Pointer — N35F — 1997 — Yorkshire Rider, 1997

44	P819YUM	46	P890TCV	48	P823YUM	50	P825YUM	55	P830YUM
45	P889TCV	47	P822YUM	49	P824YUM	54	P829YUM	56	P831YUM

MD57-68

Dennis Dart SLF — Plaxton Pointer 2 — N37F — 1997

57	R631DUS	60	R634DUS	63	R638DUS	65	R665DUS	67	R667DUS
58	R632DUS	61	R636DUS	64	R664DUS	66	R757DYS	68	R668DUS
59	R633DUS	62	R637DUS						

MD69-118

Dennis Dart SLF — Plaxton Pointer 2 — N37F — 1998

69	R301GHS	79	R312GHS	89	R670DUS	99	R759DYS	109	R290GHS
70	R302GHS	80	R313GHS	90	R671DUS	100	R641DUS	110	R291GHS
71	R303GHS	81	R314GHS	91	R672DUS	101	R642DUS	111	R292GHS
72	R304GHS	82	R315GHS	92	R673DUS	102	R643DUS	112	R293GHS
73	R305GHS	83	R316GHS	93	R674DUS	103	R644DUS	113	R294GHS
74	R307GHS	84	R319GHS	94	R675DUS	104	R645DUS	114	R295GHS
75	R308GHS	85	R321GHS	95	R676DUS	105	R646DUS	115	R296GHS
76	R309GHS	86	R322GHS	96	R677DUS	106	R647DUS	116	R297GHS
77	R310GHS	87	R324GHS	97	R678DUS	107	R288GHS	117	R298GHS
78	R311GHS	88	R669DUS	98	R758DYS	108	R289GHS	118	R299GHS

MV21-28

Volvo B6-9.9M — Alexander Dash — B40F — 1994 — 27/8 Loch Lomond Cs, 1996

21	L101WYS	23	L103WYS	25	L105XSU	27	M870DYS	28	M871DYS
22	L102WYS	24	L104WYS	26	L106XSU				

MV29-48

Volvo B6LE — Alexander ALX200 — N35F — 1997

29	P508VOS	33	P513VOS	37	P814YUM	41	P818YUM	45	P810YUM
30	P510VOS	34	P514VOS	38	P815YUM	42	P807YUM	46	P811YUM
31	P511VOS	35	P515VOS	39	P816YUM	43	P808YUM	47	P812YUM
32	P512VOS	36	P516VOS	40	P817YUM	44	P809YUM	48	P813YUM

SD11-15

Dennis Dorchester SDA804 — Alexander TS — B53F — 1983

11	A101RGE	12	A102RGE	13	A103RGE	14	A104RGE	15	A105RGE

SS1	H912HRO	Scania N113CRB	Plaxton Verde	B47F	1991	Scania demonstrator, 1993
SS2	J113XSX	Scania N113CRB	Plaxton Verde	B51F	1992	Scania demonstrator, 1993
SS3	TIB8511	Scania K93CRB	East Lancashire	BC51F	1993	
SS4	TIB8512	Scania K93CRB	East Lancashire	BC51F	1993	
SS5	TIB8513	Scania K93CRB	East Lancashire	BC51F	1993	
SS6	P106MFS	Scania L113CRL	Wright Axcess-ultralow	N47F	1996	
SS7	P107MFS	Scania L113CRL	Wright Axcess-ultralow	N47F	1996	
SS8	P108MFS	Scania L113CRL	Wright Axcess-ultralow	N47F	1996	
SS9	P109MFS	Scania L113CRL	Wright Axcess-ultralow	N47F	1996	

Fifty-two Leyland Olympians with low-height Alexander bodywork were delivered to Strathclyde Buses in 1993 and all are now in the allover red livery of First Glasgow. Pictured at Clydebank is LO76, L176UNS. In other parts of FirstGroup low-height buses such as these are being cascaded to depots where the type is needed to meet operational requirements, such as Norwich. *Billy Nicol*

The 1997 single-deck midi-buses for First Glasgow included twenty Volvo B6BLE low floor buses with Alexander ALX200 bodywork. These have entered service at Dumbarton, Knightswood and Park Head. Pictured in West Regent Street is MV32, P512VOS from the latter depot. *Murdoch Currie*

SS10-50

Scania L113CRL — Wright Axcess-ultralow — N40F — 1997

No	Reg	No	Reg	No	Reg	No	Reg	No	Reg
10	R110GSF	19	R119GSF	27	R127GSF	35	R135GSF	43	R143GSF
11	R211GSF	20	R120GSF	28	R128GSF	36	R136GSF	44	R144GSF
12	R112GSF	21	R121GSF	29	R129GSF	37	R137GSF	45	R145GSF
13	P113YSH	22	R122GSF	30	R130GSF	38	R138GSF	46	R146GSF
14	R114GSF	23	R123GSF	31	R131GSF	39	R139GSF	47	R147GSF
15	R115GSF	24	R124GSF	32	R132GSF	40	R140GSF	48	R148GSF
16	R116GSF	25	R125GSF	33	R133GSF	41	R141GSF	49	R149GSF
17	R117GSF	26	R126GSF	34	R134GSF	42	R142GSF	50	R150GSF
18	R118GSF								

SS51-83

Scania L113CRL — Wright Axcess-ultralow — N40F — 1997-98

No	Reg	No	Reg	No	Reg	No	Reg	No	Reg
51	R151GSF	58	R158GSF	65	R165GSF	72	R172GSX	78	R178GSX
52	R152GSF	59	R159GSF	66	R166GSF	73	R173GSX	79	R179GSX
53	R153GSF	60	R160GSF	67	R167GSF	74	R174GSX	80	R180GSX
54	R154GSF	61	R161GSF	68	R168GSF	75	R175GSX	81	R181GSX
55	R155GSF	62	R162GSF	69	R169GSF	76	R176GSX	82	R182GSX
56	R156GSF	63	R163GSF	70	R170GSF	77	R177GSX	83	R183GSX
57	R157GSF	64	R164GSF	71	R171GSF				

SS84-91

Scania L113CRL — Wright Axcess-ultralow — N40F — 1998

No	Reg	No	Reg	No	Reg	No	Reg	No	Reg
84	S684BFS	86	S686BFS	88	S688BFS	90	S690BFS	91	S691BFS
85	S685BFS	87	S687BFS	89	S689BFS				

SS92-100

Scania L94UB — Wright Axcess Floline — N40F* — 1998 — *95 is N43F

No	Reg	No	Reg	No	Reg	No	Reg	No	Reg
92	S692BFS	94	S694BFS	96	S686BFS	98	S698BFS	100	S701BFS
93	S693BFS	95	R195GSX	97	S697BFS	99	S699BFS		

ST333-398

Leyland Tiger TRBLXB/2RH — Alexander TS — B53F — 1984-87

No	Reg	No	Reg	No	Reg	No	Reg	No	Reg
333	A33VDS	350	A30VDS	361	B261BYS	371	B251BYS	389	D374OSU
335w	A35VDS	351	A31VDS	362w	B262BYS	372	B252BYS	390	D375OSU
338	A38VDS	353	B253BYS	363	B263BYS	373	B241BYS	391	D376OSU
339	A39VDS	354	B254BYS	364	B244BYS	374w	B242BYS	392	D377OSU
340w	A40VDS	355	B255BYS	365	B245BYS	375	B243BYS	393	D378OSU
341	A21VDS	356	B256BYS	366	B246BYS	384	D369OSU	394	D379OSU
342w	A22VDS	357	B257BYS	367	B247BYS	385	D370OSU	395	D380OSU
344	A24VDS	358	B258BYS	368	B248BYS	386	D371OSU	396	D381OSU
345	A25VDS	359	B259BYS	369	B249BYS	387	D372OSU	397	D382OSU
346	A26VDS	360	B260BYS	370	B250BYS	388	D373OSU	398	D383OSU
347	A27VDS								

SV301-310

Volvo B10B-58 — Alexander Strider — B51F — 1993

No	Reg	No	Reg	No	Reg	No	Reg	No	Reg
301	L301VSU	303	L303VSU	305	L305VSU	307	L307VSU	309	L309VSU
302	L302VSU	304	L304VSU	306	L306VSU	308	L308VSU	310	L310VSU

No	Reg	Chassis	Body	Type	Year	Notes
SV402	F706WCS	Volvo B10M-56	Duple Dominant	B53F	1988	Golden Eagle, Salsburgh, '94
SV403	F384FYS	Volvo B10M-56	Plaxton Derwent	BC46F	1988	
SV404	F385FYS	Volvo B10M-56	Plaxton Derwent	BC46F	1988	
SV405	E31BTO	Volvo B10M-56	Plaxton Derwent	BC46F	1988	Grahams, Paisley, 1990
SV406	C982KHS	Volvo B10M-61	Caetano Stagecoach	BC53F	1986	Grahams, Paisley, 1990
SV407	C983KHS	Volvo B10M-61	Caetano Stagecoach	BC53F	1986	Grahams, Paisley, 1990
SV408	C188RVV	Volvo B10M-61	Caetano Stagecoach	BC31DL	1986	Grahams, Paisley, 1990
SV409	G432UHS	Volvo B10M-55	Plaxton Derwent II	B55F	1990	Golden Eagle, Salsburgh, '94

Opposite,top:- **First Glasgow operate almost one-hundred Alexander-bodied Volvo Citybus double-decks. Numerically the last example is AH101, G545RDS, which is seen at Chalmers Street, Clydebank while operating service 11.** *Billy Nicol*
Opposite, bottom:- **The latest double-deck buses for First Glasgow comprise a large batch of Volvo Olympians with Alexander Royale bodywork in the new corporate livery. Based at Knightswood, VO119 was pictured while heading for South Nitshill.** *Paul Wigan*

SV411-428

Volvo B10M-55 | Alexander PS | BC48F | 1994 | Stagecoach, 1995

411	M778PRS	415	M765PRS	419	M769PRS	423	M773PRS	426	M776PRS
412	M779PRS	416	M766PRS	420	M770PRS	424	M774PRS	427	M877PRS
413	M780PRS	417	M767PRS	421	M771PRS	425	M775PRS	428	M428RRN
414	M781PRS	418	M768PRS	422	M772PRS				

SV429-488

Volvo B10M-55 | Alexander PS | B49F | 1995-96

429	N929LSU	441	N941LSU	453	N953LSU	465	N965LSU	477	N977LSU
430	N930LSU	442	N942LSU	454	N954LSU	466	N966LSU	478	N978LSU
431	N931LSU	443	N943LSU	455	N955LSU	467	N967LSU	479	N979LSU
432	N932LSU	444	N944LSU	456	N956LSU	468	N968LSU	480	N980LSU
433	N933LSU	445	N945LSU	457	N957LSU	469	N969LSU	481	N981LSU
434	N934LSU	446	N946LSU	458	N958LSU	470	N970LSU	482	N982LSU
435	N935LSU	447	N947LSU	459	N959LSU	471	N971LSU	483	N983LSU
436	N936LSU	448	N948LSU	460	N960LSU	472	N972LSU	484	N984LSU
437	N937LSU	449	N949LSU	461	N961LSU	473	N973LSU	485	N985LSU
438	N938LSU	450	N950LSU	462	N962LSU	474	N974LSU	486	N986LSU
439	N939LSU	451	N951LSU	463	N963LSU	475	N975LSU	487	N987LSU
440	N940LSU	452	N952LSU	464	N964LSU	476	N976LSU	488	N988LSU

SV489-518

Volvo B10M-55 | Alexander PS | B49F | 1996

489	N89OGG	495	N95OGG	501	N121OGG	507	N127OGG	513	N133OGG
490	N190OGG	496	N96OGG	502	N122OGG	508	N128OGG	514	N134OGG
491	N91OGG	497	N97OGG	503	N123OGG	509	N129OGG	515	N135OGG
492	N92OGG	498	N98OGG	504	N124OGG	510	N130OGG	516	N136OGG
493	N93OGG	499	N199OGG	505	N125OGG	511	N131OGG	517	N137OGG
494	N94OGG	500	N120OGG	506	N126OGG	512	N132OGG	518	N138OGG

SV519-549

Volvo B10M-55 | Alexander PS | B49F | 1996-97

519	P519PYS	526	P526PYS	532	P532TYS	538	P538TYS	544	P544TYS
520	P520PYS	527	P527PYS	533	P533TYS	539	P539TYS	545	P545TYS
521	P521PYS	528	P528PYS	534	P534TYS	540	P540TYS	546	P546TYS
522	P522PYS	529	P529PYS	535	P535TYS	541	P541TYS	547	P547TYS
523	P523PYS	530	P530PYS	536	P536TYS	542	P542TYS	548	P548TYS
524	P524PYS	531	P531TYS	537	P537TYS	543	P543TYS	549	P549TYS
525	P525PYS								

SV550	M10ULF	Volvo B10L	Alexander Ultra	N42F	1995	Volvo demonstrator, 1996
SV551	M394MRW	Volvo B10L	Alexander Ultra	N44F	1995	Volvo demonstrator, 1996
SV552	N141VDU	Volvo B10L	Alexander Ultra	N43F	1995	Volvo demonstrator, 1996

SV553-558

Volvo B10L | Wright Liberator | N43F | 1996

553	P188UNS	555	P190UNS	556	P191UNS	557	P192UNS	558	P193UNS
554	P189UNS								

SV559	P761XHS	Volvo B10L	Wright Liberator	N43F	1997
SV560	P762XHS	Volvo B10L	Wright Liberator	N43F	1997
SV561	P763XHS	Volvo B10L	Wright Liberator	N43F	1997
SV562	P764XHS	Volvo B10L	Wright Liberator	N43F	1997
SV563	R756DYS	Volvo B10BLE	Northern Counties	N44F	1997

SV564-576

Volvo B10BLE | Wright Renown | N43F | 1997-98

564	R326GHS	567	R330GHS	570	R334GHS	573	R337GHS	575	R339GHS
565	R327GHS	568	R331GHS	571	R335GHS	574	R338GHS	576	R340GHS
566	R329GHS	569	R332GHS	572	R336GHS				

The First Glasgow fleet includes three Alexander Ultra low floor buses all based at Possilpark . The model uses the Säffle-design, specially developed for the Volvo B10L. Säffle is a bodybuilder which is part of the Volvo group and based in the Swedish town of the same name. Pictured working route X1 in North Hamilton Street, Glasgow, is SV550, M10ULF, which was latterly a demonstrator for Volvo. *Murdoch Currie*

VO1	M939EYS	Volvo Olympian YN2RV18V3	Alexander Royale	B45/29F	1995
VO2	M940EYS	Volvo Olympian YN2RC16V3	Alexander Royale	B45/29F	1995
VO3	M941EYS	Volvo Olympian YN2RC16V3	Northern Counties Palatine2	B47/30F	1995
VO4	M942EYS	Volvo Olympian YN2RC16V3	Northern Counties Palatine2	B47/30F	1995

VO27-33
Volvo Olympian YN2RV18Z4   Alexander Royale   B45/29F   1994

| 27 | L827YGA | 29 | L829YGA | 31 | L831YGA | 32 | L832YGA | 33 | L833YGA |
| 28 | L828YGA | 30 | L830YGA | | | | | | |

VO34-43
Volvo Olympian YN2RV18Z4   Alexander Royale RL   B47/32F   1994

| 34 | M834DUS | 36 | M836DUS | 38 | M838DUS | 40 | M840DUS | 42 | WLT408 |
| 35 | M835DUS | 37 | M837DUS | 39 | M839DUS | 41 | M841DUS | 43 | WLT976 |

VO44-83
Volvo Olympian YN2RV18V3   Alexander RL   B47/32F   1996

44	N944SOS	52	N952SOS	60	N960SOS	68	N968SOS	76	P176TGD
45	N945SOS	53	N953SOS	61	N961SOS	69	N969SOS	77	P177TGD
46	N946SOS	54	N954SOS	62	N962SOS	70	N970SOS	78	P178TGD
47	N947SOS	55	N955SOS	63	N963SOS	71	N971SOS	79	P179TGD
48	N948SOS	56	N956SOS	64	N964SOS	72	N972SOS	80	P180TGD
49	N949SOS	57	N957SOS	65	N965SOS	73	N973SOS	81	P181TGD
50	N950SOS	58	N958SOS	66	N966SOS	74	P174TGD	82	P182TGD
51	N951SOS	59	N959SOS	67	N967SOS	75	P175TGD	83	P183TGD

VO84-103
Volvo Olympian YN2RV18V3   Alexander RL   B47/32F   1996

84	P184TGD	88	P188TGD	92	P192TGD	96	P196TGD	100	P201TGD
85	P185TGD	89	P189TGD	93	P193TGD	97	P197TGD	101	P202TGD
86	P186TGD	90	P190TGD	94	P194TGD	98	P198TGD	102	P203TGD
87	P187TGD	91	P191TGD	95	P195TGD	99	P199TGD	103	P204TGD

VO104-153 Volvo Olympian Alexander Royale RL B42/29F 1997

104	P585WSU	114	P595WSU	124	P606WSU	134	P616WSU	144	R144EHS
105	P586WSU	115	P596WSU	125	P607WSU	135	P617WSU	145	R145EHS
106	P587WSU	116	P597WSU	126	P608WSU	136	P618WSU	146	R146EHS
107	P588WSU	117	P598WSU	127	P609WSU	137	P619WSU	147	R147EHS
108	P589WSU	118	P599WSU	128	P610WSU	138	P620WSU	148	R148EHS
109	P590WSU	119	P601WSU	129	P611WSU	139	R139EHS	149	R149EHS
110	P591WSU	120	P602WSU	130	P612WSU	140	R140EHS	150	R150EHS
111	P592WSU	121	P603WSU	131	P613WSU	141	R141EHS	151	R151EHS
112	P593WSU	122	P604WSU	132	P614WSU	142	R142EHS	152	R152EHS
113	P594WSU	123	P605WSU	133	P615WSU	143	R143EHS	153	R153EHS

VO154-163 Volvo Olympian Northern Counties Palatine II B43/29F 1997

154	R654DUS	156	R656DUS	158	R658DUS	160	R660DUS	162	R662DUS
155	R655DUS	157	R657DUS	159	R659DUS	161	R661DUS	163	R663DUS

Ancilliary vehicles:

LA1396	RDS585W	Leyland Atlantean AN68A/1R	Alexander AL	TV	1980	
LA1399	RDS588W	Leyland Atlantean AN68A/1R	Alexander AL	TV	1990	
LA1400	RDS589W	Leyland Atlantean AN68A/1R	Alexander AL	TV	1980	
LA1402	RDS591W	Leyland Atlantean AN68A/1R	Alexander AL	TV	1980	
LA1403	RDS592W	Leyland Atlantean AN68A/1R	Alexander AL	TV	1980	
LA1416	RDS605W	Leyland Atlantean AN68A/1R	Alexander AL	TV	1980	
LA1417	RDS606W	Leyland Atlantean AN68A/1R	Alexander AL	TV	1980	
RV2	CHE540K	Leyland Leopard PSU4B/4R	Alexander	RV	1972	Yorkshire Traction, 1982
S56	HGM429E	Leyland Leopard PSU3/3R	Alexander	RV	1967	

Allocations

Cumbernauld (Glencryan Road) - Kelvin

Tiger	CT30	CT66	CT99	ST390	ST391	ST392	ST393	ST394
	ST395							
Volvo B10M	CV4	CV5	CV6	CV7	CV8	CV9	CV10	CV11
	CV12	CV13	CV14	CV15	CV16			
Scania	CS1	CS2						
Dart	MD19	MD20	MD21	MD22	MD23			
Scania	SS3	SS4	SS5					
Metrobus	DM140	DM143	DM144	DM149	DM159	DM160	DM162	DM164
	DM165	DM166	DM167	DM168	CM274	CM275	CM277	CM279
	CM281							
Olympian	CO41	CO211	CO213	CO244	LO3	LO5	LO48	LO49
	VO1	VO2	VO3	VO4	VO34	VO35	VO36	VO37
	VO38	VO40	VO42	VO43				

Dumbarton (Broadmeadow Industrial Estate) - Kelvin

Dart	MD1	MD2	MD3	MD4	MD5	MD6	MD7	MD8
	MD9	MD10	MD28					
Volvo B6	MV21	MV22	MV23	MV24	MV25	MV26	MV27	MV28
	MV29	MV30	MV34	MV39	MV40			
Olympian	CO209	CO214	CO215	CO216	LO119			

Three Caetano Stagecoach-bodied Volvo buses joined Strathclyde Buses in 1990 on the withdrawal of service work with the services of Grahams of Paisley. These are now in the red livery as shown by SV406, C982KHS, which is fitted with high-back seating. *Phillip Stephenson*

Knightswood (Great Western Road, Glasgow) - Glasgow

Mercedes-Benz	MA151	MA154	MA155	MA159	MA160	MA161	MA165	MA201
	MA202	MA203	MA204	MA205	MA206	MA207	MA208	MA209
	MA212	MA213	MA214					
Volvo B6	MV42	MV43	MV44	MV45	MV46	MV47	MV48	
Tiger	CT203							
Volvo B10M/PS	SV413	SV415	SV416	SV418	SV420	SV421	SV422	SV423
	SV242	SV425	SV435	SV438	SV439	SV462	SV500	SV482
	SV483	SV484	SV485	SV486	SV487	SV501	SV502	SV503
	SV504	SV505	SV506	SV508	SV510	SV512	SV514	SV516
	SV519	SV520	SV521					
Volvo Citybus	AH6	AH8	AH14	AH22	AH23	AH24	AH25	AH30
	AH45	AH46	AH59	AH68	AH69	AH70	AH71	AH72
	AH73	AH74	AH75	AH76	AH77	AH78	AH79	AH80
	AH81	AH82	AH83	AH84	AH85	AH86	AH87	AH88
	AH89	AH90	AH91	AH92	AH93	AH94	AH95	AH96
	AH97	AH98	AH99	AH100	AH101			
Olympian	LO1	LO2	LO4	LO34	LO43	LO44	LO124	VO44
	VO45	VO46	VO47	VO48	VO49	VO50	VO51	VO52
	VO53	VO59	VO64	VO65	VO66	VO67	VO68	VO69
	VO70	VO71	VO72	VO73	VO74	VO75	VO76	VO77
	VO82	VO83	VO84	VO85	VO86	VO87	VO96	VO99
	VO100	VO101	VO102	VO103	VO104	VO105	VO106	VO107
	VO108	VO109	VO110	VO111	VO112	VO113	VO114	VO115
	VO116	VO117	VO118	VO119	VO120	VO121	VO122	VO123
	VO124	VO125	VO126	VO127	VO128	VO129	VO130	VO131
	VO132	VO133	VO134	VO135	VO136	VO137	VO138	

Larkfield (Victoria Road, Glasgow) - Glasgow

Mercedes-Benz	MA135	MA137	MA139	MA140	MA142	MA143	MA144	MA145
	MA148	MA149	MA162	MA163	MA164	MA166	MA167	MA168
	MA210	MA211						
Dart	MD79	MD80	MD81	MD106	MD107	MD108	MD109	MD110
	MD111	MD112	MD113	MD114	MD115	MD116	MD117	MD118
Scania	SS1	SS2	SS30	SS31	SS32	SS33	SS34	SS35
	SS36	SS37	SS38	SS39	SS40	SS41	SS42	SS43
	SS44	SS45	SS46	SS47	SS48	SS49	SS50	SS51
	SS52	SS53	SS54	SS55	SS56	SS57	SS58	SS59
	SS60	SS61	SS62	SS63	SS64	SS65	SS66	SS67
	SS68	SS69	SS70	SS71	SS72	SS73	SS74	SS75
	SS76	SS77	SS78	SS79				
Volvo B10M/PS	SV411	SV412	SV417	SV419	SV426	SV427	SV428	SV431
	SV432	SV446	SV447	SV448	SV449	SV450	SV451	SV452
	SV453	SV454	SV455	SV461				
Volvo Ailsa	A2	A5	A8	A9	A11	A16	A17	A20
	A23	A27	A30	A32	A44	A45	A46	A47
	A49	A50	A51	A52	A56	A58	A59	A60
	A62	A65	A67	A74	A75	A76	A77	A78
	A79	A80	A83	A85	A86	A87	A89	A92
	A93	A94	A95	A99	A100	A101	A106	A110
	A114	A119	A120	A122	A123	A124	A125	A126
	A127	A128	A129	A132	A133			
Olympian	LO50	LO51	LO52	LO53	LO54	LO55	LO56	LO57
	LO58	LO59	LO60	LO61	LO62	LO63	LO64	LO65
	LO66	LO67	LO68	LO69	LO70	LO71	LO72	LO73
	LO74	LO75	LO76	LO77	LO78	LO79	LO80	LO81
	LO82	LO83	LO84	LO85	LO86	LO87	LO88	LO89
	LO90	LO91	LO92	LO93	LO94	LO95	LO96	LO97
	LO98	LO99	LO100	LO101	VO154	VO155	VO156	VO157
	VO158	VO159	VO160	VO161	VO162	VO163		

Motherwell (Tinker's Lane) - Kelvin

Mercedes-Benz	MA133	MA134	MA136	MA156				
Dart	MD26	MD27	MD44	MD45	MD46	MD47	MD48	MD49
	MD50	MD54	MD55	MD56	MD57	MD58	MD59	MD60
	MD61	MD62	MD63	MD64	MD65	MD66	MD67	MD68
	MD69	MD70	MD71	MD72	MD73	MD74	MD75	MD76
	MD77	MD78	MD82	MD83	MD84	MD85	MD86	MD87
	MD88	MD89						
Tiger	ST333	ST341	ST346	ST347	ST350	ST353	ST354	ST355
	ST356	ST357	ST358	ST359	ST360	ST361	ST363	ST364
	ST365	ST366	ST367	ST368	ST369	ST370	ST371	ST372
	ST373	ST375	ST384	ST385	ST386	ST387	ST388	ST389
	ST396	ST397	ST398					
Volvo B10B	SV301	SV302	SV303	SV304	SV305	SV306	SV307	SV308
	SV309	SV310						
Volvo B10M/PS	SV402	SV409	SV433	SV434	SV436	SV437	SV440	SV441
	SV442	SV443	SV444	SV445	SV456	SV457	SV458	SV459
	SV460	SV463	SV467	SV469	SV489	SV490	SV491	SV492
	SV493	SV494	SV495	SV496	SV497	SV498	SV499	SV507
	SV509	SV511	SV513	SV515	SV517	SV518	SV522	SV523
	SV524	SV525	SV526	SV527	SV528	SV529	SV530	SV531
	SV532	SV533	SV534	SV535	SV536	SV537	SV538	SV539
	SV540							
Olympian	LO102	LO103	LO104	LO105	CO40	CO57	CO212	CO245
	CO246	CO247	CO248	CO249	VO38			

Parkhead (Tollcross Road) - Glasgow

Scania	SS6	SS7	SS8	SS9	SS10	SS11	SS12	SS13
	SS14	SS15	SS16	SS17	SS18	SS19	SS20	SS21
	SS22	SS23	SS24	SS25	SS26	SS27	SS28	SS29
	SS80	SS81	SS82	SS83	SS84	SS85	SS86	SS87
	SS88	SS89	SS90	SS91	SS92	SS93	SS94	SS95
	SS96	SS97	SS98	SS99	SS100			
Tiger	ST339							
Volvo B6	MV31	MV32	MV33	MV35	MV36	MV37	MV38	MV41
Volvo B10M/PS	SV403	SV404	SV405	SV406	SV407	SV408	SV488	SV541
	SV542	SV543	SV544	SV545	SV546	SV547	SV548	SV549
Volvo B10B	SV564	SV565	SV566	SV567	SV568	SV569	SV570	SV571
	SV572	SV573	SV574	SV575	SV576			
Citybus	AH2	AH3	AH4	AH5	AH7	AH9	AH10	AH11
	AH12	AH13	AH15	AH16	AH17	AH18	AH19	AH20
	AH21	AH26	AH27	AH28	AH29	AH31	AH32	AH33
	AH34	AH35	AH36	AH37	AH38	AH39	AH40	AH42
	AH43	AH44	AH47	AH48	AH49	AH50	AH51	AH52
	AH53	AH54	AH55	AH56	AH57	AH58	AH60	AH61
	AH62	AH63	AH64	AH65	AH66	AH67		

Possilpark (Hawthorn Street) - Glasgow - Kelvin

Dart	MD13	MD14	MD15	MD16	MD17	MD18	MD90	MD91
	MD92	MD93	MD94	MD95	MD96	MD97	MD98	MD99
	MD100	MD101	MD102	MD103	MD104	MD105		
Dorchester	CD91	CD92	CD93	CD94	CD95	CD287	CD289	
Dorchester bus	SD12	SD14	SD15					
Volvo B10M/PS	SV414	SV429	SV430	SV464	SV465	SV466	SV468	SV470
	SV471	SV472	SV473	SV474	SV475	SV476	SV477	SV478
	SV479	SV480	SV481					
Volvo B10L	SV550	SV551	SV552	SV553	SV554	SV555	SV556	SV557
	SV558	SV559	SV560	SV561	SV562	SV563		
Metrobus	MB46	MB47	MB48	MB49	MB50	MB51	MB53	MB54
	MB55	MB56	MB57	MB58	MB59	MB60	MB61	MB62
	MB63	MB64	MB65	MB66	MB67	MB68	MB69	MB70
	DM135	DM136	DM137	DM139	DM146			
Volvo Ailsa	A10	A48	A55	A70	A88			
Olympian	LO26	LO45	LO115	LO117	LO123	VO27	VO28	VO29
	VO30	VO31	VO32	VO33	VO39	VO41	VO54	VO55
	VO56	VO57	VO58	VO60	VO61	VO62	VO63	VO78
	VO79	VO80	VO81	VO88	VO89	VO90	VO91	VO92
	VO93	VO94	VO95	VO97	VO98	VO139	VO140	VO141
	VO142	VO143	VO144	VO145	VO146	VO147	VO148	VO149
	VO150	VO151	VO152	VO153				

Stevenston (c/o Eagle Coaches) - Ayrshire

Dart	MD24	MD25	MD29	MD30	MD31	MD32	MD33	MD34
	MD35	MD36	MD37	MD38	MD39	MD40	MD41	MD42
	MD43							

Unallocated - Greater Glasgow - Kelvin

MetroRider	GM63							
Dorchester	CD286	CD288	CD290	SD11	SD13			
Tiger	ST338	ST344	ST345					
Ailsa	A14	A38	A39	A41	A43	A68	A71	A113
	A117	A118						
Metrobus	DM145	DM150	DM156					
Olympian	LO6	LO12	LO14	LO22	LO23	LO25	LO31	LO32
	LO35	LO41	LO42	LO125	LO126			

YORKSHIRE RIDER

Bradford - Calderline - Huddersfield - Leeds - Quickstep - Superbus- York

Yorkshire Rider Ltd, Kirkstall Garage, Kirkstall Road, Leeds, LS3 1LH

294	M294FAE	Dennis Javelin GX 12SDA2153	Plaxton Expressliner 2	C46FT	1995	Bristol (City Line), 1998
295	M295FAE	Dennis Javelin GX 12SDA2153	Plaxton Expressliner 2	C46FT	1995	Bristol (City Line), 1998
296	M296FAE	Dennis Javelin GX 12SDA2153	Plaxton Expressliner 2	C46FT	1995	Bristol (City Line), 1998
333	SWX533W	Leyland National 2 NL116AL11/1R		B52F	1981	York City & District, 1990
340	SWX540W	Leyland National 2 NL116AL11/1R		B52F	1981	York City & District, 1990
363	PNW603W	Leyland National 2 NL116L11/1R		B52F	1980	York City & District, 1990
368	UWY68X	Leyland National 2 NL116AL11/1R		B52F	1982	York City & District, 1990
371	UWY71X	Leyland National 2 NL116AL11/1R		B52F	1982	York City & District, 1990
746	PUM149W	Bristol VRT/SL3/6LXB	Eastern Coach Works	B43/31F	1980	West Yorkshire, 1989

1001-1030   Volvo B10B   Alexander Strider   B51F   1993-94

1001	K101HUM	1007	K107HUM	1013	K113HUM	1019	K119HUM	1025	L125PWR
1002	K102HUM	1008	K108HUM	1014	K114HUM	1020	K120HUM	1026	L126PWR
1003	K103HUM	1009	K109HUM	1015	K115HUM	1021	L121PWR	1027	L127PWR
1004	K104HUM	1010	K110HUM	1016	K116HUM	1022	L122PWR	1028	L128PWR
1005	K105HUM	1011	K211HUM	1017	K117HUM	1023	L123PWR	1029	L129PWR
1006	K106HUM	1012	K112HUM	1018	K118HUM	1024	L124PWR	1030	L130PWR

1031-1039   Volvo B10BLE   Wright Renown   N51F   1998

1031	R131JYG	1033	R133JYG	1035	R135JYG	1037	R137JYG	1039	R139JYG
1032	R132JYG	1034	R134JYG	1036	R136JYG	1038	R138JYG		

1040-1049   Volvo B10BLE   Wright Renown   N41F   1998   Manchester, 1998

1040	S658RNA	1042	S660RNA	1044	S662RNA	1046	S664RNA	1048	S667RNA
1041	S659RNA	1043	S661RNA	1045	S663RNA	1047	S665RNA	1049	S668RNA

1050	S674SVU	Volvo B10BLE	Wright Renown	N41F	1998	Manchester, 1999
1051	S675SVU	Volvo B10BLE	Wright Renown	N41F	1998	Manchester, 1999
1052	S676SVU	Volvo B10BLE	Wright Renown	N41F	1998	Manchester, 1999
1053	S677SVU	Volvo B10BLE	Wright Renown	N41F	1998	Manchester, 1999

1101-1115   Volvo B10BLA   Wright Fusion   AN53F   1999

1101	T101VWU	1104	T104VWU	1107	T107VWU	1110	T110VWU	1113	T113VWU
1102	T102VWU	1105	T105VWU	1108	T108VWU	1111	T211VWU	1114	T114VWU
1103	T103VWU	1106	T106VWU	1109	T109VWU	1112	T112VWU	1115	T115VWU

1201-1208   DAF SB220LC550   Ikarus CitiBus   B48F   1992

1201	J421NCP	1203	J423NCP	1205	J425NCP	1207	K527RJX	1208	K528RJX
1202	J422NCP	1204	J424NCP	1206	J426NCP				

1251-1255   DAF SB220LC550   Optare Delta   B47F   1989

1251	G251JYG	1252	G252JYG	1253	G253JYG	1254	G254JYG	1255	G255JYG

Pictured in York is Rider group's 1202, J422NCP, a DAF SB220 with Ikarus Citybus bodywork. Currently for the UK market this manufacturer is building solely on DAF chassis/underframes for and is marketed via Arriva Bus and Coach in Gomersal. *David Donati*

1317	LUA317V	Leyland National 2 NL106L11/1R		B41F	1980	WYPTE, 1986
1321	LUA321V	Leyland National 2 NL106L11/1R		B41F	1980	WYPTE, 1986
1329	LUA329V	Leyland National 2 NL106L11/1R		B41F	1980	WYPTE, 1986
1331	VWU331X	Leyland National 2 NL116AL11/1R		B49F	1981	WYPTE, 1986
1333	YWX333X	Leyland National 2 NL116AL11/1R		B49F	1982	WYPTE, 1986
1343	MNW130V	Leyland National 2 NL116L11/1R		B52F	1980	West Yorkshire, 1989
1345	PNW598W	Leyland National 2 NL116L11/1R		B49F	1980	West Yorkshire, 1989
1348	PNW601W	Leyland National 2 NL116L11/1R		B49F	1980	West Yorkshire, 1989

1349-1354

Leyland National 2 NL116AL11/1R — B52F — 1981-82 — West Yorkshire, 1989

1349	SWX537W	1351	UWY72X	1352	UWY74X	1353	UWY75X	1354	UWY90X
1350	UWY69X								

1356	PWY588W	Leyland National 2 NL106AL11/1R		B44F	1981	West Yorkshire, 1989
1367	MHJ723V	Leyland National 2 NL116AL11/1R		B49F	1980	Eastern National, 1994
1368	MHJ726V	Leyland National 2 NL116AL11/1R		B49F	1980	Eastern National, 1994
1370	STW19W	Leyland National 2 NL116AL11/1R		B49F	1980	Eastern National, 1994
1422	L22YRL	Volvo B10M-60	Jonckheere Deauville P599	C49F	1993	
1423	L511NYG	Volvo B10M-60	Plaxton Premiére 350	C49FT	1993	
1424	L541XUT	Volvo B10M-60	Plaxton Premiére 350	C49FT	1994	
1425	L542XUT	Volvo B10M-60	Plaxton Premiére 350	C49FT	1994	
1426	L546XUT	Volvo B10M-62	Plaxton Premiére 350	C49FT	1994	

1451-1460

Volvo B10M-55 — Plaxton Derwent II — B51F — 1990

1451	G451JYG	1453	G453JYG	1455	G455JYG	1457	G457JYG	1459	G459JYG
1452	G452JYG	1454	G454JYG	1456	G456JYG	1458	G458JYG	1460	G460JYG

Morley is the location of this picture of Alexander-bodied Dennis Dart 3261, M261VWW which carries the green and cream livery introduced in 1994. This batch carry the revised frontal treatment applied to the Dash before the ALX200 model was introduced. *Gerry Mead*

1595	JKW215W	Leyland Leopard PSU3G/4R	Plaxton Derwent II (1990)	B55F	1981	Reynard Buses, 1990
1596	JKW216W	Leyland Leopard PSU3G/4R	Plaxton Derwent II (1990)	B55F	1981	Reynard Buses, 1990
1610	B610VWU	Leyland Tiger TRCTL11/3RH	Plaxton Paramount 3200 IIE	C53F	1985	WYPTE, 1986
1619	F619XWY	Leyland Tiger TRCTL11/3ARZA	Plaxton Paramount 3200 III	C53F	1988	
1662	A662KUM	Leyland Tiger TRBTL11/2R	Duple Dominant	DP47F	1983	WYPTE, 1986
2121	T59BUB	Mercedes-Benz Sprinter 410	Olympus	M14	1999	

2202-2293

		Mercedes-Benz 709D		Plaxton Beaver		B25F		1994-96			

2202	M202VWU	2229	M229VWU	2253	M253VWU	2270	N270JUG	2282	N282JUG
2203	M203VWU	2230	M230VWU	2257	M257VWU	2271	N271JUG	2283	N283JUG
2204	M204VWU	2231	M231VWU	2258	M258VWU	2272	N272JUG	2284	N284JUG
2205	M205VWU	2232	M232VWU	2259	M259VWU	2273	N273JUG	2285	N285JUG
2206	M206VWU	2233	M233VWU	2262	M262VWU	2274	N274JUG	2286	N286JUG
2210	M210VWU	2235	M235VWU	2263	M263VWU	2275	N275JUG	2287	N287JUG
2216	M216VWU	2240	M240VWU	2264	N264JUG	2276	N276JUG	2288	N288JUG
2217	M217VWU	2241	M241VWU	2265	N265JUG	2277	N277JUG	2289	N289JUG
2219	M219VWU	2243	M243VWU	2266	N266JUG	2278	N278JUG	2290	N290JUG
2221	M221VWU	2250	M250VWU	2267	N267JUG	2279	N279JUG	2291	N291JUG
2222	M449VWW	2251	M251VWU	2268	N268JUG	2280	N280JUG	2292	N292JUG
2227	M227VWU	2252	M252VWU	2269	N269JUG	2281	N281JUG	2293	N293JUG
2228	M228VWU	2252	M252VWU						

Opposite, top:- First Calderline is the operation based at Halifax and features a livery of white, blue and yellow. Illustrating the batch of Volvo B10Bs, all of which are at Halifax, is 1027, L127PWR. *Paul Wigan*
Opposite, bottom:- The latest product from Optare is the Solo, and FirstGroup have taken a batch of the model for use in Leeds, where six are based, and also in the Potteries. Pictured outside the Corn Exchange in Leeds is 2302, S302EWU which carries Quickstep names. *Tony Wilson*

2301-2306

Optare Solo — Optare — N27F — 1999

2301	S301EWU	2303	S303EWU	2304	S304EWU	2305	S305EWU	2306	S306EWU
2302	S302EWU								

2405	R405WWR	Mercedes-Benz Vario O814	Plaxton Beaver 2	B27F	1998		

2406-2415

Mercedes-Benz Vario O814 — Plaxton Beaver 2 — B27F — 1998

2406	S406GUB	2408	S408GUB	2410	S410GUB	2412	S412GUB	2414	S414GUB
2407	S407GUB	2409	S409GUB	2411	S411GUB	2413	S413GUB	2415	S415GUB

3007-3018

Volvo B6BLE — Wright Crusader — N36F — 1999

3007	T307VYG	3010	T310VYG	3013	T313VYG	3015	T315VYG	3017	T317VYG
3008	T308VYG	3011	T311VYG	3014	T314VYG	3016	T316VYG	3018	T318VYG
3009	T309VYG	3012	T312VYG						

3204-3218

Dennis Dart 9.8SDL3054 — Plaxton Pointer — B40F — 1995

3204	M204VWW	3207	M207VWW	3210	M210VWW	3213	M213VWW	3216	M216VWW
3205	M205VWW	3208	M208VWW	3211	M211VWW	3214	M214VWW	3217	M217VWW
3206	M206VWW	3209	M209VWW	3212	M212VWW	3215	M215VWW	3218	M218VWW

3219-3268

Dennis Dart 9.8SDL3054 — Alexander Dash — B40F — 1995

3219	M219VWW	3229	M229VWW	3239	M239VWW	3249	M249VWW	3259	M259VWW
3220	M220VWW	3230	M230VWW	3240	M240VWW	3250	M250VWW	3260	M260VWW
3221	M221VWW	3231	M231VWW	3241	M241VWW	3251	M251VWW	3261	M261VWW
3222	M450VWW	3232	M232VWW	3242	M242VWW	3252	M252VWW	3262	M262VWW
3223	M223VWW	3233	M233VWW	3243	M243VWW	3253	M253VWW	3263	M263VWW
3224	M224VWW	3234	M234VWW	3244	M244VWW	3254	M254VWW	3264	M264VWW
3225	M225VWW	3235	M235VWW	3245	M245VWW	3255	M255VWW	3265	M265VWW
3226	M226VWW	3236	M236VWW	3246	M246VWW	3256	M256VWW	3266	M266VWW
3227	M227VWW	3237	M237VWW	3247	M247VWW	3257	M257VWW	3267	M267VWW
3228	M228VWW	3238	M238VWW	3248	M248VWW	3258	M258VWW	3268	M268VWW

3269-3298

Dennis Dart — Plaxton Pointer — B40F — 1996

3269	N269JUM	3275	N275JUM	3281	N281JUM	3287	N287JUM	3293	N293JUM
3270	N270JUM	3276	N276JUM	3282	N282JUM	3288	N288JUM	3294	N294JUM
3271	N271JUM	3277	N277JUM	3283	N283JUM	3289	N289JUM	3295	N295JUM
3272	N272JUM	3278	N278JUM	3284	N284JUM	3290	N290JUM	3296	N296JUM
3273	N273JUM	3279	N279JUM	3285	N285JUM	3291	N291JUM	3297	N297JUM
3274	N274JUM	3280	N299JUM	3286	N286JUM	3292	N292JUM	3298	N298JUM

3299	M615SBA	Dennis Dart 9.8SDL3054	Northern Counties Paladin	B39F	1995	Greater Manchester, 1996
3300	M616SBA	Dennis Dart 9.8SDL3054	Northern Counties Paladin	B39F	1995	Greater Manchester, 1996
3302	P302AUM	Dennis Dart SLF	Plaxton Pointer	N39F	1997	
3303	P303AUM	Dennis Dart SLF	Plaxton Pointer	N39F	1997	
3304	P304AUM	Dennis Dart SLF	Plaxton Pointer	N39F	1997	
3305	P305AUM	Dennis Dart SLF	Plaxton Pointer	N39F	1997	

3313-3323

Dennis Dart SLF — Plaxton Pointer — N35F — 1997-98

3313	P826YUM	3314	P827YUM	3320	P833YUM	3321	P834YUM	3323	P836YUM

3336-3340

Dennis Dart SLF — Plaxton Pointer SPD — N41F — 1998

3336	R336HYG	3337	R337HYG	3338	R338HYG	3339	R339HYG	3340	R340HYG

3341	S341EWU	Dennis Dart SLF	Plaxton Pointer 2	N33F	1998	
3342	S342EWU	Dennis Dart SLF	Plaxton Pointer 2	N37F	1998	
3343	S343EWU	Dennis Dart SLF	Plaxton Pointer 2	N38F	1998	
3344	S344EWU	Dennis Dart SLF	Plaxton Pointer 2	N39F	1998	

Recent deliveries to Yorkshire Rider include Volvo B6BLE and Dennis Dart midibuses with Wright Crusader and Alexander ALX200 bodywork respectively. Pictured at Halifax with Calderline names is 3345, S345EWU, the first to arrive and the only one to retain an 'S' index mark. *Tony Wilson*

3345-3356

Dennis Dart SLF · Alexander ALX200 · N33F · 1999

3345	S345EWU	3348	T348EUB	3351	T351EUB	3353	T353EUB	3355	T359VWU
3346	T346EUB	3349	T349EUB	3352	T352EUB	3354	T354EUB	3356	T356VWU
3347	T347EUB	3350	T350EUB						

3359-3363

Dennis Dart SLF · Plaxton Pointer SPD · N41F · 1998 · Essex Buses (EN), 1999

3359	R722HHK	3360	R723HHK	3361	R724HHK	3362	R725HHK	3363	R726HHK

4001-4048

Dennis Lance 11SDA3113 · Plaxton Verde · B49F · 1995

4001	M401VWW	4011	M411VWW	4021	M421VWW	4031	M431VWW	4040	N440VWW
4002	M402VWW	4012	M412VWW	4022	M422VWW	4032	M432VWW	4041	N441ENW
4003	M403VWW	4013	M413VWW	4023	M423VWW	4033	M433VWW	4042	N442ENW
4004	M404VWW	4014	M414VWW	4024	M424VWW	4034	M434VWW	4043	N443ENW
4005	M405VWW	4015	M415VWW	4025	M425VWW	4035	M435VWW	4044	N444ENW
4006	M406VWW	4016	M416VWW	4026	M426VWW	4036	M436VWW	4045	N445ENW
4007	M407VWW	4017	M417VWW	4027	M427VWW	4037	M437VWW	4046	N446ENW
4008	M408VWW	4018	M418VWW	4028	M428VWW	4038	M438VWW	4047	M447VWW
4009	M409VWW	4019	M419VWW	4029	M429VWW	4039	M439VWW	4048	M448VWW
4010	M410VWW	4020	M420VWW	4030	M430VWW				

4049-4078

Dennis Lance · Plaxton Verde · B49F · 1996

4049	N449JUG	4055	N455JUG	4061	N461JUG	4067	N467JUG	4073	N473JUG
4050	N450JUG	4056	N456JUG	4062	N462JUG	4068	N468JUG	4074	N474JUG
4051	N451JUG	4057	N457JUG	4063	N463JUG	4069	N469JUG	4075	N475JUG
4052	N452JUG	4058	N458JUG	4064	N464JUG	4070	N470JUG	4076	N476JUG
4053	N453JUG	4059	N459JUG	4065	N465JUG	4071	N471JUG	4077	N477JUG
4054	N454JUG	4060	N460JUG	4066	N466JUG	4072	N472JUG	4078	N478JUG

Leeds City Link adopted a livery of white with red, orange and yellow stripes and this livery was applied to the first of the Alexander Royale-bodied Olympians supplied in 1997. Shown here is 5606, R606JUB which was heading for Horsforth when seen. *Les Peters*

5018-5081

		Leyland Olympian ONLXB/1R		Roe			B47/29F	1982-83		WYPTE, 1986

5018	UWW18X	5026	CUB26Y	5034	CUB34Y	5042	CUB42Y	5052	CUB52Y
5019	UWW19X	5027	CUB27Y	5035	CUB35Y	5043	CUB43Y	5053	CUB53Y
5020	UWW20X	5028	CUB28Y	5036	CUB36Y	5044	CUB44Y	5054	CUB54Y
5021	CUB21Y	5029	CUB29Y	5037	CUB37Y	5045	CUB45Y	5055	CUB55Y
5022	CUB22Y	5030	CUB30Y	5038	CUB38Y	5046	CUB46Y	5065	CUB65Y
5023	CUB23Y	5031	CUB31Y	5039	CUB39Y	5047	CUB47Y	5077	EWY77Y
5024	CUB24Y	5032	CUB32Y	5040	CUB40Y	5048	CUB48Y	5081	EWY81Y
5025	CUB25Y	5033	CUB33Y	5041	CUB41Y	5051	CUB51Y		

5082-5127

		Leyland Olympian ONLXB/1R		Roe			B47/29F	1982-83		WYPTE, 1986

5082	A82KUM	5092	A92KUM	5101	A101KUM	5110	A110KUM	5119	A119KUM
5083	A83KUM	5093	A93KUM	5102	A102KUM	5111	A111KUM	5120	A120KUM
5084	A84KUM	5094	A94KUM	5103	A103KUM	5112	A112KUM	5121	A121KUM
5085	A85KUM	5095	A95KUM	5104	A104KUM	5113	A113KUM	5122	B122RWY
5086	A86KUM	5096	A96KUM	5105	A105KUM	5114	A114KUM	5123	B123RWY
5087	A87KUM	5097	A97KUM	5106	A106KUM	5115	A115KUM	5124	B124RWY
5088	A88KUM	5098	A98KUM	5107	A107KUM	5116	A116KUM	5125	B125RWY
5089	A89KUM	5099	A99KUM	5108	A108KUM	5117	A117KUM	5126	B126RWY
5090	A90KUM	5100	A100KUM	5109	A109KUM	5118	A118KUM	5127	B127RWY
5091	A91KUM								

5128-5145

		Leyland Olympian ONLXB/1R		Roe			B47/29F	1984		WYPTE, 1986

5128	B128RWY	5132	B132RWY	5136	B136RWY	5140	B501RWY	5143	B504RWY
5129	B129RWY	5133	B133RWY	5137	B137RWY	5141	B502RWY	5144	B505RWY
5130	B130RWY	5134	B134RWY	5138	B138RWY	5142	B503RWY	5145	B140RWY
5131	B131RWY	5135	B135RWY	5139	B139RWY				

5146	C146KBT	Leyland Olympian ONLXB/1R		Optare			CO47/29F	1985		WYPTE, 1986		
5147	C147KBT	Leyland Olympian ONLXB/1R		Optare			CO47/29F	1985		WYPTE, 1986		
5148	C148KBT	Leyland Olympian ONLXB/1R		Optare			B47/29F	1985		WYPTE, 1986		
5149	C149KBT	Leyland Olympian ONLXB/1R		Optare			B47/29F	1985		WYPTE, 1986		
5150	C150KBT	Leyland Olympian ONLXB/1R		Optare			B47/29F	1985		WYPTE, 1986		

5152-5175

Leyland Olympian ONCL10/1RZ Northern Counties B45/29F* 1988 *5165 is B43/29F
*5152 is B39/24F

5152	F152XYG	5161	F161XYG	5165	F165XYG	5169	F169XYG	5173	F173XYG
5157	F157XYG	5162	F162XYG	5166	F166XYG	5170	F170XYG	5174	F174XYG
5159	F159XYG	5163	F163XYG	5167	F167XYG	5171	F171XYG	5175	F175XYG
5160	F160XYG	5164	F164XYG	5168	F168XYG	5172	F172XYG		

5176-5185

Leyland Olympian ONCL10/1RZ Northern Counties B47/29F 1990

5176	G176JYG	5178	G178JYG	5180	G180JYG	5182	G182JYG	5184	G184JYG
5177	G177JYG	5179	G179JYG	5181	G181JYG	5183	G183JYG	5185	G185JYG

5186-5199

Leyland Olympian ONLXB/1R Eastern Coach Works B45/32F 1983-85 West Yorkshire, 1989

5186	FUM486Y	5189	FUM492Y	5194	A686MWX	5196	A600NYG	5198	C483YWY
5187	FUM487Y	5193	FUM499Y	5195	A599NYG	5197	A601NYG	5199	C484YWY
5188	FUM491Y								

5200-5222

Leyland Olympian ONCL10/1RZ Alexander RL B47/32F* 1990 *5207-13 are B47/30F

5200	G623OWR	5205	G605OWR	5210	G610OWR	5215	G615OWR	5219	G619OWR
5201	G601OWR	5206	G606OWR	5211	G611OWR	5216	G616OWR	5220	G620OWR
5202	G602OWR	5207	G607OWR	5212	G612OWR	5217	G617OWR	5221	G621OWR
5203	G603OWR	5208	G608OWR	5213	G613OWR	5218	G618OWR	5222	G622OWR
5204	G604OWR	5209	G609OWR	5214	G614OWR						

5306	L306PWR	Volvo Olympian YN2RV18Z4	Northern Counties Palatine	B47/29F	1994
5312	L312PWR	Volvo Olympian YN2RV18Z4	Northern Counties Palatine	B47/29F	1994
5313	L313PWR	Volvo Olympian YN2RV18Z4	Northern Counties Palatine	B47/29F	1994

5401-5405

Volvo Olympian YN2RC16Z4 Northern Counties Palatine B47/29F 1994

5401	L401PWR	5402	L402PWR	5403	L403PWR	5404	L404PWR	5405	L405PWR

5501	B141RWY	Leyland Olympian ONLXB/1R	Roe	B47/27F	1984	WYPTE, 1986
5502	B142RWY	Leyland Olympian ONLXB/1R	Roe	B47/27F	1984	WYPTE, 1986
5503	B143RWY	Leyland Olympian ONLXB/1R	Roe	B47/27F	1984	WYPTE, 1986
5505	B145RWY	Leyland Olympian ONLXB/1R	Roe	B47/27F	1984	WYPTE, 1986
5506	B506RWY	Leyland Olympian ONLXB/1R	Roe	B47/27F	1984	WYPTE, 1986
5507	C507KBT	Leyland Olympian ONTL11/1R	Optare	B47/27F	1985	WYPTE, 1986
5508	C508KBT	Leyland Olympian ONTL11/1R	Optare	B47/27F	1985	WYPTE, 1986
5509	C509KBT	Leyland Olympian ONTL11/1R	Optare	B47/27F	1985	WYPTE, 1986
5510	C510KBT	Leyland Olympian ONTL11/1R	Optare	B47/27F	1985	WYPTE, 1986
5511	C511KBT	Leyland Olympian ONTL11/1R	Optare	B47/27F	1985	WYPTE, 1986
5512	D512HUB	Leyland Olympian ONTL11/1R	Optare	B43/27F	1987	
5513	D513HUB	Leyland Olympian ONTL11/1R	Optare	B47/27F	1987	
5514	D514HUB	Leyland Olympian ONTL11/1R	Optare	B43/27F	1987	
5515	D515HUB	Leyland Olympian ONTL11/1R	Optare	B47/27F	1987	
5516	D516HUB	Leyland Olympian ONTL11/1R	Optare	B47/27F	1987	
5517	FUM489Y	Leyland Olympian ONLXB/1R	Eastern Coach Works	B41/29F	1983	West Yorkshire, 1989
5518	B518UWW	Leyland Olympian ONLXB/1R	Eastern Coach Works	BC42/29F	1985	West Yorkshire, 1989
5519	B519UWW	Leyland Olympian ONLXB/1R	Eastern Coach Works	BC42/29F	1985	West Yorkshire, 1989
5520	B520UWW	Leyland Olympian ONLXB/1R	Eastern Coach Works	BC42/29F	1985	West Yorkshire, 1989
5521	B523UWW	Leyland Olympian ONLXB/1R	Eastern Coach Works	BC42/29F	1985	West Yorkshire, 1989

5601-5605

Volvo Olympian YN2RV18Z4 Northern Counties Palatine B47/29F 1994

5601	L601PWR	5602	L602PWR	5603	L603PWR	5604	L604PWR	5605	L605PWR

5606-5635   Volvo Olympian   Alexander Royale RL   B43/29F   1997-98

5606	R606JUB	**5612**	R612JUB	**5618**	R618JUB	**5624**	R624JUB	**5630**	R630JUB
5607	R607JUB	**5613**	R613JUB	**5619**	R619JUB	**5625**	R625JUB	**5631**	R631JUB
5608	R608JUB	**5614**	R614JUB	**5620**	R620JUB	**5626**	R626JUB	**5632**	R632JUB
5609	R609JUB	**5615**	R615JUB	**5621**	R621JUB	**5627**	R627JUB	**5633**	R633JUB
5610	R610JUB	**5616**	R616JUB	**5622**	R622JUB	**5628**	R176HUG	**5634**	R634JUB
5611	R611JUB	**5617**	R617JUB	**5623**	R623JUB	**5629**	R629JUB	**5635**	R635JUB

5636-5659   Volvo Olympian   Alexander Royale RL   B43/29F   1998

5636	R636HYG	**5641**	R641HYG	**5646**	R646HYG	**5651**	R651HYG	**5656**	S656FWY
5637	R637HYG	**5642**	R642HYG	**5647**	R647HYG	**5652**	R652HYG	**5657**	S657FWY
5638	R638HYG	**5643**	R643HYG	**5648**	R648HYG	**5653**	R653HYG	**5658**	S658FWY
5639	R639HYG	**5644**	R644HYG	**5649**	R649HYG	**5654**	S654FWY	**5659**	S659FWY
5640	R640HYG	**5645**	R645HYG	**5650**	R650HYG	**5655**	S655FWY		

5660-5665   Volvo Olympian   Alexander Royale RL   B43/29F   1999

5660	T660VWU	**5662**	T662VWU	**5663**	T663VWU	**5664**	T664VWU	**5665**	T665VWU
5661	T661VWU								

6147-6171   Leyland Atlantean AN68/1R   Roe   B43/33F   1976-77   WYPTE, 1986

6147	SUA147R	**6158**	WNW158S	**6163**	WNW163S	**6167**	WNW167S	**6171**	WNW171S
6156	WNW156S								

6177-6191   Leyland Atlantean AN68/1R   Roe   B43/33F   1979   WYPTE, 1986

6177	GWR177T	**6182**	GWR182T	**6185**	GWR185T	**6188**	GWR188T	**6190**	GWR190T
6180	GWR180T	**6183**	GWR183T	**6187**	GWR187T	**6189**	GWR189T	**6191**	GWR191T

6195-6205   Leyland Atlantean AN68A/1R   Roe   B43/32F   1979   WYPTE, 1986

6195	JUM195V	**6198**	JUM198V	**6201**	JUM201V	**6202**	JUM202V	**6205**	JUM205V
6196	JUM196V	**6200**	JUM200V						

6208-6266   Leyland Atlantean AN68A/1R   Roe   B43/32F   1979-80   WYPTE, 1986

6208	JUM208V	**6219**	KWY219V	**6233**	KWY233V	**6246**	KWY246V	**6257**	PUA257W
6209	JUM209V	**6221**	KWY221V	**6234**	KWY234V	**6247**	KWY247V	**6258**	PUA258W
6210	JUM210V	**6222**	KWY222V	**6236**	KWY236V	**6248**	KWY248V	**6259**	PUA259W
6211	JUM211V	**6223**	KWY223V	**6237**	KWY237V	**6249**	KWY249V	**6260**	PUA260W
6212	JUM212V	**6224**	KWY224V	**6238**	KWY238V	**6250**	KWY250V	**6261**	PUA261W
6213	JUM213V	**6225**	KWY225V	**6239**	KWY239V	**6251**	KWY251W	**6262**	PUA262W
6214	JUM214V	**6226**	KWY226V	**6241**	KWY241V	**6252**	PUA252W	**6263**	PUA263W
6215	JUM215V	**6227**	KWY227V	**6242**	KWY242V	**6253**	PUA253W	**6264**	PUA264W
6216	KWY216V	**6228**	KWY228V	**6243**	KWY243V	**6254**	PUA254W	**6265**	PUA265W
6217	KWY217V	**6229**	KWY229V	**6244**	KWY244V	**6255**	PUA255W	**6266**	PUA266W
6218	KWY218V	**6230**	KWY230V	**6245**	KWY245V	**6256**	PUA256W		

Yorkshire Rider has received a batch of Volvo Olympians in corporate livery for use on prime routes. Pictured at Eastgate in Leeds is 5634, R634JUB. The picture may be compared to that shown of the inital vehicle from the batch overleaf.
Gerry Mead

6267-6326   Leyland Atlantean AN68C/1R   Roe   B43/32F   1980-81   WYPTE, 1986

6267	PUA267W	6279	PUA279W	6292	PUA292W	6303	PUA303W	6316	PUA316W
6268	PUA268W	6280	PUA280W	6293	PUA293W	6304	PUA304W	6317	PUA317W
6269	PUA269W	6282	PUA282W	6294	PUA294W	6305	PUA305W	6318	PUA318W
6271	PUA271W	6283	PUA283W	6295	PUA295W	6306	PUA306W	6319	PUA319W
6272	PUA272W	6285	PUA285W	6296	PUA296W	6307	PUA307W	6320	PUA320W
6273	PUA273W	6286	PUA286W	6297	PUA297W	6308	PUA308W	6321	PUA321W
6274	PUA274W	6287	PUA287W	6298	PUA298W	6309	PUA309W	6322	PUA322W
6275	PUA275W	6288	PUA288W	6299	PUA299W	6310	PUA310W	6323	PUA323W
6276	PUA276W	6289	PUA289W	6300	PUA300W	6311	PUA311W	6324	PUA324W
6277	PUA277W	6290	PUA290W	6301	PUA301W	6312	PUA312W	6325	PUA325W
6278	PUA278W	6291	PUA291W	6302	PUA302W	6314	PUA314W	6326	PUA326W

6327-6361   Leyland Atlantean AN68C/1R   Roe   B43/32F   1981   WYPTE, 1986

6327	VWW327X	6334	VWW334X	6341	VWW341X	6348	VWW348X	6355	VWW355X
6328	VWW328X	6335	VWW335X	6342	VWW342X	6349	VWW349X	6356	VWW356X
6329	VWW329X	6336	VWW336X	6343	VWW343X	6350	VWW350X	6357	VWW357X
6330	VWW330X	6337	VWW337X	6344	VWW344X	6351	VWW351X	6358	VWW358X
6331	VWW331X	6338	VWW338X	6345	VWW345X	6352	VWW352X	6359	VWW359X
6332	VWW332X	6339	VWW339X	6346	VWW346X	6353	VWW353X	6360	VWW360X
6333	VWW333X	6340	VWW340X	6347	VWW347X	6354	VWW354X	6361	VWW361X

6428-6435   Leyland Atlantean AN68B/1R   Roe   B43/30F   1980-81   Sovereign, 1989

6428	KPJ257W	6430	KPJ261W	6433	KPJ291W	6434	KPJ292W	6435	MPG293W

6436	ORJ356W	Leyland Atlantean AN68A/1R	Northern Counties	B43/32F	1981	Greater Manchester, 1997
6437	ORJ373W	Leyland Atlantean AN68A/1R	Northern Counties	B43/32F	1981	Greater Manchester, 1997
6438	ORJ400W	Leyland Atlantean AN68A/1R	Northern Counties	B43/32F	1981	Greater Manchester, 1997
6439	SND415X	Leyland Atlantean AN68A/1R	Northern Counties	B43/32F	1981	Greater Manchester, 1997

6443-6450   Leyland Atlantean AN68A/1R   Northern Counties   B43/32F   1980-81   Greater Manchester, 1997

6443	ORJ383W	6445	ORJ389W	6447	SND424X	6449	MNC515W	6450	MNC516W
6444	ORJ388W	6446	ORJ390W	6448	MNC505W				

6453	FVR265V	Leyland Atlantean AN68D/1R	Northern Counties	B43/32F	1979	Greater Manchester, 1998
6454	ANA536Y	Leyland Atlantean AN68D/1R	Northern Counties	B43/32F	1982	Manchester, 1998
6455	ANA557Y	Leyland Atlantean AN68D/1R	Northern Counties	B43/32F	1982	Manchester, 1998
6456	ANA560Y	Leyland Atlantean AN68D/1R	Northern Counties	B43/32F	1982	Manchester, 1998

The number of Leyland Atlanteans is now diminishing as newer buses enter Yorkshire Rider service. From the Huddersfield operation, 6271, PUA271W is seen wearing an almost all-green scheme as it works the Meltnam Circular Rider Huddersfield was known briefly as Kingfisher. *Gerry Mead*

7033	MNW33P	Leyland Fleetline FE30AGR	Roe	B43/33F	1976	WYPTE, 1986
7073	JUW73V	Leyland Fleetline FE30AGR	Northern Counties	B43/31F	1979	WYPTE, 1986
7079	JUW79V	Leyland Fleetline FE30AGR	Northern Counties	B43/31F	1979	WYPTE, 1986
7082	JUW82V	Leyland Fleetline FE30AGR	Northern Counties	B43/31F	1979	WYPTE, 1986
7156	CWU156T	Leyland Fleetline FE30AGR	Roe	B43/33F	1978	WYPTE, 1986
7203	PTD640S	Leyland Fleetline FE30AGR	Northern Counties	B43/32F	1977	G M T, 1987
7204	PTD642S	Leyland Fleetline FE30AGR	Northern Counties	B43/32F	1977	Greater Manchester, 1996
7205	PTD646S	Leyland Fleetline FE30AGR	Northern Counties	B43/32F	1977	G M T, 1987
7211	PTD658S	Leyland Fleetline FE30AGR	Northern Counties	B43/32F	1978	G M T, 1987

7216-7234

Leyland Fleetline FE30GR Northern Counties B43/32F 1978-79 G M T, 1987

7216	XBU9S	7223	ANA25T	7229	ANA40T	7230	ANA44T	7234	BVR55T
7221	XBU17S	7228	ANA34T						

7235-7243

Leyland Fleetline FE30AGR Northern Counties B43/32F 1978-80 G M T, 1987

7235	TWH690T	7237	TWH692T	7241	BCB610V	7242	BCB611V	7243	BCB612V
7236	TWH691T	7238	TWH693T						

7245-7253

Leyland Fleetline FE30GR Northern Counties B43/32F 1979 GM Buses, 1988

7245	BVR65T	7248	BVR70T	7250	BVR85T	7252	BVR92T	7253	BVR97T
7246	BVR67T								

7254	GNF16V	Leyland Fleetline FE30AGR	Northern Counties	B43/32F	1980	Greater Manchester, 1997
7255	KDB136V	Leyland Fleetline FE30AGR	Northern Counties	B43/32F	1980	Greater Manchester, 1997
7256	KDB127V	Leyland Fleetline FE30AGR	Northern Counties	B43/32F	1980	Greater Manchester, 1998
7257	BCB616V	Leyland Fleetline FE30AGR	Northern Counties	B43/32F	1980	Manchester, 1998
7258	DWH686W	Leyland Fleetline FE30AGR	Northern Counties	B43/32F	1980	Manchester, 1998
7259	DWH704W	Leyland Fleetline FE30AGR	Northern Counties	B43/32F	1980	Manchester, 1998

7521-7537

MCW Metrobus DR102/32 MCW B46/30F 1983 WYPTE, 1986

7521	CUB521Y	7525	CUB525Y	7530	CUB530Y	7534	CUB534Y	7536	CUB536Y
7522	CUB522Y	7527	CUB527Y	7531	CUB531Y	7535	CUB535Y	7537	CUB537Y
7523	CUB523Y	7529	CUB529Y						

7542-7580

MCW Metrobus DR102/38 MCW B46/30F 1984 WYPTE, 1986

7542	A542KUM	7550	A750LWY	7556	A756LWY	7563	B563RWY	7575	B575RWY
7544	A544KUM	7551	A751LWY	7558	A758LWY	7566	B566RWY	7577	B577RWY
7545	A545KUM	7552	A752LWY	7560	A760LWY	7567	B567RWY	7578	B578RWY
7549	A549KUM	7554	A754LWY	7561	B561RWY	7570	B570RWY	7580	B580RWY

7581-7595

MCW Metrobus DR102/66 MCW B46/31F 1988

7581	F581XWY	7584	F584XWY	7587	F587XWY	7590	F590XWY	7593	F593XWY
7582	F582XWY	7585	F585XWY	7588	F588XWY	7591	F591XWY	7594	F594XWY
7583	F583XWY	7586	F586XWY	7589	F589XWY	7592	F592XWY	7595	F595XWY

7596-7600

MCW Metrobus DR102/67 MCW B46/31F 1988

7596	F596XWY	7597	F597XWY	7598	F598XWY	7599	F599XWY	7600	F600XWY

7601-7605

MCW Metrobus DR102/69 MCW B46/31F 1988

7601	F601XWY	7602	F602XWY	7603	F603XWY	7604	F604XWY	7605	F605XWY

Scania double-decks joined the fleet in 1990 and while single-decks are scattered across the group only double-decks are based at Leeds and its associated operation, Quickstep. Pictured in Eastgate, Leeds is 8036, H636VNW. *Tony Wilson*

8001-8005

Scania N113DRB   Alexander RH   B47/33F   1990

8001	G801JYG	8002	G802JYG	8003	G803JYG	8004	G804JYG	8005	G805JYG

8006-8010

Scania N113DRB   Northern Counties Palatine   B43/33F   1990

8006	H806TWX	8007	H807TWX	8008	H808TWX	8009	H809TWX	8010	H810TWX

8011-8042

Scania N113DRB   Alexander RH   B47/31F   1991

8011	H611VNW	8018	H618VNW	8025	H625VNW	8031	H631VNW	8037	H637VNW
8012	H612VNW	8019	H619VNW	8026	H726VNW	8032	H632VNW	8038	H638VNW
8013	H613VNW	8020	H620VNW	8027	H627VNW	8033	H633VNW	8039	H639VNW
8014	H614VNW	8021	H621VNW	8028	H628VNW	8034	H634VNW	8040	H640VNW
8015	H615VNW	8022	H622VNW	8029	H629VNW	8035	H643VNW	8041	H641VNW
8016	H616VNW	8023	H623VNW	8030	H630VNW	8036	H636VNW	8042	H642VNW
8017	H617VNW	8024	H624VNW						

8101-8120

Scania L94UB   Wright Axcess Floline   N40F   1998-99

8101	S101CSG	8105	S105CSG	8109	S109CSG	8113	S113CSG	8117	S117CSG
8102	S102CSG	8106	S106CSG	8110	S110CSG	8114	S114CSG	8118	S118CSG
8103	S103CSG	8107	S107CSG	8111	S211CSG	8115	S115CSG	8119	S119CSG
8104	S104CSG	8108	S108CSG	8112	S112CSG	8116	S116CSG	8120	S220GKS

8192-8199

Scania L94UB   Wright Axcess Floline   N40F   1999

8192	T822SFS	8194	T824SFS	8196	T826SFS	8198	T828SFS	8199	T829SFS
8193	T823SFS	8195	T825SFS	8197	T827SFS				

8401-8405 — Scania L113CRL — Alexander Strider — N48F — 1994

8401 M401UUB	8402 M402UUB	8403 M403UUB	8404 M404UUB	8405 M405UUB

8412-8425 — Scania L113CRL — Wright Axcess-ultralow — N48F — 1995-96

8412 N412ENW	8415 N415ENW	8418 N418ENW	8421 N421MWY	8424 N424MWY
8413 N413ENW	8416 N416ENW	8419 N419ENW	8422 N422MWY	8425 N425MWY
8414 N414ENW	8417 N417ENW	8420 N420MWY	8423 N423MWY	

8426-8431 — Scania L113CRL — Wright Axcess-ultralow — N48F — 1997

8426 P426GLS	8428 P428GLS	8429 P429GLS	8430 P430GLS	8431 P431GLS
8427 P427GLS				

8432-8437 — Scania L113CRL — Wright Axcess-ultralow — N40F — 1997

8432 P432RSH	8434 R434GSF	8435 P435RSH	8436 P436RSH	8437 R437GSF
8433 P433RSH				

8438-8463 — Scania L113CRL — Wright Axcess-ultralow — N40F — 1998

8438 R438ALS	8444 S644BSG	8449 R449JSG	8454 R454JFS	8459 R459JFS
8439 R439ALS	8445 S445BSG	8450 R450JSG	8455 R455JFS	8460 R460JFS
8440 R440ALS	8446 S446BSG	8451 R451JSG	8456 R456JFS	8461 R461JFS
8441 R441ALS	8447 S447BSG	8452 R452JSG	8457 R457JFS	8462 R462JFS
8442 R442ALS	8448 S448BSG	8453 R453JFS	8458 R458JFS	8463 R463JFS
8443 S443BSG				

8534	RWT534R	Leyland Leopard PSU4D/4R	Plaxton Derwent	BC43F	1976	Ex WYPTE, 1986

8601-8634 — Scania N113CRB — Alexander Strider — B50F — 1993

8601 K601HUG	8608 K608HUG	8615 K615HUG	8622 K622HUG	8629 K629HUG
8602 K602HUG	8609 K609HUG	8616 K616HUG	8623 K623HUG	8630 K630HUG
8603 K603HUG	8610 K610HUG	8617 K617HUG	8624 K624HUG	8631 K631HUG
8604 K604HUG	8611 K611HUG	8618 K618HUG	8625 K625HUG	8632 K632HUG
8605 K605HUG	8612 K612HUG	8619 K619HUG	8626 K626HUG	8633 K633HUG
8606 K606HUG	8613 K613HUG	8620 K620HUG	8627 K627HUG	8634 K634HUG
8607 K607HUG	8614 K614HUG	8621 K621HUG	8628 K628HUG	

8635	K1YRL	Scania N113CRB	Alexander Strider	BC50F	1993

8636-8655 — Scania N113CRB — Alexander Strider — B48F — 1994

8636 L636PWR	8640 L640PWR	8644 L644PWR	8648 L648PWR	8652 L652PWR
8637 L637PWR	8641 L641PWR	8645 L645PWR	8649 L649PWR	8653 L653PWR
8638 L638PWR	8642 L642PWR	8646 L646PWR	8650 L650PWR	8654 L654PWR
8639 L639PWR	8643 L643PWR	8647 L647PWR	8651 L651PWR	8655 L655PWR

8656	8995WY	Scania N113CRL	East Lancashire European	N46F	1995	Scania demonstrator, 1997

Ancilliary vehicles:

9280	LUG115P	Leyland Atlantean AN68/1R	Roe	TV	1975	
9281	SUA128R	Leyland Atlantean AN68/1R	Roe	TV	1977	
9363	MHS18P	Leyland Leopard PSU3C/3R	Alexander AYS	TV	1976	
9389	ANA209T	Leyland Atlantean AN68/1R	Northern Counties	TV	1978	Greater Manchester, 1997
9390	JUM194V	Leyland Atlantean AN68/1R	Roe	TV	1980	
9391	JUM199V	Leyland Atlantean AN68/1R	Roe	TV	1980	
9397	ABR869S	Leyland Leopard PSU3E/4R	Plaxton Derwent II(1990)	TV	1977	Reynard Buses, 1990
9428	SUA140R	Leyland Atlantean AN68/1R	Roe	TV	1977	
9429	WNW159S	Leyland Atlantean AN68/1R	Roe	TV	1977	
9430	WNW174S	Leyland Atlantean AN68/1R	Roe	TV	1977	
9431	ANA556Y	Leyland Atlantean AN68D/1R	Northern Counties	TV	1982	Greater Manchester, 1997
9432	A737NNA	Leyland Atlantean AN68D/1R	Northern Counties	TV	1984	Greater Manchester, 1997
9973	GMS297S	Leyland Leopard PSU3E/4R	Alexander AYS	TV	1977	Greater Glasgow, ???

Previous Registrations:

8995WY	M78WKX

1993 saw the arrival of the attractive Alexander Strider-bodied single deck Scania buses,and all these are based at depots in Leeds. The type carry the white, orange and red Leeds City Link livery as illustrated by 8616, K616HUG, pictured while working route X11 to Pudsey and Chapeltown. *Tony Wilson*

Allocations:-

Bradford (Bowling Back Lane) - Bradford

Mercedes-Benz	2250	2264	2265	2266	2267	2268	2269	2270
	2271	2272	2273	2274	2275	2276	2277	2278
	2279	2280	2281	2282	2283	2284		
Volvo B10BLE	1031	1032	1033	1034	1035	1036	1037	1038
	1039	1040	1041	1042	1043	1044	1045	1046
	1047	1048	1049					
Scania L113	8438	8439	8440	8441	8442	8443	8444	8445
	8446	8447	8448					
Atlantean	6318	6319	6320	6321	6322	6323	6324	6325
	6326	6336	6352	6353	6354	6355	6356	6357
	6358	6359	6360	6361				
Olympian	5021	5022	5023	5024	5025	5026	5027	5028
	5029	5030	5031	5040	5041	5042	5043	5044
	5045	5046	5047	5048	5065	5077	5081	5082
	5083	5084	5085	5086	5087	5088	5089	5090
	5091	5097	5098	5099	5100	5101	5102	5103
	5104	5105	5106	5107	5108	5109	5110	5111
	5112	5113	5114	5115	5116	5117	5128	5129
	5130	5131	5132	5133	5134	5135	5136	5137
	5138	5139	5140	5141	5142	5145	5146	5148
	5150	5179	5180	5181	5182	5183	5184	5185
	5200	5201	5202	5203	5204	5205	5206	5207
	5208	5209	5210	5211	5212	5213	5214	5215
	5216	5217	5218	5219	5220	5221	5222	5401
	5402	5403	5404	5405	5501	5502	5503	5504
	5509	5510	5511	5515	5601	5602	5603	5604
	5605	5622	5623	5624	5625	5626	5627	5628
	5629	5646	5647	5648	5649	5650	5651	5652
	5653							

Bramley (Henconner Lane, Leeds) - Leeds

Dart	3219	3220	3221	3222	3223	3224	3225	3226
	3227	3228	3229	3230	3231	3234	3235	3244
	3245	3246	3247	3248	3254	3255	3256	3257
	3258	3259	3260	3261	3262	3263	3264	3265
	3266	3267	3268	3341				
Dennis Javelin	294	295	296					
Volvo B10M	1423	1424	1425	1426				
Scania N113	8607	8608	8609	8613	8614	8615	8616	8617
	8618	8619	8620	8621	8622	8623	8624	8625
	8626	8627	8628	8631	8635			
Scania L94	8101	8102	8103	8104	8105	8192	8192	8293
	8194	8195	8196	8197	8198	8199		
Atlantean	6182	6239	6241	6242	6243	6244	6245	6246
	6247	6248	6249	6250	6251	6252	6253	6254
	6255	6256	6257	6258	6259	6260	6261	6262
	6263	6264	6265	6266	6267	6268	6274	6275
	6276	6277	6278	6279	6280	6283	6301	6302
	6303	6304	6305	6306	6307	6308	6309	6310
	6311	6327	6328	6329	6330	6331	6332	6333
	6334	6335	6340	6341	6342	6343	6344	6345
	6346	6347	6348	6349	6428			
Olympian	5032	5033	5034	5035	5037	5051	5052	5053
	5054	5055	5143	5144	5147	5149	5152	5505
	5506	5507	5508	5512	5513	5514	5516	5609
	5610	5611	5612	5613	5614	5615	5616	5617
	5618	5619	5620	5621	5630	5631	5632	5633
	5634	5635	5654	5655	5656	5657	5658	5659

Halifax (Skircoat Lane) - Calderline

Mercedes-Benz	2202	2203	2204	2205	2206	2251	2253	2262
	2263	2292	2293	2405	2406	2407	2408	2409
	2410	2411	2412	2413	2414	2415		
National	1367							
Tiger	1610	1619	1662					
Volvo B10B	1001	1002	1003	1004	1005	1006	1007	1008
	1009	1010	1011	1012	1013	1014	1015	1016
	1017	1018	1019	1020	1021	1022	1023	1024
	1025	1026	1027	1028	1029	1030		
Volvo B10BLE	1050	1051	1052	1053				
Volvo B6BLE	3007	3008	3009	3010	3011	3012	3013	3014
	3015	3016	3017	3018				
Dart	3328	3329	3330	3331	3332	3333	3334	3335
	3345	3346	3347	3348	3349	3350	3351	3352
	3353	3354						
Fleetline	7073	7079	7082	7156	7203	7204	7211	7216
	7221	7223	7228	7229	7230	7235	7236	7237
	7238	7241	7242	7243	7245	7246	7248	7250
	7252	7253	7254	7255	7256	7257	7259	
Olympian	5018	5019	5020	5092	5093	5095	5096	
	5118	5119	5120	5121	5122	5123	5124	5125
	5126	5127	5169	5170	5198	5199	5312	5313
	5314	5315	5636	5637	5638	5639	5640	5641
	5642	5643	5644	5645	5660	5661	5662	5663
	5664	5665						

Huddersfield (Old Fieldhouse Lane) - Huddersfield

Mercedes-Benz	2121	2210	2216	2217	2219	2220	2235	2240
	2241	2243	2252					
Dart	3204	3205	3210	3211	3212	3213	3214	3336
	3337	3338	3339	3340	3359	3360	3361	3362
	3363							
Volvo B10M	1451	1452	1453	1454	1455	1456	1457	1458
	1459	1460						
Scania L113	8432	8433	8434	8435	8436	8437		
Lance	4001	4002	4003	4004	4005	4006	4007	4008
	4009	4010	4011	4012	4013	4014	4015	4016
	4017	4018	4019	4020	4021	4022	4023	4024
	4025	4026	4027	4028	4029	4031	4032	4033
	4034	4034	4036	4037	4038	4039	4040	4041
	4042	4043	4044	4045	4046	4047	4048	4050
	4051	4052	4053	4054	4055			
Atlantean	6201	6221	6224	6269	6271	6272	6273	6282
	6285	6286	6287	6288	6289	6290	6291	6292
	6293	6294	6295	6296	6297	6298	6299	6300
	6312	6314	6316	6317	6338	6339	6350	6351
	6436	6437	6438	6439	6443	6444	6446	6447
	6448	6449	6450	6454	6455	6456		

Leeds (Cherry Row, Leeds) - Leeds

Dart	3276	3277	3278	3279	3280	3281	3282	3283
	3284	3285	3286	3287	3288	3289	3290	3291
	3292	3293	3294	3295	3296	3297	3298	
Lance	4056	4057	4058	4059	4060	4061	4062	4063
	4064	4065	4066	4067	4068	4069	4070	4071
	4072	4073	4074	4075	4076	4077	4078	
Scania L113	8401	8402	8403	8404	8405	8449	8450	8451
	8452	8453	8454	8455	8456	8457	8458	8459
	8460	8461	8462	8463	8464			
Scania N113	8603	8604	8605	8606	8629	8630	8632	8633
	8634	8636	8637	8638	8639	8640	8641	8642
	8643	8644	8645	8646	8647	8648	8649	8650
	8651	8652	8653	8654	8655	8656		
Atlantean	6208	6209	6210	6211	6212	6213	6214	6215
	6216	6217	6218	6219	6222	6223	6225	6226
	6227	6228						
Olympian	5176	5177	5178	5606	5607	5608		

Leeds (Kirkstall Road, Leeds) - Leeds

Scania N113	8601	8602						
Scania L94	8106	8107	8108	8109	8110	8111	8112	8113
	8114	8115	8116	8117	8118	8119	8120	
Volvo B10BLA	1101	1102	1103	1104	1105	1106	1107	1108
	1109	1110	1111	1112	1113	1114	1115	
Atlantean	6167	6171	6177	6180	6183	6185	6188	6189
	6190	6191	6229	6230	6233	6234	6236	6237
	6238							
Metrobus	7521	7522	7523	7525	7527	7529	7530	7531
	7534	7535	7536	7537	7542	7544	7545	7549
	7550	7551	7552	7554	7556	7558	7560	7561
	7563	7566	7567	7570	7575	7577	7578	7580
	7581	7582	7583	7584	7585	7586	7587	7588
	7589	7590	7591	7592	7593	7594	7595	7596
	7597	7598	7599	7600	7601	7602	7603	7604
	7605							
Scania N113dd	8003	8004	8005	8006	8007	8008	8009	8010
	8011	8012	8013	8014	8015	8016	8017	8018
	8019	8020	8021	8022	8023	8024	8025	8026
	8027	8028	8029	8030	8031	8032	8033	8034
	8035	8036	8037	8038	8039	8040	8041	8042

Leeds (Kirkstall Road, Leeds) - Quickstep

Mercedes-Benz	2257	2258	2259					
Solo	2301	2302	2303	2304	2305	2306		
Dart	3236	3237	3238	3239	3240	3241	3242	3243
	3269	3270	3271	3272	3273	3274	3275	
Scania N113	8610	8611	8612					
Atlantean	6147	6156	6158					
Scania N113dd	8001	8002						

Todmorden (Millwood) - Calderline

Mercedes-Benz	2285	2286	2287	2288	2289	2290	2291	
Leopard	8534							
Olympian	5157	5159	5160	5161	5162	5163		
	5164	5165	5166	5167	5168	5171	5172	5173
	5174	5175	5517	5518	5519	5520		

York (James Street) - York

Mercedes-Benz	2221	2222	2227	2228	2229	2230	2231	2232
	2233							
Dart	3206	3207	3208	3209	3215	3216	3217	3218
	3231	3232	3233	3249	3250	3251	3252	3253
	3299	3300	3302	3303	3304	3305	3313	3314
	3320	3321	3323	3342	3343	3344	3355	3356
National	333	340	363	368	371	1317	1321	1329
	1333	1343	1345	1348	1349	1350	1351	1352
	1353	1354	1356	1368	1370			
Leopard	1595	1596						
DAF/Ikarus	1201	1202	1203	1204	1205	1206	1207	1208
DAF/Delta	1251	1252	1253	1254	1255			
Scania L113	8412	8413	8414	8415	8416	8417	8418	8419
	8420	8421	8422	8423	8424	8425	8426	8427
	8428	8429	8430	8431				
Bristol VR	746							
Atlantean	6430							
Olympian	5038	5039	5186	5187	5188	5189	5193	5194
	5195	5196	5197	5521				

Unallocated

National	1331							
Volvo B10	1422							
Fleetline	7033	7205	7234	7258				
Atlantean	6163	6187	6195	6196	6198	6200	6202	6205
	6313	6337	6435	6445	6453			
Olympian	5036	5094						

FIRST MAINLINE

Mainline

Mainline Group Ltd, Rotherham Garage, Midland Road, Sheffield, S61 1TF

79	HHJ379Y	Leyland Tiger TRCTL11/2R	Alexander TE	B65F	1983	Cymru, 1995

112-122		Mercedes-Benz 709D		Plaxton Beaver		BC12FL		1996	
112	N112DWE	115	N115DWE	117	N117DWE	119	N119DWE	121	N121DWE
113	N113DWE	116	N116DWE	118	N118DWE	120	N120DWE	122	N122DWE
114	N114DWE								

123-138		Mercedes-Benz Vario O810		Plaxton Beaver 2		B29F		1998	
123	R123XDT	127	R127XDT	130	R130XDT	133	R133XDT	136	R136XDT
124	R124XDT	128	R128XDT	131	R131XDT	134	R134XDT	137	R137XDT
125	R125XDT	129	R129XDT	132	R132XDT	135	R135XDT	138	R138XDT
126	R126XDT								

246	E406BCT	Renault-Dodge S56	Reeve Burgess Beaver	B25F	1988	Lincoln, 1989
287	SWB287L	Leyland Atlantean AN68/1R	Alexander AL	O43/31F	1973	

303-350		Renault-Dodge S56		Reeve Burgess Beaver		B23F		1990	
303	G303NWB	313	G313NWB	323	G323NWB	333	G333NWB	342	G342NWB
304	G304NWB	314	G314NWB	324	G324NWB	334	G334NWB	343	G343NWB
305	G305NWB	315	G315NWB	326	G326NWB	335	G335NWB	344	H344RKU
306	G306NWB	316	G316NWB	327	G327NWB	336	G336NWB	345	H345RKU
307	G307NWB	317	G317NWB	328	G328NWB	337	G337NWB	346	H346RKU
308	G308NWB	318	G318NWB	329	G329NWB	338	G338NWB	347	H347RKU
309	G309NWB	319	G319NWB	330w	G330NWB	339	G339NWB	348	H348RKU
310	G310NWB	320	G320NWB	331	G331NWB	340	G340NWB	349	H349RKU
311	G311NWB	321	G321NWB	332	G332NWB	341	G341NWB	350	H569SWJ
312	G312NWB	322	G322NWB						

351-389		Renault-Dodge S56		Reeve Burgess Beaver		B23F		1991	387-9 are B21F
351	H351UWB	359	H359UWB	367	H367UWB	375	H375UWB	383	H383UWB
352	H352UWB	360	H390UWB	368	H368UWB	376	H376UWB	384	H384UWB
353	H353UWB	361	H361UWB	369	H369UWB	377	H377UWB	385	H385UWB
354	H354UWB	362	H362UWB	370	H370UWB	378	H378UWB	386	H386UWB
355	H355UWB	363w	H363UWB	371	H371UWB	379	H379UWB	387	H387UWB
356	H356UWB	364	H364UWB	372	H372UWB	380	H380UWB	388	H388UWB
357	H357UWB	365	H365UWB	373	H373UWB	381	H381UWB	389	H389UWB
358	H358UWB	366	H366UWB	374	H374UWB	382	H382UWB		

400	M918MRW	Volvo B6BLE	Wright Crusader	N36F	1995	Volvo demonstrator, 1996
401	K401EDT	Volvo B6-8.5M	Plaxton Pointer	B34F	1992	

411-440		Volvo B6-9.9M		Plaxton Pointer		B40F		1995	
411	M411VHE	417	M417VHE	423	M423VHE	429	M429VHE	435	M435VHE
412	M412VHE	418	M418VHE	424	M424VHE	430	M430VHE	436	M436VHE
413	M413VHE	419	M419VHE	425	M425VHE	431	M431VHE	437	M437VHE
414	M414VHE	420	M420VHE	426	M426VHE	432	M432VHE	438	M438VHE
415	M415VHE	421	M421VHE	427	M427VHE	433	M433VHE	439	M439VHE
416	M416VHE	422	M422VHE	428	M428VHE	434	M434VHE	440	M440VHE

Easy Access single-deck buses have been considered for Mainline and are the forerunner to the low floor models currently entering service. Pictured leaving Sheffield interchange is 448, N448BKY, an early Volvo B6BLE with Wright Crusader bodywork. The letters OG under the fleet number indicate the depot, in this case Olive Grove in Sheffield. *Tony Wilson*

441-455

						Volvo B6-9.9			Wright Crusader		N36F*	1995-97	*450/1 are N32F
*452-5 are NC36F of which two were purchased by Tesco.

441	N441BKY	444	N144BWG	447	N447BKY	450	N450DWJ	453	P453LWE
442	N442BKY	445	N445BKY	448	N448BKY	451	N451DWJ	454	P454LWE
443	N443BKY	446	N446BKY	449	N449BKY	452	P452LWE	455	P455LWE

456-465

Volvo B6BLE   Wright Crusader   N36F   1999

456	T456JDT	458	T458JDT	460	T460JDT	462	T462JDT	464	T464JDT
457	T457JDT	459	T459JDT	461	T461JDT	463	T463JDT	465	T465JDT

500	K945JWE	Dennis Dart 9.8SDL3035	Plaxton Pointer	B36F	1993	Wilfreda-Beehive, 1997
501	K946JWE	Dennis Dart 9.8SDL3035	Plaxton Pointer	B36F	1993	Wilfreda-Beehive, 1997
502	K947JWE	Dennis Dart 9.8SDL3035	Plaxton Pointer	B36F	1993	Wilfreda-Beehive, 1997
503	K948JWE	Dennis Dart 9.8SDL3035	Plaxton Pointer	B36F	1993	Wilfreda-Beehive, 1997
504	L129OWF	Dennis Dart 9.8SDL3035	Plaxton Pointer	B36F	1994	Wilfreda-Beehive, 1997
505	L130OWF	Dennis Dart 9.8SDL3035	Plaxton Pointer	B36F	1994	Wilfreda-Beehive, 1997
506	L970NET	Dennis Dart 9.8SDL3035	Plaxton Pointer	B36F	1993	Wilfreda-Beehive, 1997
507	L971NET	Dennis Dart 9.8SDL3035	Plaxton Pointer	B36F	1993	Wilfreda-Beehive, 1997

508-538

Dennis Dart SLF   Plaxton Pointer SPD   N41F   1998

508	S508UAK	515	S515UAK	521	S521UAK	527	S527UAK	533	S533UAK
509	S509UAK	516	S516UAK	522	S522UAK	528	S528UAK	534	S534UAK
510	S510UAK	517	S517UAK	523	S523UAK	529	S529UAK	535	S535UAK
511	S511UAK	518	S518UAK	524	S524UAK	530	S530UAK	536	S536UAK
512	S512UAK	519	S519UAK	525	S525UAK	531	S531UAK	537	S537UAK
513	S513UAK	520	S520UAK	526	S526UAK	532	S532UAK	538	S538UAK
514	S514UAK								

Opposite:- Displaying Mainline's local colours are two buses that recently entered service. The upper picture shows a non-FirstGroup standard arrival, 526, S526UAK which was ordered prior to takeover. Allocated to Rotherham, this Dennis Dart carries Plaxton Pointer 2 bodywork. The lower picture shows newly-delivered 462, T462JDT, a Volvo B6BLE wlth Wrlght Crusader low floor bodywork.*Tony Wilson*

601-650

Volvo B10M-55   Alexander PS   B51F   1990   *633/4 are B37F

601	G601NWA	611	G611NWA	621	G621NWA	631	G631NWA	641	G641NWA
602	G602NWA	612	G612NWA	622	G622NWA	632	G632NWA	642	H642RKU
603	G603NWA	613	G613NWA	623	G623NWA	633	G633NWA	643	H643RKU
604	G604NWA	614	G614NWA	624	G624NWA	634	G634NWA	644	H644RKU
605	G605NWA	615	G615NWA	625	G625NWA	635	G635NWA	645	H645RKU
606	G606NWA	616	G616NWA	626	G626NWA	636	G636NWA	646	H646RKU
607	G607NWA	617	G617NWA	627	G627NWA	637	G637NWA	647	H647RKU
608	G608NWA	618	G618NWA	628	G628NWA	638	G638NWA	648	H648RKU
609	G609NWA	619	G619NWA	629	G629NWA	639	G639NWA	649	H649RKU
610	G610NWA	620	G620NWA	630	G630NWA	640	G640NWA	650	H650RKU

651-690

Volvo B10M-55   Alexander PS   B51F   1991

651	H651THL	659	H659THL	667	H667THL	675	H675THL	683	H683THL
652	H652THL	660	H660THL	668	H668THL	676	H676THL	684	H684THL
653	H653THL	661	H661THL	669	H669THL	677	H677THL	685	H685THL
654	H654THL	662	H662THL	670	H670THL	678	H678THL	686	H686THL
655	H655THL	663	H663THL	671	H671THL	679	H679THL	687	H687THL
656	H656THL	664	H664THL	672	H672THL	680	H680THL	688	H688THL
657	H657THL	665	H665THL	673	H673THL	681	H681THL	689	J689XAK
658	H658THL	666	H691THL	674	H674THL	682	H682THL	690	J690XAK

691-715

Volvo B10M-55   Alexander PS   B51F   1992

691	J691AWF	696	J696AWF	701	J701AWF	706	K706EDT	711	K711EDT
692	J692AWF	697	J697AWF	702	J702AWF	707	K707EDT	712	K712EDT
693	J693AWF	698	J698AWF	703	J703AWF	708	K708EDT	713	K713EDT
694	J694AWF	699	J699AWF	704	J704AWF	709	K709EDT	714	K714EDT
695	J695AWF	700	J794AWF	705	J705AWF	710	K710EDT	715	K715EDT

716-740

Volvo B10M-55   Alexander PS   B49F   1995

716	M716VET	721	M721VET	726	M726VET	731	M731VET	736	M736VET
717	M717VET	722	M722VET	727	M727VET	732	M732VET	737	M737VET
718	M718VET	723	M723VET	728	M728VET	733	M733VET	738	M738VET
719	M719VET	724	M724VET	729	M729VET	734	M734VET	739	M739VET
720	M720VET	725	M725VET	730	M730VET	735	M735VET	740	M740VET

741-780

Volvo B10M-55   Alexander PS   B49F*   1996   *741-8 are BC49F

741	N741CKY	749	N749CKY	757	N757CKY	765	N765CKY	773	N773CKY
742	N742CKY	750	N750CKY	758	N758CKY	766	N766CKY	774	N774CKY
743	N743CKY	751	N751CKY	759	N759CKY	767	N767CKY	775	N775CKY
744	N744CKY	752	N752CKY	760	N760CKY	768	N768CKY	776	N776CKY
745	N745CKY	753	N753CKY	761	N761CKY	769	N769CKY	777	N277CKY
746	N746CKY	754	N754CKY	762	N762CKY	770	N770CKY	778	N778CKY
747	N247CKY	755	N755CKY	763	N763CKY	771	N771CKY	779	N779CKY
748	N748CKY	756	N756CKY	764	N764CKY	772	N772CKY	780	N780CKY

781-790

Volvo B10BLE   Wright Renown   N44F   1997-98

781	R781WKW	783	R783WKW	785	R785WKW	787	R787WKW	789	R789WKW
782	R782WKW	784	R784WKW	786	R86XHL	788	R788WKW	790	R790WKW

791-814

Volvo B10BLE   Wright Renown   N41F   1998

791	S791RWG	796	S796RWG	802	S802RWG	807	S807RWG	811	S811RWG
792	S792RWG	797	S797RWG	803	S803RWG	808	S808RWG	812	S812RWG
793	S793RWG	798	S798RWG	804	S804RWG	809	S809RWG	813	S813RWG
794	S794RWG	799	S799RWG	805	S805RWG	810	S810RWG	814	S814RWG
795	S795RWG	801	S801RWG	806	S806RWG				

The First Mainline double-deck fleet now comprises just two models, the MCW Metrobus and Dennis Dominators with some withdrawals of both types occuring during 1998. The integral MCW product is represented by 1947, C947HWF, which is one of the later batches to be equipped with high-back seating for suburban services, such as the 240 to Bakewell in Derbyshire, where the vehicle was pictured.
Tony Wilson

815-884

Volvo B10BLE   Wright Renown   N41F   1999

815	T815NAK	829	T829NAK	843	T843NAK	857	T857NAK	871	T871ODT
816	T816NAK	830	T830NAK	844	T844NAK	858	T858NAK	872	T872ODT
817	T817NAK	831	T831NAK	845	T845NAK	859	T859NAK	873	T873ODT
818	T818NAK	832	T832NAK	846	T846NAK	860	T860NAK	874	T874ODT
819	T819NAK	833	T833NAK	847	T847NAK	861	T861NAK	875	T875ODT
820	T820NAK	834	T834NAK	848	T848NAK	862	T862NAK	876	T876ODT
821	T821NAK	835	T835NAK	849	T849NAK	863	T863NAK	877	T877ODT
822	T822NAK	836	T836NAK	850	T850NAK	864	T864NAK	878	T878ODT
823	T823NAK	837	T837NAK	851	T851NAK	865	T865ODT	879	T879ODT
824	T824NAK	838	T838NAK	852	T852NAK	866	T866ODT	880	T880ODT
825	T825NAK	839	T839NAK	853	T853NAK	867	T867ODT	881	T881ODT
826	T826NAK	840	T840NAK	854	T854NAK	868	T868ODT	882	T882ODT
827	T827NAK	841	T841NAK	855	T855NAK	869	T869ODT	883	T883ODT
828	T828NAK	842	T842NAK	856	T856NAK	870	T870ODT	884	T884ODT

1854	JHE154W	MCW Metrobus DR104/6	MCW	B46/31F	1981
1861	JHE161W	MCW Metrobus DR104/6	MCW	B46/31F	1981

1901-1919

MCW Metrobus DR104/11   MCW   B47/33F   1983

1901	UKY901Y	1906	A106XWE	1909	A109XWE	1912	A112XWE	1916	A116XWE
1902	UKY902Y	1907	A107XWE	1910	A110XWE	1914	A114XWE	1917	A117XWE
1903	UKY903Y	1908	A108XWE	1911	A111XWE	1915	A115XWE	1919	A119XWE
1904	UKY904Y								

1921-1940

MCW Metrobus DR104/12   MCW   B47/33F   1984-85

1921	B921CDT	1924	B924CDT	1932	B932CDT	1935	B935CDT	1940	B940CDT
1922	B922CDT	1933	B933CDT	1934	B934CDT	1937	B937CDT		

1941-1950

MCW Metrobus DR102/50   MCW   BC42/28F   1985

1941	B941FET	1943	B943FET	1947	C947HWF	1948	C948HWF	1949	C949HWF
1942	B942FET								

1951	C951LWJ	MCW Metrobus DR102/53	MCW	BC38/28F	1986
1956	C956LWJ	MCW Metrobus DR102/53	MCW	BC42/28F	1986
1957	C957LWJ	MCW Metrobus DR102/53	MCW	BC42/28F	1986

2001-2010

Leyland-DAB 07-1735B-222054   DAB   AB60T   1985

2001	C101HDT	2003	C103HDT	2005	C105HDT	2007	C107HDT	2009	C109HDT
2002	C102HDT	2004	C104HDT	2006	C106HDT	2008	C108HDT	2010	C110HDT

2011	C111HDT	Leyland-DAB 07-1735L-222054	DAB	ABC67D	1985
2012	C112HDT	Leyland-DAB 07-1735L-222054	DAB	ABC67D	1985
2013	C113HDT	Leyland-DAB 07-1735L-222054	DAB	ABC67D	1985

2102-2140

Dennis Dominator DDA133   Alexander RH   B46/32F   1981

2102	KKU102W	2108	KKU108W	2124	KKU124W	2131	MWB851W	2134	MWB854W
2103	KKU103W	2109	KKU109W	2127	KKU127W	2132	MWB852W	2136	MWB856W
2105	KKU105W	2119	KKU119W	2129	MWB849W	2133	MWB853W	2140	OWE140X
2107w	KKU107W	2120	KKU120W						

2143-2220

Dennis Dominator DDA133   Alexander RH   B46/32F   1981-82

2143	NKU143X	2164	NKU164X	2182	NKU182X	2195	NKU195X	2209	NKU209X
2146	NKU146X	2165	NKU165X	2183w	NKU183X	2198	NKU198X	2210	NKU210X
2147w	NKU147X	2167	NKU167X	2184	NKU184X	2199	NKU199X	2211	NKU211X
2148	NKU148X	2168	NKU168X	2185	NKU185X	2200	NKU200X	2212	NKU212X
2149	NKU149X	2169w	NKU169X	2186	NKU186X	2201	NKU201X	2213	NKU213X
2151	NKU151X	2170	NKU170X	2187	NKU187X	2202	NKU202X	2214	NKU214X
2154	NKU154X	2172	NKU172X	2189	NKU189X	2203	NKU203X	2215	NKU215X
2157	NKU157X	2174w	NKU174X	2190	NKU190X	2204	NKU204X	2216	NKU216X
2158w	NKU158X	2175	NKU175X	2191w	NKU191X	2205	NKU205X	2217	NKU217X
2159	NKU159X	2177	NKU177X	2192	NKU192X	2206	NKU206X	2218w	NKU218X
2160	NKU160X	2180	NKU180X	2193	NKU193X	2207	NKU207X	2219	NKU219X
2162	NKU162X	2181	NKU181X	2194	NKU194X	2208	NKU208X	2220	NKU220X
2163	NKU163X								

2221-2274

Dennis Dominator DDA133   Alexander RH   B46/32F   1982-83

2221	SDT221Y	2234	SDT234Y	2244	SDT244Y	2254	SDT254Y	2263	SDT263Y
2222	SDT222Y	2235	SDT235Y	2245	SDT245Y	2255	SDT255Y	2264	SDT264Y
2224	SDT224Y	2236	SDT236Y	2247	SDT247Y	2256	SDT256Y	2266	SDT266Y
2226	SDT226Y	2237	SDT237Y	2248	SDT248Y	2257	SDT257Y	2267	SDT267Y
2227	SDT227Y	2238	SDT238Y	2249	SDT249Y	2258	SDT258Y	2268	SDT268Y
2228	SDT228Y	2239	SDT239Y	2250	SDT250Y	2259	SDT259Y	2270	SDT270Y
2229	SDT229Y	2240	SDT240Y	2251	SDT251Y	2260	SDT260Y	2272	SDT272Y
2230	SDT230Y	2241	SDT241Y	2252	SDT252Y	2261	SDT261Y	2273	SDT273Y
2231	SDT231Y	2242	SDT242Y	2253	SDT253Y	2262	SDT262Y	2274	SDT274Y
2232	SDT232Y	2243	SDT243Y						

2275-2304

Dennis Dominator DDA165   Alexander RH   B46/32F*   1983   *2275 is B46/33F

2275	UWJ275Y	2281	UWJ281Y	2287	UWJ287Y	2293	UWJ293Y	2300	A300XAK
2276	UWJ276Y	2282	UWJ282Y	2288	UWJ288Y	2295	A295XAK	2301	A301XAK
2277	UWJ277Y	2283	UWJ283Y	2289	UWJ289Y	2296	A296XAK	2302	A302XAK
2278	UWJ278Y	2284	UWJ284Y	2290	UWJ290Y	2297	A297XAK	2303	A303XAK
2279	UWJ279Y	2285	UWJ285Y	2291	UWJ291Y	2298	A298XAK	2304	A304XAK
2280	UWJ280Y	2286	UWJ286Y	2292	UWJ292Y	2299	A299XAK		

2311-2320

Dennis Dominator DDA165   Northern Counties   B47/33F   1983

2311	A311XAK	2313	A313XAK	2315	A315XAK	2317	A317XAK	2320	A320XAK
2312	A312XAK	2314	A314XAK	2316	A316XAK	2319	A319XAK		

2351-2365   Dennis Dominator DDA901   East Lancashire   B46/33F   1984

2351	B351CDT	2354	B354CDT	2357w	B357CDT	2360	B360CDT	2364	B364CDT
2352	B352CDT	2355	B355CDT	2358	B358CDT	2361	B361CDT	2365	B365CDT
2353	B353CDT	2356	B356CDT	2359	B359CDT	2362	B362CDT		

2401-2449   Dennis Dominator DDA901   Alexander RH   B46/32F   1984

2401	A401YAK	2411	A411YAK	2419	A419YAK	2429	A429YAK	2439	B439CKW
2402	A402YAK	2412	A412YAK	2421	A421YAK	2430	A430YAK	2441	B441CKW
2403	A403YAK	2413	A413YAK	2423	A423YAK	2431	A431YAK	2442	B442CKW
2405	A405YAK	2414	A414YAK	2424	A424YAK	2433	A433YAK	2445	B445CKW
2406	A406YAK	2415	A415YAK	2425	A425YAK	2434	A434YAK	2446	B446CKW
2407	A407YAK	2416	A416YAK	2426	A426YAK	2435	A435YAK	2447	B447CKW
2408	A408YAK	2417	A417YAK	2427	A427YAK	2436	A436YAK	2448	B448CKW
2409	A409YAK	2418	A418YAK	2428	A428YAK	2438	A438YAK	2449	B449CKW
2410	A410YAK								

2451-2470   Dennis Dominator DDA910   Alexander RH   B46/32F   1986

2451	C871JWE	2455	C875JWE	2460	C880JWE	2464	C884JWE	2468	C888JWE
2452	C872JWE	2457	C877JWE	2461	C881JWE	2465	C885JWE	2469	C889JWE
2453	C873JWE	2458	C878JWE	2462	C882JWE	2466	C886JWE	2470	C890JWE
2454	C874JWE	2459	C879JWE	2463	C883JWE	2467	C887JWE		

2471-2485   Dennis Dominator DDA1011   Alexander RH   BC45/33F*   1986   *Seating varies

2471	D471OWE	2474	D474OWE	2477	D477OWE	2480	D480OWE	2483	D483OWE
2472	D472OWE	2475	D475OWE	2478	D478OWE	2481	D481OWE	2484	D484OWE
2473	D473OWE	2476	D476OWE	2479	D479OWE	2482	D482OWE	2485	D485OWE

2486	D486OWE	Dennis Dominator DDA1013	Alexander RH	BC40/33F	1986
2487	D487OWE	Dennis Dominator DDA1013	Alexander RH	BC40/33F	1986
2488	D488OWE	Dennis Dominator DDA1013	Alexander RH	BC45/24F	1986
2489	D489OWE	Dennis Dominator DDA1013	Alexander RH	BC45/33F	1986
2490	D490OWE	Dennis Dominator DDA1013	Alexander RH	BC45/24F	1986

Special Event vehicles

940	3904WE	Leyland Titan PD3/1	Roe	B39/30R	1959
1156	3156WE	Leyland Titan PD2/30	Roe	B33/26RD	1958

Allocations

Doncaster (Leger Way)

Renault-Dodge	246	311	312	313	314	327	329	339
	340	341	352	353	354	355	356	357
	358	372						
Mercedes-Benz	112	113	114	115	116			
Volvo B6	401	412	415	432	433	434	435	436
	437	438	439	440	450	451	452	453
Dart	500	501	502	503	504	505	506	507
	521	522	523	531	532	533	534	535
	536	537	538					
Volvo B10M/PS	622	640	641	642	643	644	645	646
	647	648	649	650	711	712	713	714
	715	741	742	743	744	745	746	747
	748	748	750	751	752	753	754	
Dennis Dominator	2103	2105	2211	2212	2213	2214	2215	2216
	2219	2220	2255	2258	2259	2260	2261	2262
	2263	2264	2275	2276	2277	2278	2279	2280
	2351	2352	2353	2354	2355	2356	2358	2359
	2360	2361	2362	2364	2365	2436	2438	2439
	2448	2449	2451	2452	2453	2454	2455	2461
	2471	2472	2473	2479	2480	2486	2487	

Crooks is one of the main communities to the west of Sheffield where public transport has been favoured. It is currently the route which First Mainline have chosen for one of its green routes and where the latest buses from the fleet and Yorkshire Terrier may now be found. Seen in the city while heading for Crooks is Wright-bodied Volvo B10BLE 797, S797RWG. *Tony Wilson*

Halfway (Station Road)

Renault-Dodge	344	345	346	347	348	374	375	
Mercedes-Benz	117	118	119	120	121	122		
Dart	509	510	512	519	520	524		
Volvo B10M/PS	612	613	614	615	617	618	619	620
	621	623	624	625	638	639	663	664
	665	666	667	668	669	670	680	682
	686	687	688					
Dennis Dominator	2124	2131	2140	2162	2170	2210	2252	2256
	2257	2292	2401	2407	2408	2409	2411	2412
	2415	2416	2417	2418	2445	2446	2447	2459
	2462	2463	2464	2465	2466	2467	2468	2469
	2470							

Rotherham (Midland Road)

Renault-Dodge	315	316	317	318	319	320	322	323
	326	328	331	371	373	376	381	382
Mercedes-Benz	135	136	137	138				
Volvo B6	411	419	420	421	422	426	427	428
	429	430	431					
Dart	525	526	527	528	529	530		
Volvo B10M/PS	651	652	653	654	655	656	657	658
	659	660	661	662	671	672	673	674
	675	703	704	705	706	707	708	709
	710							
Volvo B10BLE	815	816	817	818	819	820	821	822
	823	824	826	827				
Dennis Dominator	2136	2149	2151	2182	2267	2268	2270	2272

	2273	2286	2287	2288	2289	2295	2296	2297
	2298	2299	2300	2301	2302	2303	2304	2402
	2403	2405	2410	2414	2419	2421	2423	2424
	2425	2426	2427	2428	2429	2430	2431	2433
	2434	2435	2441	2442	2457	2458	2474	2475
	2476	2477	2478	2481	2482	2483	2484	2485
	2488	2489	2490					

Sheffield (Olive Grove)

Mercedes-Benz	123	124	125	126	127	128	129	130
	131	132	133	134				
Renault-Dodge	303	304	305	306	307	308	309	310
	332	333	334	335	336	337	338	342
	343	349	350	351	359	360	361	362
	364	365	366	367	368	369	370	377
	379	380	383	384	385	387	388	389
Volvo B6	400	413	414	416	417	418	423	424
	425	441	442	443	444	445	446	447
	448	449	454	455	457	462	464	
Dart	508	511	513	514	515	516	517	518
Volvo B10M/PS	601	602	603	604	605	606	607	608
	609	610	611	626	627	628	629	630
	631	632	633	634	635	636	637	676
	677	678	679	681	683	684	685	689
	690	691	692	693	694	695	696	697
	698	699	700	701	702	716	717	718
	719	720	721	722	723	724	725	726
	727	728	729	730	731	732	733	734
	735	736	737	738	739	740	755	756
	757	758	759	760	761	762	763	764
	765	766	767	768	769	770	771	772
	773	774	775	776	777	778	779	780
Volvo B10B	781	782	783	784	785	786	787	788
	789	790	791	792	793	794	795	796
	797	798	799	801	802	803	804	805
	806	807	808	809	810	811	812	813
	814							
Metrobus	1854	1861	1901	1902	1903	1904	1906	1907
	1908	1909	1910	1911	1912	1914	1915	1916
	1917	1919	1921	1922	1923	1924	1928	1932
	1933	1934	1935	1937	1939	1940	1941	1942
	1943	1947	1948	1949	1951	1956	1957	
Dennis Dominator	2108	2109	2119	2120	2132	2133	2134	2143
	2146	2154	2157	2159	2160	2163	2164	2165
	2167	2168	2172	2175	2177	2180	2181	2185
	2186	2187	2189	2192	2193	2195	2198	2199
	2200	2201	2202	2203	2204	2205	2206	2207
	2208	2209	2217	2221	2222	2224	2226	2227
	2228	2229	2230	2231	2232	2234	2235	2236
	2237	2238	2239	2240	2241	2242	2243	2244
	2245	2246	2247	2248	2249	2250	2251	2253
	2254	2266	2274	2281	2282	2283	2284	2285
	2290	2291	2311	2312	2313	2314	2315	2316
	2317	2319	2320	2406	2413			

FIRST MANCHESTER

Manchester - Pioneer

First Manchester Ltd; First Pioneer Bus Ltd,
Wallshaw Street, Oldham, OL1 3TR

101-115 Scania L94UB Wright Axcess Floline N40F 1998

101	S101TNB	104	S104TNB	107	S107TNB	110	S110TNB	113	S113TNB
102	S102TNB	105	S105TNB	108	S108TNB	111	S651RNA	114	S114TNB
103	S103TNB	106	S106TNB	109	S109TNB	112	S112TNB	115	S115TNB

116-141 Scania L94UB Wright Axcess Floline N40F 1999

116	T916SSF	122	V	127	V	132	V	137	V
117	T917SSF	123	V	128	V	133	V	138	V
118	T918SSF	124	V	129	V	134	V	139	V
119	T919SSF	125	V	120	V	135	V	140	V
121	V	126	V	131	V	136	V	141	V

301-330 Mercedes-Benz Citaro Mercedes-Benz N--F On order

301	V	307	V	313	V	319	V	325	V
302	V	308	V	314	V	320	V	326	V
303	V	309	V	315	V	321	V	327	V
304	V	310	V	316	V	322	V	328	V
305	V	311	V	317	V	323	V	329	V
306	V	312	V	318	V	324	V	330	V

401-414 Leyland Tiger TR2R62C16Z4 Alexander N B55F 1989 Timeline, 1998

401	G57RND	404	G62RND	408	G66RND	411	G69RND	413	G71RND
402	G58RND	406	G64RND	410	G68RND	412	G70RND	414	G72RND
403	G60RND	407	G65RND						

501-556 Volvo B10B-58 Wright Endurance BC50F 1994-96

501	M501PNA	512	M512PNA	523	N523WVR	534	N534WVR	545	N545WVR
502	M502PNA	513	M513PNA	524	N524WVR	535	N535WVR	546	N546WVR
503	M503PNA	514	M514PNA	525	N525WVR	536	N536WVR	547	N547WVR
504	M504PNA	515	M515PNA	526	N526WVR	537	N537WVR	548	N548WVR
505	M505PNA	516	M516PNA	527	N527WVR	538	N538WVR	549	N549WVR
506	M506PNA	517	M517PNA	528	N528WVR	539	N539WVR	550	N550WVR
507	M507PNA	518	M518PNA	529	N529WVR	540	N540WVR	551	N551WVR
508	M508PNA	519	M519PNA	530	N530WVR	541	N541WVR	552	N552WVR
509	M509PNA	520	M520PNA	531	N531WVR	542	N542WVR	553	N553WVR
510	M510PNA	521	N521WVR	532	N532WVR	543	N543WVR	554	N554WVR
511	M511PNA	522	N522WVR	533	N533WVR	544	N544WVR	556	N556WVR

557-562 Volvo B10L Wright Liberator NC41F 1996

557	N557BNF	558	N558BNF	559	N559BNF	561	N561BNF	562	N562BNF

563-568 Volvo B10L Alexander Ultra N43F 1995-96 Timeline, 1998

563	N301WNF	565	N303WNF	566	N304WNF	567	N305WNF	568	N306WNF
564	N302WNF							

Opposite:- **Two Wright-bodied buses represent the First Manchester operation. The upper picture shows 6513, P513LND in the orange colours now adopted by the company. This batch of Dennis Darts is equipped with high-back seating and was used to inaugurate the Superbus suburban services. Pictured at Stockport on service 400, the former Trans Lancs Express, the vehicle is based at Bury - indicated by the BY letters above the fleet number. The lower picture shows one of a batch of Wright Renown-bodied Volvo B10BLE low-floor buses, 623, R623CVR. This model can be found across the First Manchester operational area.** *Tony Wilson*

571-591   Volvo B10BLE   Wright Renown   N42F   1997-98

571	R571YNC	576	R576SBA	580	R580SBA	584	R584SBA	588	R588SBA
572	R572SBA	577	R577SBA	581	R581SBA	585	R585SBA	589	R589SBA
573	R573SBA	578	R578SBA	582	R582SBA	586	R586SBA	590	R590SBA
574	R574SBA	579	R579SBA	583	R583SBA	587	R587SBA	591	R591SBA
575	R575SBA								

608-618   Dennis Dart 9.8SDL3054   Northern Counties Paladin 2   B39F   1995

608	M608SBA	610	M610SBA	612	M612SBA	614	M614SBA	618	M618SBA
609	M609SBA	611	M611SBA	613	M613SBA	617	M617SBA		

621-655   Volvo B10BLE   Wright Renown   N42F   1998

621	R621CVR	628	R628CVR	635	R635CVR	642	R642CVR	649	R649CVR
622	R622CVR	629	R629CVR	636	R636CVR	643	R643CVR	650	R650CVR
623	R623CVR	630	R630CVR	637	R637CVR	644	R644CVR	651	R651CVR
624	R624CVR	631	R631CVR	638	R638CVR	645	R645CVR	652	S652RNA
625	R625CVR	632	R632CVR	639	R639CVR	646	R646CVR	653	S653RNA
626	R626CVR	633	R633CVR	640	R640CVR	647	R647CVR	654	S654RNA
627	R627CVR	634	R634CVR	641	R641CVR	648	R648CVR	655	S655RNA

656	S656RNA	Volvo B10BLE	Wright Renown	N41F	1998
657	S657RNA	Volvo B10BLE	Wright Renown	N41F	1998

669-673   Volvo B10BLE   Wright Renown   N4ˉF   1998-99

669	S669SVU	670	S670SVU	671	S671SVU	672	S672SVU	673	S673SVU

701	J461OVU	Volvo B10M-50	Northern Counties Paladin	B49F	1991	
1043	N343CJA	Volvo B6-9.9m	Alexander Dash	B36F	1996	
1044	N344CJA	Volvo B6-9.9m	Alexander Dash	B36F	1996	
1047	N347CJA	Volvo B6-9.9m	Alexander Dash	B36F	1996	
1048	N348CJA	Volvo B6-9.9m	Alexander Dash	B36F	1996	
1049	M947OVC	Volvo B6-9.9m	Alexander Dash	B40F	1995	Volvo demonstrator, 1996
1050	M260KWK	Volvo B6-9.9m	Alexander Dash	B36F	1995	Volvo demonstrator, 1996

1051-1070   Volvo B6-9.9m   Northern Counties Paladin 2   B40F   1994-95

1051	M251NVM	1055	M255NVM	1059	M259NVM	1063	M263SVU	1067	M267SVU
1052	M252NVM	1056	M256NVM	1060	M260NVM	1064	M264SVU	1068	M268SVU
1053	M253NVM	1057	M257NVM	1061	M261SVU	1065	M265SVU	1069	M269SVU
1054	M254NVM	1058	M258NVM	1062	M262SVU	1066	M266SVU	1070	M270SVU

1071	N71YNF	Volvo B6LE	Wright Crusader	N37F	1995

1072-1086   Volvo B6LE   Wright Crusader   N38F*   1996   *1072/3/7 are N36F / 1081-6 are N35F

1072	N372CJA	1075	N375CJA	1078	N378CJA	1081	N381CJA	1084	N384CJA
1073	N373CJA	1076	N376CJA	1079	N379CJA	1082	N382CJA	1085	N385CRJ
1074	N374CJA	1077	N377CJA	1080	N380CJA	1083	N383CJA	1086	N386CRJ

1087-1098   Volvo B6-9.9m   Alexander Dash   B38F   1994-95   Timeline, 1998

1087	M201LNC	1089	M203LNC	1093	N207WBA	1095	N209WBA	1097	N211WBA
1088	M202LNC	1092	M206LNC	1094	N208WBA	1096	N210WBA	1098	N212WBA

1101-1106   Dennis Dart 9.8SDL3054   Northern Counties Paladin   B39F   1995

1101	M101RRJ	1103	M103RRJ	1104	M104RRJ	1105	M105RRJ	1106	M106RRJ
1102	M102RRJ								

1119-1138   Dennis Dart 9.8SDL3054   Northern Counties Paladin   B39F   1996

1119	N619CDB	1123	N623CDB	1127	N627CDB	1131	N631CDB	1135	N635CDB
1120	N620CDB	1124	N624CDB	1128	N628CDB	1132	N632CDB	1136	N636CDB
1121	N621CDB	1125	N625CDB	1129	N629CDB	1133	N633CDB	1137	N637CDB
1122	N622CDB	1126	N626CDB	1130	N630CDB	1134	N634CDB	1138	N638CDB

1139	N742GKH	Dennis Dart 9.8SDL3054	Plaxton Pointer	B39F	1996	Ex Plaxton demonstrator, 1996

During 1998, First Manchester acquired the remaining operations of Timeline after the south Manchester and Shropshire routes had passed to Arriva. With the company came six Volvo B10Ls with Alexander Ultra bodywork and ten Optare Excel integrals. Pictured at Bury interchange is Volvo 565, N303WNF. *Cliff Beeton*

The sole Volvo B10M bus, that carries Northern Counties Palatine bodywork, has now moved to Bury. The vehicle is seen while working from its former depot, Wigan, shortly after being repainted into the deep orange colours. *Les Peters*

1140-1153		Dennis Dart 9.8SDL3054	Plaxton Pointer		B40F	1996	
1140	N640CDB	1143	N643CDB	1146	N646CDB	1149	N649CDB	1152	N652CDB
1141	N641CDB	1144	N644CDB	1147	N647CDB	1150	N650CDB	1153	N653CDB
1142	N642CDB	1145	N645CDB	1148	N648CDB	1151	N651CDB		

1161	C41HDT	Dennis Domino SDA1202	Optare	B33F	1985	Pioneer, Rochdale, 1998
1162	C46HDT	Dennis Domino SDA1202	Optare	B33F	1985	Pioneer, Rochdale, 1998
1171	P871TAV	Dennis Dart	Marshall C37	B40F	1997	Pioneer, Rochdale, 1998
1172	P872TAV	Dennis Dart	Marshall C37	B40F	1997	Pioneer, Rochdale, 1998
1401	D501LNA	Leyland Lynx LX563.6LXCTZR1	Leyland	B48F	1986	
1402	D502LNA	Leyland Lynx LX112LXCTZR1	Leyland	B48F	1986	
1403	D503LNA	Leyland Lynx LX112LXCTZR1	Leyland	B48F	1986	
1404	D504LNA	Leyland Lynx LX112LXCTZR1	Leyland	B48F	1986	
1410	M410RND	Iveco TurboDaily 59.12	Marshall C 31	B18F	1995	Citibus, Middleton, 1995
1481	C481CBU	Volvo Citybus B10M-50	Northern Counties	B46/33F	1986	
1482	C482CBU	Volvo Citybus B10M-50	Northern Counties	B46/33F	1986	
1483	C483CBU	Volvo Citybus B10M-50	Northern Counties	B46/33F	1986	
1699	E675KDG	MCW MetroRider MF150/61	MCW	BC25F	1988	Pioneer, Rochdale, 1998

1703-1714		Mercedes-Benz 811D	Plaxton Beaver		B28F	1992	Citibus, Middleton, 1995
1703	J603HMF	1706	J606HMF	1708	J608HMF	1709	J609HMF	1714	J614HMF
1704	J604HMF	1707	J607HMF						

1717	F597FAM	Mercedes-Benz 811D	Optare StarRider	BC31F	1988	MTL (Merseybus), 1995
1719	J619HMF	Mercedes-Benz 811D	Plaxton Beaver	B28F	1992	Citibus, Middleton, 1995
1721	M158LNC	Mercedes-Benz 811D	Alexander Sprint	B31F	1994	Timeline, 1998
1722	M159LNC	Mercedes-Benz 811D	Alexander Sprint	B31F	1994	Timeline, 1998
1723	M160LNC	Mercedes-Benz 811D	Alexander Sprint	B31F	1994	Timeline, 1998
1724	M161LNC	Mercedes-Benz 811D	Alexander Sprint	B31F	1994	Timeline, 1998
1731	J32KLR	Mercedes-Benz 811D	Plaxton Beaver	B33F	1991	Pioneer, Rochdale, 1998
1732	J34KLR	Mercedes-Benz 811D	Plaxton Beaver	B33F	1991	Pioneer, Rochdale, 1998
1733	J35KLR	Mercedes-Benz 811D	Plaxton Beaver	B33F	1991	Pioneer, Rochdale, 1998
1734	J36KLR	Mercedes-Benz 811D	Plaxton Beaver	B33F	1991	Pioneer, Rochdale, 1998

1801-1820		Mercedes-Benz 709D	Plaxton Beaver		B23F*	1995	Yorkshire Rider, 1996-97
							1801/3/6-10 are B20F
1801	M234VWU	1805	M239VWU	1809	M218VWU	1813	M224VWU	1817	M214VWU
1802	M236VWU	1806	M248VWU	1810	M247VWU	1814	M225VWU	1818	M213VWU
1803	M237VWU	1807	M249VWU	1811	M245VWU	1815	M209VWU	1819	M215VWU
1804	M238VWU	1808	M211VWU	1812	M223VWU	1816	M212VWU	1820	M226VWU

1821	M207VWU	Mercedes-Benz 709D	Plaxton Beaver	B21F	1995	Yorkshire Rider, 1997
1822	M244VWU	Mercedes-Benz 709D	Plaxton Beaver	B21F	1995	Yorkshire Rider, 1997

Forty Volvo B10BLA buses are being placed into FirstGroup service during 1999 with fifteen each at Bury and Leeds with the balance of ten going to Glasgow. Pictured during its first week of service on service 135 between Bury and Manchester is 2005, S995UJA.
Cliff Beeton

1831-1835   Mercedes-Benz 811D   Alexander Sprint   B31F   1994   Timeline, 1998

1831	N173WNF	1832	N174WNF	1833	N175WNF	1834	N176WNF	1835	N177WNF

1841	H372OHK	Mercedes-Benz 709D	Reeve Burgess Beaver	B23F	1991	Essex Buses (T), 1999
1842	H374OHK	Mercedes-Benz 709D	Reeve Burgess Beaver	B23F	1991	Essex Buses (T), 1999
1843	H373OHK	Mercedes-Benz 709D	Reeve Burgess Beaver	B23F	1991	Essex Buses (T), 1999
1997	F139HNC	Renault-Dodge S56	Northern Counties	B23F	1988	Pioneer, Rochdale, 1998
1998	F140HNC	Renault-Dodge S56	Northern Counties	B23F	1988	Pioneer, Rochdale, 1998
1999	E181UWF	Renault-Dodge S56	Reeve Burgess	B25F	1987	Pioneer, Rochdale, 1998

2001-2015   Volvo B10BLA   Wright Fusion   AN53F   1999

2001	S111FML	2004	S994UJA	2007	T507JNA	2010	T510JNA	2013	T513JNA
2002	S992UJA	2005	S995UJA	2008	T508JNA	2011	T511JNA	2014	T514JNA
2003	S993UJA	2006	T506JNA	2009	T509JNA	2012	T512JNA	2015	T515JNA

3011-3015   Leyland Olympian ONTL11/1R   Northern Counties   B43/30F   1983

3011	A576HDB	3012	A577HDB	3013	A578HDB	3014	A579HDB	3015	A580HDB

3037-3238   Leyland Olympian ONLXB/1R*   Northern Counties   B43/30F*   1984-86

*3038 is ONLXB/1R (LG1200)
*3218/37 are B43/26F

3037	B37PJA	3073	B73PJA	3108	B108SJA	3152	B152XNA	3202	C202CBU
3038	B38PJA	3075	B75PJA	3109	B109SJA	3157	C157YBA	3203	C203CBU
3040	B40PJA	3076	B76PJA	3111	B111SJA	3159	C159YBA	3204	C204CBU
3041	B41PJA	3078	B78PJA	3112	B112SJA	3160	C160YBA	3206	C206CBU
3042	B42PJA	3079	B79PJA	3113	B113SJA	3161	C161YBA	3209	C209CBU
3043	B43PJA	3081	B81PJA	3115	B115SJA	3162	C162YBA	3211	C211CBU
3044	B44PJA	3083	B83PJA	3116	B116TVU	3163	C163YBA	3217	C217CBU
3045	B45PJA	3085	B85PJA	3120	B120TVU	3168	C168YBA	3218	C218CBU
3046	B46PJA	3090	B90SJA	3123	B123TVU	3171	C171YBA	3219	C219CBU
3047	B47PJA	3092	B92SJA	3127	B127WNB	3177	C177YBA	3220	C220CBU
3048	B48PJA	3093	B93SJA	3128	B128WNB	3180	C180YBA	3222	C222CBU
3050	B350PJA	3096	B96SJA	3129	B129WNB	3182	C182YBA	3223	C223CBU
3051	B351PJA	3097	B97SJA	3130	B130WNB	3183	C183YBA	3225	C225CBU
3052	B52PJA	3098	B98SJA	3131	B131WNB	3186	C186YBA	3227	C227ENE
3054	B54PJA	3099	B99SJA	3134	B134WNB	3187	C187YBA	3228	C228ENE
3059	B59PJA	3100	B100SJA	3136	B136WNB	3188	C188YBA	3229	C229ENE
3061	B61PJA	3101	B101SJA	3140	B140WNB	3189	C189YBA	3231	C231ENE
3062	B62PJA	3102	B102SJA	3141	B141WNB	3190	C190YBA	3232	C232ENE
3063	B63PJA	3103	B103SJA	3142	B142WNB	3192	C192YBA	3233	C233ENE
3064	B64PJA	3104	B104SJA	3144	B144WNB	3194	C194YBA	3235	C235ENE
3066	B66PJA	3105	B105SJA	3148	B148XNA	3200	C200YBA	3237	C237EVU
3068	B68PJA	3106	B106SJA	3151	B151XNA	3201	C201CBU	3238	C238EVU
3071	B71PJA	3107	B107SJA						

The last deliveries of Metrobuses were MCW subframes completed by Northern Counties. All had high-back seating for the then limited stop services and wore a pink livery when new. many are now in normal fleet livery with all bar four based at Oldham. Typifying the type is 5302, D302JVR, which was seen outside Manchester Arndale.
Terry Wightman

3239-3276 — Leyland Olympian ONLXB/1R — Northern Counties — B43/26F — 1986-87

3239	C239EVU	3246	C246FRJ	3253	C253FRJ	3262	D262JVR	3270	D270JVR
3240	C240EVU	3247	C247FRJ	3254	C254FRJ	3263	D263JVR	3271	D271JVR
3241	C241EVU	3248	C248FRJ	3256	D256JVR	3264	D264JVR	3273	D273JVR
3242	C242EVU	3249	C249FRJ	3257	D257JVR	3265	D265JVR	3274	D274JVR
3243	C243EVU	3250	C250FRJ	3258	D258JVR	3266	D266JVR	3275	D275JVR
3244	C244EVU	3251	C251FRJ	3259	D259JVR	3267	D267JVR	3276	D276JVR
3245	C245EVU	3252	C252FRJ	3261	D261JVR				

3278-3305 — Leyland Olympian ONLXB/1RZ — Northern Counties — B43/30F — 1988-89

3278	F278DRJ	3281	F281DRJ	3287	F287DRJ	3292	F292DRJ	3302	F302DRJ
3279	F279DRJ	3284	F284DRJ	3288	F288DRJ	3293	F293DRJ	3303	F303DRJ
3280	F280DRJ	3286	F286DRJ	3290	F290DRJ	3299	F299DRJ	3305	F305DRJ

3401-3410 — Volvo Olympian — Alexander Royale RV — B43/29F — 1998

3401	S654NUG	3403	S656NUG	3405	S658NUG	3407	S660NUG	3409	S662NUG
3402	S655NUG	3404	S657NUG	3406	S659NUG	3408	S661NUG	3410	S663NUG

4401-4447 — Leyland Atlantean AN68A/1R — Northern Counties — B43/32F — 1981

4401	MRJ401W	4416	SND416X	4438	SND438X	4442	SND442X	4446	SND446X
4407	MRJ407W	4419	SND419X	4441	SND441X	4444	SND444X		

4448-4524 — Leyland Atlantean AN68B/1R* — Northern Counties — B43/32F — 1981-82
*4448/56/86/91/7-99 are AN68A/1R

4448	SND448X	4464	SND464X	4490	SND490X	4503	SND503X	4516	SND516X
4456	SND456X	4469	SND469X	4491	SND491X	4504	SND504X	4517	SND517X
4458	SND458X	4471	SND471X	4497	SND497X	4507	SND507X	4522	SND522X
4459	SND459X	4474	SND474X	4498	SND498X	4508	SND508X	4523	SND523X
4460	SND460X	4475	SND475X	4499	SND499X	4509	SND509X	4524	SND524X
4461	SND461X	4486	SND486X	4502	SND502X				

4529-4599 — Leyland Atlantean AN68D/1R — Northern Counties — B43/32F — 1982

4529	SND529X	4542	ANA542Y	4558	ANA558Y	4573	ANA573Y	4588	ANA588Y
4531	ANA531Y	4547	ANA547Y	4561	ANA561Y	4575	ANA575Y	4590	ANA590Y
4532	ANA532Y	4548	ANA548Y	4563	ANA563Y	4576	ANA576Y	4591	ANA591Y
4535	ANA535Y	4549	ANA549Y	4566	ANA566Y	4578	ANA578Y	4594	ANA594Y
4539	ANA539Y	4551	ANA551Y	4567	ANA567Y	4581	ANA581Y	4595	ANA595Y
4540	ANA540Y	4554	ANA554Y	4570	ANA570Y	4584	ANA584Y	4599	ANA599Y
4541	ANA541Y	4555	ANA555Y	4571	ANA571Y	4587	ANA587Y		

4603-4697 — Leyland Atlantean AN68D/1R — Northern Counties — B43/32F — 1982-84

4603	ANA603Y	4622	ANA622Y	4641	ANA641Y	4658	A658HNB	4677	A677HNB
4606	ANA606Y	4623	ANA623Y	4645	ANA645Y	4659	A659HNB	4681	A681HNB
4607	ANA607Y	4626	ANA626Y	4648	ANA648Y	4662	A662HNB	4682	A682HNB
4610	ANA610Y	4629	ANA629Y	4649	ANA649Y	4663	A663HNB	4686	A686HNB
4611	ANA611Y	4633	ANA633Y	4650	ANA650Y	4667	A667HNB	4689	A689HNB
4615	ANA615Y	4635	ANA635Y	4652	ANA652Y	4670	A670HNB	4691	A691HNB
4616	ANA616Y	4636	ANA636Y	4654	ANA654Y	4672	A672HNB	4692	A692HNB
4617	ANA617Y	4638	ANA638Y	4655	ANA655Y	4673	A673HNB	4697	A697HNB
4621	ANA621Y	4640	ANA640Y	4656	A656HNB	4676	A676HNB		

4701-4765 — Leyland Atlantean AN68D/1R — Northern Counties — B43/32F* — 1984
*4721 is B43/30F

4701	A701LNC	4717	A717LNC	4729	A729LNC	4739	A739NNA	4756	A756NNA
4703	A703LNC	4718	A718LNC	4732	A732LNC	4740	A740NNA	4758	A758NNA
4709	A709LNC	4720	A720LNC	4733	A733LNC	4746	A746NNA	4760	A760NNA
4712	A712LNC	4721	A721LNC	4736	A736LNC	4753	A753NNA	4763	A763NNA
4713	A713LNC	4727	A727LNC	4738	A738NNA	4755	A755NNA	4765	A765NNA
4716	A716LNC	4728	A728LNC					

5013	GBU13V	MCW Metrobus DR102/10	MCW	B43/30F	1980
5014	GBU14V	MCW Metrobus DR102/10	MCW	B43/30F	1980
5015	GBU15V	MCW Metrobus DR102/10	MCW	B43/30F	1980

5032-5104

| | | MCW Metrobus DR102/21 | MCW | | B43/30F | 1981 |

5032	MRJ32W	5050	MRJ50W	5068	MRJ68W	5085	ORJ85W	5101	SND101X
5033	MRJ33W	5056	MRJ56W	5070	MRJ70W	5089	ORJ89W	5102	SND102X
5034	MRJ34W	5058	MRJ58W	5082	ORJ82W	5096	ORJ96W	5103	SND103X
5035	MRJ35W	5060	MRJ60W	5083	ORJ83W	5097	ORJ97W	5104	SND104X
5039	MRJ39W	5064	MRJ64W	5084	ORJ84W				

5112-5188

| | | MCW Metrobus DR102/23 | MCW | | B43/30F | 1981-83 |

5112	SND112X	5133	SND133X	5148	SND148X	5168	ANA168Y	5178	ANA178Y
5114	SND114X	5136	SND136X	5149	SND149X	5169	ANA169Y	5181	ANA181Y
5115	SND115X	5137	SND137X	5150	SND150X	5171	ANA171Y	5183	ANA183Y
5122	SND122X	5138	SND138X	5151	ANA151Y	5172	ANA172Y	5184	ANA184Y
5126	SND126X	5139	SND139X	5152	ANA152Y	5174	ANA174Y	5186	ANA186Y
5129	SND129X	5140	SND140X	5166	ANA166Y	5175	ANA175Y	5187	ANA187Y
5130	SND130X	5147	SND147X	5167	ANA167Y	5176	ANA176Y	5188	ANA188Y
5131	SND131X								

5201-5210

| | | MCW Metrobus DR132/8 | Northern Counties | | BC43/29F* | 1986 | *Seating varies |

5201	C201FVU	5203	C203FVU	5205	C205FVU	5207	C207FVU	5209	C209FVU
5202	C202FVU	5204	C204FVU	5206	C206FVU	5208	C208FVU	5210	C210FVU

5301-5320

| | | MCW Metrobus DR102/51 | Northern Counties | | BC43/29F* | 1986-87 | *Seating varies |

5301	D301JVR	5305	D305JVR	5309	D309JVR	5313	D313LNB	5317	D317LNB
5302	D302JVR	5306	D306JVR	5310	D310JVR	5314	D314LNB	5318	D318LNB
5303	D303JVR	5307	D307JVR	5311	D311LNB	5315	D315LNB	5319	D319LNB
5304	D304JVR	5308	D308JVR	5312	D312LNB	5316	D316LNB	5320	D320LNB

| 5532 | CUB532Y | MCW Metrobus DR101/32 | MCW | B43/30F | 1983 | Yorkshire Rider, 1996 |

5541-5579

| | | MCW Metrobus DR102/38 | MCW | | B43/30F | 1984 | Yorkshire Rider, 1996 |

5541	A541KUM	5553	A753LWY	5564	B564RWY	5569	B569RWY	5572	B572RWY
5546	A546KUM	5555	A755LWY	5565	B565RWY	5571	B571RWY	5579	B579RWY
5547	A547KUM	5562	B562RWY	5568	B568RWY				

During 1996 several MCW Metrobuses were transferred from Yorkshire Rider to Manchester, displacing Atlanteans. Those that remain in service are now based at the Manchester depot, formerly known as Queens Road. Pictured working service 123 to Langley is 5547, A547KUM.
Richard Godfrey

During 1997, First Manchester introduced new colours for its *Gold Service* fleet, using cream and dark blue. This scheme was short-lived as many of the buses qualified for corporate livery and have been repainted. Pictured at Wigan in that scheme is Dennis Dart 6038, R238SBA. *Les Peters*

6001-6025   Dennis Dart SLF   Plaxton Pointer   N41F   1996-97

6001	P301LND	6006	P306LND	6011	P311LND	6016	P316LND	6021	P321LND
6002	P302LND	6007	P307LND	6012	P312LND	6017	P317LND	6022	P322LND
6003	P303LND	6008	P308LND	6013	P313LND	6018	P318LND	6023	P323LND
6004	P304LND	6009	P309LND	6014	P314LND	6019	P319LND	6024	P324LND
6005	P305LND	6010	P310LND	6015	P315LND	6020	P320LND	6025	P325LND

6026-6080   Dennis Dart SLF   Plaxton Pointer 2   N37F   1997

6026	R226SBA	6037	R237SBA	6048	R248SBA	6059	R259SBA	6070	R270SBA
6027	R227SBA	6038	R238SBA	6049	R249SBA	6060	R260SBA	6071	R271SBA
6028	R228SBA	6039	R239SBA	6050	R250SBA	6061	R261SBA	6072	R272SBA
6029	R229SBA	6040	R240SBA	6051	R251SBA	6062	R262SBA	6073	R273SBA
6030	R230SBA	6041	R241SBA	6052	R252SBA	6063	R263SBA	6074	R274SBA
6031	R231SBA	6042	R242SBA	6053	R253SBA	6064	R264SBA	6075	R275SBA
6032	R232SBA	6043	R243SBA	6054	R254SBA	6065	R265SBA	6076	R276SBA
6033	R233SBA	6044	R244SBA	6055	R255SBA	6066	R266SBA	6077	R277SBA
6034	R234SBA	6045	R245SBA	6056	R256SBA	6067	R267SBA	6078	R278SBA
6035	R235SBA	6046	R246SBA	6057	R257SBA	6068	R268SBA	6079	R279SBA
6036	R236SBA	6047	R247SBA	6058	R258SBA	6069	R269SBA	6080	R280SBA

6091	S395HVV	Dennis Dart SLF	Plaxton Pointer 2	N39F	1998
6092	S396HVV	Dennis Dart SLF	Plaxton Pointer 2	N39F	1998
6093	S397HVV	Dennis Dart SLF	Plaxton Pointer 2	N39F	1998
6099	P748HND	Dennis Dart SLF	Plaxton Pointer	N39F	1997

6501-6530

| | | Dennis Dart SLF | | | Wright Crusader | | NC41F* | 1996-97 | *6524-30 are NC36F |
| | | | | | | | | | * 6514 is NC38F |

6501	P501LND	6507	P507LND	6513	P513LND	6519	P519LND	6525	P525LND
6502	P502LND	6508	P508LND	6514	P514LND	6520	P520LND	6526	P526LND
6503	P503LND	6509	P509LND	6515	P515LND	6521	P521LND	6527	P527LND
6504	P504LND	6510	P510LND	6516	P516LND	6522	P522LND	6528	P528LND
6505	P505LND	6511	P511LND	6517	P517LND	6523	P523LND	6529	P529LND
6506	P506LND	6512	P512LND	6518	P518LND	6524	P524LND	6530	P530LND

6601-6610

Optare L1070 Optare Excel N37F 1996-97 Timeline, 1998

6601	P213HRJ	6603	R215SBA	6605	R217SBA	6607	R219SBA	6609	R221SBA
6602	R214SBA	6604	R216SBA	6606	R218SBA	6608	R220SBA	6610	R223SBA

6701-6708

Volvo B6BLE Wright Crusader N F 1999

6701	T701	6703	T703	6705	T705	6707	T707	6708	T708
6702	T702	6704	T704	6706	T706				

7003-7010

Volvo Citybus B10M-50 Northern Counties B45/31F* 1991-92 *7009/10 are B45/26FL

7003	H703GVM	7005	H705GVM	7008	H708GVM	7009	J709ONF	7010	J710ONF

7077	WBN955L	Leyland Atlantean AN68/1R	Park Royal	O43/32F	1972

Ancilliary vehicles:-

TV241	D241PPU	Mercedes-Benz L608D	Dormobile	TV	1986	Thamesway, 1996
TV284	HSO284V	Leyland Atlantean AN68A/1R	Alexander AL	TV	1980	Grampian 1996
TV405	G63RND	Leyland Tiger TR2R62C16Z4	Alexander N	TV	1989	Timeline, 1998
TV409	G67RND	Leyland Tiger TR2R62C16Z4	Alexander N	TV	1989	Timeline, 1998
TV1412	M412RND	Iveco TurboDaily 59.12	Marshall C 31	TV	1995	Citibus, Middleton, 1995
TV1415	M415RND	Iveco TurboDaily 59.12	Marshall C 31	TV	1995	Citibus, Middleton, 1995
TV1416	M416RND	Iveco TurboDaily 59.12	Marshall C 31	TV	1995	Citibus, Middleton, 1995
TV1421	D238PPU	Mercedes-Benz L608D	Dormobile	TV	1986	Thamesway, 1996
TV1422	DSA254T	Leyland Atlantean AN68A/1R	Alexander AL	TV	1979	Grampian, 1996
TV1423	DSA253T	Leyland Atlantean AN68A/1R	Alexander AL	TV	1979	Grampian, 1996
TV1440	TND102X	Ford R1114	Duple Dominant IV	TV	1983	Hulme Hall, Cheadle, 1994
TX1751	F636XMS	Mercedes-Benz 811D	Alexander Sprint	TV	1988	CentreWest, 1998
TX1752	F640XMS	Mercedes-Benz 811D	Alexander Sprint	TV	1988	CentreWest, 1998
TX1753	F642XMS	Mercedes-Benz 811D	Alexander Sprint	TV	1988	CentreWest, 1998
TX1754	F672XMS	Mercedes-Benz 811D	Alexander Sprint	TV	1988	CentreWest, 1998
TV4269	FVR269V	Leyland Atlantean AN68D/1R	Northern Counties	TV	1980	
TV4357	ORJ357W	Leyland Atlantean AN68D/1R	Northern Counties	TV	1981	
TV4447	SND447X	Leyland Atlantean AN68D/1R	Northern Counties	TV	1981	
TV4562	ANA562Y	Leyland Atlantean AN68D/1R	Northern Counties	TV	1980	
TV4580	ANA580Y	Leyland Atlantean AN68D/1R	Northern Counties	TV	1982	
TV4583	ANA583Y	Leyland Atlantean AN68D/1R	Northern Counties	TV	1982	
TV4642	ANA642Y	Leyland Atlantean AN68D/1R	Northern Counties	TV	1982	
TV5012	GBU12V	MCW Metrobus DR102/10	MCW	TV	1980	
TV5061	MRJ61W	MCW Metrobus DR102/21	MCW	TV	1981	
TV5062	MRJ62W	MCW Metrobus DR102/21	MCW	TV	1981	
S5086	ORJ86W	MCW Metrobus DR102/21	MCW	B43/30F	1981	
TV4768	HWT54N	Leyland Atlantean AN68/1R	Roe	TV	1975	Yorkshire Rider, 1997

Allocations

Bolton (Crook Street)

Iveco	1410							
Mercedes-Benz	1721	1722	1723	1724	1831	1832	1833	1834
	1835							
Dart	6007	6008	6009	6010	6011	6012	6013	6014
	6015	6016	6017	6018	6019	6020	6021	6022
	6023	6024	6025	6040	6041	6042	6043	6044
	6045	6046	6047	6048	6049	6061	6062	6063
	6064	6065	6066	6067	6068	6069	6070	6071
	6072	6073	6077					
Excel	6602	6603	6604	6605	6606	6607	6608	6609
	6610							
Lynx	1401	1402	1403	1404				
Tiger	401	403	404	406				
Volvo B10BLE	580	581	582	583	584	585	586	587
	588	589	590	591	634	635	636	637
	638	639	640	641	642	643	644	645
	646	647	648	649	650	651	652	653
	654	655	657					
Fleetline	4982	4990						
Atlantean	4401	4407	4416	4419	4441	4448	4456	4458
	4459	4460	4461	4464	4469	4471	4474	4475
	4486	4490	4491	4504	4508	4509	4517	4523
	4524	4529	4531	4532	4535	4539	4540	4541
	4547	4548	4549	4551	4554	4555	4561	4563
	4566	4567	4570	4573	4575	4584	4587	4588
	4594	4607	4611	4615	4617	4623	4626	4633
	4635	4640	4645	4648	4652	4713	4720	4721
	4736	4739	4740	4746	4753	4758	4763	7077
Olympian	3037	3043	3044	3046	3047	3061	3066	
	3078	3081	3083	3090	3092	3098	3099	3100
	3105	3120	3144	3151	3163	3177	3180	3190
	3192	3201	3211	3218	3219	3223	3227	3228
	3231	3232	3233	3237	3238	3239	3240	3241
	3242	3243	3244	3245	3252	3254	3256	3261
	3262	3263	3274	3275	3408	3409	3410	

Bury (Rochdale Road)

Dart	1101	1104	1123	1124	1125	1126	1127	1128
	1129	1130	1131	1132	1133	1134	1135	1136
	1137	1138	1139	1140	1141	1142	1143	1144
	1145	1146	1147	1148	1149	1150	1151	1152
	1153	6001	6002	6003	6004	6005	6006	6050
	6051	6052	6053	6054	6055	6056	6057	6058
	6059	6060						
Volvo B10B	501	504	508	509	512	519	520	521
	522	533	534	535	536	538	543	544
	545	546	547					
Volvo B10L	563	564	565	566	567	568		
Volvo B10M	701							
Volvo B10LA	2001	2002	2003	2004	2005	2006	2007	2008
	2009	2010	2011	2012	2013	2014	2015	
Atlantean	4438	4442	4444	4446	4497	4499	4507	4516
	4571	4606	4636	4677	4681	4697	4703	4717
	4718	4728	4732	4733	4755			
Olympian	3038	3052	3054	3064	3068	3076	3096	3103
	3106	3108	3109	3112	3113	3116	3127	3128
	3134	3136	3141	3142	3152	3160	3168	3182
	3183	3188	3249	3250	3251	3253	3257	3259
	3271	3273	3276					
Volvo Citybus	1481	1482	1483	7001	7002	7003	7004	7005
	7006	7007	7008	7009	7010			

The 1999 FirstGroup Bus Handbook

The number of Fleetlines and Leyland Atlanteans is now declining fast with just two of the former remain at Bolton. Pictured in Piccadilly is Queens Road's Atlantean 4578, ANA578Y. Many of these buses will be displaced during 1999 with further deliveries of Scania L94s, Volvo B10BLEs and the new Mercedes-Benz Citaro integral buses. *Les Peters*

Atherton

Volvo B6	1087	1088	1089	1090	1091	1092		

Manchester (Queens Road)

Mercedes-Benz	1801	1803	1805	1806	1807	1808	1809	1810
	1811	1812	1818	1819				
Volvo B6	1043	1044	1047	1048	1049	1050	1051	1052
	1053	1054	1055	1056	1057	1058	1059	1060
	1061	1062	1063	1064	1065	1066	1067	1068
	1069	1070	1071	1072	1073	1074	1075	1076
	1077	1078	1079	1080	1081	1082	1083	1084
	1085	1086	1093	1094	1095	1096	1097	1098
Volvo B10B	502	503	505	506	507	510	511	513
	514	515	516	517	518	550	551	552
Volvo B10BLE	621	622	623	624	625	626	627	628
	628	630	631	632	633	656		
Atlantean	4536	4558	4578	4581	4610	4614	4615	4619
	4628	4633	4634	4635	4642	4648	4650	4658
	4659	4662	4670	4676	4686	4692		
Metrobus	5013	5014	5015	5032	5033	5034	5035	5039
	5056	5082	5083	5084	5085	5096	5097	5114
	5136	5137	5138	5139	5140	5149	5152	5171
	5172	5174	5175	5316	5317	5318	5320	5532
	5541	5546	5547	5553	5555	5562	5564	5565
	5568	5569	5571	5572	5579			
Olympian	3042	3045	3050	3073	3075	3079	3093	3104
	3107	3115	3123	3129	3130	3131	3140	3157
	3159	3171	3187	3194	3222	3401	3402	3403
	3404	3405	3406	3407				

Oldham (Wallshaw Street)

Mercedes-Benz	1703	1704	1706	1707	1708	1709	1714	1719
	1802	1813	1814	1815	1816	1817	1820	
Dart	6501	6502	6503	6504	6505	6506	6507	6508
	6509	6510	6511	6512	6513	6514	6515	6516
	6517	6518	6519	6520	6521	6522	6523	6524
	6525	6526	6527	6528	6529	6530		
Volvo B10B	523	524	525	526	527	528	529	530
	531	532	537	539	540	541	542	548
	549	553	554	556	668	669	670	
Volvo B10BLE	671	672	673	674	675	676	677	
Scania	101	102	103	104	105	106	107	108
	109	110	111	112	113	114	115	116
	117	118	119					
Atlantean	4558	4581	4638	4656	4659	4663	4667	4670
	4672	4673	4676	4682	4686	4691	4692	4709
	4716	4727	4738	4765				
Metrobus	5050	5058	5060	5070	5089	5101	5102	5103
	5104	5112	5113	5114	5115	5122	5126	5129
	5130	5131	5133	5147	5148	5150	5151	5166
	5167	5168	5169	5178	5181	5183	5184	5186
	5187	5188	5201	5202	5203	5204	5205	5206
	5207	5208	5209	5210	5301	5302	5303	5304
	5305	5306	5307	5308	5309	5310	5311	5312
	5313	5314	5315	5319				
Olympian	3040	3041	3048	3051	3059	3062	3063	3085
	3097	3102	3161	3162	3186	3189	3202	3203
	3204	3206	3209	3217	3220	3225	3229	3235
	3284							

Rochdale (Miall Street) - Pioneer

MetroRider	1699							
Mercedes-Benz	1717	1731	1732	1733	1734	1841	1842	1843
Renault-Dodge	1998							
Dart	1171	1172						
Tiger	402	407	412					

Wigan (Melverley Street)

Mercedes-Benz	1804	1821	1822					
Dart	608	609	610	611	612	613	614	617
	618	1102	1103	1105	1106	1119	1120	1121
	1122	6026	6027	6028	6029	6030	6031	6032
	6033	6034	6035	6036	6037	6038	6039	6074
	6075	6076	6078	6079	6080			
Volvo B10L	557	558	559	561	562			
Volvo B10BLE	571	572	573	574	575	576	577	578
	579	587						
Tiger	408	409	410	411	413	414		
Excel	6601							
Atlantean	4374	4498	4502	4503	4522	4534	4542	4576
	4578	4590	4591	4595	4599	4603	4616	4621
	4622	4629	4641	4649	4654	4655	4689	4701
	4712	4729	4756	4760				
Olympian	3011	3012	3013	3014	3015	3071	3101	3111
	3148	3200	3246	3247	3248	3258	3264	3265
	3266	3267	3270	3278	3279	3280	3281	3286
	3287	3288	3290	3292	3293	3299	3302	3303
	3305							

Unallocated

Renault-Dodge	1997	1999	

FIRST PMT

Crosville - Flexi - Pennine - PMT - Red Rider

PMT Ltd, Hobson Street, Burslem, Stoke-on-Trent ST6 2AQ

MXP22	H202JHP	Peugeot-Talbot Pullman	Talbot	B8FL	1990	Midland Red West, 1995	
MXU23	H203JHP	Peugeot-Talbot Pullman	Talbot	B22F	1990	Midland Red West, 1995	
STL24	ERF24Y	Leyland Tiger TRCTL11/3R	Plaxton Paramount 3500	C53F	1983		
MBU25	M25YRE	Peugeot Boxer	TBP	M9	1995		
MBU26	M26YRE	Peugeot Boxer	TBP	M9	1995		
MBU27	M27YRE	Peugeot Boxer	TBP	M9	1995		
MBU28	M28YRE	Peugeot Boxer	TBP	M9	1995		
MRE29	507EXA	Renaut Master T35	Renault	M9L	1986	WYM Ambulance, 1996	
MRE30	D810NWW	Renaut Master T35	Renault	M9L	1987	WYM Ambulance, 1996	
MMM31	T131ARE	Mercedes-Benz 614	Minibus Options	M14FL	1999		
MMM32	T132ARE	Mercedes-Benz 614	Frank Guy	M14FL	1999		
MMM33	T133ARE	Mercedes-Benz 614	Frank Guy	M14FL	1999		
MMM34	T134ARE	Mercedes-Benz 614	Frank Guy	M14FL	1999		
MMM35	T135ARE	Mercedes-Benz 614	Minibus Options	M14FL	1999		
MMM36	T136ARE	Mercedes-Benz 614	Minibus Options	M14FL	1999		
STL44	FXI8653	Leyland Tiger TRCTL11/3R	Plaxton Paramount 3500 III	C53F	1988		
CTL45	WJI5239	Leyland Tiger TRCTL11/3R	Plaxton Paramount 3200 E	C53F	1984	The Shires, 1998	

MTE51-56

Tecnobus Gulliver — Tecnobus Gulliver — B9C — 1998 — LHD Electric

51	S251AFA	53	S253AFA	54	S254AFA	55	S255AFA	56	S256AFA
52	S252AFA								

IPM57-68

Optare Solo — Optare — N27F — 1999

57	T157BBF	60	T160BBF	63	T163BBF	65	T165BBF	67	T167BBF
58	T158BBF	61	T161BBF	64	T164BBF	66	T166BBF	68	T168BBF
59	T159BBF	62	T162BBF						

MMM88	C108SFP	Mercedes-Benz L307D	Reeve Burgess	M12	1985	Goldcrest, Birkenhead, 1990	
MMM100	F100UEH	Mercedes-Benz 609D	PMT	C24F	1989		
MMM101	G101EVT	Mercedes-Benz 609D	PMT	C21F	1990		
MMM102	F452YHF	Mercedes-Benz 811D	North West Coach Sales	C24F	1989	C & M, Aintree, 1992	
MMM104	F713OFH	Mercedes-Benz 307D	North West Coach Sales	M9L	1989	van, 1992	
IFF105	J328RVT	Iveco Daily 49.10	Reeve Burgess Beaver	C29F	1991	Roseville, Newcastle, 1993	
MRP106	E106LVT	Renault-Dodge S56	PMT	C24F	1988		
IMM107	XRF2X	Mercedes-Benz 811D	Optare StarRider	BC29F	1988	Leon's, Stafford, 1997	
MMM109	F217OFB	Mercedes-Benz 307D	North West Coach Sales	M12L	1989	van, 1992	
IMM110	H189CNS	Mercedes-Benz 814D	Dormobile Routemaker	C33F	1991	Executive Travel, 1994	

An unexpected arrival with PMT during 1997 was former Brewers' Tiger HHJ374Y which was acquired for a school contract. The bus has now been numbered STL297 and is seen in Newcastle.
Ciff Beeton

PMT are the second FirstGroup fleet to take a batch of Optare Solo minibuses. While the majority carry corporate livery number IPM59, T159BBF is one of a pair painted in a special *Flintshire Linxx* livery for the Deeside area. This is a result of a quality partnership between Flintshire, FirstGroup and Arriva. The vehicle was seen before its entry into service. *Cliff Beeton*

MMM112	XRF2X	Mercedes-Benz L307D	Reeve Burgess	M12	1983
MMM114	G805AAD	Mercedes-Benz 308	North West Coach Sales	M12L	1989	van, 1992
MMM115	B115NBF	Mercedes-Benz L608D	PMT Hanbridge	C21FL	1984
MFF178	F166DNT	Ford Transit VE6	Dormobile	M15L	1989	Derwen Coll, Gobowen, 1994

MPC224-230

	MCW MetroRider MF150/118	MCW		B25F*	1988	Crosville, 1990 *225/8/30 B23F

224	F88CWG	226	F106CWG	228	F108CWG	229	F109CWG	230	F110CWG
225	F95CWG	227	F107CWG

MPC231	L231NRE	Optare MetroRider	Optare	B31F	1994

MMM232-258

Mercedes-Benz Vario O810   Plaxton Beaver 2   B27F   1997

232	R232ERE	238	R238ERE	244	R244ERE	249	R249ERE	254	R254ERE
233	R233ERE	239	R239ERE	245	R245ERE	250	R250ERE	255	R255ERE
234	R234ERE	240	R240ERE	246	R246ERE	251	R251ERE	256	R256ERE
235	R235ERE	241	R241ERE	247	R247ERE	252	R252ERE	257	R257ERE
236	R236ERE	242	R242ERE	248	R248ERE	253	R253ERE	258	R258ERE
237	R237ERE	243	R243ERE

MMM259-270

Mercedes-Benz Vario O810   Plaxton Beaver 2   B27F   1998

259	S259SFA	262	S262SFA	265	S265SFA	267	S267SFA	269	S269SFA
260	S260SFA	263	S263SFA	266	S266SFA	268	S268SFA	270	S270SFA
261	S261SFA	264	S264SFA

SLL295	BVP782V	Leyland Leopard PSU3E/4R	Plaxton Supreme IV Express	C53F	1979	Midland Red West, 1996
SLL296	BVP783V	Leyland Leopard PSU3E/4R	Plaxton Supreme IV Express	C53F	1980	Midland Red West, 1996
STL297	HHJ374Y	Leyland Tiger TRCTL11/2R	Alexander TE	C49F	1983	Brewers, 1997
SNG298	GMB377T	Leyland National 11351A/1R		B49F	1978	Crosville, 1990

IWC310-318
Leyland Swift LBM6T/2RS PMT Knype BC37F* 1988-89 *312/8 are BC35F

310	F310REH	312	F312REH	313	F313REH	317	F317REH	318	G318YVT
311	F311REH								

IWC320	E342NFA	Leyland Swift LBM6T/2RS	PMT Knype	B37F	1988	PMT demonstrator, 1988
IPC321	L321HRE	Optare MetroRider	Optare	BC30F	1993	
IPC322	L269GBU	Optare MetroRider	Optare	B28F	1993	
IPC323	L323NRF	Optare MetroRider	Optare	B29F	1994	

IMM330-353
Mercedes-Benz 811D PMT Ami B28F 1989-90

330	G330XRE	335	G335XRE	340	G340XRE	345	G345CBF	350	G550ERF
331	G331XRE	336	G336XRE	341	G341XRE	346	G346CBF	351	H351HRF
332	G332XRE	337	G337XRE	342	G342CBF	347	G347ERF	352	H352HRF
333	G333XRE	338	G338XRE	343	G343CBF	348	G348ERF	353	H353HRF
334	G334XRE	339	G339XRE	344	G344CBF	349	G349ERF		

IMM354	H354HVT	Mercedes-Benz 811D	Reeve Burgess Beaver	B33F	1990
IMM355	H355HVT	Mercedes-Benz 811D	Reeve Burgess Beaver	B33F	1990
IMM356	H356HVT	Mercedes-Benz 811D	Reeve Burgess Beaver	B33F	1990
IMM357	H357HVT	Mercedes-Benz 811D	Reeve Burgess Beaver	B33F	1990

IMM358-363
Mercedes-Benz 811D PMT Ami B29F 1990

358	H358JRE	360	H160JRE	361	H361JRE	362	H362JRE	363	H363JRE
359	H359JRE								

IMM365	G495FFA	Mercedes-Benz 811D	PMT Ami	B28F	1990

IMM366-371
Mercedes-Benz 811D PMT Ami B29F 1991

366	H366LFA	368	H368LFA	369	H369LFA	370	H370LFA	371	H371LFA
367	H367LFA								

IMM372	H372MEH	Mercedes-Benz 811D	Whittaker-Europa	B31F	1991	
IMM373	H373MVT	Mercedes-Benz 811D	PMT Ami	B29F	1991	
IMM374	K374BRE	Mercedes-Benz 811D	Autobus Classique	B29F	1992	
IMM375	K375BRE	Mercedes-Benz 811D	Autobus Classique	B29F	1992	
IMM376	XRF1X	Mercedes-Benz 709D	Dormobile Routemaker	BC25F	1991	Stonier, 1994

IPC377-383
Optare MetroRider Optare B30F 1994

377	M377SRE	379	M379SRE	381	M381SRE	382	M382SRE	383	M383SRE
378	M378SRE	380	M380SRE						

IPC384-390
Optare MetroRider Optare B29F 1996

384	P384MEH	386	P386MEH	388	P388MEH	389	P389MEH	390	P390MEH
385	P385MEH	387	P387MEH						

IPC391-396
Optare MetroRider Optare B29F 1997

391	R391ERE	393	R393ERE	394	R394ERE	395	R395ERE	396	R396ERE
392	R392ERE								

MMM405-429
Mercedes-Benz 709D Plaxton Beaver B22F 1996

405	N405HVT	410	N410HVT	415	P415NFA	420	P420MEH	425	P425MEH
406	N406HVT	411	N411HVT	416	P416NFA	421	P421MEH	426	P426MEH
407	N407HVT	412	N412HVT	417	P417NFA	422	P422MEH	427	P427MEH
408	N408HVT	413	P413NFA	418	P418NFA	423	P423MEH	428	P428MEH
409	N409HVT	414	P414NFA	419	P419NFA	424	P424MEH	429	P429MEH

MMM430-448
Mercedes-Benz 709D Plaxton Beaver B24F 1992

430	J430WFA	434	K434XRF	438	K438XRF	442	K442XRF	446	K446XRF
431	J431WFA	435	K435XRF	439	K439XRF	443	K443XRF	447	K447XRF
432	K432XRF	436	K436XRF	440	K440XRF	444	K544XRF	448	K448XRF
433	K433XRF	437	K437XRF	441	K441XRF	445	K445XRF		

MXU449	K449XRF	Peugeot-Talbot Pullman	TBP	B18F	1992

MMM451-460
Mercedes-Benz L609D   PMT Hanbridge   B20F*   1987-88   *454 is B20FL

451	D451ERE	453	D453ERE	454	D454ERE	455	D455ERE	460	E760HBF
452	D452ERE								

MMM467	E767HBF	Mercedes-Benz 709D	PMT	B21F	1988	
MMM473	F473RBF	Mercedes-Benz 609D	PMT	B20F	1988	
MMM475	F475VEH	Mercedes-Benz 609D	PMT	B20F	1989	
MMM477	G477ERF	Mercedes-Benz 609D	PMT	B20F	1990	
MMM478	G478ERF	Mercedes-Benz 609D	PMT	B20F	1990	
MMM479	E384XCA	Mercedes-Benz 609D	PMT	B24F	1987	Dennis's, Ashton, 1990
MMM480	H480JRE	Mercedes-Benz 709D	PMT	B20F	1990	
MMM481	H481JRE	Mercedes-Benz 709D	PMT	B25F	1990	
MMM482	H482JRE	Mercedes-Benz 609D	Whittaker Europa	B20F	1990	
MMM483	H483JRE	Mercedes-Benz 609D	Whittaker Europa	B20F	1990	
MMM484	J484PVT	Mercedes-Benz 709D	PMT	B25F	1991	
MMM485	J485PVT	Mercedes-Benz 709D	Whittaker (PMT)	B25F	1992	
MMM486	J486PVT	Mercedes-Benz 709D	Whittaker (PMT)	B25F	1992	

MMM487-498
Mercedes-Benz 709D   Dormobile Routemaker   B24F*   1993   *488/9 are B27F

487	K487CVT	490	K490CVT	493	L493HRE	495	L495HRE	497	L497HRE
488	K488CVT	491	K491CVT	494	L494HRE	496	L496HRE	498	L498HRE
489	K489CVT	492	K492CVT						

MRP502-522
Renault-Dodge S56   Alexander AM   B20F   1987

502	E802HBF	512	E812HBF	518	E818HBF	521	E821HBF	522	E822HBF
507	E807HBF								

MRP530	E526NEH	Renault-Dodge S56	PMT	B20F	1988	
MRP532	G532CVT	Renault-Dodge S56	PMT	B25F	1990	
MRP533	H722CNC	Renault S75	Northern Counties	B17FL	1990	First Manchester, 1998
MRP534	H723CNC	Renault S75	Northern Counties	B17FL	1990	First Manchester, 1998
MRP535	H725CNC	Renault S75	Northern Counties	B17FL	1990	First Manchester, 1998
MMM550	H834GLD	Mercedes-Benz 609D	North West Coach Sales	B19F	1990	Capital, West Drayton, 1994
MMM551	H835GLD	Mercedes-Benz 609D	North West Coach Sales	B19F	1990	Capital, West Drayton, 1994
MMM552	H836GLD	Mercedes-Benz 609D	North West Coach Sales	B19F	1991	Capital, West Drayton, 1994

MMM553-563
Mercedes-Benz 709D   Marshall C19   B23F   1994

553	L553LVT	556	L556LVT	558	L558LVT	560	M660SRE	562	M562SRE
554	L554LVT	557	L557LVT	559	M559SRE	561	M561SRE	563	M563SRE
555	L455LVT								

MMM564-573
Mercedes-Benz 709D   Plaxton Beaver   B24F   1994

564	M564SRE	566	M566SRE	568	M568SRE	570	M570SRE	572	M572SRE
565	M565SRE	567	M567SRE	569	M569SRE	571	M571SRE	573	M573SRE

MMM574-594
Mercedes-Benz 709D   Plaxton Beaver   B22F   1995

574	N574CEH	579	N579CEH	583	N583CEH	587	N587CEH	591	N591CEH
575	N575CEH	580	N580CEH	584	N584CEH	588	N588CEH	592	N592CEH
576	N576CEH	581	N581CEH	585	N585CEH	589	N589CEH	593	N593CEH
577	N577CEH	582	N582CEH	586	N586CEH	590	N590CEH	594	N594CEH
578	N578CEH								

Opposite, top:- **PMT converted chassis cowls in its own workshops during the NBC minibus boom of the mid 1980s. After the sale of the company it expanded its range and markets. While these mostly comprised minibuses for its own use, some larger single-deck buses were built and many minibuses were sold to other fleets. Pictured on schools duties is IWC313 based on a Leyland Swift chassis. The body style was marketed as the Knype. As shown in the picture, the type were fitted with high-back seating and spent most of their time on less-populated, rural area services.** *Cliff Beeton*
Opposite, bottom:- **The 1998 single-deck bus intake for PMT comprised twelve Scania L113 buses fitted with Wright Axcess-ultralow bodies in corporate colours. Many are based at Adderley Green where SSS820, S820AEH was photographed.** *Cliff Beeton*

DVG607	UDM450V	Bristol VRT/SL3/501(6LXB)	Eastern Coach Works	B43/31F	1980	Crosville, 1990
DVG608	VCA452W	Bristol VRT/SL3/501(6LXB)	Eastern Coach Works	B43/31F	1980	Crosville, 1990
DVG609	VCA464W	Bristol VRT/SL3/501(6LXB)	Eastern Coach Works	B43/31F	1980	Crosville, 1990
DVG610	WTU465W	Bristol VRT/SL3/501(6LXB)	Eastern Coach Works	B43/31F	1980	Crosville, 1990
DVG614	WTU483W	Bristol VRT/SL3/501(6LXB)	Eastern Coach Works	B43/31F	1981	Crosville, 1990
DVG618	YBW489V	Bristol VRT/SL3/6LXB	Eastern Coach Works	B43/31F	1979	Thames Transit, 1989
DVG622	GBF78N	Bristol VRT/SL2/6G	Eastern Coach Works	O43/31F	1974	
DVG625	AHW203V	Bristol VRT/SL3/6LXB	Eastern Coach Works	B43/27D	1980	City Line, 1994

DVL701-731

| | | Bristol VRT/SL3/501 | Eastern Coach Works | B43/31F* | 1979-80 | *723 is BC39/28F |
| | | | | | | *728 is B39/31F |

| 701 | GRF701V | 708 | GRF708V | 715 | GRF715V | 725 | NEH725W | 729 | NEH729W |
| 707 | GRF707V | 709 | GRF709V | 723 | MFA723V | 728 | NEH728W | 731 | NEH731W |

DOG733-747

| | | Leyland Olympian ONLXB/1R | Eastern Coach Works | B45/32F* | 1983-84 | *seating varies |

733	A733GFA	736	A736GFA	739	A739GFA	742	A742GFA	745	A745JRE
734	A734GFA	737	A737GFA	740	A740GFA	743	A743JRE	746	A746JRE
735	A735GFA	738	A738GFA	741	A741GFA	744	A744JRE	747	A747JRE

DOG748	EWY78Y	Leyland Olympian ONLXB/1R	Roe	B47/29F	1983	Turner, Brown Edge, 1988
DOG749	EWY79Y	Leyland Olympian ONLXB/1R	Roe	B47/29F	1983	Turner, Brown Edge, 1988
DOG750	GFM101X	Leyland Olympian ONLXB/1R	Eastern Coach Works(1985)	B45/32F	1982	Crosville, 1990
DOG751	GFM102X	Leyland Olympian ONLXB/1R	Eastern Coach Works	B45/32F	1982	Crosville, 1990
DOG752	GFM103X	Leyland Olympian ONLXB/1R	Eastern Coach Works	B45/32F	1982	Crosville, 1990

DOC753-762

| | | Leyland Olympian ONCL11/1RZ | Leyland | B47/29F* | 1989 | *seating varies |

| 753 | G753XRE | 755 | G755XRE | 757 | G757XRE | 759 | G759XRE | 761 | G761XRE |
| 754 | G754XRE | 756 | G756XRE | 758 | G758XRE | 760 | G760XRE | 762 | G762XRE |

DOG763-782

| | | Leyland Olympian ONLXB/1R | Eastern Coach Works | B45/32F | 1982-83 | Crosville, 1990 |

763	GFM104X	767	GFM109X	770	KFM113Y	774	MTU122Y	779	A137SMA
764	GFM105X	768	KFM111Y	772	KFM115Y	775	MTU123Y	781	A143SMA
765	GFM106X	769	KFM112Y	773	MTU120Y	776	MTU124Y	782	A144SMA
766	GFM108X								

DOG784-799

| | | Leyland Olympian ONLXB/1R | Eastern Coach Works | B45/32F | 1984-85 | Crosville, 1990 |

784	A146UDM	788	A159UDM	791	A162VDM	794	A165VDM	797	A168VFM
785	A156UDM	789	A160UDM	792	A163VDM	795	A166VFM	798	A169VFM
786	A157UDM	790	A161VDM	793	A164VDM	796	A167VFM	799	A170VFM
787	A158UDM								

SAD801-809

| | | DAF SB220LC550 | Optare Delta | BC48F | 1990 | |

| 801 | H801GRE | 803 | H803GRE | 805 | H805GRE | 807 | H807GRE | 809 | H809GRE |
| 802 | H802GRE | 804 | H804GRE | 806 | H806GRE | 808 | H808GRE | | |

SSS810-821

| | | Scania L113CRL | Wright Axcess-ultralow | N40F | 1998 | |

810	R810NVT	813	S813AEH	816	S816AEH	818	S818AEH	820	S820AEH
811	R811NVT	814	S814AEH	817	S817AEH	819	S819AEH	821	S821AEH
812	R812NVT	815	S815AEH						

SLT842	D752DLO	Leyland Lynx LX112TL11ZR1S	Leyland Lynx	B49F	1987	CentreWest, 1999
SLT843	D875ELL	Leyland Lynx LX112TL11ZR1R	Leyland Lynx	B48F	1987	Essex Buses, 1999
SLC844	F102GRM	Leyland Lynx LX112L10ZR1R	Leyland Lynx	B48F	1988	CentreWest, 1999
SLC845	F361YTJ	Leyland Lynx LX112L10ZR1R	Leyland Lynx	B51F	1988	Topp-Line, Wavertree, 1994
SLC846	F362YTJ	Leyland Lynx LX112L10ZR1R	Leyland Lynx	B51F	1988	Topp-Line, Wavertree, 1994
SLC847	F363YTJ	Leyland Lynx LX112L10ZR1R	Leyland Lynx	B51F	1988	Topp-Line, Wavertree, 1994
SLC848	F364YTJ	Leyland Lynx LX112L10ZR1R	Leyland Lynx	B51F	1988	Topp-Line, Wavertree, 1994
SLC849	F608WBV	Leyland Lynx LX112L10ZR1S	Leyland Lynx	B52F	1988	Westbus, Ashford, 1993
SLC850	G136YRY	Leyland Lynx LX112L10ZR1R	Leyland Lynx	B51F	1990	Westbus, Ashford, 1993

SLC851-861

| | | Leyland Lynx LX2R11C15Z4S | Leyland Lynx | BC48F | 1990 | |

851	H851GRE	854	H854GRE	856	H856GRE	858	H858GRE	860	H860GRE
852	H852GRE	855	H855GRE	857	H857GRE	859	H859GRE	861	H861GRE
853	H853GRE								

Crosville names are carried in vehicles based at Chester and Crewe. Pictured on Chester park and ride workings is gas bus SAD882, R28GNW. Based on a DAF low floor SB220 unit it carries Northern Counties bodywork built to Plaxton's Prestige design, the current full-size bus product from Plaxton. *Cliff Beeton*

SDC862	L862HFA	Dennis Lance 11SDA3112	Northern Counties Paladin	BC47F	1993	

SDC863-867

		Dennis Lance 11SDA3113	Plaxton Verde	BC45F	1995	

863	N863CEH	864	N864CEH	865	N865CEH	866	N866CEH	867	N867CEH

SDC868	P868MBF	Dennis Lance	Northern Counties Paladin	B43F	1997
SDC869	P869MBF	Dennis Lance	Northern Counties Paladin	B43F	1997
SDC870	P870MBF	Dennis Lance	Northern Counties Paladin	B43F	1997

SSS871-878

		Scania L113CRL	Wright Axcess-ultralow	N51F	1997

871	R871ERE	873	R873ERE	875	R875ERE	877	R877ERE	878	R878ERE
872	R872ERE	874	R874ERE	876	R876ERE				

SDC879	R879HRF	Scania L113CRL	Wright Axcess-ultralow	N40F	1998	
SDC880	R880HRF	Scania L113CRL	Wright Axcess-ultralow	N40F	1998	
SDC881	R881HRF	Scania L113CRL	Wright Axcess-ultralow	N40F	1998	
SAD882	R28GNW	DAF DE02GSSB220	Northern Counties Prestige	B41F	1998	On extended loan.
SBV883	TJI4828	Volvo B10M-60	Jonckheere Deauville	C53F	1989	CentreWest (Bee Line), '98
DOC889	F156XYG	Leyland Olympian ONCL10/1RZ	Northern Counties	B45/29F	1988	Yorkshire Rider (C), 1999
DOC890	F158XYG	Leyland Olympian ONCL10/1RZ	Northern Counties	B45/29F	1988	Yorkshire Rider (C), 1999
DOG891	A171VFM	Leyland Olympian ONLXB/1R	Eastern Coach Works	B45/32F	1984	Crosville, 1990
DOG892	B181BLG	Leyland Olympian ONLXB/1R	Eastern Coach Works	B45/32F	1984	Crosville, 1990
DOG893	B182BLG	Leyland Olympian ONLXB/1R	Eastern Coach Works	B45/32F	1984	Crosville, 1990
DOG894	B188BLG	Leyland Olympian ONLXB/1R	Eastern Coach Works	B45/32F	1985	Crosville, 1990
DOG895	B195BLG	Leyland Olympian ONLXB/1R	Eastern Coach Works	B45/32F	1985	Crosville, 1990
DOG896	B199DTU	Leyland Olympian ONLXB/1R	Eastern Coach Works	B45/32F	1985	Crosville, 1990
DOG897	B200DTU	Leyland Olympian ONLXB/1R	Eastern Coach Works	BC42/32F	1985	Crosville, 1990
DOG898	B201DTU	Leyland Olympian ONLXB/1R	Eastern Coach Works	BC42/32F	1985	Crosville, 1990
DOG899	B202DTU	Leyland Olympian ONLXB/1R	Eastern Coach Works	BC42/32F	1985	Crosville, 1990

IDC901-920   Dennis Dart 9SDL3011   Plaxton Pointer   BC35F   1991-92

901	J901SEH	905	J905SEH	909	J909SEH	913	J913SEH	917	J917SEH
902	J902SEH	906	J906SEH	910	J910SEH	914	J914SEH	918	J918SEH
903	J903SEH	907	J907SEH	911	J911SEH	915	J915SEH	919	K919XRF
904	J904SEH	908	J908SEH	912	J912SEH	916	J916SEH	920	K920XRF

IDC921-929   Dennis Dart 9SDL3016   Plaxton Pointer   BC35F   1992

921	K921XRF	923	K923XRF	925	K925XRF	927	K927XRF	929	K929XRF
922	K922XRF	924	K924XRF	926	K926XRF	928	K928XRF		

IDC931	L931HFA	Dennis Dart 9SDL3034	Plaxton Pointer	BC35F	1993
IDC932	L932HFA	Dennis Dart 9SDL3034	Plaxton Pointer	BC35F	1993
IDC933	L933HFA	Dennis Dart 9SDL3034	Plaxton Pointer	BC35F	1993
IDC934	L934HFA	Dennis Dart 9SDL3034	Plaxton Pointer	BC35F	1993
IDC935	L935HFA	Dennis Dart 9.8SDL3025	Marshall C36	BC36F	1993
IDC936	L936HFA	Dennis Dart 9.8SDL3025	Marshall C36	BC36F	1993

IDC937-942   Dennis Dart 9SDL3034   Plaxton Pointer   BC35F   1994

937	L937LRF	939	L939LRF	940	L940LRF	941	L941LRF	942	L942LRF
938	L938LRF								

IDC943-952   Dennis Dart 9SDL3040   Marshall C37   BC35F   1994

943	M943SRE	945	M945SRE	947	M947SRE	949	M949SRE	952	M952SRE
944	M944SRE	946	M946SRE	948	M948SRE	951	M951SRE		

IDC953-972   Dennis Dart 9.8SDL3054   Plaxton Pointer   BC36F   1995

953	M953XVT	957	M957XVT	961	M961XVT	965	M965XVT	969	M969XVT
954	M954XVT	958	M958XVT	962	M962XVT	966	M966XVT	970	M970XVT
955	M955XVT	959	M959XVT	963	M963XVT	967	M967XVT	971	M971XVT
956	M956XVT	960	M960XVT	964	M964XVT	968	M968XVT	972	M972XVT

IDC973	P973MBF	Dennis Dart	Plaxton Pointer	B36F	1997
IDC974	P974MBF	Dennis Dart	Plaxton Pointer	B36F	1997
IDC975	P975MBF	Dennis Dart	Plaxton Pointer	B36F	1997
IDC976	P976MBF	Dennis Dart	Plaxton Pointer	B36F	1997

IDC977-981   Dennis Dart SLF   Plaxton Pointer 2   N37F   1998

977	R977NVT	978	R978NVT	979	R979NVT	980	R980NVT	981	R981NVT

Special event vehicle:-

D900	WVT900S	Foden/NC 6LXB		Northern Counties	B43/31F	1978

Ancilliary vehicles:-

TVG6	WTU472W	Bristol VRT/SL3/501(6LXB)	Eastern Coach Works	TV	1980	Crosville, 1990
TYB15	CHR194V	Bedford YMT	Duple Dominant II	TV	1980	Gregory, Netherton, 1995
TLL16	GSU845T	Leyland Leopard PSU3E/3R	Alexander AYS	Tv	1979	KCB Network, 1996
TLL17	GSU838T	Leyland Leopard PSU3E/3R	Alexander AYS	TV	1979	Greater Manchester, 1997
TLL18	EGB50T	Leyland Leopard PSU3E/3R	Alexander AY	TV	1978	Northampton, 1998
G128	C128VRE	Mercedes-Benz L608D	PMT Hanbridge	B-F	1985	
TMM146	C146WRE	Mercedes-Benz L608D	PMT Hanbridge	TV	1986	
G182	D182BEH	Mercedes-Benz L608D	PMT Hanbridge	B20F	1986	
P198	JEH198K	Bristol RESL6L	Eastern Coach Works	B F	1971	
G210	C706JMB	Mercedes-Benz L608D	Reeve Burgess	B19F	1986	Crosville, 1990
TWC314	F314REH	Leyland Swift LBM6T/2RS	PMT Knype	TV	1989	
TWC315	F315REH	Leyland Swift LBM6T/2RS	PMT Knype	TV	1989	
TWC316	F316REH	Leyland Swift LBM6T/2RS	PMT Knype	TV	1989	

SLC869, P869MBF, is a Dennis Lance with Northern Counties Paladin bodywork. Based at Burslem, it carries PMT names and livery. All the Dennis Lance buses have now migrated to this depot. *Cliff Beeton*

Previous Registrations:

507EXA	C477EUA,	TJI4828	F758OJH
D810NWW	D810NWW, FXI8653	WJI5239	A155EPA
D875ELL	D806NDW, 810DYE	XRF1X	J920HGD
FXI8653	E44JRF	XRF2X	E950LEH
GBF78N	GBF78N, 507EXA	F102GRM	F102GRM, 292CLT

Allocations

Adderley Green (Dividy Road) - PMT

Outstation:- Leek

Mercedes-Benz	MMM232	MMM260	MMM261	MMM262	MMM263	MMM264	MMM265	MMM266
	MMM267	MMM268	MMM269	MMM270	IMM352	IMM365	IMM370	IMM371
	IMM372	IMM373	MMM426	MMM427	MMM428	MMM429	MMM430	MMM431
	MMM432	MMM433	MMM437	MMM438	MMM440	MMM441	MMM445	MMM446
	MMM447	MMM448	MMM493	MMM566	MMM567	MMM568	MMM572	MMM574
	MMM575	MMM576	MMM577	MMM578	MMM579	MMM580	MMM581	MMM582
	MMM583	MMM584	MMM585	MMM586	MMM587	MMM588		
MetroRider	IPC378	IPC379	IPC380	IPC381	IPC382	IPC383	IPC391	IPC392
	IPC393	IPC394	IPC395	IPC396				
Dart	IDC902	IDC903	IDC926	IDC927	IDC928	IDC929	IDC938	IDC939
	IDC953	IDC954	IDC963	IDC964				
Swift	IWC312							
Optare Delta	SAD803	SAD804	SAD805	SAD806	SAD807			
Lynx	SLC854							
Scania L94	SSS813	SSS814	SSS815	SSS816	SSS817	SSS818	SSS819	SSS820
	SSS821							
Olypians	DOG763	DOG779						

Burslem (Scotia Road) - PMT

Mercedes-Benz	MMM247	MMM330	MMM333	MMM339	MMM353	MMM355	MMM375	MMM425
	MMM439	MMM553	MMM554	MMM555	MMM556	MMM557	MMM558	MMM559
	MMM560	MMM561	MMM562	MMM563	MMM569	MMM570	MMM571	MMM573
	MMM591							
MetroRider	IPC384	IPC385	IPC386	IPC387	IPC388	IPC389	IPC390	
Swift	IWC313	IWC317						
Dart	IDC904	IDC914	IDC915	IDC916	IDC917	IDC918	IDC932	IDC957
	IDC958	IDC959	IDC960	IDC962				
Lance	SDC863	SDC864	SDC865	SDC866	SDC867	SDC868	SDC869	SDC870
Lynx	SLC856	SLC857	SLC858	SLC859				
Bristol VR	DVL728	DVL731						
Olympian	DOC754	DOC755						

Cheadle (Brookhouse Industrial Estate) - PMT

Mercedes-Benz	MMM589	MMM590	MMM594					
Dart	IDC907	IDC909	IDC910	IDC911	IDC921	IDC922	IDC924	IDC937
	IDC940	IDC941	IDC942					
Optare Delta	SAD801	SAD802						
Olympian	DOG739	DOC758	DOC761	DOC890				

Chester (Liverpool Road) - Crosville

Mercedes-Benz	IMM349	IMM354	MMM406	MMM407	MMM408	MMM411	MMM415	MMM416
	MMM477	MMM479	MMM482	MMM485				
Talbot	MXU449							
Peugeot	MBU25	MBU26	MBU27	MBU28				
MetroRider	IPM57	IPM58	IPM59	IPM65	MPC224	MPC225	MPC226	MPC227
	MPC228	MPC229	MPC230	IPC231				
Dart	IDC912	IDC913	IDC923	IDC931	IDC933	IDC973	IDC974	IDC975
	IDC976							
Leopard	SLL295							
Tiger	STL24							
Lynx	SLC847							
DAF Gasbus	SAD882							
Scania	SSS871	SSS872	SSS873					
Bristol VR	DVG618	DVG625	DVL709	DVL729				
Olympian	DOG751	DOG769	DOG775	DOC891	DOG895	DOG898	DOG899	

PMT celebrated its centenary during 1998 and painted Leyland Lynx SLC856, H856GRE into a commemorative livery for the occasion. The scheme has been reproduced onto a model of the Lynx by Corgi. The vehicle is seen heading for Crewe one on one of the main line services, 320.
Cliff Beeton

Chester's Upton Park & Ride is operated by FirstGroup who use specially liveried Scania buses on the route.
Pictured in the city is SSS872, R872ERE, one of three buses from the batch based at Chester.
Phillip Stephenson

Crewe (Second Avenue, Crewe Gates Farm) - Crosville

Mercedes-Benz	MMM31	MMM32	MMM33	MMM34	MMM35	MMM36	IMM343	MMM495
Leopard	SLL296							
Lynx	SLC844	SLC853	SLC860	SLC861				
Bristol VR	DVL701	DVL707	DVL708	DVL715	DVL723	DVL725		
Olympian	DOC760	DOG773	DOG774	DOG786				

Dukinfield (Rothesay Garage, Broadway) - Pennine

Mercedes-Benz	IMM337	IMM357	IMM358	MMM405	MMM410	MMM435	MMM436	MMM442
	MMM443	MMM444	MMM488	MMM489	MMM496	MMM565	MMM592	
MetroRider	IPC322	IPC323						
Dart	IDC943	IDC944	IDC945	IDC946	IDC947	IDC948	IDC949	IDC951
	IDC952	IDC965	IDC966					
Olympian	DOG737	DOG740	DOG742	DOG744	DOG745	DOG746	DOG747	DOG748
	DOG749	DOG776	DOG781	DOG788	DOG789	DOG793	DOG795	DOG796
	DOG798	DOG799						

Ellesmere Port (Wellington Road) - Crosville

Mercedes-Benz	IMM359	IMM360	IMM361	IMM362	MMM409	MMM412	MMM434	MMM480
	MMM481	MMM483	MMM497					
MetroRider	IPC377							
Solo	IPM66	IPM67	IPM68					
Dart	IDC934							
Lynx	SLC846							
Bristol VR	DVG608	DVG609	DVG610	DVG614				
Olympian	DOG790	DOG897						

New arrivals in corporate livery are a batch of Optare Solo minibuses. Being prepared for service at Moreton depot, IPM62, T162BBF was photographed shortly after delivery. *Cliff Beeton*

Moreton (Tarren Way Industrial Estate) - PMT

Mercedes-Benz	MMM423							
Solo	IPM60	IPM61	IPM62	IPM63	IPM64			
Renault Master	MRE30							
Renault S75	MRP534							
MetroRider	MPC231							
Dart	IDC969	IDC970	IDC971	IDC972				
Lynx	SLC846							
Bristol VR	DVL729							
Olympian	DOG733	DOG734	DOG735	DOG736	DOG741	DOG743	DOG752	DOG753
	DOG764	DOG765	DOG766	DOG768	DOG772	DOG791	DOG792	DOG794
	DOG894							

Newcastle-under-Lyme (Liverpool Road) - Flexi

Iveco/Ford	IFF105	MFF178						
Mercedes-Benz	MMM88	MMM100	MMM101	MMM102	MMM104	IMM107	MMM109	IMM110
	MMM112	MMM114	MMM115	IMM332	IMM334	IMM376	MMM451	MMM453
	MMM454	IMM455	IMM460	IMM467	IMM494	IMM498		
Renault-Dodge	MRP533							
Talbot	MXU22							
Swift	IWC318							
Tiger	STL44	CTL45						
Bristol VR (Opentop)	DVG622							

Newcastle-under-Lyme (Liverpool Road) - PMT

Mercedes-Benz	MMM233	MMM234	MMM236	MMM237	MMM238	MMM239	MMM240	MMM241
	MMM242	MMM243	MMM244	MMM246	MMM249	MMM250	MMM251	MMM252
	MMM253	MMM254	MMM255	MMM256	IMM335	IMM336	IMM338	IMM340
	iMM341	IMM342	IMM344	IMM345	IMM346	IMM347	IMM350	IMM351
	IMM356	IMM366	IMM367	MMM413	IMM414	IMM417	MMM418	IMM419
	MMM420	IMM421	MMM484	MM487	MMM564			
Dart	IDC901	IDC925	IDC919	IDC920	IDC955			
Tiger	STL297							
Lynx	SLC845	SLC852	SLC855					
Olympian	DOG738	DOC756	DOC757	DOC759	DOC762	DOC889		

Rock Ferry (New Chester Road) - Crosville

Mercedes-Benz	MMM235	MMM245	MMM248	MMM257	MMM258	MMM259	IMM374	
Dart	IDC905	IDC906	IDC908	IDC935	IDC936	IDC956	IDC967	IDC968
	IDC977	IDC978	IDC979	IDC980	IDC981			
Lance	SDC862							
Lynx	SLC848	SLC849	SLC850	SLC851				
Olympian	DOG750	DOG767	DOG770	DOG784	DOG785	DOG787	DOG792	DOG797
	DOG892	DOG893	DOG896					

Unallocated

Mercedes-Benz	MMM112	IMM348	IMM350	IMM363	IMM368	IMM369	MMM473	MMM475
	IMM478	MMM483	MMM490	MMM491	MMM550	MMM551	MMM552	
Peugeot	MXU23							
Renault-Dodge	MRP502	MRP507	MRP512	MRP518	MRP522	MRP530	MRP532	MRP535
Swift	IWC320							
National	SNG298							
Lynx	SLT842	SLT843						
Bristol VRT	DVG607	DVL645						

Bristol VRs still play an important, but diminishing, role with many of the FirstGroup fleets. PMT are no exception with an allocation from its total of eighteen at seven depots. Currently based at Chester, DVG618 was working in Newcastle when pictured a few months ago. Interestingly, PMT perpetuate the fleet numbering system used by Crosville even though there is no duplication of actual numbers.
Cliff Beeton

FIRST MIDLAND RED

Midland Red

First Midland Red Buses Ltd, Heron Lodge, London Road, Worcester, WR5 2EU

201-237
Dennis Lance 11SDA3107 — Plaxton Verde — B49F — 1994

201	L201AAB	206	L206AAB	211	L211AAB	216	L216AAB	234	L234AAB
202	L202AAB	207	L207AAB	212	L212AAB	217	L217AAB	235	L235AAB
203	L203AAB	208	L208AAB	213	L213AAB	231	L231AAB	236	L236AAB
204	L204AAB	209	L209AAB	214	L214AAB	232	L232AAB	237	L237AAB
205	L205AAB	210	L210AAB	215	L215AAB	233	L233AAB		

238-256
Dennis Lance 11SDA3113 — Plaxton Verde — B49F — 1995

238	M238MRW	242	M242MRW	246	M246MRW	250	M250MRW	254	M254MRW
239	M239MRW	243	M243MRW	247	M247MRW	251	M251MRW	255	M255MRW
240	M240MRW	244	M244MRW	248	M248MRW	252	M252MRW	256	M256MRW
241	M241MRW	245	M245MRW	249	M249MRW	253	M253MRW		

257	P453BPH	Dennis Lance 11SDA3113	Plaxton Verde	B49F	1995	On extended loan

301-313
Dennis Dart 9.8SDL3054 — Plaxton Pointer — BC36F — 1995

301	N301XAB	304	N304XAB	307	N307XAB	310	N310XAB	312	N312XAB
302	N302XAB	305	N305XAB	308	N308XAB	311	N311XAB	313	N313XAB
303	N303XAB	306	N306XAB	309	N309XAB					

339	R739TMO	Dennis Dart SLF	Plaxton Pointer SPD	N41F	1997	On extended loan
341	N341EUY	Dennis Dart SLF	Plaxton Pointer	NC33F	1996	

501-564
Mercedes-Benz Vario O814 — Plaxton Beaver 2 — B22F — 1998

501	R501CNP	514	S514RWP	527	S527RWP	540	S540RWP	553	S553RWP
502	R502CNP	515	S515RWP	528	S528RWP	541	S541RWP	554	S554RWP
503	R503CNP	516	S516RWP	529	S529RWP	542	S542RWP	555	S955RWP
504	R504CNP	517	S517RWP	530	S530RWP	543	S543RWP	556	S556RWP
505	R505CNP	518	S518RWP	531	S531RWP	544	S544RWP	557	S557RWP
506	R506CNP	519	S519RWP	532	S532RWP	545	S545RWP	558	S558RWP
507	R507CNP	520	S520RWP	533	S533RWP	546	S546RWP	559	S559RWP
508	S508RWP	521	S521RWP	534	S534RWP	547	S547RWP	560	S560RWP
509	S509RWP	522	S522RWP	535	S535RWP	548	S548RWP	561	S561RWP
510	S510RWP	523	S523RWP	536	S536RWP	549	S549RWP	562	S562RWP
511	S511RWP	524	S524RWP	537	S537RWP	550	S550RWP	563	S563RWP
512	S512RWP	525	S525RWP	538	S538RWP	551	S551RWP	564	S564RWP
513	S513RWP	526	S526RWP	539	S539RWP	552	S552RWP		

658	SOA658S	Leyland National 11351A/1R		B49F	1977	Midland Red, 1981

722-752
Leyland National 11351A/1R — B49F — 1977-79 — Midland Red, 1981

722	WOC722T	744	XOV744T	746	XOV746T	749	XOV749T	752	XOV752T
743	XOV743T								

Opposite:- **First Midland Red mainly operate services through Herefordshire and Worcestershire while the services into south Shropshire have been reduced in recent times. In addition longer services using the Dennis Lance buses and Lynx provide trunk routes into Birmingham. Pictured on service 551 to Evesham is Dennis Lance 246, M246MRW. The lower picture shows 533, S533RWP from the recent batch of sixty-four Mercedes-Benz Vario minibuses. These are all based at Worcester. Interestingly, First Midland Red currently have no vehicles that qualify for the new corporate livery, the only fleet in the group in that predicament.** *Colin Lloyd*

755	AFJ755T	Leyland National 11351A/1R		B50F	1979	Western National, 1989
756	AFJ756T	Leyland National 11351A/1R		B50F	1979	Western National, 1990
758	XOV758T	Leyland National 11351A/1R		B49F	1979	Midland Red North, 1986
770	BVP770V	Leyland National 11351A/1R		B49F	1979	Midland Red, 1981
807	E807MOU	Mercedes-Benz 811D	Optare StarRider	B31F	1988	Western National, 1997
853	Q553UOC	Leyland Leopard PSU3F/4R	Plaxton P'mount 3200 (1984)	C49F	1982	Midland Red Coaches, 1986
854	Q276UOC	Leyland Leopard PSU3E/4R	Plaxton P'mount 3200 (1983)	C49F	1980	Midland Red, 1981
867	HUA607Y	Leyland Tiger TRCTL11/2RH	Plaxton Paramount 3200 E	C49F	1983	Rider, 1998
1003	B103JAB	Leyland Tiger TRCTL11/3RH	Plaxton Paramount 3200 II	C50FT	1985	
1005	B105JAB	Leyland Tiger TRCTL11/3RH	Plaxton Paramount 3200 II	C50FT	1985	
1006	B106JAB	Leyland Tiger TRCTL11/3RH	Plaxton Paramount 3200 II	C50FT	1985	
1007	B107JAB	Leyland Tiger TRCTL11/3RH	Plaxton Paramount 3200 II	C50FT	1985	
1010	EAH890Y	Leyland Tiger TRCTL11/3R	Plaxton Paramount 3200 E	C53F	1983	Midland Red Coaches, 1986
1011	A895KCL	Leyland Tiger TRCTL11/3R	Plaxton Paramount 3200 E	C53F	1983	Midland Red Coaches, 1986
1012	A896KCL	Leyland Tiger TRCTL11/3R	Plaxton Paramount 3200 E	C53F	1983	Midland Red Coaches, 1986

1101-1150   Leyland Lynx LX2R11C15Z4R   Leyland Lynx   B49F   1990

1101	G101HNP	1111	G111HNP	1121	G121HNP	1131	G131HNP	1141	G141HNP
1102	G102HNP	1112	G112HNP	1122	G122HNP	1132	G132HNP	1142	G142HNP
1103	G103HNP	1113	G113HNP	1123	G123HNP	1133	G133HNP	1143	G143HNP
1104	G104HNP	1114	G114HNP	1124	G124HNP	1134	G134HNP	1144	G144HNP
1105	G105HNP	1115	G115HNP	1125	G125HNP	1135	G135HNP	1145	G145HNP
1106	G106HNP	1116	G116HNP	1126	G126HNP	1136	G136HNP	1146	G146HNP
1107	G107HNP	1117	G117HNP	1127	G127HNP	1137	G137HNP	1147	G147HNP
1108	G108HNP	1118	G118HNP	1128	G128HNP	1138	G138HNP	1148	G148HNP
1109	G109HNP	1119	G119HNP	1129	G129HNP	1139	G139HNP	1149	G149HNP
1110	G110HNP	1120	G120HNP	1130	G130HNP	1140	G140HNP	1150	G150HNP

1301	C301PNP	Mercedes-Benz L608D	PMT Hanbridge	BC20F	1985
1309	C309PNP	Mercedes-Benz L608D	PMT Hanbridge	B20F	1985
1316	C316PNP	Mercedes-Benz L608D	PMT Hanbridge	B20F	1985
1319	C319PNP	Mercedes-Benz L608D	PMT Hanbridge	B20F	1985

1321-1361   Mercedes-Benz L608D   Robin Hood   B20F   1985-86

1321	C321PNP	1328	C328PNP	1332	C332PNP	1338	C338PNP	1352	C352PNP
1324	C324PNP	1331	C331PNP	1335	C335PNP	1340	C340PNP	1361	C361RUY

1362-1375   Mercedes-Benz L608D   Reeve Burgess   B20F   1986

1362	C362RUY	1364	C364RUY	1366	C366RUY	1368	C368RUY	1370	C370RUY
1363	C363RUY	1365	C365RUY	1367	C367RUY	1369	C369RUY	1375	C375RUY

1406-1439   Mercedes-Benz 609D   Reeve Burgess   B20F   1987-88

1406	E406HAB	1413	E413KUY	1420	E420KUY	1427	E427KUY	1434	E434KUY
1407	E407HAB	1414	E414KUY	1421	E421KUY	1428	E428KUY	1435	E435KUY
1408	E408HAB	1415	E415KUY	1422	E422KUY	1429	E429KUY	1436	E436KUY
1409	E409HAB	1416	E416KUY	1423	E423KUY	1430	E430KUY	1437	E437KUY
1410	E410HAB	1417	E417KUY	1424	E424KUY	1431	E431KUY	1438	E438KUY
1411	E411HAB	1418	E418KUY	1425	E425KUY	1432	E432KUY	1439	E439KUY
1412	E412KUY	1419	E419KUY	1426	E426KUY	1433	E433KUY		

1440	C475BHY	Mercedes-Benz L608D	Reeve Burgess	B20F	1986	Bristol, 1988

1441-1449   Mercedes-Benz L608D   Reeve Burgess   B20F   1986   Southdown, 1988

1441	C581SHC	1444	C584SHC	1446	C586SHC	1448	C588SHC	1449	C589SHC
1442	C582SHC	1445	C585SHC	1447	C587SHC				

1451	C790FRL	Mercedes-Benz L608D	Reeve Burgess	B20F	1986	Western National, 1989
1463	D763KWT	Mercedes-Benz 609D	Reeve Burgess	B20F	1987	SWT, 1994

The delivery of Vario minibuses during 1998 saw several of the older L608Ds displaced. During 1987-88 a single batch of 609D variants were delivered and these are represented in this picture of 1423, E423KUY taken in Dudley. *Les Peters*

1476-1499

Mercedes-Benz L608D | Reeve Burgess | B20F | 1986 | City Line, 1993
1478/80/93/4 Brewers 1997/98

1476	C476BHY	1480	C480BHY	1488	C488BHY	1492	C492BHY	1497	C497BHY
1477	C477BHY	1483	C483BHY	1490	C490BHY	1493	C213HTH	1498	C498BHY
1478	C478BHY	1487	C487BHY	1491	C491BHY	1494	C214HTH	1499	C499BHY

Ancilliary vehicles:-

2039	C339PNP	Mercedes-Benz L608D	Robin Hood	TV	1986	
2051	HHA101L	Leyland National 1151/1R/2501		TV	1972	Midland Red East, 1985
2052	MHS17P	Leyland Leopard PSU3C/3R	Alexander AY	TV	1976	Kelvin Central, 1991
2053	MHS33P	Leyland Leopard PSU3C/3R	Alexander AY	TV	1976	Kelvin Central, 1991
2054	WSU428S	Leyland Leopard PSU3C/3R	Alexander AY	TV	1977	Kelvin Central, 1991
2062	JHA230L	Leyland Leopard PSU3B/2R	Marshall	RV	1973	Midland Red, 1981
2064	NOE614R	Leyland Leopard PSU3D/4R	Plaxton Supreme III	RV	1976	Midland Red Coaches, 1986
2076	C376RUY	Mercedes-Benz L608D	Reeve Burgess	Eng	1986	

Previous Registrations:

Q276UOC	BVP804V	Q553UOC	LOA843X

Allocations:

Evesham (Abbey Road)

Tiger	867	1006	1007
Lance	Three from Worcester Allocation		
Lynx	1101	1102	+ four from Redditch Allocation

Hereford (Friar Street)

Mercedes-Benz	1301	1361	1363	1364	1365	1366	1367	1368
	1369	1370	1375	1436	1437	1438	1439	1441
	1442	1444	1445	1446	1447	1448	1449	1451
	1476	1477	1483	1487	1488	1490	1491	1492
	1497	1498	1499					
Leopard	853			Tiger	1010			
National	755			Lance	Four from Kidderminster Allocation			

Kidderminster (New Road)

Mercedes-Benz	1382	1406	1407	1408	1409	1410	1411	1412
	1413	1414	1415	1416	1417	1418	1419	1420
	1421	1422	1423	1424	1425	1426	1427	1428
	1429	1430	1431	1432	1433	1434	1435	1440
	1463	1478	1480	1493	1494			
Dart	313	339	341					
Lance	201	202	203	204	205	206	207	208
	209	210	211	212	213	214	215	216
	231	232	233	234	235	236	237	

Redditch (Plymouth Road)

Mercedes-Benz	1321	1324	1328	1331	1332	1335	1338	1340
	1352							
Dart	301	302	303	304	305	306	307	308
	309	310	311	312				
Lynx	1103	1104	1105	1106	1107	1108	1109	1110
	1111	1112	1113	1114	1115	1116	1117	1118
	1119	1120	1121	1122	1123	1124	1125	1126
	1127	1128	1129	1130	1131	1132	1133	1134
	1135	1136	1137	1138	1139	1140	1141	1142
	1143	1144	1145	1146	1147	1148	1149	1150

Worcester (Padmore Street)

Mercedes-Benz	501	502	503	504	505	506	507	508
	509	510	511	512	513	514	515	516
	517	518	519	520	521	522	523	524
	525	526	527	528	529	530	531	532
	533	534	535	536	537	538	539	540
	541	542	543	544	545	546	547	548
	549	550	551	552	553	554	555	556
	557	558	559	560	561	562	563	564
	807							
Leopard	854							
Tiger	1005	1011	1012					
National	722							
Lance	217	238	239	240	241	242	243	244
	245	246	247	248	249	250	251	252
	253	254	255	256	257			

Unallocated

Mercedes-Benz	1309	1316	1319	1362				
National	658	743	744	746	749	752	756	758
	770							
Tiger	1003							

FIRST LEICESTER

Leicester

Leicester CityBus Ltd, Abbey Park Road, Leicester, LE4 5AH

2	P176NAK	Volvo B10M-62	Plaxton Première 350	C53F	1997	Waugh, Greenhead, 1998
3	P177NAK	Volvo B10M-62	Plaxton Première 350	C53F	1997	Waugh, Greenhead, 1998
7	N378EAK	Volvo B10M-62	Plaxton Première 350	C53F	1996	Yorkshire Rider, 1998
11	SSU837	Volvo B10M-60	Plaxton Paramount 3500 III	C53F	1990	Yorkshire Rider, 1998

42-52

Dennis Dominator DDA142* East Lancashire B43/33F 1981-82 *49-52 are DDA141

42	TBC42X	45	TBC45X	49	TBC49X	50	TBC50X	52	TBC52X
43	TBC43X	46	TBC46X						

58-78

Dennis Dominator DDA155* East Lancashire B43/33F 1982-83 *70 is DDA160, 71-4 are DDA173, 75-8 are DDA168

58	VAY58X	64	XJF64Y	68	XJF68Y	72	A72FRY	76	A76FRY
61	XJF61Y	65	XJF65Y	69	XJF69Y	73	A73FRY	77	A77FRY
62	XJF62Y	66	XJF66Y	70	AUT70Y	74	A74FRY	78	A78FRY
63	XJF63Y	67	XJF67Y	71	A71FRY	75	A75FRY		

79-86

Dennis Dominator DDA1102* East Lancashire B43/33F 1984-85 *81-3 are DDA1002 *84-86 are DDA901 and B46/33F

79	B79MJF	81	B81MJF	83	B83MJF	85	B85MRY	86	B86MRY
80	B80MJF	82	B82MJF	84	B84MRY				

87-99

Dennis Dominator DDA1015 East Lancashire B46/33F 1988

87	E87HNR	90	E90HNR	93	E93HNR	96	E96HNR	98	E98HNR
88	E88HNR	91	E91HNR	94	E94HNR	97	E97HNR	99	E99HNR
89	E89HNR	92	E92HNR	95	E95HNR				

143	F143MBC	Dennis Dominator DDA1024	East Lancashire	B46/33F	1989	
144	F636BKD	Dennis Dominator DDA1025	East Lancashire	B45/31F	1989	North Western, 1997
145	F637BKD	Dennis Dominator DDA1025	East Lancashire	B45/31F	1989	North Western, 1997
146	F146MBC	Dennis Dominator DDA1024	East Lancashire	B46/33F	1989	
147	G629EKA	Dennis Dominator DDA1031	East Lancashire	B45/31F	1990	North Western, 1997
148	G667FKA	Dennis Dominator DDA1031	East Lancashire	B47/29F	1990	North Western, 1997
149	F149MBC	Dennis Dominator DDA1024	East Lancashire	B46/33F	1989	
150	F150MBC	Dennis Dominator DDA1024	East Lancashire	B46/33F	1989	

First Leicester and First Northampton share many operational and engineering facilities and plans to eliminate duplicate fleet nubers to combine the fleet have been proposed, though not yet implemented. Towards that aim, Leicester have recently been using white in place of cream as shown by East Lancashire-bodied Dennis Dominator 148, G667FKA which was acquired from North Western in 1997.
Paul Wigan

151	F151MBC	Dennis Dominator DDA1024	East Lancashire	B46/33F	1989	
152	F152MBC	Dennis Dominator DDA1024	East Lancashire	B46/33F	1989	Northampton, 1998
184	FUT184V	Dennis Dominator DDA120	East Lancashire	B43/33F	1980	Northampton, 1998
179	FUT179V	Dennis Dominator DDA120	East Lancashire	B43/33F	1979	
205	NFP205W	Dennis Dominator DDA131	East Lancashire	B43/33F	1980	
206	MUT206W	Dennis Dominator DDA131	East Lancashire	B43/33F	1980	
250	FUT250V	Dennis Dominator DDA120	East Lancashire	B43/33F	1979	
257	MUT257W	Dennis Dominator DDA120	East Lancashire	B43/33F	1981	
269	BLS443Y	MCW Metrobus DR102/33	Alexander RL	B45/33F	1983	Midland Bluebird, 1994
282	LSU717	Volvo Citybus B10M-50	Alexander RV	BC47/35F	1989	Northampton, 1997

301-310

Optare L1070 — Optare Excel — N38F — 1997

301	R1LCB	303	R3LCB	305	R5LCB	307	R7LCB	309	R9LCB
302	R2LCB	304	R4LCB	306	R6LCB	308	R8LCB	310	R10LCB

344	R344SUT	Scania L113CRL	Wright Axcess-ultralow	N40F	1998
345	R345SUT	Scania L113CRL	Wright Axcess-ultralow	N40F	1998
346	R346SUT	Scania L113CRL	Wright Axcess-ultralow	N40F	1998

347-358

Scania L113CRL — Wright Axcess-ultralow — N40F — 1998

347	S347MFP	350	S350MFP	353	S353MFP	355	S355MFP	357	S357MFP
348	S348MFP	351	S351MFP	354	S354MFP	356	S356MFP	358	S358MFP
349	S349MFP	352	S352MFP						

501-510

Mercedes-Benz O405 — Optare Prisma — B49F — 1995

501	M501GRY	503	M503GRY	505	M505GRY	507	M507GRY	509	M509GRY
502	M502GRY	504	M504GRY	506	M506GRY	508	M508GRY	510	M510GRY

611-619

Dennis Falcon HC SDA422 — East Lancashire EL2000 — B48F — 1991-92

611	H611EJF	613	H613EJF	615	H615EJF	617	K617SBC	619	K619SBC
612	H612EJF	614	H614EJF	616	H616EJF	618	K618SBC		

620-626

Dennis Falcon HC SDA422 — Northern Counties Paladin — B48F — 1993

620	K620SBC	622	K622SBC	624	L624XFP	625	L625XFP	626	L626XFP
621	K621SBC	623	L623XFP						

627	C107SDX	Dennis Falcon HC SDA416	Northern Counties	B45F	1985	Ipswich, 1997
628	C108SDX	Dennis Falcon HC SDA416	Northern Counties	B45F	1985	Ipswich, 1997
629	C109SDX	Dennis Falcon HC SDA416	Northern Counties	B45F	1986	Ipswich, 1997
630	C111SDX	Dennis Falcon HC SDA416	Northern Counties	B45F	1986	Ipswich, 1997
631	YDX100Y	Dennis Falcon HC SDA408	East Lancashire	B44D	1983	Ipswich, 1997

701	HDZ5459	Renault S75	Wright NimBus	B28F	1990	The Bee Line, 1998
702	HDZ5462	Renault S75	Wright NimBus	B28F	1990	The Bee Line, 1998
703	HDZ5475	Renault S75	Wright NimBus	B28F	1990	The Bee Line, 1998
704	HDZ5479	Renault S75	Wright NimBus	B28F	1990	The Bee Line, 1998
705	HDZ5477	Renault S75	Wright NimBus	B28F	1990	CentreWest, 1998
707	HDZ5466	Renault S75	Wright NimBus	B28F	1990	CentreWest, 1998
708	HDZ5488	Renault S75	Wright NimBus	B28F	1990	CentreWest, 1998
710	HDZ5471	Renault S75	Wright NimBus	B28F	1990	Northampton, 1998
711	HDZ5472	Renault S75	Wright NimBus	B28F	1990	Northampton, 1998

Opposite:- **Two views of First Leicester buses taken near Charles Street, Leicester provide the colour pictures for this fleet. The upper picture shows 301, R1LCB, an Optare Excel and one of ten delivered in 1997 and now repainted into corporate colours. The only other examples of this type with FirstGroup are four in service with CentreWest and a further ten with First Manchester. The lower picture shows 266, ULS642X, a MCW Metrobus new to Midland Scottish though it has subsequently moved to Northampton as part of the interchange between these two fleets that have a common management.** *Tony Wilson*

746-761

746-761	Renault-Dodge S56	Northern Counties	B25F*	1991-93	*753/4 are BC25F

746	K746VJU	750	K750VJU	753	J753MFP	756	J756MFP	759	J759NNR
748	K748VJU	751	H751ENR	754	J754MFP	757	J757MFP	760	K760SBC
749	K749VJU	752	H752ENR	755	J755MFP	758	J758NNR	761	K761SBC

776	G259LWF	Renault-Dodge S56	Reeve Burgess Beaver	B23F	1989	Yorkshire Rider, 1996

781-795

781-795	Renault S75	Wright NimBus	B28F	1990	CentreWest, 1997

781	HDZ5481	784	HDZ5484	787	HDZ5487	790	HDZ5490	793	HDZ5469
782	HDZ5482	785	HDZ5485	788	HDZ5464	791	HDZ5465	794	HDZ5440
783	HDZ5463	786	HDZ5457	789	HDZ5489	792	HDZ5467	795	HDZ5441

Special event vehicle:

154	FJF193	Leyland Titan PD2/1	Leyland	B33/29R	1950
233	UFP233S	Dennis Dominator DDA101	East Lancashire	B43/31F	1977

Ancilliary vehicle:

240	FUT240V	Dennis Dominator DDA120	East Lancashire	TV	1979

Previous Registrations:

HDZ5440 etc	From new	LSU717	F87DVV

Allocations:-

Leicester (Abbey Park Road)

Renault-Dodge	701	702	703	704	705	707	708	710
	711	746	748	750	753	760	761	781
	782	783	784	785	786	787	788	789
	790	791	792	793	794	795		
Volvo B10M Coach	2	3	7	11				
Excel	301	302	303	304	305	306	307	308
	309	310						
Dennis Falcon	611	612	613	614	615	616	617	618
	619	620	621	622	623	624	625	626
	627	628	629	630	631			
Mercedes-Benz O405	501	502	503	504	505	506	507	508
	509	510						
Metrobus	269	272						
Dominator	42	43	45	46	49	50	52	58
	61	62	63	64	65	66	67	68
	69	70	71	72	73	74	75	76
	77	78	79	80	81	82	83	84
	85	86	87	88	89	90	91	92
	93	94	95	96	97	98	99	143
	144	145	146	147	148	149	150	151
	152	206						
Volvo Citybus	282							

Unallocated:-

Renault-Dodge	749	751	752	754	755	756	757	758
	759	776						
Dominator	179	184	205	233	240	250	257	

FIRST NORTHAMPTON

Northampton

Northampton Transport Ltd, The Bus Depot, St James Road, Northampton, NN5 5JD

19	PXI8935	Leyland Tiger TRCL10/3RZA	Duple 340	C53F	1987	SMT, 1996	
20	NTL655	Leyland Tiger TRCL10/3RZA	Duple 340	C53F	1987	SMT, 1996	

31-35			MCW Metrobus DR102/35	Alexander RL	B45/33F	1983	Leicester, 1998
31	AUT31Y	32	AUT32Y	33	AUT33Y	34	AUT34Y	35	AUT35Y

41	N41RRP	Volvo B10L	Alexander Ultra	N41F	1995	
42	N42RRP	Volvo B10L	Alexander Ultra	N41F	1995	
43	N43RRP	Volvo B10L	Alexander Ultra	N41F	1995	
46	UFW40W	Bristol VRT/LL3/6LXB	East Lancashire	B50/38F	1981	RoadCar, 1997
47	UFW41W	Bristol VRT/LL3/6LXB	East Lancashire	B50/38F	1981	RoadCar, 1997

48-58			Bristol VRT/SL3/6LXB	Alexander AL	B45/27D	1978	
48	CNH48T	49	CNH49T	52	CNH52T	53	CNH53T	58	CNH58T

76	ABD76X	Bristol VRT/SL3/6LXB	East Lancashire	BC43/27D	1982	

83-88			Volvo Citybus B10M-50	Alexander RV	BC47/35F	1989	
83	F83XBD	84	F84XBD	85	F85XBD	86	F86DVV	88	F88DVV

89-94			Volvo Citybus B10M-55	Alexander RV	BC47/35F	1990	
89	H289VRP	91	H291VRP	92	H292VRP	93	H293VRP	94	H294VRP
90	H290VRP						

95-100			Volvo Citybus B10M-50	Alexander RV	BC47/35F	1991	
95	J295GNV	97	J297GNV	98	J298GNV	99	J299GNV	100	J210GNV
96	J296GNV						

Alexander-bodied Volvo Citybuses were the preferred choice for Northampton Transport from 1989 - all fitted with high-back seating and carrying names of local dignitaries. This latter feature is now being discontinued on repaint thus 97, J297GNV was still displaying one when pictured in 1998.

For a short time Northampton used second-hand Dennis saloons from Ipswich, though the last has recently been sold. Pictured in the latest livery is 627, C107SDX, a Northern Counties-bodied example. Of interest is the contrasting door types, with two-piece for the front entrance and a four-piece for the central exit. *Phillip Stephenson*

101	D101XNV	Volvo Citybus B10M-50	East Lancashire	BC47/31F	1986	
102	D102XNV	Volvo Citybus B10M-50	East Lancashire	BC47/31F	1986	
111	E111NNV	Volvo Citybus B10M-50	Duple 300	BC49F	1988	
112	G112ENV	Volvo Citybus B10M-55	Duple 300	BC49F	1989	
113	G113ENV	Volvo Citybus B10M-55	Duple 300	BC51F	1989	
114	G114ENV	Volvo Citybus B10M-55	Duple 300	BC51F	1989	
115	J115MRP	Volvo Citybus B10M-55	East Lancashire EL2000	BC47F	1992	
121	K121URP	Volvo Citybus B10M-50	Alexander RV	BC47/35F	1992	
122	WSU481	Volvo Citybus B10M-50	East Lancashire Pyoneer (98)	BC49/39F	1992	

123-132 Volvo Citybus B10M-50 Alexander RV BC47/35F 1992-93

123	K123URP	125	K125URP	127	K127GNH	129	K129GNH	131	K131GNH
124	K124URP	126	K126URP	128	K128GNH	130	K130GNH	132	K132GNH

265	ULS637X	MCW Metrobus DR102/28	Alexander RL	B45/33F	1982	Midland Bluebird, 1994
266	ULS642X	MCW Metrobus DR104/10	Alexander RL	B45/33F	1982	Midland Bluebird, 1994
267	BLS423Y	MCW Metrobus DR102/33	Alexander RL	B45/33F	1983	Midland Bluebird, 1994
268	BLS432Y	MCW Metrobus DR102/33	Alexander RL	B45/33F	1983	Midland Bluebird, 1994
270	ULS636X	MCW Metrobus DR102/28	Alexander RL	B45/33F	1982	Midland Bluebird, 1994
341	R341SUT	Scania L113CRL	Wright Axcess-ultralow	N47F	1998	
342	R342SUT	Scania L113CRL	Wright Axcess-ultralow	N47F	1998	
343	R343SUT	Scania L113CRL	Wright Axcess-ultralow	N47F	1998	

Opposite,top:- **Northampton took delivery of three Alexander Ultra buses in 1995, based on the Volvo B10L chassis. The first of these, 41, N41RRP, has now received corporate livery and is seen in the town shortly after repaint.** *Tony Wilson*
Opposite, bottom:- **In 1997 the then five year old Alexander body of 122 was badly damaged. The Volvo chassis was rebodied by East Lancashire with a new Pyoneer body the following year and was shown with other FirstGroup vehicles at Showbus.** *Phillip Stephenson*

359	S359MFP	Scania L94UB	Wright Axcess Flowline	N40F	1998	
360	S360MFP	Scania L94UB	Wright Axcess Flowline	N40F	1998	
361	S361MFP	Scania L94UB	Wright Axcess Flowline	N40F	1998	
408	EWR652Y	Leyland Tiger TRBTL11/2R	Duple Dominant	B51F	1983	Essex Buses, 1998
409	EWR651Y	Leyland Tiger TRBTL11/2R	Duple Dominant	BC47F	1983	Essex Buses, 1998
410	EWR653Y	Leyland Tiger TRBTL11/2R	Duple Dominant	BC47F	1983	Essex Buses, 1998
411	A660KUM	Leyland Tiger TRBTL11/2R	Duple Dominant	B51F	1983	Essex Buses, 1998

501-506		Volvo B10L(CNG)	Alexander Ultra	N41F	1997	
501	P501MVV	**503**	P503MVV	**504**	P504MVV	**505**	P505MVV	**506**	P506MVV
502	P502MVV								

712	HDZ5473	Renault S75	Wright NimBus	B28F	1990	Centrewest, 1998
714	HDZ5478	Renault S75	Wright NimBus	B28F	1990	Centrewest, 1998

Previous Registrations:

NTL655	E353KSF, A13SMT, WSV144	SSU837	G73RGG, 8995WY, G427PWW
PXI8935	E352KSF, A12SMT	WSU481	K122URP

Allocation:

Northampton (St James Road)

Renault-Dodge	712	714					
Tiger coach	19	20					
Tiger bus	408	409	410	411			
Volvo B10M Bus	111	112	113	114	115		
Volvo B10L	41	42	43	501	502	503	504	505
	506						
Scania L	341	342	343	359	360	361	
Bristol VR	46	47					
Metrobus	31	32	33	34	35	265	266	267
	268	270					
Volvo Citybus	83	84	85	86	88	89	90	91
	92	93	94	95	96	97	98	99
	100	101	102	121	122	123	124	125
	126	127	128	129	130	131	132	

Unallocated

Bristol VR	48	49	52	53	58	76

FIRST EASTERN COUNTIES

Blue Bus - Eastern Counties - Flying Banana

First Eastern Counties Buses Ltd; Halesworth Transit Ltd
Rouen House, Rouen Road, Norwich, NR1 1RB

19	C130HJN	Leyland Tiger TRCTL11/3R	Plaxton Paramount 3200 II E	C53F	1986	Essex Buses, 1998
20	FEH1Y	Leyland Tiger TRCTL11/3R	Plaxton Paramount 3500	C50FT	1983	Midland Red West, 1997
21	6149KP	Leyland Tiger TRCTL11/3R	Plaxton Paramount 3200 E	C53F	1983	Vanguard, 1993
22	7694VC	Leyland Tiger TRCTL11/3R	Plaxton Paramount 3200 E	C53F	1983	Vanguard, 1993
23	CSV992	Leyland Tiger TRCTL11/3R	Plaxton Paramount 3200 E	C53F	1983	Badgerline, 1996
24	CSV303	Leyland Tiger TRCTL11/3R	Plaxton Paramount 3200 E	C53F	1983	Badgerline, 1996
25	CSV524	Leyland Tiger TRCTL11/3R	Plaxton Paramount 3200 E	C53F	1983	Badgerline, 1996
26	F613XWY	Leyland Tiger TRCTL11/3ARZA	Plaxton Paramount 3200 IIIE	C53F	1988	Thamesway, 1996
27	F614XWY	Leyland Tiger TRCTL11/3ARZA	Plaxton Paramount 3200 IIIE	C53F	1988	Thamesway, 1996
28	B104JAB	Leyland Tiger TRCTL11/3RH	Plaxton Paramount 3200 II	C50F	1985	Midland Red West, 1997
29	B568BOK	Leyland Tiger TRCTL11/3RH	Duple Caribbean 2	C50FT	1984	Western National, 1997
30	P330RVG	Volvo B10M-62	Plaxton Première 320	C53F	1997	
31	P731NVG	Volvo B10M-62	Plaxton Première 320	C53F	1996	
32	P732NVG	Volvo B10M-62	Plaxton Première 320	C53F	1996	
33	P733NVG	Volvo B10M-62	Plaxton Première 320	C53F	1996	
34	P734NVG	Volvo B10M-62	Plaxton Première 320	C53F	1996	
38	HEX119Y	Volvo B10M-61	Plaxton Paramount 3200	C51F	1983	Blue Bus, 1996

40-46

		Volvo B10M-62	Plaxton Première 320	C53F	1995-96	Essex Buses (T), 1997-98

40	N616APU	42	N842DVF	44	N618APU	45	N619APU	46	N604APU
41	N841DVF	43	N617APU						

	C372CAS	Leyland Olympian ONLXB/1RH	Alexander RL	B47/25F	1986	Capital, 1999
	C373CAS	Leyland Olympian ONLXB/1RH	Alexander RL	B47/25F	1986	Capital, 1999
	C374CAS	Leyland Olympian ONLXB/1RH	Alexander RL	BC47/25F	1986	Capital, 1999
	A980OST	Leyland Olympian ONLXB/1R	Alexander RL	B45/32F	1984	Capital, 1999
68	G123YEV	Leyland Olympian ONCL10/1RZ	Alexander RL	B47/33F	1989	First Capital, 1999

69-75

		Leyland Olympian ONCL10/1RZ	Alexander RL	B47/28F	1989	Centrewest, 1999

69	G48XLO	71	G50XLO	73	G52XLO	74	G54XLO	75	G53XLO
70	G49XLO	72	G51XLO						

First Eastern Counties are increasing the number of Olympians following the transfer of low-height models from First Capital in recent months. One of Eastern Counties' own examples is 117, J625BVG which is seen at Norwich bus station.
Malcolm Flynn

76	G125YEV	Leyland Olympian ONCL10/1RZ	Alexander RL	B47/33F	1989	First Capital, 1999
77	G133ATW	Leyland Olympian ONCL10/1RZ	Northern Counties Palatine	B45/30F	1989	First Capital, 1999
78	G47XLO	Leyland Olympian ONCL10/1RZ	Alexander RL	B47/28F	1989	Centrewest, 1999
80	G46XLO	Leyland Olympian ONCL10/1RZ	Alexander RL	B47/28F	1989	Centrewest, 1999
84	F155XYG	Leyland Olympian ONCL10/1RZ	Northern Counties	B45/29F	1988	Yorkshire Rider (C), 1999
88	FUM494Y	Leyland Olympian ONLXB/1R	Eastern Coach Works	B45/32F	1983	Yorkshire Rider (C), 1999
89	F154XYG	Leyland Olympian ONCL10/1RZ	Northern Counties	B45/29F	1988	Yorkshire Rider (L), 1999
90	FUM498Y	Leyland Olympian ONLXB/1R	Eastern Coach Works	B45/32F	1983	Yorkshire Rider (C), 1999
91	FUM495Y	Leyland Olympian ONLXB/1R	Eastern Coach Works	B45/32F	1983	Yorkshire Rider (C), 1999
92	F151XYG	Leyland Olympian ONCL10/1RZ	Northern Counties	B45/29F	1988	Yorkshire Rider (L), 1998
93	F153XYG	Leyland Olympian ONCL10/1RZ	Northern Counties	B45/29F	1988	Yorkshire Rider (L), 1998
94	KGG156Y	Leyland Olympian ONTL11/1R	Eastern Coach Works	B47/31F	1983	Greater Glasgow (K), 1997
95	KGG158Y	Leyland Olympian ONTL11/1R	Eastern Coach Works	B47/31F	1983	Greater Glasgow (K), 1997
96	XAU700Y	Leyland Olympian ONLXB/1R	Eastern Coach Works	B45/32F	1983	Trent, 1998
97	A711DAU	Leyland Olympian ONLXB/1R	Eastern Coach Works	B45/32F	1983	Trent, 1998
98	KGG157Y	Leyland Olympian ONTL11/1R	Eastern Coach Works	B47/31F	1983	Greater Glasgow (K), 1997
99	KGG159Y	Leyland Olympian ONTL11/1R	Eastern Coach Works	B47/31F	1984	Greater Glasgow (K), 1997
100	KGG160Y	Leyland Olympian ONTL11/1R	Eastern Coach Works	B47/31F	1983	Greater Glasgow (K), 1997
101	XHK235X	Leyland Olympian ONLXB/1R	Eastern Coach Works	B47/31F	1981	Thamesway, 1996
102	XHK236X	Leyland Olympian ONLXB/1R	Eastern Coach Works	B47/31F	1981	Thamesway, 1996
103	XHK237X	Leyland Olympian ONLXB/1R	Eastern Coach Works	B47/31F	1981	Thamesway, 1996

104-108

		Leyland Olympian ONLXB/1RZ	Northern Counties	B40/35F*	1989	*107/8 are BC40/25F
104	F101AVG	105 F102AVG	106 F103AVG	107 F104AVG	108 F105AVG	

109	H101KVX	Leyland Olympian ON2R50G13Z4	Leyland	B45/32F	1990	Thamesway, 1996
110	H102KVX	Leyland Olympian ON2R50G13Z4	Leyland	B45/32F	1990	Thamesway, 1996
111	H103KVX	Leyland Olympian ON2R50G13Z4	Leyland	B45/32F	1990	Thamesway, 1996
112	H104KVX	Leyland Olympian ON2R50G13Z4	Leyland	B45/32F	1990	Thamesway, 1996

113-117

		Leyland Olympian ON2R50G13Z4	Leyland	B47/31F	1991-92	
113	J621BVG	114 J622BVG	115 J623BVG	116 J624BVG	117 J625BVG	

118	E40OAH	Volvo Citybus B10M-50	East Lancashire	BC45/33F	1987	Blue Bus, 1996
119	E41OAH	Volvo Citybus B10M-50	East Lancashire	BC45/33F	1987	Blue Bus, 1996

199	WPW199S	Bristol VRT/SL3/6LXB	Eastern Coach Works	B43/31F	1977	
212	WWY122S	Bristol VRT/SL3/6LXB	Eastern Coach Works	B43/31F	1977	Yorkshire Rider, 1996
213	WWY123S	Bristol VRT/SL3/6LXB	Eastern Coach Works	B43/31F	1977	Yorkshire Rider, 1996

216-229

		Bristol VRT/SL3/6LXB	Eastern Coach Works	B43/31F	1978-79	
216	BCL216T	219 BVG219T	220 BVG220T	224 BVG224T	229 DEX229T	

234	LUA719V	Bristol VRT/SL3/6LXB	Eastern Coach Works	B43/31F	1980	Yorkshire Rider, 19966

239-249

		Bristol VRT/SL3/6LXB	Eastern Coach Works	B43/31F	1979-80	246/9 Trent 1991
239	HAH239V	240 HAH240V	242 JAH242V	246 GRA842V	249 GRA847V	

253-259

		Bristol VRT/SL3/6LXB	Eastern Coach Works	B43/31F	1980	
253	PCL253W	255 PCL255W	257 PCL257W	258 RAH258W	259 RAH259W	
254	PCL254W					

Opposite:- **FirstGroup's operations in East Anglia came under common management during 1999 and plans are being made to use a common livery style for all vehicles that do not qualify for the corporate scheme. A standard yellow upper half will contrast with different colours for the skirts. Eastern Counties will use red, Eastern National green, and Thamesway pink. The upper picture shows the current scheme on Leyland National Greenway 654, NIL3954, which was new to the company. In National Bus times, Bury St Edmunds depot did not operate the National, though many are now based there. The lower picture shows the current Blue Bus livery applied to buses based at Great Yarmouth, many of which were acquired with the former municipal company. Pictured on town service is 327, PVG27W .** *Malcolm Flynn/Richard Godfrey*

During 1998 six Volvo B6 buses were transferred from Yorkshire Rider's *Kingfisher* unit to Eastern Counties. Pictured here is 394, L101PWR which is fitted with an Alexander Dash body. *Malcolm Flynn*

261	RAH261W	Bristol VRT/SL3/6LXB	Eastern Coach Works	B43/31F	1980	
262	RAH262W	Bristol VRT/SL3/6LXB	Eastern Coach Works	B43/31F	1980	
263	RAH263W	Bristol VRT/SL3/6LXB	Eastern Coach Works	B43/31F	1980	
264	GGM107W	Bristol VRT/SL3/6LXB	Eastern Coach Works	B43/31F	1980	The Bee Line, 1997
265	CJH144V	Bristol VRT/SL3/6LXB	Eastern Coach Works	B43/31F	1980	The Bee Line, 1997
266	RAH266W	Bristol VRT/SL3/6LXB	Eastern Coach Works	B43/31F	1980	
267	RAH267W	Bristol VRT/SL3/6LXB	Eastern Coach Works	B43/31F	1980	
268	PUM148W	Bristol VRT/SL3/6LXB	Eastern Coach Works	B43/31F	1980	Yorkshire Rider, 1996

269-282
Bristol VRT/SL3/6LXB Eastern Coach Works B43/31F 1980-81

| 269 | RAH269W | 271 | TAH271W | 273 | TAH273W | 276 | TAH276W | 281 | VAH281X |
| 270 | RAH270W | 272 | TAH272W | 275 | TAH275W | 277 | VAH277X | 282 | VAH282X |

283-297
Bristol VRT/SL3/6LXB Eastern Coach Works B43/31F* 1981-82 *284/5/7 are BC41/25F

| 283 | VEX283X | 285 | VEX285X | 287 | VEX287X | 290 | VEX290X | 297 | VEX297X |
| 284 | VEX284X | 286 | VEX286X | 288 | VEX288X | 294 | VEX294X | | |

303-310
Bristol VRT/SL3/6LXB Eastern Coach Works B43/31F 1981 Trent, 1991

| 303 | PRC848X | 305 | PRC851X | 307 | PRC853X | 309 | PRC855X | 310 | PRC857X |
| 304 | PRC850X | 306 | PRC852X | | | | | | |

| 318 | PWY41W | Bristol VRT/SL3/6LXB | Eastern Coach Works | B43/31F | 1980 | Yorkshire Rider (Y), 1999 |
| 319 | GGM90W | Bristol VRT/SL3/6LXB | Eastern Coach Works | B43/31F | 1980 | First Bee Line, 1998 |

Three of Great Yarmouth's Dennis Darts were supplied in 1990 with Duple Dartline bodywork, the style originally conceived for the Dennis chassis. Now as First Blue Bus, 417, G457KNG is seen on an Asda shoppers special. *Richard Godfrey*

320	CVF31T	Bristol VRT/SL3/6LXB	Eastern Coach Works	B43/31F	1979	Blue Bus, 1996	
325	PVG25W	Bristol VRT/SL3/6LXB	Eastern Coach Works	B43/31F	1981	Blue Bus, 1996	
327	PVG27W	Bristol VRT/SL3/6LXB	Eastern Coach Works	B43/31F	1981	Blue Bus, 1996	
329	CVF29T	Bristol VRT/SL3/6LXB	Eastern Coach Works	B43/31F	1979	Blue Bus, 1996	
330	CVF30T	Bristol VRT/SL3/6LXB	Eastern Coach Works	B43/31F	1979	Blue Bus, 1996	
336	ABD72X	Bristol VRT/SL2/6LX	East Lancashire	B44/28D	1982	Northampton, 1995	
337	ABD73X	Bristol VRT/SL2/6LX	East Lancashire	B44/28D	1982	Northampton, 1995	
338	ABD73X	Bristol VRT/SL2/6LX	East Lancashire	B44/28D	1982	Northampton, 1995	
340	GGM89W	Bristol VRT/SL3/6LXB	Eastern Coach Works	B43/34F	1980	The Bee Line, 1997	
355	S979JLM	Dennis Dart SLF	Marshall	N27F	1998	On loan from Centre West	

394-399
Volvo B6-9.9m — Alexander Dash — B40F — 1994 — Yorkshire Rider (K), 1998

394	L101PWR	396	L103PWR	397	L104PWR	398	L105PWR	399	L106PWR
395	L102PWR								

400	L601MWC	Volvo B6-9.9M	Northern Counties Paladin	B40F	1993	Essex Buses (EN), 1997

401-410
Volvo B6-9.9M — Plaxton Pointer — B40F — 1994

401	M584ANG	403	M586ANG	405	M588ANG	407	M590ANG	409	M592ANG
402	M585ANG	404	M587ANG	406	M589ANG	408	M591ANG	410	M593ANG

411	L807OPU	Dennis Dart 9SDL3034	Plaxton Pointer	B34F	1994	Essex Buses (EN), 1997
412	M923TEV	Dennis Dart 9.8SDL3035	Plaxton Pointer	B39F	1994	Essex Buses (T), 1997
413	N345CJA	Volvo B6-9.9m	Alexander Dash	B36F	1996	Greater Manchester, 1997
414	N346CJA	Volvo B6-9.9m	Alexander Dash	B36F	1996	Greater Manchester, 1997
415	L501VHU	Dennis Dart 9SDL3034	Plaxton Pointer	B35F	1994	Bristol (City Line), 1997
416	G456KNG	Dennis Dart 9SDL3002	Duple Dartline	B39F	1990	Blue Bus, 1996
417	G457KNG	Dennis Dart 9SDL3002	Duple Dartline	B39F	1990	Blue Bus, 1996
418	G458KNG	Dennis Dart 9SDL3002	Duple Dartline	B39F	1990	Blue Bus, 1996

First Eastern Counties has been allocated a further ten Mercedes-Benz Vario minibuses from the 1998 allocation with three being allocated to Rosemary Coaches at Kings Lynn and seven, including 825, S825TCL, shown here, to Norwich. *Phillip Stephenson*

419	K62KEX	Dennis Dart 9.8SDL3025	East Lancashire	BC43F	1993	Blue Bus, 1996
420	K63KEX	Dennis Dart 9.8SDL3025	East Lancashire	BC43F	1993	Blue Bus, 1996
421	K741JAH	Dennis Dart 9SDL3011	Plaxton Pointer	B33F	1993	
422	K742JAH	Dennis Dart 9SDL3011	Plaxton Pointer	B33F	1993	
423	K743JAH	Dennis Dart 9SDL3011	Plaxton Pointer	B33F	1993	
424	K744JAH	Dennis Dart 9SDL3011	Plaxton Pointer	B33F	1993	

425-430

		Dennis Dart 9SDL3041	Plaxton Pointer	B35F	1994	
425	M375YEX	**427** M377YEX	**428** M378YEX	**429** M379YEX	**430** M380YEX	
426	M376YEX					

| 431 | N625GAH | Dennis Dart 9SDL3041 | Plaxton Pointer | B34F | 1995 | |
| 432 | N626GAH | Dennis Dart 9SDL3041 | Plaxton Pointer | B34F | 1995 | |

433-450

		Dennis Dart SLF	Plaxton Pointer	N35F	1996-97	
433	P433NEX	**437** P437NEX	**441** P441NEX	**445** P445NEX	**448** P448NEX
434	P434NEX	**438** P438NEX	**442** P442NEX	**446** P446NEX	**449** P449NEX
435	P435NEX	**439** P439NEX	**443** P443NEX	**447** P447NEX	**450** P450NEX
436	P436NEX	**440** P440NEX	**444** P844OAH		

451	P451RPW	Dennis Dart SLF	Plaxton Pointer	N40F	1997	
452	P452RPW	Dennis Dart SLF	Plaxton Pointer	N40F	1997	
453	P453RPW	Dennis Dart SLF	Plaxton Pointer	N40F	1997	
454	M201VWW	Dennis Dart 9.8SDL3054	Plaxton Pointer	B40F	1995	Yorkshire Rider (Leeds), 1997
455	M202VWW	Dennis Dart 9.8SDL3054	Plaxton Pointer	B40F	1995	Yorkshire Rider (K), 1997
456	M203VWW	Dennis Dart 9.8SDL3054	Plaxton Pointer	B40F	1995	Yorkshire Rider (K), 1997
457	M107RRJ	Dennis Dart 9.8SDL3054	Northern Counties Paladin	B40F	1995	Yorkshire Rider (York), 1997

458-478

Dennis Dart SLF — Plaxton Pointer 2 — N37F — 1997-98

458	R458BNG	463	R463CAH	467	R467CAH	471	R471CAH	475	R475CAH
459	R459BNG	464	R464CAH	468	R468CAH	472	R472CAH	476	R476CAH
460	R460BNG	465	R465CAH	469	R469CAH	473	R473CAH	477	R477CAH
461	R461BNG	466	R466CAH	470	R470CAH	474	R474CAH	478	R478CAH
462	R462BNG								

479	L502VHU	Dennis Dart 9SDL3034	Plaxton Pointer	B35F	1994	Bristol (City Line), 1997

480-489

Dennis Dart SLF — Plaxton Pointer 2 — N37F — 1998

480	R680DPW	482	R682DPW	484	R684DPW	486	R686DPW	488	R688DPW
481	R681DPW	483	R683DPW	485	R685DPW	487	R687DPW	489	R689DPW

490-500

Dennis Dart 8.5SDL3003 — Wright Handybus — B26F — 1991 — CentreWest, 1998

490	JDZ2319	493	JDZ2376	495	JDZ2318	497	JDZ2321	499	JDZ2331
491	JDZ2337	494	JDZ2335	496	JDZ2320	498	JDZ2336	500	JDZ2332
492	JDZ2338								

501	JDZ2325	Dennis Dart 8.5SDL3003	Wright Handybus	B30F	1990	CentreWest, 1998

506-510

Dennis Javelin 11SDL1933 — Duple 300 — BC48F — 1989

506	G706JAH	507	G707JAH	508	G708JAH	509	G709JAH	510	G710JAH

511-520

Dennis Javelin 11SDL1924 — Plaxton Derwent II — BC51F — 1990

511	H611RAH	514	H614RAH	516	H616RAH	518	H618RAH	520	H620RAH
512	H612RAH	515	H615RAH	517	H617RAH	519	H619RAH		

536-540

Dennis Lance 11SDA3101 — Northern Counties Paladin — B49F — 1993

536	K736JAH	537	K737JAH	538	K738JAH	539	K739JAH	540	K740JAH

541-550

Scania L113CRL — Wright Axcess-ultralow — N47F — 1997

541	P541RNG	543	P543RNG	545	P545RNG	547	P547RNG	549	P549RNG
542	P542RNG	544	P544RNG	546	P546RNG	548	P548RNG	550	P550RNG

551-564

Scania L113CRL — Wright Axcess-ultralow — N40F — 1998

551	R551CNG	554	R554CNG	558	R258DVF	561	R261DVF	563	R263DVF
552	R552CNG	556	R556CNG	559	R259DVF	562	R262DVF	564	R264DVF
553	R553CNG	557	R257DVF	560	R260DVF				

565-574

Scania L94UB — Wright Axcess Floline — N40F — 1999

565	S565TPW	567	S567TPW	569	S569TPW	571	S571TPW	573	S573TPW
566	S566TPW	568	S568TPW	570	S570TPW	572	S572TPW	574	S574TPW

575-580

Scania L94UB — Wright Axcess Floline — N40F — 1999

575	T575JNG	577	T577JNG	578	T578JNG	579	T579JNG	580	T580JNG
576	T576JNG								

604	KVG604V	Leyland National 2 NL116L11/1R	B49F	1980	
607	KVG607V	Leyland National 2 NL116L11/1R	B49F	1980	
609	KVG609V	Leyland National 2 NL116L11/1R	B49F	1980	
611	AAE655V	Leyland National 2 NL116L11/1R	B52F	1980	Badgerline, 1996
615	PEX615W	Leyland National 2 NL116L11/1R	B49F	1980	
617	PEX617W	Leyland National 2 NL116L11/1R	B49F	1980	
624	UVF624X	Leyland National 2 NL116AL11/1R	B49F	1981	
625	UVF625X	Leyland National 2 NL116AL11/1R	B49F	1981	
628	UVF628X	Leyland National 2 NL116AL11/1R	B49F	1981	
641	A201YWP	Leyland National 2 NL116HLXCT/1R	B49F	1984	Badgerline, 1996
642	A202YWP	Leyland National 2 NL116HLXCT/1R	B52F	1984	Badgerline, 1996
644	A204YWP	Leyland National 2 NL116HLXCT/1R	B52F	1984	Badgerline, 1996

652	NIL3952	Leyland National 11351A/1R	East Lancs Greenway (1995)	B52F	1976	
653	NIL3953	Leyland National 11351A/1R	East Lancs Greenway (1994)	B52F	1976	
654	NIL3954	Leyland National 11351A/1R	East Lancs Greenway (1996)	B52F	1976	
655	NIL3955	Leyland National 11351A/1R	East Lancs Greenway (1994)	B49F	1977	
656	NIL3956	Leyland National 11351A/1R	East Lancs Greenway (1995)	B49F	1977	
657	NIL3957	Leyland National 11351A/1R	East Lancs Greenway (1995)	B52F	1977	
658	NIL3958	Leyland National 11351A/1R	East Lancs Greenway (1995)	B52F	1977	
659	NIL3959	Leyland National 11351A/1R	East Lancs Greenway (1993)	B52F	1977	
660	NIL3960	Leyland National 11351A/1R	East Lancs Greenway (1993)	B52F	1978	
661	NIL3961	Leyland National 11351A/1R	East Lancs Greenway (1995)	B52F	1978	
662	NIL3962	Leyland National 11351A/1R	East Lancs Greenway (1995)	B52F	1978	
663	NIL3963	Leyland National 11351A/1R	East Lancs Greenway (1995)	B52F	1978	
664	NIL3964	Leyland National 11351A/1R	East Lancs Greenway (1995)	B49F	1978	
665	NIL3965	Leyland National 11351A/1R	East Lancs Greenway (1994)	B52F	1978	Stagecoach South, 1993
666	NIL3966	Leyland National 11351A/1R	East Lancs Greenway (1994)	B52F	1978	Stagecoach South, 1993
667	NIL3967	Leyland National 11351A/1R	East Lancs Greenway (1994)	B52F	1978	Merseybus, 1993

694-705

		Mercedes-Benz 811D	Alexander AM	B28F	1989	CentreWest, 1997
						*703-5 are BC28F

694	F694XMS	696	F696XMS	698	F698XMS	700	F700XMS	704	F704XMS
695	F695XMS	697	F697XMS	699	F699XMS	703	F703XMS	705	F705XMS

800	H348LJN	Mercedes-Benz 709D	Reeve Burgess Beaver	B23F	1992	Essex Buses (EN), 1998
801	N627GAH	Mercedes-Benz 711D	Alexander Sprint	B25F	1995	
802	N628GAH	Mercedes-Benz 711D	Alexander Sprint	B25F	1995	
803	H411BVR	Mercedes-Benz 709D	Carlyle	B27F	1991	Waylands, Beccles, 1996
804	M242AEX	Mercedes-Benz 711D	Marshall C19	B29F	1995	Waylands, Beccles, 1996
805	N887FVF	Mercedes-Benz 709D	Marshall C19	B29F	1995	Waylands, Beccles, 1996

806-822

		Mercedes-Benz Vario O810	Plaxton Beaver 2	B27F	1997

806	P806REX	810	P810REX	814	P814REX	817	P817REX	820	P820SCL
807	P807REX	811	P811REX	815	P815REX	818	P818REX	821	P821SCL
808	P808REX	812	P812REX	816	P816REX	819	P819REX	822	P822SCL
809	P809REX	813	P813REX						

823-832

		Mercedes-Benz Vario O810	Plaxton Beaver 2	B27F	1998

823	S823TCL	825	S825TCL	827	S827TCL	829	S829TCL	831	S831TCL
824	S824TCL	826	S826TCL	828	S828TCL	830	S830TCL	832	S832TCL

B833	P692HND	Mercedes-Benz Vario O810	Plaxton Beaver 2	B31F	1997	Flying Banana, 1998
B834	P693HND	Mercedes-Benz Vario O810	Plaxton Beaver 2	B31F	1997	Flying Banana, 1998
B861	H347LJN	Mercedes-Benz 709D	Reeve Burgess Beaver	B23F	1992	Essex Buses (EN), 1998
B862	H349LJN	Mercedes-Benz 709D	Reeve Burgess Beaver	B23F	1990	Essex Buses (EN), 1998
B863	H343LJN	Mercedes-Benz 709D	Reeve Burgess Beaver	B23F	1992	Essex Buses (EN), 1998
B864	H307LJN	Mercedes-Benz 709D	Reeve Burgess Beaver	B23F	1992	Essex Buses (EN), 1998
B865	H351LJN	Mercedes-Benz 709D	Reeve Burgess Beaver	B23F	1990	Essex Buses (EN), 1998
B866	M384KVR	Mercedes-Benz 709D	Alexander Sprint	B27F	1995	Flying Banana, 1998
B867	N589WND	Mercedes-Benz 709D	Alexander Sprint	B27F	1996	Flying Banana, 1998
B868	P681HND	Mercedes-Benz 709D	Alexander Sprint	B27F	1996	Flying Banana, 1998
B869	P682HND	Mercedes-Benz 709D	Alexander Sprint	B27F	1996	Flying Banana, 1998
870	H378OHK	Mercedes-Benz 709D	Reeve Burgess Beaver	B23F	1991	Essex Buses (EN), 1998
871	H361LJN	Mercedes-Benz 709D	Reeve Burgess Beaver	B23F	1991	Essex Buses (EN), 1998
872	H359LJN	Mercedes-Benz 709D	Reeve Burgess Beaver	B23F	1991	Essex Buses (EN), 1998
873	H384OHK	Mercedes-Benz 709D	Reeve Burgess Beaver	B23F	1991	Essex Buses (EN), 1998
874	H376OHK	Mercedes-Benz 709D	Reeve Burgess Beaver	B23F	1991	Essex Buses (EN), 1998
875	H354LJN	Mercedes-Benz 709D	Reeve Burgess Beaver	B23F	1991	Essex Buses (EN), 1998
876	H357LJN	Mercedes-Benz 709D	Reeve Burgess Beaver	B23F	1991	Essex Buses (EN), 1998
877	F633XMS	Mercedes-Benz 811D	Alexander Sprint	B28F	1989	CentreWest, 1998
878	F638XMS	Mercedes-Benz 811D	Alexander Sprint	B28F	1989	CentreWest, 1998
880	H335LAN	Mercedes-Benz 811D	Reeve Burgess Beaver	B33F	1991	Porthcawl Omnibus, 1997
881	G52GEX	Mercedes-Benz 811D	Reeve Burgess Beaver	BC33F	1989	Blue Bus, 1996
882	G53GEX	Mercedes-Benz 811D	Reeve Burgess Beaver	BC33F	1989	Blue Bus, 1996
883	G54GEX	Mercedes-Benz 811D	Reeve Burgess Beaver	B33F	1989	Blue Bus, 1996
884	G55GEX	Mercedes-Benz 811D	Reeve Burgess Beaver	B33F	1989	Blue Bus, 1996
885	G833RDS	Mercedes-Benz 811D	Reeve Burgess Beaver	B31F	1990	Blue Bus, 1996
886	G453SGB	Mercedes-Benz 811D	Reeve Burgess Beaver	B31F	1990	Blue Bus, 1996
887	G834RDS	Mercedes-Benz 811D	Reeve Burgess Beaver	B33F	1990	Blue Bus, 1996

Pictures passing through Wisbech is Eastern Counties' 42, R842DVF, one of the new Volvo coaches employed on Express services for which the *excel* name is used. The vehicle has a Plaxton Premiere 320 body. *Paul Wigan*

888	G395OWB	Mercedes-Benz 811D	Whittaker Europa	B26F	1990	Blue Bus, 1996	
889	J404WDA	Mercedes-Benz 811D	Whittaker Europa	B31F	1992	Blue Bus, 1996	
890	M68XVF	Mercedes-Benz 811D	Marshall C16	B33F	1994	Blue Bus, 1996	
891	M69XVF	Mercedes-Benz 811D	Marshall C16	B33F	1994	Blue Bus, 1996	
895	G645YVS	Mercedes-Benz 709D	Reeve Burgess Beaver	B25F	1990	The Bee Line, 1997	
896	G646YVS	Mercedes-Benz 709D	Reeve Burgess Beaver	B25F	1990	The Bee Line, 1997	
897	G647YVS	Mercedes-Benz 709D	Reeve Burgess Beaver	B25F	1990	The Bee Line, 1997	
898	J31KLR	Mercedes-Benz 811D	Plaxton Beaver	B28F	1991	The Bee Line, 1997	
899	J37KLR	Mercedes-Benz 811D	Plaxton Beaver	B28F	1991	The Bee Line, 1997	

909-914   Mercedes-Benz 609D   Dormobile   B20F   1992-93

909	J530FCL	**911**	K732JAH	**913**	K734JAH	**912**	K733JAH	**914** K735JAH
910	K731JAH							

915-944   Mercedes-Benz 609D   Frank Guy   B20F   1993-94

915	L245PAH	**923**	L253PAH	**929**	L259PAH	**935**	M365XEX	**940** M370XEX
916	L246PAH	**924**	L254PAH	**930**	M360XEX	**936**	M366XEX	**941** M371XEX
917	L247PAH	**925**	L255PAH	**931**	M361XEX	**937**	M367XEX	**942** M372XEX
919	L249PAH	**926**	L256PAH	**932**	M362XEX	**938**	M368XEX	**943** M373XEX
921	L251PAH	**927**	L257PAH	**933**	M363XEX	**939**	M369XEX	**944** M374XEX
922	L252PAH	**928**	L258PAH	**934**	M364XEX			

945-964   Mercedes-Benz 609D   Frank Guy   B20F   1995

945	N605GAH	**949**	N609GAH	**953**	N613GAH	**957**	N617GAH	**961** N621GAH
946	N606GAH	**950**	N610GAH	**954**	N614GAH	**958**	N618GAH	**962** N622GAH
947	N607GAH	**951**	N611GAH	**955**	N615GAH	**959**	N619GAH	**963** N623GAH
948	N608GAH	**952**	N612GAH	**956**	N616GAH	**960**	N620GAH	**964** N624GAH

965	F34TJN	Mercedes-Benz 609D	Reeve Burgess Beaver	B19F	1989	Waylands, Beccles, 1996
966	M883XVG	Mercedes-Benz 609D	Cymric	B20F	1995	Waylands, Beccles, 1996
967	M884XVG	Mercedes-Benz 609D	Cymric	B20F	1995	Waylands, Beccles, 1996
	D227OOJ	Freight-Rover Sherpa	Carlyle	O20F	1987	Flying Banana, 1998
	D70TLV	Freight-Rover Sherpa	Carlyle	O20F	1987	Flying Banana, 1998

Special Event vehicle:-

LFL57	557BNG	Bristol Lodekka FL6B (6LW)	Eastern Coach Works	B37/33R	1963	preservation, 1997

Ancilliary vehicles:-

35	4750WY	Volvo B10M-61	Plaxton Paramount 3200 II	C53F	1986	Blue Bus, 1996
207	XNG207S	Bristol VRT/SL3/6LXB	Eastern Coach Works	TV	1977	
853	E853PEX	Ford Transit 190	Robin Hood	B16F	1987	
9410	SUM129W	Bedford YMT	Plaxton Supreme IV	TV	1981	Yorkshire Rider, 1998
9037	HEX118Y	Volvo B10M-61	Plaxton Paramount 3200	TV	1983	Blue Bus, 1996
9039	JTY926P	Bedford YRT	Plaxton Supreme III	TV	1975	Rosemary Cs, Terrington, '93
9042	EHE234V	Bedford YMT	Duple Dominant II	TV	1980	Rosemary Cs, Terrington, '93

Previous registrations:-

557BNG	From new		NIL3955	TVF620R
4750WY	C517DND		NIL3956	WAH587S
6149KP	WWA300Y, 9258VC, GAC98Y		NIL3957	WAH588S
7694VC	FWH37Y		NIL3958	WAH590S
A908OST	A183WEV		NIL3959	WAH593S
CSV303	A207SAE		NIL3960	WAH599S
CSV524	A208SAE		NIL3961	XNG765S
CSV992	A209SAE		NIL3962	XNG766S
FEH1Y	?		NIL3963	XNG768S
HEX119Y	FUA385Y, 4750WY		NIL3964	DPW782T
J404WDA	J11OPY		NIL3965	VFX981S
NIL3952	PVF367R		NIL3966	UFX854S
NIL3953	PVF368R		NIL3967	YFY7M
NIL3954	PVF369R			

Allocations

Bury St Edmunds (Cotton Lane)

Mercedes-Benz	805	885	896	897	898	899		
Tiger	26	27						
National	652	654	655	658	660	661	665	666
Olympian	84	88	89	90	91	92	93	
Bristol VR	304	307						

Great Yarmouth (Caister Road) - Blue Bus

Mercedes-Benz	881	882	883	884	886	887	888	889
	890	891						
Dart	411	412	416	417	418	419	420	421
	422	423	424	451	452	453	479	496
	498							
National	615	617						
Scania	551	552	553	554	556			
Bristol VR	219	262	320	327	329	330	338	
Volvo Citybus	118	119						
Olympian	104							

Halesworth () Flying Banana

Mercedes-Benz	B833	B834	B861	B862	B863	B864	B865	B866
	B867	B868	B869	B877	B878			

East Lancashire built up a clientele mostly comprising municipal authorties and small independents. After a period when the firm was part of British Bus the bodybuilder is gaining orders especially from the London area, and large independents, such as Yorkshire Traction. The products in Firstgroup have mostly been acquired with businesses, such as Blue Bus' K62KEX which is now numbered 417 with First Eastern Counties. The vehicle is seen in its home town of Great Yarmouth. *Richard Godfrey*

Ipswich (Foundation Street)

Mercedes-Benz	800	880	928					
Volvo B6	394	395	396	397	401	402	403	404
	405	406	407	408	409	410		
Dart	415	425	426	427	428	429	430	431
	432							
Javelin	512	514	517	518	519			
Lance	536	537	538	539	540			
Scania	541	542	543	544	545	546	547	548
	549	550	567	569	570	572	573	574
	607	611	653	656	657	662		
Bristol VR	242	264	265	275	287	290	306	309
Olympian	94	95	96	97	98	99	101	102
	103	106						

Kings Lynn (Vancouver Avenue)

Mercedes-Benz	895	921	940	941	943	955	956	958
	959	960	961	964				
Volvo B10Mcoach	30	31	32	33	34	40	41	42
	46							
Dart	454	455	480	481	482			
Scania	575	576	577	578				
Bristol VR	229	239	255	283	285			

Kings Lynn (St Michael's Road) - Rosemary Coaches

Mercedes-Benz	820	821	822	830	831	832		
Tiger	19	20	21	22	23	24	25	28
	29							
Volvo	38							
Dart	449							
Bristol VR	199	213	224	270	318	319	336	340

Lowestoft (Gas Works Road)

Mercedes-Benz	801	802	870	912	913	914	915	916
	917	930	931	934	942	951	952	954
	957							
Volvo B10M	43	44	45					
Dart	460	461	462					
National	604	609						
Javelin	520							
Bristol VR	216	234	263	284	286	294	310	
Olympian	107	108						

Norwich (Vulcan Road and Roundtree Way)

Mercedes-Benz	694	695	696	697	698	699	700	703
	704	705	806	807	808	809	810	811
	812	813	814	815	816	817	818	819
	823	824	825	826	827	828	829	919
	922	923	924	925	926	927	928	929
	932	933	935	936	937	938	939	945
	946	947	948	949	950	953	962	963
Volvo B6	398	399	400					
Dart	413	414	433	434	435	436	437	438
	439	440	441	442	443	444	445	446
	447	448	450	456	457	458	459	463
	464	465	466	467	468	469	470	471
	472	473	474	475	476	477	478	483
	484	485	486	487	488	489		
Javelin	506	507	508	509	510	515	516	
Scania L	557	558	559	560	561	562	563	564
	565	566	567	568	571	579	580	
National	624	628	641	642	644	659	663	664
	667							
Bristol VR	212	220	246	249	253	254	257	258
	259	261	266	267	271	272	273	276
	277	282	288	297	305			
Olympian	100	105	109	110	111	112	113	114
	115	116	117					

Worlingham (College Lane) - Waylands

Mercedes-Benz	803	804	944	965	966	967
Javelin	511					
National	625					

Unallocated

National	642

ESSEX BUSES

Eastern National - Thameswas

Eastern National - Thameswas

Essex Buses Ltd, Stapleford Close, New Writtle Street, Chelmsford CM2 0SD

308-356		Mercedes-Benz 709D		Reeve Burgess Beaver		B23F		1991	
308	H308LPU	316	H319LJN	325	H332LJN	332	H341LJN	348	H358LJN
309	H310LPU	317	H321LJN	326	H334LJN	333	H342LJN	351	H362LJN
310	H311LJN	318	H322LJN	327	H335LJN	335	H344LJN	352	H363LJN
311	H312LJN	319	H324LJN	328	H336LJN	342	H352LJN	353	H364LJN
312	H313LJN	320	H326LJN	329	H337LJN	343	H353LJN	354	H365LJN
313	H314LJN	321	H327LJN	330	H338LJN	345	H355LJN	355	H366LJN
314	H315LJN	323	H320LJN	331	H339LJN	346	H356LJN	356	H367LJN
315	H317LJN	324	H331LJN						

357-387		Mercedes-Benz 709D		Reeve Burgess Beaver		B23F		1991	
357	H368OHK	366	H377OHK	372	H383OHK	378	H389OHK	383	H394OHK
358	H369OHK	368	H379OHK	374	H385OHK	379	H390OHK	384	H395OHK
359	H370OHK	369	H380OHK	375	H386OHK	380	H391OHK	385	H396OHK
360	H371OHK	370	H381OHK	376	H387OHK	381	H392OHK	386	H397OHK
364	H375OHK	371	H382OHK	377	H388OHK	382	H393OHK	387	H398OHK

397	K397KHJ	Mercedes-Benz 709D		Plaxton Beaver		B23F		1993	
398	K398KHJ	Mercedes-Benz 709D		Plaxton Beaver		B23F		1993	

401-410		Mercedes-Benz 711D		Plaxton Beaver		B23F		1996	
401	P401HPU	403	P403HPU	405	P405HPU	407	P407HPU	409	P409HPU
402	P402HPU	404	P404HPU	406	P406HPU	408	P408HPU	410	P410HPU

601-615		Volvo B10M-62		Plaxton Première 320		C53F		1995-96	
601	N601APU	605	N605APU	608	N608APU	611	N611APU	614	N614APU
602	N602APU	606	N606APU	609	N609APU	612	N612APU	615	N615APU
603	N603APU	607	N607APU	610	N610APU	613	N613APU		

650-654		Scania L94UB		Wright Axcess Floline		N43F		1999	
650	T650SSF	651	T651SSF	652	T652SSF	653	T653SSF	654	T654SSF

701	N701CPU	Dennis Dart SLF		Plaxton Pointer		N37F		1995	

702-711		Dennis Dart		Plaxton Pointer		B37F		1996	
702	P702HPU	704	P704HPU	706	P706HPU	708	P708HPU	710	P710HPU
703	P703HPU	705	P705HPU	707	P707HPU	709	P709HPU	711	P711HPU

712-721		Dennis Dart SLF		Plaxton Pointer 2		N37F		1998	
712	R712DJN	714	R714DJN	716	R716DJN	718	R718DJN	720	R720DJN
713	R713DJN	715	R715DJN	717	R717DJN	719	R719DJN	721	R721DJN

729-738		Dennis Dart SLF		Plaxton Pointer 2		N37F		1998	
729	S729TWC	731	S731TWC	733	S733TWC	735	S735TWC	737	S737TWC
730	S730TWC	732	S732TWC	734	S734TWC	736	S737TWC	738	S738TWC

Thamesway's operation has reduced since the last edition of this book with the Ponders End depot and services transferring to First Capital. As we go to press it has been announced that Essex Buses and Eastern Counties are to come under a common management and that liveries for those buses not qualifying for the corporate scheme will be yellow and pink for Thamesway, yellow and green for Eastern National, while yellow and red will be applied to the Eastern Counties fleet. Shown in the older raspberry and custard scheme is Dart 711, P711HPU. *Phillip Stephenson*

805-811   Mercedes-Benz 811D   Plaxton Beaver   B31F   1992

805	K805DJN	807	K807DJN	809	K809DJN	810	K810DJN	811	K811DJN
806	K806DJN	808	K808DJN						

851	N851CPU	Dennis Dart 9SDL3040	Marshall C36	BC17FL	1995
852	N852CPU	Dennis Dart 9SDL3040	Marshall C36	BC17FL	1995
853	N853CPU	Dennis Dart 9SDL3040	Marshall C36	BC17FL	1995
854	N854CPU	Dennis Dart 9SDL3040	Marshall C36	BC17FL	1995

907-917   Dennis Dart 9SDL3016   Plaxton Pointer   B35F   1992

907	K907CVW	910	K910CVW	912	K912CVW	914	K914CVW	916	K916CVW
908	K908CVW	911	K911CVW	913	K913CVW	915	K915CVW	917	K917CVW
909	K909CVW								

918-943   Dennis Dart 9.8SDL3035   Plaxton Pointer   B39F   1994

918	M918TEV	925	M925TEV	930	M930TEV	935	M935TEV	940	M940TEV
919	M919TEV	926	M926TEV	931	M931TEV	936	M936TEV	941	M941TEV
920	M920TEV	927	M927TEV	932	M932TEV	937	M937TEV	942	M942TEV
921	M921TEV	928	M928TEV	933	M933TEV	938	M938TEV	943	M943TEV
922	M922TEV	929	M929TEV	934	M934TEV	939	M939TEV		
924	M924TEV								

Opposite, top:- **Thamesway provide Mobility buses for London Transport contracts. Shown here is Marshall-bodied Dart 853, N853CPU.** *Phillip Stephenson*
Opposite, bottom:- **The** *City Saver* **service between Southend and London is provided by Essex Buses using coaches in a livery of yellow, orange and blue. Pictured at the eastern terminus is 615, N615APU. The route includes stops at Basildon and Lakeside shopping centre.** *Richard Godfrey*

This last year has seen the number of Lynx with Thamesway increase following the transfer of four buses from sister FirstGroup fleets. One of the original batch, 1404, F404LTW, is seen heading for Hullbridge on route 20. *Phillip Stephenson*

944-972

Dennis Dart 9.8SDL3054   Plaxton Pointer   B39F*   1995   *959-72 are B37F

944	N944CPU	950	N950CPU	956	N956CPU	962	N962CPU	968	N968CPU
945	N945CPU	951	N951CPU	957	N957CPU	963	N963CPU	969	N969CPU
946	N946CPU	952	N952CPU	958	N958CPU	964	N964CPU	970	N970CPU
947	N947CPU	953	N953CPU	959	N959CPU	965	N965CPU	971	N971CPU
948	N948CPU	954	N954CPU	960	N960CPU	966	N966CPU	972	N972CPU
949	N949CPU	955	N955CPU	961	N961CPU	967	N967CPU		

1400-1429

Leyland Lynx LX112L10ZR/1R   Leyland Lynx   B49F*   1988   *1427-9 are B47F

1400	E400HWC	1406	F406LTW	1412	F412MNO	1418	F418MWC	1424	F424MJN
1401	E401HWC	1407	F407LTW	1413	F413MNO	1419	F419MWC	1425	F425MJN
1402	F402LTW	1408	F408LTW	1414	F414MNO	1420	F420MJN	1426	F426MJN
1403	F403LTW	1409	F409LTW	1415	F415MWC	1421	F421MJN	1427	F427MJN
1404	F404LTW	1410	F410MNO	1416	F416MWC	1422	F422MJN	1428	F428MJN
1405	F405LTW	1411	F411MNO	1417	F417MWC	1423	F423MJN	1429	F429MJN

1430	D755DLO	Leyland Lynx LX112TL11ZR1S	Leyland Lynx	B49F	1987	CentreWest (B), 1997
1431	D754DLO	Leyland Lynx LX112TL11ZR1R	Leyland Lynx	B49F	1987	CentreWest (B), 1998
1432	D876ELL	Leyland Lynx LX112TL11ZR1R	Leyland Lynx	BC48F	1987	Eastern Counties, 1998
1433	D756DLO	Leyland Lynx LX112TL11ZR1R	Leyland Lynx	B49F	1987	CentreWest (B), 1999

1501-1513

Dennis Lance   Northern Counties Paladin   B49F   1997

1501	P501MNO	1504	P504MNO	1507	P507MNO	1510	P510MNO	1512	P512MNO
1502	P502MNO	1505	P505MNO	1508	P508MNO	1511	P511MNO	1513	P513MNO
1503	P503MNO	1506	P506MNO	1509	P509MNO				

1601	D497NYS	Volvo B10M-61	Duple Dominant	B55F	1986	First Capital, 1999
1602	D499NYS	Volvo B10M-61	Duple Dominant	B55F	1986	First Capital, 1999

Eastern National 4304, L304PWR, pictured in Colchester bus station, joined Essex Buses from Yorkshire Rider during 1998. One of twelve to be transferred south, these buses operated with Calderline, the trading name used for vehicles based at Halifax. With Eastern National, the buses are shared between Colchester and Harwich.
Mark Lyons

1803-1924
Leyland National 11351A/1R   B49F*   1977-79   *1803/70 are B52F

| 1803 | TJN502R | 1870 | YEV328S | 1916 | JHJ142V | 1924 | JHJ150V |
| 1850 | YEV308S | 1886 | BNO676T | 1921 | JHJ147V | | |

2601-2617
Mercedes-Benz 709D   Reeve Burgess Beaver   B23F   1991

2601	H601OVW	2605	H605OVW	2609	H609OVW	2612	J612UTW	2615	J615UTW
2602	H602OVW	2606	H606OVW	2610	J610UTW	2613	J613UTW	2616	J616UTW
2603	H603OVW	2607	H607OVW	2611	J611UTW	2614	J614UTW	2617	J617UTW
2604	H604OVW	2608	H608OVW						

2618-2630
Mercedes-Benz 709D   Plaxton Beaver   B23F   1991

2618	J618UTW	2621	J621UTW	2624	J624UTW	2627	J627UTW	2629	J629UTW
2619	J619UTW	2622	J622UTW	2625	J625UTW	2628	J628UTW	2630	J630UTW
2620	J620UTW	2623	J623UTW	2626	J626UTW				

2631-2656
Mercedes-Benz 709D   Plaxton Beaver   B23F   1993-94

2631	K631GVX	2637	K637GVX	2642	K642GVX	2647	L647MEV	2652	L652MEV
2632	K632GVX	2638	K638GVX	2643	K643GVX	2648	L648MEV	2653	L653MEV
2633	K633GVX	2639	K639GVX	2644	K644GVX	2649	L649MEV	2654	L654MEV
2634	K634GVX	2640	K640GVX	2645	K645GVX	2650	L650MEV	2655	L655MEV
2635	K635GVX	2641	K641GVX	2646	K646GVX	2651	L651MEV	2656	L656MEV
2636	K636GVX								

2657-2676
Mercedes-Benz 709D   Plaxton Beaver   B23F   1995

2657	M657VJN	2661	M661VJN	2665	M665VJN	2669	M669VJN	2673	M673VJN
2658	M658VJN	2662	M662VJN	2666	M166VJN	2670	M670VJN	2674	M674VJN
2659	M659VJN	2663	M663VJN	2667	M667VJN	2671	M671VJN	2675	M675VJN
2660	M660VJN	2664	M664VJN	2668	M668VJN	2672	M672VJN	2676	M676VJN

| 2677 | L21AHA | Mercedes-Benz 709D | Plaxton Beaver | B23F | 1993 | Frontline, 1995 |

2678-2682

Mercedes-Benz 709D — Plaxton Beaver — B23F — 1996

2678	P678HPU	2679	P679HPU	2680	P680HPU	2681	P681HPU	2682	P682HPU

2801-2822

Dennis Dart 9SDL3034 — Plaxton Pointer — B34F — 1993-94

2801	L801MEV	2806	L806OPU	2811	L811OPU	2815	L815OPU	2819	L819OPU
2802	L802MEV	2808	L808OPU	2812	L812OPU	2816	L816OPU	2820	L820OPU
2803	L803OPU	2809	L809OPU	2813	L813OPU	2817	L817OPU	2821	L821OPU
2804	L804OPU	2810	L810OPU	2814	L814OPU	2818	L818OPU	2822	L822OPU
2805	L805OPU								

2823-2830

Dennis Dart 9.8SDL3054 — Plaxton Pointer — B39F — 1995

2823	N823APU	2825	N825APU	2827	N827APU	2829	N829APU	2830	N830APU
2824	N824APU	2826	N826APU	2828	N828APU					

3069-3094

Bristol VRT/SL3/6LXB — Eastern Coach Works — B43/31F* — 1980-81 — *3069/71 are B39/31F

3069	KOO787V	3076	KOO794V	3079	STW23W	3084	STW28W	3093	STW37W
3071	KOO789V	3077	STW21W	3083	STW27W	3092	STW36W	3094	STW38W
3072	KOO790V	3078	STW22W						

3101	UAR591W	Bristol VRT/SL3/6LXB	Eastern Coach Works	B43/31F	1981
3103	UAR593W	Bristol VRT/SL3/6LXB	Eastern Coach Works	B43/31F	1981
3106	UAR596W	Bristol VRT/SL3/6LXB	Eastern Coach Works	B43/34F	1981
3109	UAR599W	Bristol VRT/SL3/6LXB	Eastern Coach Works	B43/31F	1981
3110	XHK215X	Bristol VRT/SL3/6LXB	Eastern Coach Works	B43/31F	1981
3112	XHK217X	Bristol VRT/SL3/6LXB	Eastern Coach Works	B43/34F	1981
3113	XHK218X	Bristol VRT/SL3/6LXB	Eastern Coach Works	B43/31F	1981
3219	VTH941T	Bristol VRT/SL3/501	Eastern Coach Works	B43/31F	1978	Brewers, 1990
3220	WTH949T	Bristol VRT/SL3/501	Eastern Coach Works	B43/31F	1979	Brewers, 1990
3222	BEP963V	Bristol VRT/SL3/501(6LXB)	Eastern Coach Works	B43/31F	1980	Brewers, 1990
3226	DWU298T	Bristol VRT/SL3/6LXB	Eastern Coach Works(1979)	B43/31F	1978	Yorkshire Rider, 1994
3227	LUA716V	Bristol VRT/SL3/6LXB	Eastern Coach Works	B43/31F	1979	Yorkshire Rider, 1994
3228	LWU469V	Bristol VRT/SL3/6LXB	Eastern Coach Works	B43/31F	1979	Yorkshire Rider, 1994
3230	PWY44W	Bristol VRT/SL3/6LXB	Eastern Coach Works	B43/31F	1981	Yorkshire Rider, 1994
4003	B698BPU	Leyland Olympian ONLXB/1R	Eastern Coach Works	B45/32F	1984	
4004	B699BPU	Leyland Olympian ONLXB/1R	Eastern Coach Works	B45/32F	1984	
4005	C711GEV	Leyland Olympian ONLXB/1R	Eastern Coach Works	B45/32F	1985	

4007-4021

Leyland Olympian ONLXB/1R — Eastern Coach Works — BC42/30F — 1986

4007	C407HJN	4010	C410HJN	4014	C414HJN	4017	C417HJN	4019	C419HJN
4008	C408HJN	4012	C412HJN	4015	C415HJN	4018	C418HJN	4021	C421HJN
4009	C409HJN	4013	C413HJN	4016	C416HJN				

4024	B960WRN	Leyland Olympian ONLXB/1R	Eastern Coach Works	B45/32F	1985	Arriva North West, 1998
4025	A147UDM	Leyland Olympian ONLXB/1R	Eastern Coach Works	B45/32F	1983	Arriva North West, 1998

4026-4031

Leyland Olympian ONLXB/1R — Eastern Coach Works — B45/32F — 1983-85 — Keighley & District, 1999

4026	FUM485Y	4028	FUM496Y	4029	FUM497Y	4030	FUM500Y	4031	A92KWW
4027	FUM493Y								

4301-4315

Volvo Olympian YN2RV18Z4 — Northern Counties Palatine — B47/29F — 1994 — Yorkshire Rider (C), 1998

4301	L301PWR	4304	L304PWR	4308	L308PWR	4310	L310PWR	4314	L314PWR
4302	L302PWR	4305	L305PWR	4309	L309PWR	4311	L311PWR	4315	L315PWR
4303	L303PWR	4307	L307PWR						

Special Event vehicles:-

2383	WNO479	Bristol KSW5G	Eastern Coach Works	O33/28R	1953	Westcliffe-on-Sea, 1955
9001	AJN825	Bristol K5G	Eastern Coach Works	B27/26R	1939	

Ancilliary vehicles:-

9016	XYK761T	Bedford YLQ	Duple Dominant II	TV	1978	
9017	YYL794T	Bedford YLQ	Duple Dominant II	TV	1978	
9020	VIB9308	Bedford YMT	Plaxton Supreme III	TV	1978	Chalkwell, Sittingbourne, '98
9018	D228PPU	Mercedes-Benz L608D	Reeve Burgess	TV	1986	
9411	FTO549U	Bedford YMT	Plaxton Supreme III	TV	1978	Yorkshire Rider, 1999

High Street, Colchester, is the setting for this picture of two similar Eastern Counties Olympians. The leading vehicle is 4021, C421HJN. *Mark Lyons*

Previous Registrations

D876ELL	D111NDW, 811DYE		VIB9308	JJK938S

Allocations

Basildon (Cherrydown) - Thamesway

Mercedes-Benz	345	348	356	357	359	364	366	368
	369	371	372	374	375	376	377	379
	380	381	810	811	2660	2661	2662	
Dart	711	734	735	736	737	738	851	852
	853	854	914	915	916	918	919	920
	921	922	924	925	926	927	928	929
	930	931	932	933	934	935	936	937
	938	939	940	941	942	943	959	960
	961	962	963	964	965	966	967	968
	969	970	971	972				
Volvo B10M Coach	601	602	603	605	607	608	609	610
	611	612	613	614	615			
Bristol VRT	3069	3109	3222	3226				
Olympian	4026							

Thirteen Dennis Lance single-deck buses were supplied to Eastern National in 1997 and these were fitted with Northern Counties Paladin bodywork. Representing the batch is 1510, P510MNO, seen arriving in Colchester. *Mark Lyons*

Braintree (Fairfield Road) - Eastern National

Mercedes-Benz	346	352	2601	2626	2627	2628	2629	2630
	2663	2664	2665	2666				
Dart	2808	2811	2812	2817	2818	2819	2820	2827
Bristol VRT	3092							

Chelmsford (Duke Street) - Eastern National

Outstations: Bishops Stortford; Dunmow and Maldon.

Mercedes-Benz	382	383	384	385	386	387	2602	2603
	2604	2605	2606	2607	2608	2609	2610	2611
	2612	2613	2614	2615	2616	2617	2618	2619
	2620	2621	2622	2623	2624	2625	2631	2632
	2633	2634	2635	2636	2637	2638	2639	2640
	2641	2642	2643	2644	2645	2646	2667	2668
	2670	2671	2672	2677				
Dart	712	713	714	715	716	729	730	731
	732	733	2802	2813	2814	2815	2816	2821
	2822	2826	2823	2824	2825			
Volvo	1601	1602						
Lynx	1401	1402	1403	1407	1408	1413	1414	1415
	1416	1425	1426	1427	1428	1429		
National	1850	1916	1924					
Bristol VR	3071	3077	3083	3084	3103	3110	3112	
Olympian	4007	4008	4010	4012	4013	4014	4015	4019
	4021	4024	4025	4029				

Clacton-on-Sea (Telford Road) - Eastern National

Mercedes-Benz	308	328	329	330	331	332	333	335
	358	370	378	2647	2648	2649	2650	2651
	2652	2653	2654					
Lance	1510	1511						
Dart	2828	2829	2830					
Bristol VR	3227							
Olympian	4009	4016	4017	4018				

Colchester (Queen Street & Haven Road) - Eastern National

Mercedes-Benz	2673	2674	2675	2676	2678	2679	2680	
Dart	907	908	909	910	911	912	2801	2803
	2804	2805	2806	2809	2810			
Lance	1501	1502	1503	1504	1505	1506	1507	1508
	1509							
Scania	650	651	652	653	654			
Bristol VR	3072	3079	3093	3094	3101	3106	3220	3228
	3230							
Olympian	4301	4302	4303	4304	4305	4307	4309	4315

Hadleigh (London Road) - Thamesway

Mercedes-Benz	309	310	311	312	313	314	315	316
	317	318	319	320	321	323	324	325
	326	327						
Dart	701	702	703	704	705	706	707	708
	709	710	717	718	719	720	721	944
	945	946	947	948	949	950	951	952
	953	954	955	956	957	958	987	
Volvo B10M	606							
National	1803	1870						
Lynx	1400	1404	1405	1406	1409	1410	1411	1412
	1417	1418	1419	1420	1421	1422	1423	1424
	1430	1431	1432	1433				
Bristol VR	3113							
Olympian	4003	4004	4005	4027				

Harwich (Station Road) - Eastern National

Mercedes-Benz	2655	2656	2669	2681	2682
Lance	1512	1513			
Bristol VR	3076	3078	3219		
Olympian	4308	4310	4311	4314	

Romford (Bryant Avenue, Harold Wood) - Thamesway

Mercedes-Benz	351	353	354	355	397	398	401	402
	403	404	405	406	407	408	409	410
	805	806	807	808	809			
Dart	913							

Unallocated

Mercedes-Benz	342	343	360			
National	1870	1886	1921			
Bristol VR	3110	3219	3220	3228	3235	3236
Olympian	4028	4030	4031			

FIRST CAPITAL

Capital

Capital Citybus Ltd, Chequers Lane, Dagenham, Essex RM9 6QD

100	JHE144W	MCW Metrobus DR104/6	MCW	B46/31F	1981	Merseybus, 1996
101	JHE171W	MCW Metrobus DR104/6	MCW	B46/31F	1981	South Yorkshire, 1991
102	JHE172W	MCW Metrobus DR104/6	MCW	B46/31F	1981	South Yorkshire, 1991
104	JHE194W	MCW Metrobus DR104/6	MCW	B46/31F	1981	Mainline, 1994
105	JHE138W	MCW Metrobus DR104/6	MCW	B46/31F	1981	Steveneons, 1995
106	JHE157W	MCW Metrobus DR104/6	MCW	B46/31F	1981	South Yorkshire, 1991
107	G107FJW	MCW Metrobus DR102/70	MCW	B43/30F	1989	Optare, Leeds, 1991
109	JHE152W	MCW Metrobus DR104/6	MCW	B46/31F	1981	MTL, 1996
110	JHE170W	MCW Metrobus DR104/6	MCW	B46/31F	1981	South Yorkshire, 1991

115-120   MCW Metrobus DR104/6   MCW   B46/31F   1981   South Yorkshire, 1991-92

115	JHE182W	117	JHE147W	118	JHE148W	119	JHE149W	120	JHE150W
116	JHE146W								

121-128   Leyland Olympian ON2R50C13Z4 Northern Counties Palatine   B47/30F   1990   CentreWest, 1999

121	H141FLX	123	H130FLX	125	H135FLX	127	H137FLX	128	H145FLX
122	H142FLX	124	H144FLX	126	H136FLX				

129	J129YRM	Leyland Olympian ON2R50C13Z4 Northern Counties Palatine	B47/30F	1991	
130	J130YRM	Leyland Olympian ON2R50C13Z4 Northern Counties Palatine	B47/30F	1991	
131	J131YRM	Leyland Olympian ON2R50C13Z4 Northern Counties Palatine	B47/30F	1991	
132	J132YRM	Leyland Olympian ON2R50C13Z4 Northern Counties Palatine	B47/30F	1991	
133	H132FLX	Leyland Olympian ON2R50C13Z4 Northern Counties Palatine	B47/30F	1990	CentreWest, 1999
134	J134YRM	Leyland Olympian ON2R50C13Z4 Northern Counties Palatine	B47/30F	1991	
135	J135YRM	Leyland Olympian ON2R50C13Z4 Northern Counties Palatine	B47/30F	1991	

136-158   Leyland Olympian ON2R50C13Z4   Leyland   B47/29F   1991

136	J136YRM	141	J141YRM	146	J146YRM	151	J151YRM	155	J155YRM
137	J137YRM	142	J142YRM	147	J247YRM	152	J152YRM	156	J156YRM
138	J138YRM	143	J143YRM	148	J148YRM	153	J153YRM	157	J157YRM
139	J139YRM	144	J144YRM	149	J149YRM	154	J154YRM	158	J158YRM
140	J140YRM	145	J145YRM	150	J150YRM				

159-165   Leyland Olympian ON2R50C13Z4   Northen Counties Palatine   B47/30F   1992

159	K888TTT	161	K888TWY	163	K888PFD	164	K888BFG	165	K888BWU
160	K888ELR	162	K888LAD						

166	K888TKS	Leyland Olympian ON2R50C13Z4 Northen Counties Palatine 2	B46/29F	1993	
167	L888YTT	Volvo Olympian YN2RV18Z4	Northen Counties Palatine 2	B47/29F	1993	
168	L888TTT	Volvo Olympian YN2RV18Z4	Northen Counties Palatine 2	B47/29F	1993	
169	E964PME	Leyland Olympian ONLXB/1RH	Optare	B47/29F	1988	Ensign, Rainham, 1994
170	E470SON	MCW Metrobus DR102/63	MCW	B45/30F	1989	London Buses, 1992
171	E461SON	MCW Metrobus DR102/63	MCW	B45/30F	1989	London Buses, 1992
173	H129FLX	Leyland Olympian ON2R50C13Z4 Northern Counties Palatine	B47/30F	1990	CentreWest, 1999
176	DAE512W	MCW Metrobus DR103/4	MCW	BC43/29F	1989	MTL (Liverpool), 1996
177	DAE513W	MCW Metrobus DR103/4	MCW	BC43/29F	1989	MTL (Liverpool), 1996
178	E478SON	MCW Metrobus DR102/63	MCW	B45/30F	1989	London Buses, 1992
179	H139FLX	Leyland Olympian ON2R50C13Z4 Northern Counties Palatine	B47/30F	1990	CentreWest, 1999
180	H140FLX	Leyland Olympian ON2R50C13Z4 Northern Counties Palatine	B47/30F	1990	CentreWest, 1999

Opposite, top:- **First Capital have adopted a livery similar to CentreWest, the other FirstGroup company that serves London. Pictured in its new colours is Northern Counties-bodied Olympian 168, L888TTT. The vehicle is seen at Leyton while working London Transport route 158 to Stratford.** *Gerry Mead*
Opposite, bottom:- **Pictured at Southgate is First Capital's Wright-bodied Dart 645, JDZ2373 which joined the fleet from CentreWest during 1998. Originally a large order placed by London Buses, the batch is now being displaced to other fleets within the group.** *Colin Lloyd*

181	J181HME	Dennis Dominator DDA2004	Northern Counties	B45/29F	1991	
182	J182HME	Dennis Dominator DDA2004	Northern Counties	B45/29F	1991	
183	B443CKW	Dennis Dominator DDA901	Alexander RH	B46/32F	1984	Mainline, Sheffield, 1994
184	B444CKW	Dennis Dominator DDA901	Alexander RH	B46/32F	1984	Mainline, Sheffield, 1994
190	B440CKW	Dennis Dominator DDA901	Alexander RH	B46/32F	1984	Mainline, Sheffield, 1994

191-198
Dennis Dominator DDA1023   East Lancashire   B45/31F   1988   Citybus, Southampton, 1992

191	F291PTP	193	F293PTP	195	F295PTP	197	F297PTP	198	F298PTP
192	F292PTP	194	F294PTP	196	F296PTP				

202	B102WUW	Dennis Dominator DDA1001	Northern Counties	B43/31F	1984	London Coaches, 1993
203	B103WUW	Dennis Dominator DDA1001	Northern Counties	B43/31F	1984	London Coaches, 1993

206-222
Volvo Olympian   Northen Counties Palatine II   B47/27D   1998

206	S206LLO	210	S210LLO	214	S214LLO	217	S217LLO	220	S220LLO
207	S207LLO	211	S211LLO	215	S215LLO	218	S218LLO	221	S221LLO
208	S208LLO	212	S212LLO	216	S216LLO	219	S219LLO	222	S422LLO
209	S209LLO	213	S213LLO						

223-238
Volvo Olympian   Alexander RH   B47/25D   1997

223	P223MPU	227	P227MPU	230	P230MPU	233	P233MPU	236	P236MPU
224	P224MPU	228	P228MPU	231	P231MPU	234	P234MPU	237	P237MPU
225	P225MPU	229	P229MPU	232	P232MPU	235	P235MPU	238	P238MPU
226	P226MPU								

239-249
Volvo Olympian   Northern Counties Palatine   B47/27D   1996

239	P239HMD	242	P242HMD	244	N244CMP	246	P246HMD	248	P248HMD
240	P240HMD	243	P243HMD	245	P245HMD	247	N247CMP	249	P249HMD
241	N241CMP								

250	J135PVC	Leyland Olympian ON2R50C13Z4 Leyland		B47/25D	1991	Volvo demonstrator, 1991

251-274
Dennis Dominator DDA2001   Northern Counties   B47/29D   1990

251	H251KVX	257	H257KVX	262	H262KVX	267	H267KVX	271	'H271KVX
252	H252KVX	258	H258KVX	263	H263KVX	268	H268KVX	272	H272KVX
253	H253KVX	259	H259KVX	264	H264KVX	269	H269KVX	273	H273KVX
254	H254KVX	260	H460KVX	265	H265KVX	270	H270KVX	274	H274KVX
255	H255KVX	261	H461KVX	266	H266KVX				

279-294
MCW Metrobus DR102/71*   MCW   B46/27F   1988   *294 is DR102/73

279	F279NHJ	282	F282NHJ	285	F285NHJ	288	F288NHJ	291	F291NHJ
280	F280NHJ	283	F283NHJ	286	F286NHJ	289	F289NHJ	293	F293NHJ
281	F281NHJ	284	F284NHJ	287	F287NHJ	290	F290NHJ	294	F294NHJ

295-299
MCW Metrobus DR104/3   MCW   B46/30F   1980   South Yorkshire, 1988

295	JWF495W	296	JWF496W	297	JWF497W	298	JWF498W	299	JWF499W

301	GYE379W	MCW Metrobus DR101/12	MCW	B43/28D	1980	London General, 1998
302	GYE479W	MCW Metrobus DR101/12	MCW	B43/28D	1980	London General, 1998
303	GYE546W	MCW Metrobus DR101/12	MCW	B43/28D	1980	London General, 1998
304	BYX284X	MCW Metrobus DR101/12	MCW	B43/28D	1980	London General, 1998
305	GYE405W	MCW Metrobus DR101/12	MCW	B43/28D	1980	London General, 1998
306	KYO606X	MCW Metrobus DR101/12	MCW	B43/28D	1980	London General, 1998
307	BYX287V	MCW Metrobus DR101/12	MCW	B43/28D	1980	London General, 1998
308	GYE498W	MCW Metrobus DR101/12	MCW	B43/28D	1980	CentreWest, 1998
309	BYX249V	MCW Metrobus DR101/12	MCW	B43/28D	1980	London General, 1998
310	GYE369W	MCW Metrobus DR101/12	MCW	B43/28D	1980	CentreWest, 1998
311	BYX311V	MCW Metrobus DR101/12	MCW	B43/28D	1980	CentreWest, 1998
312	EYE339V	MCW Metrobus DR101/12	MCW	B43/28D	1980	CentreWest, 1998
313	EYE343V	MCW Metrobus DR101/12	MCW	B43/28D	1980	CentreWest, 1998
314	GYE434W	MCW Metrobus DR101/12	MCW	B43/28D	1980	London General, 1998
315	GYE355W	MCW Metrobus DR101/12	MCW	B43/28D	1980	London General, 1998

In 1996 Capital Citybus purchased sixteen Dennis Arrows with Northern Counties Palatine 2 bodywork. These were followed in 1997 and 1998 by further batches though with the new East Lancashire Pyoneer body. One of the latest of the type is 451, S451SLL which is seen in First Capital livery at Edmonton Green bus station. *Colin Lloyd*

316	GYE416W	MCW Metrobus DR101/12	MCW	B43/28D	1980	London General, 1998
317	GYE457W	MCW Metrobus DR101/12	MCW	B43/28D	1980	London General, 1998
318	KYV668X	MCW Metrobus DR101/12	MCW	B43/28D	1980	London General, 1998
319	KYV769X	MCW Metrobus DR101/12	MCW	B43/28D	1980	CentreWest, 1998
321	GYE451W	MCW Metrobus DR101/12	MCW	B43/28D	1980	CentreWest, 1998
322	GYE487W	MCW Metrobus DR101/12	MCW	B43/28D	1980	CentreWest, 1998
323	OJD843Y	MCW Metrobus DR101/12	MCW	B43/28D	1980	CentreWest, 1998
324	GYE348W	MCW Metrobus DR101/12	MCW	B43/28D	1980	London General, 1999
328	GYE418W	MCW Metrobus DR101/12	MCW	B43/28D	1980	CentreWest, 1998
330	EYE330V	MCW Metrobus DR101/12	MCW	B43/28D	1980	Citybus, Leicester, 1998
332	EYE332V	MCW Metrobus DR101/12	MCW	B43/28D	1980	Citybus, Leicester, 1998
333	GYE413W	MCW Metrobus DR101/12	MCW	B43/28D	1980	Citybus, Leicester, 1999
334	GYE484W	MCW Metrobus DR101/12	MCW	B43/28D	1980	London General, 1999
338	GYE488W	MCW Metrobus DR101/12	MCW	B43/28D	1980	Citybus, Leicester, 1999

340-348

		Dennis Dominator DDA1024		East Lancashire		B46/33F		1989		Leicester Citybus, 1996

340	F140MBC	342	F142MBC	345	F145MBC	347	F147MBC	348	F148MBC
341	F141MBC	344	F144MBC						

401-416

		Dennis Arrow		Northern Counties Palatine 2		B47/35F*		1996		*413-6 are B47/33F

401	P401PLE	405	P405PLE	408	P408PLE	411	P411PLE	414	P414PLE
402	P402PLE	406	P406PLE	409	P409PLE	412	P412PLE	415	P415PLE
403	P403PLE	407	P407PLE	410	P410PLE	413	P413PLE	416	P416PLE
404	P404PLE								

417-426

		Dennis Arrow		East Lancashire Pyoneer		B49/28D*		1997		*426 is B49/27D

417	P417PVW	419	P419PVW	421	P421PVW	423	P423PVW	425	P425PVW
418	P418PVW	420	P420PVW	422	P422PVW	424	P424PVW	426	R426SOY

The Thamesway depot at Ponders End together with buses and routes were transferred from Essex Buses to First Capital during 1998. Now numbered 776, N976EHJ is seen at Enfield Town working service 191 to Brimsdown Station having received First Capital livery. *Colin Lloyd*

427-454

								East Lancashire Pyoneer	B49/25D	1998		

Dennis Arrow

427	R427ULE	433	R433ULE	439	R439ULE	445	R445ULE	450	R450ULE
428	R428ULE	434	R434ULE	440	R440ULE	446	R446ULE	451	S451SLL
429	R429ULE	435	R435ULE	441	R441ULE	447	R447ULE	452	S452SLL
430	R430ULE	436	R436ULE	442	R442ULE	448	R448ULE	453	S453SLL
431	R431ULE	437	R437ULE	443	R443ULE	449	R449ULE	454	S454SLL
432	R432ULE	438	R438ULE	444	R844YLC						

561	F251NJN	Mercedes-Benz 709D	Reeve Burgess Beaver	B23F	1988	Essex Buses, 1998
562	F255RHK	Mercedes-Benz 709D	Reeve Burgess Beaver	B23F	1989	Essex Buses, 1998
564	D764KWT	Mercedes-Benz 609D	Robin Hood	B20F	1987	Essex Buses, 1998

565-570

		Mercedes-Benz 709D		Reeve Burgess Beaver		B23F		1988-89		Essex Buses, 1998

565	F245MVW	567	F257RHK	568	F258RHK	569	F264MVW	570	F254RHK
566	F256RHK								

571-579

		Mercedes-Benz Vario O814		Marshall Master		B27F		1997-98		Essex Buses, 1998

571	R411VPU	573	R413VPU	575	R415VPU	577	R417VPU	579	R419VPU
572	R412VPU	574	R414VPU	576	R416VPU	578	R418VPU		

581-586

		Mercedes-Benz 709D		Reeve Burgess Beaver		B23F		1991		Essex Buses, 1998

581	H301LPU	583	H303LPU	584	H304LPU	585	H305LPU	586	H306LPU
582	H302LPU								

588-595

		Mercedes-Benz 709D		Reeve Burgess Beaver		B23F		1991		Essex Buses, 1998

588	H388MAR	590	H390MAR	592	H392MAR	594	H394MAR	595	H395MAR
589	H389MAR	591	H391MAR	593	H393MAR				

Capital Citybus won the tender to provide replacement bus services while the Docklands Light Rail was being enhanced. For the contract, and in the livery is Optare Excel 701, P701HMT. *Colin Lloyd*

596	K396KHJ	Mercedes-Benz 709D	Plaxton Beaver	B23F	1993	Essex Buses, 1998
600	F800RHK	Mercedes-Benz 811D	Reeve Burgess Beaver	B31F	1989	Essex Buses, 1998
601	J601HMF	Mercedes-Benz 811D	Plaxton Beaver	B28F	1992	
602	J602HMF	Mercedes-Benz 811D	Plaxton Beaver	B28F	1992	
603	F803RHK	Mercedes-Benz 811D	Reeve Burgess Beaver	B31F	1989	Essex Buses, 1998
604	F804RHK	Mercedes-Benz 811D	Reeve Burgess Beaver	B31F	1989	Essex Buses, 1998
605	J605HMF	Mercedes-Benz 811D	Plaxton Beaver	B28F	1992	
606	F801RHK	Mercedes-Benz 811D	Reeve Burgess Beaver	B31F	1989	Essex Buses, 1998
607	F802RHK	Mercedes-Benz 811D	Reeve Burgess Beaver	B31F	1989	Essex Buses, 1998

610-620

Mercedes-Benz 811D — Plaxton Beaver — B28F — 1992

610	J610HMF	612	J612HMF	615	J615HMF	617	J617HMF	620	J620HMF
611	J611HMF	613	J613HMF	616	J616HMF	618	J618HMF		

621-630

Optare MetroRider — Optare — B28F — 1992

621	J621HMH	623	J623HMH	625	J625HMH	627	J627HMH	629	J629HMH
622	J622HMH	624	J624HMH	626	J626HMH	628	J628HMH	630	J630HMH

631	J631HMH	Mercedes-Benz 811D	Alexander Sprint	B28F	1992
632	J632HMH	Mercedes-Benz 811D	Alexander Sprint	B28F	1992
633	J633HMH	Mercedes-Benz 811D	Alexander Sprint	B28F	1992

639-645

Dennis Dart 8.5SDL3003 — Wright Handybus — B26F — 1991 — CentreWest, 1998

639	JDZ2339	641	JDZ2341	643	JDZ2343	644	JDZ2372	645	JDZ2373
640	JDZ2340	642	JDZ2342						

DMS646-651

Dennis Dart SLF — Marshall Capital — N25F — On order

646	T646	648	T648	649	T649	650	T650	651	T651
647	T647								

669	J459JOW	Dennis Dart 9SDL3011	Wadham Stringer Portsdown	B37F	1991	Wealden Beeline, 1995
670	L670SMC	Dennis Dart 9SDL3034	Northen Counties Paladin	B31F	1994	

671-680

		Volvo B6-9.9		Alexander Dash		B31F		1994	

671	L671RMD	673	L673RMD	675	L675RMD	677	L677RMD	679	L679RMD
672	L672RMD	674	L674RMD	676	L676RMD	678	L678RMD	680	L680RMD

681	L281RML	Volvo B6-9.9	Northen Counties Paladin	B39F	1994	
682	L888JTC	Volvo B6-9.9	Northen Counties Paladin	B39F	1994	
683	L888AMY	Volvo B6-9.9	Northen Counties Paladin	B39F	1994	
684	L4GML	Volvo B6-9.9	Northen Counties Paladin	B31F	1994	Flightparks, Horley, 1996
685	L5GML	Volvo B6-9.9	Northen Counties Paladin	B31F	1994	Flightparks, Horley, 1996
686	L6GML	Volvo B6-9.9	Northen Counties Paladin	B31F	1994	Flightparks, Horley, 1996

691-696

		Dennis Dart 9SDL3016		Plaxton Pointer		B35F		1992	Essex Buses, 1998

691	K901CVW	693	K903CVW	694	K904CVW	695	K905CVW	696	K906CVW
692	K902CVW								

701	P701HMT	Optare L1070	Optare Excel	N33F	1996
702	P702HMT	Optare L1070	Optare Excel	N33F	1996
703	P703HMT	Optare L1070	Optare Excel	N33F	1996
704	P704HMT	Optare L1070	Optare Excel	N33F	1996

705-717

		Dennis Dart SLF		East Lancashire Spryte		N37F		1998	

705	R705VLA	708	R708VLA	711	R711VLA	714	R714VLA	716	R716VLA
706	R706VLA	709	R709VLA	712	R712VLA	715	R715VLA	717	R717VLA
707	R707VLA	710	R710VLA	713	R713VLA				

DML718-740

		Dennis Dart SLF		Marshall Capital		N--F		On order	

718	T718	723	T723	728	T728	733	T733	737	T737
719	T719	724	T724	729	T729	734	T734	738	T738
720	T720	725	T725	730	T730	735	T735	739	T739
721	T721	726	T726	731	T731	736	T736	740	T740
722	T722	727	T727	732	T732				

739	KRS539V	Leyland National 2 NL106L11/1R	B44F	1980	Bluebird Buses, 1993
744	GUW454W	Leyland National 2 NL106AL11/1R	B41F	1981	London Buses, 1994
749	B359LOY	Leyland National 2 NL116TL11/3R	B48F	1984	British Airways, 1993
750	NLP839V	Leyland National 2 NL116L11/1R	B49F	1980	Bluebird Buses, 1993

773-786

		Dennis Dart		Plaxton Pointer		B40F		1996	Essex Buses, 1998

773	N973EHJ	776	N976EHJ	779	N979EHJ	782	N982EHJ	785	N985EHJ
774	N974EHJ	777	N977EHJ	780	N980EHJ	783	N983EHJ	786	N986EHJ
775	N975EHJ	778	N978EHJ	781	N981EHJ	784	N984EHJ		

796	M796MPM	Dennis Lance	Alexander PS	B46F	1995	Dennis demonstrator, 1998
798	S838VAG	Dennis Dart SLF	Plaxton Pointer SPD	N38F	1998	On extended loan

TN801-TN822

		Dennis Trident		Plaxton President		N (--)D		1999	

801	T801LLC	806	T706LLC	811	T711LLC	815	T714LLC	819	T719LLC
802	T802LLC	807	T707LLC	812	T712LLC	816	T715LLC	820	T720LLC
803	T803LLC	808	T708LLC	813	T713LLC	817	T717LLC	821	T721LLC
804	T804LLC	809	T709LLC	814	T714LLC	818	T718LLC	822	T722LLC
805	T805LLC	810	T710LLC						

TN854-TN887

		Dennis Trident		Plaxton President		N (--)D		On order	

854	861	868	875	882
855	862	869	876	883
856	863	870	877	884
857	864	871	878	885
858	865	872	879	886
859	866	873	880	887
860	867	874	881	

Special Event vehicles owned by Capital Citybus TV Ltd:-

913	ALD913B	AEC Routemaster 6RM	Park Royal		B36/28R	1959	
920	VLT120	AEC Routemaster 6RM	Park Royal		O36/28R	1959	LBPG, Cobham, 199-

Ancilliary vehicles:-

175	DAE510W	MCW Metrobus DR103/4	MCW		TV	1989	MTL, Liverpool, 1996
276	FUT36V	MCW Metrobus DR102/14	MCW		TV	1980	Leicester, 1990
277	FUT37V	MCW Metrobus DR102/14	MCW		TV	1980	Leicester, 1990

Previous Registrations:

KRS539V	GSO5V	P405PLE	P905HMH	P409PLE	P909HMH
P401PLE	P901HMH	P406PLE	P906HMH	P410PLE	P910HMH
P402PLE	P902HMH	P407PLE	P907HMH	P411PLE	P911HMH
P403PLE	P903HMH	P408PLE	P908HMH	P412PLE	P912HMH
P404PLE	P904HMH				

Allocations:-

Dagenham (Chequers Lane)

Dart	691	692	693	694	695	696	717	780
Optare Excel	701	702	703	704				
National	739	744	749	750				
Lance	796							
Metrobus	107	170	171	176	178	179	279	280
	281	282	283	284	285	286	287	288
	289	290	291	293	294	308	310	311
	312	313	314	317	321	322	323	324
	328	330	332	333	334	338		
Olympian	136	137	138	139	140	141	142	143
	144	145	146	147	148	149	150	151
	152	153	154	155	156	157	158	159
	160	161	162	163	164	165	169	
Dominator	196	197	251	252	253	254	255	257
	258	259	260	261	262	263		
Arrow	401	407	408	409	410	411	412	417
	418	419	420	421	422	423	424	453
	454							

Hackney (Waterden Road)

Mercedes-Benz	601	602	605	610	611	612	613	615
	616	617	618	620	631	632	633	
Dart	669	670	705	706	707	708	709	710
	711	712	713	714	715	716		
Volvo B6	671	672	673	674	675	676	677	678
	679	680	681	682	683	684	685	686
Metrobus	100	104	105	106	109	117	177	
Dominator	181	182	183	184	190	191	192	193
	194	195	198	202	203	340	341	342
	344	345	347	348				
Olympian	125	127	128	129	166	167	168	173
	179	180						
Arrow	402	403	404	405	406	413	414	415
	416							
Special Event vehicles	913	920						

Northumberland Park (Marsh Lane)

Mercedes-Benz	565	566	567	568	569	570	594	
MetroRider	621	622	624	625	626	627	628	629
	630							
Dart	639	640	641	642	643	644	645	
Mertrobus	101	102	110	115	116	118	119	120
	295	296	297	298	299	301	302	303
	304	305	306	307	309	315	316	318
	319							

The integral MetroRider currently being produced by Optare was the choice of minibus for Capital Citybus in 1992 when ten joined the fleet. The type is illustrated by 627, J627HMH, seen on London Buses route W6 in Edmonton. *Colin Lloyd*

Dominator	264	265	266	267	268	269	270	271
	272	273	274					
Olympian	121	122	124	126	130	131	132	133
	134	135	206	207	208	209	210	211
	212	213	214	215	216	217	218	219
	220	221	222	223	224	225	226	227
	228	229	230	231	232	233	234	235
	236	237	238	239	240	241	242	243
	244	245	246	247	248	249	250	
Arrow	425	426	427	428	429	430	431	432
	433	434	435	436	437	438	439	440
	441	442	443	444	445	446	447	448
	449	450	451	452				

Ponders End (Moreson Road)

Mercedes-Benz	561	562	564	571	572	573	574	575
	576	577	578	579	581	582	583	584
	585	586	588	589	590	591	592	593
	595	596	600	603	604	606	607	
Dart	773	774	775	776	777	778	779	781
	782	783	784	785	786			

Unallocated

MetroRider	623	625

FIRST CENTREWEST

Bee Line - Ealing Buses - Challenger - Gold Arrow - London Buslines

Orpington Buses - Uxbridge Buses

CentreWest London Buses Ltd; The Berks Bucks Bus Co Ltd;
London Buslines Ltd,
Macmillan House, Paddington Station, London W2 1TY

D33-41

		Dennis Dart		Plaxton Pointer		B37F	1996		
33	133CLT	**35**	N635ACF	**37**	N637ACF	**39**	P409MLA	**41**	P411MLA
34	N634ACF	**36**	N636ACF	**38**	P408MLA	**40**	P410MLA		

D201	K279XJB	Dennis Dart 9.8SDL3017	Plaxton Pointer	B40F	1993
D202	K281XJB	Dennis Dart 9.8SDL3017	Plaxton Pointer	B40F	1993
D203	K282XJB	Dennis Dart 9.8SDL3017	Plaxton Pointer	B40F	1993
D204	K283XJB	Dennis Dart 9.8SDL3017	Plaxton Pointer	B40F	1993
D205	L205GMO	Dennis Dart 9.8SDL3035	Plaxton Pointer	B37F	1993
D206	L206GMO	Dennis Dart 9.8SDL3035	Plaxton Pointer	B37F	1993
D207	L207GMO	Dennis Dart 9.8SDL3035	Plaxton Pointer	B37F	1993
D208	L208GMO	Dennis Dart 9.8SDL3035	Plaxton Pointer	B37F	1993

D601-632

		Dennis Dart		Plaxton Pointer		B37F		1996			
601	N601XJM	**608**	N608XJM	**615**	N615XJM	**621**	N621XJM	**627**	P627CGM
602	N602XJM	**609**	N609XJM	**616**	N616XJM	**622**	N622XJM	**628**	P628CGM
603	N603XJM	**610**	N610XJM	**617**	N617XJM	**623**	N623XJM	**629**	P629CGM
604	N604XJM	**611**	N611XJM	**618**	N618XJM	**624**	N624XJM	**630**	P630CGM
605	N605XJM	**612**	N612XJM	**619**	N619XJM	**625**	N625XJM	**631**	P631CGM
606	N606XJM	**613**	N613XJM	**620**	N620XJM	**626**	N626XJM	**632**	P632CGM
607	N607XJM	**614**	N614XJM						

First CentreWest DW126, LDZ9126 is the last of the 1992 intake of Wright Handybus-bodied Dennis Dart and is seen heading for Wandsworth on tendered route 28. *Gold Arrow* names are used by CentreWest on services operated by the Westbourne Park depot.
Phillip Stephenson

DM117-157

Dennis Dart SLF Marshall Capital N31F 1997

117	P117NLW	126	P126NLW	134	P134NLW	142	P142NLW	150	P150NLW
118	P118NLW	127	P127NLW	135	P135NLW	143	P143NLW	151	P151NLW
119	P119NLW	128	P128NLW	136	P136NLW	144	P144NLW	152	P152NLW
120	P120NLW	129	P129NLW	137	P137NLW	145	P145NLW	153	P153NLW
121	P121NLW	130	P130NLW	138	P138NLW	146	P146NLW	154	P154NLW
122	P122NLW	131	P131NLW	139	P139NLW	147	P247OEW	155	P255RFL
123	P123NLW	132	P132NLW	140	P140NLW	148	P148NLW	156	P156NLW
124	P124NLW	133	P133NLW	141	P141NLW	149	P149NLW	157	P157NLW
125	P125NLW								

DM158-164

Dennis Dart SLF Marshall Capital N31F 1998

158	R158TLM	160	R160TLM	162	R162TLM	163	R163TLM	164	R164TLM
159	R159TLM	161	R161TLM						

DML165-190

Dennis Dart SLF Marshall Capital N35F* 1997-98 179-190 are N37F

165	R165TLM	171	R171TLM	176	R176TLM	181	R181TLM	186	R186TLM
166	R166TLM	172	R172TLM	177	R177TLM	182	R182TLM	187	R187TLM
167	R167TLM	173	R173TLM	178	R178TLM	183	R183TLM	188	R188TLM
168	R168TLM	174	R174TLM	179	R179TLM	184	R184TLM	189	R189TLM
169	R169TLM	175	R175TLM	180	R180TLM	185	R185TLM	190	R190TLM
170	R170TLM								

DML191-200

Dennis Dart SLF Marshall Capital N37F 1998

191	R191VLD	193	R193VLD	195	R195VLD	197	S197KLM	199	S199KLM
192	R192VLD	194	R194VLD	196	R196VLD	198	S198KLM	200	S220KLM

DM201-234

Dennis Dart SLF Marshall Capital N23D 1998

201	R201TLM	208	R208TLM	215	R215TLM	222	R322TLM	229	R229TLM
202	R202TLM	209	R209TLM	216	R216TLM	223	R223TLM	230	R230TLM
203	R203TLM	210	R210TLM	217	R217TLM	224	R224TLM	231	R231TLM
204	R204TLM	211	R211TLM	218	R218TLM	225	R225TLM	232	R232TLM
205	R205TLM	212	R212TLM	219	R219TLM	226	R226TLM	233	R233TLM
206	R206TLM	213	R213TLM	220	R220TLM	227	R227TLM	234	R234TLM
207	R207TLM	214	R214TLM	221	R221TLM	228	R228TLM		

DML235-256

Dennis Dart SLF Marshall Capital N28D* 1998 *249-52 are N24D

235	S235KLM	240	S240KLM	245	S245KLM	249	809DYE	253	S253JLP
236	S236KLM	241	S241KLM	246	S246KLM	250	810DYE	254	S254JLP
237	S237KLM	242	S242KLM	247	S247KLM	251	811DYE	255	S255JLP
238	S238KLM	243	S243KLM	248	S248KLM	252	292CLT	256	S256JLP
239	S239KLM	244	S244KLM						

DMS257-263

Dennis Dart SLF Marshall Capital N25F 1999

257	T257JLD	259	T259JLD	261	T261JLD	262	T262JLD	263	T263JLD
258	T258JLD	260	T260JLD						

DM264-306

Dennis Dart SLF Marshall Capital N--D On order

264	T264JLD	273	T273JLD	282	T282JLD	291	T291JLD	299	T299JLD
265	T265JLD	274	T274JLD	283	T283JLD	292	T292JLD	300	T430JLD
266	T266JLD	275	T275JLD	284	T284JLD	293	T293JLD	301	T301JLD
267	T267JLD	276	T276JLD	285	T285JLD	294	T294JLD	302	T302JLD
268	T268JLD	277	T277JLD	286	T286JLD	295	T295JLD	303	T303JLD
269	T269JLD	278	T278JLD	287	T287JLD	296	T296JLD	304	T304JLD
270	T270JLD	279	T279JLD	288	T288JLD	297	T297JLD	305	T305JLD
271	T271JLD	280	T280JLD	289	T289JLD	298	T298JLD	306	T306JLD
272	T272JLD	281	T281JLD	290	T290JLD					

Opposite:- **Recent arrivals at Golders Green station where the** *Challenger* **name dominates are DML241, S241KLM, a Marshall-bodied Dennis Dart and VN891, T891KLF, one of the last Volvo Olympians to enter service with a UK operator. The Volvo Olympian has been replaced by new low-floor double-deck, the B7 which was introduced during 1999. Interestingly, production of the Northern Counties Palatine '1' body continued for several weeks after the last Palatine 2 was completed.** *Tony Wilson*

DML336	V		Dennis Dart SLF		Marshall Capital		N25F	On order		

DMS337-361

Dennis Dart SLF — Marshall Capital — N25F — On order

337	V	342	V	347	V	352	V	357	V
338	V	343	V	348	V	353	V	358	V
339	V	344	V	349	V	354	V	359	V
340	V	345	V	350	V	355	V	360	V
341	V	346	V	351	V	356	V	361	V

DML633-653

Dennis Dart SLF — Marshall Capital — N37F — 1997-98

633	R633VLX	638	R638VLX	642	R642TLM	646	R646TLM	650	R650TLM
634	R634VLX	639	R639VLX	643	R643TLM	647	R647TLM	651	R651TLM
635	R835VLX	640	R640VLX	644	R644TLM	648	R648TLM	652	R652TLM
636	R636VLX	641	R641VLX	645	R645TLM	649	R649TLM	653	R653TLM
637	R637VLX								

DP1-32

Dennis Dart 9SDL3053 — Plaxton Pointer — B32F — 1995

1	N801FLW	8	N808FLW	15	N815FLW	21	N821FLW	27	N827FLW
2	N802FLW	9	N809FLW	16	N816FLW	22	N822FLW	28	N828FLW
3	N803FLW	10	N810FLW	17	N817FLW	23	N823FLW	29	N829FLW
4	N804FLW	11	N811FLW	18	N818FLW	24	N824FLW	30	N830FLW
5	N805FLW	12	N812FLW	19	N819FLW	25	N825FLW	31	N831FLW
6	N806FLW	13	N813FLW	20	N820FLW	26	N826FLW	32	N832FLW
7	N807FLW	14	N814FLW						

DW1-14

Dennis Dart 8.5SDL3003 — Wright Handybus — B30F — 1990 — London Buses, 1994

1	JDZ2301	4	JDZ2304	7	JDZ2307	10	JDZ2310	13	JDZ2313
2	JDZ2302	5	JDZ2305	8	JDZ2308	11	JDZ2311	14	JDZ2314
3	JDZ2303	6	JDZ2306	9	JDZ2309	12	JDZ2312		

DW15-91

Dennis Dart 8.5SDL3003 — Wright Handybus — B26F* — 1991 — London Buses, 1994
26-32 are B30F

15	JDZ2315	26	JDZ2326	32w	JDZ2332	80	JDZ2380	86	JDZ2386
16	JDZ2316	27	JDZ2327	74	JDZ2374	81	JDZ2381	87	JDZ2387
17	JDZ2317	28	JDZ2328	75	JDZ2375	82	JDZ2382	88	JDZ2388
22	JDZ2322	29	JDZ2329	77	JDZ2377	83	JDZ2383	89	JDZ2389
23	JDZ2323	30	JDZ2330	78	JDZ2378	84	JDZ2384	90	JDZ2390
24	JDZ2324	31w	JDZ2331	79	JDZ2379	85	JDZ2385	91	JDZ2391

DW92-126

Dennis Dart 8.5SDL3010* — Wright Handybus — B26F — 1991-92 — London Buses, 1994
*100 is 8.5SDL3003; 115-25 are 8.5SDL3015; 126 is 8.5SDL3018

92	JDZ2392	99	JDZ2399	106	KDZ5106	113	LDZ9113	120	LDZ9120
93	JDZ2393	100	JDZ2300	107	KDZ5107	114	LDZ9114	121	LDZ9121
94	JDZ2394	101	KDZ5101	108	KDZ5108	115	LDZ9115	122	LDZ9122
95	JDZ2395	102	KDZ5102	109	KDZ5109	116	LDZ9116	123	LDZ9123
96	JDZ2396	103	KDZ5103	110	KDZ5110	117	LDZ9117	124	LDZ9124
97	JDZ2397	104	KDZ5104	111	KDZ5111	118	LDZ9118	125	LDZ9125
98	JDZ2398	105	KDZ5105	112	KDZ5112	119	LDZ9119	126	LDZ9126

DW162-170

Dennis Dart 8.5SDL3015 — Wright Handybus — B29F* — 1993 — London Buses, 1994
*169/70 are B26F

162	NDZ3162	164	NDZ3164	166	NDZ3166	168	NDZ3168	170	NDZ3170
163	NDZ3163	165	NDZ3165	167	NDZ3167	169	NDZ3169		

L1-7

Dennis Dart SLF — Plaxton Pointer — N34F — 1996

1	P401MLA	3	P403MLA	5	P405MLA	6	P406MLA	7	P407MLA
2	P402MLA	4	P404MLA						

Vehicles at Greenford depot carry *Ealing Buses* names. Pictured on the E1 is MCW Metrobus M1422, C422BUV. Several of the Metrobuses perform a dual role that includes driver training. A livery of yellow and red is carried by M1422. *Gerry Mead*

Marshall-bodied Dennis Darts have fulfilled CentreWest's midibus needs since 1997, with lengths of batches being varied to suit specific tenders. One of the longer examples is DML168, R168TLM. *Bob Stanger*

L211-217 | Dennis Dart SLF | Plaxton Pointer | N37F | 1996

211	N211WRD	**213**	N213WRD	**215**	N215WRD	**216**	N216WRD	**217**	N217WRD
212	N212WRD	**214**	N214WRD						

L237	P237NLW	Dennis Dart SLF	Plaxton Pointer	N37F	1997
L238	P238NLW	Dennis Dart SLF	Plaxton Pointer	N37F	1997
L239	P239NLW	Dennis Dart SLF	Plaxton Pointer	N37F	1997

LA24-28 | Leyland Olympian ON2R50C13Z4 Alexander RH | B45/29F | 1993

24	L24GAN	**25**	L25GAN	**26**	L26GAN	**27**	L27GAN	**28**	L28GAN

LA506	G55XLO	Leyland Olympian ONCL10/1RZ Alexander RL		B47/28F	1989
LA507	G56XLO	Leyland Olympian ONCL10/1RZ Alexander RL		B47/28F	1989

LC1	N921LUF	LDV 400	Crystals	M10L	1995
LC2	N922LUF	LDV 400	Crystals	M10L	1995
LC3	N923LUF	LDV 400	Crystals	M10L	1995

LLW11-24 | Dennis Lance SLF | Wright Pathfinder 320 | N34D* | 1993-94 | London Buses, 1994 *13 is B31D

11	ODZ8911	**14**	ODZ8914	**17**	ODZ8917	**20**	ODZ8920	**23**	ODZ8923
12	ODZ8912	**15**	ODZ8915	**18**	ODZ8918	**21**	ODZ8921	**24**	ODZ8924
13	ODZ8913	**16**	ODZ8916	**19**	ODZ8919	**22**	ODZ8922		

LLW31	M221EAF	Dennis Lance SLF	Wright Pathfinder 320	N34F	1995	Yorkshire Rider, 1998

LN31-43 | Leyland Olympian ON2R50C13Z4 Northern Counties Palatine | B47/30F | 1990

31	H131FLX	**33**	H133FLX	**34**	H134FLX	**38**	H138FLX	**43**	H143FLX

LN501-505 | Leyland Olympian ONCL10/1RZ Northern Counties | B45/29F | 1989

501	F172LBL	**502**	F173LBL	**503**	F174LBL	**504**	F175LBL	**505**	F176LBL

LX800	F101GRM	Leyland Lynx LX112L10ZR1R	Leyland Lynx	BC48F	1988	
LX801	K801CAN	Leyland Lynx LX2R11V18Z4S	Leyland Lynx 2	B51F	1992	Stagecoach South, 1992
LX802	K802CAN	Leyland Lynx LX2R11V18Z4S	Leyland Lynx 2	B51F	1992	Stagecoach South, 1992
LX803	D751DLO	Leyland Lynx LX112TL11ZR1S	Leyland Lynx	B49F	1987	
LX805	D753DLO	Leyland Lynx LX112TL11ZR1S	Leyland Lynx	B49F	1987	
LX807	D105NDW	Leyland Lynx LX112TL11ZR1R	Leyland Lynx	BC48F	1988	

M285-583 | MCW Metrobus DR101/12* | MCW | B43/28D | 1980 | 523/83 are DR104/14
London Buses, 1994 except 385 which was London General, 1996.

285	BYX285V	**340**	EYE340V	**371**	GYE371W	**414**	GYE414W	**489**	GYE489W
291	BYX291V	**347**	GYE347W	**374**	GYE374W	**425**	GYE425W	**494**	GYE494W
305	BYX305V	**349**	GYE349W	**383**	GYE383W	**427**	GYE427W	**497**	GYE497W
308	BYX308V	**358**	GYE358W	**385**	GYE385W	**442**	GYE442W	**499**	GYE499W
316	EYE316V	**360**	GYE360W	**390**	GYE390W	**452**	GYE452W	**504**	GYE504W
319	EYE319V	**362**	GYE362W	**393**	GYE393W	**465**	GYE465W	**505**	GYE505W
329	EYE329V	**364**	GYE364W	**397**	GYE397W	**470**	GYE470W	**523**	GYE523W
337	EYE337V	**368**	GYE368W	**406**	GYE406W	**486**	GYE486W	**583**	GYE583W
338	EYE338V	**370**	GYE370W						

M851-952 | MCW Metrobus DR101/16 | MCW | B43/28D | 1983 | London Buses, 1994

851	OJD851Y	**866**	OJD866Y	**883**	OJD883Y	**892**	A892SUL	**938**	A938SUL
857	OJD857Y	**872**	OJD872Y	**884**	OJD884Y	**893**	A893SUL	**941**	A941SUL
859	OJD859Y	**874**	OJD874Y	**885**	OJD885Y	**898**	A898SUL	**943**	A943SUL
860	OJD860Y	**875**	OJD875Y	**886**	OJD886Y	**901**	A901SUL	**952**	A952SUL
861	OJD861Y	**882**	OJD882Y	**887**	OJD887Y				

M979	A979SYF	MCW Metrobus DR101/17	MCW	B43/28D	1984	London Buses, 1994
M1049	A749THV	MCW Metrobus DR101/19	MCW	B43/28D	1985	London Buses, 1994
M1051	A751THV	MCW Metrobus DR101/19	MCW	B43/28D	1985	London Buses, 1994
M1054	A754THV	MCW Metrobus DR101/19	MCW	B43/28D	1985	London Buses, 1994

BeeLine is operated as a separate unit within CentreWest as their duties extend into the area covered by the former Royal County of Berkshire, away from the London Transport tendering area. Pictured in Windsor while working the Reading service is Scania L113 816, M816PGM. The bodywork on this batch is Northern Counties Paladin. *Colin Lloyd*

M1144-1438
MCW Metrobus DR101/17 MCW B43/28D 1985-86 London Buses, 1994

1144	B144WUL	1256	B257WUL	1338	C338BUV	1380	C380BUV	1418	C418BUV
1199	B199WUL	1258	B258WUL	1340	C340BUV	1382	C382BUV	1419	C419BUV
1201	B201WUL	1259	B259WUL	1375	C375BUV	1384	C384BUV	1420	C420BUV
1244	B244WUL	1260	B260WUL	1376	C376BUV	1400	C400BUV	1421	C421BUV
1245	B245WUL	1267	B267WUL	1377	C377BUV	1412	C412BUV	1422	C422BUV
1246	B246WUL	1328	C328BUV	1378	C378BUV	1415	C415BUV	1438	C438BUV
1247	B247WUL	1335	C335BUV						

ML103-116
Marshall Minibus MM2 Marshall N26F 1997-98

103	R103VLX	107	R107VLX	109	R109VLX	112	R112VLX	114	R114VLX
105	R105VLX	108	R108VLX	111	R211VLX	113	R113VLX	116	R116VLX

MM1-10
Mercedes-Benz 811D Marshall C16 B28F 1995-96

1	N521REW	3	N523REW	5	N525REW	7	N527REW	9	P489CEG
2	N522REW	4	N524REW	6	N526REW	8	P488CEG	10	P490CEG

MM25	P825NAV	Mercedes-Benz Vario O814	Marshall Master	B28F	1997	
MM26	P826NAV	Mercedes-Benz Vario O814	Marshall Master	B28F	1997	
MT8	G538GBD	Mercedes-Benz 709D	Reeve Burgess Beaver	B18FL	1989	London Buses, 1994
RML885	WLT885	AEC Routemaster 7RM(Cummins) Park Royal		B40/32R	1961	London Buses, 1994

Orpington Buses' V3, N303JBV was one of twelve vehicles supplied by Northern Counties in 1995 and registered at the Preston DVLO. The batch are based at Orpington and are the only double-decks at the garage. *Phillip Stephenson*

RML2268-2740			AEC Routemaster 7RM(Cummins) Park Royal				B40/32R	1965-67		Ex London Buses, 1994
2268	CUV268C	2374	JJD374D	2476	JJD476D	2542	JJD542D	2664	SMK664F
2278	CUV278C	2378	JJD378D	2480	JJD480D	2553	JJD553D	2667	SMK667F
2281	CUV281C	2379	JJD379D	2486	JJD486D	2555	JJD555D	2672	SMK672F
2291	CUV291C	2388	JJD388D	2490	JJD490D	2559	JJD559D	2677	SMK677F
2309	CUV309C	2390	JJD390D	2498	JJD498D	2602	NML602E	2687	SMK687F
2313	CUV313C	2405	JJD405D	2501	JJD501D	2609	NML609E	2717	SMK717F
2352	CUV352C	2428	JJD428D	2506	JJD506D	2623	NML623E	2724	SMK724F
2357	CUV357C	2442	JJD442D	2522	JJD522D	2647	NML647E	2735	SMK735F
2365	JJD365D	2467	JJD467D	2530	JJD530D	2656	NML656E	2740	SMK740F
2369	JJD369D	2473	JJD473D						

RB551	K651DBL	Renault S75		Plaxton Beaver		B18FL	1992
RB552	K652DBL	Renault S75		Plaxton Beaver		B18FL	1992
RB553	K653DBL	Renault S75		Plaxton Beaver		B18FL	1992

RW4-83			Renault S75		Wright		B28F	1990
4	HDZ5404	18	HDZ5418	26	HDZ5426	37	HDZ5437	49	HDZ5449
5	HDZ5405	19	HDZ5419	27	HDZ5427	38	HDZ5438	50	HDZ5450
6	HDZ5406	20	HDZ5420	29	HDZ5429	39	HDZ5439	51	HDZ5451
7	HDZ5407	21	HDZ5421	30	HDZ5430	42	HDZ5442	52	HDZ5452
8	HDZ5408	22	HDZ5422	31	HDZ5431	43	HDZ5443	53	HDZ5453
9	HDZ5409	23	HDZ5423	33	HDZ5433	45	HDZ5445	58	HDZ5458
15	HDZ5415	24	HDZ5424	34	HDZ5434	47	HDZ5447	60	HDZ5460
17	HDZ5417	25	HDZ5425	35	HDZ5435	48	HDZ5448	83	HDZ5483

Opposite,top:- Gold Arrow use AEC Routemasters for some London Transport tenders that serve central London. The type is illustrated by RML2490, JJD490D, seen in wet weather. *Phillip Stephenson*
Opposite, bottom:- Waiting time at Golders Green station VN892, T892KLF illustrates the nearside styling of this last batch of Volvo Olympians. Production of vehicles at the Northern Counties plant will in future carry Plaxton badging since the assembly unit has been renamed Plaxton (Wigan). *Tony Wilson*

SB740-746

Scania K113CRB — Berkhof Excellence 2000 — C53F — 1991

740	TJI4830	742	TJI4832	744	TJI4834	745	TJI4835	746	TJI4836
741	TJI4831	743	TJI4833						

SB791-798

Scania K113CRB — Berkhof Excellence 1000LD — C53F — 1995

791	M791TCF	793	M793TCF	795	N795WAN	797	N797WAN	798	N798WAN
792	M792TCF	794	M794TCF	796	N796WAN				

SN810-819

Scania L113CRL* — Northern Counties Paladin — B51F — 1988 — *810 is type L113CLL

810	M810PGM	812	M812PGM	814	M814PGM	816	M816PGM	818	M818PGM
811	M811PGM	813	M813PGM	815	M815PGM	817	M817PGM	819	M819PGM

SW820-825

Scania L94UB — Wright Axcess Floline — N40F — 1999

820	T820JBL	822	T822JBL	823	T823JBL	824	T824JBL	825	T825JBL
821	T821JBL								

TN823-853

Dennis Trident II — Plaxton President — N../..F — On order

823	T823LLC	830	T830LLC	836	T836LLC	842	T842LLC	848	T848LLC
824	T824LLC	831	T831LLC	837	T837LLC	843	T843LLC	849	T849LLC
825	T825LLC	832	T832LLC	838	T838LLC	844	T844LLC	850	T850LLC
826	T826LLC	833	T833LLC	839	T839LLC	845	T845LLC	851	T851LLC
827	T827LLC	834	T834LLC	840	T840LLC	846	T846LLC	852	T852LLC
828	T828LLC	835	T835LLC	841	T841LLC	847	T847LLC	853	T853LLC
829	T829LLC								

V1-12

Volvo Olympian YN2RV18Z4 — Northern Counties Palatine II B43/29F — 1995

1	N301JBV	4	N304JBV	7	N307JBV	9	N309JBV	11	N311JBV
2	N302JBV	5	N305JBV	8	N308JBV	10	N310JBV	12	N312JBV
3	N303JBV	6	N306JBV						

V41-55

Volvo Olympian — Northern Counties Palatine II BC43/27F — 1996

41	P241UCW	44	P244UCW	47	P247UCW	50	P250UCW	53	P253UCW
42	P242UCW	45	P245UCW	48	P248UCW	51	P251UCW	54	P254UCW
43	P243UCW	46	P246UCW	49	P249UCW	52	P252UCW	55	P255UCW

VJ782	TJI4822	Volvo B10M-60	Jonckheere Deauville P50	C55F	1989	Ex Alder Valley, 1992
VJ783	TJI4823	Volvo B10M-60	Jonckheere Deauville P50	C55F	1989	Ex Alder Valley, 1992
VJ786	TJI4826	Volvo B10M-60	Jonckheere Deauville P50	C55F	1989	Ex Alder Valley, 1992
VJ789	TJI4829	Volvo B10M-60	Jonckheere Deauville P50	C55F	1989	Ex Alder Valley, 1992
VJ790	TJI4820	Volvo B10M-60	Jonckheere Deauville P50	C55F	1989	Ex Alder Valley, 1992

VP701-707

Volvo B12T — Plaxton Excalibur — C F — On order

701	T701JLD	703	T703JLD	705	T705JLD	706	T706JLD	707	T707JLD
702	T702JLD	704	T704JLD						

VN888-907

Volvo Olympian — Northern Counties Palatine I B47/27D — 1999

888	T988KLF	892	T892KLF	896	T896KLF	900	T990KLF	904	T904KLF
889	T889KLF	893	T893KLF	897	T897KLF	901	T901KLF	905	T905KLF
890	T890KLF	894	T894KLF	898	T898KLF	902	T902KLF	906	T906KLF
891	T891KLF	895	T895KLF	899	T899KLF	903	T903KLF	907	T907KLF

Special Event vehicles:-

MA1	F601XMS	Mercedes-Benz 811D	Alexander Sprint	B26F	1988	London Buses, 1994
RF326	MLL963	AEC Regal IV 9821LT	Metro-Cammell	B39F	1952	preservation, 1996
RMC1510	510CLT	AEC Routemaster 6RM(Cummins) Park Royal		O32/25R	1962	London Buses, 1994

Ancilliary vehicles:-

LS470	GUW470W	Leyland National 2 NL106AL11/1R(Volvo)	BC43F	1981	London Buses, 1994
LS472	GUW472W	Leyland National 2 NL106AL11/1R(Volvo)	BC43F	1981	London Buses, 1994
LS497	GUW497W	Leyland National 2 NL106AL11/1R(Volvo)	BC43F	1981	London Buses, 1994
LS503	GUW503W	Leyland National 2 NL106AL11/1R(Volvo)	BC43F	1981	London Buses, 1994
LS504	GUW504W	Leyland National 2 NL106AL11/1R(Volvo)	BC43F	1981	London Buses, 1994

Note:- twelve Metrobuses are also driver trainers. See allocations below

Previous Registrations:

133CLT	N633ACF	TJI4820	F760OJH	TJI4831	J741TDP
292CLT	R650MEW	TJI4822	F772OJH	TJI4832	J742TDP
809DYE	R677MEW	TJI4823	F773OJH	TJI4833	J743TDP
810DYE	R678MEW	TJI4826	F756OJH	TJI4834	J744TDP
811DYE	R679MEW	TJI4829	F759OJH	TJI4835	J745TDP
D105NDW	D105NDW, 809DYE	TJI4830	J740TDP	TJI4836	J746TDP
GUW503W	GUW503W, 503CLT				

Allocations

Acton (High Street) - Uxbridge Buses

Metrobus	M285	M305	M308	M337	M347	M362	M364	M371
	M390	M414	M425	M442	M486	M489	M497	M504
	M523	M583	M851	M859	M860	M938	M943	M1244
	M1256	M1258	M1375	M1421				

Alperton (Ealing Road) - Challenger

Dart	D601	D602	D603	D604	D605	D606	D607	D608
	D609	D610	DML235	DML236	DML237	DML238	DML239	DML240
	DML241	DML242	DML243	DML244	DML245	DML246	DML247	DML248
	DML253	DML254	DML255	DML256	DW1	DW2	DW3	DW4
	DW5	DW6	DW7	DW8	DW9	DW10	DW11	DW12
	DW13	DW14	DW15	DW16	DW17	DW22	DW23	DW74
	DW75	DW162	DW163	DW164	DW165	DW166	DW167	DW168
Metrobus	M1245	M1377	M1378	M1382				
Olympian	VN888	VN889	VN890	VN891	VN892	VN893	VN894	VN895
	VN896	VN897	VN898	VN899	VN900	VN901	VN902	VN903
	VN904	VN905	VN906	VN907				

London Buslines now operate an all-single-deck fleet from Southall, and with the exception of four Renault S75s the fleet is now all Dennis Dart of varying specifications. Seen working route 105 is Plaxton-bodied L238, P238NLW, one of seventeen Darts that carry an L-prefix.
Phillip Stephenson

Bracknell (Market Street) - The Bee Line

Renault	RW42	RW43	RW45	RW47	RW48	RW49	RW50	RW52
	RW53							
Dart	L211	L212						
Lynx	LX800	LX803						
Scania Coach	SB740	SB741	SB742	SB743	SB744	SB745	SB746	SB791
	SB792	SB793	SB794	SB795	SB796	SB797	SB798	
Scania Bus	SN810	SN811	SN812	SN813	SN814	SN815	SN816	SN817
	SN818	SN819	SW820	SW821	SW822	SW823	SW824	SW825
Volvo Coach	VJ782	VJ783	VJ786	VJ789	VJ790			
Olympian	LN501	LN502	LN503	LN504	LN505	LA506	LA507	

Greenford (Greenford Road) - Ealing Buses

Dart	DM117	DM118	DM119	DM120	DM121	DM122	DM123	DM124
	DM125	DM126	DM127	DM128	DM129	DM130	DM131	DM132
	DM133	DM134	DM135	DM136	DM137	DM138	DM139	DM140
	DM141	DM142	DM143	DM144	DM145	DM146	DM147	DM148
	DM149	DM150	DM151	DM152	DM153	DM154	DM155	DM156
	DM157	DM158	DM159	DM160	DM161	DM162	DM163	DM164
	DML165	DML166	DML167	DML168	DML169	DML170	DML171	DML172
	DML173	DML174	DML175	DML176	DML177	DML178	DMS258	DMS259
	DMS260	DMS261	DMS262	DMS263				
Olympian	LA24	LA25	LA26	LA27	LA28	LN31	LN33	LN34
	LN38	LN43						
Marshall Mini	ML103	ML105	ML107	ML108	ML109	ML111	ML112	ML113
	ML114	ML116						

Orpington (Faraday Way, St Mary Cray) - Orpington Buses

Mercedes-Benz	MM1	MM2	MM3	MM4	MM5	MM6	MM7	MM8
	MM9	MM10						
Dart	DP1	DP2	DP3	DP4	DP5	DP6	DP7	DP8
	DP9	DP10	DP11	DP12	DP13	DP14	DP15	DP16
	D38	D39	D40	D41	DMS257			
Olympian	V1	V2	V3	V4	V5	V6	V7	V8
	V9	V10	V11	V12				

Slough (Stanley Cottages) - The Bee Line

Renault	RW4	RW5	RW6	RW8	RW9	RW15	RW18	RW20
	RW22	RW24	RW25	RW26	RW27	RW29	RW30	RW31
	RW33	RW35	RW37	RW38	RW39	RW51		
Dart	D201	D202	D203	D204	D205	D206	D207	D208
	L213	L214	L215	L216	L217	DP218	DP219	DP220
	DP221	DP222	DP223	DP224	DP225	DP226	DP227	DP228
	DP229	DP230	DP231	DP232				
Lynx	LX801	LX802	LX805	LX807				

Southall (Bridge Road) - London Buslines

Renault	RB551	RB552	RB553	RW34				
Dart	D611	D612	D613	D614	D615	D616	D617	D618
	D619	D620	D621	D622	D623	D624	D625	D626
	D627	D628	D629	D630	D631	D632	DML633	DML634
	DML635	DML636	DML637	DML638	DML639	DML640	DML641	DML642
	DML643	DML644	DML645	DML646	DML647	DML648	DML649	DML650
	DML651	DML652	DML653	L7	L237	L238	L239	

Uxbridge (Bakers Road) - Uxbridge Buses

Mercedes-Benz	MM25	MM26					
Dart	L1	L2	L3	L4	L5	L6	DP17	DW26
	DW27	DW28	DW29	DW30	DW31	DW32	D33	D34
	D35	D36	D37	DML179	DML180	DML181	DML182	DML183
	DML184	DML185	DML186	DML187	DML188	DML189	DML190	DML191
	DML192	DML193	DML194	DML195	DML196	DML197	DML198	DML199
	DML200							
Lance	LLW11	LLW12	LLW13	LLW14	LLW15	LLW16	LLW17	LLW18
	LLW19	LLW20	LLW21	LLW22	LLW23	LLW24	LLW31	
Metrobus	M291	M338	M349	M358	M368	M370	M374	M383
	M385	M393	M406	M470	M882	M979	M1199	M1201
	M1246	M1247	M1259	M1400	M1438			
Olympian	V41	V42	V43	V44	V45	V46	V47	V48
	V49	V50	V51	V52	V53	V54	V55	

Westbourne Park (Great Western Road) - Gold Arrow

LDV400	LC1	LC2	LC3					
Mercedes-Benz	MT8							
Dart	DW74	DW77	DW78	DW79	DW80	DW81	DW82	DW83
	DW84	DW85	DW86	DW87	DW88	DW89	DW90	DW91
	DW92	DW93	DW94	DW95	DW96	DW97	DW98	DW99
	DW100	DW101	DW102	DW103	DW104	DW105	DW106	DW107
	DW108	DW109	DW110	DW111	DW112	DW113	DW114	DW115
	DW116	DW117	DW118	DW119	DW120	DW121	DW122	DW123
	DW124	DW125	DW126	DW169	DW170	DM201	DM202	DM203
	DM204	DM205	DM206	DM207	DM208	DM209	DM210	DM211
	DM212	DM213	DM214	DM215	DM216	DM217	DM218	DM219
	DM220	DM221	DM222	DM223	DM224	DM225	DM226	DM227
	DM228	DM229	DM230	DM231	DM232	DM233	DM234	DML249
	DML250	DML251	DML252					
Routemaster	RML885	RML2268	RML2278	RML2281	RML2291	RML2309	RML2313	RML2352
	RML2357	RML2365	RML2369	RML2374	RML2378	RML2379	RML2388	RML2390
	RML2405	RML2428	RML2442	RML2467	RML2473	RML2476	RML2480	RML2486
	RML2490	RML2498	RML2501	RML2506	RML2522	RML2530	RML2542	RML2553
	RML2555	RML2559	RML2602	RML2609	RML2623	RML2647	RML2656	RML2664
	RML2667	RML2672	RML2677	RML2687	RML2717	RML2724	RML2735	RML2740
Metrobus	M316	M319	M329	M340	M397	M465	M494	M499
	M505	M857	M861	M866	M872	M874	M875	M883
	M884	M886	M887	M892	M893	M898	M901	M941
	M952	M1049	M1051	M1054	M1144	M1267	M1376	M1415

Training fleet (Acton High Street)

National	LS470	LS472	LS497	LS503	LS504			
Metrobus	M1260	M1328	M1335	M1338	M1340	M1380	M1384	M1412
	M1418	M1419	M1420	M1422				

Unallocated

Heritage	MA1	RF326	RMC1510			
Renault	RW7	RW17	RW19	RW21	RW23	RW60
Metrobus	M360	M427	M452	M885		

TRAMLINK

Tramlink

Tram Operations Ltd, Macmillan House, Paddington Station, London W2 1TY

2530-2553		Bombardier		Bombardier		AB70T	1998-99		
2530	2533	2536	2539	2542	2544	2546	2548	2550	2552
2531	2534	2537	2540	2543	2545	2547	2549	2551	2553
2532	2535	2538	2541						

Depot: Therapia Lane, Croydon

When Croydon Tramlink opens in Autumn 1999 Tram Operations Ltd will be running the system. This company has been set up in Croydon as part of First CentreWest. Tramlink will radiate from Croydon to terminals at Wimbledon, Beckenham Junction, Elmers End and New Addington. The fleet numbers allocated continue on from the highest tram number used in London Transport days. Pictured on test is Bombardier-built 2536. The trams were assembled in Vienna before being shipped to England.
First CentreWest

HAMPSHIRE

Provincial - Citybus

First Hampshire Ltd; First Provincial Ltd,
226 Portswood Road, Southampton, SO17 2BE

100	VCL461	Mercedes-Benz 609D	Reeve Burgess Beaver	BC20F	1988	Diesel-electric Hybrid vehicle

160-165   Iveco TurboDaily 59.12   WS Coachbuilders Wessex II   B27F   1993

160	K160PPO	162	K162PPO	163	K163PPO	164	K164PPO	165	K165PPO
161	K161PPO								

166-207   Iveco TurboDaily 59.12   Marshall C31   B27F   1993-95

166	L166TRV	175	L175TRV	183	M183XTR	191	M191XTR	199	M199XTR
167	L167TRV	176	L176TRV	184	M184XTR	192	M192XTR	201	M201XTR
168	L168TRV	177	L177TRV	185	M185XTR	193	M193XTR	202	M202XTR
169	L169TRV	178	L178TRV	186	M186XTR	194	M194XTR	203	M203XTR
170	L170TRV	179	M179XTR	187	M187XTR	195	M195XTR	204	M204BPO
171	L171TRV	180	M180XTR	188	M188XTR	196	M196XTR	205	M205BPO
172	L172TRV	181	M181XTR	189	M189XTR	197	M197XTR	206	M206BPO
173	L173TRV	182	M182XTR	190	M190XTR	198	M198XTR	207	M207BPO
174	L174TRV								

208-213   Iveco TurboDaily 59-12   Marshall C31   B26D   1994   Blue Admiral, 1996

208	M642HDV	210	M644HDV	211	M645HDV	212	M646HDV	213	M647HDV
209	M643HDV								

222-259   Iveco TurboDaily 59-12   Mellor Duet   B26D*   1992-93   Blue Admiral, 1996
   *229 is B28F

222	K703UTT	237	K802WFJ	243	K633XOD	249	K917VDV	255	K923VDV
229	K710UTT	238	K819WFJ	244	K911VDV	250	K9182VDV	256	K928VDV
233	K723UTT	239	K619XOD	245	K912VDV	251	K919VDV	257	K929VDV
234	K728UTT	240	K621XOD	246	K914VDV	252	K920VDV	258	K930VDV
235	K729UTT	241	K622XOD	247	K915VDV	253	K921VDV	259	K931VDV
236	K801WFJ	242	K623XOD	248	K916VDV	254	K922VDV		

In early 1999 Provincial and Southampton Citybus were formed into one management unit now called First Hampshire. Pictured at Portsmouth is a new experimental livery on National, 332 UFX848S. As we go to press various livery experiments for older vehicles are taking place.
David Heath

Provincial operates some open-top Bristol VRs. Dual-doored version 504, RHT504S came from Bristol City Line and is seen in Provincial's cream and red livery. The Hoeford and Hilsea depots are due to be replaced by a single facility in the near future. *Phillip Stephenson*

260-271		Iveco TurboDaily 59-12		Mellor-Duet		B26D*	1993	Blue Admiral, 1996 *263-5 are B28F
260	L311BOD	263	L314BOD	266	L317BOD	268	L320BOD	270	L323BOD
261	L312BOD	264	L315BOD	267	L319BOD	269	L322BOD	271	L324BOD
262	L313BOD	265	L316BOD						

312	JBP129P	Leyland National 11351/2R	B44D	1975	
315	JBP133P	Leyland National 11351/2R	B44D	1975	
316	MJT880P	Leyland National 11351/1R	B49F	1976	Hants & Dorset, 1983
319	SPR40R	Leyland National 11351A/1R	B49F	1977	Hants & Dorset, 1983
320	SPR41R	Leyland National 11351A/1R	B49F	1977	Hants & Dorset, 1983
321	RJT147R	Leyland National 11351A/1R	B49F	1977	Hants & Dorset, 1983
322	RJT148R	Leyland National 11351A/1R	B49F	1977	Hants & Dorset, 1983
323	LTP634R	Leyland National 11351A/2R	B44D	1977	
324	MOW636R	Leyland National 11351A/2R	B44D	1977	
329	WFX257S	Leyland National 11351A/1R	BC48F	1978	Hants & Dorset, 1983
330	SBK740S	Leyland National 11351A/2R	B44D	1978	
331	UFX847S	Leyland National 11351A/1R	B49F	1977	Hants & Dorset, 1983
332	UFX848S	Leyland National 11351A/1R	B49F	1977	Hants & Dorset, 1983
333	VFX980S	Leyland National 11351A/1R	B49F	1978	Hants & Dorset, 1983
334	TPX41T	Leyland National 11351A/2R	B44D	1979	
336	UPO443T	Leyland National 11351A/2R	B44D	1979	
337	UPO444T	Leyland National 11351A/2R	B44D	1979	
338	EEL893V	Leyland National 11351A/1R(Volvo)	B52F	1979	Hants & Dorset, 1983

Opposite:- **Both of First Hampshire's constituent operations use red and cream liveries, the Provincial fleet having more cream. The upper picture shows this scheme on Iveco 196, M196XTR, which is bodied by Marshall. The lower picture shows Southampton's colours on Volvo B10B 1114, K114PRV. At the time the picture was taken the renumbering of the Southampton fleet had not taken place.** *Phillip Stephenson*

351-363 Volvo B10BLE · Wright Renown · N44F · 1998-99

351	S351NPO	354	S354NPO	357	S357XCR	360	S360XCR	362	S362XCR
352	S352NPO	355	S355XCR	358	S358XCR	361	S361XCR	363	S363XCR
353	S353NPO	356	S356XCR	359	S359XCR					

401	A301KJT	Leyland National 2 NL116L11/1R		BC47F	1984
402	A302KJT	Leyland National 2 NL116L11/1R		BC47F	1984

403-411 Leyland National 2 NL116L11/1R · B49F* · 1980-81 · KCB Network, 1996 · *403/4 are B52F

403	MDS855V	405	MDS857V	408	MDS867V	410	SNS827W	411	YFS306W
404	MDS856V	406	MDS863V	409	WAS766V					

413-418 Leyland National 2 NL116L11/1R · B49F · 1981 · KCB Network, 1996

413	AST151W	415	AST154W	416	AST156W	417	AST158W	418	AST159W
414	AST153W								

419	SWX534W	Leyland National 2 NL116AL11/1R		B52F	1981	KCB Network, 1996
420	UWY66X	Leyland National 2 NL116AL11/1R		B52F	1981	KCB Network, 1996
421	AAE645V	Leyland National 2 NL116L11/1R		B52F	1980	City Line, 1997
422	AAE652V	Leyland National 2 NL116L11/1R		B52F	1980	City Line, 1997
424	BOU3V	Leyland National 2 NL116L11/1R		B52F	1980	Badgerline, 1998
427	BOU4V	Leyland National 2 NL116L11/1R		B52F	1980	Badgerline, 1998
428	AAE653V	Leyland National 2 NL116L11/1R		B52F	1980	Brewers, 1997
429	AAE663V	Leyland National 2 NL116L11/1R		B52F	1980	Brewers, 1997
501	SFJ101R	Bristol VRT/SL3/6LXB	Eastern Coach Works	B43/31F	1977	Western National, 1993
504	RHT504S	Bristol VRT/SL3/6LXB	Eastern Coach Works	CO43/27D	1978	City Line, 1994
507	UTO836S	Bristol VRT/SL3/501(6LXB)	Eastern Coach Works	B43/31F	1977	Western National, 1993
509	AFJ748T	Bristol VRT/SL3/6LXB	Eastern Coach Works	B43/31F	1979	Western National, 1993
510	AFJ752T	Bristol VRT/SL3/6LXB	Eastern Coach Works	B43/31F	1979	Western National, 1993
511	AFJ763T	Bristol VRT/SL3/6LXB	Eastern Coach Works	B43/31F	1979	Western National, 1993
512	AHU514V	Bristol VRT/SL3/6LXB	Eastern Coach Works	B43/27D	1980	Southampton Citybus, 1997
513	LWU471V	Bristol VRT/SL3/6LXB	Eastern Coach Works	B39/31F	1980	Rider York, 1995
594	MOD571P	Bristol VRT/SL3/6LXB	Eastern Coach Works	O43/31F	1976	Western National, 1993

600	H523CTR	Ace Cougar	Wadham Stringer Portsdown	B41F	1990	

601-607 Dennis Dart 9.8SDL3054 · UVG Urban Star · B40F · 1995

601	N601EBP	603	N603EBP	605	N605EBP	606	N606EBP	607	N607EBP
602	N602EBP	604	N604EBP						

608-623 Dennis Dart SLF · Plaxton Pointer 2 · N37F · 1997-98

608	R608YCR	612	R612YCR	615	R615YCR	618	R618YCR	621	R621YCR
609	R609YCR	613	R613YCR	616	R616YCR	619	R619YCR	622	R622YCR
610	R610YCR	614	R614YCR	617	R617YCR	620	R620YCR	623	R623YCR
611	R611YCR								

624-634 Dennis Dart SLF · Plaxton Pointer 2 · N37F · 1998-99

624	S624KTP	627	S627KTP	629	S629KTP	631	S631KTP	633	S633KTP
625	S625KTP	628	S628KTP	630	S630KTP	632	S632KTP	634	S634KTP
626	S626KTP								

635-642 Dennis Dart SLF · Plaxton Pointer 2 · N37F · 1999

635	S635XCR	637	S637XCR	639	S639XCR	641	S641XCR	642	S642XCR
636	S636XCR	638	S638XCR	640	S640XCR					

710-729 Mercedes-Benz 709D · Plaxton Beaver · B27F · 1996

710	N710GRV	714	N714GRV	718	N718GRV	723	P723KCR	727	P727KCR
711	N711GRV	715	N715GRV	720	N720GRV	724	P724KCR	728	P728KCR
712	N712GRV	716	N716GRV	721	N721GRV	725	P725KCR	729	P729KCR
713	N713GRV	717	N717GRV	722	P722KCR	726	P726KCR		

801	H171GTA	Mercedes-Benz 811D	Carlyle	B29F	1991	
806	H176GTA	Mercedes-Benz 811D	Carlyle	B29F	1991	
811	H783GTA	Mercedes-Benz 811D	Carlyle	B29F	1991	
812	H787GTA	Mercedes-Benz 811D	Carlyle	B29F	1991	
815	H991FTT	Mercedes-Benz 811D	Carlyle	B29F	1991	
821	H997FTT	Mercedes-Benz 811D	Carlyle	B29F	1991	

1102	F102RTR	Leyland Lynx LX112L10ZR1S	Leyland Lynx	B47F	1989	
1104	G104WRV	Leyland Lynx LX2R11C15Z4R	Leyland Lynx	B47F	1990	
1105	G105WRV	Leyland Lynx LX2R11C15Z4R	Leyland Lynx	B47F	1990	
1106	G106WRV	Leyland Lynx LX2R11C15Z4R	Leyland Lynx	B47F	1990	
1108	G108WRV	Leyland Lynx LX2R11C15Z4R	Leyland Lynx	B47F	1990	

1109-1113

		Leyland Lynx LX2R11C15Z4R	Leyland Lynx	B47F*	1990	*1113 is B51F		
1109	G109XOW	1110	G110XOW	1111	G111XOW	1112	G112XOW	1113	G113XOW

1114	K114PRV	Volvo B10B	Northern Counties Paladin	BC47F	1993	
1115	M967GDU	Volvo B10B	Plaxton Verde	B51F	1994	Plaxton demonstrator, 1995

1116-1122

		Volvo B10BLE		Wright Renown	B41F	1998-99		
1116	S116JTP	1118	S118JTP	1120	S120JTP	1121	S121JTP	1122	S122UOT
1117	S117JTP	1119	S119JTP					

1224-1231

		Leyland Atlantean AN68A/1R	East Lancashire	B45/31F	1977-78		
1224	PBP224S	1228	PBP228S	1229	PBP229S	1230	PBP230S	1231	PBP231S
1225	PBP225S						

1232-1266

		Leyland Atlantean AN68A/1R	East Lancashire	B45/31F	1979-81	1265/6 are B40/31F
1232	UPO232T	1239	UPO239T	1247	YRV247V	1254	YRV254V	1261	YRV261V
1233	UPO233T	1240	UPO240T	1248	YRV248V	1255	YRV255V	1262	DBK262W
1234	UPO234T	1242	UPO242T	1249	YRV249V	1256	YRV256V	1263	DBK263W
1235	UPO235T	1243	UPO243T	1250	YRV250V	1257	YRV257V	1264	DBK264W
1236	UPO236T	1244	UPO244T	1251	YRV251V	1258	YRV258V	1265	DBK265W
1237	UPO237T	1245	UPO245T	1252	YRV252V	1259	YRV259V	1266	DBK266W
1238	UPO238T	1246	UPO246T	1253	YRV253V	1260	YRV260V		

1267-1276

		Leyland Atlantean AN68C/1R	East Lancashire	B40/31F	1981-82		
1267	FTR267X	1269	FTR269X	1271	FTR271X	1273	KOW273Y	1275	KOW275Y
1268	FTR268X	1270	FTR270X	1272	KOW272Y	1274	KOW274Y	1276	KOW276Y

Southampton was a keen supporter of East Lancashire products and shared the development of the Atlantean body with municipals such as Bolton and Blackburn. Pictured with its old number, 1267, FTR267X shows the all-over red livery latterly applied to the Southampton fleet.
Phillip Stephenson

1277	A277ROW	Dennis Dominator DDA171	East Lancashire	B46/30F	1984	
1289	E289HRV	Leyland Olympian ONLXB/1RH	East Lancashire	BC43/27F	1987	
1290	E290HRV	Leyland Olympian ONLXB/1RH	East Lancashire	BC43/27F	1987	

1291-1296

Volvo Olympian YN2RV18Z4 — Northern Counties Palatine — B47/30F — 1996

1291	P291KPX	1293	P293KPX	1294	P294KPX	1295	P295KPX	1296	P296KPX
1292	P292KPX								

| 1307 | G895XPX | Dennis Dart 8.5SDL3003 | Wadham Stringer Portsdown | B31F | 1990 | Wadham Stringer, 1990 |
| 1308 | H308DRV | Dennis Dart 9SDL3002 | Reeve Burgess Pointer | B35F | 1991 | |

1309-1313

Dennis Dart 9SDL3011 — Plaxton Pointer — B35F — 1993

1309	L309RTP	1310	L310RTP	1311	L311RTP	1312	L312RTP	1313	L313RTP

1314-329

Dennis Dart 9SDL3051* — Plaxton Pointer — B35F — 1994-95 — *1314/5 are 9SDL3031

1314	M314YOT	1318	M318YOT	1321	M321YOT	1324	N324ECR	1327	N327ECR
1315	M315YOT	1319	M319YOT	1322	M322YOT	1325	N325ECR	1328	N328ECR
1316	M316YOT	1320	M320YOT	1323	M323YOT	1326	N326ECR	1329	N329ECR
1317	M317YOT								

1350	OJI1870	Leyland Atlantean AN68/1R	East Lancashire EL2000(1991)	B35F	1974	
1351	OJI1871	Leyland Atlantean AN68/1R	East Lancashire EL2000(1991)	B35F	1974	
1352	OJI1872	Leyland Atlantean AN68/1R	East Lancashire EL2000(1991)	B35F	1974	
1353	OJI1873	Leyland Atlantean AN68/1R	East Lancashire EL2000(1991)	B29F	1975	
1354	OJI1874	Leyland Atlantean AN68/1R	East Lancashire EL2000(1991)	B35F	1975	
1400	N615DWY	Dennis Dart 9.8SDL3054	Plaxton Pointer	B40F	1995	Hughes-DAF, 1996
1401	N465ETR	Dennis Dart 9.8SDL3054	Plaxton Pointer	B40F	1995	
1402	N466ETR	Dennis Dart 9.8SDL3054	Plaxton Pointer	B40F	1995	
1403	N467ETR	Dennis Dart 9.8SDL3054	Plaxton Pointer	B40F	1995	
1404	P404KOW	Dennis Dart SLF	Plaxton Pointer	N37F	1996	
1405	P405KOW	Dennis Dart SLF	Plaxton Pointer	N37F	1996	
1406	P406KOW	Dennis Dart SLF	Plaxton Pointer	N37F	1996	
1407	P407KOW	Dennis Dart SLF	Plaxton Pointer	N37F	1996	

1408-1427

Dennis Dart SLF — Plaxton Pointer 2 — N37F — 1998

1408	R408WPX	1412	R412WPX	1416	R416WPX	1420	R420WPX	1424	R424WPX
1409	R409WPX	1413	R413WPX	1417	R417WPX	1421	R421WPX	1425	R425WPX
1410	R410WPX	1414	R414WPX	1418	R418WPX	1422	R422WPX	1426	R426WPX
1411	R411WPX	1415	R415WPX	1419	R419WPX	1423	R423WPX	1427	R427WPX

2301-2305

Dennis Dart 9SDL3002 — Duple Dartline — B36F — 1990

2301	G301XCR	2302	G302XCR	2303	G303XCR	2304	G304XCR	2305	G305XCR

| 2306 | H306DRV | Dennis Dart 9SDL3002 | Carlyle Dartline | B35F | 1990 | |

2330-2339

Dennis Dart — Plaxton Pointer — B35F — 1996

2330	N159GOT	2332	N161GOT	2334	N163GOT	2336	N165GOT	2338	N167GOT
2331	N160GOT	2333	N162GOT	2335	N164GOT	2337	N166GOT	2339	N168GOT

Ancilliary vehicles:

002	C433BHY	Ford Transit 190	Dormobile	TV	1986	White Horse Ferries, Hythe, 95
949	B449WTC	Ford Transit 190	Dormobile	B16F	1985	Badgerline, 1995
950	C443BHY	Ford Transit 190	Dormobile	B16F	1985	White Horse Ferries, Hythe, 95
966	D562HPO	Dodge Commando G13	Wadham Stringer Vanguard	TV	1986	MoD, 1997 (80KF30)
967	B631XOW	Dodge Commando G13	Reeve Burgess	TV	1985	MoD, 1997 (?)

Previous Registrations:

OJI1870	PCR299M		OJI1873	HTR570P
OJI1871	HTR567P		OJI1874	HTR568P
OJI1872	EOW398L		VCL461	E350AMR

Allocations

Hilsea (London Road) - Provincial

Iveco	184	185	186	187	188	189	190	191
	192	193	194	195	196	197	198	199
	201	202	203	204	205	206	207	208
	209	210	211	212	213	222	229	235
	236	237	238	239	240	241	242	243
	244	245	246	247	248	249	250	251
	252	253	254	255	256	258	259	260
	261	262	263	264	265	266	267	268
	269	270	271		Hybrid	100		
Volvo B10B	351	352	353	354	355	356	357	358
	359	360	361	362	363			

Hoeford (Gosport Road) - Provincial

Iveco	160	161	162	163	164	165	166	167
	168	169	170	171	172	173	174	175
	176	177	178	179	180	181	182	183
Mercedes-Benz	710	711	712	713	714	715	716	717
	718	720	721	722	723	724	725	726
	727	728	729					
Dart	601	602	603	604	605	606	607	608
	609	610	611	612	613	614	615	616
	617	618	619	620	621	622	623	624
	625	626	627	628	629	630	631	632
	633	634	635	636	637	638	639	640
	642	642						
National	315	316	320	321	322	323	324	329
	330	331	332	333	334	336	337	338
	401	402	403	404	405	406	408	409
	410	411	413	414	415	415	417	418
	419	420	421	422	424	427	428	429
ACE	600							
Bristol VR	501	504	506	507	509	510	511	512
	513	594						

Southampton (Portswood Road) - Citybus

Mercedes-Benz	806	811	812	815	821			
Dart	1307	1308	1309	1310	1311	1312	1313	1314
	1315	1316	1317	1318	1319	1320	1321	1322
	1323	1324	1325	1326	1327	1328	1329	1400
	1401	1402	1403	1404	1405	1406	1407	1408
	1409	1410	1411	1412	1413	1414	1415	1416
	1417	1418	1419	1420	1421	1422	1423	1424
	1425	1426	14271	2301	2302	2303	2304	2305
	2306	2330	2331	2332	2333	2334	2335	2336
	2337	2338	2339					
Lynx	1102	1104	1105	1106	1108	1109	1110	1111
	1112	1113						
Volvo B10B	1114	1115	1116	1117	1118	1119	1120	1121
	1122							
Atlantean	1224	1225	1228	1229	1230	1231	1230	1231
	1232	1233	1234	1235	1236	1237	1238	1239
	1240	1242	1243	1244	1245	1246	1247	1248
	1249	1250	1251	1252	1253	1254	1255	1256
	1257	1258	1259	1260	1261	1262	1263	1264
	1265	1266	1267	1268	1269	1270	1271	1272
	1273	1274	1275	1276				
Dominator	1277							
Olympians	1289	1290	1291	1292	1293	1294	1295	1296

Unallocated

Iveco	233	234	257		National	312	319	
Mercedes-Benz	801	Atlantean SD		1350	1351	1352	1353	1354

FIRST CYMRU

SWT - Brewers - United Welsh Coaches

First Cymru Ltd, Heol Gwyrosydd, Penlan, Swansea, SA5 7BN

101	T102XDE	Dennis Javelin GX	Plaxton Expressliner 2	C44FT	1999	
102	T102XDE	Dennis Javelin GX	Plaxton Expressliner 2	C44FT	1999	
103	T103XDE	Dennis Javelin GX	Plaxton Expressliner 2	C44FT	1999	
106	L506GEP	Volvo B10M-60	Plaxton Expressliner 2	C46FT	1993	
107	M107NEP	Dennis Javelin GX 12SDA2132	Plaxton Expressliner 2	C44FT	1994	
108	M108NEP	Dennis Javelin GX 12SDA2132	Plaxton Expressliner 2	C44FT	1994	
109	M109PWN	Dennis Javelin GX 12SDA2133	Plaxton Expressliner 2	C44FT	1995	
110	M110PWN	Dennis Javelin GX 12SDA2133	Plaxton Expressliner 2	C44FT	1995	
111	M111PWN	Dennis Javelin GX 12SDA2133	Plaxton Expressliner 2	C44FT	1995	
112	N112EWJ	Dennis Javelin GX 12SDA2153	Plaxton Expressliner 2	C44FT	1996	
113	N113VWN	Dennis Javelin GX 12SDA2153	Plaxton Expressliner 2	C44FT	1996	
114	N114VWN	Dennis Javelin GX 12SDA2153	Plaxton Expressliner 2	C44FT	1996	
115	N115VWN	Dennis Javelin GX 12SDA2153	Plaxton Expressliner 2	C44FT	1996	
116	S116RKG	Dennis Javelin GX	Plaxton Expressliner 2	C44FT	1999	
124	NIL2455	Leyland Tiger TRCTL11/3R	Plaxton Paramount 3500	C48FT	1983	Midland Red West, 1996
125	NIL2456	Leyland Tiger TRCTL11/3R	Plaxton Paramount 3500	C48FT	1983	Midland Red West, 1996
126	NIL2454	Leyland Tiger TRCTL11/3R	Plaxton Paramount 3500	C48FT	1983	Midland Red West, 1996
131	C312KTH	Hestair-Duple SDA1510	Duple 425	C53FT	1986	
132	ACY178A	Hestair-Duple SDA1510	Duple 425	C48FT	1986	
133	MKH487A	Hestair-Duple SDA1510	Duple 425	C48FT	1986	
134	F134DEP	Hestair-Duple SDA1510	Duple 425	C48FT	1989	
135	F135DEP	Hestair-Duple SDA1510	Duple 425	C48FT	1989	
136	F99CEP	Hestair-Duple SDA1510	Duple 425	C46FT	1989	
137	F100CEP	Hestair-Duple SDA1512	Duple 425	C46FT	1989	
139	E206BOD	Hestair-Duple SDA1510	Duple 425	C53FT	1988	Western National, 1995
150	L538XUT	Toyota Coaster HDB30R	Caetano Optimo II	C18F	1994	Grampian, 1997
153	WSV410	Leyland Tiger TRCTL11/2RH	Plaxton Paramount 3200	C49F	1984	Yorkshire Rider (York), 1997
159	UOI4323	Volvo B10M-61	East Lancashire (1993)	B51F	1982	Yorkshire Rider (York), 1997
160	F229FSU	Leyland Tiger TRBTL11/2RP	Plaxton Derwent II	B54F	1988	Yorkshire Rider (York), 1997
161	F300GNS	Leyland Tiger TRBTL11/2RP	Plaxton Derwent II	B54F	1988	Yorkshire Rider (York), 1997
162	EWW945Y	Leyland Tiger TRCTL11/3R	Plaxton Paramount 3200 E	C53F	1983	Yorkshire Rider (York), 1996
166	HUA606Y	Leyland Tiger TRCTL11/3R	Plaxton Paramount 3200 E	C49F	1984	Yorkshire Rider (York), 1997
171	K13BMS	Dennis Javelin 12SDA2117	Plaxton Premiére 320	C50FT	1993	
172	L6BMS	Dennis Javelin 12SDA2131	Plaxton Premiére 320	C50FT	1993	
173	L8BMS	Dennis Javelin 12SDA2131	Plaxton Premiére 320	C53F	1993	
174	L14BMS	Dennis Javelin 12SDA2135	Plaxton Premiére 350	C53F	1993	
175	R175VWN	Dennis Javelin GX	Plaxton Premiére 350	C53F	1998	
176	R176VWN	Dennis Javelin GX	Plaxton Premiére 350	C53F	1998	
177	R177VWN	Dennis Javelin GX	Plaxton Premiére 350	C53F	1998	
178	R178VWN	Dennis Javelin GX	Plaxton Premiére 350	C53F	1998	
180	F618XWY	Leyland Tiger TRCTL11/3ARZA	Plaxton Paramount 3200 IIIE	C53F	1988	Yorkshire Rider (York), 1996
185	A693OHJ	Leyland Tiger TRCTL11/2AR	Alexander TE	C49F	1983	Thamesway, 1991
188	278TNY	DAF MB230LT615	Plaxton Paramount 3500 III	C49FT	1989	
189	LIL5069	DAF MB200DKFL600	Plaxton Paramount 3500 II	C53FT	1986	Western National, 1995
190	LIL5070	DAF MB230DKFL615	Duple 340	C50FT	1987	Western National, 1995
191	LIL5071	DAF MB230DKFL615	Duple 340	C53F	1987	Western National, 1995
192	948RJO	DAF MB230LB615	Plaxton Paramount 3500 III	C49FT	1989	
195	H202CRH	Volvo B10M-60	Plaxton Expressliner	C46FT	1991	York Pullman, 1998
196	H326DTR	Volvo B10M-60	Plaxton Expressliner	C49FT	1991	Priory Coaches, Gosport, 1998
197	GSU388	Volvo B10M-61	Jonckheere Jubilee P599	C51FT	1987	Yorkshire Rider, 1997
198	PSU626	Volvo B10M-60	Plaxton Paramount 3500 III	C49FT	1989	Grampian (Mairs), 1997

Opposite, top:- **SWT's Coaching Unit, separately from United Welsh Coaches, operate many National Express contracts. Vehicles used on airport related services carry Flightlink livery and this is shown on Dennis Javelin 111, M111PWN as it passes through Chepstow.** *John Jones*
Opposite, bottom:- **The latest minibuses with First Cymru are a batch of Mercedes-Benz Vario O814s with Plaxton Beaver 2 bodywork. From that batch 484, R484EDW is heading for Talbot Green. The vehicle is based at Brewer's new depot near Bridgend.** *Byron Gage*

201-216

Iveco TurboDaily 59-12 | Mellor Duet | B26D | 1992-93 | Hampshire , 1999

201	K701UTT	205	K705UTT	207	K707UTT	209	K709UTT	215	K715UTT
204	K704UTT	206	K706UTT	208	K708UTT	212	K712UTT	216	K716UTT

287-322

Mercedes-Benz 709D | Reeve Burgess Beaver | B23F | 1988 | 294 rebodied 1997

287	E287UCY	295	E295VEP	302	E302VEP	309	F309AWN	316	F316AWN
289	E289VEP	296	E296VEP	303	E303VEP	310	F310AWN	317	F317AWN
290	E290VEP	297	E297VEP	304	E304VEP	311	F311AWN	319	F319AWN
291	E291VEP	298	E298VEP	305	E305VEP	312	F312AWN	320	F320AWN
292	E292VEP	299	E299VEP	306	E306VEP	313	F313AWN	321	F321AWN
293	E293VEP	300	E300VEP	307	F307AWN	314	F314AWN	322	F322AWN
294	E294VEP	301	E301VEP	308	F308AWN	315	F315AWN		

323-327

Mercedes-Benz 811D | Reeve Burgess Beaver | B23F | 1989

323	F323DCY	324	F324DCY	325	F325DCY	326	F326DCY	327	F327DCY

329-347

Mercedes-Benz 814D | Robin Hood | B31F | 1989

329	F329FCY	333	F333FCY	337	F337FCY	341	F341FCY	345	G345GEP
330	F330FCY	334	F334FCY	338	F338FCY	342	F342FCY	346	G346GEP
331	F331FCY	335	F335FCY	339	F339FCY	343	F343FCY	347	G347GEP
332	F332FCY	336	F336FCY	340	F340FCY	344	G344GEP		

348-361

Mercedes-Benz 814D | Phoenix | B31F | 1989

348	G348JTH	351	G351JTH	354	G354JTH	357	G357JTH	360	G360JTH
349	G349JTH	352	G352JTH	355	G355JTH	358	G358JTH	361	G361JTH
350	G350JTH	353	G353JTH	356	G356JTH	359	G359JTH		

365-371

Mercedes-Benz 814D | Phoenix | B31F | 1990

365	G365JTH	367	G367MEP	369	G369MEP	370	G370MEP	371	G371MEP
366	G366JTH	368	G368MEP						

372	G372MEP	Mercedes-Benz 814D	Plaxton Beaver (1992)	B31F	1990

373-381

Mercedes-Benz 814D | Phoenix | B31F | 1990

373	G373MEP	375	H375OTH	377	H377OTH	379	H379OTH	381	H381OTH
374	H374OTH	376	H376OTH	378	H378OTH	380	H380OTH		

382	H382TTH	Mercedes-Benz 814D	Reeve Burgess Beaver	B31F	1991	
383	M997CYS	Mercedes-Benz 811D	WS Wessex II	B31F	1994	Pullman, Crofty, 1995
384	L364GTH	Mercedes-Benz 609D	Cymric	B22F	1993	Rees & Williams, 1996
385	H852OWN	Mercedes-Benz 811D	Reeve Burgess Beaver	B31F	1990	Rees & Williams, 1996
386	H853OWN	Mercedes-Benz 811D	Reeve Burgess Beaver	B31F	1990	Rees & Williams, 1996
394	F607AWN	Mercedes-Benz 709D	Reeve Burgess Beaver	BC25F	1988	
395	J581VTH	Dennis Dart 9.8SDL3012	Plaxton Pointer	B40F	1992	Rees & Williams, 1996
396	J582VTH	Dennis Dart 9.8SDL3012	Plaxton Pointer	B40F	1992	Rees & Williams, 1996
397	J580VTH	Dennis Dart 9.8SDL3012	Plaxton Pointer	B40F	1992	Rees & Williams, 1996
398	L844JCY	Dennis Dart 9.8SDL3035	Plaxton Pointer	B40F	1994	Rees & Williams, 1996
399	K82BWN	Dennis Dart 9.8SDL3017	Alexander Dash	B40F	1993	Rees & Williams, 1996

401-410

Mercedes-Benz 811D | Plaxton Beaver | B31F | 1993

401	K401BAX	403	K403BAX	405	K405BAX	407	K407BAX	409	K409BAX
402	K402BAX	404	K404BAX	406	K406BAX	408	K408BAX	410	K410BAX

411	F601AWN	Mercedes-Benz 709D	Reeve Burgess Beaver	B25F	1988	
412	F602AWN	Mercedes-Benz 709D	Reeve Burgess Beaver	B25F	1988	
413	F603AWN	Mercedes-Benz 709D	Reeve Burgess Beaver	B25F	1988	
415	F605AWN	Mercedes-Benz 709D	Reeve Burgess Beaver	B25F	1988	
417	F618AWN	Mercedes-Benz 709D	Reeve Burgess Beaver	B25F	1988	
418	F608AWN	Mercedes-Benz 709D	Reeve Burgess Beaver	B25F	1988	
419	F546EJA	Mercedes-Benz 709D	PMT	BC25F	1988	Yorkshire Rider, 1996
429	J901MAF	Mercedes-Benz 709D	Wadham Stringer Wessex	B21F	1991	Western National, 1996

431-438

Mercedes-Benz 709D | Reeve Burgess Beaver | BC25F | 1988 | Provincial, 1996

431	F713FDV	433	F725FDV	435	F749FDV	437	F712FDV	438	F739FDV
432	F721FDV	434	F727FDV	436	F761FDV				

170

440-450

						Mercedes-Benz 811D	Carlyle	BC29F	1991	Ex Provincial, 1997

440	H172GTA	443	H178GTA	445	H990FTT	447	H993FTT	449	H995FTT
441	H174GTA	444	H782GTA	446	H992FTT	448	H994FTT	450	H996FTT
442	H177GTA								

451	H173GTA	Mercedes-Benz 811D	Carlyle	B29F	1991	Hampshire, 1999
452	H175GTA	Mercedes-Benz 811D	Carlyle	B29F	1991	Hampshire, 1999
453	H179GTA	Mercedes-Benz 811D	Carlyle	B29F	1991	Hampshire, 1999
454	H788GTA	Mercedes-Benz 811D	Carlyle	B29F	1991	Hampshire, 1999

481-490

						Mercedes-Benz Vario O810	Plaxton Beaver 2	B27F	1998

481	R481EDW	483	R483EDW	485	R485EDW	487	R487EDW	489	R489EDW
482	R482EDW	484	R484EDW	486	R486EDW	488	R488EDW	490	R490EDW

501-524

						Dennis Dart 9SDL3034	Plaxton Pointer	B31F	1993

501	L501HCY	506	L506HCY	511	L511HCY	516	L516HCY	521	L521HCY
502	L502HCY	507	L507HCY	512	L512HCY	517	L517HCY	522	L522HCY
503	L503HCY	508	L508HCY	513	L513HCY	518	L518HCY	523	L523HCY
504	L504HCY	509	L509HCY	514	L514HCY	519	L519HCY	524	L524HCY
505	L505HCY	510	L510HCY	515	L515HCY	520	L520HCY		

525-550

						Dennis Dart 9SDL3034	Plaxton Pointer	B31F	1994

525	L525JEP	531	L531JEP	536	L536JEP	541	L541JEP	546	L546JEP
526	L526JEP	532	L532JEP	537	L537JEP	542	L542JEP	547	L547JEP
527	L527JEP	533	L533JEP	538	L538JEP	543	L543JEP	548	L548JEP
528	L528JEP	534	L534JEP	539	L539JEP	544	L544JEP	549	L549JEP
529	L529JEP	535	L535JEP	540	L540JEP	545	L545JEP	550	L550JEP
530	L530JEP								

551-568

						Dennis Dart 9SDL3034	Plaxton Pointer	B31F	1995

551	N551UCY	555	N555UCY	559	N559UCY	563	N563UCY	566	N566UCY
552	N552UCY	556	N556UCY	561	N561UCY	564	N564UCY	567	N567UCY
553	N553UCY	557	N557UCY	562	N562UCY	565	N565UCY	568	N568UCY
554	N554UCY	558	N558UCY						

569-580

						Dennis Dart SLF	Plaxton Pointer	N31F	1996

569	P569BTH	572	P572BTH	575	P575BTH	577	P577BTH	579	P579BTH
570	P570BTH	573	P573BTH	576	P576BTH	578	P578BTH	580	P580BTH
571	P571BTH	574	P574BTH						

581-599

						Dennis Dart SLF	Plaxton Pointer 2	N26F	1998

581	R581SWN	585	R585SWN	589	R589SWN	593	R593SWN	597	R597SWN
582	R582SWN	586	R586SWN	590	R590SWN	594	R594SWN	598	R598SWN
583	R583SWN	587	R587SWN	591	R591SWN	595	R595SWN	599	R599SWN
584	R584SWN	588	R588SWN	592	R592SWN	596	R596SWN		

601-608

						Dennis Dart 9.8SDL3035	Plaxton Pointer	B40F	1994

601	L601FKG	603	L603FKG	605	L605FKG	607	L607FKG	608	L608FKG
602	L602FKG	604	L604FKG	606	L606FKG				

609-618

						Dennis Dart 9.8SDL3054	Plaxton Pointer	BC40F*	1995	*616 is BC36F

609	N609MHB	611	N611MHB	613	N613MHB	615	N615MHB	617	N617MHB
610	N610MHB	612	N612MHB	614	N614MHB	616	N616MHB	618	N618MHB

619	P619VDW	Dennis Dart	Plaxton Pointer	B40F	1997
620	P620VDW	Dennis Dart	Plaxton Pointer	B40F	1997
621	P621VDW	Dennis Dart	Plaxton Pointer	B40F	1997

622-637

						Dennis Dart SLF	Alexander ALX200	N37F	1999

622	T622CEJ	626	T626CEJ	629	T629CEJ	632	T632CEJ	635	T635CEJ
623	T623CEJ	627	T627CEJ	630	T630CEJ	633	T633CEJ	636	T636CEJ
624	T624CEJ	628	T628CEJ	631	T631CEJ	634	T634CEJ	637	T637CEJ
625	T625CEJ								

Until this year's batch, all Dennis Darts purchased new by SWT had been bodied by Plaxton. Representing the type is 612, N612MHB seen passing through Castle Street, Cardiff in the summer of 1998. This batch are fitted with high-back seating for its express service role. *John Jones*

701	CSU244	Leyland Leopard PSU3D/4R	Plaxton Derwent (1987)	B51F	1977	Yorkshire Rider (Y), 1996
702	LOI6690	Leyland Leopard PSU3D/4R	Plaxton Derwent (1987)	B51F	1977	Yorkshire Rider (Y), 1996
703	VDH244S	Leyland Leopard PSU3E/4R	Duple Dominant (1985)	B51F	1977	Yorkshire Rider (Y), 1996
704	BVP781V	Leyland Leopard PSU3E/4R	Plaxton Supreme IV Express	C49F	1980	Midland Red West, 1996
705	BVP776V	Leyland Leopard PSU3E/4R	Plaxton Supreme IV Express	C49F	1980	Midland Red West, 1996
706	BVP778V	Leyland Leopard PSU3E/4R	Plaxton Supreme IV Express	C49F	1980	Midland Red West, 1996
797	AAE654V	Leyland National 2 NL116L11/1R		B49F	1980	Bristol (City Line), 1998
798	BOU5V	Leyland National 2 NL116L11/1R		B49F	1980	Bristol (Bagerline), 1998
799	BOU8V	Leyland National 2 NL116L11/1R		B49F	1980	Bristol (Bagerline), 1998
813	AWN813V	Leyland National 11351A/1R		B49F	1979	
815	AWN815V	Leyland National 11351A/1R		B49F	1979	

816-825

		Dennis Lance 11SDA3112	Plaxton Verde	BC45F	1993	

| 816 | L816HCY | 818 | L818HCY | 820 | L820HCY | 822 | L822HCY | 824 | L824HCY |
| 817 | L817HCY | 819 | L819HCY | 821 | L821HCY | 823 | L823HCY | 825 | L825HCY |

826	L218AAB	Dennis Lance 11SDA3107	Plaxton Verde	B49F	1994	Midland Red West, 1998
827	L219AAB	Dennis Lance 11SDA3107	Plaxton Verde	B49F	1994	Midland Red West, 1998
828	L220AAB	Dennis Lance 11SDA3107	Plaxton Verde	B49F	1994	Midland Red West, 1998
836	G841PNW	Van Hool A600	Van Hool	B52F	1990	Yorkshire Rider (Q), 1994
838	J916WVC	Leyland Lynx LX2R11V18245	Leyland Lynx	B51F	1992	Volvo demonstrator, 1992
839	J375WWK	Leyland Lynx LX2R11V18245	Leyland Lynx	B47F	1992	Volvo demonstrator, 1992
840	K10BMS	Leyland Lynx LX2R11C15Z4A	Leyland Lynx	B47F	1992	
841	K11BMS	Leyland Lynx LX2R11C15Z4A	Leyland Lynx	B47F	1992	
842	K12BMS	Leyland Lynx LX2R11C15Z4A	Leyland Lynx	B47F	1992	
851	AAL516A	Leyland Tiger TRCTL11/3R	Plaxton Paramount 3200	C53F	1983	Stagecoach Red & White, '98
852	AAX529A	Leyland Tiger TRCTL11/3R	Plaxton Paramount 3200	C53F	1983	Stagecoach Red & White, '97
853	AAX450A	Leyland Tiger TRCTL11/3R	Plaxton Paramount 3200E	C53F	1983	Stagecoach Red & White, '97
854	AAX466A	Leyland Tiger TRCTL11/3R	Plaxton Paramount 3200E	C53F	1983	Stagecoach Red & White, '97
855	AAX515A	Leyland Tiger TRCTL11/3R	Plaxton Paramount 3200	C53F	1983	Stagecoach Red & White, '97
856	OIL3796	Leyland Tiger TRCTL11/3R	Plaxton Paramount 3200E	C53F	1984	The Shires, 1998

WS' Wessex II bodywork is fitted to Mercedes-Benz 383, M997CYS. Vehicles built at this factory are now produced under the Caetano name. The vehicle came into the fleet from Pullman of Crofty after a short time in use on a West Glamorgan sponsored Rail-link service on the Gower. It now carries Rail-link livery for similar duties at Maesteg. *John Jones*

901-907

Leyland Olympian ONCL10/1RV Eastern Coach Works B45/30F 1985

901	C901FCY	903	C903FCY	905	C905FCY	906	C906FCY	907	C907FCY
902	C902FCY	904	C904FCY						

920	ANA189Y	MCW Metrobus DR102/23	MCW	B43/30F	1983	Manchester, 1998
921	ANA182Y	MCW Metrobus DR102/23	MCW	B43/30F	1983	Manchester, 1998
922	SND135X	MCW Metrobus DR102/23	MCW	B43/30F	1983	Manchester, 1998
946	XHK234X	Bristol VRT/SL3/6LXB	Eastern Coach Works	B43/31F	1981	
947	UAR587W	Bristol VRT/SL3/6LXB	Eastern Coach Works	B43/31F	1981	
948	UAR588W	Bristol VRT/SL3/6LXB	Eastern Coach Works	B43/31F	1981	
949	UAR598W	Bristol VRT/SL3/6LXB	Eastern Coach Works	B43/31F	1981	
950	ANA630Y	Leyland Atlantean AN68D/1R	Northern Counties	B43/32F	1983	Greater Manchester, 1997
951	ANA624Y	Leyland Atlantean AN68D/1R	Northern Counties	B43/32F	1983	Greater Manchester, 1997
952	TGG739R	Leyland Atlantean AN68A/1R	Alexander AL	B45/31F	1977	Greater Glasgow, 1997
955	LSU381V	Leyland Atlantean AN68A/1R	Alexander AL	B45/33F	1979	Greater Glasgow, 1997
956	A748NNA	Leyland Atlantean AN68D/1R	Northern Counties	B43/32F	1984	Greater Manchester, 1997
957	A675HNB	Leyland Atlantean AN68D/1R	Northern Counties	B43/32F	1984	Greater Manchester, 1997
958	A688HNB	Leyland Atlantean AN68D/1R	Northern Counties	B43/32F	1984	Greater Manchester, 1997
960	EWS744W	Bristol VRT/SL3/680	Eastern Coach Works	B43/31F	1981	Badgerline, 1997
962	LSU379V	Leyland Atlantean AN68A/1R	Alexander AL	B45/33F	1979	Greater Glasgow, 1997
963	A694HNB	Leyland Atlantean AN68D/1R	Northern Counties	B43/32F	1984	Greater Manchester, 1997

976-994

Bristol VRT/SL3/501 Eastern Coach Works B43/31F 1979-80

976	BEP976V	980	BEP980V	984w	BEP984V	990	ECY990V	994	EWN994W
978	BEP978V	981	BEP981V	989	ECY989V	992	EWN992W	995	EWN995W

Special event vehicle:

| 1114 | AKG219A | Leyland Leopard L1 | Weymann | B44F | 1961 | Ex Llynfi, Maesteg, 1988 |

Ancilliary vehicles:

38	LJN648P	Bristol VRT/SL3/501	Eastern Coach Works	TV	1976	Skillplace, Port Talbot, 1997
56	B124PEL	Bedford YNT	Plaxton Paramount 3200 E	TV	1976	Skillplace, Port Talbot, 1997
207	C207HTH	Mercedes-Benz L608D	Robin Hood	B20F	1986	Publicity
414	F604AWN	Mercedes-Benz 709D	Reeve Burges Beaver	B25F	1988	
416	F606AWN	Mercedes-Benz 709D	Reeve Burges Beaver	B25F	1988	
430	H825ERV	Mercedes-Benz 709D	Wadham Stringer Wessex	B25F	1991	Western National, 1996
988w	ECY988V	Bristol VRT/SL3/501	Eastern Coach Works	B43/31F	1979	
—	SHO628P	Bedford SB5	Plaxton Panorama	C41F	1976	

Previous Registrations:

278TNY	F200EEP	LIL5070	E340WTT
300CUH	YR3939, E218WWW	LIL5071	E978WTA
948RJO	G500JEP	LOI6690	REL400R,
AAL516A	SDW927Y	MKH487A	from new
AAX450A	SDW914Y	NIL2450	F618XWY
AAX466A	SDW917Y	NIL2451	C985HOX
AAX515A	SDW929Y	NIL2452	C986HOX
AAX529A	SDW931Y	NIL2453	C987HOX
ACY178A	From new	NIL2454	A678KDV
AKG219A	YBK132	NIL2455	A656VDA
C312KTH	999BCY	NIL2456	A657VDA
CSU244	REL402R	NIL2459	C976GCV
G841PNW	G680TKE, A6RLR	NIL2461	C975GCV
GSU388	E405RWR	OIL3796	A151EPA
J901MAF	J6EDE	PSU626	F986HGE
K386DWN	J4SWT	UOI4323	BKH129X, VOI4323
K388DWN	J5SWT	WCY701	L538XUT
LIL5069	C792MVH	WSV410	A608KYG

Allocations:

Coaching unit (Pentregethin Road, Ravenhill) - SWT

Volvo Expressliner	106							
Javelin Expressliner	101	102	103	107	108	109	110	111
	112	113	114	115	116			
Duple 425	131	132	133	134	135	136	137	139

Coaching unit (Acacia Avenue, Sandfields Estate, Port Talbot) - United Welsh Coaches

Toyota/Optimo	150							
Tiger coach	124	125	126	153	166	179	180	
DAF coach	188	189	191	192				
Javelin coach	171	172	173	174	175	176	177	178
Volvo coach	195	196	197	198				
Mercedes-Benz	304	370	386	450				
Leopard coach	702	704	705	706				
Atlantean	952	955	956	957	958	963		
Bristol VR	946	947	948	960	963			

Leyland Leopard 702, LOI6690 was re-bodied in 1987 with a Plaxton Derwent body but joined First Cymru in 1996 from Yorkshire Rider to undertake school contract duties. As illustrated, the vehicle carries Brewers' names. *Phillip Stephenson*

Ammanford (Pontardulais Road, Tycroes) - SWT

Mercedes-Benz	332	333	342	378	379	380	381
Dart	395	396	397	398	399		

Bridgend (Aneurin Bevan Avenue, Brynmenyn Ind Est) - Brewers

Mercedes-Benz	306	401	402	403	404	405	406	408
	409	410	413	431	432	435	481	482
	483	484	485					
Dart	507	508	509	510	606	607	608	609
	610	611	615	616	617	618	619	620
	621							
Lynx	840	841	842					
Atlantean	950	951						

Haverfordwest (Withybush Industrial Estate) - SWT

Outstation: Pembroke Dock

Mercedes-Benz	294	297	301	302	326	327	329	330
	335	343	347	348	360	365		

Llanelli (Inkerman Street) - SWT

Outstation: Carmarthen

Mercedes-Benz	291	292	293	296	298	300	313	316
	317	319	322	323	324	325	331	334
	336	337	338	339	340	341	344	345
	366	367	368	369	371	374	375	377
	394	412	451	452	453	454		
Dart	501	502	503	504	505	506		
National	815							
Tiger	851	852	853	854	855	856		

Maesteg (Heol Ty Gwyn Industrial Estate, Tyle Teg) - Brewers

Mercedes-Benz	295	383	418	434	436	437	438	486
	487	488	489	490				
Tiger bus	160	161	162					
Dart	601	602	603	604				
Leopard bus	701	703						
Van Hool A600	836							
National	798	799						
Lynx	838	839						

Pontardawe (Tawe Terrace) - Valley Link - SWT

Mercedes-Benz	310	311	346	349	350	351	352	353
	354	355	356	357	358	359	361	372
	373	382						
Dart	581	582	583	584	585	586	587	588
	589	590	591	592	593	594	595	596
	597	598	599	614				
Lance	818	819	820	821	822	823	824	825
Bristol VR	978	980	984	990	994			

Port Talbot (Acacia Avenue, Sandfields Estate) - Brewers

Mercedes-Benz	385	407	440	441	442	443	444	445
	446	447	448	449				
Dart	605	612	613					
Lance	816	817	826	827	828			
Volvo bus	159							
Metrobus	920	921	922					

First Cymru currently operate only a small double-deck fleet with a mixture of types transferred into Wales for school duties. From Manchester have come MCW Metrobuses and Atlanteans. The fleet contains only seven Leyland Olympians - the last double-decks bought new by South Wales Transport - and all are based at the SWT depot at Ravenhill. From that batch, 902 is seen on local service. *Cliff Beeton*

Ravenhill (Pentregethin Road) - SWT

Outstation: Ludchurch

Mercedes-Benz	287	289	290	299	303	305	307	308
	309	312	314	315	320	321	384	
Dart	511	512	513	514	515	516	517	518
	519	520	521	522	523	524	525	526
	527	528	529	530	531	532	533	534
	535	536	537	538	539	540	541	542
	543	544	545	546	547	548	549	550
	551	552	553	554	555	556	557	558
	559	561	562	563	564	565	566	567
	568	569	570	571	572	573	574	575
	576	577	578	579	580			
Olympian	901	902	903	904	905	906	907	
Bristol VR	976	989	992	995				

Unallocated

Mercedes-Benz	376	411	415	417	419	429
Tiger	185					
DAF	190					
National	797	813				
Heritage	1114					
Bristol VR	949	981				
Atlantean	962					

Note: - 5 Leyland Nationals not shown in the fleet list were held for disposal at the time of publication.

FIRST BRISTOL

Badgerline - City Line - Durbins - Streamline - Wessex - Southern National

Comfylux - Dorchester Coachways - Dorset Transit - Smiths - Taylors

First Bristol Buses Ltd, Enterprise House, Easton Road, Bristol BS5 0DZ
Southern National Ltd, 4 Hamilton Road, Taunton, Somerset, TA1 2EH
First Wessex National Ltd, Croydon Street, Lawrence Hill, Bristol, BS5 0DY

100-113
Volvo B10M-56   Alexander P   BC53F   1987

100	D100GHY	103	D103GHY	106	D106GHY	109	D109GHY	112	D112GHY
101	D101GHY	104	D104GHY	107	D107GHY	110	D110GHY	113	D113GHY
102	D102GHY	105	D105GHY	108	D108GHY	111	D111GHY		

121-136
Dennis Lance 11SDA3112   Plaxton Verde   B49F   1993-94

121	L121TFB	125	L125TFB	128	L128TFB	131	L131TFB	134	L134TFB
122	L122TFB	126	L126TFB	129	L129TFB	132	L132TFB	135	L135TFB
123	L123TFB	127	L127TFB	130	L130TFB	133	L133TFB	136	L136TFB
124	L124TFB								

137-142
Dennis Lance SLF   Wright Pathfinder 320   N38F   1995

137	M137FAE	138	M138FAE	140	M140FAE	141	M141FAE	142	M142FAE

201-225
Dennis Dart 9.8SDL3035   Plaxton Pointer   B40F   1993-94

201	L201SHW	206	L206SHW	211	L211VHU	216	L216VHU	221	L221VHU
202	L202SHW	207	L207SHW	212	L212VHU	217	L217VHU	223	L223VHU
203	L203SHW	208	L208SHW	213	L213VHU	218	L218VHU	224	L224VHU
204	L204SHW	209	L209SHW	214	L214VHU	219	L219VHU	225	L225VHU
205	L205SHW	210	L210VHU	215	L215VHU	220	L220VHU		

226-242
Dennis Dart 9.8SDL3054   Plaxton Pointer   B40F   1995

226	N226KAE	230	N230KAE	234	N234KAE	237	N237KAE	240	N240KAE
227	N227KAE	231	N231KAE	235	N235KAE	238	N238KAE	241	N241KAE
228	N228KAE	232	N232KAE	236	N236KAE	239	N239KAE	242	N242KAE
229	N229KAE	233	N233KAE						

243-250
Dennis Dart 9.8SDL3054   Plaxton Pointer   B40F   1996

243	N243LHT	245	N245LHT	247	N247LHT	249	N249LHT	250	N250LHT
244	N244LHT	246	N246LHT	248	N248LHT				

251-257
Dennis Dart   Plaxton Pointer   B40F   1996

251	P251PAE	253	P253PAE	255	P255PAE	256	P256PAE	257	P257PAE
252	P252PAE	254	P254PAE						

258-264
Dennis Dart SLF   Plaxton Pointer   N39F   1996

258	P258PAE	260	P260PAE	262	P262PAE	263	P263PAE	264	P264PAE
259	P259PAE	261	P261PAE						

Opposite, top:- **Badgerline, from being the name of a 'major group' now exists only as the operational name of First Bristol for rural services in the North Somerset area. Nineteen Volvo B10Bs with Wright Renown bodywork joined the fleet in 1998 and these are based at Bath and Wells with three retained at Marlborough Street depot in Bristol. Based at Bath, 1917, R917BOU is seen heading for Bristol on limited stop service X39.** *Phillip Stephenson*
Opposite, bottom:- **Durbins operation was acquired by Badgerline in 1996 and the vehicles are now housed at the Lawrence Hill depot in Bristol. Bristol VR 5560, STW33W, which was transferred into First Bristol from Essex Buses, is seen in Durbins colours of light and mid blue.** *Phillip Stephenson*

290-299

Dennis Javelin GX 12SDA2153 — Plaxton Expressliner 2 — C46FT — 1995-98

290	M290FAE	292	M292FAE	297	R297AYB	298	R298AYB	299	R299AYB
291	M291FAE	293	M293FAE						

1221-1230

Dennis Lance 11SDA3107 — Plaxton Verde — B49F — 1994 — Midland Red West, 1997

1221	L221AAB	1223	L223AAB	1225	L225AAB	1227	L227AAB	1229	L229AAB
1222	L322AAB	1224	L224AAB	1226	L226AAB	1228	L228AAB	1230	L230AAB

1503-1508

Dennis Dart 9SDL3034 — Plaxton Pointer — B35F — 1994

1503	L503VHU	1505	L505VHU	1506	L506VHU	1507	L507VHU	1508	L508VHU
1504	L504VHU								

1509-1547

Dennis Dart 9SDL3053 — Plaxton Pointer — B35F — 1995

1509	M509DHU	1517	M517DHU	1525	M525FFB	1533	M533FFB	1541	N541HAE
1510	M510DHU	1518	M518DHU	1526	M526FFB	1534	M534FFB	1542	N542HAE
1511	M511DHU	1519	M519DHU	1527	M527FFB	1535	M535FFB	1543	N543HAE
1512	M512DHU	1520	M520FFB	1528	M528FFB	1536	M536FFB	1544	N544HAE
1513	M513DHU	1521	M521FFB	1529	M529FFB	1537	M537FFB	1545	N545HAE
1514	M514DHU	1522	M522FFB	1530	M530FFB	1538	M538FFB	1546	N546HAE
1515	M515DHU	1523	M523FFB	1531	M531FFB	1539	N539HAE	1547	N547HAE
1516	M516DHU	1524	M524FFB	1532	M532FFB	1540	N540HAE		

1548	N548HAE	Dennis Dart 9SDL3053	Plaxton Pointer	B35F	1996	CNG development unit.	

1549-1559

Dennis Dart — Plaxton Pointer — B35F — 1996

1549	N549LHU	1551	N551LHU	1553	N553LHU	1556	N556LHU	1558	N558LHU
1550	N550LHU	1552	N552LHU	1554	N554LHU	1557	N557LHU	1559	N559LHU

1600-1662

Leyland Lynx LX2R11C15Z4R — Leyland Lynx — B49F — 1989-90

1600	F600RTC	1613	F613RTC	1626	F626RTC	1639	H639YHT	1651	H651YHT
1601	F601RTC	1614	F614RTC	1627	F627RTC	1640	H640YHT	1652	H652YHT
1602	F602RTC	1615	F615RTC	1628	F628RTC	1641	H641YHT	1653	H653YHT
1603	F603RTC	1616	F616RTC	1629	F629RTC	1642	H642YHT	1654	H654YHT
1604	F604RTC	1617	F617RTC	1630	F630RTC	1643	H643YHT	1655	H655YHT
1605	F605RTC	1618	F618RTC	1631	F631RTC	1644	H644YHT	1656	H656YHT
1606	F606RTC	1619	F619RTC	1632	F632RTC	1645	H645YHT	1657	H657YHT
1607	F607RTC	1620	F620RTC	1633	H633YHT	1646	H646YHT	1658	H658YHT
1608	F608RTC	1621	F621RTC	1634	H634YHT	1647	H647YHT	1659	H659YHT
1609	F609RTC	1622	F622RTC	1636	H636YHT	1648	H648YHT	1660	H660YHT
1610	F610RTC	1623	F623RTC	1637	H637YHT	1649	H649YHT	1661	H661YHT
1611	F611RTC	1624	F624RTC	1638	H638YHT	1650	H650YHT	1662	H662YHT
1612	F612RTC	1625	F625RTC						

1701-1718

Dennis Dart SLF — Plaxton Pointer 2 — N26F — 1997

1701	R701BAE	1705	R705BAE	1709	R709BAE	1713	R713BAE	1716	R716BAE
1702	R702BAE	1706	R706BAE	1710	R710BAE	1714	R714BAE	1717	R717BAE
1703	R703BAE	1707	R707BAE	1711	R711BAE	1715	R715BAE	1718	R718BAE
1704	R704BAE	1708	R708BAE	1712	R712BAE				

1719	R719RAD	Dennis Dart SLF (CNG)	Plaxton Pointer MPD	N29F	1998		

1720-1729

Dennis Dart SLF — Plaxton Pointer SPD — N35F — 1998-99

1720	S720AFB	1722	S722AFB	1724	S724AFB	1726	T726REU	1728	T728REU
1721	S721AFB	1723	S723AFB	1725	S725AFB	1727	T727REU	1729	T729REU

1730	T730REU	Dennis Dart SLF	Alexander ALX200	N37F	1999	
1731	T731REU	Dennis Dart SLF	Alexander ALX200	N37F	1999	

1901-1920

Volvo B10BLE — Wright Renown — B47F — 1998

1901	R901BOU	1905	R905BOU	1909	R909BOU	1914	R914BOU	1918	R918BOU
1902	R902BOU	1906	R906BOU	1910	R910BOU	1915	R915BOU	1919	R919BOU
1903	R903BOU	1907	R907BOU	1912	R912BOU	1916	R916BOU	1920	R920COU
1904	R904BOU	1908	R908BOU	1913	R913BOU	1917	R917BOU		

City Line vehicles carry a livery of yellow, red and blue. Initially a devotee of the Leyland Lynx, with 62 operate for City Line and a further seven with Badgerline. By the time further full-size saloons were ordered Lynx production had ceased. Representing the type is 1610, F610RTC. For many years TC index marks were issued by Lancashire and appeared on many Leyland buses before that mark was transferred to the Bristol Office in the 1970s. *T S Powell*

2203	A203RHT	Leyland Tiger TRCTL11/3R	Plaxton Paramount 3200 E	C57F	1983	
2500	D500GHY	Volvo B10M-61	Van Hool Alizée	C48FT	1987	
2501	D501GHY	Volvo B10M-61	Van Hool Alizée	C53F	1987	
2502	D502GHY	Volvo B10M-61	Van Hool Alizée	C48FT	1987	
2503	D503GHY	Volvo B10M-61	Van Hool Alizée	C48FT	1987	
2504	ODT232	Volvo B10M-61	Van Hool Alizée	C48FT	1987	Western National, 1997
2510	PSU527	Volvo B10M-61	Van Hool Alizée	C48FT	1987	Western National, 1997
2600	WYY752	Volvo B10M-61	Van Hool Alizée	C57F	1987	
2601	LSU788	Volvo B10M-61	Van Hool Alizée	C57F	1987	

3610-3616

	Leyland Lynx LX2R11C15Z4R	Leyland Lynx	B49F	1990	

3610	H610YTC	3612	H612YTC	3614	H614YTC	3615	H615YTC	3616	H616YTC
3611	H611YTC	3613	H613YTC						

3800-3823

	Mercedes-Benz 811D	Optare StarRider	B31F*	1988	*3819/21-3 are BC29F

3800	E800MOU	3804	E804MOU	3810	E810MOU	3815	E815MOU	3819	E819MOU
3801	E801MOU	3805	E805MOU	3811	E811MOU	3816	E816MOU	3821	E821MOU
3802	E802MOU	3806	E806MOU	3813	E813MOU	3817	E817MOU	3822	E822MOU
3803	E803MOU	3809	E809MOU	3814	E814MOU	3818	E818MOU	3823	E823MOU

3824	F695AWW	Mercedes-Benz 811D	Optare StarRider	B33F	1988	Clapton Cs, Radstock, 1994

3850-3866

	Mercedes-Benz 709D	Reeve Burgess Beaver	B23F	1991-92	

3850	J850FTC	3854	J854FTC	3858	J858FTC	3861	J861HWS	3864	J864HWS
3851	J851FTC	3855	J855FTC	3859	J859FTC	3862	J862HWS	3865	J865HWS
3852	J852FTC	3856	J856FTC	3860	J860HWS	3863	J863HWS	3866	J866HWS
3853	J853FTC	3857	J857FTC						

3867-3876   Mercedes-Benz 709D   Plaxton Beaver   B23F   1993

3867	K867NEU	3869	K869NEU	3871	K871NEU	3873	K873NEU	3875	K875NEU
3868	K868NEU	3870	K870NEU	3872	K872NEU	3874	K874NEU	3876	K876NEU

3877	L877TFB	Mercedes-Benz 711D	Plaxton Beaver	B23F	1993

3878-3911   Mercedes-Benz 709D   Plaxton Beaver   B23F   1994

3878	L878VHT	3885	L885VHT	3893	L893VHT	3899	L899VHT	3906	L906VHT
3879	L879VHT	3886	L886VHT	3894	L894VHT	3901	L901VHT	3907	L907VHT
3880	L880VHT	3887	L887VHT	3895	L895VHT	3902	L902VHT	3908	L908VHT
3881	L881VHT	3889	L889VHT	3896	L896VHT	3903	L903VHT	3909	L909VHT
3882	M882BEU	3890	L890VHT	3897	L897VHT	3904	L904VHT	3910	L910VHT
3883	L883VHT	3891	L891VHT	3898	L898VHT	3905	L905VHT	3911	L911VHT
3884	L884VHT	3892	L892VHT						

3912	E694UND	Mercedes-Benz 609D	Made-to-Measure	B21F	1987	Durbin, 1996
3913	F850TCW	Mercedes-Benz 609D	Reeve Burgess Beaver	B20F	1988	Clapton Cs, Radstock, 1994
3914	J850OBV	Mercedes-Benz 709D	Plaxton Beaver	B23F	1992	Clapton Cs, Radstock, 1994
3915	L390UHU	Mercedes-Benz 709D	Plaxton Beaver	B23F	1993	Clapton Cs, Radstock, 1994
3916	K29OEU	Mercedes-Benz 709D	Wright NimBus	B29F	1993	Somerbus, Poulton, 1994
5000	C28EUH	Leyland Olympian ONTL11/2R	East Lancashire	C47/31F	1985	G&G, Leamington, 1989
5001	C29EUH	Leyland Olympian ONTL11/2R	East Lancashire	C47/31F	1985	G&G, Leamington, 1989
5073	MOU747R	Bristol VRT/SL3/6LXB	Eastern Coach Works	B43/27D	1976	
5147	AHW198V	Bristol VRT/SL3/6LXB	Eastern Coach Works	B43/27D	1980	
5531	EWS739W	Bristol VRT/SL3/680(6LXB)	Eastern Coach Works	B43/31F	1981	Western National, 1997
5534	EWS742W	Bristol VRT/SL3/680(6LXB)	Eastern Coach Works	B43/31F	1981	
5541	EWS749W	Bristol VRT/SL3/680(6LXB)	Eastern Coach Works	B43/31F	1981	
5551	KOO792V	Bristol VRT/SL3/6LXB	Eastern Coach Works	B39/31F	1980	Thamesway, 1991
5560	STW33W	Bristol VRT/SL3/6LXB	Eastern Coach Works	B39/31F	1981	Thamesway, 1992
5562	XHK221X	Bristol VRT/SL3/6LXB	Eastern Coach Works	B43/31F	1981	Thamesway, 1992
5564	XHK224X	Bristol VRT/SL3/6LXB	Eastern Coach Works	B43/31F	1981	Thamesway, 1992

5700-5711   Volvo Citybus B10M-50   Alexander RH   BC47/35F   1987

5700	D700GHY	5703	D703GHY	5706	D706GHY	5708	D708GHY	5710	D710GHY
5701	D701GHY	5704	D704GHY	5707	D707GHY	5709	D709GHY	5711	D711GHY
5702	D702GHY	5705	D705GHY						

5714	E217BTA	Volvo Citybus B10M-50	Alexander RH	BC47/35F	1988	Western National, 1989

6130	K461PNR	Volvo B10M-60	Plaxton Première 350	C51FT	1993	
6131	L65UOU	Volvo B10M-62	Plaxton Première 350	C49FT	1994	
6138	K65OHT	Volvo B10M-60	Plaxton Première 350	C49FT	1993	
6139	K67OHT	Volvo B10M-60	Plaxton Première 350	C49FT	1993	
6145	H201JHP	Peugeot-Talbot Pullman	Talbot	B19F	1990	Midland Red West, 1995
6154	J429GHT	Volvo B10M-60	Plaxton Expressliner	C46FT	1991	
6157	J203HWS	Volvo B10M-60	Plaxton Expressliner	C46FT	1991	
6158	J204HWS	Volvo B10M-60	Plaxton Expressliner	C46FT	1991	
6159	K509NOU	Volvo B10M-60	Plaxton Expressliner 2	C46FT	1993	
6160	K991OEU	Volvo B10M-60	Plaxton Première 350	C49FT	1993	
6161	K792OTC	Volvo B10M-60	Plaxton Expressliner 2	C46FT	1993	
6162	K793OTC	Volvo B10M-60	Plaxton Expressliner 2	C46FT	1993	
6163	K794OTC	Volvo B10M-60	Plaxton Expressliner 2	C46FT	1993	
6166	L64UOU	Volvo B10M-60	Plaxton Expressliner 2	C46FT	1993	
6167	L67UOU	Volvo B10M-60	Plaxton Expressliner 2	C46FT	1993	
6169	M92BOU	Volvo B10M-62	Plaxton Expressliner 2	C46FT	1994	
6174	M763CWS	Volvo B10M-62	Plaxton Expressliner 2	C44FT	1994	
6175	M764CWS	Volvo B10M-62	Plaxton Expressliner 2	C44FT	1994	
6176	M765CWS	Volvo B10M-62	Plaxton Expressliner 2	C49FT	1994	
6177	M413DEU	Volvo B10M-62	Plaxton Expressliner 2	C44FT	1995	
6178	M439FHW	Volvo B10M-62	Plaxton Expressliner 2	C49FT	1995	
6179	M440FHW	Volvo B10M-62	Plaxton Expressliner 2	C49FT	1995	
6180	M41FTC	Volvo B10M-62	Plaxton Expressliner 2	C44FT	1995	
6181	P944RWS	Volvo B10M-62	Plaxton Expressliner 2	C46FT	1996	
6182	P945RWS	Volvo B10M-62	Plaxton Expressliner 2	C49FT	1996	
6183	P946RWS	Volvo B10M-62	Plaxton Expressliner 2	C49FT	1996	
6184	R813HWS	Volvo B10M-62	Plaxton Expressliner 2	C44FT	1995	
6185	R814HWS	Volvo B10M-62	Plaxton Expressliner 2	C49FT	1996	

Bristol VR 8622, LEU263P, is one of three dual-doored open-top buses to be used by Badgerline. The vehicle is seen working at Weston-super-Mare. *Phillip Stephenson*

6201-6212

Dennis Javelin GX 12SDA2153 Plaxton Expressliner 2 C49FT 1995-96

6201	N471KHU	6204	N474KHU	6207	N821KWS	6209	N319NHY	6211	N321NHY
6202	N472KHU	6205	N913KHW	6208	N822KWS	6210	N320NHY	6212	N322NHY
6203	N473KHU	6206	N914KHW						

6301	R71GNW	DAF DE33WSSB3000	Plaxton Premiere 350	C51F	1998	
6302	R72GNW	DAF DE33WSSB3000	Plaxton Premiere 350	C51F	1998	
6303	R73GNW	DAF DE33WSSB3000	Plaxton Premiere 350	C51F	1998	
6707	NFB599R	Leyland National 11351A/1R		B52F	1976	
6710	OHW489R	Leyland National 11351A/1R		B52F	1976	
6712	TTC537T	Leyland National 11351A/1R		B52F	1978	
6713	YFB969V	Leyland National 11351A/1R		B52F	1978	
6801	RKA869T	Leyland National 11351A/1R(Volvo)		B49F	1978	Yorkshire Rider (Q), 1997
6802	SKF11T	Leyland National 11351A/1R(Volvo)		B49F	1979	Yorkshire Rider (YR), 1997
6803	BOK258T	Leyland National 11351A/1R(Volvo)		B49F	1979	Yorkshire Rider (YR), 1997
6804	JUB646V	Leyland National 11351A/1R(Volvo)		B49F	1979	Yorkshire Rider (YR), 1997
6805	JUB647V	Leyland National 11351A/1R(Volvo)		B49F	1979	Yorkshire Rider (YR), 1997
7591	F591OHT	Iveco Daily 49.10	Dormobile Routemaker	B20F	1989	
7592	F592OHT	Iveco Daily 49.10	Dormobile Routemaker	B20F	1989	
7596	F596OHT	Iveco Daily 49.10	Dormobile Routemaker	B20F	1989	
7610	F610PWS	Iveco Daily 49.10	Dormobile Routemaker	B20F	1989	
7615	M411RND	Iveco TurboDaily 59-12	Marshall C31	B25F	1995	Greater Manchester, 1997
7616	M248NNF	Iveco TurboDaily 59-12	Marshall C31	B25F	1995	Greater Manchester, 1997
7617	M249NNF	Iveco TurboDaily 59-12	Marshall C31	B27F	1995	Greater Manchester, 1997
7618	M414RND	Iveco TurboDaily 59-12	Marshall C31	B20F	1995	Greater Manchester, 1997
7619	M413RND	Iveco TurboDaily 59-12	Marshall C31	B20F	1995	Greater Manchester, 1997

7801-7826   Mercedes-Benz 709D   Plaxton Beaver   B22F   1993

7801	L801SAE	7807	L807SAE	7812	L812SAE	7817	L817SAE	7822	L822SAE
7802	L802SAE	7808	L808SAE	7813	L813SAE	7818	L818SAE	7823	L823SAE
7803	L803SAE	7809	L809SAE	7814	L814SAE	7819	L819SAE	7824	L824SAE
7804	L804SAE	7810	L810SAE	7815	L815SAE	7820	L820SAE	7825	L825SAE
7805	L805SAE	7811	L811SAE	7816	L816SAE	7821	L821SAE	7826	L826SAE
7806	L806SAE								

7827-7874   Mercedes-Benz 709D   Plaxton Beaver   B22F   1994

7827	L827WHY	7837	M837ATC	7847	M847ATC	7857	M857ATC	7866	M866ATC
7828	L828WHY	7838	M838ATC	7848	M848ATC	7858	M858ATC	7867	M867ATC
7829	L829WHY	7839	M839ATC	7849	M849ATC	7859	M859ATC	7868	M868ATC
7830	L830WHY	7840	M840ATC	7850	M850ATC	7860	M860ATC	7869	M869ATC
7831	M831ATC	7841	M841ATC	7851	M851ATC	7861	M861ATC	7870	M870ATC
7832	M832ATC	7842	M842ATC	7852	M852ATC	7862	M862ATC	7871	M871ATC
7833	M833ATC	7843	M843ATC	7853	M853ATC	7863	M863ATC	7872	M872ATC
7834	M834ATC	7844	M844ATC	7854	M854ATC	7864	M864ATC	7873	M873ATC
7835	M835ATC	7845	M845ATC	7855	M855ATC	7865	M865ATC	7874	M874ATC
7836	M836ATC	7846	M846ATC	7856	M856ATC				

7875-7907   Mercedes-Benz 709D   Plaxton Beaver   B22F   1995

7875	N875HWS	7882	N882HWS	7889	N889HWS	7895	N895HWS	7902	N902HWS
7876	N876HWS	7883	N883HWS	7890	N890HWS	7896	N896HWS	7903	N903HWS
7877	N877HWS	7884	N884HWS	7891	N891HWS	7897	N897HWS	7904	N904HWS
7878	N878HWS	7885	N885HWS	7892	N892HWS	7898	N898HWS	7905	N905HWS
7879	N879HWS	7886	N886HWS	7893	N893HWS	7899	N899HWS	7906	N906HWS
7880	N880HWS	7887	N887HWS	7894	N894HWS	7901	N901HWS	7907	N907HWS
7881	N881HWS								

8101	R101DTC	Tecnobus Gulliver O500ESP	Tecnobus	B9C	1996	LHD electric	
8102	R102DTC	Tecnobus Gulliver O500ESP	Tecnobus	B9C	1996	LHD electric	
8144	J144KPX	Iveco Daily 49.10	Marshall C29	B23F	1992	Provincial, 1997	
8200	SSU437	DAF MB200DKFL600	Plaxton Paramount 3500	C53F	1984	Durbin, 1996	
8205	RJI2720	DAF SB2300DHS585	Plaxton Paramount 3500	C53F	1984	Durbin, 1996	
8212	OIL9262	Leyland Tiger TRCTL11/3ARZA	Plaxton Paramount 3200 IIIE	C53F	1988	Brewers, 1998	
8213	OIL9263	Leyland Tiger TRCTL11/3ARZA	Plaxton Paramount 3200 IIIE	C53F	1988	Brewers, 1998	
8214	OIL9264	Leyland Tiger TRCTL11/3ARZA	Plaxton Paramount 3200 III	C53F	1988	Brewers, 1998	
8300	P829KTP	Iveco TurboDaily 59-12	UVG CitiStar	B25F	1996	Streamline, Bath, 1997	
8301	P828KTP	Iveco TurboDaily 59-12	UVG CitiStar	B25F	1996	Streamline, Bath, 1997	
8302	N34FWU	DAF DE02LTSB220	Ikarus Citibus	B49F	1996	Streamline, Bath, 1997	
8303	N28FWU	DAF DE02LTSB220	Ikarus Citibus	B49F	1996	Streamline, Bath, 1997	
8304	N29FWU	DAF DE02LTSB220	Ikarus Citibus	B49F	1996	Streamline, Bath, 1997	
8305	M606RCP	DAF SB220LT550	Ikarus Citibus	B49F	1995	Streamline, Bath, 1997	
8306	M968USC	Mercedes-Benz 814D	Plaxton Beaver	C33F	1994	Streamline, Bath, 1997	
8307	M45BEG	Mercedes-Benz 811D	Marshall C16	B31F	1994	Streamline, Bath, 1997	
8308	M46BEG	Mercedes-Benz 811D	Marshall C16	B31F	1994	Streamline, Bath, 1997	
8309	M857XHY	Mercedes-Benz 811D	Marshall C16	B31F	1994	Streamline, Bath, 1997	
8310	M48BEG	Mercedes-Benz 811D	Marshall C16	B31F	1994	Streamline, Bath, 1997	
8311	K690UFV	Mercedes-Benz 709D	Plaxton Beaver	B23F	1993	Streamline, Bath, 1997	
8312	K691UFV	Mercedes-Benz 709D	Plaxton Beaver	B23F	1993	Streamline, Bath, 1997	
8313	K692UFV	Mercedes-Benz 709D	Plaxton Beaver	B23F	1993	Streamline, Bath, 1997	
8314	K693UFV	Mercedes-Benz 709D	Plaxton Beaver	B23F	1993	Streamline, Bath, 1997	
8315	K694UFV	Mercedes-Benz 709D	Plaxton Beaver	B23F	1993	Streamline, Bath, 1997	
8316	K695RNR	Toyota Coaster HDB30R	Caetano Optimo II	C21F	1992	Streamline, Bath, 1997	
8320	ESK812	Kässbohrer Setra S213H	Kässbohrer	C53F	1982	Streamline, Bath, 1997	
8342	J142KPX	Iveco Daily 49.10	Marshall C29	B23F	1992	Provincial, 1997	
8343	J143KPX	Iveco Daily 49.10	Marshall C29	B23F	1992	Provincial, 1997	
8345	J145KPX	Iveco Daily 49.10	Marshall C29	B23F	1992	Provincial, 1997	
8346	J146KPX	Iveco Daily 49.10	Marshall C29	B23F	1992	Provincial, 1997	

Opposite:- **1998 saw the introduction of the CENTAUR (Clean and Efficient Transport Approach for Urban Rationalisation) experiment, a European Union funded project covering several cities across Europe. First City Line is operating two Italian-built Technobus electric battery-powered buses on the 905 service between Tollgate car park and the Broadmead shopping centre. The upper picture shows 102, R102DTC while the lower picture shows Marshall-bodied Iveco 7618, M414RND, which also carries the livery.**
Dennis Lewis/Dominic McCall

8583	GHT127	Bristol K5G	Eastern Coach Works	O33/26R	1941	
8600	RTH931S	Bristol VRT/SL3/501(6LXB)	Eastern Coach Works	CO43/31F	1977	SWT, 1991
8605	VDV143S	Bristol VRT/SL3/6LXB	Eastern Coach Works	CO43/31F	1978	Western National, 1993
8606	VDV137S	Bristol VRT/SL3/6LXB	Eastern Coach Works	CO43/31F	1977	Western National, 1990
8608	UFX860S	Bristol VRT/SL3/6LXB	Eastern Coach Works	CO43/31F	1977	Southern Vectis, 1983

8609-8614

Leyland Olympian ONLXB/1R   Roe   CO47/29F   1984

8609	A809THW	8611	A811THW	8612	A812THW	8613	A813THW	8614	A814THW
8610	A810THW								

8615	JHW107P	Bristol VRT/SL3/6LXB	Eastern Coach Works	O43/29F	1975	
8616	JHW108P	Bristol VRT/SL3/6LXB	Eastern Coach Works	O43/29F	1975	
8617	JHW109P	Bristol VRT/SL3/6LXB	Eastern Coach Works	O43/29F	1975	
8619	JHW114P	Bristol VRT/SL3/6LXB	Eastern Coach Works	O43/29F	1976	
8620	LEU256P	Bristol VRT/SL3/6LXB	Eastern Coach Works	O43/27D	1976	
8621	LEU269P	Bristol VRT/SL3/6LXB	Eastern Coach Works	O43/27D	1976	
8622	LEU263P	Bristol VRT/SL3/6LXB	Eastern Coach Works	O43/27D	1976	
8656	A756VAF	Leyland Olympian ONLXB/1R	Eastern Coach Works	BC43/31F	1983	Western National, 1997
8657	A757VAF	Leyland Olympian ONLXB/1R	Eastern Coach Works	BC43/31F	1983	Western National, 1997

9001-9010

Leyland Olympian ONCL10/1RZ Leyland   B47/31F*   1989   *9009/10 are BC43/29F

9001	G901TWS	9003	G903TWS	9005	G905TWS	9007	G907TWS	9009	G909TWS
9002	G902TWS	9004	G904TWS	9006	G906TWS	9008	G908TWS	9010	G910TWS

9501-9544

Leyland Olympian ONLXB/1R   Roe   B47/29F   1982-83

9501	JHU900X	9508	JHU907X	9516	LWS32Y	9532	NTC131Y	9539	NTC138Y
9502	JHU901X	9509	JHU908X	9526	LWS42Y	9534	NTC133Y	9540	NTC139Y
9503	JHU902X	9510	JHU909X	9527	LWS43Y	9535	NTC134Y	9541	NTC140Y
9504	JHU903X	9511	JHU910X	9528	LWS44Y	9536	NTC135Y	9542	NTC141Y
9505	JHU904X	9512	JHU911X	9529	LWS45Y	9537	NTC136Y	9543	NTC142Y
9506	JHU905X	9514	JHU913X	9530	NTC129Y	9538	NTC137Y	9544	NTC143Y
9507	JHU906X	9515	JHU914X	9531	NTC130Y				

9545-9568

Leyland Olympian ONLXB/1R   Roe   B47/29F   1983-84

9545	A945SAE	9550	A950SAE	9555	A955THW	9560	A960THW	9565	A965THW
9546	A946SAE	9551	A951SAE	9556	A956THW	9561	A961THW	9566	A966THW
9547	A947SAE	9552	A952SAE	9557	A957THW	9562	A962THW	9567	A967THW
9548	A948SAE	9553	A953SAE	9558	A958THW	9563	A963THW	9568	A968THW
9549	A949SAE	9554	A954SAE	9559	A959THW	9564	A964THW		

9601-9630

Leyland Olympian ON2R56C16Z4 Northern Counties Palatine   B44/32F   1992-93

9601	K601LAE	9607	K607LAE	9613	K613LAE	9619	K619LAE	9625	K625LAE
9602	K602LAE	9608	K608LAE	9614	K614LAE	9620	K620LAE	9626	K626LAE
9603	K603LAE	9609	K609LAE	9615	K615LAE	9621	K621LAE	9627	K627LAE
9604	K604LAE	9610	K610LAE	9616	K616LAE	9622	K622LAE	9628	K628LAE
9605	K605LAE	9611	K611LAE	9617	K617LAE	9623	K623LAE	9629	K629LAE
9606	K606LAE	9612	K612LAE	9618	K618LAE	9624	K624LAE	9630	K630LAE

9631-9654

Volvo Olympian YN2RC16Z4*   Northern Counties Palatine II B47/29F   1993-94   *9645-8 are YN2RC16Z5

9631	L631SEU	9636	L636SEU	9641	L641SEU	9646	L646SEU	9651	L651SEU
9632	L632SEU	9637	L637SEU	9642	L642SEU	9647	L647SEU	9652	L652SEU
9633	L633SEU	9638	L638SEU	9643	L643SEU	9648	L648SEU	9653	L653SEU
9634	L634SEU	9639	L639SEU	9644	L644SEU	9649	L649SEU	9654	L654SEU
9635	L635SEU	9640	L640SEU	9645	L645SEU	9650	L650SEU		

9655-9664

Volvo Olympian   Northern Counties Palatine II B43/29F   1997

9655	P655UFB	9657	P657UFB	9659	P659UFB	9661	R661NHY	9663	R663NHY
9656	P656UFB	9658	P658UFB	9660	P660UFB	9662	R662NHY	9664	R664NHY

9665-9691 Volvo Olympian — Northern Counties Palatine II B43/29F* 1998 — *9688-91 are BC47/29F

9665	S665AAE	9672	S672AAE	9677	S677AAE	9682	S682AAE	9687	S687AAE
9667	S667AAE	9673	S673AAE	9678	S678AAE	9683	S683AAE	9688	S688AAE
9668	S668AAE	9674	S674AAE	9679	S679AAE	9684	S684AAE	9689	S689AAE
9669	S669AAE	9675	S675AAE	9680	S680AAE	9685	S685AAE	9690	S690AAE
9670	S670AAE	9676	S676AAE	9681	S681AAE	9686	S686AAE	9691	S691AAE
9671	S671AAE								

9978	P87BPL	Dennis Lance	Northern Counties	B F	1988	On extended loan

Southern National

5	B895YYD	Leyland Tiger TRCTL11/3RH	Plaxton Paramount 3200 II	C48FT	1985	
11	4384LJ	Leyland Tiger TRCTL11/3R	Plaxton Paramount 3500	C49F	1983	Yelloway, Rochdale, 1985
12	620HOD	Leyland Tiger TRCTL11/3R	Plaxton Paramount 3200 E	C53F	1983	Eastern Counties, 1992
50	D50ERV	Iveco Daily 49.10	Robin Hood City Nippy	B21F	1987	Southampton Citybus, 1990
52	D52ERV	Iveco Daily 49.10	Robin Hood City Nippy	B21F	1987	Southampton Citybus, 1990
53	D53ERV	Iveco Daily 49.10	Robin Hood City Nippy	B21F	1987	Southampton Citybus, 1990
54	D54ERV	Iveco Daily 49.10	Robin Hood City Nippy	B21F	1987	Southampton Citybus, 1990
94	FDV789V	Bristol LHS6L	Eastern Coach Works	B35F	1979	Devon General, 1985
113	D113ERV	Iveco Daily 49.10	Robin Hood City Nippy	B21F	1986	People's Provincial, 1989
124	D124ERV	Iveco Daily 49.10	Robin Hood City Nippy	B21F	1986	People's Provincial, 1989
125	D125ERV	Iveco Daily 49.10	Robin Hood City Nippy	B21F	1986	People's Provincial, 1989

150-191 Ford Transit VE6 — Mellor — B16F 1987-89 — Provincial, 1996

150	E196BDV	158	E208BDV	167	E807WDV	176	D106PTT	184	E214BDV
151	E201BDV	159	E199BDV	168	E808WDV	177	E817WDV	185	E215BDV
152	E202BDV	160	E197BDV	169	E809WDV	178	E198BDV	186	D793NDV
153	E203BDV	161	E811BDV	170	E220BDV	179	E819WDV	187	E217BDV
154	E204BDV	163	E803WDV	171	E221BDV	180	E820WDV	188	E218BDV
155	F751FDV	164	E814WDV	172	E222BDV	181	D788NDV	189	E219BDV
156	E206BDV	165	E805WDV	173	F773FDV	182	D782NDV	190	D643NOD
157	E207BDV	166	F752FDV	174	F753FDV	183	D783NDV	191	D645NOD

221-232 Iveco Daily 49.10 — Robin Hood City Nippy — B21F 1986 — Brighton & Hove, 1989

221	D221VCD	222	D222VCD	223	D223VCD	227	D227VCD	232	D232VCD

280	DAD254T	Leyland Leopard PSU5C/4R	Plaxton Supreme IV	C57F	1979	Black & White, 1985

Bristol's Park & Ride services have liveries for each specific route. Illustrating that for Long Ashton is Volvo Olympian 9660, P660UFB which carries a red and silver scheme. FirstGroup have entered into several partnerships with local authorities to provide special services, and this example is typical.
Les Peters

300-325

			Ford Transit 190		Robin Hood		B16F		1985	
300	C862DYD	306	C868DYD	314	C876DYD	318	C880DYD	323	C885DYD	
304	C866DYD	307	C869DYD	315	C877DYD	319	C881DYD	325	C887DYD	
305	C867DYD	312w	C874DYD	316	C878DYD	322	C884DYD			

331-377

			Ford Transit 190		Dormobile		B16F		1986	
331w	C893GYD	338	C900GYD	351	C913GYD	363	C925GYD	371	C933GYD
332	C894GYD	339	C901GYD	352	C914GYD	364	C926GYD	372	C934GYD
333	C895GYD	340	C902GYD	359	C921GYD	365	C927GYD	373	C935GYD
334	C896GYD	341	C903GYD	360	C922GYD	367	C929GYD	374	C936GYD
336w	C898GYD	345	C907GYD	361	C923GYD	368	C930GYD	377	C939GYD
337	C899GYD	347	C909GYD	362	C924GYD	369	C931GYD		

380-393

			Ford Transit 190		Dormobile		B16F		1986	*389 is B6FL
380	C942GYD	383	C945GYD	385	C947GYD	389	C951GYD	393	C955GYD

397	D112DRV	Iveco Daily 49.10		Robin Hood City Nippy		B21F		1986		People's Provincial, 1988

415-436

			Ford Transit 190		Robin Hood		B16F		1986	
415	C336GFJ	426	C347GFJ	428	C349GFJ	432	C353GFJ	436	C357GFJ

448	B460BHY	Ford Transit 190	Dormobile	B16F	1986	Bristol, 1989
449	B461BHY	Ford Transit 190	Dormobile	B16F	1986	Bristol, 1989
450	B462BHY	Ford Transit 190	Dormobile	B16F	1986	Bristol, 1989
451	B106XJO	Ford Transit 190	Carlyle	B16F	1986	Devon General, 1992
506	D114DRV	Iveco Daily 49.10	Robin Hood City Nippy	B21F	1986	People's Provincial, 1989
508	D508OTA	Iveco Daily 49.10	Robin Hood City Nippy	BC21F	1986	
511	D228VCD	Iveco Daily 49.10	Robin Hood City Nippy	B21F	1987	Brighton & Hove, 1989
512	D233VCD	Iveco Daily 49.10	Robin Hood City Nippy	B21F	1987	Brighton & Hove, 1989
513	D225VCD	Iveco Daily 49.10	Robin Hood City Nippy	B21F	1987	Brighton & Hove, 1989
514	D224VCD	Iveco Daily 49.10	Robin Hood City Nippy	B21F	1987	Brighton & Hove, 1989
520	D116DRV	Iveco Daily 49.10	Robin Hood City Nippy	B21F	1986	People's Provincial, 1989
522	E963HTP	Iveco Daily 49.10	Robin Hood City Nippy	B21F	1986	W & H, Horley, 1990
523	F908FHE	Iveco Daily 49.10	Carlyle Dailybus 2	B19F	1989	East Midland, 1990
524	F905FHE	Iveco Daily 49.10	Carlyle Dailybus 2	B19F	1989	East Midland, 1990
529	F588OOU	Iveco Daily 49.10	Dormobile	B25F	1987	Cityline, 1996
530	F590OHT	Iveco Daily 49.10	Dormobile	B25F	1987	Cityline, 1996
549	D510MJA	Iveco Daily 49.10	Robin Hood City Nippy	B21F	1986	GM Buses, 1990
555	ATL555L	Bristol VRT/SL2/6LX	Eastern Coach Works	O43/32F	1973	Western National, 1983
559	ATL559L	Bristol VRT/SL2/6LX	Eastern Coach Works	O43/32F	1973	Western National, 1983
560	MBZ7140	Bristol VRT/SL3/501	Eastern Coach Works	O--/--F	1976	Stephenson, Rochford,1998
574	VOD594S	Bristol VRT/SL3/6LXB	Eastern Coach Works	B43/31F	1978	Western National, 1983

601-608

			Bristol VRT/SL3/501(6LXB)		Eastern Coach Works		B43/31F		1976	Western National, 1983
601	LWG844P	603	LWG846P	604	LWG847P	605	OWE848P	608	OWE851P

650	D146VRP	Mercedes-Benz L608D	Alexander AM	BC19F	1986	Buckinghamshire Road, 1995
651	D151VRP	Mercedes-Benz L608D	Alexander AM	BC19F	1986	Buckinghamshire Road, 1995
652	D149VRP	Mercedes-Benz L608D	Alexander AM	BC19F	1986	MK Metro, 1995

701-710

			Mercedes-Benz 709D		Carlyle		B29F		1991	
701	H906WYB	703	H908WYB	705	H910WYB	707	H913WYB	709	H915WYB
702	H907WYB	704	H909WYB	706	H912WYB	708	H914WYB	710	H916WYB

719	J969EYD	Mercedes-Benz 709D	Carlyle	B29F	1992
720	J241FYA	Mercedes-Benz 709D	Carlyle	B29F	1992
721	J580FYA	Mercedes-Benz 709D	Carlyle	B29F	1992
722	J601FYA	Mercedes-Benz 709D	Carlyle	B29F	1992
725	M305TSF	Mercedes-Benz 709D	Alexander Sprint	B29F	1994

Southern National, latterly part of the Cawlett Group which was acquired by FirstGroup in the spring of 1999 is now, along with its associated local operations under First Bristol mangement while the North Devon/Red Bus operation is now under the control of Western National. Southern National's 605, OWB48P, had a revised livery for route 31. The vehicle is seen near Askerswell on that service. *DWR Picture Library*

726-735

			Mercedes-Benz 709D		Alexander Sprint		B29F	1994-95	
726	M804UYA	728	M805UYA	730	M278UYD	732	M281UYD	734	M239VYA
727	M803UYA	729	M802UYA	731	M279UYD	733	M282UYD	735	M240VYA

736	M220PMS	Mercedes-Benz 709D	Alexander Sprint	B29F	1995
737	TDZ3265	Mercedes-Benz 709D	Alexander Sprint	B29F	1995

738-742

			Mercedes-Benz 709D		Alexander Sprint		B29F	1996	
738	N556EYB	739	N557EYB	740	N558EYB	741	N559EYB	742	N561EYB

743	L26LSG	Mercedes-Benz 709D	Alexander Sprint	B25F	1995	Bryans, Denny, 1995
744	865GAT	Mercedes-Benz 709D	Alexander AM	B29F	1988	Glyn Williams, Crosskeys, 97
745	L23LSG	Mercedes-Benz 709D	Alexander Sprint	B25F	1995	Henderson, Hamilton, 1997
746	L24LSG	Mercedes-Benz 709D	Alexander Sprint	B25F	1995	Henderson, Hamilton, 1997
747	M14ABC	Mercedes-Benz 709D	Alexander Sprint	B29F	1995	Stonehouse Coaches, 1997
748	M19ABC	Mercedes-Benz 709D	Alexander Sprint	B29F	1995	Stonehouse Coaches, 1997
749	L92LSG	Mercedes-Benz 709D	Alexander Sprint	B25F	1995	Henderson, Hamilton, 1997

751-762

			Mercedes-Benz 811D		Wright NimBus		B33F	1993-94	
751	K751VFJ	757	L651CJT	759	L329MYC	761	L67EPR	762	L68EPR
756	L650CJT	758	L652CJT	760	L330MYC				

766	M766FTT	Mercedes-Benz 811D	Marshall C16	B33F	1994
770	M241VYA	Mercedes-Benz 811D	Wright NimBus	B33F	1995
771	M242VYA	Mercedes-Benz 811D	Wright NimBus	B33F	1995
772	M508VYA	Mercedes-Benz 811D	Wright NimBus	B33F	1995
773	M509VYA	Mercedes-Benz 811D	Wright NimBus	B33F	1995

774	F154RHK	Mercedes-Benz 811D	Reeve Burgess Beaver	B33F	1989	Jackson, Bicknacre, 1995
775	J185LGE	Mercedes-Benz 811D	Alexander Sprint	B29F	1992	Harte, Greenock, 1997
776	K776AFS	Mercedes-Benz 711D	Alexander Sprint	B31F	1992	

780-785
Mercedes-Benz 711D Alexander Sprint B29F 1996

780	P442KYC	782	P445KYC	783	P446KYC	784	P447KYC	785	P448KYC
781	P443KYC								

786-790
Mercedes-Benz 711D Plaxton Beaver B29F 1997

786	P179LYB	787	P180LYB	788	P181LYB	789	P182LYB	790	P183LYB

791	N806CRJ	Mercedes-Benz 711D	Plaxton Beaver	BC25F	1996	Hayton, Burnage, 1998
802	H802GDV	Dennis Dart 9.8SDL3004	Carlyle Dartline	B40F	1991	
806	K328KYC	Dennis Dart 9.8SDL3017	Wright Handybus	BC37F	1993	
807	K329KYC	Dennis Dart 9.8SDL3017	Wright Handybus	BC37F	1993	
808	K330KYC	Dennis Dart 9.8SDL3017	Wright Handybus	BC37F	1993	

817-823
Dennis Dart SLF Plaxton Pointer 2 N39F 1998

817	S817KPR	819	S819KPR	821	S821KPR	822	S822KPR	823	S823KPR
818	S818KPR	820	S820KPR						

824	S824WYD	Dennis Dart SLF	East Lancashire Spryte	N35F	1999
825	S825WYD	Dennis Dart SLF	East Lancashire Spryte	N35F	1999
826	T826AFX	Dennis Dart SLF	Plaxton Pointer 2	N39F	1999
827	T827AFX	Dennis Dart SLF	Plaxton Pointer 2	N39F	1999
828	T828AFX	Dennis Dart SLF	Plaxton Pointer 2	N39F	1999
829	T829AFX	Dennis Dart SLF	Plaxton Pointer 2	N39F	1999

854-864
Mercedes-Benz Vario O810* Plaxton Beaver 2 B27F 1998 *857/60/1 are O814

854	R501NPR	857	R504NPR	859	R506NPR	861	R508NPR	863	S863LRU
855	R502NPR	858	R505NPR	860	R507NPR	862	S340WYB	864	S864LRU
856	R503NPR								

934	VDV134S	Bristol VRT/SL3/6LXB	Eastern Coach Works	CO43/31F	1977	Western National, 1983
942	VDV142S	Bristol VRT/SL3/6LXB	Eastern Coach Works	CO43/31F	1978	Devon General, 1983
950	M392KVR	Mercedes-Benz 709D	Alexander Sprint	B27F	1995	Glossopdale, 1997
951	M393KVR	Mercedes-Benz 709D	Alexander Sprint	B27F	1995	Beeline, West Bromwich,97
952	M386KVR	Mercedes-Benz 709D	Alexander Sprint	B27F	1994	Little Red Bus, Smethwick, 97
953	M674RAJ	Mercedes-Benz 709D	Alexander Sprint	B25F	1994	Go-Ahead (OK), 1998
954	M675RAJ	Mercedes-Benz 709D	Alexander Sprint	B25F	1994	Go-Ahead (OK), 1998
958	M381KVR	Mercedes-Benz 709D	Alexander Sprint	B29F	1995	Eastern Counties, 1998
959	M382KVR	Mercedes-Benz 709D	Alexander Sprint	B29F	1995	Essex Buses (T), 1998

960-967
Mercedes-Benz 709D Reeve Burgess Beaver B25F 1990-91 Plymouth Citybus, 1997-98

960	H684BTA	962	J220KTT	964	J205KTT	966	J213KTT	967	J210KTT
961	J208KTT	963	J217KTT	965	H683KTA				

968	N585WND	Mercedes-Benz 709D	Reeve Burgess Beaver	B25F	1995	Western Buses(AA), 1998
969	N584WND	Mercedes-Benz 709D	Reeve Burgess Beaver	B25F	1995	Williamsons, Shrewsbury, 98
970	N586WND	Mercedes-Benz 709D	Reeve Burgess Beaver	B25F	1995	Thompson, South Bank, 1998
971	N583WND	Mercedes-Benz 709D	Reeve Burgess Beaver	B25F	1995	Epsom Coaches, 1999
1097	PTT97R	Bristol VRT/SL3/6LXB	Eastern Coach Works	B43/31F	1977	Western National, 1983
1110	VDV110S	Bristol VRT/SL3/6LXB	Eastern Coach Works	B43/31F	1978	Western National, 1983
1111	VDV111S	Bristol VRT/SL3/6LXB	Eastern Coach Works	B43/31F	1978	Western National, 1983
1121	BFX576T	Bristol VRT/SL3/6LXB	Eastern Coach Works	B43/31F	1979	Solent Blue Line, 1997

1125-1193
Bristol VRT/SL3/6LXB Eastern Coach Works B43/31F 1978 Western National, 1983

1125	XDV605S	1159	AFJ766T	1163	AFJ770T	1168	FDV780V	1192	FDV836V
1157	AFJ764T	1160	AFJ767T	1166	AFJ773T	1169	FDV781V	1193	FDV837V
1158	AFJ765T	1161	AFJ768T	1167	FDV779V	1170	FDV782V		

1634	REU326S	Bristol LH6L	Eastern Coach Works	B43F	1978	Western National, 1983
1813	A685KDV	Leyland Olympian ONLXB/1R	Eastern Coach Works	B45/32F	1983	Devon General, 1990
2213	A590AHB	Leyland Tiger TRCTL11/3R	Marshall Campaigner	B57F	1983	MoD, 1996 (20KB57)
2214	A696YOX	Leyland Tiger TRCTL11/3R	Marshall Campaigner	B54F	1983	MoD, 1995 (20KB47)
2215	UOB366Y	Leyland Tiger TRCTL11/3R	Marshall Campaigner	B54F	1983	MoD, 1996 (20KB53)
2216	B591FOG	Leyland Tiger TRCTL11/3R	Marshall Campaigner	B57F	1984	MoD, 1996 (20KB61)

2217	A649YOX	Leyland Tiger TRCTL11/3R	Marshall Campaigner	B56F	1983	MoD, 1996 (20KB77)		
2218	A624YOX	Leyland Tiger TRCTL11/3R	Marshall Campaigner	B57F	1983	MoD, 1996 (20KB66)		
2219	A622YOX	Leyland Tiger TRCTL11/3R	Marshall Campaigner	B57F	1983	MoD, 1996 (20KB53)		
2220	LIL5851	Leyland Tiger TRCTL11/3R	Plaxton Paramount 3200 E	C53F	1983	Lancaster, 1993		
2221	HHJ372Y	Leyland Tiger TRCTL11/2R	Alexander TE	C53F	1983	Eastern Counties, 1998		
2222	RIL1055	Leyland Tiger TRCTL11/2R	Plaxton Paramount 3500	C49F	1983	Yelloway, Rochdale, 1985		
2223	A695OHJ	Leyland Tiger TRCTL11/2R	Alexander TE	C53F	1983	SWT, 1998		
2224	A691OHJ	Leyland Tiger TRCTL11/2R	Alexander TE	C53F	1983	SWT, 1998		
2228	595JPU	Volvo B10M-60	Plaxton Expressliner	C46FT	1991			
2229	UFX330	Volvo B10M-60	Plaxton Expressliner	C46FT	1991			
2812	WDR665M	Leyland National 11351/2R		BC41F	1974	Plymouth Citybus, 1989		
2814	MOD814P	Leyland National 11351/1R		B50F	1975	Western National, 1983		
2820	MOD820P	Leyland National 11351/1R		B50F	1975	Western National, 1983		
2821	MOD821P	Leyland National 11351/1R		B50F	1975	Western National, 1983		

2823-2882

		Leyland National 11351A/1R		B50F	1976-80	Western National, 1983		
2823	MOD823P	2829	MOD829P	2879	FDV775V	2880	FDV776V	2882	FDV778V
2828	MOD828P	2830	MOD852P					

2884	KPA362P	Leyland National 11351/1R		B49F	1975	Red Bus Services, 1997		
2919	OJF419P	Leyland National 10351/1R		B41F	1976	County Bus, Atherington, 1990		

2920	VBG114V	Leyland National 2 NL116AL11/1R		B52F	1980	MTL (North),1998		
2921	VBG127V	Leyland National 2 NL116AL11/1R		B49F	1980	MTL (North),1998		
2923	XLV143W	Leyland National 2 NL116AL11/1R		B53F	1981	MTL (Liverbus),1998		
2924	VBG120V	Leyland National 2 NL116AL11/1R		B53F	1980	MTL (North),1998		
2925	VBG118V	Leyland National 2 NL116AL11/1R		B53F	1980	HMB, Gateshead,1998		
2926	LRB211W	Leyland National 2 NL116AL11/1R		B49F	1981	Border, Burnley,1998		
2927	DOC44V	Leyland National 2 NL116AL11/1R		B50F	1980	Border, Burnley,1998		
2928	AFM3W	Leyland National 2 NL116AL11/1R		B52F	1981	Arriva North West (M),1998		
2929	LRB202W	Leyland National 2 NL116AL11/1R		B52F	1980	Stephenson, Rochford,1998		
2930	HHH370V	Leyland National 2 NL116AL11/1R		B52F	1980	Stagecoach Ribble,1998		
2931	DMS22V	Leyland National 2 NL116AL11/1R		B52F	1980	Stagecoach Red & White,1998		
2932	RSG815V	Leyland National 2 NL116AL11/1R		B52F	1980	Stagecoach Red & White,1998		

3131	AFJ692T	Bristol LH6L	Plaxton Supreme III Express	C41F	1979	Western National, 1983		
3306	AFJ726T	Bristol LH6L	Plaxton Supreme III Express	C41F	1979	Western National, 1983		
3307	AFJ727T	Bristol LH6L	Plaxton Supreme III Express	C41F	1979	Western National, 1983		
3308	AFJ728T	Bristol LH6L	Plaxton Supreme III Express	C41F	1979	Western National, 1983		
3309	AFJ729T	Bristol LH6L	Plaxton Supreme III Express	C41F	1979	Western National, 1983		
3551	GMS280S	Leyland Leopard PSU3E/4R	Alexander AYS	B53F	1978	Moffat & Williamson, 1994		
3553	GWV925V	Leyland Leopard PSU3E/4R	Plaxton Supreme IV Express	C53F	1980	Clews, Perry Barr, 1996		
3554	YSF85S	Leyland Leopard PSU3E/4R	Alexander AYS	B53F	1977	Stevensons, 1996		
3555	GMS295S	Leyland Leopard PSU3E/4R	Alexander AYS	B53F	1978	Stevensons, 1996		
3556	MFR18P	Leyland Leopard PSU3C/4R	Alexander AYS	B53F	1976	Stevensons, 1996		
3558	PRA114R	Leyland Leopard PSU3C/4R	Alexander AT	C49F	1976	Blue Bus, Horwich, 1996		
3559	PRA115R	Leyland Leopard PSU3C/4R	Alexander AT	B53F	1976	Blue Bus, Horwich, 1996		
3561	GLS267S	Leyland Leopard PSU3E/4R	Alexander AT	B53F	1978	Blue Bus, Horwich, 1996		
3562	GLS275S	Leyland Leopard PSU3E/4R	Alexander AT	B49F	1978	Blue Bus, Horwich, 1996		
3563	TSJ74S	Leyland Leopard PSU3D/4R	Alexander AYS	B53F	1978	Blue Bus, Horwich, 1997		
3564	YSF97S	Leyland Leopard PSU3E/4R	Alexander AYS	B53F	1978	Blue Bus, Horwich, 1997		
3565	YSF99S	Leyland Leopard PSU3E/4R	Alexander AYS	B53F	1977	Blue Bus, Horwich, 1997		
3566	GMS291S	Leyland Leopard PSU3E/4R	Alexander AYS	BC53F	1977	Stevensons, 1996		
3567	GMS310S	Leyland Leopard PSU3E/4R	Alexander AYS	BC53F	1977	Stevensons, 1996		

6000	TJI4681	Leyland Tiger TRCTL11/3RH	Berkhof Everest 370	C51FT	1986	Smith's, Portland, 1998		
6001	TJI4682	Bedford YNV Venturer	Jonckheere Jubilee P50	C53F	1985	Smith's, Portland, 1998		
6002	TJI4683	Leyland Tiger TRCTL11/3RZ	Plaxton Paramount 3500	C50F	1984	Smith's, Portland, 1998		
6003	CAV624V	Volvo B58-56	Duple Dominant II Express	C53F	1979	Smith's, Portland, 1998		
6004	AHT206J	Bristol RELL6L	Eastern Coach Works	B50F	1971	Smith's, Portland, 1998		
6005	E96OUH	Freight Rover Sherpa(Ford)	Carlyle Citybus 2	B20F	1987	Smith's, Portland, 1998		
6007	E158RNY	Freight Rover Sherpa(Ford)	Carlyle Citybus 2	B20F	1988	Smith's, Portland, 1998		
6008	F202YKG	Freight Rover Sherpa(Ford)	Carlyle Citybus 2	B20F	1988	Smith's, Portland, 1998		
6009	C333GFJ	Ford Transit 190	Robin Hood	B16F	1986	Smith's, Portland, 1998		
6010	C314DRH	Ford Transit 190	Carlyle	B20F	1986	Smith's, Portland, 1998		

7001	TXI2426	Volvo B10M-61	Van Hool Alizée	C53F	1988	Allisons Cs, Dunfermline, 1994
7002	RIL1057	Volvo B10M-61	Van Hool Alizée	C53F	1988	Taylors Travel, Tintinhull, 1993
7003	KDU648	Volvo B10M-61	Van Hool Alizée	C49FT	1983	Taylors Travel, Tintinhull, 1993
7004	RIL1056	Volvo B10M-61	Plaxton Paramount 3200 II	C53F	1985	Taylors Travel, Tintinhull, 1993
7005	RIL1058	Volvo B10M-61	LAG Galaxy	C39FT	1982	Taylors Travel, Tintinhull, 1993
7010	FYD864T	AEC Reliance 6U3ZR	Plaxton Supreme IV	C53F	1979	Taylors Travel, Tintinhull, 1993
7018	KIW5940	Leyland Leopard PSU5D/4R	Plaxton Supreme IV	C53F	1981	Birmingham Omnibus, 1995
7019	CSU993	Leyland Leopard PSU5C/4R	Plaxton Supreme V	C53F	1981	Birmingham Coach Co, 1995
7020	YSV739	Leyland Leopard PSU5C/4R	Plaxton Supreme V	C53F	1981	Birmingham Coach Co, 1995
7022	RIL1053	Dennis Javelin 12SDA1907	Plaxton Paramount 3200 III	C53F	1989	Beeline, Warminster, 1996
7023	UFX940	Leyland Tiger TRCTL11/2R	Alexander TE	C53F	1983	Eastern Counties, 1998
7024	HHJ375Y	Leyland Tiger TRCTL11/2R	Alexander TE	C53F	1983	Essex Buses (T), 1998
7025	HHJ376Y	Leyland Tiger TRCTL11/2R	Alexander TE	C53F	1983	Essex Buses (T), 1998
7026	A694OHJ	Leyland Tiger TRCTL11/2R	Alexander TE	C53F	1983	Eastern Counties, 1998
8001	EYP29V	Bedford YMT (Cummins)	Plaxton Supreme IV	C53F	1980	ComfyLux, Cattistock, 1990
8002	YNF348T	Bedford YMT	Plaxton Supreme IV	C53F	1978	ComfyLux, Cattistock, 1990
8003	CMJ2T	Bedford YMT (Cummins)	Plaxton Supreme III	C53F	1978	ComfyLux, Cattistock, 1990
8004	RBW176P	Bedford YRT	Duple Dominant	C53F	1976	ComfyLux, Cattistock, 1990
8006	PYD427P	Bedford YRT	Plaxton Supreme III	C45F	1975	ComfyLux, Cattistock, 1990
8007	KYC604N	Bedford YRQ	Plaxton Elite III	C45F	1975	ComfyLux, Cattistock, 1990
8008	NEJ26R	Bedford YMT (Cummins)	Duple Dominant	C53F	1977	ComfyLux, Cattistock, 1990
8013	KFX791	Leyland Tiger TRCTL11/3R	Plaxton Paramount 3200	C50FT	1983	Arlington demonstrator, 1983
8014	PUS157W	Leyland Leopard PSU3F/4R	Alexander AYS	B53F	1981	Smith's, Portland, 1990
8015	RIL1069	Leyland Tiger TRCTL11/3ARZM	Plaxton Paramount 3500 III	C45FT	1990	Hill's of Tredegar, 1991
8016	USV821	Leyland Tiger TRCTL11/3R	Plaxton Paramount 3200	C46FT	1984	
8017	XOJ431T	Bedford YMT (Cummins)	Plaxton Supreme IV Express	C53F	1979	Bowen, Birmingham, 1991
8018	EUK547V	Bedford YMT (Cummins)	Plaxton Supreme IV Express	C53F	1980	Bowen, Birmingham, 1991
8019	XOJ432T	Bedford YMT (Cummins)	Plaxton Supreme IV Express	C53F	1979	Bowen, Birmingham, 1991
8020	EUK546V	Bedford YMT (Cummins)	Plaxton Supreme IV Express	C53F	1980	Bowen, Birmingham, 1991
8021	IIL2490	Leyland Tiger TRCTL11/2RH	Plaxton Paramount 3200 IIE	C53F	1986	Lancaster, 1993
8023	FDC418V	Leyland Leopard PSU3E/4R	Plaxton Supreme IV Exp	B53F	1980	Cleveland Transit, 1994
8025	8683LJ	Dennis Javelin 11SDL1905	Duple 320	C53F	1988	Brighton & Hove, 1997
8026	OJI8786	Dennis Javelin 11SDL1905	Duple 320	C53F	1988	Brighton & Hove, 1997
8027	HHJ381Y	Leyland Tiger TRCTL11/3R	Alexander TE	C53F	1983	Eastern Counties, 1999
8028	HHJ382Y	Leyland Tiger TRCTL11/3R	Alexander TE	C53F	1983	Eastern Counties, 1999
8057	TPR34	Leyland Tiger TRCTL11/3R	Plaxton Supreme V	C53F	1982	, 1998
9001	GIL1684	Volvo B10M-61	Van Hool Alizée	C53F	1988	Allisons, Dunfermline, 1994
9002	TJI3135	Volvo B10M-61	Ikarus Blue Danube	C53F	1988	Bere Regis & District, 1994
9003	TJI3136	Volvo B10M-61	Ikarus Blue Danube	C53F	1988	Bere Regis & District, 1994
9004	TJI3137	Volvo B10M-61	Ikarus Blue Danube	C53F	1988	Bere Regis & District, 1994
9005	TJI3138	Volvo B10M-61	Ikarus Blue Danube	C53F	1988	Bere Regis & District, 1994
9007	TJI3134	Volvo B10M-61	Duple Caribbean	C55F	1984	Bere Regis & District, 1994
9008	USV823	Volvo B10M-61	Duple Dominant IV	C53F	1983	Bere Regis & District, 1994
9010	ENF568Y	Volvo B10M-61	Duple Dominant IV	C53F	1983	Bere Regis & District, 1994
9011	ENF564Y	Volvo B10M-61	Duple Dominant IV	C53F	1983	Bere Regis & District, 1994
9023	SFX785R	Bedford YMT	Plaxton Supreme VIII	C53F	1977	Bere Regis & District, 1994
9039	BGS292X	Bedford YNT	Plaxton Supreme V Express	C53F	1982	Dorset CC, 1996
9040	YKW655T	Bedford YMT	Duple Dominant II	C53F	1979	Dorset CC, 1996
9041	FDU805T	Bedford YMT	Plaxton Supreme IV Express	C53F	1979	Dorset CC, 1996
9044	YEU6V	Bedford YMT	Plaxton Supreme IV	C53F	1979	Scarlet Cs, Minehead, 1997
9045	D659WEY	Bedford YNT	Plaxton Paramount 3200 II	C53F	1986	Nefyn Coaches, 1997
9046	ENJ913V	Leyland National 11351/2R		B52F	1979	Stagecoach South (SC), 1998
9047	ORX107X	Bedford YMT	Plaxton Supreme V Express	C53F	1982	Horesman, Reading, 1998
9048	KGM328W	Leyland Leopard PSU3F/4R	Duple Dominant	C53F	1981	Horseman, Reading, 1998
9052	YPD116Y	Leyland Tiger TRCTL11/3R	Duple Dominant	C53F	1983	Dorset CC, 1998
9053	AHG947R	Leyland Leopard PSU3E/4R	Plaxton Supreme III	C53F	1977	Travelmate, Wareham, 1998
9054	XFG28Y	Leyland National 2 NL116AL11/1R		B49F	1983	Brighton & Hove, 1998
9055	XFG27Y	Leyland National 2 NL116AL11/1R		B49F	1983	Brighton & Hove, 1998
9056	XFG26Y	Leyland National 2 NL116AL11/1R		B49F	1983	Brighton & Hove, 1998
9057	J732KBC	Dennis Javelin 11SDL1921	Plaxton Paramount 3200 III	C53F	1982	Jones, Login, 1998
9058	G802XLO	Volvo B10M-60	Plaxton Paramount 3200 III	C53F	1990	Capital West Drayton, 1998
9059	G803XLO	Volvo B10M-60	Plaxton Paramount 3200 III	C53F	1990	Channel, Bow, 1998
9060	J329LLK	Volvo B10M-60	Plaxton Paramount 3200 III	C53F	1992	Capital West Drayton, 1998

Ancilliary vehicles:-

43	HRO987V	Bedford YMT	Duple Dominant II	TV	1979	
45	KKW525W	Bedford YMT	Duple Dominant II	TV	1981	
46	EKU75V	Bedford YMT	Duple Dominant II	TV	1980	Billies, Mexborough, 1992
329	C891GYD	Ford Transit 190	Dormobile	RV	1986	Western National, 1983
4944	E944LAE	Iveco Daily 49.10	Robin Hood City Nippy	TV	1987	Wessex, 1998
7468	C468BHY	Mercedes-Benz L608D	Reeve Burgess	TV	1986	
7473	C473BHY	Mercedes-Benz L608D	Reeve Burgess	TV	1986	
8158	C158TLF	Volvo B9M	Plaxton Paramount 3200 II	TV	1985	Capital, West Drayton, 1997
8159	C159TLF	Volvo B9M	Plaxton Paramount 3200 II	TV	1985	Capital, West Drayton, 1997
8317	G229EOA	Iveco Daily 49.10	Carlyle Dailybus 2	TV	1989	
8752	E752YDY	Volvo B9M	Plaxton Paramount 3200 III	TV	1988	Hallmark, 1998
8939	AFJ739T	Bristol LH6L	Plaxton Supreme III Express	TV	1979	Provincial, 1997

Previous Registrations:

595JPU	H227CFJ, H228CFJ	M802UYA	M805UYA	RJI2720	A463HJF
620HOD	A897KCL	M804UYA	M802UYA	SSU437	A985UFB
865GAT	E814XHS	M805UYA	M804UYA	TDZ3265	From new
4384LJ	A580KVU	M857XHY	M47BEG	TJI3134	A600LJT
8683LJ	E474FWV	MBZ7140	OTO151R	TJI3135	E221GCG
BOK258T	SKF1T	NEJ26R	PDY42R, 279NDE	TJI3136	E222GCG
CSU993	SND291X	ODT232	D504GHY	TJI3137	E223GCG
D659WEY	D933XWP, 610LYB	OIL9262	F615XWY	TJI3138	E224GCG
ESK812	VWX362X 452WAL YNA483X	OIL9264	F620XWY	TJI4681	C137SPB
GIL1684	E631UNE, LSK813	OIL9263	F617XWY	TJI4682	465YUR
IIL2490	C90MHG	OJI8768	E475FWV	TJI4683	A33FVN
J185LGE	J259WFS, IIB1618	PSU527	D510HHW	TXI2426	E643UNE, LSK873
KDU648	MSU612Y	PYD427P	LPA76P, 865GAT	UFX330	H226CFJ, H229CFJ
KFX791	FNM854Y	RBW176P	RBW176P, 595JPU	UFX940	A696OHJ
KIW5940	PNW340W	RIL1053	F173TRU, RJI8602, F576AEL, 40FER	USV821	A679KDV
KTA986V	FDV803V, 925GTA	RIL1055	A68GBN, 10TV	USV823	ENF560Y
KYC604N	JNR885N, 620HOD	RIL1056	B904SPR, RFP6	WYY752	D600GHY
LIL5851	A620ATV	RIL1057	E313OPR, 8TEN	YSV739	SND294X
LSU788	D601GHY	RIL1058	B829BYA, GDS3	YTA792S	VOD613S, 925GTA
M19ABC	M496JRY	RIL1059	G155JBO, 10HR		

Allocations:

Bath (London Road) - Badgerline - Streamline

Outstations: - Chippenham, Colerne, Devizes, Frome, Melksham, Radstock and Trowbridge

Iveco	8300	8301	8346						
Mercedes-Benz	3805	3806	3809	3810	3811	3813	3814	3815	
	3816	3817	3818	3819	3821	3822	3868	3870	
	3871	3872	3873	3874	3875	3876	3877	3878	
	3879	3880	3881	3882	3883	3884	3885	3886	
	3887	3889	3890	3891	3892	3893	3894	3895	
	3896	3897	3898	3912	3913	3914	3915	7802	
	8306	8307	8308	8310	8311	8312	8314	8315	
Dart	206	209	210	211	212	213	214	215	
	216	217	218	219	220	221	223	224	
	225	232	233	234	235	236	237	238	
	239	240	241	1726	1727	1728	1729	1730	
	1731								
Lance	134	135	136	137	138	140	141	142	
	1221	1222	1223	1225	1228	1229	1230	9978	
Volvo B10M bus	107	108	109	110	111	112	113		
Volvo B10B	1914	1915	1916	1917	1918	1919	1920		
DAF/Ikarus	8302	8303	8304	8305					
Javelin Expressliner	290	291	292	293	297	298	299		
Volvo B10M coach	2501	2502	2503						
Volvo B9	8752								
Bristol K	8583								
Bristol VR	5534	5551	5562	8600	8605	8606	8608	8615	
	8616	8620	8621						
Olympian	8656	8657	9001	9002	9003	9004	9005	9006	
	9007	9008	9009	9010	9540	9501	9502	9503	
	9504	9505	9515	9526	9527	9535	9536	9538	
	9541	9542							

Bristol (Easton Road, Lawrence Hill) - City Line - Durbins

Iveco	7591	7592	7596	7610	7615	7618		
Mercedes-Benz	3817	7801	7837	7875	7876	7877	7878	7879
	7880	7881	7882	7883	7884	7885	7886	7887
	7889	7890	7891	7892	7893	7894	7895	7896
Tecnobus	8101	8102						
Dart	1503	1504	1506	1507	1508	1509	1510	
	1511	1512	1513	1514	1515	1516	1520	1521
	1522	1523	1524	1525	1526	1527	1528	1529
	1530	1531	1532	1533	1534	1535	1536	1537
	1538	1547	1548	1549	1550	1551	1552	1553
	1554	1556	1557	1558	1559	1719		
Lynx	1646	1647	1648	1649	1650	1651	1652	1653
	1654	1655	1656	1657	1658	1659	1660	1661
	1662							
Leopard /Tiger	2203	8212	8213	8214				
Toyota-Optimo	8316							
DAF coach	8200	8205						
Setra coach	8320							
Volvo B10M coach	2504	2600	2601					
Bristol VR	5073	5147	5531	5541	5560	5564		
Olympian	5000	5001	9529	9537	9539	9543	9544	9545
	9546	9547	9548	9549	9550	9551	9552	9553
	9554	9555	9556	9557	9558	9559	9560	9561
	9562	9563	9565	9567	9661	9662	9663	9664
	9665	9667	9968	9669	9670	9671	9672	9673
	9674	9675	9676	9677	9678	9679	9680	9681
	9682	9683	9684	9685	9686	9687		

Bristol (Marlborough Street Bus Station) - Badgerline

Iveco	8342	8343	8345					
Mercedes-Benz	3822	3823	3824	3916	8313			
Dart	201	202	203	204	205	207	208	226
	242	243	244	245	246	247	248	249
	250	251	252	253	254	255		
Volvo B10M Bus	102							
Volvo B10B	1910	1912	1913					
Lance	121	122	123	124	125	126	127	128
	129	130	131	132	133	1224	1226	1227
Volvo B10M coach	2500	2510						
Citybus	5708	5709	5710	5711	5714			
Olympian	8610	8613	8614	9506	9507	9508	9509	9510
	9511	9512	9514	9516	9530	9531	9532	9534
	9655	9656	9657	9658	9659	9660	9566	

Bristol (Muller Road, Horfield) - City Line

Iveco	7616	7617	7619					
Mercedes-Benz	3909	3910	3911	7803	7804	7805	7806	7807
	7808	7809	7810	7811	7812	7813	7814	7815
	7816	7817	7818	7819	7820	7821	7822	7823
	7824	7825	7826	7827	7828	7829	7830	7831
	7832	7833	7834	7835	7836	7854	7855	7856
	7857	7871	7872	7873	7874			
Dart	1517	1518	1519	1539	1540	1541	1542	1543
	1544	1545	1546					
Lynx	1600	1619	1620	1621	1622	1623	1624	1625
	1626	1627	1628	1629	1630	1631	1643	1645
Olympian	9528	9564	9568	9601	9602	9603	9604	9605
	9606	9607	9608	9609	9610	9611	9612	9613
	9614	9615	9616	9617	9618	9619	9620	9621
	9622	9623	9624	9625	9626	9627	9628	9629
	9630	9631	9632	9638				

City Line 9664, R664NHY, is a Northern Counties Palatine II seen in Penn Street, Bristol shortly after delivery. It is based at Lawrence Hill depot. In 1999 a new depot will open at Hengrove to replace Muller Road and Winterstoke Road. *Mark Lyons*

Bristol (Easton Road, Lawrence Hill) - Wessex - Sky Blue Buses

Dennis Javelin	6201	6202	6203	6204	6205	6206	6207	6208
	6209	6210	6211	6212				
DAF coach	6301	6302	6303					
Volvo B10M coach	6130	6131	6138	6139	6154	6157	6158	6159
	6160	6161	6162	6163	6166	6167	6169	6174
	6175	6176	6177	6178	6179	6180	6181	6182
	6183	6184	6185					
National	6707	6710	6712	6801	6802	6803	6804	6805
	6806							
Volvo B6								

Bristol (Winterstoke Road, Ashton) - City Line

Mercedes-Benz	7838	7839	7840	7841	7842	7843	7844	7845
	7846	7847	7848	7849	7850	7851	7852	7853
	7858	7859	7860	7861	7862	7863	7864	7865
	7866	7867	7868	7869	7870	7897	7898	7901
	7902	7903	7904	7905	7906	7907		
Dart	1701	1702	1703	1704	1705	1706	1707	1708
	1709	1710	1711	1712	1713	1718	1720	1721
	1722	1723	1724	1725				
Lynx	1601	1602	1603	1604	1605	1606	1607	1608
	1609	1610	1611	1612	1613	1614	1615	1616
	1617	1618	1632	1633	1634	1636	1637	1638
	1639	1640	1641	1642				
Olympian	9633	9634	9635	9636	9637	9639	9640	9641
	9642	9643	9644	9645	9646	9647	9648	
	9649	9650	9651	9652	9653	9654		

Wells (Prior Road) - Badgerline

Mercedes-Benz	3801	3802	3803	3804	3899	3904	3905	3906
	3907	3908						
Dart	228							
Lynx	3614	3615	3616					
Volvo B10M Bus	103	104						
Volvo B10BLE	1901	1902	1903	1904	1905	1906	1907	1908
	1909							

Weston-super-Mare (Searle Crescent) - Badgerline

Mercedes-Benz	3800	3850	3851	3852	3853	3854	3855	3856
	3857	3858	3859	3860	3861	3862	3863	3864
	3865	3866	3867	3869	3901	3902	3903	
Dart	227	229	230	231	256	257	258	259
	260	261	262	263	264	1644	1714	1715
	1716	1717						
Lynx	3610	3611	3612	3613				
Volvo B10M bus	100	101	105	106				
Bristol VR	8617	8619	8622					
Olympian	8609	8611	8612	9688	9689	9690	9691	
Citybus	5700	5701	5702	5703	5704	5705	5706	5707

Unallocated (Bristol)

MercedesBenz	3912	7899			Peugeot		6145
Iveco	7610				Olympian		9503
Dart	1721	1722	1723	1724	1725		

Southern National

Bridgwater (East Quay) - Southern National

Transit	153	154	155	160	173	174	176	183
	186	316	373					
Iveco	523	549						
Mercedes-Benz	727	733	748	772	780	968	971	
Leopard	3553	3554	3555	3562	3563			
Tiger	2214	2215	2217	2220				
Bristol VR	1097	1125		1157	1166		1168	1169	1193

Bridport (Tannery Road) - Southern National

Transit	448	449			
Iveco	221				
Mercedes-Benz	650	651	766	863	864
Volvo coach	9058	9059	9060		
Bristol LH	94	3131			
Dart	802	817	818	819	820
National	2828				
Tiger	5				
Bristol VR	605	1161	1163		

Dorchester (Grove Trading Estate) - Southern National

Outstations - Bere Regis; Bovington; Sherborne and Hazelbury Bryan

Transit	161	333	341	369	371	383	450	
Mercedes-Benz	775							
Bedford	8004	8020	9023	9039	9040	9041	9044	9047
Dart	826	827	828	829				
Leopard	9053							
National	2823	2830	2884	2921	2923	2924	9046	
Volvo	9001	9002	9003	9004	9005	9007	9008	9010
	9011							
Bristol VR	1121							

Martock (A38) - Southern National (Comfylux Travel)

Tiger	12	8013	8027	8028	8057
Leopard	8023				
Javelin	8025	8026			
Bedford	8001	8002	8003	8006	8007	8017	8018	8019

Portland (Victoria Square) - Smiths Coaches

Ivecot	6011	6012	6013	6014	6015
Bedford	6001				
Tiger	6000	6002			
Bristol RE	6004				
Volvo coach	2228	2229	6003		

Taunton (Hamilton Road) - Southern National

Outstation - Bridgwater

Iveco	50	53	124	529				
Transit	150	151	157	158	159	163	166	167
	179	184	185	187	305	319	323	325
	367							
Mercedes-Benz	728	731	732	734	735	736	737	740
	741	742	743	744	757	758	760	761
	762	773	781	782	783	784	786	787
	788	789	790	862	953	954	958	959
	969	970						
Bristol LH	3307	3309						
Dart	806	807	808	824	825			
Leopard	3551	3558	3561	3566	3567	8014		
National	2928	2929	2931					
Tiger	11	2213	2216	2218	2219	2221	2222	2223
	2224	8015	8016	8020	8021			
Bristol VR	1110	1111	1192					
Olympian	1813							

Streamline's livery of red and white is seen on Iveco minibus 8343, J143KPX, one of four of the type transferred from Provincial in 1997, shortly after the operation was acquired by Badgerline. The Streamline operation includes larger single-deck buses in the form of Ikarus-bodied DAF single-decks.
TS Powell

Tintinhull (Townsend Garage) - Taylors

Iveco	52	514			
Mercedes-Benz	730	791			
AEC	7010				
Leopard	280	7018	7019	7020	
Javelin	7022				
Tiger	7023	7024	7025	7026	
Volvo	7001	7002	7003	7004	7005

Weymouth (Edward Street) - Southern National - Dorset Transit

Transit	152	165	169	191	304	315	337	339
	340	345	347	360	361	368	374	377
	380	385	393	415	432	451		
Mercedes-Benz	701	702	703	704	705	706	707	708
	709	710	719	720	721	722	774	776
	854	855	856	857	858	859	860	861
	950	951						
Dart	821	822	823					
Bristol LHS	1634							
Javelin	9057							
National	2882	2919	2926	2927	2930	9054	9055	9056
Bristol VR	555	559	560	574	601	603	604	608
	934	942	1158	1159	1170			

Yeovil (Reckleford) - Southern National

Transit	300	307	314	318	332	359	362	365
	426	428	436					
Iveco	222	513	522	530				
Mercedes-Benz	725	726	729	738	739	745	746	747
	749	751	756	759	770	771	785	952
	960	961	962	963	964	965	966	967
Bedford	9045							
Bristol LH	3306							
Leopard	3556	3559	3564	3565				
National	2812	2814	2820	2821	2879	2880	2920	2925
	2932							
Bristol VR	1122	1167						

Unallocated (Southern National) including group store.

Transit	156	161	164	168	170	171	172	177
	178	180	181	182	188	189	190	306
	322	334	338	342	352	363	364	372
	389	6009	6010					
Sherpa	6005	6007	6008					
Mercedes-Benz	652							
Iveco	54	113	125	223	227	232	397	506
	508	511	512	520	524			
Bedford	8008	9030	9043					
Bristol LH	3308							
National	2829	2850						
Bristol VR	1111	1160						

Note: All vehicles were new to Bristol Omnibus Co (until 1986), City Line or Badgerline (until 1996) except where shown.

Named Vehicles: 6157 *Spirit of Cardiff*; 6158 *Spirit of Newport*; 6182 *Spirit of Glastonbury*; 6183 *Spirit of Burnham-on-Sea*; 6201 *Spirit of Clevedon*; 6202 *Spirit of Weston-super-Mare*; 6203 *Spirit of Keynsham*; 6204 *Spirit of Kingswood*; 6205 *Spirit of Worle*; 6206 *Spirit of Gordano*; 6207 *Spirit of Portishead*; 6208 *Spirit of Bristol*; 6209 *Spirit of Wells*; 6210 *Spirit of Clifton*; 6211 *Spirit of Eastville*; 6212 *Spirit of Street.*: 8583 *Prince Bladud*, 8600 *I.K.Brunel*, 8601 *William Herschel*, 8605 *Jane Austen*, 8606 *Minerva*, 8608 *John Wood*, 8615 *Sally Lunn*, 8616 *Beau Nash*, 8617 *Ralph Allen*, 8620 *King Edgar*, 8621 *Dr William Oliver*.

FIRST WESTERN NATIONAL

Western National - Red Bus

First Western National Buses Ltd, Western House, 38 Lemon Street, Truro, TR1 2NS

1000	BFR302R	Leyland Atlantean AN68A/2R	East Lancashire	B50/36F	1977	Partridge, Hadleigh, 1995	
1001	JFV311S	Leyland Atlantean AN68A/2R	East Lancashire	B50/36F	1978	Blackpool, 1991	
1002	JFV312S	Leyland Atlantean AN68A/2R	East Lancashire	B50/36F	1978	Blackpool, 1991	
1003	VDV141S	Bristol VRT/SL3/6LXB	Eastern Coach Works	CO43/31F	1978		
1006	VDV144S	Bristol VRT/SL3/6LXB	Eastern Coach Works	CO43/31F	1978		
1083	JNU138N	Bristol VRT/SL2/6LX(6LXB)	Eastern Coach Works	B39/31F	1975	Badgerline, 1988	
1084	HTC728N	Bristol VRT/SL2/6LX(6LXB)	Eastern Coach Works	B43/31F	1975	Badgerline, 1988	
1085	HTC726N	Bristol VRT/SL2/6LX	Eastern Coach Works	B43/31F	1975	Durbins, 1996	
1100	SFJ100R	Bristol VRT/SL3/6LXB	Eastern Coach Works	B43/31F	1977	Devon General, 1987	
1105	SFJ105R	Bristol VRT/SL3/6LXB	Eastern Coach Works	B43/31F	1977	Devon General, 1987	
1106	SFJ106R	Bristol VRT/SL3/6LXB	Eastern Coach Works	B43/31F	1977		
1108	VDV108S	Bristol VRT/SL3/6LXB	Eastern Coach Works	B43/31F	1977		
1109	UTO832S	Bristol VRT/SL3/501(6LXB)	Eastern Coach Works	B43/31F	1977	Devon General, 1987	

1114-1131

Bristol VRT/SL3/6LXB — Eastern Coach Works — B43/31F — 1977-78

1114	VDV114S	1118	VDV118S	1120	VDV120S	1123	XDV603S	1129	XDV609S
1116	VDV116S	1119	VDV119S	1121	VDV121S	1128	XDV608S	1131	XDV601S
1117	VDV117S								

1132-1183

Bristol VRT/SL3/6LXB — Eastern Coach Works — B43/31F — 1978-80

1132	AFJ697T	1137	AFJ702T	1142	AFJ744T	1148	AFJ750T	1174	FDV806V
1133	AFJ698T	1138	AFJ703T	1143	AFJ745T	1149	AFJ751T	1175	FDV807V
1134	AFJ699T	1139	AFJ704T	1144	AFJ746T	1153	AFJ760T	1176	FDV808V
1135	AFJ700T	1140	AFJ705T	1145	AFJ747T	1154	AFJ761T	1182	FDV814V
1136	AFJ701T	1141	AFJ706T	1147	AFJ749T	1155	AFJ762T	1183	FDV815V

1187	BEP968V	Bristol VRT/SL3/501(6LXB)	Eastern Coach Works	B43/31F	1979	South Wales, 1989

1197-1226

Bristol VRT/SL3/6LXB — Eastern Coach Works — B43/31F — 1980-81

1197	LFJ841W	1200	LFJ844W	1202	LFJ846W	1220	LFJ867W	1225	LFJ872W
1198	LFJ842W	1201	LFJ845W	1203	LFJ847W	1224	LFJ871W	1226	LFJ873W
1199	LFJ843W								

The Mercedes-Benz minibus, Dennis Dart and Bristol VR dominate the Western National fleet. Photographed in Penzance bus station is Mercedes-Benz 6332, K332OAF, an 811 model dating from 1992. The red and blue flag vinyls have been removed from the buses in recent months.
Tony Wilson

Dennis Dart 4452, R452CCV is seen at Plymouth with route branding for service to the north Devon town of Barnstaple through Tavistock and Okehampton. The majority of the Darts are allocated to the Devon engineering area from where vehicles are allocated to outstations. In addition to those listed, many of these have sub-bases. One example is Kingsbridge, which houses vehicles from the Dartmouth outstation.
Phillip Stephenson

1227	EWS747W	Bristol VRT/SL3/680(6LXB)	Eastern Coach Works	BC43/31F	1981	Badgerline, 1990

1228-1237

Bristol VRT/SL3/501(6LXB)* Eastern Coach Works B43/31F 1978-79 South Wales, 1990
*1232 is VRT/SL3/501

1228	RTH929S	1230	WTH942T	1232	WTH945T	1234	WTH950T	1236	WTH961T
1229	TWN936S	1231	WTH943T	1233	WTH946T	1235	WTH951T	1237	BEP966V

1238-1251

Bristol VRT/SL3/6LXB Eastern Coach Works R43/31F* 1980-81 Thamesway. 1991-92
*1238 is B39/31F

1238	KOO785V	1241w	XHK231X	1244	UAR589W	1248	UAR590W	1250	XHK220X
1239	UAR595W	1242	XHK228X	1245	UAR594W	1249	XHK223X	1251	XHK230X
1240	XHK225X	1243	UAR586W	1246	UAR597W				

1252	PHY697S	Bristol VRT/SL3/6LXB	Eastern Coach Works	B43/31F	1977	City Line, 1994
1253	TWS915T	Bristol VRT/SL3/6LXB	Eastern Coach Works	B43/31F	1979	City Line, 1994
1254	AHU516V	Bristol VRT/SL3/6LXB	Eastern Coach Works	B43/31F	1980	City Line, 1994
1256	JWT758V	Bristol VRT/SL3/6LXB	Eastern Coach Works	B43/31F	1979	Yorkshire Rider, 1996
1257	PWY38W	Bristol VRT/SL3/6LXB	Eastern Coach Works	B43/31F	1980	Yorkshire Rider, 1996
1258	STW34W	Bristol VRT/SL3/6LXB	Eastern Coach Works	B43/31F	1981	City Line, 1996
1259	URF668S	Bristol VRT/SL3/501(6LXB)	Eastern Coach Works	B43/31F	1978	Durbins, 1992
1260	PEU518R	Bristol VRT/SL3/6LXB	Eastern Coach Works	B43/31F	1977	Bristol, 1998
1261	RHT503S	Bristol VRT/SL3/6LXB	Eastern Coach Works	B43/27D	1978	Hampshire (P), 1999
1262	NTC573R	Bristol VRT/SL3/6LXB	Eastern Coach Works	B43/27D	1977	Hampshire (P), 1999
1300	OCK997K	Bristol VRT/SL2/6LX	Eastern Coach Works	B39/31F	1972	Crosville Cymru, 1987
1301	PTT99R	Bristol VRT/SL3/6LXB	Eastern Coach Works	B43/31F	1977	Western National, 1983
1302	RTH926S	Bristol VRT/SL3/6LXB	Eastern Coach Works	B43/31F	1972	SWT, 1989
1303	FDV785V	Bristol VRT/SL3/6LXB	Eastern Coach Works	B43/31F	1978	Western National, 1983
1304	XAN431T	Bristol VRT/SL3/6LXB	Eastern Coach Works	B43/34F	1978	Berry's Taunton, 1998
1305	AJH855T	Bristol VRT/SL3/6LXB	Eastern Coach Works	B43/34F	1978	Berry's Taunton, 1998
1306	LFJ860W	Bristol VRT/SL3/6LXB	Eastern Coach Works	B43/31F	1981	Devon General, 1990

The Bristol VR still dominates the Western National double-deck fleet having been allocated a high proportion of production towards the end of the model. Indeed, with one-hundred and one of First group's 181 remaining VRs itw ill be of interest to see what will replace them. Seen at Falmouth Moor is 1145, AFJ745T from the 1978 delivery. The type are used to cater for the numbers of school children who use the services as well as high numbers of summer visitors. *Tony Wilson*

1750-1755

		Leyland Olympian ONLXB/1R	Eastern Coach Works	DPH44/33F	1983	
1750	A750VAF	1752	A752VAF	1753	A753VAF	1754 A754VAF	1755 A755VAF
1751	A751VAF						

1790	E215BTA	Volvo Citybus B10M-50	Alexander RH	BC47/35F	1988	Bristol (Badgerline), 1997
1791	E216BTA	Volvo Citybus B10M-50	Alexander RH	BC47/35F	1988	Bristol (Badgerline), 1997
1801	K801ORL	Volvo Olympian YN2RV18Z4	Northern Counties Palatine	BC39/30F	1993	
1802	K802ORL	Volvo Olympian YN2RV18Z4	Northern Counties Palatine	BC39/30F	1993	
1803	K803ORL	Volvo Olympian YN2RV18Z4	Northern Counties Palatine	BC39/30F	1993	
1804	K804ORL	Volvo Olympian YN2RV18Z4	Northern Counties Palatine	BC39/30F	1993	
1815	L815CFJ	Volvo Olympian YN2RV18Z4	Northern Counties Palatine	B47/29F	1993	
1816	L816CFJ	Volvo Olympian YN2RV18Z4	Northern Counties Palatine	B47/29F	1993	
1817	L817CFJ	Volvo Olympian YN2RV18Z4	Northern Counties Palatine	B47/29F	1993	
2101	M101ECV	Volvo B12(T)	Van Hool Astrobel	C57/14CT	1995	
2102	M102ECV	Volvo B12(T)	Van Hool Astrobel	C57/14CT	1995	
2103	M103ECV	Volvo B12(T)	Van Hool Astrobel	C57/14CT	1995	
2203	TLJ372	Leyland Tiger TRCTL11/3R	Plaxton Paramount 3500	C51F	1983	
2206	PJY551	Leyland Tiger TRCTL11/3R	Plaxton Paramount 3200	C53F	1984	
2207	VOD372	Leyland Tiger TRCTL11/3R	Plaxton Paramount 3200	C57F	1983	Ford's, Gunnislake, 1997
2208	DOF708	Leyland Tiger TRCTL11/3R	Plaxton Paramount 3200	C53F	1984	
2209	530OHU	Leyland Tiger TRCTL11/3R	Plaxton Paramount 3200	C53F	1983	Badgerline, 1996
2210	VPM642	Leyland Tiger TRCTL11/3R	Plaxton Paramount 3200	C53F	1983	Badgerline, 1996
2211	WSV408	Leyland Tiger TRCTL11/3R	Plaxton Paramount 3200	C53F	1983	Yorkshire Rider, 1996
2212	WSV409	Leyland Tiger TRCTL11/3R	Plaxton Paramount 3200	C53F	1983	Yorkshire Rider, 1996
2213	HVJ716	Leyland Tiger TRCTL11/3R	Plaxton Paramount 3200	C50FT	1983	Midland Red West, 1997
2214	481FPO	Leyland Tiger TRCTL11/3R	Plaxton Paramount 3200	C53F	1984	M C Travel, Melksham, 1997
2215	FNR923	Leyland Tiger TRCTL11/3RH	Plaxton Paramount 3200 II	C51F	1985	Wealden, Five Oak Green, '96
2216	NER621	Leyland Tiger TRCTL11/3RH	Plaxton Paramount 3200 II	C51F	1985	Wealden, Five Oak Green, '96
2217	B194BAF	Leyland Tiger TRCTL11/3RH	Plaxton Paramount 3200 II	C46FT	1985	
2218	B195BAF	Leyland Tiger TRCTL11/3RH	Plaxton Paramount 3200 II	C46FT	1985	
2219	B196BAF	Leyland Tiger TRCTL11/3RH	Plaxton Paramount 3200 II	C46FT	1985	

Four Volvo Olympians joined Western National in 1993 and, being fitted with high-back seating, are used on rural limited stop services such as the X80 on which 1803, K803ORL was operating when caught by the camera. As can be seen from the picture, now that the 'flags' have been removed, the only red remaining is that around the destination box and the doors. *Dominic McCall*

2220	B197BAF	Leyland Tiger TRCTL11/3RH	Plaxton Paramount 3200 II	C46FT	1985	
2221	UKT552	Leyland Tiger TRCTL11/3RH	Plaxton Paramount 3200 II	C50FT	1985	Midland Red West, 1997
2222	A204RHT	Leyland Tiger TRCTL11/3R	Plaxton Paramount 3200E	C53F	1983	Bristol (Badgerline), 1997
2223	A206SAE	Leyland Tiger TRCTL11/3R	Plaxton Paramount 3200E	C53F	1983	Bristol (Badgerline), 1997
2224	HHJ373Y	Leyland Tiger TRCTL11/2R	Alexander TE	C53F	1983	Essex Buses (EN), 1998
2225	A128ESG	Leyland Tiger TRCTL11/3RH	Plaxton Paramount 3200 E	C53F	1984	Glasgow (Kelvin), 1998
2226	TJI4838	Leyland Tiger TRCTL11/3ARZA	Plaxton Paramount 3200 II	C53F	1984	CentreWest (B),1998
2227	A665KUM	Leyland Tiger TRCTL11/2R	Duple Dominant	BC47F	1984	Essex Buses (EN), 1998
2228	EWW946Y	Leyland Tiger TRCTL11/3R	Plaxton Paramount 3200 E	C53F	1983	Essex Buses (EN), 1998
2247	HFN769	Volvo B10M-61	Plaxton Paramount 3500 III	C48FT	1989	Wallace Arnold, 1992
2248	FNJ905	Volvo B10M-61	Plaxton Paramount 3500 III	C48FT	1989	Wallace Arnold, 1992
2252	TJY761	Volvo B10M-60	Plaxton Paramount 3500 III	C51FT	1989	Wallace Arnold, 1993
2253	WNN734	Volvo B10M-60	Plaxton Paramount 3500 III	C51FT	1990	Wallace Arnold, 1993
2258	H613UWR	Volvo B10M-60	Plaxton Paramount 3500 III	C46FT	1991	Wallace Arnold, 1994
2259	H614UWR	Volvo B10M-60	Plaxton Paramount 3500 III	C46FT	1991	Wallace Arnold, 1994
2260	H615UWR	Volvo B10M-60	Plaxton Paramount 3500 III	C46FT	1991	Wallace Arnold, 1994
2261	FDZ980	Volvo B10M-60	Plaxton Paramount 3500 III	C49FT	1990	Wallace Arnold, 1994
2301	M301BRL	Volvo B10M-62	Plaxton Expressliner 2	C46FT	1994	
2302	M302BRL	Volvo B10M-62	Plaxton Expressliner 2	C46FT	1994	
2303	M303BRL	Volvo B10M-62	Plaxton Expressliner 2	C46FT	1994	
2304	R304JAF	Volvo B10M-62	Plaxton Expressliner 2	C44FT	1998	
2305	R305JAF	Volvo B10M-62	Plaxton Expressliner 2	C44FT	1998	
2307	R307JAF	Volvo B10M-62	Plaxton Expressliner 2	C44FT	1998	
2308	R308JAF	Volvo B10M-62	Plaxton Expressliner 2	C44FT	1998	
2309	R309JAF	Volvo B10M-62	Plaxton Expressliner 2	C44FT	1998	
2310	R310JAF	Volvo B10M-62	Plaxton Expressliner 2	C44FT	1998	
2311	S311SCV	Volvo B10M-62	Plaxton Expressliner 2	C44FT	1998	
2312	S312SCV	Volvo B10M-62	Plaxton Expressliner 2	C44FT	1998	
2313	S313SCV	Volvo B10M-62	Plaxton Expressliner 2	C44FT	1998	
2314	S314SRL	Volvo B10M-62	Plaxton Interurban	BC53F	1999	
2315	S315SRL	Volvo B10M-62	Plaxton Interurban	BC53F	1999	
2316	T316KCV	Volvo B10M-62	Plaxton Expressliner 2	C44FT	1999	
2401	J701CWT	Volvo B10M-60	Plaxton Première 350	C36FT	1992	Wallace Arnold, 1995
2402	J703CWT	Volvo B10M-60	Plaxton Première 350	C46FT	1992	Wallace Arnold, 1995

2505	XFF283	Volvo B10M-61	Van Hool Alizée	C48FT	1987	Badgerline, 1995
2506	EWV665	Volvo B10M-61	Van Hool Alizée	C48FT	1987	Badgerline, 1995
2507	RUH346	Volvo B10M-61	Van Hool Alizée	C48FT	1987	Badgerline, 1995
2508	UWB183	Volvo B10M-61	Van Hool Alizée	C53F	1987	Badgerline, 1991
2509	OWB243	Volvo B10M-61	Van Hool Alizée	C48FT	1987	Badgerline, 1991
2511	UHW661	Volvo B10M-61	Van Hool Alizée	C48FT	1987	Badgerline, 1991
2521	P521PRL	Volvo B10M-62	Van Hool Alizée	C44FT	1996	
2522	P522PRL	Volvo B10M-62	Van Hool Alizée	C44FT	1996	

2600-2605

	Leyland Lynx LX112TL11R1R	Leyland Lynx	B51F	1988		

2600	E200BOD	2602	E202BOD	2603	E203BOD	2604	E204BOD	2605	E205BOD
2601	E201BOD								

2606	G261LUG	Leyland Lynx LX112L10ZR1R	Leyland Lynx	B51F	1989	Brewers, 1996
2800	THX187S	Leyland National 10351A/2R		B44F	1978	Thames Transit, 1991
2801	THX220S	Leyland National 10351A/2R		B44F	1978	Thames Transit, 1991
2802	HTA844N	Leyland National 11351/1R(DAF)		B49F	1975	Western National, 1983
2803	PTT75R	Leyland National 11351A/1R		B50F	1977	Western National, 1983
2804	AFJ707T	Leyland National 11351A/1R		B50F	1978	Western National, 1983
2805	FDV774V	Leyland National 11351A/1R		B50F	1979	Western National, 1983
2806	FDV777V	Leyland National 11351A/1R		B50F	1980	Western National, 1983
2807	VBG115V	Leyland National 2 NL116L11/1R		B49F	1980	MTL (North) , 1998
2808	RSG325V	Leyland National 2 NL116L11/1R		B52F	1980	Stagecoach Red & White, 98
2820	RIL1172	Leyland Tiger TRCTL11/3RH	Plaxton Paramount 3500 II	C49FT	1986	
2821	920GTA	Volvo B10M-60	Plaxton Expressliner	C39FT	1990	Premier Travel, 1993
2822	GIL2967	Volvo B10M-61	Van Hool Alizée	C53F	1988	Allisons, Dunfermline, 1994
2850	N232WFJ	Dennis Javelin GX12SDA2161	Plaxton Expressliner 2	C44FT	1996	
2851	N233WFJ	Dennis Javelin GX12SDA2161	Plaxton Expressliner 2	C44FT	1996	
2852	P234BFJ	Volvo B10M-62	Plaxton Expressliner 2	C49FT	1996	
2853	P235CTA	Dennis Javelin GX12SDA2153	Plaxton Expressliner 2	C44FT	1997	
2854	P236CTA	Dennis Javelin GX12SDA2153	Plaxton Expressliner 2	C44FT	1997	

3444	SFJ144R	Leyland Leopard PSU3E/4R	Plaxton Supreme III	C47F	1977	Provincial, 1997
3450	SFJ150R	Leyland Leopard PSU3E/4R	Plaxton Supreme III	C47F	1977	
3500	KTT808P	Leyland Leopard PSU3B/4R	Plaxton Supreme III Express	BC53F	1975	
3508	SFJ158R	Leyland Leopard PSU3E/4R	Plaxton Supreme III	C47F	1977	
3510	KUB548V	Leyland Leopard PSU3C/4R	Plaxton Supreme IV Express	C49F	1980	Yorkshire Rider, 1996
3512	ELJ208V	Leyland Leopard PSU3C/4R(Vo)	Plaxton Supreme IV Express	C53F	1979	Wealden, Five Oak Green, '96
3513	GWU529T	Leyland Leopard PSU3E/4R(Vo)	Plaxton Supreme III Express	C53F	1979	Wealden, Five Oak Green, '96
3514	URL992S	Leyland Leopard PSU3E/4R(Vo)	Plaxton Supreme III Express	C49F	1978	Thomas, Relubbus, 1995

3516-3523

	Leyland Leopard PSU3E/4R(DAF) Plaxton Supreme III Express	C49F	1978-79	

3516	VOD616S	3517	VOD617S	3522	AFJ714T	3523	AFJ715T

3530-3546

	Leyland Leopard PSU3E/4R(Vo) Plaxton Supreme IV Express	C49F	1980	

3530	FDV821V	3538	FDV794V	3544	FDV800V	3545	FDV801V	3546	FDV802V
3535	FDV826V	3542	FDV798V						

3549	FDV805V	Leyland Leopard PSU3F/5R(Vo)	Plaxton Supreme IV Express	C49F	1980	
3550	JTH44W	Leyland Leopard PSU3F/5R	Plaxton Supreme IV Express	C53F	1982	Brewers, 1994
3551	NTH156X	Leyland Leopard PSU3F/5R	Plaxton Supreme IV Express	C53F	1982	Brewers, 1994
3553	JWE243W	Leyland Leopard PSU5D/4R	Plaxton Supreme IV	C46FT	1980	Brewers, 1995
3580	VJT738	Leyland Leopard PSU3E/4R	Plaxton P'mount 3200E(1983)	C49F	1977	Brewers, 1995
3581	HVG803V	Leyland Leopard PSU3E/4R	Duple Dominant II Express	C49F	1979	Northampton, 1998

4000	H801GDV	Dennis Dart 9.8SDL3004	Carlyle Dartline	B40F	1991	
4001	J803PFJ	Dennis Dart 9.8SDL3012	Wright Handybus	B39F	1992	
4002	K804WTT	Dennis Dart 9.8SDL3017	Wright Handybus	B40F	1993	
4003	K805WTT	Dennis Dart 9.8SDL3017	Wright Handybus	B39F	1993	
4004	M809FTT	Dennis Dart 9.8SDL3040	Marshall C37	B40F	1994	
4005	N810NOD	Dennis Dart SLF	Plaxton Pointer	B36F	1996	
4006	N811NOD	Dennis Dart SLF	Plaxton Pointer	B36F	1996	
4007	P853DTT	Dennis Dart SLF	Plaxton Pointer	B37F	1997	
4008	N22BLU	Dennis Dart 9.8SDL3054	Marshall C37	B40F	1997	Bluebird, Middleton, 1997
4009	N608WND	Dennis Dart 9.8SDL3054	Plaxton Pointer	B41F	1996	Swanbrooke, Cheltenham, 98
4010	N610WND	Dennis Dart 9.8SDL3054	Plaxton Pointer	B40F	1996	Western Buses (AA), 1998
4011	N612WND	Dennis Dart 9.8SDL3054	Plaxton Pointer	B40F	1996	Western Buses (AA), 1998

4401-4406 — Dennis Dart 9.8SDL3035 — Plaxton Pointer — B40F — 1994

4401	L401VCV	4403	L403VCV	4404	L404VCV	4405	L405VCV	4406	L406VCV
4402	L402VCV								

4407-4426 — Dennis Dart 9.8SDL3054 — Plaxton Pointer — B38F — 1995 — 4422-6 are BC37F

4407	M407CCV	4411	M411CCV	4415	M415CCV	4419	M419CCV	4423	M423CCV
4408	M408CCV	4412	M412CCV	4416	M416CCV	4420	M420CCV	4424	M424CCV
4409	M409CCV	4413	M413CCV	4417	M417CCV	4421	M421CCV	4425	M425CCV
4410	M410CCV	4414	M414CCV	4418	M418CCV	4422	M422CCV	4426	M426CCV

4427-4440 — Dennis Dart SLF — Plaxton Pointer — NC35F — 1996

4427	P427ORL	4430	P430ORL	4433	P433ORL	4436	P436ORL	4439	P439ORL
4428	P428ORL	4431	P431ORL	4434	P434ORL	4437	P437ORL	4440	P440ORL
4429	P429ORL	4432	P432ORL	4435	P435ORL	4438	P438ORL		

4441-4446 — Dennis Dart SLF — Plaxton Pointer — N35F — 1997

4441	P441TCV	4443	P443TCV	4444	P444TCV	4445	P445TCV	4446	P446TCV
4442	P442TCV								

4447-4464 — Dennis Dart SLF — Plaxton Pointer 2 — N35F — 1997-98

4447	R447CCV	4451	R451CCV	4455	R445CCV	4459	R459CCV	4462	R462CCV
4448	R448CCV	4452	R452CCV	4456	R456CCV	4460	R460CCV	4463	R463CCV
4449	R449CCV	4453	R453CCV	4457	R457CCV	4461	R461CCV	4464	R464CCV
4450	R450CCV	4454	R454CCV	4458	R458CCV				

4465	N561LHU	Dennis Dart	Plaxton Pointer	B35F	1996	Bristol (Cityline), 1998
4466	N562LHU	Dennis Dart	Plaxton Pointer	B35F	1996	Bristol (Cityline), 1998
4467	N563LHU	Dennis Dart	Plaxton Pointer	B35F	1996	Bristol (Cityline), 1998
4468	N564LHU	Dennis Dart	Plaxton Pointer	B35F	1996	Bristol (Cityline), 1998
4469	T469JCV	Dennis Dart SLF	Alexander ALX200	N37F	1999	
4470	T470JCV	Dennis Dart SLF	Alexander ALX200	N37F	1999	
4471	T471JCV	Dennis Dart SLF	Alexander ALX200	N37F	1999	
4472	T472YTT	Dennis Dart SLF	Alexander ALX200	N37F	1999	
4473	T473YTT	Dennis Dart SLF	Alexander ALX200	N37F	1999	
4501	M501CCV	Dennis Dart 9SDL3053	Plaxton Pointer	B35F	1995	
4502	M502CCV	Dennis Dart 9SDL3053	Plaxton Pointer	B35F	1995	
4503	M503CCV	Dennis Dart 9SDL3053	Plaxton Pointer	B35F	1995	

6000	D105PTT	Ford Transit VE6	Mellor	B16F	1987-89	Ex Provincial, 1996
6001	C890GYD	Ford Transit 190	Dormobile	B16F	1986	

6002-6016 — Ford Transit 190 — Robin Hood — B16F — 1986

6002	C56FDV	6005	C327GFJ	6008	C337GFJ	6011	C342GFJ	6014	C346GFJ
6003	C325GFJ	6006	C331GFJ	6009	C338GFJ	6012	C343GFJ	6015	C348GFJ
6004	C326GFJ	6007	C334GFJ	6010	C341GFJ	6013	C344GFJ	6016	C350GFJ

6051	B38AAF	Mercedes-Benz L608D	Reeve Burgess	B16FL	1984
6054	B41AAF	Mercedes-Benz L608D	Reeve Burgess	B16FL	1984
6056	B43AAF	Mercedes-Benz L608D	Reeve Burgess	B19FL	1984

6059	C674ECV	Mercedes-Benz L608D	Reeve Burgess	B19F	1985

Opposite,top:- **Western National provide vehicles for many of the National Express services from the west country. Pictured at Hanley while heading for Liverpool is Van Hool Alizée-bodied Volvo 2522, P522PRL.** *Cliff Beeton*
Opposite, bottom:- **Pictured leaving Barnstaple for Newquay is Dennis Dart 4417, M417CCV. The principal depot and operation of Red bus is also at Barnstaple. Red Bus, the trading name of North Devon, was acquired by FirstGroup during the spring of 1999 and placed under Western National management. As we went to press the renumbering of Red Bus vehicles into the Western National series is being implemented. Most of the Western National fleet and all the North Devon vehicles were renumbered during June 1999 to form a single sequence. The scheme was being implemented as this book went to press.** *Tony Wilson*

6061-6124   Mercedes-Benz L608D   Reeve Burgess   B19F*   1985-86   *6119/22/4 are BC19F

6061	C676ECV	6090	C787FRL	6099	C796FRL	6105	C802FRL	6113	C956GAF
6074	C686ECV	6094	C791FRL	6100	C797FRL	6107	C950GAF	6116	C959GAF
6075	C690ECV	6095	C792FRL	6101	C798FRL	6109	C952GAF	6119	C965GCV
6076	C691ECV	6097	C794FRL	6103	C800FRL	6111	C954GAF	6122	C968GCV
6087	C784FRL	6098	C795FRL	6104	C801FRL	6112	C955GAF	6124	C970GCV
6088	C785FRL								

6145-6156   Mercedes-Benz L608D   Reeve Burgess   B20F   1986

6145	C98HGL	6147	C100HGL	6151	C104HGL	6153	C106HGL	6156	C109HGL
6146	C99HGL	6150	C103HGL	6152	C105HGL	6155	C108HGL		

6158-6174   Mercedes-Benz L608D   Reeve Burgess   B20F   1986   Eastern National, 1994

6158	C208HJN	6168	C218HJN	6170	C220HJN	6173	C223HJN	6174	C224HJN
6166	C216HJN	6169	C219HJN						

6177	C377RUY	Mercedes-Benz L608D	Reeve Burgess	B20F	1986	Midland Red West, 1996
6178	C378RUY	Mercedes-Benz L608D	Reeve Burgess	B20F	1986	Midland Red West, 1996
6179	C379RUY	Mercedes-Benz L608D	Reeve Burgess	B20F	1986	Midland Red West, 1996
6180	C380RUY	Mercedes-Benz L608D	Reeve Burgess	B20F	1986	Midland Red West, 1996

6270-6293   Mercedes-Benz 811D   Alexander AM   B28F   1988   CentreWest, 1998

6270	F689XMS	6275	F668XMS	6280	F683XMS	6286	F657XMS	6290	F652BMS
6271	F666XMS	6276	F455TOY	6281	F683XMS	6287	F667XMS	6291	F658BMS
6272	F677XMS	6277	F948BMS	6283	F643XMS	6288	F602XMS	6292	F669XMS
6273	F706XMS	6278	F680XMS	6284	F949BMS	6289	F946BMS	6293	F707XMS
6274	F645XMS	6279	F684XMS	6285	F954BMS				

6301-6326   Mercedes-Benz 811D   Carlyle   B31F*   1990-91   *6301/2/11 are BC31F
     6325/6 are B33F

6301	G151GOL	6307	H892LOX	6312	H712HGL	6317	H717HGL	6322	H722HGL
6302	G152GOL	6308	H893LOX	6313	H713HGL	6318	H718HGL	6323	H723HGL
6303	G153GOL	6309	H894LOX	6314	H714HGL	6319	H719HGL	6324	H724HGL
6304	G154GOL	6310	H895LOX	6315	H715HGL	6320	H720HGL	6325	H725HGL
6305	G155GOL	6311	H896LOX	6316	H716HGL	6321	H721HGL	6326	H726HGL
6306	H891LOX								

6328	E808MOU	Mercedes-Benz 811D	Optare StarRider	B33F	1988	Badgerline, 1991
6329	E812MOU	Mercedes-Benz 811D	Optare StarRider	B31F	1988	Badgerline, 1991
6330	E820MOU	Mercedes-Benz 811D	Optare StarRider	B31F	1988	Badgerline, 1991

6331-6343   Mercedes-Benz 811D   Plaxton Beaver   B31F   1992

6331	K331OAF	6334	K334OAF	6337	K337OAF	6340	K340OAF	6342	K342OAF
6332	K332OAF	6335	K335OAF	6338	K338OAF	6341	K341OAF	6343	K343OAF
6333	K333OAF	6336	K336OAF	6339	K339OAF				

6344-6360   Mercedes-Benz 811D   Plaxton Beaver   B31F   1993-94

6344	K344ORL	6348	K348ORL	6352	K352ORL	6355	L355VCV	6358	L358VCV
6345	K345ORL	6349	K349ORL	6353	K353ORL	6356	L356VCV	6359	L359VCV
6346	K346ORL	6350	K350ORL	6354	K354ORL	6357	L357VCV	6360	L360VCV
6347	K347ORL	6351	K351ORL						

6370	J610PTA	Mercedes-Benz 811D	Marshall C16	B33F	1992

6371-6375   Mercedes-Benz 811D   Wright NimBus   B33F   1993-94

6371	K752XTA	6372	K753XTA	6373	K754XTA	6374	K755XTA	6375	L69EPR

6376	M764FTT	Mercedes-Benz 811D	Marshall C16	B33F	1994
6377	M765FTT	Mercedes-Benz 811D	Marshall C16	B33F	1994
6378	M767FTT	Mercedes-Benz 811D	Marshall C16	DP33F	1994
6379	M768FTT	Mercedes-Benz 811D	Marshall C16	DP33F	1994
6380	M769FTT	Mercedes-Benz 811D	Marshall C16	DP33F	1994

Plaxton Expressliner II number 2312, S312SCV, is seen heading to London in heavy rain. The Expressliner was the principal choice of coach for National Express at one time, though recently the number of model that qualify has increased, the latest example being an integral Mercedes-Benz coach which Yorkshire Traction are using on their Rapide service from Barnsley. *Phillip Stephenson*

6500	H324HVT	Mercedes-Benz 609D	PMT	BC24F	1990	Plymouth Argyle AFC, 1994

6520-6528

		Mercedes-Benz 709D		Wrigth NimBus	B29F	1992		
6520	J140SJT	6522	J142SJT	6524	J144SJT	6527	J146SJT	6528	J148SJT
6521	J141SJT	6523	J143SJT	6526	J145SJT				

6529	K723WTT	Mercedes-Benz 709D	Wright NimBus	B29F	1993	
6530	L649CJT	Mercedes-Benz 709D	Wright NimBus	B29F	1993	
6531	M901LTT	Mercedes-Benz 609D	Frank Guy	B19F	1995	
6532	M902LTT	Mercedes-Benz 609D	Frank Guy	B19F	1995	
6533	M676RAJ	Mercedes-Benz 709D	Alexander Sprint	B25F	1994	Go-Ahead (Gateshead), 1998
6534	M677RAJ	Mercedes-Benz 709D	Alexander Sprint	B25F	1994	Go-Ahead (Gateshead), 1998
6535	M678RAJ	Mercedes-Benz 709D	Alexander Sprint	B25F	1994	Go-Ahead (Gateshead), 1998

6601-6625

		Mercedes-Benz 709D		Plaxton Beaver	B23F*	1993	*6602/20-5 are B25F	
6601	K601ORL	6606	K606ORL	6611	K611ORL	6616	K616ORL	6621	K621ORL
6602	K602ORL	6607	K607ORL	6612	K612ORL	6617	K617ORL	6622	K622ORL
6603	K603ORL	6608	K608ORL	6613	K613ORL	6618	K618ORL	6623	K623ORL
6604	K604ORL	6609	K609ORL	6614	K614ORL	6619	K619ORL	6624	K624ORL
6605	K605ORL	6610	K610ORL	6615	K615ORL	6620	K620ORL	6625	K625ORL

6628-651

		Mercedes-Benz 709D		Plaxton Beaver	B23F	1994		
6628	L628VCV	6633	L633VCV	6638	L638VCV	6643	L643VCV	6648	L648VCV
6629	L629VCV	6634	L634VCV	6639	L639VCV	6644	L644VCV	6649	L649VCV
6630	L630VCV	6635	L635VCV	6640	L640VCV	6645	L645VCV	6650	L650VCV
6631	L631VCV	6636	L636VCV	6641	L641VCV	6646	L646VCV	6651	L651VCV
6632	L632VCV	6637	L637VCV	6642	L642VCV	6647	L647VCV		

6652	M246VWU	Mercedes-Benz 709D	Plaxton Beaver	B23F	1995	Yorkshire Rider, 1996
6653	M226VWU	Mercedes-Benz 709D	Plaxton Beaver	B23F	1995	Yorkshire Rider (RY), 1996

6654-6658

		Mercedes-Benz 709D	Reeve Burgess Beaver	B25F	1988	Cymru (SWT), 1998

6654	E283UCY	6655	E284UCY	6656	E285UCY	6657	E286UCY	6658	E288VEP

6659	N719GRV	Mercedes-Benz 709D	Plaxton Beaver	B27F	1996	Hampshire, 1999

6700	R650TDV	Mercedes-Benz Vario O810	Plaxton Beaver 2	B29F	1997	
6701	R851YDV	Mercedes-Benz Vario O810	Plaxton Beaver 2	B29F	1997	
6702	R852TFJ	Mercedes-Benz Vario O810	Plaxton Beaver 2	B27F	1998	
6703	R853TFJ	Mercedes-Benz Vario O810	Plaxton Beaver 2	B27F	1998	

6704-6711

		Mercedes-Benz Vario O810	Plaxton Beaver 2	B29F*	1999	*6704 is B33F, 6707 is B27F

6704	S865NOD	6706	S867NOD	6708	S869NOD	6710	S871NOD	6711	S872NOD
6705	S866NOD	6707	S868NOD	6709	S870NOD				

9700	RUF40R	Leyland National 11351/1R		B23F	1977	Bike Bus
9701	AFJ708T	Leyland National 11351A/1R		B21F	1978	Bike Bus
9702	L548CDV	Dennis Dart 8.5SDL	Wright Handybus	B28FL	1993	Operated on behalf of South Devon Council
9703	RHE987R	Bristol LHS6L	Plaxton Supreme III Express	C33F	1977	County Bus, Atherington, 1990

9813	N326HUA	Volvo B6-9.9	Alexander Dash	B40F	1995	Yorkshire Travel, 1999
9814	N390EUG	Volvo B6-9.9	Alexander Dash	B40F	1995	Yorkshire Travel, 1999

Special Event vehicles:

1056	OTA290G	Bristol VRT/SL/6LX	Eastern Coach Works	B39/31F	1969	
1255	VOD125K	Bristol LHS6L	Marshall	B33F	1972	
1420	270KTA	Bristol SUL4A	Eastern Coach Works	BC33F	1962	Willis, Bodmin, 1994
2019	824KDV	Bristol Lodekka FLF6G	Eastern Coach Works	B38/30F	1963	preservation
9432	LBP500	Bedford OB	Duple Vista	C29F	1949	Roberts Cs, Plympton, 1988

Ancilliary vehicles

1100w	SFJ100R	Bristol VRT/SL3/6LXB	Eastern Coach Works	B43/31F	1977	
2202	894GUO	Leyland Tiger TRCTL11/3R	Plaxton Paramount 3500	C55F	1983	Grampian (Mair's), 1997
3312	RHE986R	Bristol LHS6L	Plaxton Supreme III Express	C33F	1977	County Bus, Atherington, 1990
3551	NTH156X	Leyland Leopard PSU3F/5RT	Duple Dominant IV Express	C53F	1981	Brewers, 1994

Previous Registrations:

270KTA	From new	OWB243	D509HHW
481FPO	B826KRY	PJY551	A530WRL
530OHU	A205SAE	RIL1172	C923HYA, 7ACL
824KDV	From new	RUH346	D507GHY
894GUO	FNM863Y, SCV426,	T.II4538	E322OMG
	C50544Y	TJY761	F445DUG
920GTA	G326GEW	TLJ372	A749VAF
C686ECV	C689ECV	UHW661	D511HHW
DOF708	A532WRL	UKT552	B102JAB
EWV665	D506GHY	URL992S	UWE89S, GUN162
FDZ980	G521LWU	URL94Y	OHM832Y, FDZ980
FNJ905	F446DUG	UWB183	D508HHW
FNR923	B291KPF	VJT738	PWS492S
GIL2967	E634UNE, LSK819	VOD372	A101JJT
HFN769	F444DUG	VPM642	A210SAE
HVJ716	A658VDA	WNN734	G541LWU
JTH44W	GTH536W, 948RJO	WSV408	HUA604Y
LBP500	From new	WSV409	HUA605Y
NER621	B295KPF	XFF283	D505GHY
NTH156X	MEP969X, YBK132		

Allocations and special liveries

Barnstaple (Coney Avenue) - Red Bus

Outstations - Bideford; Exeter; Ilfracombe and Tiverton

Ford Transit	6000	6001	6002	6003	6004	6005	6006	6007
	6008	6009	6010	6011	6012	6013	6014	6015
	6016							
Mercedes-Benz	6370	6371	6372	6373	6374	6375	6376	6377
	6378	6379	6380	6520	6521	6522	6523	6524
	6525	6526	6527	6528	6529	6530	6531	6532
	6533	6534	6535	6700	6701	6702	6703	6704
	6705	6707	6706	6708	6709	6710	6711	
Dart	4000	4001	4002	4003	4004	4005	4006	4007
	4008	4009	4010	4011				
Tiger	2820							
Volvo B10M	2821	2822	2852					
Javelin	2850	2851	2853	2854				
Bristol LH	9702	9703						
National	9700	9701	2800	2801	2802	2803	2804	2805
	2806	2807	2808					
Bristol VR	1300	1301	1302	1303	1304	1305		
Atlantean	1000	1001	1002					
Olympian	1815	1816	1817					

Camborne (Union Street) - Western National

Outstations: Flambards, Helston; Trecerus Ind Est, Padstow; Long Rock Ind Est, Penzance and Lemon Quay, Truro.

Mercedes-Benz	6099	6105	6107	6109	6112	6113	6116	6145
	6146	6147	6151	6166	6168	6170	6174	6301
	6302	6303	6305	6329	6331	6332	6333	6334
	6335	6336	6337	6338	6339	6341	6342	6343
	6355	6356	6357	6358	6359	6360	6603	6639
	6640	6641	6642	6643	6644	6645	6646	6271
	6272	6273	6274	6276	6278	6279	6280	6281
	6283	6285	6286	6287	6288	6289	6291	
Dart	4413	4414	4415	4416	4417	4418	4419	4420
	4421	4422	4423	4424	4425	4426	4454	4455
	4456	4457	4458	4459	4463	4464	4469	4470
	4471							
Leopard	3544	3550						
Tiger	2213	2215	2217	2218	2219	2220	2222	2223
	2226	2228						
Volvo B10	2252	2505	2511					
Volvo NX	2301	2302	2303	2304	2305	2307	2308	2309
	2310	2311	2312	2402	2521	2522		
Volvo B12	2101	2102	2103					
Bristol VR	1003	1123	1128	1131	1135	1136	1144	1145
	1147	1148	1149	1153	1182	1233	1238	1240
	1242	1243	1244	1249	1251	1256	1258	1262
Olympian	1754	1755						

Plymouth (Laira Bridge Road) - Western National

Outstations - New Road, Callington; Little Cotton Farm, Dartmouth; Crowndale Road, Tavistock; Wills Road Ind Est, Totnes and Trevol Road, Torpoint.

Mercedes-Benz	6056	6103	6119	6124	6156	6177	6328	6330
	6344	6345	6346	6347	6348	6349	6350	6351
	6352	6353	6354	6520	6601	6602	6604	6605
	6606	6607	6608	6609	6610	6611	6612	6613
	6614	6615	6616	6617	6618	6619	6620	6621
	6622	6623	6624	6625	6647	6648	6649	6650
	6651	6652	6653	6654	6655	6656	6657	6658
	6659	6275	6277					
Dart	4401	4402	4403	4404	4405	4406	4407	4408
	4409	4410	4411	4412	4433	4434	4435	4436
	4437	4438	4439	4440	4441	4442	4443	4444
	4445	4446	4447	4448	4449	4450	4451	4452
	4453	4460	4461	4462	4465	4466	4467	4468
	4501	4502	4503					
Lynx	2600	2601	2602	2603	2604	2605	2606	
Leopard	3508	3513	3580					
Tiger	2203	2206	2207	2208	2209	2210	2211	2212
	2214	2216	2221	2224	2227			
Volvo B10	2247	2248	2253	2258	2259	2260	2261	2314
	2315	2401	2506	2507	2508			
Bristol VR	1006	1137	1155	1174	1175	1176	1183	1187
	1197	1198	1199	1200	1202	1203	1220	1227
	1228	1229	1230	1232	1236	1239	1248	1252
	1253	1254	1259	1260				
Olympian	1750	1751	1752	1753	1801	1802	1803	1804
Citybus	1790	1791						

St Austell (Elliot Road) - Western National

Outstations - Bodmin; Camworthy Water; Delabole; Tregonnigie Industrial Estate, Falmouth; Launceston; Liskeard; Tolcarne Street, Newquay; North Petherwin; Pelynt and Tregony

Mercedes-Benz	6061	6090	6094	6104	111	152	153	155
	6306	6308	6309	6310	311	318	321	322
	6323	6326	6628	629	630	631	632	6633
	6634	6635	6636	637	638			
Dart	4427	4428	4429	4430	4431	4432		
Leopard	3512	3514	3538	3542	3545	3546	3549	
Bristol VR	1106	1114	1116	1117	1118	1119	1120	1121
	1129	1132	1133	1134	1138	1139	1140	1141
	1142	1143	1154	1201	1224	1225	1226	1231
	1234	1237	1245	1246	1250	1257		

Unallocated

Mercedes-Benz	6051	6054	6059	6074	6075	6076	6087	6088
	6095	6097	6098	6100	6101	6122	6150	6158
	6169	6173	6178	6179	6180	6304	6307	6312
	6313	6314	6315	6316	6317	6319	6320	6324
	6325	6270	6284	6290	6292	6293		
Leopard	3444	3500	3510	3516	3517	3522	3551	3553
Tiger	2200	2202	2225					
Bristol VR	1083	1085	1100	1105	1108	1109	1235	1261
Heritage	1056	1255	1420	2019	9432			

New World First Bus

New World First Bus Services Ltd, 25th Floor Eight Commercial Tower,
8 Sun Yip Street, Chai Wan, Hong Kong

DA1-12

Dennis Condor DDA1809   Duple Metsec   B66/41D   1990

DA1	EM8539	DA4	EM8645	DA7	EN2946	DA9	EN5953	DA11	EN6522
DA2	EM8983	DA5	EN1721	DA8	EN2924	DA10	EN8287	DA12	EN9804
DA3	EN275	DA6	EN758						

DA13-36

Dennis Condor DDA1809   Duple Metsec   B66/41D   1991

DA13	EU7418	DA18	EV1394	DA23	EV7489	DA28	EW724	DA33	EW4639
DA14	EU7840	DA19	EV1016	DA24	EV7207	DA29	EW1940	DA34	EW5006
DA15	EU8719	DA20	EV2743	DA25	EV9195	DA30	EW1691	DA35	EW8101
DA16	EV352	DA21	EV2652	DA26	EV9176	DA31	EW4319	DA36	EW6985
DA17	EV2009	DA22	EV6409	DA27	EW1256	DA32	EW4321		

DA37-56

Dennis Condor DDA1817   Duple Metsec   B66/41D   1993

DA37	FS3024	DA41	FS7967	DA45	FT3674	DA49	FT5696	DA53	FU1457
DA38	FS3241	DA42	FS6573	DA46	FT2896	DA50	FT5059	DA54	FU684
DA39	FS5635	DA43	FT336	DA47	FT5168	DA51	FT8465	DA55	FU3477
DA40	FS5294	DA44	FS8718	DA48	FT5295	DA52	FT7484	DA56	FU4461

DA57-66

Dennis Condor DDA1822   Duple Metsec   B64/41D   1996

DA57	GX7529	DA59	GX7099	DA61	GY572	DA63	GY3754	DA65	DB550
DA58	GX7580	DA60	GX9848	DA62	GY2016	DA64	GY2679	DA66	GY4478

DA67-92

Dennis Condor DDA1822   Duple Metsec   B64/41D   1997

DA67	HA1470	DA73	HA9736	DA78	HB4359	DA83	HG4178	DA88	HH4157
DA68	HA551	DA74	HA9516	DA79	HB4954	DA84	HG4712	DA89	HH6355
DA69	HA4051	DA75	HB2179	DA80	HB5648	DA85	HG9458	DA90	HH6198
DA70	HA2599	DA76	HB925	DA81	HB7365	DA86	HB4359	DA91	HH8093
DA71	HA8204	DA77	HB2564	DA82	HB8095	DA87	HH2711	DA92	HH7687
DA72	HA8337								

DC1	EU3821	Dennis Dart 98SDL3008	Carlyle	BC37F	1991	

DC2-20

Dennis Dart 98SDL3014*   Carlyle   BC43F**   1991   * DC2-8 are 98SDL3008
** DC2-4 are BC37F

DC2	EX1835	DC6	EX3655	DC10	EZ548	DC14	EZ5493	DC18	EZ8889
DC3	EX1241	DC7	EX3833	DC11	EZ1810	DC15	EZ7136	DC19	FA2285
DC4	EX4327	DC8	EX2604	DC12	EZ1337	DC16	EZ6900	DC20	FB904
DC5	EX3840	DC9	EZ597	DC13	EZ4951	DC17	EZ9823		

DL1	CV4990	Dennis Condor DDA602	Duple Metsec	H75/33D	1982	
DL2	CW3359	Dennis Condor DDA602	Alexander RH	H73/35D	1982	

DL3-48

Dennis Condor DDA1702   Duple Metsec   H72/35D   1989-90

DL3	EE8750	DL17	EG1700	DL25	EG7583	DL33	EH5561	DL41	EH9876
DL4	EE9168	DL18	EG2166	DL26	EG9356	DL34	EH6321	DL42	EJ2225
DL5	EF2202	DL19	EG2545	DL27	EG9386	DL35	EH6403	DL43	EJ1293
DL8	EF3349	DL20	EG3419	DL28	EH1530	DL36	EH7956	DL44	EJ2261
DL9	EF6489	DL21	EG5131	DL29	EH2206	DL37	EH6884	DL45	EJ3194
DL13	EF7027	DL22	EG4627	DL30	EH2014	DL38	EH7098	DL46	EJ3811
DL14	EF9534	DL23	EG5851	DL31	EH4324	DL39	EH7436	DL47	EJ4042
DL15	EG1787	DL24	EG6964	DL32	EH3444	DL40	EH9604	DL48	EJ4800
DL16	EG857								

DM1-28

Dennis Condor DDA1810 · Duple Metsec · B69/41D · 1990

DM1	EP8262	DM7	ER3652	DM13	ER8470	DM19	ES2015	DM24	ES5032
DM2	EP7995	DM8	ER4467	DM14	ER7882	DM20	ES2546	DM25	ES5063
DM3	EP9931	DM9	ER4914	DM15	ER8931	DM21	ES4494	DM26	ES5317
DM4	EP9611	DM10	ER4920	DM16	ER8581	DM22	ES2559	DM27	ES7966
DM5	ER1604	DM11	ER5034	DM17	ES997	DM23	ES3299	DM28	ES6657
DM6	ER1474	DM12	ER7054	DM18	ES1970				

DS1-27

Dennis Jubilant DD205 · Alexander · B60/42D · 1980

DS1	CD2198	DS6	CD3693	DS11	CD9268	DS18	CE4950	DS24	CE7114
DS2	CD2237	DS7	CD3729	DS13	CE204	DS19	CE3627	DS27	CE8285
DS4	CD3524	DS9	CD4725	DS15	CE3491	DS20	CE3680		

LA1-5

Leyland Olympian ON3R49C18Z4 Alexander RH · B64/40D · 1991

LA1	EX9383	LA2	EY6303	LA3	EY7405	LA4	EZ1236	LA5	EZ4168

LA6-25

Leyland Olympian ON3R49C18Z4 Alexander RH · B64/40D · 1992

LA6	FF3170	LA10	FF7409	LA14	FG3725	LA18	FH1086	LA22	FH6751
LA7	FF2854	LA11	FF7869	LA15	FG4346	LA19	FH2405	LA23	FH7208
LA8	FF3551	LA12	FF8835	LA16	FG8663	LA20	FH4562	LA24	FJ1017
LA9	FF4163	LA13	FF8735	LA17	FG9004	LA21	FH5136	LA25	FJ853

LF13	BG1222	Daimler Fleetline CRG6LXB-33 Alexander AL (1988)	B61/41D	1974

LF18-46

Leyland Fleetline FE33AGR · Alexander AL (1988) · B61/41D · 1974

LF18	BG1911	LF21	BG2294	LF26	BG2977	LF28	BG3633	LF46	DW6399

LF105	BL482	Leyland Fleetline FE33AGR Metal Sections*	B61/41D	1976

LF107-304

Leyland Fleetline FE33AGR · Alexander AL · B61/41D · 1976-79

LF107	BL483	LF116	BL7948	LF126	BM2340	LF248	BT8284	LF260	BU7565
LF109	BL3422	LF118	BL8603	LF160	BN4296	LF249	BT8285	LF272	BV9450
LF110	BL3423	LF119	BL8604	LF217	BR8985	LF252	BU4108	LF278	BW4603
LF111	BL4959	LF120	BL8605	LF223	BS4522	LF254	BU4840	LF281	BW4606
LF113	BL5497	LF121	BM2335	LF237	BS9858	LF255	BU4841	LF291	BW9124
LF114	BL5498	LF125	BM2339	LF243	BT5156	LF256	BU5820	LF304	CB1479
LF115	BL7957								

LM1-10

Leyland Olympian ON3R49C18Z4 Alexander RH · B69/40D · 1993

LM1	FV6607	LM3	FW739	LM5	FW2286	LM7	FW3152	LM9	FW2788
LM2	FV7737	LM4	FW2045	LM6	FW1878	LM8	FW2508	LM10	FW3858

LV1	CA9169	Leyland Victory Mk2 ser2 Alexander	B60/42D	1979

LV2-33

Leyland Victory Mk2 Ser2 · Alexander · B60/42D · 1980

LV2	CF4179	LV9	CF6739	LV15	CG1064	LV20	CG5483	LV29	CH5815
LV3	CF4279	LV11	CF6215	LV16	CG3647	LV22	CH1205	LV30	CH5001
LV4	CF4280	LV12	CF9655	LV17	CG3934	LV24	CH1603	LV32	CH5075
LV5	CF5482	LV13	CF9879	LV18	CG4376	LV27	CH3916	LV33	CH6982
LV6	CF5483	LV14	CG729	LV19	CG4861				

Opposite:- **New World First Bus is a joint venture between FirstGroup and New World Development Group in which FirstGroup have a 26% shareholding and undertake the mangement of the new company. It was awarded a five year franchise commencing 1st September 1998 and took over many of the buses that the former franchise operator, China Motor Bus, previously used. A livery of white, orange and green has been chosen and is being applied to those vehicles acquired. The initial batch of Alexander-bodied Dennis Tridents carry the colour split across the vehicle side using the NW of New World as the line. This is illustrated on 1038, HX853, seen at Siu Sai Win. The lower picture shows the conventional livery applied to former CMB Dennis Dragon DA7, EN2946.** *Paul Wigan*

LV70-112

Leyland Victory Mk2 Ser2 Alexander B60/42D 1980-81

LV70	CK6178	LV83	CM2681	LV91	CM6212	LV98	CM7019	LV105	CN2492
LV71	CK6299	LV84	CM2206	LV92	CM6715	LV99	CM7107	LV106	CN2635
LV72	CK9234	LV85	CM2512	LV93	CM6762	LV100	CM7448	LV107	CN2644
LV75	CL8082	LV86	CM2659	LV94	CM6263	LV101	CM7569	LV109	CN8415
LV80	CM2014	LV87	CM2735	LV95	CM6463	LV102	CM9145	LV110	CN8509
LV81	CM2105	LV88	CM3278	LV96	CM6743	LV103	CM9204	LV111	CN9574
LV82	CM2355	LV90	CM6061	LV97	CM7009	LV104	CM9386	LV112	HX6588

LV113-147

Leyland Victory Mk2 Ser2 Alexander B60/42D 1981

LV113	CP340	LV120	CP3371	LV126	CP5021	LV133	CP9172	LV140	CR2820
LV114	CP521	LV121	CP3647	LV127	CP5123	LV134	CP9372	LV142	CR4353
LV115	CP1443	LV122	CP3867	LV128	CP6036	LV135	CP9873	LV143	CR4703
LV116	CP1298	LV123	CP4382	LV129	CP6142	LV137	CR1140	LV144	CR4786
LV117	CP1910	LV124	CP4423	LV130	CP7065	LV138	CR1343	LV145	CR5875
LV118	CP2209	LV125	CP4727	LV132	CP7514	LV139	CR2381	LV147	CR6191
LV119	CP2372								

LV158-166

Leyland Victory Mk2 Ser2 Duple Metsec H60/38D 1982

LV158	CT6092	LV160w	CT6297	LV164	CU3263	LV165	CU4517	LV166	CU4529

MB5-40

MCW Metrobus DR105/1 MCW B70/48D 1979

MB5	BY8149	MB15	BZ3679	MB23	BZ8414	MB31	CA2256	MB35	CA3343
MB10	BY9490	MB18	BZ3869	MB25	BZ8416	MB32	CA2257	MB38	CA3347
MB11	BY9491	MB19	BZ6109	MB26	BZ8417	MB33	CA2258	MB39	CA6001
MB13	BZ3677	MB20	BZ6110	MB27	CA471	MB34	CA3342	MB40	CA6002
MB14	BZ3678	MB22	BZ6112	MB30	CA475				

MC2-12

MCW Metrobus DR102/2 MCW BC43/29F 1978

MC3	BT9142	MC7	BV205	MC10	BVB2053	MC11	BV2054	MC12	BV20550
MC4	BU2257	MC9	BV2052						

ML1	CM8935	MCW Metrobus DR115/1	MCW	H77/33D	1981
ML2	CR4882	MCW Metrobus DR115/1	MCW	H76/33D	1981

ML3-44

MCW Metrobus DR115/1 MCW H75/33D 1983-84

ML3	CY2674	ML12	CY7152	ML21	CZ2806	ML29	CZ8125	ML37	DA4520
ML4	CY3083	ML13	CY7986	ML22	CZ4476	ML30	CZ9920	ML38	DA6377
ML5w	CY3562	ML14	CY6555	ML23	CZ2627	ML31	CZ8947	ML39	DA7025
ML6	CY4197	ML15	CY7533	ML24	CZ3659	ML32	DA397	ML40	DA8454
ML7w	CY3642	ML16	CY9638	ML25	CZ5554	ML33	DA2590	ML41	DA8239
ML8w	CY4401	ML17	CZ894	ML26	CZ5864	ML34	DA3002	ML42	DB1623
ML9	CY3741	ML18	CZ2276	ML27	CZ6319	ML35	DA2952	ML43	DB1959
ML10w	CY8361	ML19	CZ664	ML28	CZ7579	ML36	DA4121	ML44	DB1342
ML11	CY6656	ML20	CZ4050						

ML45-64

MCW Metrobus DR115/4 MCW H75/33D 1987-88

ML45	DT4549	ML49	DT9375	ML53	DU4314	ML57	DU8346	ML61	DV542
ML46	DT7029	ML50	DU154	ML54	DU3460	ML58	DU8506	ML62	DV3433
ML47	DT7256	ML51	DU1637	ML55	DU5325	ML59	DV471	ML63	DV2896
ML48	DT9187	ML52	DU3481	ML56	DU7765	ML60	DV704	ML64	DV4883

ML65-84

MCW Metrobus DR115/5 MCW H75/33D 1988

ML65	DY8312	ML69	DY7398	ML73	DZ3015	ML77	DZ7095	ML81	EA4389
ML66	DY6756	ML70	DZ956	ML74	DZ3401	ML78	DZ8263	ML82	EA3926
ML67	DY7388	ML71	DZ2444	ML75	DZ7066	ML79	DZ6532	ML83	EA6156
ML68	DY8172	ML72	DZ1845	ML76	DZ7166	ML80	EA1844	ML84	EA4952

SF3-31 — Leyland Fleetline FE31AGR — Alexander — H56/36D — 1979-80

SF3	CB5930	SF7	CB8043	SF13	CD1098	SF19	CD2957	SF25	CD9724
SF4	CB5574	SF8	CB8696	SF14	CD1169	SF20	CD2229	SF30	CE2444
SF5	CB6089	SF9	CB8820	SF15	CD1446	SF21	CD2248	SF31	CE2543
SF6	CB6090	SF10	CB8909	SF16	CD1532	SF24	CD9071		

VA1-30 — Volvo Olympian YN3RC18Z4 — Alexander RH — B64/40D — 1994-95

VA1	GD7476	VA7	GE3255	VA13	GE9574	VA19	GF8254	VA25	GG8241
VA2	GD6917	VA8	GE3588	VA14	GE9536	VA20	GF7258	VA26	GG5629
VA3	GD7590	VA9	GE6431	VA15	GF2817	VA21	GF8579	VA27	GG4586
VA4	GD6958	VA10	GE5908	VA16	GF2620	VA22	GF9086	VA28	GG4658
VA5	GE1766	VA11	GE6588	VA17	GF6345	VA23	GF8727	VA29	GG8152
VA6	GE1769	VA12	GE7388	VA18	GF5094	VA24	GG3083	VA30	GG8455

VA31-50 — Volvo Olympian YN3RC18Z4 — Alexander RH — B65/40D — 1996

VA31	GV1897	VA35	GV6267	VA39	GV7288	VA43	GW1735	VA47	GW5011
VA32	GV1386	VA36	GV6348	VA40	GP8588	VA44	GW1562	VA48	GW5878
VA33	GV4297	VA37	GV5740	VA41	GV9359	VA45	GW2762	VA49	GW8435
VA34	GR295	VA38	GV6192	VA42	GV9212	VA46	GW3191	VA50	GW8272

VA51-63 — Volvo Olympian YN3RC18Z4 — Alexander RH — B65/40D — 1998

VA51	HN8481	VA54	HN8897	VA57	HP6260	VA59	HP7236	VA61	HP8961
VA52	HN6509	VA55	HP3851	VA58	HP7236	VA60	HP8260	VA63	HR2439
VA53	HN9798	VA56	HP3011						

Many of the VA class of Volvo Olympian are liveried with advertisements. Seen in a purple and white scheme is VA10, GE5908, with Alexander bodywork. A model of this product has been extensively liveried by Corgi with several in the colours of NWFB and its predecessor, China Motor Bus. *Ken MacKenzie*

1001-1160   Dennis Trident   Alexander ALX400   N59/34D   1998-99

1001	HU8370	1033	HX548	1065	HX9538	1097	HY4544	1129	HZ958
1002	HV3176	1034	HX2026	1066	HY2017	1098	HY4562	1130	HZ9312
1003	HV4273	1035	HX1640	1067	HY763	1099	HY6092	1131	HZ1665
1004	HV3406	1036	HX804	1068	HY1796	1100	HY6455	1132	HZ2128
1005	HV2854	1037	HX1323	1069	HY543	1101	HY4273	1133	HZ2393
1006	HV2808	1038	HX853	1070	HY1376	1102	HY3544	1134	HZ2143
1007	HV2560	1039	HX703	1071	HY671	1103	HY3782	1135	HZ1539
1008	HV6531	1040	HX615	1072	HY2330	1104	HY4099	1136	HZ1562
1009	HV8318	1041	HX1585	1073	HY1835	1105	HY3813	1137	HZ2286
1010	HV7249	1042	HX1860	1074	HY1266	1106	HY3082	1138	HZ1597
1011	HV6812	1043	HX1120	1075	HY1740	1107	HY3334	1139	HZ2132
1012	HV8027	1044	HX905	1076	HY2400	1108	HY3979	1140	HZ3713
1013	HV7187	1045	HX1995	1077	HY2483	1109	HY2877	1141	HZ7612
1014	HV7225	1046	HX2174	1078	HY1121	1110	HY4363	1142	HZ6781
1015	HV7992	1047	HX4754	1079	HY1231	1111	HY2509	1143	HZ9742
1016	HV6921	1048	HX5793	1080	HY2385	1112	HY3130	1144	HZ9257
1017	HV8316	1049	HX6151	1081	HY2053	1113	HY4399	1145	JA4277
1018	HV7798	1050	HX5917	1082	HY1988	1114	HY5393	1146	JA3533
1019	HV6927	1051	HX5473	1083	HY2177	1115	HY6444	1147	JA4944
1020	HW3836	1052	HX5851	1084	HY2249	1116	HY5356	1148	JA4946
1021	HW3545	1053	HX5293	1085	HY1072	1117	HZ936	1149	JA7142
1022	HW9107	1054	HX5595	1086	HY2326	1118	HZ752	1150	JA7544
1023	HW9139	1055	HX6009	1087	HY1631	1119	HZ654	1151	JA8108
1024	HX273	1056	HX6393	1088	HY1582	1120	HZ1179	1152	JA7923
1025	HW8505	1057	HX6061	1089	HY1164	1121	HZ590	1153	JB1384
1026	HW9403	1058	HX4736	1090	HY2563	1122	HZ2136	1154	JB1626
1027	HW9945	1059	HX6181	1091	HY7048	1123	HZ1518	1155	JB3160
1028	HX217	1060	HX6341	1092	HY4017	1124	HZ1064	1156	JB2960
1029	HW8963	1061	HX5031	1093	HY2755	1125	HZ1891	1157	JB6196
1030	HW1396	1062	HX5242	1094	HY2653	1126	HZ1908	1158	JB4590
1031	HX501	1063	HX8852	1095	HY2716	1127	HZ830	1159	JB8416
1032	HX574	1064	HX9093	1096	HY3161	1128	HZ2032	1160	JB5808

1161-1172   Dennis Trident   Alexander ALX400   N59/34D   1999

1161	JB9953	1164	JB9941	1167	JB9643	1169	JB9727	1171	JB9156
1162	JB9544	1165	JB9980	1168	JB9058	1170	JB8843	1172	JC240
1163	JB8699	1166	JB8937						

1401-1414   Dennis Trident   Alexander ALX400   N--/--D   1999

1401	JC1103	1404	JC1359	1407	JC1874	1410		1413	
1402	JC2381	1405	JC1696	1408	JC2185	1411	JC2161	1414	JC1578
1403	JC1621	1406	JC2470	1409	JC582	1412	JC1886		

2001-2042   Dennis Dart SLF 10.7m   Plaxton Pointer 2   N39D   1998-99

2001	HV3127	1010	HV4863	1019	HV8029	1027	HV6817	1035	HW2439
2002	HV6302	1011	HV7513	1020	HV6940	1028	HV7556	1036	HW354
2003	HV4733	1012	HV6710	1021	HV7615	1029	HV7025	1037	HV8607
2004	HV5822	1013	HV7180	1022	HV8246	1030	HV8435	1038	HW584
2005	HV6137	1014	HV8186	1023	HV7858	1031	HV8152	1039	HW2481
2006	HV5087	1015	HV7615	1024	HV8137	1032	HV6952	1040	HV8986
2007	HV5609	1016	HV8269	1025	HV8337	1033	HV6769	1041	HV9990
2008	HV5346	1017	HV6815	1026	HV7008	1034	HV8910	1042	HW7962
2009	HV5864	1018	HV6963						

Opposite, top:- **New single-deck buses for New World First Bus comprise Plaxton-bodied Dennis Darts which, as with all the new buses being delivered, are fitted with airconditioning. Pictured passing through the Admiralty district is 2016, HV8269.** *Paul Wigan*
Opposite, bottom:- **The latest buses taken into stock by CMB were Alexander-bodied Volvo Olympians with three batches being supplied between 1994 and 1998. One of the 1996 delivery is VA47, GW5011, seen at Causeway Bay on Hong Kong island. Fleet details of the previous CMB fleet, and the other operators in Hong Kong at the time of tranfer to China are included in the sister publication the Hong Kong Bus Handbook.** *Paul Wigan*

FirstGroup provide the operational management for New World First Bus and have been instrumental in providing the supply of new vehicles needed for this franchise. Pictured on service 691 is Dennis Dominators 3004, HX5101. *Ken Mackenzie*

2061-2094 Dennis Dart SLF 10.3m   Plaxton Pointer 2   N--D   1999

2061	HY7390	2068	HY7438	2075	HY8973	2082	HY9708	2089	
2062	HY7281	2069	HY6798	2076	HY9848	2083	HY8839	2090	
2063	HY7985	2070	HZ220	2077	HY9246	2084	HY9275	2091	
2064	HY9159	2071	HY9064	2078	HY8521	2085	HY8681	2092	
2065	HY6371	2072	HY9322	2079	HY8993	2086	HZ1973	2093	
2066	HY8116	2073	HY9996	2080	HY9603	2087	HZ1586	2094	
2067	HY9565	2074	HY8369	2081	HY324	2088			

3001-3042 Dennis Trident 12m   Duple Metsec   N--/--D   1998-99

3001	HX5993	3010	HY726	3019	HY6227	3027	HZ3648	3035	HZ5090
3002	HX5636	3011	HY2077	3020	HZ1156	3028	HZ3150	3036	HZ6313
3003	HX6064	3012	HY3075	3021	HZ691	3029	HZ4001	3037	HZ6761
3004	HX5101	3013	HY3650	3022	HZ706	3030	HZ2867	3038	HZ6800
3005	HY2357	3014	HY3792	3023	HZ802	3031	HZ4237	3039	HZ8453
3006	HY2230	3015	HY3524	3024	HZ1453	3032	HZ5937	3040	HZ9312
3007	HY1508	3016	HY4142	3025	HZ2509	3033	HZ5518	3041	JA2047
3008	HY2190	3017	HY2530	3026	HZ1770	3034	HZ4843	3042	HZ9589
3009	HY1426	3018	HY4596						

3043-3062 Dennis Trident 12m   Duple Metsec   N--/--D   1998-99

3043	JB3937	3047	JB5486	3051	JB6704	3055	JB7656	3059	JB7484
3044	JB3385	3048	JB4830	3052	JB6491	3056	JB7199	3060	
3045	JB5584	3049	JB4604	3053	JB7236	3057	JB5423	3061	
3046	JB4752	3050	JB6402	3054	JB6897	3058	JB7507	3062	

Index to UK vehicles

2GRT	Aberdeen	A75FRY	Leicester	A117XWE	Mainline	A329BSC	Midland/Lowland
101ASV	Midland/Lowland	A76FRY	Leicester	A118KUM	Yorkshire	A371TGB	Glasgow
110ASV	Midland/Lowland	A77FRY	Leicester	A119GLS	Midland/Lowland	A372TGB	Glasgow
133CLT	CentreWest	A77RRP	Midland/Lowland	A119KUM	Yorkshire	A373TGB	Glasgow
143ASV	Midland/Lowland	A78FRY	Leicester	A119XWE	Mainline	A374TGB	Glasgow
144ASV	Midland/Lowland	A78RRP	Midland/Lowland	A120KUM	Yorkshire	A401YAK	Mainline
156ASV	Midland/Lowland	A79RRP	Midland/Lowland	A121KUM	Yorkshire	A402YAK	Mainline
270KTA	Western National	A80RRP	Midland/Lowland	A128ESG	Western National	A403YAK	Mainline
278TNY	Cymru	A81RRP	Midland/Lowland	A136BSC	Midland/Lowland	A405YAK	Mainline
292CLT	CentreWest	A82RRP	Midland/Lowland	A137BSC	Midland/Lowland	A406YAK	Mainline
365UMY	Midland/Lowland	A82KUM	Yorkshire	A137SMA	PMT	A407YAK	Mainline
481FPO	Western National	A83KUM	Yorkshire	A138BSC	Midland/Lowland	A408YAK	Mainline
487GFR	Midland/Lowland	A84KUM	Yorkshire	A139BSC	Midland/Lowland	A409YAK	Mainline
507EXA	PMT	A85KUM	Yorkshire	A140BSC	Midland/Lowland	A410YAK	Mainline
510CLT	CentreWest	A86KUM	Yorkshire	A141BSC	Midland/Lowland	A411YAK	Mainline
530OHU	Western National	A87KUM	Yorkshire	A142BSC	Midland/Lowland	A412YAK	Mainline
557BNG	Eastern Counties	A88KUM	Yorkshire	A143BSC	Midland/Lowland	A413YAK	Mainline
595JPU	Southern National	A89KUM	Yorkshire	A143SMA	PMT	A414YAK	Mainline
620HOD	Southern National	A90KUM	Yorkshire	A144SMA	PMT	A415YAK	Mainline
624BVG	Eastern Counties	A91KUM	Yorkshire	A146UDM	PMT	A416YAK	Mainline
692FFC	Midland/Lowland	A92KUM	Yorkshire	A147UDM	Essex Buses	A417YAK	Mainline
693AFU	Midland/Lowland	A93KUM	Yorkshire	A156UDM	PMT	A418YAK	Mainline
737ABD	Aberdeen	A94KUM	Yorkshire	A157UDM	PMT	A419YAK	Mainline
781GRT	Aberdeen	A95KUM	Yorkshire	A158UDM	PMT	A421YAK	Mainline
809DYE	CentreWest	A96KUM	Yorkshire	A159UDM	PMT	A423YAK	Mainline
810DYE	CentreWest	A97KUM	Yorkshire	A160UDM	PMT	A424YAK	Mainline
811DYE	CentreWest	A98KUM	Yorkshire	A161VDM	PMT	A425YAK	Mainline
824KDV	Western National	A99KUM	Yorkshire	A162VDM	PMT	A426YAK	Mainline
865GAT	Southern National	A100KUM	Yorkshire	A163VDM	PMT	A427YAK	Mainline
894GUO	Western National	A101FSA	Aberdeen	A164VDM	PMT	A428YAK	Mainline
920GTA	Western National	A101KUM	Yorkshire	A165VDM	PMT	A429YAK	Mainline
948RJO	Cymru	A101RGE	Glasgow	A166VFM	PMT	A430YAK	Mainline
3156WE	Mainline	A102FPL	Glasgow	A167VFM	PMT	A431YAK	Mainline
3904WE	Mainline	A102FSA	Aberdeen	A168VFM	PMT	A433YAK	Mainline
4384LJ	Southern National	A102KUM	Yorkshire	A169VFM	PMT	A434YAK	Mainline
4750WY	Eastern Counties	A102RGE	Glasgow	A170VFM	PMT	A435YAK	Mainline
6149KP	Eastern Counties	A103FSA	Aberdeen	A171VFM	PMT	A436YAK	Mainline
7694VC	Eastern Counties	A103KUM	Yorkshire	A201YWP	Eastern Counties	A438YAK	Mainline
7881UA	Midland/Lowland	A103RGE	Glasgow	A202UYS	Glasgow	A470GMS	Midland/Lowland
8683LJ	Southern National	A104FSA	Aberdeen	A202YWP	Eastern Counties	A475GMS	Glasgow
8995WY	Yorkshire	A104KUM	Yorkshire	A203RHT	Bristol	A477GMS	Midland/Lowland
A9SMT	Midland/Lowland	A104RGE	Glasgow	A203UYS	Glasgow	A483UYS	Glasgow
A10SMT	Midland/Lowland	A105FSA	Aberdeen	A204RHT	Western National	A484UYS	Glasgow
A12SMT	Midland/Lowland	A105KUM	Yorkshire	A204UYS	Glasgow	A541KUM	Manchester
A13SMT	Midland/Lowland	A105RGE	Glasgow	A204YWP	Eastern Counties	A542KUM	Yorkshire
A14SMT	Midland/Lowland	A106FSA	Aberdeen	A205UYS	Glasgow	A544KUM	Yorkshire
A15SMT	Midland/Lowland	A106KUM	Yorkshire	A206SAE	Western National	A545KUM	Yorkshire
A16SMT	Midland/Lowland	A106UYS	Glasgow	A206UYS	Glasgow	A546KUM	Manchester
A17SMT	Midland/Lowland	A106XWE	Mainline	A277ROW	Hampshire	A547KUM	Manchester
A18SMT	Midland/Lowland	A107FSA	Aberdeen	A295XAK	Mainline	A549KUM	Yorkshire
A19SMT	Midland/Lowland	A107KUM	Yorkshire	A296XAK	Mainline	A562SGA	Glasgow
A20SMT	Midland/Lowland	A107UYS	Glasgow	A297XAK	Mainline	A563SGA	Glasgow
A21VDS	Glasgow	A107XWE	Mainline	A298XAK	Mainline	A564SGA	Glasgow
A22VDS	Glasgow	A108FSA	Aberdeen	A299XAK	Mainline	A566SGA	Glasgow
A22VDS	Midland/Lowland	A108KUM	Yorkshire	A300XAK	Mainline	A568SGA	Glasgow
A23VDS	Midland/Lowland	A108UYS	Glasgow	A301KJT	Hampshire	A576HDB	Manchester
A24VDS	Glasgow	A108XWE	Mainline	A301XAK	Mainline	A577HDB	Manchester
A25VDS	Glasgow	A109FSA	Aberdeen	A302KJT	Hampshire	A578HDB	Manchester
A26VDS	Glasgow	A109KUM	Yorkshire	A302XAK	Mainline	A579HDB	Manchester
A27VDS	Glasgow	A109UYS	Glasgow	A303XAK	Mainline	A580HDB	Manchester
A29VDS	Midland/Lowland	A109XWE	Mainline	A304XAK	Mainline	A590AHB	Southern National
A30VDS	Glasgow	A110FSA	Aberdeen	A311XAK	Mainline	A599NYG	Yorkshire
A31VDS	Glasgow	A110KUM	Yorkshire	A312XAK	Mainline	A600NYG	Yorkshire
A32VDS	Midland/Lowland	A110UYS	Glasgow	A313XAK	Mainline	A600TNS	Glasgow
A33VDS	Glasgow	A110XWE	Mainline	A314XAK	Mainline	A601NYG	Yorkshire
A34VDS	Midland/Lowland	A111KUM	Yorkshire	A315XAK	Mainline	A601TNS	Glasgow
A35VDS	Glasgow	A111XWE	Mainline	A316XAK	Mainline	A602TNS	Glasgow
A35VDS	Midland/Lowland	A112KUM	Yorkshire	A317XAK	Mainline	A603TNS	Glasgow
A36VDS	Midland/Lowland	A112XWE	Mainline	A319XAK	Mainline	A604TNS	Glasgow
A37VDS	Midland/Lowland	A113KUM	Yorkshire	A320XAK	Mainline	A622YOX	Southern National
A38VDS	Glasgow	A114KUM	Yorkshire	A322BSC	Midland/Lowland	A624YOX	Southern National
A39VDS	Glasgow	A114XWE	Mainline	A323BSC	Midland/Lowland	A649YOX	Southern National
A40VDS	Midland/Lowland	A115KUM	Yorkshire	A324BSC	Midland/Lowland	A656HNB	Manchester
A71FRY	Leicester	A115XWE	Mainline	A325BSC	Midland/Lowland	A658HNB	Manchester
A72FRY	Leicester	A116KUM	Yorkshire	A326BSC	Midland/Lowland	A659HNB	Manchester
A73FRY	Leicester	A116XWE	Mainline	A327BSC	Midland/Lowland	A659KUM	Midland/Lowland
A74FRY	Leicester	A117KUM	Yorkshire	A328BSC	Midland/Lowland	A660KUM	Northampton

Reg	Operator	Reg	Operator	Reg	Operator	Reg	Operator
A661KUM	Midland/Lowland	A753LWY	Manchester	ACY178A	Cymru	ANA169Y	Manchester
A662HNB	Manchester	A753NNA	Manchester	AFJ692T	Southern National	ANA171Y	Manchester
A662KUM	Yorkshire	A753VAF	Western National	AFJ697T	Western National	ANA172Y	Manchester
A663HNB	Manchester	A754LWY	Yorkshire	AFJ698T	Western National	ANA174Y	Manchester
A665KUM	Western National	A754THV	CentreWest	AFJ699T	Western National	ANA175Y	Manchester
A667HNB	Manchester	A754VAF	Western National	AFJ700T	Western National	ANA176Y	Manchester
A669KUM	Midland/Lowland	A755LWY	Manchester	AFJ701T	Western National	ANA178Y	Manchester
A670HNB	Manchester	A755NNA	Manchester	AFJ702T	Western National	ANA181Y	Manchester
A672HNB	Manchester	A755VAF	Western National	AFJ703T	Western National	ANA182Y	Cymru
A673HNB	Manchester	A756LWY	Yorkshire	AFJ704T	Western National	ANA183Y	Manchester
A675HNB	Cymru	A756NNA	Manchester	AFJ705T	Western National	ANA184Y	Manchester
A676HNB	Manchester	A756VAF	Bristol	AFJ706T	Western National	ANA186Y	Manchester
A677HNB	Manchester	A757VAF	Bristol	AFJ707T	Western National	ANA187Y	Manchester
A681HNB	Manchester	A758LWY	Yorkshire	AFJ708T	Western National	ANA188Y	Manchester
A682HNB	Manchester	A758NNA	Manchester	AFJ714T	Western National	ANA189Y	Cymru
A685KDV	Southern National	A760LWY	Yorkshire	AFJ715T	Western National	ANA209T	Yorkshire
A686HNB	Manchester	A760NNA	Manchester	AFJ726T	Southern National	ANA531Y	Manchester
A686MWX	Yorkshire	A763NNA	Manchester	AFJ727T	Southern National	ANA532Y	Manchester
A688HNB	Cymru	A765NNA	Manchester	AFJ728T	Southern National	ANA535Y	Manchester
A689HNB	Manchester	A809THW	Bristol	AFJ729T	Southern National	ANA536Y	Manchester
A691HNB	Manchester	A810THW	Bristol	AFJ730T	Southern National	ANA539Y	Yorkshire
A691OHJ	Southern National	A811THW	Bristol	AFJ739T	Southern National	ANA540Y	Manchester
A692HNB	Manchester	A812THW	Bristol	AFJ744T	Western National	ANA541Y	Manchester
A694HNB	Cymru	A813THW	Bristol	AFJ745T	Western National	ANA542Y	Manchester
A694OHJ	Southern National	A814THW	Bristol	AFJ746T	Western National	ANA547Y	Manchester
A695OHJ	Southern National	A892SUL	CentreWest	AFJ747T	Western National	ANA548Y	Manchester
A696YOX	Southern National	A893SUL	CentreWest	AFJ748T	Hampshire	ANA549Y	Manchester
A697HNB	Manchester	A895KCL	Midland Red	AFJ749T	Western National	ANA551Y	Manchester
A701LNC	Manchester	A896KCL	Midland Red	AFJ750T	Western National	ANA554Y	Manchester
A703LNC	Manchester	A898SUL	CentreWest	AFJ751T	Western National	ANA555Y	Manchester
A709LNC	Manchester	A901SUL	CentreWest	AFJ752T	Hampshire	ANA556Y	Yorkshire
A711DAU	Eastern Counties	A92KWW	Essex Buses	AFJ755T	Midland Red	ANA557Y	Yorkshire
A712LNC	Manchester	A938SUL	CentreWest	AFJ756T	Midland Red	ANA558Y	Manchester
A713LNC	Manchester	A941SUL	CentreWest	AFJ760T	Western National	ANA560Y	Yorkshire
A716LNC	Manchester	A943SUL	CentreWest	AFJ761T	Western National	ANA561Y	Manchester
A717LNC	Manchester	A945SAE	Bristol	AFJ762T	Western National	ANA563Y	Manchester
A718LNC	Manchester	A946SAE	Bristol	AFJ763T	Hampshire	ANA566Y	Manchester
A720LNC	Manchester	A947SAE	Bristol	AFJ764T	Southern National	ANA567Y	Manchester
A721LNC	Manchester	A948SAE	Bristol	AFJ765T	Southern National	ANA570Y	Manchester
A727LNC	Manchester	A949SAE	Bristol	AFJ766T	Southern National	ANA571Y	Manchester
A728LNC	Manchester	A950SAE	Bristol	AFJ767T	Southern National	ANA573Y	Manchester
A729LNC	Manchester	A951SAE	Bristol	AFJ768T	Southern National	ANA575Y	Manchester
A732LNC	Manchester	A952SAE	Bristol	AFJ770T	Southern National	ANA576Y	Manchester
A732PSU	Glasgow	A952SUL	CentreWest	AFJ773T	Southern National	ANA578Y	Manchester
A733GFA	PMT	A953SAE	Bristol	AFM3W	Southern National	ANA580Y	Manchester
A733LNC	Manchester	A954SAE	Bristol	AHG947R	Southern National	ANA581Y	Manchester
A733PSU	Glasgow	A955THW	Bristol	AHT206J	Southern National	ANA584Y	Manchester
A734GFA	PMT	A956THW	Bristol	AHU514V	Hampshire	ANA587Y	Manchester
A734PSU	Glasgow	A957THW	Bristol	AHU516V	Western National	ANA588Y	Manchester
A735GFA	PMT	A958THW	Bristol	AHW198V	Bristol	ANA590Y	Manchester
A735PSU	Glasgow	A959THW	Bristol	AHW203V	PMT	ANA591Y	Manchester
A736GFA	PMT	A960THW	Bristol	AJH855T	Western National	ANA594Y	Manchester
A736LNC	Manchester	A961THW	Bristol	AJN825	Essex Buses	ANA595Y	Manchester
A736PSU	Glasgow	A962THW	Bristol	AKG219A	Cymru	ANA599Y	Manchester
A737GFA	PMT	A963THW	Bristol	ALD913B	Capital	ANA603Y	Manchester
A737NNA	Yorkshire	A964THW	Bristol	ALS104Y	Midland/Lowland	ANA606Y	Manchester
A737PSU	Glasgow	A965THW	Bristol	ALS116Y	Midland/Lowland	ANA607Y	Manchester
A738GFA	PMT	A966THW	Bristol	ALS117Y	Midland/Lowland	ANA610Y	Manchester
A738NNA	Manchester	A967THW	Bristol	ALS118Y	Midland/Lowland	ANA611Y	Manchester
A739GFA	PMT	A968THW	Bristol	ALS119Y	Midland/Lowland	ANA615Y	Manchester
A739NNA	Manchester	A979SYF	CentreWest	ALS120Y	Glasgow	ANA616Y	Manchester
A739PSU	Glasgow	A980OST	Eastern Counties	ALS122Y	Midland/Lowland	ANA617Y	Manchester
A740GFA	PMT	A981FLS	Glasgow	ALS123Y	Midland/Lowland	ANA621Y	Manchester
A740NNA	Manchester	A982FLS	Glasgow	ALS124Y	Midland/Lowland	ANA622Y	Manchester
A741GFA	PMT	A983FLS	Glasgow	ALS125Y	Midland/Lowland	ANA623Y	Manchester
A741PSU	Glasgow	A984FLS	Glasgow	ALS126Y	Midland/Lowland	ANA624Y	Cymru
A742GFA	PMT	AAE645V	Hampshire	ALS127Y	Midland/Lowland	ANA626Y	Manchester
A742PSU	Glasgow	AAE652V	Hampshire	ALS128Y	Midland/Lowland	ANA629Y	Manchester
A743JRE	PMT	AAE653V	Hampshire	ALS129Y	Midland/Lowland	ANA630Y	Cymru
A743PSU	Glasgow	AAE654V	Cymru	ALS130Y	Glasgow	ANA633Y	Manchester
A744JRE	PMT	AAE655V	Eastern Counties	ALS131Y	Glasgow	ANA635Y	Manchester
A745JRE	PMT	AAE663V	Hampshire	ALS132Y	Midland/Lowland	ANA636Y	Manchester
A746JRE	PMT	AAL516A	Cymru	ALS133Y	Midland/Lowland	ANA638Y	Manchester
A746NNA	Manchester	AAX450A	Cymru	ALS134Y	Midland/Lowland	ANA640Y	Manchester
A747JRE	PMT	AAX466A	Cymru	ALS135Y	Midland/Lowland	ANA641Y	Manchester
A748NNA	Cymru	AAX515A	Cymru	ANA25T	Yorkshire	ANA645Y	Manchester
A749THV	CentreWest	AAX529A	Cymru	ANA34T	Yorkshire	ANA648Y	Manchester
A750LWY	Yorkshire	ABD72X	Eastern Counties	ANA40T	Yorkshire	ANA649Y	Manchester
A750VAF	Western National	ABD73X	Eastern Counties	ANA44T	Yorkshire	ANA650Y	Manchester
A751LWY	Yorkshire	ABD73X	Eastern Counties	ANA152Y	Manchester	ANA652Y	Manchester
A751THV	CentreWest	ABD74X	Northampton	ANA166Y	Manchester	ANA654Y	Manchester
A751VAF	Western National	ABD75X	Northampton	ANA167Y	Manchester	ANA655Y	Manchester
A752LWY	Yorkshire	ABD76X	Northampton	ANA168Y	Manchester	AST151W	Hampshire
A752VAF	Western National	ABR869S	Yorkshire			AST153W	Hampshire

Reg	Fleet	Reg	Fleet	Reg	Fleet	Reg	Fleet
AST154W	Hampshire	B100PKS	Midland/Lowland	B151XNA	Manchester	B440CKW	Capital
AST156W	Hampshire	B100SJA	Manchester	B152GSC	Midland/Lowland	B441CKW	Mainline
AST158W	Hampshire	B101PKS	Midland/Lowland	B152XNA	Manchester	B442CKW	Mainline
AST159W	Hampshire	B101SJA	Manchester	B153GSC	Midland/Lowland	B443CKW	Capital
ATL555L	Southern National	B102PKS	Midland/Lowland	B154GSC	Midland/Lowland	B444CKW	Capital
ATL559L	Southern National	B102SJA	Manchester	B155GSC	Midland/Lowland	B445CKW	Mainline
AUT31Y	Northampton	B102WUW	Capital	B156GSC	Midland/Lowland	B446CKW	Mainline
AUT32Y	Northampton	B103JAB	Midland Red	B157GSC	Midland/Lowland	B447CKW	Mainline
AUT33Y	Northampton	B103PKS	Midland/Lowland	B158GSC	Midland/Lowland	B448CKW	Mainline
AUT34Y	Northampton	B103SJA	Manchester	B159KSC	Midland/Lowland	B449CKW	Mainline
AUT35Y	Northampton	B103WUW	Capital	B160KSC	Midland/Lowland	B449WTC	Hampshire
AUT70Y	Leicester	B104JAB	Eastern Counties	B161KSC	Midland/Lowland	B460BHY	Southern National
AWG623	Midland/Lowland	B104PKS	Midland/Lowland	B162KSC	Midland/Lowland	B461BHY	Southern National
AWN813V	Cymru	B104SJA	Manchester	B169KSC	Midland/Lowland	B462BHY	Southern National
AWN815V	Cymru	B105JAB	Midland Red	B170KSC	Midland/Lowland	B501RWY	Yorkshire
B21YYS	Glasgow	B105PKS	Midland/Lowland	B171KSC	Midland/Lowland	B502RWY	Yorkshire
B23YYS	Glasgow	B105SJA	Manchester	B172KSC	Midland/Lowland	B503RWY	Yorkshire
B24YYS	Glasgow	B106JAB	Midland Red	B173KSC	Midland/Lowland	B504RWY	Yorkshire
B25YYS	Glasgow	B106PKS	Midland/Lowland	B181BLG	PMT	B505RWY	Yorkshire
B26YYS	Glasgow	B106SJA	Manchester	B182BLG	PMT	B506RWY	Yorkshire
B27YYS	Glasgow	B106XJO	Southern National	B188BLG	PMT	B518UWW	Yorkshire
B28YYS	Glasgow	B107JAB	Midland Red	B194BAF	Western National	B519UWW	Yorkshire
B29YYS	Glasgow	B107SJA	Manchester	B195BAF	Western National	B520UWW	Yorkshire
B30YYS	Glasgow	B108SJA	Manchester	B195BLG	PMT	B523UWW	Yorkshire
B31YYS	Glasgow	B108XJO	Southern National	B196BAF	Western National	B561RWY	Yorkshire
B33YYS	Glasgow	B109SJA	Manchester	B197BAF	Western National	B562RWY	Manchester
B34YYS	Glasgow	B111SJA	Manchester	B199DTU	PMT	B563RWY	Yorkshire
B37PJA	Manchester	B112MSO	Aberdeen	B199WUL	CentreWest	B564RWY	Manchester
B38AAF	Western National	B112SJA	Manchester	B200DGG	Glasgow	B565RWY	Manchester
B38PJA	Manchester	B113MSO	Aberdeen	B200DTU	PMT	B566RWY	Yorkshire
B40PJA	Manchester	B113SJA	Manchester	B201DTU	PMT	B567RWY	Yorkshire
B41AAF	Western National	B114MSO	Aberdeen	B201WUL	CentreWest	B568BOK	Eastern Counties
B41PJA	Manchester	B115MSO	Aberdeen	B202DTU	PMT	B568RWY	Manchester
B43AAF	Western National	B115NBF	PMT	B241BYS	Glasgow	B569RWY	Manchester
B43PJA	Manchester	B115SJA	Manchester	B242BYS	Midland/Lowland	B570RWY	Yorkshire
B44PJA	Manchester	B116MSO	Aberdeen	B243BYS	Glasgow	B571RWY	Manchester
B45PJA	Manchester	B116TVU	Manchester	B244BYS	Glasgow	B572RWY	Manchester
B46PJA	Manchester	B117MSO	Aberdeen	B244WUL	CentreWest	B575RWY	Yorkshire
B47PJA	Manchester	B118MSO	Aberdeen	B245BYS	Glasgow	B577RWY	Yorkshire
B48PJA	Manchester	B119MSO	Aberdeen	B245WUL	CentreWest	B578RWY	Yorkshire
B52PJA	Manchester	B120MSO	Aberdeen	B246BYS	Glasgow	B579MLS	Glasgow
B54PJA	Manchester	B120TVU	Manchester	B246WUL	CentreWest	B579RWY	Manchester
B59PJA	Manchester	B121MSO	Aberdeen	B247BYS	Glasgow	B580MLS	Glasgow
B61PJA	Manchester	B122RWY	Yorkshire	B247WUL	CentreWest	B580RWY	Yorkshire
B62PJA	Manchester	B123RWY	Yorkshire	B248BYS	Glasgow	B581MLS	Midland/Lowland
B63PJA	Manchester	B123TVU	Manchester	B249BYS	Glasgow	B582MLS	Midland/Lowland
B64PJA	Manchester	B124PEL	Cymru	B250BYS	Glasgow	B583MLS	Midland/Lowland
B66PJA	Manchester	B124RWY	Yorkshire	B251BYS	Glasgow	B584MLS	Midland/Lowland
B68PJA	Manchester	B125RWY	Yorkshire	B252BYS	Glasgow	B585MLS	Midland/Lowland
B71PJA	Manchester	B126RWY	Yorkshire	B253BYS	Glasgow	B586MLS	Glasgow
B73PJA	Manchester	B127RWY	Yorkshire	B254BYS	Glasgow	B587MLS	Midland/Lowland
B75PJA	Manchester	B127WNB	Manchester	B255BYS	Glasgow	B588MLS	Midland/Lowland
B76PJA	Manchester	B128RWY	Yorkshire	B256BYS	Glasgow	B591FOG	Southern National
B78PJA	Manchester	B128WNB	Manchester	B257BYS	Glasgow	B610VWU	Yorkshire
B79MJF	Leicester	B129RWY	Yorkshire	B257WUL	CentreWest	B631XOW	Hampshire
B79PJA	Manchester	B129WNB	Manchester	B258BYS	Glasgow	B697BPU	Glasgow
B80MJF	Leicester	B130RWY	Yorkshire	B258WUL	CentreWest	B698BPU	Essex Buses
B81MJF	Leicester	B130WNB	Manchester	B259BYS	Glasgow	B699BPU	Essex Buses
B81PJA	Manchester	B131RWY	Yorkshire	B259WUL	CentreWest	B86MRY	Leicester
B82MJF	Leicester	B131WNB	Manchester	B260BYS	Glasgow	B895YYD	Southern National
B83MJF	Leicester	B132RWY	Yorkshire	B260WUL	CentreWest	B921CDT	Mainline
B83PJA	Manchester	B133RWY	Yorkshire	B261BYS	Glasgow	B922CDT	Mainline
B84MRY	Leicester	B134RWY	Yorkshire	B262BYS	Midland/Lowland	B924CDT	Mainline
B85MRY	Leicester	B134WNB	Manchester	B263BYS	Glasgow	B932CDT	Mainline
B85PJA	Manchester	B135RWY	Yorkshire	B267WUL	CentreWest	B933CDT	Mainline
B88PKS	Midland/Lowland	B136WNB	Manchester	B287KPF	Midland/Lowland	B934CDT	Mainline
B89PKS	Glasgow	B137RWY	Yorkshire	B350PJA	Manchester	B935CDT	Mainline
B90PKS	Glasgow	B138RWY	Yorkshire	B351CDT	Mainline	B937CDT	Mainline
B90SJA	Manchester	B139RWY	Yorkshire	B351PJA	Manchester	B940CDT	Mainline
B91PKS	Glasgow	B140RWY	Yorkshire	B352CDT	Mainline	B941FET	Mainline
B92PKS	Glasgow	B140WNB	Manchester	B353CDT	Mainline	B942FET	Mainline
B92SJA	Manchester	B141RWY	Yorkshire	B354CDT	Mainline	B943FET	Mainline
B93PKS	Midland/Lowland	B141WNB	Manchester	B355CDT	Mainline	B960WRN	Essex Buses
B93SJA	Manchester	B142RWY	Yorkshire	B356CDT	Mainline	B999YUS	Glasgow
B94PKS	Midland/Lowland	B142WNB	Manchester	B357CDT	Mainline	BCB610V	Yorkshire
B95PKS	Midland/Lowland	B143RWY	Yorkshire	B358CDT	Mainline	BCB611V	Yorkshire
B96PKS	Midland/Lowland	B144WNB	Manchester	B359CDT	Mainline	BCB612V	Yorkshire
B96SJA	Manchester	B144WUL	CentreWest	B359LOY	Capital	BCB616V	Yorkshire
B97SJA	Manchester	B145RWY	Yorkshire	B360CDT	Mainline	BCL216T	Eastern Counties
B98PKS	Midland/Lowland	B148XNA	Manchester	B361CDT	Mainline	BEP963V	Essex Buses
B98SJA	Manchester	B149GSC	Midland/Lowland	B362CDT	Mainline	BEP966V	Western National
B99PKS	Midland/Lowland	B150GSC	Midland/Lowland	B364CDT	Mainline	BEP968V	Western National
B99SJA	Manchester	B151GSC	Midland/Lowland	B365CDT	Mainline	BEP976V	Cymru
				B439CKW	Mainline	BEP978V	Cymru

BEP980V	Cymru	C112BTS	Glasgow	C224HJN	Western National	C376RUY	Midland Red
BEP981V	Cymru	C112HDT	Mainline	C225CBU	Manchester	C377BUV	CentreWest
BEP984V	Cymru	C113BTS	Glasgow	C227ENE	Manchester	C377RUY	Western National
BFR302R	Western National	C113HDT	Mainline	C228ENE	Manchester	C378BUV	CentreWest
BFX576T	Southern National	C114BTS	Glasgow	C229ENE	Manchester	C378RUY	Western National
BGS292X	Southern National	C115BTS	Glasgow	C231ENE	Manchester	C379RUY	Western National
BLS423Y	Northampton	C128VRE	PMT	C232ENE	Manchester	C380BUV	CentreWest
BLS426Y	Glasgow	C130HJN	Eastern Counties	C233ENE	Manchester	C380RUY	Western National
BLS427Y	Glasgow	C146KBT	Yorkshire	C235ENE	Manchester	C382BUV	CentreWest
BLS428Y	Glasgow	C146WRE	PMT	C237EVU	Manchester	C384BUV	CentreWest
BLS430Y	Glasgow	C147KBT	Yorkshire	C238EVU	Manchester	C400BUV	CentreWest
BLS431Y	Glasgow	C148KBT	Yorkshire	C239EVU	Manchester	C407HJN	Essex Buses
BLS432Y	Northampton	C149KBT	Yorkshire	C240EVU	Manchester	C408HJN	Essex Buses
BLS436Y	Glasgow	C150KBT	Yorkshire	C241EVU	Manchester	C409HJN	Essex Buses
BLS437Y	Midland/Lowland	C157YBA	Manchester	C242EVU	Manchester	C410HJN	Essex Buses
BLS438Y	Glasgow	C158TLF	Southern National	C243EVU	Manchester	C412BUV	CentreWest
BLS439Y	Glasgow	C159TLF	Southern National	C244EVU	Manchester	C412HJN	Essex Buses
BLS440Y	Glasgow	C159YBA	Manchester	C245EVU	Manchester	C413HJN	Essex Buses
BLS443Y	Leicester	C160YBA	Manchester	C246FRJ	Manchester	C414HJN	Essex Buses
BLS444Y	Glasgow	C161YBA	Manchester	C247FRJ	Manchester	C415BUV	CentreWest
BLS445Y	Glasgow	C162YBA	Manchester	C248FRJ	Manchester	C415HJN	Essex Buses
BLS446Y	Midland/Lowland	C163YBA	Manchester	C249FRJ	Manchester	C416HJN	Essex Buses
BNO676T	Essex Buses	C168YBA	Manchester	C250FRJ	Manchester	C417HJN	Essex Buses
BOK258T	Bristol	C171YBA	Manchester	C251FRJ	Manchester	C418BUV	CentreWest
BOU3V	Hampshire	C174VSF	Midland/Lowland	C252FRJ	Manchester	C418HJN	Essex Buses
BOU4V	Hampshire	C175VSF	Midland/Lowland	C253FRJ	Manchester	C419BUV	CentreWest
BOU5V	Cymru	C176VSF	Midland/Lowland	C254FRJ	Manchester	C419HJN	Essex Buses
BOU8V	Cymru	C177VSF	Midland/Lowland	C301PNP	Midland Red	C420BUV	CentreWest
BSS76	Midland/Lowland	C177YBA	Manchester	C309PNP	Midland Red	C421BUV	CentreWest
BSV807	Midland/Lowland	C178VSF	Midland/Lowland	C312KTH	Cymru	C421HJN	Essex Buses
BVG219T	Eastern Counties	C179VSF	Midland/Lowland	C314DRH	Southern National	C422BUV	CentreWest
BVG220T	Eastern Counties	C180VSF	Midland/Lowland	C316PNP	Midland Red	C433BHY	Hampshire
BVG224T	Eastern Counties	C180YBA	Manchester	C319PNP	Midland Red	C438BUV	CentreWest
BVP770V	Midland Red	C181VSF	Midland/Lowland	C321PNP	Midland Red	C443BHY	Hampshire
BVP776V	Cymru	C182VSF	Midland/Lowland	C324PNP	Midland Red	C448BKM	Glasgow
BVP778V	Cymru	C182YBA	Manchester	C325GFJ	Western National	C468BHY	Southern National
BVP781V	Cymru	C183VSF	Midland/Lowland	C326GFJ	Western National	C46HDT	Manchester
BVP782V	PMT	C183YBA	Manchester	C327GFJ	Western National	C473BHY	Southern National
BVP783V	PMT	C186YBA	Manchester	C328BUV	CentreWest	C475BHY	Midland Red
BVR55T	Yorkshire	C187YBA	Manchester	C328PNP	Midland Red	C476BHY	Midland Red
BVR65T	Yorkshire	C188RVV	Glasgow	C331GFJ	Western National	C477BHY	Midland Red
BVR67T	Yorkshire	C188YBA	Manchester	C331PNP	Midland Red	C478BHY	Midland Red
BVR70T	Yorkshire	C189YBA	Manchester	C332PNP	Midland Red	C480BHY	Midland Red
BVR85T	Yorkshire	C190YBA	Manchester	C333GFJ	Southern National	C481BHY	Cymru
BVR92T	Yorkshire	C192YBA	Manchester	C334GFJ	Western National	C481CBU	Manchester
BVR97T	Yorkshire	C194YBA	Manchester	C335BUV	CentreWest	C482CBU	Manchester
BYX249V	Capital	C200YBA	Manchester	C335PNP	Midland Red	C483BHY	Midland Red
BYX284X	Capital	C201CBU	Manchester	C336GFJ	Southern National	C483CBU	Manchester
BYX285V	CentreWest	C201FVU	Manchester	C337GFJ	Western National	C483YWY	Yorkshire
BYX287V	Capital	C202CBU	Manchester	C338BUV	CentreWest	C484YWY	Yorkshire
BYX291V	CentreWest	C202FVU	Manchester	C338GFJ	Western National	C487BHY	Midland Red
BYX305V	CentreWest	C202HTH	Cymru	C338PNP	Midland Red	C488BHY	Midland Red
BYX308V	CentreWest	C203CBU	Manchester	C339PNP	Midland Red	C489HCV	Western National
BYX311V	Capital	C203FVU	Manchester	C340BUV	CentreWest	C490BHY	Midland Red
C28EUH	Bristol	C204CBU	Manchester	C340PNP	Midland Red	C491BHY	Midland Red
C29EUH	Bristol	C204FVU	Manchester	C341GFJ	Western National	C492BHY	Midland Red
C41HDT	Manchester	C205FVU	Manchester	C342GFJ	Western National	C497BHY	Midland Red
C56FDV	Western National	C206CBU	Manchester	C343GFJ	Western National	C498BHY	Midland Red
C98HGL	Western National	C206FVU	Manchester	C344GFJ	Western National	C499BHY	Midland Red
C99HGL	Western National	C207FVU	Manchester	C346GFJ	Western National	C507KBT	Yorkshire
C100HGL	Western National	C207HTH	Cymru	C347GFJ	Southern National	C508KBT	Yorkshire
C101HDT	Mainline	C208FVU	Manchester	C348GFJ	Western National	C509KBT	Yorkshire
C102HDT	Mainline	C208HJN	Western National	C349GFJ	Southern National	C510KBT	Yorkshire
C103HDT	Mainline	C209CBU	Manchester	C350GFJ	Western National	C511BFB	Essex Buses
C103HGL	Western National	C209FVU	Manchester	C352PNP	Midland Red	C511KBT	Yorkshire
C104HDT	Mainline	C210FVU	Manchester	C353GFJ	Southern National	C581SHC	Midland Red
C104HGL	Western National	C211CBU	Manchester	C357GFJ	Southern National	C582SHC	Midland Red
C105HDT	Mainline	C211UPD	Glasgow	C361RUY	Midland Red	C584SHC	Midland Red
C105HGL	Western National	C212UPD	Glasgow	C362RUY	Midland Red	C585SHC	Midland Red
C106HDT	Mainline	C213HTH	Midland Red	C363RUY	Midland Red	C586SHC	Midland Red
C106HGL	Western National	C213UPD	Glasgow	C364RUY	Midland Red	C587SHC	Midland Red
C107HDT	Mainline	C214HTH	Midland Red	C365GFJ	Southern National	C588SHC	Midland Red
C107HGL	Midland/Lowland	C215UPD	Glasgow	C365RUY	Midland Red	C589SHC	Midland Red
C107SDX	Leicester	C216HJN	Western National	C366RUY	Midland Red	C674ECVF	Western National
C108HDT	Mainline	C217CBU	Manchester	C367RUY	Midland Red	C676ECV	Western National
C108HGL	Western National	C218CBU	Manchester	C368RUY	Midland Red	C678ECV	Midland/Lowland
C108SDX	Leicester	C218HJN	Western National	C369RUY	Midland Red	C686ECV	Western National
C108SFP	PMT	C219CBU	Manchester	C370RUY	Midland Red	C690ECV	Western National
C109HDT	Mainline	C219HJN	Western National	C372CAS	Eastern Counties	C691ECV	Western National
C109HGL	Western National	C220CBU	Manchester	C373CAS	Eastern Counties	C695ECV	Midland/Lowland
C109SDX	Leicester	C220HJN	Western National	C374CAS	Eastern Counties	C695ECV	Midland/Lowland
C110HDT	Mainline	C222CBU	Manchester	C375BUV	CentreWest	C698ECV	Midland/Lowland
C111HDT	Mainline	C223CBU	Manchester	C375RUY	Midland Red	C698ECV	Midland/Lowland
C111SDX	Leicester	C223HJN	Western National	C376BUV	CentreWest	C706JMB	PMT

Reg	Operator	Reg	Operator	Reg	Operator	Reg	Operator
C711GEV	Essex Buses	C923GYD	Southern National	CUB38Y	Yorkshire	D182BEH	PMT
C784FRL	Western National	C924GYD	Southern National	CUB39Y	Yorkshire	D184ESC	Midland/Lowland
C785FRL	Western National	C925GYD	Southern National	CUB40Y	Yorkshire	D185ESC	Midland/Lowland
C787FRL	Western National	C926GYD	Southern National	CUB41Y	Yorkshire	D186ESC	Midland/Lowland
C790FRL	Midland Red	C927GYD	Southern National	CUB42Y	Yorkshire	D221VCD	Southern National
C791FRL	Western National	C929GYD	Southern National	CUB43Y	Yorkshire	D222VCD	Southern National
C792FRL	Western National	C930GYD	Southern National	CUB44Y	Yorkshire	D223VCD	Southern National
C794FRL	Western National	C931GYD	Southern National	CUB45Y	Yorkshire	D224VCD	Southern National
C795FRL	Western National	C933GYD	Southern National	CUB46Y	Yorkshire	D225VCD	Southern National
C796FRL	Western National	C934GYD	Southern National	CUB47Y	Yorkshire	D226UHC	Midland/Lowland
C797FRL	Western National	C935GYD	Southern National	CUB48Y	Yorkshire	D227OOJ	Eastern Counties
C798FRL	Western National	C936GYD	Southern National	CUB51Y	Yorkshire	D227UHC	Midland/Lowland
C800FRL	Western National	C939GYD	Southern National	CUB52Y	Yorkshire	D227VCD	Southern National
C801FRL	Western National	C942GYD	Southern National	CUB53Y	Yorkshire	D228PPU	Essex Buses
C801KHS	Glasgow	C945GYD	Southern National	CUB54Y	Yorkshire	D228VCD	Southern National
C802FRL	Western National	C947GYD	Southern National	CUB55Y	Yorkshire	D232UHC	Midland/Lowland
C802KHS	Glasgow	C947HWF	Mainline	CUB65Y	Yorkshire	D232VCD	Southern National
C803KHS	Glasgow	C948HWF	Mainline	CUB521Y	Yorkshire	D233VCD	Southern National
C804KHS	Glasgow	C949HWF	Mainline	CUB522Y	Yorkshire	D238PPU	Manchester
C805KHS	Glasgow	C950GAF	Western National	CUB523Y	Yorkshire	D241PPU	Manchester
C806KHS	Glasgow	C951GYD	Southern National	CUB525Y	Yorkshire	D256JVR	Manchester
C807KHS	Glasgow	C951LWJ	Mainline	CUB527Y	Yorkshire	D257JVR	Manchester
C808KHS	Glasgow	C952GAF	Western National	CUB529Y	Yorkshire	D258JVR	Manchester
C809KHS	Glasgow	C954GAF	Western National	CUB530Y	Yorkshire	D259JVR	Manchester
C810KHS	Glasgow	C955GAF	Western National	CUB531Y	Yorkshire	D261JVR	Manchester
C812SDY	Midland/Lowland	C955GYD	Southern National	CUB532Y	Manchester	D262JVR	Manchester
C821SDY	Midland/Lowland	C956GAF	Western National	CUB534Y	Yorkshire	D263JVR	Manchester
C862DYD	Southern National	C956LWJ	Mainline	CUB535Y	Yorkshire	D264JVR	Manchester
C866DYD	Southern National	C957LWJ	Mainline	CUB536Y	Yorkshire	D265JVR	Manchester
C867DYD	Southern National	C959GAF	Western National	CUB537Y	Yorkshire	D266JVR	Manchester
C868DYD	Southern National	C965GCV	Western National	CUV268C	CentreWest	D267JVR	Manchester
C869DYD	Southern National	C968GCV	Western National	CUV278C	CentreWest	D270JVR	Manchester
C871JWE	Mainline	C970GCV	Western National	CUV281C	CentreWest	D271JVR	Manchester
C872JWE	Mainline	C982KHS	Glasgow	CUV291C	CentreWest	D273JVR	Manchester
C873JWE	Mainline	C983KHS	Glasgow	CUV309C	CentreWest	D274JVR	Manchester
C874DYD	Southern National	CAV624V	Southern National	CUV313C	CentreWest	D275JVR	Manchester
C874JWE	Mainline	CGG835X	Glasgow	CUV352C	CentreWest	D276FAS	Midland/Lowland
C875JWE	Mainline	CGG837X	Glasgow	CUV357C	CentreWest	D276JVR	Manchester
C876DYD	Southern National	CHE540K	Glasgow	CVF29T	Eastern Counties	D301JVR	Manchester
C877DYD	Southern National	CHR194V	PMT	CVF30T	Eastern Counties	D302JVR	Manchester
C877JWE	Mainline	CJH144V	Eastern Counties	CVF31T	Eastern Counties	D303JVR	Manchester
C878DYD	Southern National	CMJ2T	Southern National	CWG273	Aberdeen	D304JVR	Manchester
C878JWE	Mainline	CNH48T	Northampton	CWG720V	Midland/Lowland	D305JVR	Manchester
C879JWE	Mainline	CNH49T	Northampton	CWU156T	Yorkshire	D306JVR	Manchester
C880DYD	Southern National	CNH52T	Northampton	D50ERV	Southern National	D307JVR	Manchester
C880JWE	. Mainline	CNH53T	Northampton	D52ERV	Southern National	D308JVR	Manchester
C881DYD	Southern National	CNH58T	Northampton	D53ERV	Southern National	D309JVR	Manchester
C881JWE	Mainline	CRG325C	Aberdeen	D54ERV	Southern National	D310JVR	Manchester
C882JWE	Mainline	CSF155W	Midland/Lowland	D70TLV	Eastern Counties	D311LNB	Manchester
C883JWE	Mainline	CSG29C	Midland/Lowland	D100GHY	Bristol	D312LNB	Manchester
C884DYD	Southern National	CSU219X	Glasgow	D101GHY	Bristol	D313LNB	Manchester
C884JWE	Mainline	CSU224X	Glasgow	D101XNV	Northampton	D314LNB	Manchester
C885DYD	Southern National	CSU225X	Glasgow	D102GHY	Bristol	D315LNB	Manchester
C885JWE	Mainline	CSU228X	Glasgow	D102XNV	Northampton	D316LNB	Manchester
C886JWE	Mainline	CSU231X	Glasgow	D103GHY	Bristol	D317LNB	Manchester
C887DYD	Southern National	CSU235X	Glasgow	D104GHY	Bristol	D318LNB	Manchester
C887JWE	Mainline	CSU238X	Glasgow	D105GHY	Bristol	D319LNB	Manchester
C888JWE	Mainline	CSU240X	Glasgow	D105NDW	CentreWest	D320LNB	Manchester
C889JWE	Mainline	CSU244	Cymru	D105PTT	Midland/Lowland	D328DKS	Midland/Lowland
C890GYD	Western National	CSU246X	Glasgow	D105PTT	Western National	D329DKS	Midland/Lowland
C890JWE	Mainline	CSU247X	Glasgow	D106GHY	Bristol	D330DKS	Midland/Lowland
C893GYD	Southern National	CSU932	Glasgow	D106PTT	Southern National	D349ESC	Midland/Lowland
C894GYD	Southern National	CSU993	Southern National	D107GHY	Bristol	D350ESC	Midland/Lowland
C895GYD	Southern National	CSV303	Eastern Counties	D108ELS	Midland/Lowland	D351ESC	Midland/Lowland
C896GYD	Southern National	CSV524	Eastern Counties	D108GHY	Bristol	D369OSU	Glasgow
C898GYD	Southern National	CSV992	Eastern Counties	D109ELS	Midland/Lowland	D370OSU	Glasgow
C899GYD	Southern National	CTM406T	Hampshire	D109GHY	Bristol	D371OSU	Glasgow
C900GYD	Southern National	CUB21Y	Yorkshire	D110ELS	Midland/Lowland	D372OSU	Glasgow
C901FCY	Cymru	CUB22Y	Yorkshire	D110GHY	Bristol	D373OSU	Glasgow
C901GYD	Southern National	CUB23Y	Yorkshire	D111ELS	Midland/Lowland	D374OSU	Glasgow
C902FCY	Cymru	CUB24Y	Yorkshire	D111GHY	Bristol	D375OSU	Glasgow
C902GYD	Southern National	CUB25Y	Yorkshire	D112DRV	Southern National	D376OSU	Glasgow
C903FCY	Cymru	CUB26Y	Yorkshire	D112GHY	Bristol	D377OSU	Glasgow
C903GYD	Southern National	CUB27Y	Yorkshire	D113ERV	Southern National	D378OSU	Glasgow
C904FCY	Cymru	CUB28Y	Yorkshire	D113GHY	Bristol	D379OSU	Glasgow
C905FCY	Cymru	CUB29Y	Yorkshire	D114DRV	Southern National	D380OSU	Glasgow
C906FCY	Cymru	CUB30Y	Yorkshire	D115ELS	Midland/Lowland	D381OSU	Glasgow
C907FCY	Cymru	CUB31Y	Yorkshire	D116DRV	Southern National	D382OSU	Glasgow
C907GYD	Southern National	CUB32Y	Yorkshire	D116ELS	Midland/Lowland	D383OSU	Glasgow
C909GYD	Southern National	CUB33Y	Yorkshire	D124ERV	Southern National	D402ASF	Midland/Lowland
C913GYD	Southern National	CUB34Y	Yorkshire	D125ERV	Southern National	D420ASF	Midland/Lowland
C914GYD	Southern National	CUB35Y	Yorkshire	D146VRP	Southern National	D451ERE	PMT
C921GYD	Southern National	CUB36Y	Yorkshire	D149VRP	Southern National	D452ERE	PMT
C922GYD	Southern National	CUB37Y	Yorkshire	D151VRP	Southern National	D453ERE	PMT

Reg	Operator	Reg	Operator	Reg	Operator	Reg	Operator
D454ERE	PMT	DAE513W	Capital	E218BDV	Southern National	E802MOU	Bristol
D455ERE	PMT	DBK262W	Hampshire	E219BDV	Southern National	E803BDV	Southern National
D471OWE	Mainline	DBK263W	Hampshire	E220BDV	Southern National	E803MOU	Bristol
D472OWE	Mainline	DBK264W	Hampshire	E221BDV	Southern National	E804MOU	Bristol
D473OWE	Mainline	DBK265W	Hampshire	E222BDV	Southern National	E805MOU	Bristol
D474OWE	Mainline	DBK266W	Hampshire	E283UCY	Western National	E805WDV	Southern National
D475OWE	Mainline	DDB157C	Midland/Lowland	E284UCY	Western National	E806MOU	Bristol
D476OWE	Mainline	DEX229T	Eastern Counties	E285UCY	Western National	E807HBF	PMT
D477OWE	Mainline	DMS22V	Southern National	E286UCY	Western National	E807MOU	Midland Red
D478OWE	Mainline	DMS348C	Midland/Lowland	E287UCY	Cymru	E807WDV	Southern National
D479OWE	Mainline	DOC44V	Southern National	E288VEP	Western National	E808MOU	Western National
D480OWE	Mainline	DOF708	Western National	E289HRV	Hampshire	E808WDV	Southern National
D481OWE	Mainline	DSA244T	Midland/Lowland	E289VEP	Cymru	E809MOU	Bristol
D482OWE	Mainline	DSA248T	Midland/Lowland	E290HRV	Hampshire	E809WDV	Southern National
D483OWE	Mainline	DSA249T	Midland/Lowland	E290VEP	Cymru	E810MOU	Bristol
D484OWE	Mainline	DSA250T	Midland/Lowland	E291VEP	Cymru	E811MOU	Bristol
D485OWE	Mainline	DSA253T	Manchester	E292VEP	Cymru	E811WDV	Southern National
D486OWE	Mainline	DSA254T	Manchester	E293VEP	Cymru	E812HBF	PMT
D487OWE	Mainline	DSD965V	Midland/Lowland	E294VEP	Cymru	E812MOU	Western National
D488OWE	Mainline	DWH686W	Yorkshire	E295VEP	Cymru	E813MOU	Bristol
D489OWE	Mainline	DWH704W	Yorkshire	E296VEP	Cymru	E814MOU	Bristol
D490OWE	Mainline	DWU298T	Essex Buses	E297VEP	Cymru	E814WDV	Southern National
D497NYS	Essex Buses	E31BTO	Glasgow	E298VEP	Cymru	E815MOU	Bristol
D499NYS	Essex Buses	E40OAH	Eastern Counties	E299VEP	Cymru	E816MOU	Bristol
D500GHY	Bristol	E41OAH	Eastern Counties	E300VEP	Cymru	E817MOU	Bristol
D501GHY	Bristol	E60MMT	Midland/Lowland	E301VEP	Cymru	E817WDV	Southern National
D501 NA	Manchester	E87HNR	Leicester	E302VEP	Cymru	E818HBF	PMT
D502GHY	Bristol	E88HNR	Leicester	E303VEP	Cymru	E818MOU	Bristol
D502LNA	Manchester	E89HNR	Leicester	E304VEP	Cymru	E819MOU	Bristol
D503GHY	Bristol	E90HNR	Leicester	E305VEP	Cymru	E819WDV	Southern National
D503LNA	Manchester	E91HNR	Leicester	E306VEP	Cymru	E820MOU	Western National
D504LNA	Manchester	E92HNR	Leicester	E342NFA	PMT	E820WDV	Southern National
D508OTA	Southern National	E93HNR	Leicester	E384XCA	PMT	E821HBF	PMT
D510MJA	Southern National	E94HNR	Leicester	E400HWC	Essex Buses	E821MOU	Bristol
D512HUB	Yorkshire	E95HNR	Leicester	E401HWC	Essex Buses	E822HBF	PMT
D513HUB	Yorkshire	E96HNR	Leicester	E404BCT	Mainline	E822MOU	Bristol
D514HUB	Yorkshire	E96OUH	Southern National	E406BCT	Mainline	E823MOU	Bristol
D515HUB	Yorkshire	E97HNR	Leicester	E406HAB	Midland Red	E853PEX	Eastern Counties
D516HUB	Yorkshire	E98HNR	Leicester	E407HAB	Midland Red	E944LAE	Southern National
D534KGL	Midland/Lowland	E99HNR	Leicester	E408HAB	Midland Red	E963HTP	Southern National
D562HPO	Hampshire	E106LVT	PMT	E409HAB	Midland Red	E964PME	Capital
D591MVR	Midland/Lowland	E108JNH	Aberdeen	E410HAB	Midland Red	EAH890Y	Midland Red
D599MVR	Midland/Lowland	E111NNV	Northampton	E411HAB	Midland Red	ECY988V	Cymru
D643NOD	Southern National	E122DRS	Aberdeen	E412KUY	Midland Red	ECY989V	Cymru
D645NOD	Southern National	E123DRS	Aberdeen	E413KUY	Midland Red	ECY990V	Cymru
D659WEY	Southern National	E124DRS	Aberdeen	E414KUY	Midland Red	EEL893V	Hampshire
D674MHS	Glasgow	E125DRS	Aberdeen	E415KUY	Midland Red	EGB50T	PMT
D675MHS	Glasgow	E126DRS	Aberdeen	E416KUY	Midland Red	EHE234V	Eastern Counties
D677MHS	Glasgow	E127DRS	Aberdeen	E417KUY	Midland Red	EKU75V	Southern National
D679MHS	Glasgow	E128DRS	Aberdeen	E418KUY	Midland Red	ELJ208V	Western National
D681MHS	Glasgow	E130DRS	Aberdeen	E419KUY	Midland Red	ENF561Y	Southern National
D700GHY	Bristol	E131DRS	Aberdeen	E420KUY	Midland Red	ENF564Y	Southern National
D701GHY	Bristol	E158RNY	Southern National	E421KUY	Midland Red	ENF568Y	Southern National
D702GHY	Bristol	E181UWF	Manchester	E422KUY	Midland Red	ENJ913V	Southern National
D703GHY	Bristol	E187HSF	Midland/Lowland	E423KUY	Midland Red	ERF24Y	PMT
D704GHY	Bristol	E188HSF	Midland/Lowland	E424KUY	Midland Red	ESK812	Bristol
D705GHY	Bristol	E189HSF	Midland/Lowland	E425KUY	Midland Red	ESK955	Aberdeen
D706GHY	Bristol	E190HSF	Midland/Lowland	E426KUY	Midland Red	ESK956	Aberdeen
D707GHY	Bristol	E196BDV	Southern National	E427KUY	Midland Red	ESK957	Aberdeen
D708GHY	Bristol	E197BDV	Southern National	E428KUY	Midland Red	ESK958	Midland/Lowland
D709GHY	Bristol	E198BDV	Southern National	E429KUY	Midland Red	ESX257	Midland/Lowland
D710GHY	Bristol	E199BDV	Southern National	E430KUY	Midland Red	EUK546V	Southern National
D711GHY	Bristol	E200BOD	Western National	E431KUY	Midland Red	EUK547V	Southern National
D751DLO	CentreWest	E201BDV	Southern National	E432KUY	Midland Red	EWN992W	Cymru
D752DLO	PMT	E201BOD	Western National	E433KUY	Midland Red	EWN994W	Cymru
D753DLO	CentreWest	E202BDV	Southern National	E434KUY	Midland Red	EWN995W	Cymru
D753DSH	Midland/Lowland	E202BOD	Western National	E435KUY	Midland Red	EWR651Y	Northampton
D754DLO	Essex Buses	E203BDV	Southern National	E436KUY	Midland Red	EWR652Y	Northampton
D755DLO	Essex Buses	E203BOD	Western National	E437KUY	Midland Red	EWR653Y	Northampton
D756DLO	Essex Buses	E204BDV	Southern National	E438KUY	Midland Red	EWS739W	Bristol
D763KWT	Midland Red	E204BOD	Western National	E439KUY	Midland Red	EWS742W	Bristol
D764KWT	Capital	E205BOD	Western National	E461SON	Capital	EWS744W	Cymru
D782NDV	Southern National	E206BDV	Southern National	E467JSG	Midland/Lowland	EWS747W	Western National
D783NDV	Southern National	E206BOD	Cymru	E470SON	Capital	EWS749W	Bristol
D788NDV	Southern National	E207BDV	Southern National	E478SON	Capital	EWV665	Western National
D793NDV	Southern National	E208BDV	Southern National	E526NEH	PMT	EWW945Y	Cymru
D810NWW	PMT	E209JKS	Midland/Lowland	E675KDG	Manchester	EWW946Y	Western National
D875ELL	PMT	E214BDV	Southern National	E694UND	Bristol	EWY77Y	Yorkshire
D876ELL	Essex Buses	E215BDV	Southern National	E752YDY	Southern National	EWY78Y	PMT
D901CSH	Midland/Lowland	E215BTA	Western National	E760HBF	PMT	EWY79Y	PMT
D902CSH	Midland/Lowland	E216BTA	Western National	E767HBF	PMT	EWY81Y	Yorkshire
DAD254T	Southern National	E217BDV	Southern National	E800MOU	Bristol	EYE316V	CentreWest
DAE510W	Capital	E217BTA	Bristol	E801MOU	Bristol	EYE319V	CentreWest
DAE512W	Capital			E802HBF	PMT	EYE329V	CentreWest

Reg	Operator	Reg	Operator	Reg	Operator	Reg	Operator
EYE330V	Capital	F170XYG	Yorkshire	F324DCY	Cymru	F600XWY	Yorkshire
EYE332V	Capital	F171XYG	Yorkshire	F325DCY	Cymru	F601AWN	Cymru
EYE337V	CentreWest	F172LBL	CentreWest	F326DCY	Cymru	F601RTC	Bristol
EYE338V	CentreWest	F172XYG	Yorkshire	F327DCY	Cymru	F601XMS	CentreWest
EYE339V	Capital	F173LBL	CentreWest	F329FCY	Cymru	F601XWY	Yorkshire
EYE340V	CentreWest	F173XYG	Yorkshire	F330FCY	Cymru	F602AWN	Cymru
EYE343V	Capital	F174LBL	CentreWest	F331FCY	Cymru	F602RTC	Bristol
EYP29V	Southern National	F174XYG	Yorkshire	F332FCY	Cymru	F602XMS	Western National
F34TJN	Eastern Counties	F175LBL	CentreWest	F333FCY	Cymru	F602XWY	Yorkshire
F37ENF	Midland/Lowland	F175XYG	Yorkshire	F334FCY	Cymru	F603AWN	Cymru
F38ENF	Midland/Lowland	F202YKG	Southern National	F335FCY	Cymru	F603RTC	Bristol
F50BMS	Midland/Lowland	F217OFB	PMT	F336FCY	Cymru	F603XWY	Yorkshire
F50ENF	Midland/Lowland	F229FSU	Cymru	F337FCY	Cymru	F604RTC	Bristol
F83XBD	Northampton	F245MVW	Capital	F338FCY	Cymru	F604XWY	Yorkshire
F84XBD	Northampton	F251NJN	Capital	F339FCY	Cymru	F605AWN	Cymru
F85XBD	Northampton	F254RHK	Capital	F340FCY	Cymru	F605RTC	Bristol
F86DVV	Northampton	F255RHK	Capital	F341FCY	Cymru	F605XWY	Yorkshire
F88CWG	PMT	F256RHK	Capital	F342FCY	Cymru	F606RTC	Bristol
F88DVV	Northampton	F257RHK	Capital	F343FCY	Cymru	F607AWN	Cymru
F89JYS	Glasgow	F258RHK	Capital	F361YTJ	PMT	F607RTC	Bristol
F90JYS	Glasgow	F264MVW	Capital	F362YTJ	PMT	F608AWN	Cymru
F91JYS	Glasgow	F278DRJ	Manchester	F363YTJ	PMT	F608RTC	Bristol
F92JYS	Glasgow	F279DRJ	Manchester	F364YTJ	PMT	F608WBV	PMT
F93JYS	Glasgow	F279NHJ	Capital	F384FYS	Glasgow	F609RTC	Bristol
F94JYS	Glasgow	F280DRJ	Manchester	F385FYS	Glasgow	F610PWS	Bristol
F95JYS	Glasgow	F280NHJ	Capital	F402LTW	Essex Buses	F610RTC	Bristol
F96JYS	Glasgow	F281DRJ	Manchester	F403LTW	Essex Buses	F610XMS	Midland/Lowland
F97JYS	Glasgow	F281NHJ	Capital	F404LTW	Essex Buses	F611RTC	Bristol
F98JYS	Glasgow	F282NHJ	Capital	F405LTW	Essex Buses	F611XMS	Glasgow
F99CEP	Cymru	F283NHJ	Capital	F406LTW	Essex Buses	F612RTC	Bristol
F99JYS	Glasgow	F284DRJ	Manchester	F407LTW	Essex Buses	F612XMS	Midland/Lowland
F100CEP	Cymru	F284NHJ	Capital	F408LTW	Essex Buses	F613RTC	Bristol
F100UEH	PMT	F285NHJ	Capital	F409LTW	Essex Buses	F613XMS	Glasgow
F101AVG	Eastern Counties	F286DRJ	Manchester	F410MNO	Essex Buses	F613XWY	Eastern Counties
F101GRM	CentreWest	F286NHJ	Capital	F411MNO	Essex Buses	F614RTC	Bristol
F102AVG	Eastern Counties	F287DRJ	Manchester	F412MNO	Essex Buses	F614XWY	Eastern Counties
F102GRM	PMT	F287NHJ	Capital	F413MNO	Essex Buses	F615RTC	Bristol
F102RTR	Hampshire	F288DRJ	Manchester	F414MNO	Essex Buses	F616RTC	Bristol
F103AVG	Eastern Counties	F288NHJ	Capital	F415MWC	Essex Buses	F616XWY	Midland/Lowland
F104AVG	Eastern Counties	F289NHJ	Capital	F416MWC	Essex Buses	F617RTC	Bristol
F105AVG	Eastern Counties	F290DRJ	Manchester	F417MWC	Essex Buses	F618RTC	Bristol
F106CWG	PMT	F290NHJ	Capital	F418MWC	Essex Buses	F618XMS	Glasgow
F107CWG	PMT	F291NHJ	Capital	F419MWC	Essex Buses	F618XWY	Cymru
F108CWG	PMT	F291PTP	Capital	F420MJN	Essex Buses	F619RTC	Bristol
F109CWG	PMT	F292DRJ	Manchester	F421MJN	Essex Buses	F619XWY	Yorkshire
F110CWG	PMT	F292PTP	Capital	F422MJN	Essex Buses	F620RTC	Bristol
F134DEP	Cymru	F293DRJ	Manchester	F423MJN	Essex Buses	F621RTC	Bristol
F135DEP	Cymru	F293NHJ	Capital	F424MJN	Essex Buses	F621XWY	Midland/Lowland
F139HNC	Manchester	F293PTP	Capital	F425MJN	Essex Buses	F622RTC	Bristol
F140HNC	Manchester	F294NHJ	Capital	F426MJN	Essex Buses	F622XMS	Glasgow
F140MBC	Capital	F294PTP	Capital	F427MJN	Essex Buses	F622XWY	Midland/Lowland
F141MBC	Capital	F295PTP	Capital	F428MJN	Essex Buses	F623RTC	Bristol
F142MBC	Capital	F296PTP	Capital	F429MJN	Essex Buses	F623XMS	Midland/Lowland
F143MBC	Leicester	F297PTP	Capital	F452YHF	PMT	F624RTC	Bristol
F144MBC	Capital	F298PTP	Capital	F455TOY	Western National	F625RTC	Bristol
F145MBC	Capital	F299DRJ	Manchester	F473RBF	PMT	F626RTC	Bristol
F146MBC	Leicester	F300GNS	Cymru	F475VEH	PMT	F626XMS	Midland/Lowland
F147MBC	Capital	F302DRJ	Manchester	F546EJA	Cymru	F627RTC	Bristol
F148MBC	Capital	F303DRJ	Manchester	F581XWY	Yorkshire	F627XMS	Glasgow
F149MBC	Leicester	F305DRJ	Manchester	F582XWY	Yorkshire	F628RTC	Bristol
F150MBC	Leicester	F307AWN	Cymru	F583XWY	Yorkshire	F629RTC	Bristol
F151MBC	Leicester	F308AWN	Cymru	F584XWY	Yorkshire	F630RTC	Bristol
F151XYG	Eastern Counties	F309AWN	Cymru	F585XWY	Yorkshire	F631RTC	Bristol
F152MBC	Leicester	F310AWN	Cymru	F586XWY	Yorkshire	F632RTC	Bristol
F152XYG	Yorkshire	F310REH	PMT	F587XWY	Yorkshire	F632XMS	Glasgow
F153XYG	Eastern Counties	F311AWN	Cymru	F588OOU	Southern National	F633XMS	Eastern Counties
F154RHK	Southern National	F311REH	PMT	F588XWY	Yorkshire	F634JSO	Aberdeen
F154XYG	Eastern Counties	F312AWN	Cymru	F589XWY	Yorkshire	F636BKD	Leicester
F155XYG	Eastern Counties	F312REH	PMT	F590OHT	Southern National	F636XMS	Manchester
F156XYG	PMT	F313AWN	Cymru	F590XWY	Yorkshire	F637BKD	Leicester
F157XYG	Yorkshire	F313REH	PMT	F591OHT	Bristol	F638XMS	Eastern Counties
F158XYG	PMT	F314AWN	Cymru	F591XWY	Yorkshire	F639XMS	Glasgow
F159XYG	Yorkshire	F314REH	PMT	F592OHT	Bristol	F640XMS	Manchester
F160XYG	Yorkshire	F315AWN	Cymru	F592XWY	Yorkshire	F642XMS	Manchester
F161XYG	Yorkshire	F315REH	PMT	F593XWY	Yorkshire	F643XMS	Western National
F162XYG	Yorkshire	F316AWN	Cymru	F594XWY	Yorkshire	F645XMS	Western National
F163XYG	Yorkshire	F316REH	PMT	F595XWY	Yorkshire	F656XMS	Midland/Lowland
F164XYG	Yorkshire	F317AWN	Cymru	F596OHT	Bristol	F657XMS	Western National
F165XYG	Yorkshire	F317REH	PMT	F596XWY	Yorkshire	F658XMS	Glasgow
F166DNT	PMT	F319AWN	Cymru	F597FAM	Manchester	F659XMS	Glasgow
F166XYG	Yorkshire	F320AWN	Cymru	F597XWY	Yorkshire	F660XMS	Glasgow
F167XYG	Yorkshire	F321AWN	Cymru	F598XWY	Yorkshire	F661XMS	Glasgow
F168XYG	Yorkshire	F322AWN	Cymru	F599XWY	Yorkshire	F663XMS	Glasgow
F169XYG	Yorkshire	F323DCY	Cymru	F600RTC	Bristol	F666XMS	Western National

Reg	Operator	Reg	Operator	Reg	Operator	Reg	Operator
F668XMS	Western National	FDV801V	Western National	G66RND	Manchester	G181JYG	Yorkshire
F671XMS	Midland/Lowland	FDV802V	Western National	G68RND	Manchester	G182JYG	Yorkshire
F672XMS	Manchester	FDV805V	Western National	G69RND	Manchester	G183JYG	Yorkshire
F675XMS	Midland/Lowland	FDV806V	Western National	G70RND	Manchester	G184JYG	Yorkshire
F676XMS	Glasgow	FDV807V	Western National	G71RND	Manchester	G185JYG	Yorkshire
F677XMS	Western National	FDV808V	Western National	G72RND	Manchester	G229EOA	Southern National
F679XMS	Midland/Lowland	FDV814V	Western National	G101EVT	PMT	G251JYG	Yorkshire
F680XMS	Western National	FDV815V	Western National	G101HNP	Midland Red	G252JYG	Yorkshire
F682XMS	Western National	FDV836V	Southern National	G102HNP	Midland Red	G253JYG	Yorkshire
F683XMS	Western National	FDV837V	Southern National	G103HNP	Midland Red	G254JYG	Yorkshire
F684XMS	Western National	FDZ980	Western National	G104HNP	Midland Red	G255JYG	Yorkshire
F687XMS	Glasgow	FEH1Y	Eastern Counties	G104WRV	Hampshire	G259LWF	Leicester
F688XMS	Midland/Lowland	FFS10X	Midland/Lowland	G105HNP	Midland Red	G261LUG	Western National
F689XMS	Western National	FGG603X	Glasgow	G105WRV	Hampshire	G280OGE	Glasgow
F690XMS	Glasgow	FJF193	Leicester	G106HNP	Midland Red	G281OGE	Glasgow
F691XMS	Glasgow	FNJ905	Western National	G106WRV	Hampshire	G282OGE	Glasgow
F692XMS	Glasgow	FNM868Y	Midland/Lowland	G107FJW	Capital	G283OGE	Glasgow
F693XMS	Glasgow	FNR923	Western National	G107HNP	Midland Red	G284OGE	Glasgow
F694XMS	Eastern Counties	FSU302	Midland/Lowland	G108HNP	Midland Red	G285OGE	Glasgow
F695AWW	Bristol	FSU308	Midland/Lowland	G108WRV	Hampshire	G286OGE	Glasgow
F695XMS	Eastern Counties	FSU315	Midland/Lowland	G109HNP	Midland Red	G287OGE	Glasgow
F696XMS	Eastern Counties	FSU333	Aberdeen	G109XOW	Hampshire	G288OGE	Glasgow
F697XMS	Eastern Counties	FSU334	Midland/Lowland	G110HNP	Midland Red	G290OGE	Glasgow
F698XMS	Eastern Counties	FSU335	Aberdeen	G110XOW	Hampshire	G291OGE	Glasgow
F699XMS	Eastern Counties	FSU380	Midland/Lowland	G111HNP	Midland Red	G292OGE	Glasgow
F700XMS	Eastern Counties	FSU381	Midland/Lowland	G111XOW	Hampshire	G293OGE	Glasgow
F702XMS	Glasgow	FSU382	Midland/Lowland	G112ENV	Northampton	G294OGE	Glasgow
F703XMS	Eastern Counties	FSU383	Midland/Lowland	G112HNP	Midland Red	G295OGE	Glasgow
F704XMS	Eastern Counties	FSV634	Midland/Lowland	G112XOW	Hampshire	G296OGE	Glasgow
F705XMS	Eastern Counties	FTO549V	Essex Buses	G113ENV	Northampton	G297OGE	Glasgow
F706WCS	Glasgow	FTR267X	Hampshire	G113HNP	Midland Red	G298OGE	Glasgow
F706XMS	Western National	FTR268X	Hampshire	G113XOW	Hampshire	G299OGE	Glasgow
F707XMS	Western National	FTR269X	Hampshire	G114ENV	Northampton	G300OGE	Glasgow
F712FDV	Cymru	FTR270X	Hampshire	G114HNP	Midland Red	G301OGE	Glasgow
F713FDV	Cymru	FTR271X	Hampshire	G115HNP	Midland Red	G301XCR	Hampshire
F713OFH	PMT	FTU240V	Leicester	G116HNP	Midland Red	G302OGE	Glasgow
F721FDV	Cymru	FUM485Y	Essex Buses	G117HNP	Midland Red	G302XCR	Hampshire
F725FDV	Cymru	FUM486Y	Yorkshire	G118HNP	Midland Red	G303NWB	Mainline
F727FDV	Cymru	FUM487Y	Yorkshire	G119HNP	Midland Red	G303OGE	Glasgow
F739FDV	Cymru	FUM489Y	Yorkshire	G120HNP	Midland Red	G303XCR	Hampshire
F749FDV	Cymru	FUM491Y	Yorkshire	G121HNP	Midland Red	G304NWB	Mainline
F751FDV	Southern National	FUM492Y	Yorkshire	G122HNP	Midland Red	G304OGE	Glasgow
F752FDV	Southern National	FUM493Y	Essex Buses	G123HNP	Midland Red	G304XCR	Hampshire
F753FDV	Southern National	FUM494Y	Eastern Counties	G123YEV	Eastern Counties	G305NWB	Mainline
F761FDV	Cymru	FUM495Y	Eastern Counties	G124HNP	Midland Red	G305XCR	Hampshire
F773FDV	Southern National	FUM496Y	Essex Buses	G125HNP	Midland Red	G306NWB	Mainline
F790LSU	Glasgow	FUM497Y	Essex Buses	G125YEV	Eastern Counties	G307NWB	Mainline
F791LSU	Glasgow	FUM498Y	Eastern Counties	G126HNP	Midland Red	G308NWB	Mainline
F792LSU	Glasgow	FUM499Y	Yorkshire	G127HNP	Midland Red	G309NWB	Mainline
F793LSU	Glasgow	FUM500Y	Essex Buses	G128HNP	Midland Red	G310NWB	Mainline
F794LSU	Glasgow	FUT36V	Capital	G129HNP	Midland Red	G311NWB	Mainline
F795LSU	Glasgow	FUT37V	Capital	G130HNP	Midland Red	G312NWB	Mainline
F800RHK	Capital	FUT179V	Leicester	G131HNP	Midland Red	G313NWB	Mainline
F801RHK	Capital	FUT184V	Leicester	G132HNP	Midland Red	G314NWB	Mainline
F802RHK	Capital	FUT250V	Leicester	G133ATW	Eastern Counties	G315NWB	Mainline
F803HHK	Capital	FVR265V	Yorkshire	G133HNP	Midland Red	G316NWB	Mainline
F804RHK	Capital	FVR269V	Manchester	G134HNP	Midland Red	G317NWB	Mainline
F850TCW	Bristol	FXI8653	PMT	G135HNP	Midland Red	G318NWB	Mainline
F905FHE	Southern National	FYD864T	Southern National	G136HNP	Midland Red	G318YVT	PMT
F908FHE	Southern National	G46XLO	Eastern Counties	G136YRY	PMT	G319NWB	Mainline
F946BMS	Western National	G47XLO	Eastern Counties	G137HNP	Midland Red	G320NWB	Mainline
F947BMS	Glasgow	G48XLO	Eastern Counties	G138HNP	Midland Red	G321NWB	Mainline
F948BMS	Western National	G49XLO	Eastern Counties	G139HNP	Midland Red	G322NWB	Mainline
F951BMS	Western National	G50XLO	Eastern Counties	G140HNP	Midland Red	G323NWB	Mainline
F952BMS	Western National	G51XLO	Eastern Counties	G141HNP	Midland Red	G324NWB	Mainline
F953BMS	Western National	G52GEX	Eastern Counties	G142HNP	Midland Red	G326NWB	Mainline
F954BMS	Western National	G52XLO	Eastern Counties	G143HNP	Midland Red	G327NWB	Mainline
F95CWG	PMT	G53GEX	Eastern Counties	G144HNP	Midland Red	G328NWB	Mainline
FDC418V	Southern National	G53XLO	Eastern Counties	G145HNP	Midland Red	G329NWB	Mainline
FDU805T	Southern National	G54GEX	Eastern Counties	G146HNP	Midland Red	G330NWB	Mainline
FDV774V	Western National	G54RND	Midland/Lowland	G147HNP	Midland Red	G330XRE	PMT
FDV775V	Southern National	G54XLO	Eastern Counties	G148HNP	Midland Red	G331NWB	Mainline
FDV776V	Southern National	G55GEX	Eastern Counties	G149HNP	Midland Red	G331XRE	PMT
FDV777V	Western National	G55RND	Midland/Lowland	G150HNP	Midland Red	G332NWB	Mainline
FDV778V	Southern National	G55RND	Midland/Lowland	G151GOL	Western National	G332XRE	PMT
FDV779V	Southern National	G55XLO	CentreWest	G152GOL	Western National	G333NWB	Mainline
FDV780V	Southern National	G56RND	Midland/Lowland	G153GOL	Western National	G333XRE	PMT
FDV781V	Southern National	G56XLO	CentreWest	G154GOL	Western National	G334NWB	Mainline
FDV782V	Southern National	G57RND	Manchester	G155GOL	Western National	G334XRE	PMT
FDV785V	Western National	G58RND	Manchester	G176JYG	Yorkshire	G335NWB	Mainline
FDV789V	Southern National	G60RND	Manchester	G177JYG	Yorkshire	G335XRE	PMT
FDV794V	Western National	G62RND	Manchester	G178JYG	Yorkshire	G336NWB	Mainline
FDV798V	Western National	G64RND	Manchester	G179JYG	Yorkshire	G336XRE	PMT
FDV800V	Western National	G65RND	Manchester	G180JYG	Yorkshire	G337NWB	Mainline

226

Registration	Operator
G337XRE	PMT
G338NWB	Mainline
G338XRE	PMT
G339NWB	Mainline
G339XRE	PMT
G340NWB	Mainline
G340XRE	PMT
G341NWB	Mainline
G341XRE	PMT
G342CBF	PMT
G342NWB	Mainline
G343CBF	PMT
G343NWB	Mainline
G344CBF	PMT
G344GEP	Cymru
G345CBF	PMT
G345GEP	Cymru
G346CBF	PMT
G346GEP	Cymru
G347ERF	PMT
G347GEP	Cymru
G348ERF	PMT
G348JTH	Cymru
G349ERF	PMT
G349JTH	Cymru
G350JTH	Cymru
G351JTH	Cymru
G352JTH	Cymru
G353JTH	Cymru
G354JTH	Cymru
G355JTH	Cymru
G356JTH	Cymru
G357JTH	Cymru
G358JTH	Cymru
G359JTH	Cymru
G360JTH	Cymru
G361JTH	Cymru
G365JTH	Cymru
G366JTH	Cymru
G367MEP	Cymru
G368MEP	Cymru
G369MEP	Cymru
G370MEP	Cymru
G371MEP	Cymru
G372MEP	Cymru
G373MEP	Cymru
G384OGD	Glasgow
G385OGD	Glasgow
G386OGD	Glasgow
G387OGD	Glasgow
G388OGD	Glasgow
G389OGD	Glasgow
G390OGD	Glasgow
G391OGD	Glasgow
G392OGD	Glasgow
G393OGD	Glasgow
G394OGD	Glasgow
G395OGD	Glasgow
G395OWB	Eastern Counties
G396OGD	Glasgow
G397OGD	Glasgow
G398OGD	Glasgow
G399OGD	Glasgow
G400OGD	Glasgow
G401OGD	Glasgow
G402OGD	Glasgow
G403OGD	Glasgow
G404OGD	Glasgow
G405OGD	Glasgow
G406OGD	Glasgow
G407OGD	Glasgow
G408OGD	Glasgow
G409OGD	Glasgow
G410OGD	Glasgow
G411OGD	Glasgow
G412OGD	Glasgow
G413OGD	Glasgow
G414OGD	Glasgow
G415OGD	Glasgow
G416OGD	Glasgow
G432UHS	Glasgow
G451JYG	Yorkshire
G452JYG	Yorkshire
G453JYG	Yorkshire
G453SGB	Eastern Counties
G454JYG	Yorkshire
G455JYG	Yorkshire
G456JYG	Yorkshire
G456KNG	Eastern Counties
G457JYG	Yorkshire
G457KNG	Eastern Counties
G458JYG	Yorkshire
G458KNG	Eastern Counties
G459JYG	Yorkshire
G460JYG	Yorkshire
G477ERF	PMT
G478ERF	PMT
G495FFA	PMT
G521RDS	Glasgow
G522RDS	Glasgow
G523RDS	Glasgow
G524RDS	Glasgow
G525RDS	Glasgow
G526RDS	Glasgow
G527RDS	Glasgow
G528RDS	Glasgow
G529RDS	Glasgow
G530RDS	Glasgow
G531RDS	Glasgow
G532CVT	PMT
G532RDS	Glasgow
G533RDS	Glasgow
G534RDS	Glasgow
G535RDS	Glasgow
G536RDS	Glasgow
G537RDS	Glasgow
G538GBD	CentreWest
G538RDS	Glasgow
G539RDS	Glasgow
G540RDS	Glasgow
G541RDS	Glasgow
G542RDS	Glasgow
G543RDS	Glasgow
G544RDS	Glasgow
G545RDS	Glasgow
G550ERF	PMT
G601NWA	Mainline
G601OSH	Midland/Lowland
G601OWR	Yorkshire
G602NWA	Mainline
G602OWR	Yorkshire
G603NWA	Mainline
G603OWR	Yorkshire
G604NWA	Mainline
G604OWR	Yorkshire
G605NWA	Mainline
G605OWR	Yorkshire
G606NWA	Mainline
G606OWR	Yorkshire
G607NWA	Mainline
G607OWR	Yorkshire
G608NWA	Mainline
G608OWR	Yorkshire
G609NWA	Mainline
G609OWR	Yorkshire
G610NWA	Mainline
G610OWR	Yorkshire
G611NWA	Mainline
G611OWR	Yorkshire
G612NWA	Mainline
G612OWR	Yorkshire
G613NWA	Mainline
G613OWR	Yorkshire
G614NWA	Mainline
G614OWR	Yorkshire
G615NWA	Mainline
G615OWR	Yorkshire
G616NWA	Mainline
G616OWR	Yorkshire
G617NWA	Mainline
G617OWR	Yorkshire
G618NWA	Mainline
G618OWR	Yorkshire
G619NWA	Mainline
G619OWR	Yorkshire
G620NWA	Mainline
G620OWR	Yorkshire
G621NWA	Mainline
G621OWR	Yorkshire
G622NWA	Mainline
G622OWR	Yorkshire
G623NWA	Mainline
G623OWR	Yorkshire
G624NWA	Mainline
G625NWA	Mainline
G626NWA	Mainline
G627NWA	Mainline
G628NWA	Mainline
G629EKA	Leicester
G629NWA	Mainline
G630NWA	Mainline
G631NWA	Mainline
G632NWA	Mainline
G633NWA	Mainline
G634NWA	Mainline
G635NWA	Mainline
G636NWA	Mainline
G637NWA	Mainline
G638NWA	Mainline
G639NWA	Mainline
G640NWA	Mainline
G641NWA	Mainline
G645YVS	Eastern Counties
G646YVS	Eastern Counties
G647YVS	Eastern Counties
G667FKA	Leicester
G685PNS	Glasgow
G686PNS	Glasgow
G687PNS	Glasgow
G688PNS	Glasgow
G689PNS	Glasgow
G690PNS	Glasgow
G691PNS	Glasgow
G692PNS	Glasgow
G693PNS	Glasgow
G694PNS	Glasgow
G695PNS	Glasgow
G696PNS	Glasgow
G697PNS	Glasgow
G698PNS	Glasgow
G699PNS	Glasgow
G700PNS	Glasgow
G701PNS	Glasgow
G702PNS	Glasgow
G703PNS	Glasgow
G704PNS	Glasgow
G706JAH	Eastern Counties
G707JAH	Eastern Counties
G708JAH	Eastern Counties
G709JAH	Eastern Counties
G710JAH	Eastern Counties
G715OSH	Midland/Lowland
G753XRE	PMT
G754XRE	PMT
G755XRE	PMT
G756XRE	PMT
G757XRE	PMT
G758XRE	PMT
G759XRE	PMT
G760XRE	PMT
G761XRE	PMT
G762XRE	PMT
G801JYG	Yorkshire
G802JYG	Yorkshire
G802XLO	Southern National
G803JYG	Yorkshire
G803XLO	Southern National
G804JYG	Yorkshire
G805AAD	PMT
G805JYG	Yorkshire
G833RDS	Eastern Counties
G834RDS	Eastern Counties
G841PNW	Cymru
G895XPX	Hampshire
G901TWS	Bristol
G902TWS	Bristol
G903TWS	Bristol
G904TWS	Bristol
G905TWS	Bristol
G906TWS	Bristol
G907TWS	Bristol
G908TWS	Bristol
G909TWS	Bristol
G910TWS	Bristol
GBF78N	PMT
GBU12V	Manchester
GBU13V	Manchester
GBU14V	Manchester
GBU15V	Manchester
GFM101X	PMT
GFM102X	PMT
GFM103X	PMT
GFM104X	PMT
GFM105X	PMT
GFM106X	PMT
GFM108X	PMT
GFM109X	PMT
GGM89W	Eastern Counties
GGM90W	Eastern Counties
GGM107W	Eastern Counties
GHT127	Bristol
GIL1684	Southern National
GIL2967	Western National
GLS267S	Southern National
GLS275S	Southern National
GMB377T	PMT
GMS280S	Southern National
GMS291S	Southern National
GMS295S	Southern National
GMS297S	Yorkshire
GMS310S	Southern National
GNF13V	Capital
GNF16V	Yorkshire
GRA842V	Eastern Counties
GRA847V	Eastern Counties
GRF701V	PMT
GRF707V	PMT
GRF708V	PMT
GRF709V	PMT
GRF715V	PMT
GSO80V	Midland/Lowland
GSU338	Midland/Lowland
GSU339	Midland/Lowland
GSU388	Cymru
GSU390	Aberdeen
GSU838T	PMT
GSU845T	PMT
GUW454W	Capital
GUW470W	CentreWest
GUW472W	CentreWest
GUW497W	CentreWest
GUW503W	CentreWest
GUW504W	CentreWest
GWR177T	Yorkshire
GWR180T	Yorkshire
GWR182T	Yorkshire
GWR183T	Yorkshire
GWR185T	Yorkshire
GWR187T	Yorkshire
GWR188T	Yorkshire
GWR189T	Yorkshire
GWR190T	Yorkshire
GWR191T	Yorkshire
GWU529T	Western National
GWV925V	Southern National
GYE347W	CentreWest
GYE348W	Capital
GYE349W	CentreWest
GYE355W	Capital
GYE358W	CentreWest
GYE360W	CentreWest
GYE362W	CentreWest
GYE364W	CentreWest
GYE368W	CentreWest
GYE369W	Capital
GYE370W	CentreWest
GYE371W	CentreWest
GYE374W	CentreWest
GYE379W	Capital
GYE383W	CentreWest
GYE385W	CentreWest
GYE390W	CentreWest
GYE393W	CentreWest
GYE397W	CentreWest
GYE405W	Capital
GYE406W	CentreWest

Reg	Operator	Reg	Operator	Reg	Operator
GYE413W	Capital	H269KVX	Capital	H359JRE	PMT
GYE414W	CentreWest	H270KVX	Capital	H359LJN	Eastern Counties
GYE416W	Capital	H271KVX	Capital	H359UWB	Mainline
GYE418W	Capital	H272KVX	Capital	H361JRE	PMT
GYE425W	CentreWest	H273KVX	Capital	H361LJN	Eastern Counties
GYE427W	CentreWest	H274KVX	Capital	H361UWB	Mainline
GYE434W	Capital	H289VRP	Northampton	H362JRE	PMT
GYE442W	CentreWest	H290VRP	Northampton	H362LJN	Essex Buses
GYE451W	Capital	H291VRP	Northampton	H362UWB	Mainline
GYE452W	CentreWest	H292VRP	Northampton	H363JRE	PMT
GYE457W	Capital	H293VRP	Northampton	H363LJN	Essex Buses
GYE465W	CentreWest	H294VRP	Northampton	H363UWB	Mainline
GYE470W	CentreWest	H301LPU	Capital	H364LJN	Essex Buses
GYE479W	Capital	H302LPU	Capital	H364UWB	Mainline
GYE484W	Capital	H303LPU	Capital	H365LJN	Essex Buses
GYE486W	CentreWest	H304LPU	Capital	H365UWB	Mainline
GYE487W	Capital	H305LPU	Capital	H366LFA	PMT
GYE488W	CentreWest	H306DRV	Hampshire	H366LJN	Essex Buses
GYE489W	CentreWest	H306LPU	Capital	H366UWB	Mainline
GYE494W	CentreWest	H307LJN	Eastern Counties	H367LFA	PMT
GYE497W	CentreWest	H308DRV	Hampshire	H367LJN	Essex Buses
GYE498W	Capital	H308LPU	Essex Buses	H367UWB	Mainline
GYE499W	CentreWest	H310LPU	Essex Buses	H368LFA	PMT
GYE504W	CentreWest	H311LJN	Essex Buses	H368OHK	Essex Buses
GYE505W	CentreWest	H312LJN	Essex Buses	H368UWB	Mainline
GYE523W	CentreWest	H313LJN	Essex Buses	H369LFA	PMT
GYE546W	Capital	H314LJN	Essex Buses	H369OHK	Essex Buses
GYE583W	CentreWest	H315LJN	Essex Buses	H369UWB	Mainline
H34USO	Aberdeen	H317LJN	Essex Buses	H370OHK	Essex Buses
H35USO	Aberdeen	H319LJN	Essex Buses	H370UWB	Mainline
H36USO	Aberdeen	H320LJN	Essex Buses	H371OHK	Essex Buses
H37USO	Aberdeen	H321LJN	Essex Buses	H371UWB	Mainline
H39USO	Aberdeen	H322LJN	Essex Buses	H372MEH	PMT
H101KVX	Eastern Counties	H324HVT	Western National	H372OHK	Manchester
H102KVX	Eastern Counties	H324LJN	Essex Buses	H372UWB	Mainline
H103KVX	Eastern Counties	H326DTR	Cymru	H373MVT	PMT
H104KVX	Eastern Counties	H326LJN	Essex Buses	H373OHK	Manchester
H129FLX	Capital	H327LJN	Essex Buses	H373UWB	Mainline
H130FLX	Capital	H331LJN	Essex Buses	H374OHK	Manchester
H130FLX	CentreWest	H332LJN	Essex Buses	H374OTH	Cymru
H131FLX	CentreWest	H334LJN	Essex Buses	H374UWB	Mainline
H132FLX	Capital	H335LAN	Eastern Counties	H375OHK	Essex Buses
H133FLX	CentreWest	H335LJN	Essex Buses	H375OTH	Cymru
H134FLX	CentreWest	H336LJN	Essex Buses	H375UWB	Mainline
H135FLX	Capital	H337LJN	Essex Buses	H376OHK	Eastern Counties
H136FLX	Capital	H338LJN	Essex Buses	H376UWB	Mainline
H137FLX	Capital	H339LJN	Essex Buses	H377OHK	Essex Buses
H138FLX	CentreWest	H341LJN	Essex Buses	H377OTH	Cymru
H139FLX	Capital	H342LJN	Essex Buses	H377UWB	Mainline
H140FLX	Capital	H343LJN	Eastern Counties	H378OHK	Eastern Counties
H141FLX	Capital	H344LJN	Essex Buses	H378OTH	Cymru
H142FLX	Capital	H344RKU	Mainline	H378UWB	Mainline
H144FLX	Capital	H345RKU	Mainline	H379OHK	Essex Buses
H145FLX	Capital	H346RKU	Mainline	H379OTH	Cymru
H160JRE	PMT	H347LIN	Eastern Countioc	IJ079UWB	Mainline
H171GTA	Hampshire	H347RKU	Mainline	H380OHK	Essex Buses
H172GTA	Cymru	H348LJN	Eastern Counties	H380OTH	Cymru
H173GTA	Cymru	H348RKU	Mainline	H380UWB	Mainline
H174GTA	Cymru	H349LJN	Eastern Counties	H381OHK	Essex Buses
H175GTA	Cymru	H349RKU	Mainline	H381OTH	Cymru
H176GTA	Hampshire	H351HRF	PMT	H381UWB	Mainline
H177GTA	Cymru	H351LJN	Eastern Counties	H382OHK	Essex Buses
H178GTA	Cymru	H351UWB	Mainline	H382TTH	Cymru
H179GTA	Cymru	H352HRF	PMT	H382UWB	Mainline
H189CNS	PMT	H352LJN	Essex Buses	H383OHK	Essex Buses
H201JHP	Bristol	H352UWB	Mainline	H383UWB	Mainline
H202CRH	Cymru	H353HRF	PMT	H384OHK	Eastern Counties
H202JHP	PMT	H353LJN	Essex Buses	H384UWB	Mainline
H203JHP	PMT	H353UWB	Mainline	H385OHK	Essex Buses
H251KVX	Capital	H354HVT	PMT	H385UWB	Mainline
H252KVX	Capital	H354LJN	Eastern Counties	H386OHK	Essex Buses
H253KVX	Capital	H354UWB	Mainline	H386UWB	Mainline
H254KVX	Capital	H355HVT	PMT	H387OHK	Essex Buses
H255KVX	Capital	H355LJN	Essex Buses	H387UWB	Mainline
H257KVX	Capital	H355UWB	Mainline	H388MAR	Capital
H258KVX	Capital	H356HVT	PMT	H388OHK	Essex Buses
H259KVX	Capital	H356LJN	Essex Buses	H388UWB	Mainline
H262KVX	Capital	H356UWB	Mainline	H389MAR	Capital
H263KVX	Capital	H357HVT	PMT	H389OHK	Essex Buses
H264KVX	Capital	H357LJN	Eastern Counties	H389UWB	Mainline
H265KVX	Capital	H357UWB	Mainline	H390MAR	Capital
H266KVX	Capital	H358JRE	PMT	H390OHK	Essex Buses
H267KVX	Capital	H358LJN	Essex Buses	H390UWB	Mainline
H268KVX	Capital	H358UWB	Mainline	H391MAR	Capital

Reg	Operator
H391OHK	Essex Buses
H392MAR	Capital
H392OHK	Essex Buses
H393MAR	Capital
H393OHK	Essex Buses
H394MAR	Capital
H394OHK	Essex Buses
H395MAR	Capital
H395OHK	Essex Buses
H396OHK	Essex Buses
H397OHK	Essex Buses
H398OHK	Essex Buses
H411BVR	Eastern Counties
H460KVX	Capital
H461KVX	Capital
H471OSC	Midland/Lowland
H472OSC	Midland/Lowland
H473OSC	Midland/Lowland
H474OSC	Midland/Lowland
H475OSC	Midland/Lowland
H476OSC	Midland/Lowland
H477OSC	Midland/Lowland
H478OSC	Midland/Lowland
H479OSC	Midland/Lowland
H480JRE	PMT
H481JRE	PMT
H481OSC	Midland/Lowland
H482JRE	PMT
H482OSC	Midland/Lowland
H483JRE	PMT
H483OSC	Midland/Lowland
H484OSC	Midland/Lowland
H485OSC	Midland/Lowland
H486OSC	Midland/Lowland
H487OSC	Midland/Lowland
H488OSC	Midland/Lowland
H489OSC	Midland/Lowland
H490OSC	Midland/Lowland
H491OSC	Midland/Lowland
H492OSC	Midland/Lowland
H493OSC	Midland/Lowland
H494OSC	Midland/Lowland
H495OSC	Midland/Lowland
H496OSC	Midland/Lowland
H497OSC	Midland/Lowland
H498OSC	Midland/Lowland
H499OSC	Midland/Lowland
H501OSC	Midland/Lowland
H502OSC	Midland/Lowland
H523CTR	Hampshire
H569SWJ	Mainline
H601OVW	Essex Buses
H602OVW	Essex Buses
H603OVW	Essex Buses
H604OVW	Essex Buses
H605OVW	Essex Buses
H606OVW	Essex Buses
H607OVW	Essex Buses
H608OVW	Essex Buses
H609OVW	Essex Buses
H610YTC	Bristol
H611EJF	Leicester
H611RAH	Eastern Counties
H611VNW	Yorkshire
H611YTC	Bristol
H612EJF	Leicester
H612RAH	Eastern Counties
H612VNW	Yorkshire
H612YTC	Bristol
H613EJF	Leicester
H613UWR	Western National
H613VNW	Yorkshire
H613YTC	Bristol
H614EJF	Leicester
H614RAH	Eastern Counties
H614UWR	Western National
H614VNW	Yorkshire
H614YTC	Bristol
H615EJF	Leicester
H615RAH	Eastern Counties
H615UWR	Western National
H615VNW	Yorkshire
H615YTC	Bristol
H616EJF	Leicester

Reg	Operator	Reg	Operator	Reg	Operator	Reg	Operator
H616RAH	Eastern Counties	H663THL	Mainline	H852GRE	PMT	HDZ5452	CentreWest
H616VNW	Yorkshire	H664THL	Mainline	H852OWN	Cymru	HDZ5453	CentreWest
H616YTC	Bristol	H665THL	Mainline	H853GRE	PMT	HDZ5457	Leicester
H617RAH	Eastern Counties	H667THL	Mainline	H853OWN	Cymru	HDZ5458	CentreWest
H617VNW	Yorkshire	H668THL	Mainline	H854GRE	PMT	HDZ5459	Leicester
H618RAH	Eastern Counties	H669THL	Mainline	H855GRE	PMT	HDZ5460	CentreWest
H618VNW	Yorkshire	H670THL	Mainline	H856GRE	PMT	HDZ5462	Leicester
H619RAH	Eastern Counties	H671THL	Mainline	H857GRE	PMT	HDZ5463	Leicester
H619VNW	Yorkshire	H672THL	Mainline	H858GRE	PMT	HDZ5464	Leicester
H620RAH	Eastern Counties	H673THL	Mainline	H859GRE	PMT	HDZ5465	Leicester
H620VNW	Yorkshire	H674THL	Mainline	H860GRE	PMT	HDZ5466	Leicester
H621VNW	Yorkshire	H675THL	Mainline	H861GRE	PMT	HDZ5467	Leicester
H622VNW	Yorkshire	H676THL	Mainline	H891LOX	Western National	HDZ5469	Leicester
H623VNW	Yorkshire	H677THL	Mainline	H892LOX	Western National	HDZ5471	Leicester
H624VNW	Yorkshire	H678THL	Mainline	H893LOX	Western National	HDZ5472	Leicester
H625VNW	Yorkshire	H679THL	Mainline	H894LOX	Western National	HDZ5473	Northampton
H627VNW	Yorkshire	H67RND	Manchester	H895LOX	Western National	HDZ5475	Leicester
H628VNW	Yorkshire	H680THL	Mainline	H896LOX	Western National	HDZ5477	Leicester
H629VNW	Yorkshire	H681THL	Mainline	H906WYB	Southern National	HDZ5478	Northampton
H630VNW	Yorkshire	H682THL	Mainline	H907WYB	Southern National	HDZ5479	Leicester
H631VNW	Yorkshire	H683BTA	Southern National	H908WYB	Southern National	HDZ5480	Midland/Lowland
H632VNW	Yorkshire	H683THL	Mainline	H909WYB	Southern National	HDZ5481	Leicester
H633VNW	Yorkshire	H684BTA	Southern National	H910WYB	Southern National	HDZ5482	Leicester
H633YHT	Bristol	H684THL	Mainline	H912HRO	Glasgow	HDZ5483	CentreWest
H634VNW	Yorkshire	H685THL	Mainline	H912WYB	Southern National	HDZ5484	Leicester
H634YHT	Bristol	H686THL	Mainline	H913WYB	Southern National	HDZ5485	Leicester
H636VNW	Yorkshire	H687THL	Mainline	H914WYB	Southern National	HDZ5487	Leicester
H636YHT	Bristol	H688THL	Mainline	H915WYB	Southern National	HDZ5488	Leicester
H637VNW	Yorkshire	H691THL	Mainline	H916WYB	Southern National	HDZ5489	Leicester
H637YHT	Bristol	H701GVM	Midland/Lowland	H925PMS	Midland/Lowland	HDZ5490	Leicester
H638VNW	Yorkshire	H702GVM	Midland/Lowland	H926PMS	Midland/Lowland	HEX118Y	Eastern Counties
H638YHT	Bristol	H703GVM	Manchester	H972RSG	Midland/Lowland	HEX119Y	Eastern Counties
H639VNW	Yorkshire	H704GVM	Midland/Lowland	H973RSG	Midland/Lowland	HFN769	Western National
H639YHT	Bristol	H705GVM	Manchester	H974RSG	Midland/Lowland	HGM429E	Glasgow
H63RND	Manchester	H706GVM	Midland/Lowland	H975RSG	Midland/Lowland	HHA101L	Midland Red
H640VNW	Yorkshire	H707GVM	Midland/Lowland	H976RSG	Midland/Lowland	HHH370V	Southern National
H640YHT	Bristol	H708GVM	Manchester	H990FTT	Cymru	HHJ372Y	Southern National
H641VNW	Yorkshire	H712HGL	Western National	H991FTT	Hampshire	HHJ373Y	Western National
H641YHT	Bristol	H713HGL	Western National	H992FTT	Cymru	HHJ374Y	PMT
H642RKU	Mainline	H714HGL	Western National	H993FTT	Cymru	HHJ375Y	Southern National
H642VNW	Yorkshire	H715HGL	Western National	H994FTT	Cymru	HHJ376Y	Southern National
H642YHT	Bristol	H716HGL	Western National	H995FTT	Cymru	HHJ379Y	Mainline
H643RKU	Mainline	H717HGL	Western National	H996FTT	Cymru	HHJ381Y	Southern National
H643VNW	Yorkshire	H718HGL	Western National	H997FTT	Hampshire	HHJ382Y	Southern National
H643YHT	Bristol	H719HGL	Western National	HAH239V	Eastern Counties	HRO987V	Southern National
H644RKU	Mainline	H720HGL	Western National	HAH240V	Eastern Counties	HRS261V	Midland/Lowland
H644YHT	Bristol	H721HGL	Western National	HDZ5404	CentreWest	HRS262V	Aberdeen
H645RKU	Mainline	H722CNC	PMT	HDZ5405	CentreWest	HRS265V	Midland/Lowland
H645YHT	Bristol	H722HGL	Western National	HDZ5406	CentreWest	HRS267V	Midland/Lowland
H646RKU	Mainline	H723CNC	PMT	HDZ5407	CentreWest	HRS268V	Aberdeen
H646YHT	Bristol	H723HGL	Western National	HDZ5408	CentreWest	HRS269V	Aberdeen
H647RKU	Mainline	H724HGL	Western National	HDZ5409	CentreWest	HRS271V	Aberdeen
H647YHT	Bristol	H725CNC	PMT	HDZ5415	CentreWest	HRS273V	Midland/Lowland
H648RKU	Mainline	H725HGL	Western National	HDZ5417	CentreWest	HRS274V	Midland/Lowland
H648YHT	Bristol	H726HGL	Western National	HDZ5418	CentreWest	HRS276V	Midland/Lowland
H649RKU	Mainline	H726VNW	Yorkshire	HDZ5419	CentreWest	HRS278V	Aberdeen
H649USH	Midland/Lowland	H751ENR	Leicester	HDZ5420	CentreWest	HRS280V	Aberdeen
H649YHT	Bristol	H752ENR	Leicester	HDZ5421	CentreWest	HRS288V	Midland/Lowland
H650RKU	Mainline	H782GTA	Cymru	HDZ5422	CentreWest	HSF76X	Midland/Lowland
H650YHT	Bristol	H783GTA	Hampshire	HDZ5423	CentreWest	HSF77X	Midland/Lowland
H651THL	Mainline	H787GTA	Hampshire	HDZ5424	CentreWest	HSF78X	Midland/Lowland
H651YHT	Bristol	H788GTA	Cymru	HDZ5425	CentreWest	HSF80X	Midland/Lowland
H652THL	Mainline	H801GDV	Western National	HDZ5426	CentreWest	HSF81X	Midland/Lowland
H652YHT	Bristol	H801GRE	PMT	HDZ5427	CentreWest	HSF82X	Midland/Lowland
H653THL	Mainline	H802GDV	Southern National	HDZ5429	CentreWest	HSF83X	Midland/Lowland
H653YHT	Bristol	H802GRE	PMT	HDZ5430	CentreWest	HSF84X	Midland/Lowland
H654THL	Mainline	H803GRE	PMT	HDZ5431	CentreWest	HSF85X	Midland/Lowland
H654YHT	Bristol	H804GRE	PMT	HDZ5433	CentreWest	HSF86X	Midland/Lowland
H655THL	Mainline	H805GRE	PMT	HDZ5434	CentreWest	HSF87X	Midland/Lowland
H655YHT	Bristol	H806GRE	PMT	HDZ5435	CentreWest	HSF88X	Midland/Lowland
H656THL	Mainline	H806TWX	Yorkshire	HDZ5437	CentreWest	HSF91X	Midland/Lowland
H656YHT	Bristol	H807GRE	PMT	HDZ5438	CentreWest	HSF92X	Midland/Lowland
H657THL	Mainline	H807TWX	Yorkshire	HDZ5439	CentreWest	HSF93X	Midland/Lowland
H657YHT	Bristol	H808GRE	PMT	HDZ5440	Leicester	HSF94X	Midland/Lowland
H658THL	Mainline	H808TWX	Yorkshire	HDZ5441	Leicester	HSF95X	Midland/Lowland
H658YHT	Bristol	H809GRE	PMT	HDZ5442	CentreWest	HSO61N	Aberdeen
H659THL	Mainline	H809TWX	Yorkshire	HDZ5443	CentreWest	HSO284V	Manchester
H659YHT	Bristol	H810TWX	Yorkshire	HDZ5445	CentreWest	HSO287V	Midland/Lowland
H660THL	Mainline	H825ERV	Cymru	HDZ5446	Midland/Lowland	HSU247	Midland/Lowland
H660YHT	Bristol	H834GLD	PMT	HDZ5447	CentreWest	HSU273	Midland/Lowland
H661THL	Mainline	H835GLD	PMT	HDZ5448	CentreWest	HSU301	Midland/Lowland
H661YHT	Bristol	H836GLD	PMT	HDZ5449	CentreWest	HTA844N	Western National
H662THL	Mainline	H844UUA	Glasgow	HDZ5450	CentreWest	HTC726N	Western National
H662YHT	Bristol	H851GRE	PMT	HDZ5451	CentreWest	HTC728N	Western National

Reg	Operator	Reg	Operator	Reg	Operator	Reg	Operator
HUA606Y	Cymru	J310XLS	Midland/Lowland	J625BVG	Eastern Counties	J916SEH	PMT
HUA607Y	Midland Red	J328RVT	PMT	J625HMH	Capital	J916WVC	Cymru
HVG803V	Western National	J329LLK	Southern National	J625UTW	Essex Buses	J917SEH	PMT
HVJ716	Western National	J375WWK	Cymru	J626HMH	Capital	J918SEH	PMT
HWT54N	Manchester	J404WDA	Eastern Counties	J626UTW	Essex Buses	J969EYD	Southern National
IIL2490	Southern National	J421NCP	Yorkshire	J627HMH	Capital	JAH242V	Eastern Counties
J8SMT	Midland/Lowland	J422NCP	Yorkshire	J627UTW	Essex Buses	JBP129P	Hampshire
J11AFC	Aberdeen	J423NCP	Yorkshire	J628HMH	Capital	JBP133P	Hampshire
J11GRT	Aberdeen	J424NCP	Yorkshire	J628UTW	Essex Buses	JDZ2300	CentreWest
J31KLR	Eastern Counties	J425NCP	Yorkshire	J629HMH	Capital	JDZ2301	CentreWest
J32KLR	Manchester	J426NCP	Yorkshire	J629UTW	Essex Buses	JDZ2302	CentreWest
J34KLR	Manchester	J429GHT	Bristol	J630HMH	Capital	JDZ2303	CentreWest
J35KLR	Manchester	J430WFA	PMT	J630UTW	Essex Buses	JDZ2304	CentreWest
J36KLR	Manchester	J431WFA	PMT	J631HMH	Capital	JDZ2305	CentreWest
J37KLR	Eastern Counties	J459JOW	Capital	J632HMH	Capital	JDZ2306	CentreWest
J113XSX	Glasgow	J461OVU	Manchester	J633HMH	Capital	JDZ2307	CentreWest
J115MRP	Northampton	J484PVT	PMT	J689XAK	Mainline	JDZ2308	CentreWest
J129YRM	Capital	J485PVT	PMT	J690XAK	Mainline	JDZ2309	CentreWest
J130YRM	Capital	J486PVT	PMT	J691AWF	Mainline	JDZ2310	CentreWest
J131YRM	Capital	J503WSX	Midland/Lowland	J692AWF	Mainline	JDZ2311	CentreWest
J132YRM	Capital	J504WSX	Midland/Lowland	J693AWF	Mainline	JDZ2312	CentreWest
J134YRM	Capital	J505WSX	Midland/Lowland	J694AWF	Mainline	JDZ2313	CentreWest
J135PVC	Capital	J506WSX	Midland/Lowland	J695AWF	Mainline	JDZ2314	CentreWest
J135YRM	Capital	J507WSX	Midland/Lowland	J696AWF	Mainline	JDZ2315	CentreWest
J136YRM	Capital	J508WSX	Midland/Lowland	J697AWF	Mainline	JDZ2316	CentreWest
J137FYS	Glasgow	J509WSX	Midland/Lowland	J698AWF	Mainline	JDZ2317	CentreWest
J137YRM	Capital	J510WSX	Midland/Lowland	J699AWF	Mainline	JDZ2318	Eastern Counties
J138FYS	Glasgow	J511WSX	Midland/Lowland	J701AWF	Mainline	JDZ2319	Eastern Counties
J138YRM	Capital	J512WSX	Midland/Lowland	J701CWT	Western National	JDZ2320	Eastern Counties
J139YRM	Capital	J513FPS	Glasgow	J702AWF	Mainline	JDZ2321	Eastern Counties
J140SJT	Western National	J514FPS	Glasgow	J703AWF	Mainline	JDZ2322	CentreWest
J140YRM	Capital	J515FPS	Glasgow	J703CWT	Western National	JDZ2323	CentreWest
J141SJT	Western National	J516FPS	Glasgow	J704AWF	Mainline	JDZ2324	CentreWest
J141YRM	Capital	J517FPS	Glasgow	J705AWF	Mainline	JDZ2325	Eastern Counties
J142KPX	Bristol	J518FPS	Glasgow	J709ONF	Manchester	JDZ2326	CentreWest
J142SJT	Western National	J530FCL	Eastern Counties	J710ONF	Manchester	JDZ2327	CentreWest
J142YRM	Capital	J580FYA	Southern National	J753MFP	Leicester	JDZ2328	CentreWest
J143KPX	Bristol	J580VTH	Cymru	J754MFP	Leicester	JDZ2329	CentreWest
J143SJT	Western National	J581VTH	Cymru	J755MFP	Leicester	JDZ2330	CentreWest
J143YRM	Capital	J582VTH	Cymru	J756MFP	Leicester	JDZ2331	Eastern Counties
J144KPX	Bristol	J601FYA	Southern National	J757MFP	Leicester	JDZ2332	Eastern Counties
J144SJT	Western National	J601HMF	Capital	J758NNR	Leicester	JDZ2335	Eastern Counties
J144YRM	Capital	J602HMF	Capital	J759NNR	Leicester	JDZ2336	Eastern Counties
J145KPX	Bristol	J603HMF	Manchester	J774WLS	Midland/Lowland	JDZ2337	Eastern Counties
J145SJT	Western National	J604HMF	Manchester	J775WLS	Midland/Lowland	JDZ2338	Eastern Counties
J145YRM	Capital	J605HMF	Capital	J776WLS	Midland/Lowland	JDZ2339	Capital
J146KPX	Bristol	J606HMF	Manchester	J778WLS	Midland/Lowland	JDZ2340	Capital
J146SJT	Western National	J607HMF	Manchester	J779WLS	Midland/Lowland	JDZ2341	Capital
J146YRM	Capital	J608HMF	Manchester	J794AWF	Mainline	JDZ2342	Capital
J148SJT	Western National	J609HMF	Manchester	J803PFJ	Western National	JDZ2343	Capital
J148YRM	Capital	J610HMF	Capital	J850FTC	Bristol	JDZ2372	Capital
J149YRM	Capital	J610PTA	Western National	J850OBV	Bristol	JDZ2373	Capital
J150YRM	Capital	J610UTW	Essex Buses	J851FTC	Bristol	JDZ2374	CentreWest
J151YRM	Capital	J611HMF	Capital	J852FTC	Bristol	JDZ2375	CentreWest
J152YRM	Capital	J611UTW	Essex Buses	J853FTC	Bristol	JDZ2376	Eastern Counties
J153YRM	Capital	J612HMF	Capital	J854FTC	Bristol	JDZ2377	CentreWest
J154YRM	Capital	J612UTW	Essex Buses	J855FTC	Bristol	JDZ2378	CentreWest
J155YRM	Capital	J613HMF	Capital	J856FTC	Bristol	JDZ2379	CentreWest
J156YRM	Glasgow	J613UTW	Essex Buses	J857FTC	Bristol	JDZ2380	CentreWest
J157YRM	Capital	J614HMF	Manchester	J858FTC	Bristol	JDZ2381	CentreWest
J158YRM	Capital	J614UTW	Essex Buses	J859FTC	Bristol	JDZ2382	CentreWest
J181HME	Capital	J615HMF	Capital	J860HWS	Bristol	JDZ2383	CentreWest
J182HME	Capital	J615UTW	Essex Buses	J861HWS	Bristol	JDZ2384	CentreWest
J185LGE	Southern National	J616HMF	Capital	J862HWS	Bristol	JDZ2385	CentreWest
J203HWS	Bristol	J616UTW	Essex Buses	J863HWS	Bristol	JDZ2386	CentreWest
J204HWS	Bristol	J617HMF	Capital	J864HWS	Bristol	JDZ2387	CentreWest
J205KTT	Southern National	J617UTW	Essex Buses	J865HWS	Bristol	JDZ2388	CentreWest
J208KTT	Southern National	J618HMF	Capital	J866HWS	Bristol	JDZ2389	CentreWest
J210GNV	Northampton	J618UTW	Essex Buses	J901MAF	Cymru	JDZ2390	CentreWest
J210KTT	Southern National	J619HMF	Manchester	J901SEH	PMT	JDZ2391	CentreWest
J213KTT	Southern National	J619UTW	Essex Buses	J902SEH	PMT	JDZ2392	CentreWest
J217KTT	Southern National	J620HMF	Capital	J903SEH	PMT	JDZ2393	CentreWest
J220KTT	Southern National	J620UTW	Essex Buses	J904SEH	PMT	JDZ2394	CentreWest
J241FYA	Southern National	J621BVG	Eastern Counties	J905SEH	PMT	JDZ2395	CentreWest
J247YRM	Capital	J621HMH	Capital	J906SEH	PMT	JDZ2396	CentreWest
J295GNV	Northampton	J621UTW	Essex Buses	J907SEH	PMT	JDZ2397	CentreWest
J296GNV	Northampton	J622BVG	Eastern Counties	J908SEH	PMT	JDZ2398	CentreWest
J297GNV	Northampton	J622HMH	Capital	J909SEH	PMT	JDZ2399	CentreWest
J298GNV	Northampton	J622UTW	Essex Buses	J910SEH	PMT	JFS983X	Midland/Lowland
J299GNV	Northampton	J623BVG	Eastern Counties	J911SEH	PMT	JFS986X	Midland/Lowland
J301ASH	Midland/Lowland	J623HMH	Capital	J912SEH	PMT	JFV311S	Western National
J302ASH	Midland/Lowland	J623UTW	Essex Buses	J913SEH	PMT	JFV312S	Western National
J303ASH	Midland/Lowland	J624HMH	Capital	J914SEH	PMT	JFX232N	Southern National
J304ASH	Midland/Lowland	J624UTW	Essex Buses	J915SEH	PMT	JHA230L	Midland Red

Reg	Operator	Reg	Operator	Reg	Operator	Reg	Operator
JHE138W	Capital	JUM211V	Yorkshire	K339OAF	Western National	K603LAE	Bristol
JHE146W	Capital	JUM212V	Yorkshire	K340OAF	Western National	K603ORL	Western National
JHE147W	Capital	JUM213V	Yorkshire	K341OAF	Western National	K604HUG	Yorkshire
JHE148W	Capital	JUM214V	Yorkshire	K342OAF	Western National	K604LAE	Bristol
JHE149W	Capital	JUM215V	Yorkshire	K343OAF	Western National	K604ORL	Western National
JHE150W	Capital	JUW73V	Yorkshire	K344ORL	Western National	K605HUG	Yorkshire
JHE152W	Capital	JUW79V	Yorkshire	K345ORL	Western National	K605LAE	Bristol
JHE154W	Mainline	JUW82V	Yorkshire	K346ORL	Western National	K605ORL	Western National
JHE157W	Capital	JWE243W	Western National	K347ORL	Western National	K606HUG	Yorkshire
JHE161W	Mainline	JWF495W	Capital	K348ORL	Western National	K606LAE	Bristol
JHE170W	Capital	JWF496W	Capital	K349ORL	Western National	K606ORL	Western National
JHE171W	Capital	JWF497W	Capital	K350ORL	Western National	K607HUG	Yorkshire
JHE172W	Capital	JWF498W	Capital	K350SDS	Glasgow	K607LAE	Bristol
JHE182W	Capital	JWF499W	Capital	K351ORL	Western National	K607ORL	Western National
JHE194W	Capital	JWT758V	Western National	K352ORL	Western National	K608HUG	Yorkshire
JHJ142V	Essex Buses	K1GRT	Aberdeen	K353ORL	Western National	K608LAE	Bristol
JHJ147V	Essex Buses	K1YRL	Yorkshire	K354ORL	Western National	K608ORL	Western National
JHJ150V	Essex Buses	K3GRT	Aberdeen	K374BRE	PMT	K609HUG	Yorkshire
JHU900X	Bristol	K4GRT	Aberdeen	K375BRE	PMT	K609LAE	Bristol
JHU901X	Bristol	K10BMS	Cymru	K396KHJ	Capital	K609ORL	Western National
JHU902X	Bristol	K11BMS	Cymru	K397KHJ	Essex Buses	K610HUG	Yorkshire
JHU903X	Bristol	K12BMS	Cymru	K398KHJ	Essex Buses	K610LAE	Bristol
JHU904X	Bristol	K13BMS	Cymru	K401BAX	Cymru	K610ORL	Western National
JHU905X	Bristol	K29OEU	Bristol	K401EDT	Mainline	K611HUG	Yorkshire
JHU906X	Bristol	K62KEX	Eastern Counties	K401HRS	Aberdeen	K611LAE	Bristol
JHU907X	Bristol	K63KEX	Eastern Counties	K402BAX	Cymru	K611ORL	Western National
JHU908X	Bristol	K65OHT	Bristol	K402HRS	Aberdeen	K612HUG	Yorkshire
JHU909X	Bristol	K67HSA	Aberdeen	K403BAX	Cymru	K612LAE	Bristol
JHU910X	Bristol	K67OHT	Bristol	K403HRS	Aberdeen	K612ORL	Western National
JHU911X	Bristol	K82BWN	Cymru	K404BAX	Cymru	K613HUG	Yorkshire
JHU913X	Bristol	K101HUM	Yorkshire	K404HRS	Aberdeen	K613LAE	Bristol
JHU914X	Bristol	K102HUM	Yorkshire	K405BAX	Cymru	K613ORL	Western National
JHW107P	Bristol	K103HUM	Yorkshire	K405HRS	Aberdeen	K614HUG	Yorkshire
JHW108P	Bristol	K104HUM	Yorkshire	K406BAX	Cymru	K614LAE	Bristol
JHW109P	Bristol	K105HUM	Yorkshire	K406HRS	Aberdeen	K614ORL	Western National
JHW114P	Bristol	K106HUM	Yorkshire	K407BAX	Cymru	K615HUG	Yorkshire
JJD365D	CentreWest	K107HUM	Yorkshire	K407HRS	Aberdeen	K615LAE	Bristol
JJD369D	CentreWest	K108HUM	Yorkshire	K408BAX	Cymru	K615ORL	Western National
JJD374D	CentreWest	K109HUM	Yorkshire	K408HRS	Aberdeen	K616HUG	Yorkshire
JJD378D	CentreWest	K110HUM	Yorkshire	K409BAX	Cymru	K616LAE	Bristol
JJD379D	CentreWest	K112HUM	Yorkshire	K409HRS	Aberdeen	K616ORL	Western National
JJD388D	CentreWest	K113HUM	Yorkshire	K410BAX	Cymru	K617HUG	Yorkshire
JJD390D	CentreWest	K114HUM	Yorkshire	K432XRF	PMT	K617LAE	Bristol
JJD405D	CentreWest	K114PRV	Hampshire	K433XRF	PMT	K617ORL	Western National
JJD428D	CentreWest	K115HUM	Yorkshire	K434XRF	PMT	K617SBC	Leicester
JJD442D	CentreWest	K116HUM	Yorkshire	K435XRF	PMT	K618HUG	Yorkshire
JJD467D	CentreWest	K117HUM	Yorkshire	K436XRF	PMT	K618LAE	Bristol
JJD473D	CentreWest	K118HUM	Yorkshire	K437XRF	PMT	K618ORL	Western National
JJD476D	CentreWest	K119HUM	Yorkshire	K438XRF	PMT	K618SBC	Leicester
JJD480D	CentreWest	K120HUM	Yorkshire	K439XRF	PMT	K619HUG	Yorkshire
JJD486D	CentreWest	K121URP	Northampton	K440XRF	PMT	K619LAE	Bristol
JJD490D	CentreWest	K123URP	Northampton	K441XRF	PMT	K619ORL	Western National
JJD498D	CentreWest	K124URP	Northampton	K442XRF	PMT	K619SBC	Leicester
JJD501D	CentreWest	K125URP	Northampton	K443XRF	PMT	K619XOD	Hampshire
JJD506D	CentreWest	K126URP	Northampton	K445XRF	PMT	K620HUG	Yorkshire
JJD522D	CentreWest	K127GNH	Northampton	K446XRF	PMT	K620LAE	Bristol
JJD530D	CentreWest	K128GNH	Northampton	K447XRF	PMT	K620ORL	Western National
JJD542D	CentreWest	K129GNH	Northampton	K448XRF	PMT	K620SBC	Leicester
JJD553D	CentreWest	K130GNH	Northampton	K449XRF	PMT	K621HUG	Yorkshire
JJD555D	CentreWest	K131GNH	Northampton	K461PNR	Bristol	K621LAE	Bristol
JJD559D	CentreWest	K132GNH	Northampton	K473EDT	Midland/Lowland	K621ORL	Western National
JKW215W	Yorkshire	K160PPO	Hampshire	K487CVT	PMT	K621SBC	Leicester
JKW216W	Yorkshire	K161PPO	Hampshire	K488CVT	PMT	K621XOD	Hampshire
JNU138N	Western National	K162PPO	Hampshire	K489CVT	PMT	K622HUG	Yorkshire
JSF927T	Midland/Lowland	K163PPO	Hampshire	K490CVT	PMT	K622LAE	Bristol
JSF929T	Midland/Lowland	K164PPO	Hampshire	K491CVT	PMT	K622ORL	Western National
JSF930T	Midland/Lowland	K165PPO	Hampshire	K492CVT	PMT	K622SBC	Leicester
JSV426	Aberdeen	K175YVC	Midland/Lowland	K509NOU	Bristol	K622XOD	Hampshire
JTH44W	Yorkshire	K211HUM	Yorkshire	K513BSX	Midland/Lowland	K623HUG	Yorkshire
JTY926P	Eastern Counties	K279XJB	CentreWest	K514BSX	Midland/Lowland	K623LAE	Bristol
JUB646V	Bristol	K281XJB	CentreWest	K515BSX	Midland/Lowland	K623ORL	Western National
JUB647V	Bristol	K282XJB	CentreWest	K516BSX	Midland/Lowland	K623XOD	Hampshire
JUM194V	Yorkshire	K283XJB	CentreWest	K517BSX	Midland/Lowland	K624HUG	Yorkshire
JUM195V	Yorkshire	K328KYC	Southern National	K527RJX	Yorkshire	K624LAE	Bristol
JUM196V	Yorkshire	K329KYC	Southern National	K528RJX	Yorkshire	K624ORL	Western National
JUM198V	Yorkshire	K330KYC	Southern National	K535RJX	Midland/Lowland	K625HUG	Yorkshire
JUM199V	Yorkshire	K331OAF	Western National	K544XRF	PMT	K625LAE	Bristol
JUM200V	Yorkshire	K332OAF	Western National	K601HUG	Yorkshire	K625ORL	Western National
JUM201V	Yorkshire	K333OAF	Western National	K601LAE	Bristol	K626HUG	Yorkshire
JUM202V	Yorkshire	K334OAF	Western National	K601ORL	Western National	K626LAE	Bristol
JUM205V	Yorkshire	K335OAF	Western National	K602HUG	Yorkshire	K627HUG	Yorkshire
JUM208V	Yorkshire	K336OAF	Western National	K602LAE	Bristol	K627LAE	Bristol
JUM209V	Yorkshire	K337OAF	Western National	K602ORL	Western National	K628HUG	Yorkshire
JUM210V	Yorkshire	K338OAF	Western National	K603HUG	Yorkshire	K628LAE	Bristol

Reg	Operator	Reg	Operator	Reg	Operator	Reg	Operator
K629HUG	Yorkshire	K750VJU	Leicester	K923VDV	Hampshire	KGG159Y	Eastern Counties
K629LAE	Bristol	K751VFJ	Southern National	K923XRF	PMT	KGG160Y	Eastern Counties
K630HUG	Yorkshire	K752XTA	Southern National	K924RGE	Midland/Lowland	KGG161Y	Glasgow
K630LAE	Bristol	K752XTA	Western National	K924XRF	PMT	KGM328Y	Southern National
K631GVX	Essex Buses	K753XTA	Southern National	K925XRF	PMT	KIW5940	Southern National
K631HUG	Yorkshire	K753XTA	Western National	K926XRF	PMT	KKU102W	Mainline
K632GVX	Essex Buses	K754XTA	Southern National	K927XRF	PMT	KKU103W	Mainline
K632HUG	Yorkshire	K754XTA	Western National	K928VDV	Hampshire	KKU105W	Mainline
K633GVX	Essex Buses	K755XTA	Southern National	K928XRF	PMT	KKU107W	Mainline
K633HUG	Yorkshire	K755XTA	Western National	K929VDV	Hampshire	KKU108W	Mainline
K633XOD	Hampshire	K760SBC	Leicester	K929XRF	PMT	KKU109W	Mainline
K634GVX	Essex Buses	K761SBC	Leicester	K930VDV	Hampshire	KKU119W	Mainline
K634HUG	Yorkshire	K776AFS	Southern National	K931VDV	Hampshire	KKU120W	Mainline
K635GVX	Essex Buses	K792OTC	Bristol	K945JWE	Mainline	KKU124W	Mainline
K636GVX	Essex Buses	K793OTC	Bristol	K946JWE	Mainline	KKU127W	Mainline
K637GVX	Essex Buses	K794OTC	Bristol	K947JWE	Mainline	KKW525W	Southern National
K638GVX	Essex Buses	K801CAN	CentreWest	K948JWE	Mainline	KOO785V	Western National
K639GVX	Essex Buses	K801ORL	Western National	K991OEU	Bristol	KOO787V	Essex Buses
K640GVX	Essex Buses	K801WFJ	Hampshire	KBZ3627	Midland/Lowland	KOO789V	Essex Buses
K641GVX	Essex Buses	K802CAN	CentreWest	KBZ3628	Midland/Lowland	KOO790V	Essex Buses
K642GVX	Essex Buses	K802ORL	Western National	KBZ3629	Midland/Lowland	KOO792V	Bristol
K643GVX	Essex Buses	K802WFJ	Hampshire	KCB758	Glasgow	KOO794V	Essex Buses
K644GVX	Essex Buses	K803ORL	Western National	KDB127V	Yorkshire	KOW272Y	Hampshire
K645GVX	Essex Buses	K804ORL	Western National	KDB136V	Yorkshire	KOW273Y	Hampshire
K646GVX	Essex Buses	K804WTT	Western National	KDU648	Southern National	KOW274Y	Hampshire
K651DBL	CentreWest	K805DJN	Essex Buses	KDZ5101	CentreWest	KOW275Y	Hampshire
K651DLS	Midland/Lowland	K805WTT	Western National	KDZ5102	CentreWest	KOW276Y	Hampshire
K652DBL	CentreWest	K806DJN	Essex Buses	KDZ5103	CentreWest	KPA360P	Cymru
K652DLS	Midland/Lowland	K807DJN	Essex Buses	KDZ5104	CentreWest	KPA362P	Southern National
K653DBL	CentreWest	K808DJN	Essex Buses	KDZ5105	CentreWest	KPJ257W	Yorkshire
K653DLS	Midland/Lowland	K809DJN	Essex Buses	KDZ5106	CentreWest	KPJ261W	Yorkshire
K654DLS	Midland/Lowland	K810DJN	Essex Buses	KDZ5107	CentreWest	KPJ291W	Yorkshire
K655DLS	Midland/Lowland	K811DJN	Essex Buses	KDZ5108	CentreWest	KPJ292W	Yorkshire
K656DLS	Midland/Lowland	K819WFJ	Hampshire	KDZ5109	CentreWest	KRS539V	Capital
K657DLS	Midland/Lowland	K867NEU	Bristol	KDZ5110	CentreWest	KSU388	Midland/Lowland
K658DLS	Midland/Lowland	K868NEU	Bristol	KDZ5111	CentreWest	KSU389	Midland/Lowland
K659DLS	Midland/Lowland	K869NEU	Bristol	KDZ5112	CentreWest	KSU390	Midland/Lowland
K690UFV	Bristol	K870NEU	Bristol	KEX532	Midland/Lowland	KSU391	Midland/Lowland
K691UFV	Bristol	K871NEU	Bristol	KFM111Y	PMT	KSU392	Midland/Lowland
K692UFV	Bristol	K872NEU	Bristol	KFM112Y	PMT	KSU393	Midland/Lowland
K693UFV	Bristol	K873NEU	Bristol	KFM113Y	PMT	KSU394	Midland/Lowland
K694UFV	Bristol	K874NEU	Bristol	KFM115Y	PMT	KSU834	Midland/Lowland
K695RNR	Bristol	K875NEU	Bristol	KFX791	Southern National	KTA986V	Southern National
K701UTT	Cymru	K876NEU	Bristol	KGG101Y	Glasgow	KTT808P	Western National
K703UTT	Hampshire	K888BFG	Capital	KGG102Y	Glasgow	KUB548V	Western National
K704UTT	Cymru	K888BWU	Capital	KGG103Y	Glasgow	KVG604V	Eastern Counties
K705UTT	Cymru	K888ELR	Capital	KGG104Y	Glasgow	KVG607V	Eastern Counties
K706EDT	Mainline	K888LAD	Capital	KGG105Y	Glasgow	KVG609V	Eastern Counties
K706UTT	Cymru	K888PFD	Capital	KGG106Y	Glasgow	KWY216V	Yorkshire
K707EDT	Mainline	K888TKS	Capital	KGG107Y	Glasgow	KWY217V	Yorkshire
K707UTT	Cymru	K888TTT	Capital	KGG108Y	Glasgow	KWY218V	Yorkshire
K708EDT	Mainline	K888TWY	Capital	KGG109Y	Glasgow	KWY219V	Yorkshire
K708UTT	Cymru	K901CVW	Capital	KGG110Y	Glasgow	KWY221V	Yorkshire
K709EDT	Mainline	K902CVW	Capital	KGG111Y	Glasgow	KWY222V	Yorkshire
K709UTT	Cymru	K903CVW	Capital	KGG112Y	Glasgow	KWY223V	Yorkshire
K710EDT	Mainline	K904CVW	Capital	KGG115Y	Glasgow	KWY224V	Yorkshire
K710UTT	Hampshire	K905CVW	Capital	KGG116Y	Glasgow	KWY225V	Yorkshire
K711EDT	Mainline	K906CVW	Capital	KGG118Y	Glasgow	KWY226V	Yorkshire
K712EDT	Mainline	K907CVW	Essex Buses	KGG119Y	Glasgow	KWY227V	Yorkshire
K712UTT	Cymru	K908CVW	Essex Buses	KGG122Y	Glasgow	KWY228V	Yorkshire
K713EDT	Mainline	K909CVW	Essex Buses	KGG125Y	Glasgow	KWY229V	Yorkshire
K714EDT	Mainline	K910CVW	Essex Buses	KGG127Y	Glasgow	KWY230V	Yorkshire
K715EDT	Mainline	K911CVW	Essex Buses	KGG128Y	Glasgow	KWY233V	Yorkshire
K715UTT	Cymru	K911VDV	Hampshire	KGG130Y	Glasgow	KWY234V	Yorkshire
K716UTT	Cymru	K912CVW	Essex Buses	KGG131Y	Glasgow	KWY236V	Yorkshire
K723UTT	Hampshire	K912VDV	Hampshire	KGG134Y	Glasgow	KWY237V	Yorkshire
K723WTT	Western National	K913CVW	Essex Buses	KGG135Y	Glasgow	KWY238V	Yorkshire
K728UTT	Hampshire	K914CVW	Essex Buses	KGG136Y	Glasgow	KWY239V	Yorkshire
K729UTT	Hampshire	K914VDV	Hampshire	KGG137Y	Glasgow	KWY241V	Yorkshire
K731JAH	Eastern Counties	K915CVW	Essex Buses	KGG138Y	Glasgow	KWY242V	Yorkshire
K732JAH	Eastern Counties	K915VDV	Hampshire	KGG139Y	Glasgow	KWY243V	Yorkshire
K734JAH	Eastern Counties	K916CVW	Essex Buses	KGG140Y	Glasgow	KWY244V	Yorkshire
K736JAH	Eastern Counties	K916VDV	Hampshire	KGG141Y	Glasgow	KWY245V	Yorkshire
K737JAH	Eastern Counties	K917CVW	Essex Buses	KGG142Y	Glasgow	KWY246V	Yorkshire
K738JAH	Eastern Counties	K917VDV	Hampshire	KGG143Y	Glasgow	KWY247V	Yorkshire
K739JAH	Eastern Counties	K918VDV	Hampshire	KGG145Y	Glasgow	KWY248V	Yorkshire
K740JAH	Eastern Counties	K919VDV	Hampshire	KGG146Y	Glasgow	KWY249V	Yorkshire
K741JAH	Eastern Counties	K919XRF	PMT	KGG151Y	Glasgow	KWY250V	Yorkshire
K742JAH	Eastern Counties	K920VDV	Hampshire	KGG152Y	Glasgow	KWY251W	Yorkshire
K743JAH	Eastern Counties	K920XRF	PMT	KGG154Y	Glasgow	KYC604N	Southern National
K744JAH	Eastern Counties	K921VDV	Hampshire	KGG155Y	Glasgow	KYO606X	Capital
K746VJU	Leicester	K921XRF	PMT	KGG156Y	Eastern Counties	KYV668X	Capital
K748VJU	Leicester	K922VDV	Hampshire	KGG157Y	Eastern Counties	KYV769X	Capital
K749VJU	Leicester	K922XRF	PMT	KGG158Y	Eastern Counties	L4GML	Capital

The 1999 FirstGroup Bus Handbook

Reg	Operator	Reg	Operator	Reg	Operator	Reg	Operator
L5GML	Capital	L169TRV	Hampshire	L213KSX	Midland/Lowland	L314PWR	Essex Buses
L6BMS	Cymru	L169UNS	Glasgow	L213VHU	Bristol	L315BOD	Hampshire
L6GML	Capital	L170TRV	Hampshire	L214AAB	Midland Red	L315PWR	Essex Buses
L8BMS	Cymru	L170UNS	Glasgow	L214VHU	Bristol	L316BOD	Hampshire
L14BMS	Cymru	L171TRV	Hampshire	L215AAB	Midland Red	L317BOD	Hampshire
L21AHA	Essex Buses	L171UNS	Glasgow	L215VHU	Bristol	L319BOD	Hampshire
L22YRL	Yorkshire	L172TRV	Hampshire	L216AAB	Midland Red	L320BOD	Hampshire
L23LSG	Southern National	L172UNS	Glasgow	L216VHU	Bristol	L321HRE	PMT
L24GAN	CentreWest	L173TRV	Hampshire	L217AAB	Midland Red	L322AAB	Bristol
L24LSG	Southern National	L173UNS	Glasgow	L217VHU	Bristol	L322BOD	Hampshire
L25GAN	CentreWest	L174TRV	Hampshire	L218AAB	Cymru	L323BOD	Hampshire
L26GAN	CentreWest	L174UNS	Glasgow	L218VHU	Bristol	L323NRF	PMT
L26LSG	Southern National	L175TRV	Hampshire	L219AAB	Cymru	L324BOD	Hampshire
L27GAN	CentreWest	L175UNS	Glasgow	L219VHU	Bristol	L329MYC	Southern National
L28GAN	CentreWest	L176TRV	Hampshire	L220AAB	Cymru	L330MYC	Southern National
L60HMS	Midland/Lowland	L176UNS	Glasgow	L220VHU	Bristol	L355VCV	Western National
L64UOU	Bristol	L177TRV	Hampshire	L221AAB	Bristol	L356VCV	Western National
L65UOU	Bristol	L177UNS	Glasgow	L221VHU	Bristol	L357VCV	Western National
L67EPR	Southern National	L178TRV	Hampshire	L223AAB	Bristol	L358VCV	Western National
L67UOU	Bristol	L178UNS	Glasgow	L223VHU	Bristol	L359VCV	Western National
L68EPR	Southern National	L179UNS	Glasgow	L224AAB	Bristol	L360VCV	Western National
L69EPR	Southern National	L180UNS	Glasgow	L224VHU	Bristol	L364GTH	Cymru
L69EPR	Western National	L181UNS	Glasgow	L225AAB	Bristol	L390UHU	Bristol
L92NSG	Southern National	L182UNS	Glasgow	L225VHU	Bristol	L401PWR	Yorkshire
L101PWR	Eastern Counties	L183UNS	Glasgow	L226AAB	Bristol	L401VCV	Western National
L101WYS	Glasgow	L184UNS	Glasgow	L227AAB	Bristol	L402PWR	Yorkshire
L102PWR	Eastern Counties	L185UNS	Glasgow	L228AAB	Bristol	L402VCV	Western National
L102WYS	Glasgow	L186UNS	Glasgow	L229AAB	Bristol	L403PWR	Yorkshire
L103PWR	Eastern Counties	L187UNS	Glasgow	L230AAB	Bristol	L403VCV	Western National
L103WYS	Glasgow	L188UNS	Glasgow	L231AAB	Midland Red	L404PWR	Yorkshire
L104PWR	Eastern Counties	L189UNS	Glasgow	L231NRE	PMT	L404VCV	Western National
L104WYS	Glasgow	L190UNS	Glasgow	L232AAB	Midland Red	L405PWR	Yorkshire
L105PWR	Eastern Counties	L191UNS	Glasgow	L233AAB	Midland Red	L405VCV	Western National
L105XSU	Glasgow	L192UNS	Glasgow	L234AAB	Midland Red	L406VCV	Western National
L106PWR	Eastern Counties	L193UNS	Glasgow	L235AAB	Midland Red	L455LVT	PMT
L106XSU	Glasgow	L194UNS	Glasgow	L236AAB	Midland Red	L493HRE	PMT
L109OSX	Midland/Lowland	L195UNS	Glasgow	L237AAB	Midland Red	L494HRE	PMT
L110OSX	Midland/Lowland	L196UNS	Glasgow	L245PAH	Eastern Counties	L495HRE	PMT
L121PWR	Yorkshire	L197UNS	Glasgow	L246PAH	Eastern Counties	L496HRE	PMT
L121TFB	Bristol	L198UNS	Glasgow	L247PAH	Eastern Counties	L497HRE	PMT
L122PWR	Yorkshire	L199UNS	Glasgow	L249PAH	Eastern Counties	L498HRE	PMT
L122TFB	Bristol	L201AAB	Midland Red	L251PAH	Eastern Counties	L501HCY	Cymru
L123PWR	Yorkshire	L201KFS	Midland/Lowland	L252PAH	Eastern Counties	L501KSA	Aberdeen
L123TFB	Bristol	L201SHW	Bristol	L253PAH	Eastern Counties	L501VHU	Eastern Counties
L124PWR	Yorkshire	L201UNS	Glasgow	L254PAH	Eastern Counties	L502HCY	Cymru
L124TFB	Bristol	L202AAB	Midland Red	L255PAH	Eastern Counties	L502KSA	Aberdeen
L125PWR	Yorkshire	L202KFS	Midland/Lowland	L256PAH	Eastern Counties	L502VHU	Eastern Counties
L125TFB	Bristol	L202SHW	Bristol	L257PAH	Eastern Counties	L503HCY	Cymru
L126PWR	Yorkshire	L202UNS	Glasgow	L258PAH	Eastern Counties	L503KSA	Aberdeen
L126TFB	Bristol	L203AAB	Midland Red	L259PAH	Eastern Counties	L503VHU	Bristol
L127PWR	Yorkshire	L203KSX	Midland/Lowland	L269GBU	PMT	L504HCY	Cymru
L127TFB	Bristol	L203SHW	Bristol	L281RML	Capital	L504KSA	Aberdeen
L128PWR	Yorkshire	L204AAB	Midland Red	L301PWR	Essex Buses	L504VHU	Bristol
L128TFB	Bristol	L204KSX	Midland/Lowland	L301VSU	Glasgow	L505HCY	Cymru
L129OWF	Mainline	L204SHW	Bristol	L302PWR	Essex Buses	L505KSA	Aberdeen
L129PWR	Yorkshire	L205AAB	Midland Red	L302VSU	Glasgow	L505VHU	Bristol
L129TFB	Bristol	L205GMO	CentreWest	L303PWR	Essex Buses	L506GEP	Cymru
L130OWF	Mainline	L205KSX	Midland/Lowland	L303VSU	Glasgow	L506HCY	Cymru
L130PWR	Yorkshire	L205SHW	Bristol	L304PWR	Essex Buses	L506KSA	Aberdeen
L130TFB	Bristol	L206AAB	Midland Red	L304VSU	Glasgow	L506VHU	Bristol
L131TFB	Bristol	L206GMO	CentreWest	L305PWR	Essex Buses	L507HCY	Cymru
L132TFB	Bristol	L206KSX	Midland/Lowland	L305VSU	Glasgow	L507KSA	Aberdeen
L133TFB	Bristol	L206SHW	Bristol	L306PWR	Yorkshire	L507VHU	Bristol
L134TFB	Bristol	L207AAB	Midland Red	L306VSU	Glasgow	L508HCY	Cymru
L135TFB	Bristol	L207GMO	CentreWest	L307PWR	Essex Buses	L508KSA	Aberdeen
L136TFB	Bristol	L207KSX	Midland/Lowland	L307VSU	Glasgow	L508VHU	Bristol
L140MAK	Midland/Lowland	L207SHW	Bristol	L308PWR	Essex Buses	L509HCY	Cymru
L155UNS	Glasgow	L208AAB	Midland Red	L308VSU	Glasgow	L509KSA	Aberdeen
L156UNS	Glasgow	L208GMO	CentreWest	L309PWR	Essex Buses	L510HCY	Cymru
L157UNS	Glasgow	L208KSX	Midland/Lowland	L309RTP	Hampshire	L510KSA	Aberdeen
L158UNS	Glasgow	L208SHW	Bristol	L309VSU	Glasgow	L511HCY	Cymru
L159UNS	Glasgow	L209AAB	Midland Red	L310PWR	Essex Buses	L511KSA	Aberdeen
L160UNS	Glasgow	L209KSX	Midland/Lowland	L310RTP	Hampshire	L511NYG	Yorkshire
L161UNS	Glasgow	L209SHW	Bristol	L310VSU	Glasgow	L512HCY	Cymru
L162UNS	Glasgow	L210AAB	Midland Red	L311BOD	Hampshire	L512KSA	Aberdeen
L163UNS	Glasgow	L210KSX	Midland/Lowland	L311PWR	Essex Buses	L513HCY	Cymru
L164UNS	Glasgow	L210VHU	Bristol	L311RTP	Hampshire	L513KSA	Aberdeen
L165UNS	Glasgow	L211AAB	Midland Red	L312BOD	Hampshire	L514HCY	Cymru
L166TRV	Hampshire	L211KSX	Midland/Lowland	L312PWR	Yorkshire	L514KSA	Aberdeen
L166UNS	Glasgow	L211VHU	Bristol	L312RTP	Hampshire	L515HCY	Cymru
L167TRV	Hampshire	L212AAB	Midland Red	L313BOD	Hampshire	L516HCY	Cymru
L167UNS	Glasgow	L212KSX	Midland/Lowland	L313PWR	Yorkshire	L517HCY	Cymru
L168TRV	Hampshire	L212VHU	Bristol	L313RTP	Hampshire	L518HCY	Cymru
L168UNS	Glasgow	L213AAB	Midland Red	L314BOD	Hampshire	L518KSX	Midland/Lowland

Reg	Operator	Reg	Operator	Reg	Operator	Reg	Operator
L519HCY	Cymru	L604FKG	Cymru	L653MEV	Essex Buses	L824HCY	Cymru
L519KSX	Midland/Lowland	L604PWR	Yorkshire	L653PWR	Yorkshire	L824SAE	Bristol
L520HCY	Cymru	L605FKG	Cymru	L653SEU	Bristol	L825HCY	Cymru
L520KSX	Midland/Lowland	L605PWR	Yorkshire	L654MEV	Essex Buses	L825SAE	Bristol
L521EHD	Midland/Lowland	L606FKG	Cymru	L654PWR	Yorkshire	L826SAE	Bristol
L521HCY	Cymru	L607FKG	Cymru	L654SEU	Bristol	L827WHY	Bristol
L521KSX	Midland/Lowland	L608FKG	Cymru	L655MEV	Essex Buses	L827YGA	Glasgow
L522HCY	Cymru	L623XFP	Leicester	L655PWR	Yorkshire	L828WHY	Bristol
L522KSX	Midland/Lowland	L624XFP	Leicester	L656MEV	Essex Buses	L828YGA	Glasgow
L523HCY	Cymru	L625XFP	Leicester	L670SMC	Capital	L829WHY	Bristol
L523KSX	Midland/Lowland	L626XFP	Leicester	L671RMD	Capital	L829YGA	Glasgow
L524HCY	Cymru	L628VCV	Western National	L672RMD	Capital	L830WHY	Bristol
L524KSX	Midland/Lowland	L629VCV	Western National	L673RMD	Capital	L830YGA	Glasgow
L525JEP	Cymru	L630VCV	Western National	L674RMD	Capital	L844JCY	Cymru
L525KSX	Midland/Lowland	L631SEU	Bristol	L675RMD	Capital	L862HFA	PMT
L526JEP	Cymru	L631VCV	Western National	L676RMD	Capital	L877TFB	Bristol
L526KSX	Midland/Lowland	L632SEU	Bristol	L677RMD	Capital	L878VHT	Bristol
L527JEP	Cymru	L632VCV	Western National	L678RMD	Capital	L879VHT	Bristol
L527KSX	Midland/Lowland	L633SEU	Bristol	L679RMD	Capital	L880VHT	Bristol
L528JEP	Cymru	L633VCV	Western National	L680RMD	Capital	L881VHT	Bristol
L529JEP	Cymru	L634SEU	Bristol	L720JKS	Midland/Lowland	L883VHT	Bristol
L530JEP	Cymru	L634VCV	Western National	L721JKS	Midland/Lowland	L884VHT	Bristol
L531JEP	Cymru	L635SEU	Bristol	L722JKS	Midland/Lowland	L885VHT	Bristol
L532JEP	Cymru	L635VCV	Western National	L723JKS	Midland/Lowland	L886VHT	Bristol
L533JEP	Cymru	L636PWR	Yorkshire	L724JKS	Midland/Lowland	L887VHT	Bristol
L534JEP	Cymru	L636SEU	Bristol	L725JKS	Midland/Lowland	L888AMY	Capital
L535JEP	Cymru	L636VCV	Western National	L726JKS	Midland/Lowland	L888JTC	Capital
L536JEP	Cymru	L637PWR	Yorkshire	L727JKS	Midland/Lowland	L888TTT	Capital
L537JEP	Cymru	L637SEU	Bristol	L801MEV	Essex Buses	L888YTT	Capital
L538JEP	Cymru	L637VCV	Western National	L801SAE	Bristol	L889VHT	Bristol
L538XUT	Cymru	L638PWR	Yorkshire	L802MEV	Essex Buses	L890VHT	Bristol
L539JEP	Cymru	L638SEU	Bristol	L802SAE	Bristol	L891VHT	Bristol
L540JEP	Cymru	L638VCV	Western National	L803OPU	Essex Buses	L892VHT	Bristol
L541JEP	Cymru	L639PWR	Yorkshire	L803SAE	Bristol	L893VHT	Bristol
L541XUT	Yorkshire	L639SEU	Bristol	L804OPU	Essex Buses	L894VHT	Bristol
L542JEP	Cymru	L639VCV	Western National	L804SAE	Bristol	L895VHT	Bristol
L542XUT	Yorkshire	L640PWR	Yorkshire	L805OPU	Essex Buses	L896VHT	Bristol
L543JEP	Cymru	L640SEU	Bristol	L805SAE	Bristol	L897VHT	Bristol
L544JEP	Cymru	L640VCV	Western National	L806OPU	Essex Buses	L898VHT	Bristol
L545JEP	Cymru	L641PWR	Yorkshire	L806SAE	Bristol	L899VHT	Bristol
L546JEP	Cymru	L641SEU	Bristol	L807OPU	Eastern Counties	L901VHT	Bristol
L546XUT	Yorkshire	L641VCV	Western National	L807SAE	Bristol	L902VHT	Bristol
L547JEP	Cymru	L642PWR	Yorkshire	L808OPU	Essex Buses	L903VHT	Bristol
L548CDV	Western National	L642SEU	Bristol	L808SAE	Bristol	L904VHT	Bristol
L548JEP	Cymru	L642VCV	Western National	L809OPU	Essex Buses	L905VHT	Bristol
L549JEP	Cymru	L643PWR	Yorkshire	L809SAE	Bristol	L906VHT	Bristol
L550JEP	Cymru	L643SEU	Bristol	L810OPU	Essex Buses	L907VHT	Bristol
L551HMS	Midland/Lowland	L643VCV	Western National	L810SAE	Bristol	L908VHT	Bristol
L551USU	Glasgow	L644PWR	Yorkshire	L811OPU	Essex Buses	L909VHT	Bristol
L552GMS	Midland/Lowland	L644SEU	Bristol	L811SAE	Bristol	L910VHT	Bristol
L552HMS	Midland/Lowland	L644VCV	Western National	L812OPU	Essex Buses	L911VHT	Bristol
L552USU	Glasgow	L645PWR	Yorkshire	L812SAE	Bristol	L931HFA	PMT
L553GMS	Midland/Lowland	L645SEU	Bristol	L813OPU	Essex Buses	L932HFA	PMT
L553HMS	Midland/Lowland	L645VCV	Western National	L813SAE	Bristol	L933HFA	PMT
L553LVT	PMT	L646PWR	Yorkshire	L814OPU	Essex Buses	L934HFA	PMT
L553USU	Glasgow	L646SEU	Bristol	L814SAE	Bristol	L935HFA	PMT
L554GMS	Midland/Lowland	L646VCV	Western National	L815CFJ	Western National	L936HFA	PMT
L554HMS	Midland/Lowland	L647MEV	Essex Buses	L815OPU	Essex Buses	L937LRF	PMT
L554LVT	PMT	L647PWR	Yorkshire	L815SAE	Bristol	L938LRF	PMT
L554USU	Glasgow	L647SEU	Bristol	L816CFJ	Western National	L939LRF	PMT
L555GMS	Midland/Lowland	L647VCV	Western National	L816HCY	Cymru	L940LRF	PMT
L555HMS	Midland/Lowland	L648MEV	Essex Buses	L816OPU	Essex Buses	L941LRF	PMT
L556GMS	Midland/Lowland	L648PWR	Yorkshire	L816SAE	Bristol	L942LRF	PMT
L556HMS	Midland/Lowland	L648SEU	Bristol	L817CFJ	Western National	L970NET	Mainline
L556LVT	PMT	L648VCV	Western National	L817HCY	Cymru	L971NET	Mainline
L557GMS	Midland/Lowland	L649CJT	Western National	L817OPU	Essex Buses	LAT662	Midland/Lowland
L557JLS	Midland/Lowland	L649MEV	Essex Buses	L817SAE	Bristol	LBP500	Western National
L557LVT	PMT	L649PWR	Yorkshire	L818HCY	Cymru	LDZ9113	CentreWest
L558JLS	Midland/Lowland	L649SEU	Bristol	L818OPU	Essex Buses	LDZ9114	CentreWest
L558LVT	PMT	L649VCV	Western National	L818SAE	Bristol	LDZ9115	CentreWest
L559JLS	Midland/Lowland	L650CJT	Southern National	L819HCY	Cymru	LDZ9116	CentreWest
L561JLS	Midland/Lowland	L650MEV	Essex Buses	L819OPU	Essex Buses	LDZ9117	CentreWest
L562JLS	Midland/Lowland	L650PWR	Yorkshire	L819SAE	Bristol	LDZ9118	CentreWest
L563JLS	Midland/Lowland	L650SEU	Bristol	L820HCY	Cymru	LDZ9119	CentreWest
L564JLS	Midland/Lowland	L650VCV	Western National	L820OPU	Essex Buses	LDZ9120	CentreWest
L565JLS	Midland/Lowland	L651CJT	Southern National	L820SAE	Bristol	LDZ9121	CentreWest
L566JLS	Midland/Lowland	L651MEV	Essex Buses	L821HCY	Cymru	LDZ9122	CentreWest
L601FKG	Cymru	L651PWR	Yorkshire	L821OPU	Essex Buses	LDZ9123	CentreWest
L601MWC	Eastern Counties	L651SEU	Bristol	L821SAE	Bristol	LDZ9124	CentreWest
L601PWR	Yorkshire	L651VCV	Western National	L822HCY	Cymru	LDZ9125	CentreWest
L602FKG	Cymru	L652CJT	Southern National	L822OPU	Essex Buses	LDZ9126	CentreWest
L602PWR	Yorkshire	L652MEV	Essex Buses	L822SAE	Bristol	LEU256P	Bristol
L603FKG	Cymru	L652PWR	Yorkshire	L823HCY	Cymru	LEU263P	Bristol
L603PWR	Yorkshire	L652SEU	Bristol	L823SAE	Bristol	LEU269P	Bristol

Reg	Fleet	Reg	Fleet	Reg	Fleet	Reg	Fleet
LFJ841W	Western National	M106PKS	Midland/Lowland	M217VWU	Yorkshire	M249VWW	Yorkshire
LFJ842W	Western National	M106RRJ	Manchester	M217VWW	Yorkshire	M250MRW	Midland Red
LFJ843W	Western National	M107NEP	Cymru	M218VWU	Manchester	M250VWU	Yorkshire
LFJ844W	Western National	M107RRJ	Eastern Counties	M218VWW	Yorkshire	M250VWW	Yorkshire
LFJ845W	Western National	M108NEP	Cymru	M219VWU	Yorkshire	M251MRW	Midland Red
LFJ846W	Western National	M109PWN	Cymru	M219VWW	Yorkshire	M251NVM	Manchester
LFJ847W	Western National	M110PWN	Cymru	M220PMS	Southern National	M251VWU	Yorkshire
LFJ860W	Western National	M111PWN	Cymru	M220VWU	Yorkshire	M251VWW	Yorkshire
LFJ867W	Western National	M137FAE	Bristol	M220VWW	Yorkshire	M252MRW	Midland Red
LFJ871W	Western National	M138FAE	Bristol	M221EAF	CentreWest	M252NVM	Manchester
LFJ872W	Western National	M140FAE	Bristol	M221VWU	Yorkshire	M252VWU	Yorkshire
LFJ873W	Western National	M141FAE	Bristol	M221VWW	Yorkshire	M252VWW	Yorkshire
LIL5069	Cymru	M142FAE	Bristol	M223VWU	Manchester	M253MRW	Midland Red
LIL5070	Cymru	M151PKS	Midland/Lowland	M223VWW	Yorkshire	M253NVM	Manchester
LIL5071	Cymru	M152PKS	Midland/Lowland	M224VWU	Manchester	M253VWU	Yorkshire
LIL5851	Southern National	M158LNC	Manchester	M224VWW	Yorkshire	M253VWW	Yorkshire
LJN648P	Cymru	M159LNC	Manchester	M225VWU	Manchester	M254MRW	Midland Red
LMS374W	Midland/Lowland	M160LNC	Manchester	M225VWW	Yorkshire	M254NVM	Manchester
LMS376W	Midland/Lowland	M161LNC	Manchester	M226VWU	Manchester	M254VWU	Glasgow
LMS386W	Midland/Lowland	M166VJN	Essex Buses	M226VWU	Western National	M254VWW	Yorkshire
LOA832X	Western National	M179XTR	Hampshire	M226VWW	Yorkshire	M255MRW	Midland Red
LOI6690	Cymru	M180XTR	Hampshire	M227VWU	Yorkshire	M255NVM	Manchester
LRB121W	Southern National	M181XTR	Hampshire	M227VWW	Yorkshire	M255VWU	Glasgow
LRB202W	Southern National	M182XTR	Hampshire	M228VWU	Yorkshire	M255VWW	Yorkshire
LRS292W	Aberdeen	M183XTR	Hampshire	M228VWW	Yorkshire	M256MRW	Midland Red
LRS295W	Aberdeen	M184XTR	Hampshire	M229VWU	Yorkshire	M256NVM	Manchester
LRS296W	Aberdeen	M185XTR	Hampshire	M229VWW	Yorkshire	M256VWU	Glasgow
LRS299W	Aberdeen	M186XTR	Hampshire	M230VWU	Yorkshire	M256VWW	Yorkshire
LRS300W	Aberdeen	M187XTR	Hampshire	M230VWW	Yorkshire	M257NVM	Manchester
LSC936T	Midland/Lowland	M188XTR	Hampshire	M231VWU	Yorkshire	M257VWU	Yorkshire
LSK475	Aberdeen	M189XTR	Hampshire	M231VWW	Yorkshire	M257VWW	Yorkshire
LSK476	Aberdeen	M190XTR	Hampshire	M232VWU	Yorkshire	M258NVM	Manchester
LSK529	Aberdeen	M191XTR	Hampshire	M232VWW	Yorkshire	M258VWU	Yorkshire
LSK530	Aberdeen	M192XTR	Hampshire	M233VWU	Yorkshire	M258VWW	Yorkshire
LSK546	Aberdeen	M193XTR	Hampshire	M233VWW	Yorkshire	M259NVM	Manchester
LSK570	Aberdeen	M194XTR	Hampshire	M234VWU	Manchester	M259VWU	Yorkshire
LSK571	Aberdeen	M195XTR	Hampshire	M234VWW	Yorkshire	M259VWW	Yorkshire
LSK572	Aberdeen	M196XTR	Hampshire	M235VWU	Yorkshire	M260KWK	Manchester
LSK573	Aberdeen	M197XTR	Hampshire	M235VWW	Yorkshire	M260NVM	Manchester
LSU379V	Cymru	M198XTR	Hampshire	M236VWU	Manchester	M260VWU	Glasgow
LSU381V	Cymru	M199XTR	Hampshire	M236VWW	Yorkshire	M260VWW	Yorkshire
LSU717	Leicester	M201LNC	Manchester	M237VWU	Manchester	M261SVU	Manchester
LSU788	Bristol	M201VWU	Glasgow	M237VWW	Yorkshire	M261VWU	Glasgow
LSU917	Aberdeen	M201VWW	Eastern Counties	M238MRW	Midland Red	M261VWW	Yorkshire
LTP634R	Hampshire	M201XTR	Hampshire	M238VWU	Manchester	M262SVU	Manchester
LUA317V	Yorkshire	M202LNC	Manchester	M238VWW	Yorkshire	M262VWU	Yorkshire
LUA321V	Yorkshire	M202VWU	Yorkshire	M239MRW	Midland Red	M262VWW	Yorkshire
LUA329V	Yorkshire	M202VWW	Eastern Counties	M239VWU	Manchester	M263SVU	Manchester
LUA716V	Essex Buses	M202XTR	Hampshire	M239VWW	Yorkshire	M263VWU	Yorkshire
LUA719V	Eastern Counties	M203LNC	Manchester	M239VYA	Southern National	M263VWW	Yorkshire
LUG115P	Yorkshire	M203VWU	Yorkshire	M240MRW	Midland Red	M264SVU	Manchester
LWG844P	Southern National	M203VWW	Eastern Counties	M240VWU	Yorkshire	M264VWW	Yorkshire
LWG846P	Southern National	M203XTR	Hampshire	M240VWW	Yorkshire	M265SVU	Manchester
LWG847P	Southern National	M204BPO	Hampshire	M240VYA	Southern National	M265VWW	Yorkshire
LWS32Y	Bristol	M204VWU	Yorkshire	M241MRW	Midland Red	M266SVU	Manchester
LWS42Y	Bristol	M204VWW	Yorkshire	M241VWU	Yorkshire	M266VWW	Yorkshire
LWS43Y	Bristol	M205BPO	Hampshire	M241VWW	Yorkshire	M267SVU	Manchester
LWS44Y	Bristol	M205VWU	Yorkshire	M241VYA	Southern National	M267VWW	Yorkshire
LWS45Y	Bristol	M205VWW	Yorkshire	M242AEX	Eastern Counties	M268SVU	Manchester
LWU469V	Essex Buses	M206BPO	Hampshire	M242MRW	Midland Red	M268VWW	Yorkshire
LWU471V	Hampshire	M206LNC	Manchester	M242VWW	Yorkshire	M269SVU	Manchester
M1GRT	Aberdeen	M206VWU	Yorkshire	M242VYA	Southern National	M270SVU	Manchester
M10ULF	Glasgow	M206VWW	Yorkshire	M243MRW	Midland Red	M278UYD	Southern National
M14ABC	Southern National	M207BPO	Hampshire	M243VWU	Yorkshire	M279UYD	Southern National
M19ABC	Southern National	M207VWU	Manchester	M243VWW	Yorkshire	M281UYD	Southern National
M25YRE	PMT	M207VWW	Yorkshire	M244MRW	Midland Red	M282UYD	Southern National
M26YRE	PMT	M208VWU	Glasgow	M244VWU	Manchester	M284SMS	Midland/Lowland
M27YRE	PMT	M208VWW	Yorkshire	M244VWW	Yorkshire	M290FAE	Bristol
M28YRE	PMT	M209VWU	Manchester	M245MRW	Midland Red	M291FAE	Bristol
M41FTC	Bristol	M209VWW	Yorkshire	M245VWU	Manchester	M292FAE	Bristol
M45BEG	Bristol	M210VWU	Yorkshire	M245VWW	Yorkshire	M293FAE	Bristol
M46BEG	Bristol	M210VWW	Yorkshire	M246MRW	Midland Red	M294FAE	Yorkshire
M48BEG	Bristol	M211VWU	Manchester	M246VWU	Western National	M295FAE	Yorkshire
M68XVF	Eastern Counties	M211VWW	Yorkshire	M246VWW	Yorkshire	M296FAE	Yorkshire
M69XVF	Eastern Counties	M212VWU	Manchester	M247MRW	Midland Red	M301BRL	Western National
M92BOU	Bristol	M212VWW	Yorkshire	M247VWU	Manchester	M302BRL	Western National
M101ECV	Western National	M213VWU	Manchester	M247VWW	Yorkshire	M303BRL	Western National
M101RRJ	Manchester	M213VWW	Yorkshire	M248MRW	Midland Red	M305TSF	Southern National
M102ECV	Western National	M214VWU	Manchester	M248NNF	Bristol	M314YOT	Hampshire
M102RRJ	Manchester	M214VWW	Yorkshire	M248VWU	Manchester	M315YOT	Hampshire
M103ECV	Western National	M215VWU	Manchester	M248VWW	Yorkshire	M316YOT	Hampshire
M103RRJ	Manchester	M215VWW	Yorkshire	M249MRW	Midland Red	M317YOT	Hampshire
M104RRJ	Manchester	M216VWU	Yorkshire	M249NNF	Bristol	M318YOT	Hampshire
M105RRJ	Manchester	M216VWW	Yorkshire	M249VWU	Manchester	M319YOT	Hampshire

Reg	Operator	Reg	Operator	Reg	Operator	Reg	Operator
M320YOT	Hampshire	M416VWW	Yorkshire	M508VYA	Southern National	M606RCP	Bristol
M321YOT	Hampshire	M417CCV	Western National	M509DHU	Bristol	M608SBA	Manchester
M322YOT	Hampshire	M417VHE	Mainline	M509GRY	Leicester	M609SBA	Manchester
M323YOT	Hampshire	M417VWW	Yorkshire	M509PNA	Manchester	M610SBA	Manchester
M360XEX	Eastern Counties	M418CCV	Western National	M509VYA	Southern National	M611SBA	Manchester
M361XEX	Eastern Counties	M418VHE	Mainline	M510DHU	Bristol	M612SBA	Manchester
M362XEX	Eastern Counties	M418VWW	Yorkshire	M510GRY	Leicester	M613SBA	Manchester
M363XEX	Eastern Counties	M419CCV	Western National	M510PNA	Manchester	M614SBA	Manchester
M364XEX	Eastern Counties	M419VHE	Mainline	M511DHU	Bristol	M615SBA	Yorkshire
M365XEX	Eastern Counties	M419VWW	Yorkshire	M511PNA	Manchester	M616SBA	Yorkshire
M366XEX	Eastern Counties	M420CCV	Western National	M512DHU	Bristol	M617SBA	Manchester
M367XEX	Eastern Counties	M420VHE	Mainline	M512PNA	Manchester	M618SBA	Manchester
M368XEX	Eastern Counties	M420VWW	Yorkshire	M513DHU	Bristol	M642HDV	Hampshire
M369XEX	Eastern Counties	M421CCV	Western National	M513PNA	Manchester	M643HDV	Hampshire
M370XEX	Eastern Counties	M421VHE	Mainline	M514DHU	Bristol	M644HDV	Hampshire
M371XEX	Eastern Counties	M421VWW	Yorkshire	M514PNA	Manchester	M645HDV	Hampshire
M372XEX	Eastern Counties	M422CCV	Western National	M515DHU	Bristol	M646HDV	Hampshire
M373XEX	Eastern Counties	M422VHE	Mainline	M515PNA	Manchester	M647HDV	Hampshire
M374XEX	Eastern Counties	M422VWW	Yorkshire	M516DHU	Bristol	M657VJN	Essex Buses
M375YEX	Eastern Counties	M423CCV	Western National	M516PNA	Manchester	M658VJN	Essex Buses
M376YEX	Eastern Counties	M423VHE	Mainline	M516RSS	Aberdeen	M659VJN	Essex Buses
M377SRE	PMT	M423VWW	Yorkshire	M517DHU	Bristol	M660SRE	PMT
M377YEX	Eastern Counties	M424CCV	Western National	M517PNA	Manchester	M660VJN	Essex Buses
M378SRE	PMT	M424VHE	Mainline	M517RSS	Aberdeen	M661VJN	Essex Buses
M378YEX	Eastern Counties	M424VWW	Yorkshire	M518DHU	Bristol	M662VJN	Essex Buses
M379SRE	PMT	M425CCV	Western National	M518PNA	Manchester	M663VJN	Essex Buses
M379YEX	Eastern Counties	M425VHE	Mainline	M518RSS	Aberdeen	M664VJN	Essex Buses
M380SRE	PMT	M425VWW	Yorkshire	M519DHU	Bristol	M665VJN	Essex Buses
M380YEX	Eastern Counties	M426CCV	Western National	M519PNA	Manchester	M667VJN	Essex Buses
M381KVR	Southern National	M426VHE	Mainline	M519RSS	Aberdeen	M668VJN	Essex Buses
M381SRE	PMT	M426VWW	Yorkshire	M520FFB	Bristol	M669VJN	Essex Buses
M382KVR	Southern National	M427VHE	Mainline	M520PNA	Manchester	M670VJN	Essex Buses
M382SRE	PMT	M427VWW	Yorkshire	M520RSS	Aberdeen	M671VJN	Essex Buses
M383SRE	PMT	M428RRN	Glasgow	M521FFB	Bristol	M672VJN	Essex Buses
M384KVR	Eastern Counties	M428VHE	Mainline	M521RSS	Aberdeen	M673VJN	Essex Buses
M386KVR	Southern National	M428VWW	Yorkshire	M522FFB	Bristol	M674RAJ	Southern National
M392KVR	Southern National	M429VHE	Mainline	M522RSS	Aberdeen	M674VJN	Essex Buses
M393KVR	Southern National	M429VWW	Yorkshire	M523FFB	Bristol	M675RAJ	Southern National
M394MRW	Glasgow	M430VHE	Mainline	M523RSS	Aberdeen	M675VJN	Essex Buses
M399OMS	Midland/Lowland	M430VWW	Yorkshire	M524FFB	Bristol	M676RAJ	Southern National
M401UUB	Yorkshire	M431VHE	Mainline	M524RSS	Aberdeen	M676VJN	Western National
M401VWW	Yorkshire	M431VWW	Yorkshire	M525FFB	Bristol	M677RAJ	Western National
M402UUB	Yorkshire	M432VHE	Mainline	M526FFB	Bristol	M678RAJ	Western National
M402VWW	Yorkshire	M432VWW	Yorkshire	M527FFB	Bristol	M716VET	Mainline
M403UUB	Yorkshire	M433VHE	Mainline	M528FFB	Bristol	M717VET	Mainline
M403VWW	Yorkshire	M433VWW	Yorkshire	M529FFB	Bristol	M718VET	Mainline
M404UUB	Yorkshire	M434VHE	Mainline	M530FFB	Bristol	M719VET	Mainline
M404VWW	Yorkshire	M434VWW	Yorkshire	M531FFB	Bristol	M720VET	Mainline
M405UUB	Yorkshire	M435VHE	Mainline	M532FFB	Bristol	M721VET	Mainline
M405VWW	Yorkshire	M435VWW	Yorkshire	M533FFB	Bristol	M722VET	Mainline
M406VWW	Yorkshire	M436VHE	Mainline	M534FFB	Bristol	M723VET	Mainline
M407CCV	Western National	M436VWW	Yorkshire	M535FFB	Bristol	M724VET	Mainline
M407VWW	Yorkshire	M437VHE	Mainline	M536FFB	Bristol	M725VET	Mainline
M408CCV	Western National	M437VWW	Yorkshire	M537FFB	Bristol	M726VET	Mainline
M408VWW	Yorkshire	M438VHE	Mainline	M538FFB	Bristol	M727VET	Mainline
M409CCV	Western National	M438VWW	Yorkshire	M559SRE	PMT	M728VET	Mainline
M409VWW	Yorkshire	M439FHW	Bristol	M561SRE	PMT	M729VET	Mainline
M410CCV	Western National	M439VHE	Mainline	M562SRE	PMT	M730VET	Mainline
M410RND	Manchester	M439VWW	Yorkshire	M563SRE	PMT	M731VET	Mainline
M410VWW	Yorkshire	M440FHW	Bristol	M564SRE	PMT	M732VET	Mainline
M411CCV	Western National	M440VHE	Mainline	M565SRE	PMT	M733VET	Mainline
M411RND	Bristol	M447VWW	Yorkshire	M566SRE	PMT	M734VET	Mainline
M411VHE	Mainline	M448VWW	Yorkshire	M567RMS	Midland/Lowland	M735VET	Mainline
M411VWW	Yorkshire	M449VWW	Yorkshire	M567SRE	PMT	M736VET	Mainline
M412CCV	Western National	M450VWW	Yorkshire	M568RMS	Midland/Lowland	M737VET	Mainline
M412RND	Manchester	M501CCV	Western National	M568SRE	PMT	M738VET	Mainline
M412VHE	Mainline	M501GRY	Leicester	M569RMS	Midland/Lowland	M739VET	Mainline
M412VWW	Yorkshire	M501PNA	Manchester	M569SRE	PMT	M740VET	Mainline
M413CCV	Western National	M502CCV	Western National	M570RMS	Midland/Lowland	M763CWS	Bristol
M413DEU	Bristol	M502GRY	Leicester	M570SRE	PMT	M764CWS	Bristol
M413RND	Bristol	M502PNA	Manchester	M571RMS	Midland/Lowland	M765CWS	Bristol
M413VHE	Mainline	M503CCV	Western National	M571SRE	PMT	M765FTT	Western National
M413VWW	Yorkshire	M503GRY	Leicester	M572SRE	PMT	M765PRS	Glasgow
M414CCV	Western National	M503PNA	Manchester	M573SRE	PMT	M766FTT	Southern National
M414RND	Bristol	M504GRY	Leicester	M584ANG	Eastern Counties	M766PRS	Glasgow
M414VHE	Mainline	M504PNA	Manchester	M585ANG	Eastern Counties	M767FTT	Western National
M414VWW	Yorkshire	M505GRY	Leicester	M586ANG	Eastern Counties	M767PRS	Glasgow
M415CCV	Western National	M505PNA	Manchester	M587ANG	Eastern Counties	M768FTT	Western National
M415RND	Manchester	M506GRY	Leicester	M588ANG	Eastern Counties	M768PRS	Glasgow
M415VHE	Mainline	M506PNA	Manchester	M589ANG	Eastern Counties	M769FTT	Western National
M415VWW	Yorkshire	M507GRY	Leicester	M590ANG	Eastern Counties	M769PRS	Glasgow
M416CCV	Western National	M507PNA	Manchester	M591ANG	Eastern Counties	M770PRS	Glasgow
M416RND	Manchester	M508PNA	Manchester	M592ANG	Eastern Counties		
M416VHE	Mainline			M593ANG	Eastern Counties		

The 1999 FirstGroup Bus Handbook

M771PRS	Glasgow	M874ATC	Bristol	MHS33P	Midland Red	N116DWE	Mainline
M772PRS	Glasgow	M877PRS	Glasgow	MJT880P	Hampshire	N117DWE	Mainline
M773PRS	Glasgow	M882BEU	Bristol	MKH487A	Cymru	N118DWE	Mainline
M774PRS	Glasgow	M883XVG	Eastern Counties	MLL963	CentreWest	N119DWE	Mainline
M775PRS	Glasgow	M884XVG	Eastern Counties	MNC505W	Yorkshire	N120DWE	Mainline
M776PRS	Glasgow	M901LTT	Western National	MNC515W	Yorkshire	N120OGG	Glasgow
M778PRS	Glasgow	M902LTT	Western National	MNC516W	Yorkshire	N121DWE	Mainline
M779PRS	Glasgow	M918MRW	Mainline	MNW33P	Yorkshire	N121OGG	Glasgow
M780PRS	Glasgow	M918TEV	Essex Buses	MNW130V	Yorkshire	N122DWE	Mainline
M781PRS	Glasgow	M919TEV	Essex Buses	MOD571P	Hampshire	N122OGG	Glasgow
M791TCF	CentreWest	M920TEV	Essex Buses	MOD814P	Southern National	N123OGG	Glasgow
M792TCF	CentreWest	M921TEV	Essex Buses	MOD820P	Southern National	N124OGG	Glasgow
M793TCF	CentreWest	M922TEV	Essex Buses	MOD821P	Southern National	N125OGG	Glasgow
M794TCF	CentreWest	M923TEV	Eastern Counties	MOD823P	Southern National	N126OGG	Glasgow
M796MPM	Capital	M924TEV	Essex Buses	MOD828P	Southern National	N127OGG	Glasgow
M802UYA	Southern National	M925TEV	Essex Buses	MOD829P	Southern National	N128OGG	Glasgow
M803UYA	Southern National	M926TEV	Essex Buses	MOD852P	Southern National	N129OGG	Glasgow
M804UYA	Southern National	M927TEV	Essex Buses	MOW636R	Hampshire	N130OGG	Glasgow
M805UYA	Southern National	M928TEV	Essex Buses	MPG293W	Yorkshire	N131OGG	Glasgow
M809FTT	Western National	M929TEV	Essex Buses	MRJ32W	Manchester	N132OGG	Glasgow
M810PGM	CentreWest	M930TEV	Essex Buses	MRJ33W	Manchester	N133OGG	Glasgow
M811PGM	CentreWest	M931TEV	Essex Buses	MRJ34W	Manchester	N134OGG	Glasgow
M812PGM	CentreWest	M932TEV	Essex Buses	MRJ35W	Manchester	N135OGG	Glasgow
M813PGM	CentreWest	M933TEV	Essex Buses	MRJ39W	Manchester	N136OGG	Glasgow
M814PGM	CentreWest	M934TEV	Essex Buses	MRJ50W	Manchester	N137OGG	Glasgow
M815PGM	CentreWest	M935TEV	Essex Buses	MRJ56W	Manchester	N138OGG	Glasgow
M816PGM	CentreWest	M936TEV	Essex Buses	MRJ58W	Manchester	N141VDU	Glasgow
M817PGM	CentreWest	M937TEV	Essex Buses	MRJ60W	Manchester	N144BWG	Mainline
M818PGM	CentreWest	M938TEV	Essex Buses	MRJ61W	Manchester	N159GOT	Hampshire
M819PGM	CentreWest	M939EYS	Glasgow	MRJ62W	Manchester	N160GOT	Hampshire
M831ATC	Bristol	M939TEV	Essex Buses	MRJ64W	Manchester	N161GOT	Hampshire
M832ATC	Bristol	M940EYS	Glasgow	MRJ68W	Manchester	N162GOT	Hampshire
M833ATC	Bristol	M940TEV	Essex Buses	MRJ70W	Manchester	N163GOT	Hampshire
M834ATC	Bristol	M941EYS	Glasgow	MRJ401W	Manchester	N164GOT	Hampshire
M834DUS	Glasgow	M941TEV	Essex Buses	MRJ407W	Manchester	N165GOT	Hampshire
M835ATC	Bristol	M942EYS	Glasgow	MTU120Y	PMT	N166GOT	Hampshire
M835DUS	Glasgow	M942TEV	Essex Buses	MTU122Y	PMT	N167GOT	Hampshire
M836ATC	Bristol	M943SRE	PMT	MTU123Y	PMT	N168GOT	Hampshire
M836DUS	Glasgow	M943TEV	Essex Buses	MTU124Y	PMT	N173WNF	Manchester
M837ATC	Bristol	M944SRE	PMT	MUH747R	Bristol	N174WNF	Manchester
M837DUS	Glasgow	M945SRE	PMT	MUT206W	Leicester	N175WNF	Manchester
M838ATC	Bristol	M946SRE	PMT	MUT257W	Leicester	N176WNF	Manchester
M838DUS	Glasgow	M947OVC	Manchester	MWB849W	Mainline	N177WNF	Manchester
M839ATC	Bristol	M947SRE	PMT	MWB851W	Mainline	N190OGG	Glasgow
M839DUS	Glasgow	M948SRE	PMT	MWB852W	Mainline	N199OGG	Glasgow
M840ATC	Bristol	M949SRE	PMT	MWB853W	Mainline	N201VSA	Aberdeen
M840DUS	Glasgow	M951SRE	PMT	MWB854W	Mainline	N202VSA	Aberdeen
M841ATC	Bristol	M952SRE	PMT	MWB856W	Mainline	N203VSA	Aberdeen
M841DUS	Glasgow	M953XVT	PMT	N22BLU	Western National	N204VSA	Aberdeen
M842ATC	Bristol	M954XVT	PMT	N28FWU	Bristol	N205VSA	Aberdeen
M843ATC	Bristol	M955XVT	PMT	N29FWU	Bristol	N206VSA	Aberdeen
M844ATC	Bristol	M956XVT	PMT	N41RRP	Northampton	N207WBA	Manchester
M845ATC	Bristol	M957XVT	PMT	N42RRP	Northampton	N208WBA	Manchester
M846ATC	Bristol	M958XVT	PMT	N43RRP	Northampton	N209WBA	Manchester
M847ATC	Bristol	M959XVT	PMT	N49FWU	Midland/Lowland	N210WBA	Manchester
M848ATC	Bristol	M960XVT	PMT	N61CSC	Midland/Lowland	N211WBA	Manchester
M849ATC	Bristol	M961XVT	PMT	N62CSC	Midland/Lowland	N211WRD	CentreWest
M850ATC	Bristol	M962XVT	PMT	N63CSC	Midland/Lowland	N212WBA	Manchester
M851ATC	Bristol	M963XVT	PMT	N64CSC	Midland/Lowland	N212WRD	CentreWest
M852ATC	Bristol	M964XVT	PMT	N65CSC	Midland/Lowland	N213WRD	CentreWest
M853ATC	Bristol	M965XVT	PMT	N66CSC	Midland/Lowland	N214WRD	CentreWest
M854ATC	Bristol	M966XVT	PMT	N67CSC	Midland/Lowland	N215WRD	CentreWest
M855ATC	Bristol	M967GDU	Hampshire	N68CSC	Midland/Lowland	N216WRD	CentreWest
M856ATC	Bristol	M967XVT	PMT	N69CSC	Midland/Lowland	N217WRD	CentreWest
M857ATC	Bristol	M968USC	Bristol	N70CSC	Midland/Lowland	N226KAE	Bristol
M857XHY	Bristol	M968XVT	PMT	N71YNF	Manchester	N227KAE	Bristol
M858ATC	Bristol	M969XVT	PMT	N89OGG	Glasgow	N228KAE	Bristol
M859ATC	Bristol	M970XVT	PMT	N91OGG	Glasgow	N229KAE	Bristol
M860ATC	Bristol	M971XVT	PMT	N92OGG	Glasgow	N230KAE	Bristol
M861ATC	Bristol	M972XVT	PMT	N93OGG	Glasgow	N231KAE	Bristol
M862ATC	Bristol	M997CYS	Cymru	N94OGG	Glasgow	N232KAE	Bristol
M863ATC	Bristol	MBZ7140	Southern National	N95OGG	Glasgow	N232WFJ	Western National
M864ATC	Bristol	MDS855V	Hampshire	N96OGG	Glasgow	N233KAE	Bristol
M865ATC	Bristol	MDS856V	Hampshire	N97OGG	Glasgow	N233WFJ	Western National
M866ATC	Bristol	MDS857V	Hampshire	N98OGG	Glasgow	N234KAE	Bristol
M867ATC	Bristol	MDS862V	Midland/Lowland	N107VKS	Midland/Lowland	N235KAE	Bristol
M868ATC	Bristol	MDS863V	Hampshire	N112DWE	Mainline	N236KAE	Bristol
M869ATC	Bristol	MDS867V	Hampshire	N112EWJ	Cymru	N237KAE	Bristol
M870ATC	Bristol	MFA723V	PMT	N113DWE	Mainline	N238KAE	Bristol
M870DYS	Glasgow	MFR18P	Southern National	N113VWN	Cymru	N239KAE	Bristol
M871ATC	Bristol	MHJ723V	Yorkshire	N114DWE	Mainline	N240KAE	Bristol
M871DYS	Glasgow	MHJ726V	Yorkshire	N114VWN	Cymru	N241CMP	Capital
M872ATC	Bristol	MHS17P	Midland Red	N115DWE	Mainline	N241KAE	Bristol
M873ATC	Bristol	MHS18P	Yorkshire	N115VWN	Cymru	N242KAE	Bristol

N243LHT	Bristol	N305JBV	CentreWest	N441BKY	Mainline	N535WVR	Manchester
N244CMP	Capital	N305WNF	Manchester	N441ENW	Yorkshire	N536VSA	Aberdeen
N244LHT	Bristol	N305XAB	Midland Red	N442BKY	Mainline	N536WVR	Manchester
N245LHT	Bristol	N306JBV	CentreWest	N442ENW	Yorkshire	N537VSA	Aberdeen
N246LHT	Bristol	N306WNF	Manchester	N443BKY	Mainline	N537WVR	Manchester
N247CKY	Mainline	N306XAB	Midland Red	N443ENW	Yorkshire	N538VSA	Aberdeen
N247CMP	Capital	N307JBV	CentreWest	N445BKY	Mainline	N538WVR	Manchester
N247LHT	Bristol	N307XAB	Midland Red	N445ENW	Yorkshire	N539HAE	Bristol
N248LHT	Bristol	N308JBV	CentreWest	N446BKY	Mainline	N539VSA	Aberdeen
N249LHT	Bristol	N308XAB	Midland Red	N446ENW	Yorkshire	N539WVR	Manchester
N250LHT	Bristol	N309JBV	CentreWest	N447BKY	Mainline	N540HAE	Bristol
N264JUG	Yorkshire	N309XAB	Midland Red	N448BKY	Mainline	N540WVR	Manchester
N265JUG	Yorkshire	N310JBV	CentreWest	N449BKY	Mainline	N541HAE	Bristol
N266JUG	Yorkshire	N310XAB	Midland Red	N449JUG	Yorkshire	N541WVR	Manchester
N267JUG	Yorkshire	N311JBV	CentreWest	N450DWJ	Mainline	N542HAE	Bristol
N268JUG	Yorkshire	N311XAB	Midland Red	N450JUG	Yorkshire	N542WVR	Manchester
N269JUG	Yorkshire	N312JBV	CentreWest	N451DWJ	Mainline	N543HAE	Bristol
N269JUM	Yorkshire	N312XAB	Midland Red	N451JUG	Yorkshire	N543WVR	Manchester
N270JUG	Yorkshire	N313XAB	Midland Red	N452JUG	Yorkshire	N544ENW	Yorkshire
N270JUM	Yorkshire	N319NHY	Bristol	N453JUG	Yorkshire	N544HAE	Bristol
N271JUG	Yorkshire	N320NHY	Bristol	N454JUG	Yorkshire	N544WVR	Manchester
N271JUM	Yorkshire	N321NHY	Bristol	N455JUG	Yorkshire	N545HAE	Bristol
N272JUG	Yorkshire	N322NHY	Bristol	N456JUG	Yorkshire	N545WVR	Manchester
N272JUM	Yorkshire	N324ECR	Hampshire	N457JUG	Yorkshire	N546HAE	Bristol
N273JUG	Yorkshire	N325ECR	Hampshire	N458JUG	Yorkshire	N546WVR	Manchester
N273JUM	Yorkshire	N326ECR	Hampshire	N459JUG	Yorkshire	N547HAE	Bristol
N274JUG	Yorkshire	N326HUA	Western National	N460JUG	Yorkshire	N547WVR	Manchester
N274JUM	Yorkshire	N327ECR	Hampshire	N461JUG	Yorkshire	N548HAE	Bristol
N275JUG	Yorkshire	N328ECR	Hampshire	N462JUG	Yorkshire	N548WVR	Manchester
N275JUM	Yorkshire	N329ECR	Hampshire	N463JUG	Yorkshire	N549LHU	Bristol
N276JUG	Yorkshire	N341EUY	Midland Red	N464JUG	Yorkshire	N549WVR	Manchester
N276JUM	Yorkshire	N343CJA	Manchester	N465ETR	Hampshire	N550LHU	Bristol
N277CKY	Mainline	N344CJA	Manchester	N465JUG	Yorkshire	N550WVR	Manchester
N277JUG	Yorkshire	N345CJA	Eastern Counties	N466ETR	Hampshire	N551LHU	Bristol
N277JUM	Yorkshire	N346CJA	Eastern Counties	N466JUG	Yorkshire	N551UCY	Cymru
N278JUG	Yorkshire	N347CJA	Manchester	N467ETR	Hampshire	N551WVR	Manchester
N278JUM	Yorkshire	N348CJA	Manchester	N467JUG	Yorkshire	N552LHU	Bristol
N279JUG	Yorkshire	N34FWU	Bristol	N468JUG	Yorkshire	N552UCY	Cymru
N279JUM	Yorkshire	N372CJA	Manchester	N469JUG	Yorkshire	N552WVR	Manchester
N280JUG	Yorkshire	N373CJA	Manchester	N470JUG	Yorkshire	N553LHU	Bristol
N281JUG	Yorkshire	N374CJA	Manchester	N471JUG	Yorkshire	N553UCY	Cymru
N281JUM	Yorkshire	N375CJA	Manchester	N471KHU	Bristol	N553WVR	Manchester
N282JUG	Yorkshire	N376CJA	Manchester	N472JUG	Yorkshire	N554LHU	Bristol
N282JUM	Yorkshire	N377CJA	Manchester	N472KHU	Bristol	N554UCY	Cymru
N283JUG	Yorkshire	N378CJA	Manchester	N473JUG	Yorkshire	N554WVR	Manchester
N283JUM	Yorkshire	N378EAK	Leicester	N473KHU	Bristol	N555UCY	Cymru
N284JUG	Yorkshire	N379CJA	Manchester	N474JUG	Yorkshire	N556EYB	Southern National
N284JUM	Yorkshire	N380CJA	Manchester	N474KHU	Bristol	N556LHU	Bristol
N285JUG	Yorkshire	N381CJA	Manchester	N475JUG	Yorkshire	N556UCY	Cymru
N285JUM	Yorkshire	N382CJA	Manchester	N476JUG	Yorkshire	N556WVR	Manchester
N286JUG	Yorkshire	N383CJA	Manchester	N477JUG	Yorkshire	N557BNF	Manchester
N286JUM	Yorkshire	N384CJA	Manchester	N478JUG	Yorkshire	N557EYB	Southern National
N287JUG	Yorkshire	N385CRJ	Manchester	N521REW	CentreWest	N557LHU	Bristol
N287JUM	Yorkshire	N386CRJ	Manchester	N521WVR	Manchester	N557UCY	Cymru
N288JUG	Yorkshire	N390EUG	Western National	N522REW	CentreWest	N558BNF	Manchester
N288JUM	Yorkshire	N405HVT	PMT	N522WVR	Manchester	N558EYB	Southern National
N289JUG	Yorkshire	N406HVT	PMT	N523REW	CentreWest	N558LHU	Bristol
N289JUM	Yorkshire	N406MWY	Midland/Lowland	N523WVR	Manchester	N558UCY	Cymru
N290JUG	Yorkshire	N407ENW	Midland/Lowland	N524REW	CentreWest	N559BNF	Manchester
N290JUM	Yorkshire	N407HVT	PMT	N524WVR	Manchester	N559EYB	Southern National
N291JUG	Yorkshire	N408ENW	Midland/Lowland	N525REW	CentreWest	N559LHU	Bristol
N291JUM	Yorkshire	N408HVT	PMT	N525VSA	Aberdeen	N559UCY	Cymru
N292JUG	Yorkshire	N409ENW	Midland/Lowland	N525WVR	Manchester	N561BNF	Manchester
N292JUM	Yorkshire	N409HVT	PMT	N526REW	CentreWest	N561EYB	Southern National
N293JUG	Yorkshire	N410ENW	Midland/Lowland	N526VSA	Aberdeen	N561LHU	Western National
N293JUM	Yorkshire	N410HVT	PMT	N526WVR	Manchester	N561UCY	Cymru
N294JUM	Yorkshire	N411ENW	Midland/Lowland	N527REW	CentreWest	N562BNF	Manchester
N295JUM	Yorkshire	N411HVT	PMT	N527VSA	Aberdeen	N562LHU	Western National
N296JUM	Yorkshire	N412ENW	Yorkshire	N527WVR	Manchester	N562UCY	Cymru
N297JUM	Yorkshire	N412HVT	PMT	N528VSA	Aberdeen	N563LHU	Western National
N298JUM	Yorkshire	N413ENW	Yorkshire	N528WVR	Manchester	N563UCY	Cymru
N299JUM	Yorkshire	N414ENW	Yorkshire	N529VSA	Aberdeen	N564LHU	Western National
N301JBV	CentreWest	N415ENW	Yorkshire	N529WVR	Manchester	N564UCY	Cymru
N301WNF	Manchester	N416ENW	Yorkshire	N530VSA	Aberdeen	N565UCY	Cymru
N301XAB	Midland Red	N417ENW	Yorkshire	N530WVR	Manchester	N566UCY	Cymru
N302JBV	CentreWest	N418ENW	Yorkshire	N531VSA	Aberdeen	N567UCY	Cymru
N302WNF	Manchester	N419ENW	Yorkshire	N531WVR	Manchester	N568UCY	Cymru
N302XAB	Midland Red	N420MWY	Yorkshire	N532VSA	Aberdeen	N572VMS	Midland/Lowland
N303JBV	CentreWest	N421MWY	Yorkshire	N532WVR	Manchester	N573VMS	Midland/Lowland
N303WNF	Manchester	N422MWY	Yorkshire	N533VSA	Aberdeen	N574CEH	PMT
N303XAB	Midland Red	N423MWY	Yorkshire	N533WVR	Manchester	N574VMS	Midland/Lowland
N304JBV	CentreWest	N424MWY	Yorkshire	N534VSA	Aberdeen	N575CEH	PMT
N304WNF	Manchester	N425MWY	Yorkshire	N534WVR	Manchester	N576CEH	PMT
N304XAB	Midland Red	N440VWW	Yorkshire	N535VSA	Aberdeen	N577CEH	PMT

Reg	Operator	Reg	Operator	Reg	Operator	Reg	Operator
N578CEH	PMT	N617GAH	Eastern Counties	N742GKH	Manchester	N831FLW	CentreWest
N579CEH	PMT	N617MHB	Cymru	N743CKY	Mainline	N832FLW	CentreWest
N580CEH	PMT	N617XJM	CentreWest	N744CKY	Mainline	N841DVF	Eastern Counties
N581CEH	PMT	N618APU	Eastern Counties	N745CKY	Mainline	N842DVF	Eastern Counties
N582CEH	PMT	N618GAH	Eastern Counties	N746CKY	Mainline	N851CPU	Essex Buses
N583CEH	PMT	N618MHB	Cymru	N748CKY	Mainline	N852CPU	Essex Buses
N583WND	Southern National	N618XJM	CentreWest	N749CKY	Mainline	N853CPU	Essex Buses
N584CEH	PMT	N619APU	Eastern Counties	N750CKY	Mainline	N854CPU	Essex Buses
N584WND	Southern National	N619CDB	Manchester	N751CKY	Mainline	N863CEH	PMT
N585CEH	PMT	N619GAH	Eastern Counties	N752CKY	Mainline	N864CEH	PMT
N585WND	Southern National	N619XJM	CentreWest	N753CKY	Mainline	N865CEH	PMT
N586CEH	PMT	N620CDB	Manchester	N754CKY	Mainline	N866CEH	PMT
N586WND	Southern National	N620GAH	Eastern Counties	N755CKY	Mainline	N867CEH	PMT
N587CEH	PMT	N620XJM	CentreWest	N756CKY	Mainline	N875HWS	Bristol
N588CEH	PMT	N621CDB	Manchester	N757CKY	Mainline	N876HWS	Bristol
N589CEH	PMT	N621GAH	Eastern Counties	N758CKY	Mainline	N877HWS	Bristol
N589WND	Eastern Counties	N621XJM	CentreWest	N759CKY	Mainline	N878HWS	Bristol
N590CEH	PMT	N622CDB	Manchester	N760CKY	Mainline	N879HWS	Bristol
N591CEH	PMT	N622GAH	Eastern Counties	N761CKY	Mainline	N880HWS	Bristol
N592CEH	PMT	N622XJM	CentreWest	N762CKY	Mainline	N881HWS	Bristol
N593CEH	PMT	N623CDB	Manchester	N763CKY	Mainline	N882HWS	Bristol
N594CEH	PMT	N623GAH	Eastern Counties	N764CKY	Mainline	N883HWS	Bristol
N601APU	Essex Buses	N623XJM	CentreWest	N765CKY	Mainline	N884HWS	Bristol
N601EBP	Hampshire	N624CDB	Manchester	N766CKY	Mainline	N885HWS	Bristol
N601XJM	CentreWest	N624GAH	Eastern Counties	N767CKY	Mainline	N886HWS	Bristol
N602APU	Essex Buses	N624XJM	CentreWest	N768CKY	Mainline	N887FVF	Eastern Counties
N602EBP	Hampshire	N625CDB	Manchester	N769CKY	Mainline	N887HWS	Bristol
N602XJM	CentreWest	N625GAH	Eastern Counties	N771CKY	Mainline	N889HWS	Bristol
N603APU	Essex Buses	N625XJM	CentreWest	N772CKY	Mainline	N890HWS	Bristol
N603EBP	Hampshire	N626CDB	Manchester	N773CKY	Mainline	N891HWS	Bristol
N603XJM	CentreWest	N626GAH	Eastern Counties	N774CKY	Mainline	N892HWS	Bristol
N604APU	Eastern Counties	N626XJM	CentreWest	N775CKY	Mainline	N893HWS	Bristol
N604EBP	Hampshire	N627CDB	Manchester	N776CKY	Mainline	N894HWS	Bristol
N604XJM	CentreWest	N627GAH	Eastern Counties	N778CKY	Mainline	N895HWS	Bristol
N605APU	Essex Buses	N628CDB	Manchester	N779CKY	Mainline	N896HWS	Bristol
N605EBP	Hampshire	N628GAH	Eastern Counties	N780CKY	Mainline	N897HWS	Bristol
N605GAH	Eastern Counties	N629CDB	Manchester	N795WAN	CentreWest	N898HWS	Bristol
N605XJM	CentreWest	N630CDB	Manchester	N796WAN	CentreWest	N899HWS	Bristol
N606APU	Essex Buses	N631CDB	Manchester	N797WAN	CentreWest	N901HWS	Bristol
N606GAH	Eastern Counties	N632CDB	Manchester	N798WAN	CentreWest	N902HWS	Bristol
N606XJM	CentreWest	N633CDB	Manchester	N801FLW	CentreWest	N903HWS	Bristol
N607APU	Essex Buses	N634ACF	CentreWest	N802FLW	CentreWest	N904HWS	Bristol
N607GAH	Eastern Counties	N634CDB	Manchester	N803FLW	CentreWest	N905HWS	Bristol
N607XJM	CentreWest	N635ACF	CentreWest	N804FLW	CentreWest	N906HWS	Bristol
N608APU	Essex Buses	N635CDB	Manchester	N805FLW	CentreWest	N907HWS	Bristol
N608GAH	Eastern Counties	N636ACF	CentreWest	N806CRJ	Southern National	N913KHW	Bristol
N608WND	Western National	N636CDB	Manchester	N806FLW	CentreWest	N914KHW	Bristol
N608XJM	CentreWest	N637ACF	CentreWest	N807FLW	CentreWest	N921LUF	CentreWest
N609APU	Essex Buses	N637CDB	Manchester	N808FLW	CentreWest	N922LUF	CentreWest
N609GAH	Eastern Counties	N638CDB	Manchester	N809FLW	CentreWest	N923LUF	CentreWest
N609MHB	Cymru	N640CDB	Manchester	N810FLW	CentreWest	N929LSU	Glasgow
N609XJM	CentreWest	N641CDB	Manchester	N810NOD	Western National	N930LSU	Glasgow
N610APU	Essex Buses	N642CDB	Manchester	N811FLW	CentreWest	N931LSU	Glasgow
N610GAH	Eastern Counties	N643CDB	Manchester	N811NOD	Western National	N932LSU	Glasgow
N610MHB	Cymru	N644CDB	Manchester	N812FLW	CentreWest	N933LSU	Glasgow
N610WND	Western National	N645CDB	Manchester	N813FLW	CentreWest	N934LSU	Glasgow
N610XJM	CentreWest	N646CDB	Manchester	N814FLW	CentreWest	N935LSU	Glasgow
N611APU	Essex Buses	N647CDB	Manchester	N815FLW	CentreWest	N936LSU	Glasgow
N611GAH	Eastern Counties	N648CDB	Manchester	N816FLW	CentreWest	N937LSU	Glasgow
N611MHB	Cymru	N649CDB	Manchester	N817FLW	CentreWest	N938LSU	Glasgow
N611XJM	CentreWest	N650CDB	Manchester	N818FLW	CentreWest	N939LSU	Glasgow
N612APU	Essex Buses	N651CDB	Manchester	N819FLW	CentreWest	N940LSU	Glasgow
N612GAH	Eastern Counties	N652CDB	Manchester	N820FLW	CentreWest	N941LSU	Glasgow
N612MHB	Cymru	N653CDB	Manchester	N821FLW	CentreWest	N942LSU	Glasgow
N612WND	Western National	N686WLS	Midland/Lowland	N821KWS	Bristol	N943LSU	Glasgow
N612XJM	CentreWest	N687WLS	Midland/Lowland	N822FLW	CentreWest	N944CPU	Essex Buses
N613APU	Essex Buses	N688WLS	Midland/Lowland	N822KWS	Bristol	N944LSU	Glasgow
N613GAH	Eastern Counties	N689WLS	Midland/Lowland	N823APU	Essex Buses	N944SOS	Essex Buses
N613MHB	Cymru	N690WLS	Midland/Lowland	N823FLW	CentreWest	N945CPU	Essex Buses
N613XJM	CentreWest	N701CPU	Essex Buses	N824APU	Essex Buses	N945LSU	Glasgow
N614APU	Essex Buses	N710GRV	Hampshire	N824FLW	CentreWest	N945SOS	Glasgow
N614GAH	Eastern Counties	N711GRV	Hampshire	N825APU	Essex Buses	N946CPU	Essex Buses
N614MHB	Cymru	N712GRV	Hampshire	N825FLW	CentreWest	N946LSU	Glasgow
N614XJM	CentreWest	N713GRV	Hampshire	N826APU	Essex Buses	N946SOS	Glasgow
N615APU	Essex Buses	N714GRV	Hampshire	N826FLW	CentreWest	N947CPU	Essex Buses
N615DWY	Hampshire	N715GRV	Hampshire	N827APU	Essex Buses	N947LSU	Glasgow
N615GAH	Eastern Counties	N716GRV	Hampshire	N827FLW	CentreWest	N947SOS	Glasgow
N615MHB	Cymru	N717GRV	Hampshire	N828APU	Essex Buses	N948CPU	Essex Buses
N615XJM	CentreWest	N718GRV	Hampshire	N828FLW	CentreWest	N948LSU	Glasgow
N616APU	Eastern Counties	N719GRV	Western National	N829APU	Essex Buses	N948SOS	Glasgow
N616GAH	Eastern Counties	N720GRV	Hampshire	N829FLW	CentreWest	N949CPU	Essex Buses
N616MHB	Cymru	N721GRV	Hampshire	N830APU	Essex Buses	N949LSU	Glasgow
N616XJM	CentreWest	N741CKY	Mainline	N830FLW	CentreWest	N949SOS	Glasgow
N617APU	Eastern Counties	N742CKY	Mainline			N950CPU	Essex Buses

The 1999 FirstGroup Bus Handbook

Reg	Operator	Reg	Operator	Reg	Operator	Reg	Operator
N950LSU	Glasgow	N980LSU	Glasgow	NKU189X	Mainline	OGG184Y	Glasgow
N950SOS	Glasgow	N981EHJ	Capital	NKU190X	Mainline	OGG185Y	Glasgow
N951CPU	Essex Buses	N981LSU	Glasgow	NKU191X	Mainline	OGG186Y	Glasgow
N951LSU	Glasgow	N982EHJ	Capital	NKU192X	Mainline	OGG188Y	Glasgow
N951SOS	Glasgow	N982LSU	Glasgow	NKU193X	Mainline	OGG189Y	Glasgow
N952CPU	Essex Buses	N983EHJ	Capital	NKU194X	Mainline	OGG190Y	Glasgow
N952LSU	Glasgow	N983LSU	Glasgow	NKU195X	Mainline	OGG191Y	Glasgow
N952SOS	Glasgow	N984EHJ	Capital	NKU198X	Mainline	OHW489R	Bristol
N953CPU	Essex Buses	N984LSU	Glasgow	NKU199X	Mainline	OIL3796	Cymru
N953LSU	Glasgow	N985EHJ	Capital	NKU200X	Mainline	OIL9262	Bristol
N953SOS	Glasgow	N985LSU	Glasgow	NKU201X	Mainline	OIL9263	Bristol
N954CPU	Essex Buses	N986EHJ	Capital	NKU202X	Mainline	OIL9264	Bristol
N954LSU	Glasgow	N986LSU	Glasgow	NKU203X	Mainline	OJD843Y	Capital
N954SOS	Glasgow	N987LSU	Glasgow	NKU204X	Mainline	OJD851Y	CentreWest
N955CPU	Essex Buses	N988LSU	Glasgow	NKU205X	Mainline	OJD857Y	CentreWest
N955LSU	Glasgow	NBD107Y	Midland/Lowland	NKU206X	Mainline	OJD859Y	CentreWest
N955SOS	Glasgow	NDZ3162	CentreWest	NKU207X	Mainline	OJD860Y	CentreWest
N956CPU	Essex Buses	NDZ3163	CentreWest	NKU208X	Mainline	OJD861Y	CentreWest
N956LSU	Glasgow	NDZ3164	CentreWest	NKU209X	Mainline	OJD866Y	CentreWest
N956SOS	Glasgow	NDZ3165	CentreWest	NKU210X	Mainline	OJD872Y	CentreWest
N957CPU	Essex Buses	NDZ3166	CentreWest	NKU211X	Mainline	OJD874Y	CentreWest
N957LSU	Glasgow	NDZ3167	CentreWest	NKU212X	Mainline	OJD875Y	CentreWest
N957SOS	Glasgow	NDZ3168	CentreWest	NKU213X	Mainline	OJD882Y	CentreWest
N958CPU	Essex Buses	NDZ3169	CentreWest	NKU214X	Mainline	OJD883Y	CentreWest
N958LSU	Glasgow	NDZ3170	CentreWest	NKU215X	Mainline	OJD884Y	CentreWest
N958SOS	Glasgow	NEH725W	PMT	NKU216X	Mainline	OJD885Y	CentreWest
N959CPU	Essex Buses	NEH728W	PMT	NKU217X	Mainline	OJD886Y	CentreWest
N959LSU	Glasgow	NEH729W	PMT	NKU218X	Mainline	OJD887Y	CentreWest
N959SOS	Glasgow	NEH731W	PMT	NKU219X	Mainline	OJF419P	Southern National
N960CPU	Essex Buses	NEJ26R	Southern National	NKU220X	Mainline	OJI1870	Hampshire
N960LSU	Glasgow	NER621	Western National	NLP839V	Capital	OJI1871	Hampshire
N960SOS	Glasgow	NFB599R	Bristol	NML602E	CentreWest	OJI1872	Hampshire
N961CPU	Essex Buses	NFP205W	Leicester	NML609E	CentreWest	OJI1873	Hampshire
N961LSU	Glasgow	NFS984T	Midland/Lowland	NML623E	CentreWest	OJI1874	Hampshire
N961SOS	Glasgow	NIL2454	Cymru	NML647E	CentreWest	OJI8786	Southern National
N962CPU	Essex Buses	NIL2455	Cymru	NML656E	CentreWest	ORJ82W	Manchester
N962LSU	Glasgow	NIL2456	Cymru	NOE614R	Midland Red	ORJ83W	Manchester
N962SOS	Glasgow	NIL3952	Eastern Counties	NRS301W	Aberdeen	ORJ84W	Manchester
N963CPU	Essex Buses	NIL3953	Eastern Counties	NRS302W	Aberdeen	ORJ85W	Manchester
N963LSU	Glasgow	NIL3954	Eastern Counties	NRS305W	Aberdeen	ORJ89W	Manchester
N963SOS	Glasgow	NIL3955	Eastern Counties	NRS307W	Aberdeen	ORJ96W	Manchester
N964CPU	Essex Buses	NIL3956	Eastern Counties	NRS308W	Midland/Lowland	ORJ97W	Manchester
N964LSU	Glasgow	NIL3957	Eastern Counties	NRS310W	Aberdeen	ORJ356W	Yorkshire
N964SOS	Glasgow	NIL3958	Eastern Counties	NRS311W	Aberdeen	ORJ357W	Manchester
N965CPU	Essex Buses	NIL3959	Eastern Counties	NRS312W	Aberdeen	ORJ373W	Yorkshire
N965LSU	Glasgow	NIL3960	Eastern Counties	NRS313W	Aberdeen	ORJ383W	Yorkshire
N965SOS	Glasgow	NIL3961	Eastern Counties	NRS314W	Aberdeen	ORJ388W	Yorkshire
N966CPU	Essex Buses	NIL3962	Eastern Counties	NRS315W	Aberdeen	ORJ389W	Yorkshire
N966LSU	Glasgow	NIL3963	Eastern Counties	NTC129Y	Bristol	ORJ390W	Yorkshire
N966SOS	Glasgow	NIL3964	Eastern Counties	NTC130Y	Bristol	ORJ400W	Yorkshire
N967CPU	Essex Buses	NIL3965	Eastern Counties	NTC131Y	Bristol	ORS205R	Midland/Lowland
N967LSU	Glasgow	NIL3966	Eastern Counties	NTC133Y	Bristol	ORS208R	Midland/Lowland
N967SOS	Glasgow	NIL3967	Eastern Counties	NTC134Y	Bristol	ORS209R	Midland/Lowland
N968CPU	Essex Buses	NKU143X	Mainline	NTC135Y	Bristol	ORS215R	Midland/Lowland
N968LSU	Glasgow	NKU146X	Mainline	NTC136Y	Bristol	ORX107X	Southern National
N968SOS	Glasgow	NKU147X	Mainline	NTC137Y	Bristol	OTA290G	Western National
N969CPU	Essex Buses	NKU148X	Mainline	NTC138Y	Bristol	OUS11Y	Midland/Lowland
N969LSU	Glasgow	NKU149X	Mainline	NTC139Y	Bristol	OUS12Y	Midland/Lowland
N969SOS	Glasgow	NKU151X	Mainline	NTC140Y	Bristol	OUS13Y	Midland/Lowland
N970CPU	Essex Buses	NKU154X	Mainline	NTC141Y	Bristol	OUS14Y	Midland/Lowland
N970LSU	Glasgow	NKU157X	Mainline	NTC142Y	Bristol	OUS15Y	Midland/Lowland
N970SOS	Glasgow	NKU158X	Mainline	NTC143Y	Bristol	OUS16Y	Midland/Lowland
N971CPU	Essex Buses	NKU159X	Mainline	NTC573R	Western National	OUS17Y	Midland/Lowland
N971LSU	Glasgow	NKU160X	Mainline	NTH156X	Western National	OUS18Y	Midland/Lowland
N971SOS	Glasgow	NKU162X	Mainline	NTL655	Northampton	OUS19Y	Midland/Lowland
N972CPU	Essex Buses	NKU163X	Mainline	NVS485	Capital	OUS20Y	Midland/Lowland
N972LSU	Glasgow	NKU164X	Mainline	OCK997K	Western National	OVT798	Midland/Lowland
N972SOS	Glasgow	NKU165X	Mainline	ODT232	Bristol	OWB243	Western National
N973EHJ	Capital	NKU167X	Mainline	ODZ8911	CentreWest	OWE140X	Mainline
N973LSU	Glasgow	NKU168X	Mainline	ODZ8912	CentreWest	OWE848P	Southern National
N973SOS	Glasgow	NKU169X	Mainline	ODZ8913	CentreWest	OWE851P	Southern National
N974EHJ	Capital	NKU170X	Mainline	ODZ8914	CentreWest	P2GRT	Aberdeen
N974LSU	Glasgow	NKU172X	Mainline	ODZ8915	CentreWest	P2UVG	Glasgow
N975EHJ	Capital	NKU174X	Mainline	ODZ8916	CentreWest	P4GRT	Aberdeen
N975LSU	Glasgow	NKU175X	Mainline	ODZ8917	CentreWest	P25RFS	Glasgow
N976EHJ	Capital	NKU177X	Mainline	ODZ8918	CentreWest	P26RFS	Glasgow
N976LSU	Glasgow	NKU180X	Mainline	ODZ8919	CentreWest	P87BPL	Bristol
N977EHJ	Capital	NKU181X	Mainline	ODZ8920	CentreWest	P106MFS	Glasgow
N977LSU	Glasgow	NKU182X	Mainline	ODZ8921	CentreWest	P107MFS	Glasgow
N978EHJ	Capital	NKU183X	Mainline	ODZ8922	CentreWest	P108MFS	Glasgow
N978LSU	Glasgow	NKU184X	Mainline	OGG179Y	Glasgow	P109MFS	Glasgow
N979EHJ	Capital	NKU185X	Mainline	OGG181Y	Glasgow	P113YSH	Glasgow
N979LSU	Glasgow	NKU186X	Mainline	OGG182Y	Glasgow	P117NI W	CentreWest
N980EHJ	Capital	NKU187X	Mainline	OGG183Y	Glasgow	P118NLW	CentreWest

Reg	Operator	Reg	Operator	Reg	Operator	Reg	Operator
P119NLW	CentreWest	P203NSC	Midland/Lowland	P294KPX	Hampshire	P416PLE	Capital
P120NLW	CentreWest	P203TGD	Glasgow	P295KPX	Hampshire	P417NFA	PMT
P121NLW	CentreWest	P204NSC	Midland/Lowland	P296KPX	Hampshire	P417PVW	Capital
P122NLW	CentreWest	P204TGD	Glasgow	P301LND	Manchester	P418NFA	PMT
P123NLW	CentreWest	P205NSC	Midland/Lowland	P302AUM	Yorkshire	P418PVW	Capital
P124NLW	CentreWest	P206NSC	Midland/Lowland	P302LND	Manchester	P419NFA	PMT
P125NLW	CentreWest	P207NSC	Midland/Lowland	P303AUM	Yorkshire	P419PVW	Capital
P126NLW	CentreWest	P208NSC	Midland/Lowland	P303LND	Manchester	P420MEH	PMT
P127NLW	CentreWest	P209NSC	Midland/Lowland	P304AUM	Yorkshire	P420PVW	Capital
P128NLW	CentreWest	P20GRT	Aberdeen	P304LND	Manchester	P421MEH	PMT
P129NLW	CentreWest	P210NSC	Midland/Lowland	P305AUM	Yorkshire	P421PVW	Capital
P130NLW	CentreWest	P211NSC	Midland/Lowland	P305LND	Manchester	P422MEH	PMT
P131NLW	CentreWest	P212NSC	Midland/Lowland	P306LND	Manchester	P422PVW	Capital
P132NLW	CentreWest	P213HRJ	Manchester	P307LND	Manchester	P423MEH	PMT
P133NLW	CentreWest	P213NSC	Midland/Lowland	P308LND	Manchester	P423PVW	Capital
P134NLW	CentreWest	P214NSC	Midland/Lowland	P309LND	Manchester	P424MEH	PMT
P135NLW	CentreWest	P215NSC	Midland/Lowland	P310LND	Manchester	P424PVW	Capital
P136NLW	CentreWest	P216YSH	Midland/Lowland	P311LND	Manchester	P425MEH	PMT
P137NLW	CentreWest	P217YSH	Midland/Lowland	P312LND	Manchester	P425PVW	Capital
P138NLW	CentreWest	P218YSH	Midland/Lowland	P313LND	Manchester	P426GLS	Yorkshire
P139NLW	CentreWest	P223MPU	Capital	P314LND	Manchester	P426MEH	PMT
P140NLW	CentreWest	P224MPU	Capital	P315LND	Manchester	P427GLS	Yorkshire
P141NLW	CentreWest	P225MPU	Capital	P316LND	Manchester	P427MEH	PMT
P142NLW	CentreWest	P226MPU	Capital	P317LND	Manchester	P427ORL	Western National
P143NLW	CentreWest	P227MPU	Capital	P318LND	Manchester	P428GLS	Yorkshire
P144NLW	CentreWest	P228MPU	Capital	P319LND	Manchester	P428MEH	PMT
P145NLW	CentreWest	P229MPU	Capital	P320LND	Manchester	P428ORL	Western National
P146NLW	CentreWest	P230MPU	Capital	P321LND	Manchester	P429GLS	Yorkshire
P148NLW	CentreWest	P231MPU	Capital	P322LND	Manchester	P429MEH	PMT
P149NLW	CentreWest	P232MPU	Capital	P323LND	Manchester	P429ORL	Western National
P150NLW	CentreWest	P233MPU	Capital	P324LND	Manchester	P430GLS	Yorkshire
P151NLW	CentreWest	P234BFJ	Western National	P325LND	Manchester	P430ORL	Western National
P152NLW	CentreWest	P234MPU	Capital	P330RVG	Eastern Counties	P431GLS	Yorkshire
P153NLW	CentreWest	P235CTA	Western National	P384MEH	PMT	P431ORL	Western National
P154NLW	CentreWest	P235MPU	Capital	P385MEH	PMT	P432ORL	Western National
P156NLW	CentreWest	P236CTA	Western National	P386MEH	PMT	P432RSH	Yorkshire
P157NLW	CentreWest	P236MPU	Capital	P387MEH	PMT	P433NEX	Eastern Counties
P171DMS	Midland/Lowland	P237MPU	Capital	P388MEH	PMT	P433ORL	Western National
P172DMS	Midland/Lowland	P237NLW	CentreWest	P389MEH	PMT	P433RSH	Yorkshire
P173DMS	Midland/Lowland	P238MPU	Capital	P390MEH	PMT	P434NEX	Eastern Counties
P174DMS	Midland/Lowland	P238NLW	CentreWest	P401HPU	Essex Buses	P434ORL	Western National
P174TGD	Glasgow	P239HMD	Capital	P401MLA	CentreWest	P435NEX	Eastern Counties
P175TGD	Glasgow	P239NLW	CentreWest	P401PLE	Capital	P435ORL	Western National
P176NAK	Leicester	P240HMD	Capital	P402HPU	Essex Buses	P435RSH	Yorkshire
P176TGD	Glasgow	P241UCW	CentreWest	P402MLA	CentreWest	P436NEX	Eastern Counties
P177NAK	Leicester	P242HMD	Capital	P402PLE	Capital	P436ORL	Western National
P177TGD	Glasgow	P242UCW	CentreWest	P403HPU	Essex Buses	P436RSH	Yorkshire
P178TGD	Glasgow	P243HMD	Capital	P403MLA	CentreWest	P437NEX	Eastern Counties
P179LYB	Southern National	P243UCW	CentreWest	P403PLE	Capital	P437ORL	Western National
P179TGD	Glasgow	P244UCW	CentreWest	P404HPU	Essex Buses	P438NEX	Eastern Counties
P180LYB	Southern National	P245HMD	Capital	P404KOW	Hampshire	P438ORL	Western National
P180TGD	Glasgow	P245UCW	CentreWest	P404MLA	CentreWest	P439NEX	Eastern Counties
P181LYB	Southern National	P246HMD	Capital	P404PLE	Capital	P439ORL	Western National
P181TGD	Glasgow	P246UCW	CentreWest	P405HPU	Essex Buses	P440NEX	Eastern Counties
P182LYB	Southern National	P247OEW	CentreWest	P405KOW	Hampshire	P440ORL	Western National
P182TGD	Glasgow	P247UCW	CentreWest	P405MLA	CentreWest	P441NEX	Eastern Counties
P183LYB	Southern National	P248HMD	Capital	P406HPU	Essex Buses	P441TCV	Western National
P183TGD	Glasgow	P248UCW	CentreWest	P406KOW	Hampshire	P442KYC	Southern National
P184TGD	Glasgow	P249HMD	Capital	P406MLA	CentreWest	P442NEX	Eastern Counties
P185TGD	Glasgow	P249UCW	CentreWest	P406PLE	Capital	P442TCV	Western National
P186TGD	Glasgow	P250UCW	CentreWest	P407HPU	Essex Buses	P443KYC	Southern National
P187TGD	Glasgow	P251PAE	Bristol	P407KOW	Hampshire	P443NEX	Eastern Counties
P188TGD	Glasgow	P251UCW	CentreWest	P407MLA	CentreWest	P443TCV	Western National
P188UNS	Glasgow	P252PAE	Bristol	P407PLE	Capital	P444TCV	Western National
P189TGD	Glasgow	P252UCW	CentreWest	P408HPU	Essex Buses	P445KYC	Southern National
P189UNS	Glasgow	P253PAE	Bristol	P408MLA	CentreWest	P445NEX	Eastern Counties
P190TGD	Glasgow	P253UCW	CentreWest	P408PLE	Capital	P445TCV	Western National
P190UNS	Glasgow	P254PAE	Bristol	P409HPU	Essex Buses	P446KYC	Southern National
P191TGD	Glasgow	P254UCW	CentreWest	P409MLA	CentreWest	P446NEX	Eastern Counties
P191UNS	Glasgow	P255PAE	Bristol	P409PLE	Capital	P446TCV	Western National
P192TGD	Glasgow	P255RFL	CentreWest	P410HPU	Essex Buses	P447KYC	Southern National
P192UNS	Glasgow	P255UCW	CentreWest	P410MLA	CentreWest	P447NEX	Eastern Counties
P193TGD	Glasgow	P256PAE	Bristol	P410PLE	Capital	P448KYC	Southern National
P193UNS	Glasgow	P257PAE	Bristol	P411MLA	CentreWest	P448NEX	Eastern Counties
P194TGD	Glasgow	P258PAE	Bristol	P411PLE	Capital	P449NEX	Eastern Counties
P195TGD	Glasgow	P259PAE	Bristol	P412PLE	Capital	P450NEX	Eastern Counties
P196TGD	Glasgow	P260PAE	Bristol	P413NFA	PMT	P451RPW	Eastern Counties
P197TGD	Glasgow	P261PAE	Bristol	P413PLE	Capital	P452LWE	Mainline
P198TGD	Glasgow	P262PAE	Bristol	P414NFA	PMT	P452RPW	Eastern Counties
P199TGD	Glasgow	P263PAE	Bristol	P414PLE	Capital	P453BPH	Midland Red
P201NSC	Midland/Lowland	P264PAE	Bristol	P415NFA	PMT	P453LWE	Mainline
P201TGD	Glasgow	P291KPX	Hampshire	P415PLE	Capital	P453RPW	Eastern Counties
P202NSC	Midland/Lowland	P292KPX	Hampshire	P416NFA	PMT	P454LWE	Mainline
P202TGD	Glasgow	P293KPX	Hampshire			P455LWE	Mainline

Reg	Operator	Reg	Operator	Reg	Operator	Reg	Operator
P488CEG	CentreWest	P537TYS	Glasgow	P613WSU	Glasgow	P756XUS	Glasgow
P489CEG	CentreWest	P538TYS	Glasgow	P614WSU	Glasgow	P757XUS	Glasgow
P490CEG	CentreWest	P538YSH	Midland/Lowland	P615WSU	Glasgow	P758XUS	Glasgow
P501LND	Manchester	P539TYS	Glasgow	P616WSU	Glasgow	P759XUS	Glasgow
P501MNO	Essex Buses	P539YSH	Midland/Lowland	P617WSU	Glasgow	P760XUS	Glasgow
P501MVV	Northampton	P540BSS	Aberdeen	P618WSU	Glasgow	P761XHS	Glasgow
P502LND	Manchester	P540TYS	Glasgow	P619VDW	Cymru	P761XUS	Glasgow
P502MNO	Essex Buses	P540YSH	Midland/Lowland	P619WSU	Glasgow	P762XHS	Glasgow
P502MVV	Northampton	P541BSS	Aberdeen	P620VDW	Cymru	P762XUS	Glasgow
P503LND	Manchester	P541RNG	Eastern Counties	P620WSU	Glasgow	P763XHS	Glasgow
P503MNO	Essex Buses	P541TYS	Glasgow	P621VDW	Cymru	P764XHS	Glasgow
P503MVV	Northampton	P541YSH	Midland/Lowland	P626WSU	Glasgow	P765XHS	Glasgow
P503XSH	Midland/Lowland	P542BSS	Aberdeen	P627CGM	CentreWest	P766XHS	Glasgow
P504LND	Manchester	P542RNG	Eastern Counties	P627WSU	Glasgow	P767XHS	Bristol
P504MNO	Essex Buses	P542TYS	Glasgow	P628CGM	CentreWest	P768XHS	Glasgow
P504MVV	Northampton	P542YHS	Midland/Lowland	P628WSU	Glasgow	P769XHS	Glasgow
P504XSH	Midland/Lowland	P543BSS	Aberdeen	P629CGM	CentreWest	P770XHS	Glasgow
P505LND	Manchester	P543RNG	Eastern Counties	P629WSU	Glasgow	P771XHS	Glasgow
P505MNO	Essex Buses	P543TYS	Glasgow	P630CGM	CentreWest	P806REX	Eastern Counties
P505MVV	Northampton	P544BSS	Aberdeen	P630WSU	Glasgow	P807REX	Eastern Counties
P505XSH	Midland/Lowland	P544RNG	Eastern Counties	P631CGM	CentreWest	P807YUM	Glasgow
P506LND	Manchester	P544TYS	Glasgow	P631WSU	Glasgow	P808REX	Eastern Counties
P506MNO	Essex Buses	P545BSS	Aberdeen	P632CGM	CentreWest	P808YUM	Glasgow
P506MVV	Northampton	P545RNG	Eastern Counties	P632WSU	Glasgow	P809REX	Eastern Counties
P506XSH	Midland/Lowland	P545TYS	Glasgow	P633WSU	Glasgow	P809YUM	Glasgow
P507LND	Manchester	P546BSS	Aberdeen	P634WSU	Glasgow	P810REX	Eastern Counties
P507MNO	Essex Buses	P546RNG	Eastern Counties	P635WSU	Glasgow	P810YUM	Glasgow
P508LND	Manchester	P546TYS	Glasgow	P655UFB	Bristol	P811REX	Eastern Counties
P508MNO	Essex Buses	P547BSS	Aberdeen	P656UFB	Bristol	P811YUM	Glasgow
P508VOS	Glasgow	P547RNG	Eastern Counties	P657UFB	Bristol	P812REX	Eastern Counties
P509LND	Manchester	P547TYS	Glasgow	P658UFB	Bristol	P812YUM	Glasgow
P509MNO	Essex Buses	P548BSS	Aberdeen	P659UFB	Bristol	P813REX	Eastern Counties
P510LND	Manchester	P548RNG	Eastern Counties	P660UFB	Bristol	P813YUM	Glasgow
P510MNO	Essex Buses	P548TYS	Glasgow	P678HPU	Essex Buses	P814REX	Eastern Counties
P510VOS	Glasgow	P549BSS	Aberdeen	P679HPU	Essex Buses	P814YUM	Glasgow
P511LND	Manchester	P549RNG	Eastern Counties	P680HPU	Essex Buses	P815REX	Eastern Counties
P511MNO	Essex Buses	P549TYS	Glasgow	P681HND	Eastern Counties	P815YUM	Glasgow
P511VOS	Glasgow	P550RNG	Eastern Counties	P681HPU	Essex Buses	P816REX	Eastern Counties
P512LND	Manchester	P569BTH	Cymru	P682HND	Eastern Counties	P816YUM	Glasgow
P512MNO	Essex Buses	P570BTH	Cymru	P682HPU	Essex Buses	P817REX	Eastern Counties
P512VOS	Glasgow	P571BTH	Cymru	P692HND	Eastern Counties	P817YUM	Glasgow
P513LND	Manchester	P572BTH	Cymru	P693HND	Eastern Counties	P818REX	Eastern Counties
P513MNO	Essex Buses	P573BTH	Cymru	P701HMT	Capital	P818YUM	Glasgow
P513VOS	Glasgow	P574BTH	Cymru	P701PWC	Glasgow	P819REX	Eastern Counties
P514LND	Manchester	P575BTH	Cymru	P702HMT	Capital	P819YUM	Glasgow
P514VOS	Glasgow	P575DMS	Midland/Lowland	P702HPU	Essex Buses	P820SCL	Eastern Counties
P515LND	Manchester	P576BTH	Cymru	P702PWC	Glasgow	P821SCL	Eastern Counties
P515VOS	Glasgow	P576DMS	Midland/Lowland	P703HMT	Capital	P822SCL	Eastern Counties
P516LND	Manchester	P577BTH	Cymru	P703HPU	Essex Buses	P822YUM	Glasgow
P516VOS	Glasgow	P577DMS	Midland/Lowland	P703PWC	Glasgow	P823YUM	Glasgow
P517LND	Manchester	P578BTH	Cymru	P704HMT	Capital	P824YUM	Glasgow
P518LND	Manchester	P578DMS	Midland/Lowland	P704HPU	Essex Buses	P825NAV	CentreWest
P519LND	Manchester	P579BTH	Cymru	P704PWC	Glasgow	P825YUM	Glasgow
P519PYS	Glasgow	P579DMS	Midland/Lowland	P705HPU	Essex Buses	P826NAV	CentreWest
P520LND	Manchester	P580BTH	Cymru	P705PWC	Glasgow	P826YUM	Yorkshire
P520PYS	Glasgow	P580DMS	Midland/Lowland	P706HPU	Essex Buses	P827YUM	Yorkshire
P521LND	Manchester	P581DMS	Midland/Lowland	P706PWC	Glasgow	P828KTP	Bristol
P521PRL	Western National	P585WSU	Glasgow	P707HPU	Essex Buses	P828YUM	Midland/Lowland
P521PYS	Glasgow	P586WSU	Glasgow	P707PWC	Glasgow	P829KTP	Bristol
P522LND	Manchester	P587WSU	Glasgow	P708HPU	Essex Buses	P829YUM	Glasgow
P522PRL	Western National	P588WSU	Glasgow	P708PWC	Glasgow	P830YUM	Glasgow
P522PYS	Glasgow	P589WSU	Glasgow	P709HPU	Essex Buses	P831YUM	Glasgow
P523LND	Manchester	P590WSU	Glasgow	P710HPU	Essex Buses	P832YUM	Midland/Lowland
P523PYS	Glasgow	P591WSU	Glasgow	P711HPU	Essex Buses	P833YUM	Yorkshire
P524LND	Manchester	P592WSU	Glasgow	P722KCR	Hampshire	P834YUM	Yorkshire
P524PYS	Glasgow	P593WSU	Glasgow	P723KCR	Hampshire	P835YUM	Midland/Lowland
P525LND	Manchester	P594WSU	Glasgow	P724KCR	Hampshire	P836YUM	Yorkshire
P525PYS	Glasgow	P595WSU	Glasgow	P725KCR	Hampshire	P844OAH	Eastern Counties
P526LND	Manchester	P596WSU	Glasgow	P726KCR	Hampshire	P852VUS	Glasgow
P526PYS	Glasgow	P597WSU	Glasgow	P727KCR	Hampshire	P853DTT	Western National
P527LND	Manchester	P598WSU	Glasgow	P728KCR	Hampshire	P853VUS	Glasgow
P527PYS	Glasgow	P599WSU	Glasgow	P729KCR	Hampshire	P854VUS	Glasgow
P528LND	Manchester	P601WSU	Glasgow	P731NVG	Eastern Counties	P855VUS	Glasgow
P528PYS	Glasgow	P602WSU	Glasgow	P732NVG	Eastern Counties	P856VUS	Glasgow
P529LND	Manchester	P603WSU	Glasgow	P733NVG	Eastern Counties	P857VUS	Glasgow
P529PYS	Glasgow	P604WSU	Glasgow	P734NVG	Eastern Counties	P858VUS	Glasgow
P530LND	Manchester	P605WSU	Glasgow	P748HND	Manchester	P859VUS	Glasgow
P530PYS	Glasgow	P606WSU	Glasgow	P748XUS	Glasgow	P860VUS	Glasgow
P531TYS	Glasgow	P607WSU	Glasgow	P749XUS	Glasgow	P861VUS	Glasgow
P532TYS	Glasgow	P608WSU	Glasgow	P750XUS	Glasgow	P868MBF	PMT
P533TYS	Glasgow	P609WSU	Glasgow	P751XUS	Glasgow	P869MBF	PMT
P534TYS	Glasgow	P610WSU	Glasgow	P752XUS	Glasgow	P870MBF	PMT
P535TYS	Glasgow	P611WSU	Glasgow	P753XUS	Glasgow	P871TAV	Manchester
P536TYS	Glasgow	P612WSU	Glasgow	P754XUS	Glasgow	P872TAV	Manchester

Reg	Operator	Reg	Operator	Reg	Operator	Reg	Operator
P875YKS	Midland/Lowland	PUA263W	Yorkshire	R28GNW	PMT	R146EHS	Glasgow
P876YKS	Midland/Lowland	PUA264W	Yorkshire	R71GNW	Bristol	R146GSF	Glasgow
P877YKS	Midland/Lowland	PUA265W	Yorkshire	R72GNW	Bristol	R147EHS	Glasgow
P878YKS	Midland/Lowland	PUA266W	Yorkshire	R73GNW	Bristol	R147GSF	Glasgow
P879YKS	Midland/Lowland	PUA267W	Yorkshire	R81GNW	Midland/Lowland	R148EHS	Glasgow
P889TCV	Glasgow	PUA268W	Yorkshire	R82GNW	Midland/Lowland	R148GSF	Glasgow
P890TCV	Glasgow	PUA269W	Yorkshire	R86XHL	Mainline	R149EHS	Glasgow
P944RWS	Bristol	PUA271W	Yorkshire	R101DTC	Bristol	R149GSF	Glasgow
P945RWS	Bristol	PUA272W	Yorkshire	R102DTC	Bristol	R150EHS	Glasgow
P946RWS	Bristol	PUA273W	Yorkshire	R103VLX	CentreWest	R150GSF	Glasgow
P973MBF	PMT	PUA274W	Yorkshire	R105VLX	CentreWest	R151EHS	Glasgow
P974MBF	PMT	PUA275W	Yorkshire	R107VLX	CentreWest	R151GSF	Glasgow
P975MBF	PMT	PUA276W	Yorkshire	R108VLX	CentreWest	R152EHS	Glasgow
P976MBF	PMT	PUA277W	Yorkshire	R109VLX	CentreWest	R152GSF	Glasgow
PBP224S	Hampshire	PUA278W	Yorkshire	R110GSF	Glasgow	R153EHS	Glasgow
PBP225S	Hampshire	PUA279W	Yorkshire	R112GSF	Glasgow	R153GSF	Glasgow
PBP228S	Hampshire	PUA280W	Yorkshire	R112VLX	CentreWest	R154GSF	Glasgow
PBP229S	Hampshire	PUA282W	Yorkshire	R113VLX	CentreWest	R155GSF	Glasgow
PBP230S	Hampshire	PUA285W	Yorkshire	R114GSF	Glasgow	R156GSF	Glasgow
PBP231S	Hampshire	PUA286W	Yorkshire	R114VLX	CentreWest	R157GSF	Glasgow
PCL253W	Eastern Counties	PUA287W	Yorkshire	R115GSF	Glasgow	R158GSF	Glasgow
PCL254W	Eastern Counties	PUA288W	Yorkshire	R116GSF	Glasgow	R158TLM	CentreWest
PCL255W	Eastern Counties	PUA289W	Yorkshire	R116VLX	CentreWest	R159GSF	Glasgow
PCL257W	Eastern Counties	PUA290W	Yorkshire	R117GSF	Glasgow	R159TLM	CentreWest
PEU518R	Western National	PUA291W	Yorkshire	R118GSF	Glasgow	R160GSF	Glasgow
PEX615W	Eastern Counties	PUA292W	Yorkshire	R119GSF	Glasgow	R160TLM	CentreWest
PEX617W	Eastern Counties	PUA293W	Yorkshire	R120GSF	Glasgow	R161GSF	Glasgow
PHY697S	Western National	PUA294W	Yorkshire	R121GSF	Glasgow	R161TLM	CentreWest
PJY551	Western National	PUA295W	Yorkshire	R122GSF	Glasgow	R162GSF	Glasgow
PNW598W	Yorkshire	PUA296W	Yorkshire	R123GSF	Glasgow	R162TLM	CentreWest
PNW601W	Yorkshire	PUA297W	Yorkshire	R123XDT	Mainline	R163GSF	Glasgow
PNW603W	Yorkshire	PUA298W	Yorkshire	R124GSF	Glasgow	R163TLM	CentreWest
PRA114R	Southern National	PUA299W	Yorkshire	R124XDT	Mainline	R164GSF	Glasgow
PRA115R	Southern National	PUA300W	Yorkshire	R125GSF	Glasgow	R164TLM	CentreWest
PRC848X	Eastern Counties	PUA301W	Yorkshire	R125XDT	Mainline	R165GSF	Glasgow
PRC850X	Eastern Counties	PUA302W	Yorkshire	R126GSF	Glasgow	R165TLM	CentreWest
PRC851X	Eastern Counties	PUA303W	Yorkshire	R126XDT	Mainline	R166GSF	Glasgow
PRC852X	Eastern Counties	PUA304W	Yorkshire	R127GSF	Glasgow	R166TLM	CentreWest
PRC853X	Eastern Counties	PUA305W	Yorkshire	R127XDT	Mainline	R167GSF	Glasgow
PRC855X	Eastern Counties	PUA306W	Yorkshire	R128GSF	Glasgow	R167TLM	CentreWest
PRC857X	Eastern Counties	PUA307W	Yorkshire	R128XDT	Mainline	R168GSF	Glasgow
PSF311Y	Midland/Lowland	PUA308W	Yorkshire	R129GSF	Glasgow	R168TLM	CentreWest
PSF313Y	Midland/Lowland	PUA309W	Yorkshire	R129XDT	Mainline	R169GSF	Glasgow
PSF314Y	Midland/Lowland	PUA310W	Yorkshire	R130GSF	Glasgow	R169TLM	CentreWest
PSF315Y	Midland/Lowland	PUA311W	Yorkshire	R130XDT	Mainline	R170GSF	Glasgow
PSF316Y	Midland/Lowland	PUA312W	Yorkshire	R131GSF	Glasgow	R170TLM	CentreWest
PSU314	Midland/Lowland	PUA314W	Yorkshire	R131JYG	Yorkshire	R171GSF	Glasgow
PSU315	Midland/Lowland	PUA316W	Yorkshire	R131XDT	Mainline	R171TLM	CentreWest
PSU316	Midland/Lowland	PUA317W	Yorkshire	R132GSF	Glasgow	R172GSX	Glasgow
PSU317	Midland/Lowland	PUA318W	Yorkshire	R132JYG	Yorkshire	R172TLM	CentreWest
PSU320	Midland/Lowland	PUA319W	Yorkshire	R132XDT	Mainline	R173GSX	Glasgow
PSU321	Midland/Lowland	PUA320W	Yorkshire	R133GSF	Glasgow	R173TLM	CentreWest
PSU322	Midland/Lowland	PUA321W	Yorkshire	R133JYG	Yorkshire	R174GSX	Glasgow
PSU527	Bristol	PUA322W	Yorkshire	R133XDT	Mainline	R174TLM	CentreWest
PSU609	Aberdeen	PUA323W	Yorkshire	R134GSF	Glasgow	R175GSX	Glasgow
PSU622	Midland/Lowland	PUA324W	Yorkshire	R134JYG	Yorkshire	R175TLM	CentreWest
PSU623	Aberdeen	PUA325W	Yorkshire	R134XDT	Mainline	R175VWN	Cymru
PSU624	Aberdeen	PUA326W	Yorkshire	R135GSF	Glasgow	R176GSX	Glasgow
PSU625	Midland/Lowland	PUM148W	Eastern Counties	R135JYG	Yorkshire	R176HUG	Yorkshire
PSU626	Cymru	PUM149W	Yorkshire	R135XDT	Mainline	R176TLM	CentreWest
PSU627	Aberdeen	PUS157W	Southern National	R136GSF	Glasgow	R176VWN	Cymru
PSU628	Aberdeen	PVG25W	Eastern Counties	R136XDT	Mainline	R177GSX	Glasgow
PSU629	Aberdeen	PVG27W	Eastern Counties	R137GSF	Glasgow	R177TLM	CentreWest
PSU631	Midland/Lowland	PWY38W	Western National	R137JYG	Yorkshire	R177VWN	Cymru
PSU968	Aberdeen	PWY41W	Eastern Counties	R137XDT	Mainline	R178GSX	Glasgow
PTD640S	Yorkshire	PWY44W	Essex Buses	R138GSF	Glasgow	R178TLM	CentreWest
PTD642S	Yorkshire	PWY588W	Yorkshire	R138JYG	Yorkshire	R178VWN	Cymru
PTD646S	Yorkshire	PXI8935	Northampton	R138XDT	Mainline	R179GSX	Glasgow
PTD658S	Yorkshire	PYD427P	Southern National	R139EHS	Glasgow	R179TLM	CentreWest
PTT75R	Western National	Q276UOC	Midland Red	R139GSF	Glasgow	R180GSX	Glasgow
PTT90R	Southern National	Q553UOC	Midland Red	R139JYG	Yorkshire	R180TLM	CentreWest
PTT97R	Southern National	R1LCB	Leicester	R140EHS	Glasgow	R181GSX	Glasgow
PTT99R	Western National	R2LCB	Leicester	R140GSF	Glasgow	R181TLM	CentreWest
PUA252W	Yorkshire	R3FAL	Aberdeen	R141EHS	Glasgow	R182GSX	Glasgow
PUA253W	Yorkshire	R3LCB	Leicester	R141GSF	Glasgow	R182TLM	CentreWest
PUA254W	Yorkshire	R4LCB	Leicester	R142EHS	Glasgow	R183GSX	Glasgow
PUA255W	Yorkshire	R5FAL	Aberdeen	R142GSF	Glasgow	R183TLM	CentreWest
PUA256W	Yorkshire	R5LCB	Leicester	R143EHS	Glasgow	R184TLM	CentreWest
PUA257W	Yorkshire	R6LCB	Leicester	R143GSF	Glasgow	R185TLM	CentreWest
PUA258W	Yorkshire	R7LCB	Leicester	R144EHS	Glasgow	R186TLM	CentreWest
PUA259W	Yorkshire	R8LCB	Leicester	R144GSF	Glasgow	R187TLM	CentreWest
PUA260W	Yorkshire	R9LCB	Leicester	R145EHS	Glasgow	R188TLM	CentreWest
PUA261W	Yorkshire	R10LCB	Leicester	R145GSF	Glasgow	R189TLM	CentreWest
PUA262W	Yorkshire					R190TLM	CentreWest

Reg	Depot	Reg	Depot	Reg	Depot	Reg	Depot
R191VLD	CentreWest	R233SBA	Manchester	R289GHS	Glasgow	R341HYG	Yorkshire
R192VLD	CentreWest	R233TLM	CentreWest	R290GHS	Glasgow	R341SUT	Northampton
R193VLD	CentreWest	R234ERE	PMT	R291GHS	Glasgow	R342GHS	Glasgow
R194VLD	CentreWest	R234SBA	Manchester	R292GHS	Glasgow	R342HYG	Yorkshire
R195GSX	Glasgow	R234TLM	CentreWest	R293GHS	Glasgow	R342SUT	Northampton
R195VLD	CentreWest	R235ERE	PMT	R294GHS	Glasgow	R343GHS	Glasgow
R196VLD	CentreWest	R235SBA	Manchester	R295GHS	Glasgow	R343HYG	Yorkshire
R201TLM	CentreWest	R236ERE	PMT	R296GHS	Glasgow	R343SUT	Northampton
R202TLM	CentreWest	R236SBA	Manchester	R297AYB	Bristol	R344GHS	Glasgow
R203TLM	CentreWest	R237ERE	PMT	R297GHS	Glasgow	R344SUT	Leicester
R204TLM	CentreWest	R237SBA	Manchester	R298AYB	Bristol	R345GHS	Glasgow
R205TLM	CentreWest	R238ERE	PMT	R298GHS	Glasgow	R345SUT	Leicester
R206TLM	CentreWest	R238SBA	Manchester	R299AYB	Bristol	R346GHS	Glasgow
R207MSA	Aberdeen	R239ERE	PMT	R299GHS	Glasgow	R346SUT	Leicester
R207TLM	CentreWest	R239SBA	Manchester	R301GHS	Glasgow	R391ERE	PMT
R208MSA	Aberdeen	R240ERE	PMT	R301LKS	Midland/Lowland	R392ERE	PMT
R208TLM	CentreWest	R240SBA	Manchester	R302GHS	Glasgow	R393ERE	PMT
R209MSA	Aberdeen	R241ERE	PMT	R302LKS	Midland/Lowland	R394ERE	PMT
R209TLM	CentreWest	R241SBA	Manchester	R303GHS	Glasgow	R395ERE	PMT
R210MSA	Aberdeen	R242ERE	PMT	R303LKS	Midland/Lowland	R396ERE	PMT
R210TLM	CentreWest	R242SBA	Manchester	R304GHS	Glasgow	R401HYG	Glasgow
R211GSF	Glasgow	R243ERE	PMT	R304JAF	Western National	R402HYG	Glasgow
R211MSA	Aberdeen	R243SBA	Manchester	R304LKS	Midland/Lowland	R403HYG	Glasgow
R211TLM	CentreWest	R244ERE	PMT	R305GHS	Glasgow	R404HYG	Glasgow
R211VLX	CentreWest	R244SBA	Manchester	R305JAF	Western National	R405WWR	Yorkshire
R212MSA	Aberdeen	R245ERE	PMT	R305LKS	Midland/Lowland	R408WPX	Hampshire
R212TLM	CentreWest	R245SBA	Manchester	R306LKS	Midland/Lowland	R409WPX	Hampshire
R213MSA	Aberdeen	R246ERE	PMT	R307GHS	Glasgow	R410WPX	Hampshire
R213TLM	CentreWest	R246SBA	Manchester	R307JAF	Western National	R411VPU	Capital
R214MSA	Aberdeen	R247ERE	PMT	R307LKS	Midland/Lowland	R411WPX	Hampshire
R214SBA	Manchester	R247SBA	Manchester	R308GHS	Glasgow	R412VPU	Capital
R214TLM	CentreWest	R248ERE	PMT	R308JAF	Western National	R412WPX	Hampshire
R215MSA	Aberdeen	R248SBA	Manchester	R308LKS	Midland/Lowland	R413VPU	Capital
R215SBA	Manchester	R249ERE	PMT	R309GHS	Glasgow	R413WPX	Hampshire
R215TLM	CentreWest	R249SBA	Manchester	R309JAF	Western National	R414VPU	Capital
R216MSA	Aberdeen	R250ERE	PMT	R309LKS	Midland/Lowland	R414WPX	Hampshire
R216SBA	Manchester	R250SBA	Manchester	R310GHS	Glasgow	R415VPU	Capital
R216TLM	CentreWest	R251ERE	PMT	R310JAF	Western National	R415WPX	Hampshire
R217MSA	Aberdeen	R251SBA	Manchester	R310LKS	Midland/Lowland	R416RMS	Midland/Lowland
R217SBA	Manchester	R252ERE	PMT	R311GHS	Glasgow	R416VPU	Capital
R217TLM	CentreWest	R252SBA	Manchester	R311LKS	Midland/Lowland	R416WPX	Hampshire
R218MSA	Aberdeen	R253ERE	PMT	R312GHS	Glasgow	R417VPU	Capital
R218SBA	Manchester	R253SBA	Manchester	R312LKS	Midland/Lowland	R417WPX	Hampshire
R218TLM	CentreWest	R254ERE	PMT	R313GHS	Glasgow	R417YMS	Midland/Lowland
R219GFS	Midland/Lowland	R254SBA	Manchester	R313LKS	Midland/Lowland	R418VPU	Capital
R219MSA	Aberdeen	R255ERE	PMT	R314GHS	Glasgow	R418WPX	Hampshire
R219SBA	Manchester	R255SBA	Manchester	R314LKS	Midland/Lowland	R418YMS	Midland/Lowland
R219TLM	CentreWest	R256ERE	PMT	R315GHS	Glasgow	R419VPU	Capital
R220GFS	Midland/Lowland	R256SBA	Manchester	R315LKS	Midland/Lowland	R419WPX	Hampshire
R220MSA	Aberdeen	R257DVF	Eastern Counties	R316GHS	Glasgow	R419YMS	Midland/Lowland
R220SBA	Manchester	R257ERE	PMT	R319GHS	Glasgow	R420WPX	Hampshire
R220TLM	CentreWest	R257SBA	Manchester	R321GHS	Glasgow	R420YMS	Midland/Lowland
R221GFS	Midland/Lowland	R258DVF	Eastern Counties	R322GHS	Glasgow	R421WPX	Hampshire
R221MSA	Aberdeen	R258ERE	PMT	R322TLM	CentreWest	R421YMS	Midland/Lowland
R221SBA	Manchester	R258SBA	Manchester	R324GHS	Glasgow	R422WPX	Hampshire
R221TLM	CentreWest	R259DVF	Eastern Counties	R324HYG	Yorkshire	R422YMS	Midland/Lowland
R222MSA	Aberdeen	R259SBA	Manchester	R326GHS	Glasgow	R423WPX	Hampshire
R223GFS	Midland/Lowland	R260DVF	Eastern Counties	R326HYG	Yorkshire	R423YMS	Midland/Lowland
R223SBA	Manchester	R260SBA	Manchester	R327GHS	Glasgow	R424WPX	Hampshire
R223TLM	CentreWest	R261DVF	Eastern Counties	R327HYG	Yorkshire	R425WPX	Hampshire
R224GFS	Midland/Lowland	R261SBA	Manchester	R329GHS	Glasgow	R426SOY	Capital
R224TLM	CentreWest	R262DVF	Eastern Counties	R329HYG	Yorkshire	R426WPX	Hampshire
R225GFS	Midland/Lowland	R262SBA	Manchester	R330GHS	Glasgow	R427ULE	Capital
R225TLM	CentreWest	R263DVF	Eastern Counties	R330HYG	Yorkshire	R427WPX	Hampshire
R226GFS	Midland/Lowland	R263SBA	Manchester	R331GHS	Glasgow	R428ULE	Capital
R226SBA	Manchester	R264DVF	Eastern Counties	R331HYG	Yorkshire	R429ULE	Capital
R226TLM	CentreWest	R264SBA	Manchester	R332GHS	Glasgow	R430PSH	Midland/Lowland
R227GFS	Midland/Lowland	R265SBA	Manchester	R332HYG	Yorkshire	R430ULE	Capital
R227SBA	Manchester	R266SBA	Manchester	R334GHS	Glasgow	R431PSH	Midland/Lowland
R227TLM	CentreWest	R267SBA	Manchester	R334HYG	Yorkshire	R431ULE	Capital
R228GFS	Midland/Lowland	R268SBA	Manchester	R335GHS	Glasgow	R432PSH	Midland/Lowland
R228SBA	Manchester	R269SBA	Manchester	R335HYG	Yorkshire	R432ULE	Capital
R228TLM	CentreWest	R270SBA	Manchester	R336GHS	Glasgow	R433PSH	Midland/Lowland
R229GFS	Midland/Lowland	R271SBA	Manchester	R336HYG	Yorkshire	R433ULE	Capital
R229SBA	Manchester	R272SBA	Manchester	R337GHS	Glasgow	R434GSF	Yorkshire
R229TLM	CentreWest	R273SBA	Manchester	R337HYG	Yorkshire	R434PSH	Midland/Lowland
R230SBA	Manchester	R274SBA	Manchester	R338GHS	Glasgow	R434ULE	Capital
R230TLM	CentreWest	R275SBA	Manchester	R338HYG	Yorkshire	R435ULE	Capital
R231SBA	Manchester	R276SBA	Manchester	R339GHS	Glasgow	R436ULE	Capital
R231TLM	CentreWest	R277SBA	Manchester	R339HYG	Yorkshire	R437GSF	Yorkshire
R232ERE	PMT	R278SBA	Manchester	R340GHS	Glasgow	R437ULE	Capital
R232SBA	Manchester	R279SBA	Manchester	R340HYG	Yorkshire	R438ALS	Yorkshire
R232TLM	CentreWest	R280SBA	Manchester			R438ULE	Capital
R233ERE	PMT	R288GHS	Glasgow				

Reg	Area	Reg	Area	Reg	Area	Reg	Area
R439ALS	Yorkshire	R489EDW	Cymru	R611JUB	Yorkshire	R643CVR	Manchester
R439ULE	Capital	R490EDW	Cymru	R611YCR	Hampshire	R643DUS	Glasgow
R440ALS	Yorkshire	R501CNP	Midland Red	R612JUB	Yorkshire	R643HYG	Yorkshire
R440ULE	Capital	R501NPR	Southern National	R612YCR	Hampshire	R643TLM	CentreWest
R441ALS	Yorkshire	R502CNP	Midland Red	R613JUB	Yorkshire	R644CVR	Manchester
R441ULE	Capital	R502NPR	Southern National	R613YCR	Hampshire	R644DUS	Glasgow
R442ALS	Yorkshire	R503CNP	Midland Red	R614JUB	Yorkshire	R644HYG	Yorkshire
R442ULE	Capital	R503NPR	Southern National	R614YCR	Hampshire	R644TLM	CentreWest
R443ALS	Midland/Lowland	R504CNP	Midland Red	R615JUB	Yorkshire	R645CVR	Manchester
R443ULE	Capital	R504NPR	Southern National	R615YCR	Hampshire	R645DUS	Glasgow
R445ALS	Midland/Lowland	R505CNP	Midland Red	R616JUB	Yorkshire	R645HYG	Yorkshire
R445CCV	Western National	R505NPR	Southern National	R616YCR	Hampshire	R645TLM	CentreWest
R445ULE	Capital	R506CNP	Midland Red	R617JUB	Yorkshire	R646CVR	Manchester
R446ALS	Midland/Lowland	R506NPR	Southern National	R617YCR	Hampshire	R646DUS	Glasgow
R446ULE	Capital	R507CNP	Midland Red	R618JUB	Yorkshire	R646HYG	Yorkshire
R447ALS	Midland/Lowland	R507NPR	Southern National	R618YCR	Hampshire	R646TLM	CentreWest
R447CCV	Western National	R508NPR	Southern National	R619JUB	Yorkshire	R647CVR	Manchester
R447ULE	Capital	R521BMS	Midland/Lowland	R619YCR	Hampshire	R647DUS	Glasgow
R448ALS	Midland/Lowland	R522BMS	Midland/Lowland	R620JUB	Yorkshire	R647HYG	Yorkshire
R448CCV	Western National	R524BMS	Midland/Lowland	R620YCR	Hampshire	R647TLM	CentreWest
R448ULE	Capital	R544ALS	Midland/Lowland	R621CVR	Manchester	R648CVR	Manchester
R449ALS	Midland/Lowland	R551CNG	Eastern Counties	R621JUB	Yorkshire	R648HYG	Yorkshire
R449CCV	Western National	R552CNG	Eastern Counties	R621YCR	Hampshire	R648TLM	CentreWest
R449JSG	Yorkshire	R553CNG	Eastern Counties	R622CVR	Manchester	R649CVR	Manchester
R449ULE	Capital	R554CNG	Eastern Counties	R622JUB	Yorkshire	R649HYG	Yorkshire
R450CCV	Western National	R556CNG	Eastern Counties	R622YCR	Hampshire	R649TLM	CentreWest
R450JSG	Yorkshire	R571YNC	Manchester	R623CVR	Manchester	R650CVR	Manchester
R450ULE	Capital	R572SBA	Manchester	R623JUB	Yorkshire	R650HYG	Yorkshire
R451CCV	Western National	R573SBA	Manchester	R623YCR	Hampshire	R650TDV	Western National
R451JSG	Yorkshire	R574SBA	Manchester	R624CVR	Manchester	R650TLM	CentreWest
R452CCV	Western National	R575SBA	Manchester	R624JUB	Yorkshire	R651CVR	Manchester
R452JSG	Yorkshire	R576SBA	Manchester	R625CVR	Manchester	R651HYG	Yorkshire
R453CCV	Western National	R577SBA	Manchester	R625JUB	Yorkshire	R651TLM	CentreWest
R453JFS	Yorkshire	R578SBA	Manchester	R626CVR	Manchester	R652HYG	Yorkshire
R454CCV	Western National	R579SBA	Manchester	R626JUB	Yorkshire	R652TLM	CentreWest
R454JFS	Yorkshire	R580SBA	Manchester	R627CVR	Manchester	R653HYG	Yorkshire
R455JFS	Yorkshire	R581SWN	Cymru	R627JUB	Yorkshire	R653TLM	CentreWest
R456CCV	Western National	R582SBA	Manchester	R628CVR	Manchester	R654DUS	Glasgow
R456JFS	Yorkshire	R582YMS	Cymru	R629CVR	Manchester	R655DUS	Glasgow
R457CCV	Western National	R582YMS	Midland/Lowland	R629JUB	Yorkshire	R656DUS	Glasgow
R457JFS	Yorkshire	R583SBA	Manchester	R630CVR	Manchester	R657DUS	Glasgow
R458BNG	Eastern Counties	R583SWN	Cymru	R630JUB	Yorkshire	R658DUS	Glasgow
R458CCV	Western National	R583YMS	Midland/Lowland	R631CVR	Manchester	R659DUS	Glasgow
R458JFS	Yorkshire	R584SBA	Manchester	R631DUS	Glasgow	R660DUS	Glasgow
R459BNG	Eastern Counties	R584SWN	Cymru	R631JUB	Yorkshire	R661DUS	Glasgow
R459CCV	Western National	R584YMS	Midland/Lowland	R632CVR	Manchester	R661NHY	Bristol
R459JFS	Yorkshire	R585SBA	Manchester	R632DUS	Glasgow	R662DUS	Glasgow
R460BNG	Eastern Counties	R585SWN	Cymru	R632JUB	Yorkshire	R662NHY	Bristol
R460CCV	Western National	R585YMS	Midland/Lowland	R633CVR	Manchester	R663DUS	Glasgow
R460JFS	Yorkshire	R586SBA	Manchester	R633DUS	Glasgow	R663NHY	Bristol
R461BNG	Eastern Counties	R586SWN	Cymru	R633JUB	Yorkshire	R664DUS	Glasgow
R461CCV	Western National	R586YMS	Midland/Lowland	R633VLX	CentreWest	R664NHY	Bristol
R461JFS	Yorkshire	R587BMS	Midland/Lowland	R634CVR	Manchester	R665DUS	Glasgow
R462BNG	Eastern Counties	R587SBA	Manchester	R634DUS	Glasgow	R667DUS	Glasgow
R462CCV	Western National	R587SWN	Cymru	R634JUB	Yorkshire	R668DUS	Glasgow
R462JFS	Yorkshire	R588BMS	Midland/Lowland	R634VLX	CentreWest	R669DUS	Glasgow
R463CAH	Eastern Counties	R588SBA	Manchester	R635CVR	Manchester	R670DUS	Glasgow
R463CCV	Western National	R588SWN	Cymru	R635JUB	Yorkshire	R671DUS	Glasgow
R463JFS	Yorkshire	R589BMS	Midland/Lowland	R636CVR	Manchester	R672DUS	Glasgow
R464CAH	Eastern Counties	R589SBA	Manchester	R636DUS	Glasgow	R673DUS	Glasgow
R464CCV	Western National	R589SWN	Cymru	R636HYG	Yorkshire	R674DUS	Glasgow
R464JFS	Midland/Lowland	R590BMS	Midland/Lowland	R636VLX	CentreWest	R675DUS	Glasgow
R465CAH	Eastern Counties	R590SBA	Manchester	R637CVR	Manchester	R676DUS	Glasgow
R466CAH	Eastern Counties	R590SWN	Cymru	R637DUS	Glasgow	R677DUS	Glasgow
R467CAH	Eastern Counties	R591BMS	Midland/Lowland	R637HYG	Yorkshire	R678DUS	Glasgow
R468CAH	Eastern Counties	R591SBA	Manchester	R637VLX	CentreWest	R680DPW	Eastern Counties
R469CAH	Eastern Counties	R591SWN	Cymru	R638CVR	Manchester	R681DPW	Eastern Counties
R470CAH	Eastern Counties	R592SWN	Cymru	R638DUS	Glasgow	R682DPW	Eastern Counties
R471CAH	Eastern Counties	R593SWN	Cymru	R638HYG	Yorkshire	R683DPW	Eastern Counties
R472CAH	Eastern Counties	R594SWN	Cymru	R638VLX	CentreWest	R684DPW	Eastern Counties
R473CAH	Eastern Counties	R595SWN	Cymru	R639CVR	Manchester	R685DPW	Eastern Counties
R474CAH	Eastern Counties	R596SWN	Cymru	R639HYG	Yorkshire	R686DPW	Eastern Counties
R475CAH	Eastern Counties	R597SWN	Cymru	R639VLX	CentreWest	R687DPW	Eastern Counties
R476CAH	Eastern Counties	R598SWN	Cymru	R640CVR	Manchester	R688DPW	Eastern Counties
R477CAH	Eastern Counties	R599SWN	Cymru	R640HYG	Yorkshire	R689DPW	Eastern Counties
R478CAH	Eastern Counties			R640VLX	CentreWest	R701BAE	Bristol
R481EDW	Cymru	R606JUB	Yorkshire	R641CVR	Manchester	R702BAE	Bristol
R482EDW	Cymru	R607JUB	Yorkshire	R641DUS	Glasgow	R703BAE	Bristol
R483EDW	Cymru	R608JUB	Yorkshire	R641HYG	Yorkshire	R704BAE	Bristol
R484EDW	Cymru	R608YCR	Hampshire	R641VLX	CentreWest	R705BAE	Bristol
R485EDW	Cymru	R609JUB	Yorkshire	R642CVR	Manchester	R705VLA	Capital
R486EDW	Cymru	R609YCR	Hampshire	R642DUS	Glasgow	R706BAE	Bristol
R487EDW	Cymru	R610JUB	Yorkshire	R642HYG	Yorkshire	R706VLA	Capital
R488EDW	Cymru	R610YCR	Hampshire	R642TLM	CentreWest	R707BAE	Bristol

Reg	Operator	Reg	Operator	Reg	Operator	Reg	Operator
R707VLA	Capital	R913BOU	Bristol	S114TNB	Manchester	S270SFA	PMT
R708BAE	Bristol	R914BOU	Bristol	S115CSG	Yorkshire	S271LGA	Glasgow
R708VLA	Capital	R915BOU	Bristol	S115TNB	Manchester	S272LGA	Glasgow
R709BAE	Bristol	R916BOU	Bristol	S116CSG	Yorkshire	S301EWU	Yorkshire
R709VLA	Capital	R917BOU	Bristol	S116JTP	Hampshire	S302EWU	Yorkshire
R710BAE	Bristol	R918BOU	Bristol	S116RKG	Cymru	S303EWU	Yorkshire
R710VLA	Capital	R919BOU	Bristol	S117CSG	Yorkshire	S304EWU	Yorkshire
R711BAE	Bristol	R920COU	Bristol	S117JTP	Hampshire	S305EWU	Yorkshire
R711VLA	Capital	R977NVT	PMT	S118CSG	Yorkshire	S306EWU	Yorkshire
R712BAE	Bristol	R978NVT	PMT	S118JTP	Hampshire	S311SCV	Western National
R712DJN	Essex Buses	R979NVT	PMT	S119CSG	Yorkshire	S312SCV	Western National
R712VLA	Capital	R980NVT	PMT	S119JTP	Hampshire	S313SCV	Western National
R713BAE	Bristol	R981NVT	PMT	S120JTP	Hampshire	S314SRL	Western National
R713DJN	Essex Buses	RAH258W	Eastern Counties	S121JTP	Hampshire	S315SRL	Western National
R713VLA	Capital	RAH259W	Eastern Counties	S122UOT	Hampshire	S340WYB	Southern National
R714BAE	Bristol	RAH261W	Eastern Counties	S197KLM	CentreWest	S341EWU	Yorkshire
R714DJN	Essex Buses	RAH262W	Eastern Counties	S198KLM	CentreWest	S342EWU	Yorkshire
R714VLA	Capital	RAH263W	Eastern Counties	S199KLM	CentreWest	S343EWU	Yorkshire
R715BAE	Bristol	RAH266W	Eastern Counties	S206LLO	Capital	S344EWU	Yorkshire
R715DJN	Essex Buses	RAH267W	Eastern Counties	S207LLO	Capital	S345EWU	Yorkshire
R715VLA	Capital	RAH269W	Eastern Counties	S208LLO	Capital	S347MFP	Leicester
R716BAE	Bristol	RAH270W	Eastern Counties	S209LLO	Capital	S348MFP	Leicester
R716DJN	Essex Buses	RBW176P	Southern National	S210LLO	Capital	S349MFP	Leicester
R716VLA	Capital	RDS585W	Glasgow	S211CSG	Yorkshire	S350MFP	Leicester
R717BAE	Bristol	RDS588W	Glasgow	S211LLO	Capital	S351MFP	Leicester
R717DJN	Essex Buses	RDS589W	Glasgow	S212LLO	Capital	S351NPO	Hampshire
R717VLA	Capital	RDS591W	Glasgow	S213LLO	Capital	S352MFP	Leicester
R718BAE	Bristol	RDS592W	Glasgow	S214LLO	Capital	S352NPO	Hampshire
R718DJN	Essex Buses	RDS605W	Glasgow	S215LLO	Capital	S353MFP	Leicester
R719DJN	Essex Buses	RDS606W	Glasgow	S216LLO	Capital	S353NPO	Hampshire
R719RAD	Bristol	REU326S	Southern National	S217LLO	Capital	S354MFP	Leicester
R720DJN	Essex Buses	RG1173	Aberdeen	S218LLO	Capital	S354NPO	Hampshire
R721DJN	Essex Buses	RHE986R	Western National	S219LLO	Capital	S355MFP	Leicester
R722HHK	Yorkshire	RHE987R	Western National	S220GKS	Yorkshire	S355XCR	Hampshire
R723HHK	Yorkshire	RHT503S	Western National	S220KLM	CentreWest	S356MFP	Leicester
R724HHK	Yorkshire	RHT504S	Hampshire	S220LLO	Capital	S356XCR	Hampshire
R725HHK	Yorkshire	RIL1053	Southern National	S221LLO	Capital	S357MFP	Leicester
R726HHK	Yorkshire	RIL1055	Southern National	S235KLM	CentreWest	S357XCR	Hampshire
R739TMO	Midland Red	RIL1056	Southern National	S236KLM	CentreWest	S358MFP	Leicester
R756DYS	Glasgow	RIL1057	Southern National	S237KLM	CentreWest	S358XCR	Hampshire
R757DYS	Glasgow	RIL1058	Southern National	S238KLM	CentreWest	S359MFP	Northampton
R758DYS	Glasgow	RIL1059	Southern National	S239KLM	CentreWest	S359XCR	Hampshire
R759DYS	Glasgow	RIL1172	Western National	S240CSF	Midland/Lowland	S360MFP	Northampton
R781WKW	Mainline	RJ2720	Bristol	S240KLM	CentreWest	S360XCR	Hampshire
R782WKW	Mainline	RJT147R	Hampshire	S241CSF	Midland/Lowland	S361MFP	Northampton
R783WKW	Mainline	RJT148R	Hampshire	S241KLM	CentreWest	S361XCR	Hampshire
R784WKW	Mainline	RKA869T	Bristol	S242CSF	Midland/Lowland	S362XCR	Hampshire
R785WKW	Mainline	RMS398W	Midland/Lowland	S242KLM	CentreWest	S363XCR	Hampshire
R787WKW	Mainline	RMS400W	Midland/Lowland	S243CSF	Midland/Lowland	S395HVV	Manchester
R788WKW	Mainline	RSG325V	Western National	S243KLM	CentreWest	S396HVV	Manchester
R789WKW	Mainline	RSG815V	Southern National	S244CSF	Midland/Lowland	S397HVV	Manchester
R790WKW	Mainline	RSX84J	Midland/Lowland	S244KLM	CentreWest	S406GUB	Yorkshire
R810NVT	PMT	RTH926S	Western National	S245CSF	Midland/Lowland	S407GUB	Yorkshire
R811NVT	PMT	RTH929S	Western National	S245KLM	CentreWest	S408GUB	Yorkshire
R812NVT	PMT	RTH931S	Bristol	S246CSF	Midland/Lowland	S409GUB	Yorkshire
R814HWS	Bristol	RUF40R	Western National	S246KLM	CentreWest	S410GUB	Yorkshire
R818HWS	Bristol	RUH346	Western National	S247CSF	Midland/Lowland	S411GUB	Yorkshire
R835VLX	CentreWest	RWT534R	Yorkshire	S247KLM	CentreWest	S412GUB	Yorkshire
R844YLC	Capital	S101CSG	Yorkshire	S248CSF	Midland/Lowland	S413GUB	Yorkshire
R851YDV	Western National	S101TNB	Manchester	S248KLM	CentreWest	S414GUB	Yorkshire
R852TFJ	Western National	S102CSG	Yorkshire	S249CSF	Midland/Lowland	S415GUB	Yorkshire
R853TFJ	Western National	S102TNB	Manchester	S250CSF	Midland/Lowland	S422LLO	Capital
R871ERE	PMT	S103CSG	Yorkshire	S251AFA	PMT	S443BSG	Yorkshire
R872ERE	PMT	S103TNB	Manchester	S251CSF	Midland/Lowland	S445BSG	Yorkshire
R873ERE	PMT	S104CSG	Yorkshire	S252AFA	PMT	S446BSG	Yorkshire
R874ERE	PMT	S104TNB	Manchester	S253AFA	PMT	S447BSG	Yorkshire
R875ERE	PMT	S105CSG	Yorkshire	S253JLP	CentreWest	S448BSG	Yorkshire
R876ERE	PMT	S105TNB	Manchester	S254AFA	PMT	S451SLL	Capital
R877ERE	PMT	S106CSG	Yorkshire	S254JLP	CentreWest	S452SLL	Capital
R878ERE	PMT	S106TNB	Manchester	S255AFA	PMT	S453SLL	Capital
R879HRF	PMT	S107CSG	Yorkshire	S255JLP	CentreWest	S454SLL	Capital
R880HRF	PMT	S107TNB	Manchester	S256AFA	PMT	S508RWP	Midland Red
R881HRF	PMT	S108CSG	Yorkshire	S256JLP	CentreWest	S508UAK	Mainline
R901BOU	Bristol	S108TNB	Manchester	S259SFA	PMT	S509RWP	Midland Red
R902BOU	Bristol	S109CSG	Yorkshire	S260SFA	PMT	S509UAK	Mainline
R903BOU	Bristol	S109TNB	Manchester	S261SFA	Cymru	S510RWP	Midland Red
R904BOU	Bristol	S110CSG	Yorkshire	S262SFA	PMT	S510UAK	Mainline
R905BOU	Bristol	S110TNB	Manchester	S263SFA	PMT	S511RWP	Midland Red
R906BOU	Bristol	S111FML	Manchester	S264SFA	PMT	S511UAK	Mainline
R907BOU	Bristol	S112CSG	Yorkshire	S265SFA	PMT	S512RWP	Midland Red
R908BOU	Bristol	S112TNB	Manchester	S266SFA	PMT	S512UAK	Mainline
R909BOU	Bristol	S113CSG	Yorkshire	S267SFA	PMT	S513RWP	Midland Red
R910BOU	Bristol	S113TNB	Manchester	S268SFA	PMT	S513UAK	Mainline
R912BOU	Bristol	S114CSG	Yorkshire	S269SFA	PMT	S514RWP	Midland Red

Registration	Operator	Registration	Operator	Registration	Operator	Registration	Operator
S514UAK	Mainline	S560RWP	Midland Red	S675AAE	Bristol	S819AEH	PMT
S515RWP	Midland Red	S561JSE	Aberdeen	S675SVU	Yorkshire	S819KPR	Southern National
S515UAK	Mainline	S561RWP	Midland Red	S676AAE	Bristol	S820AEH	PMT
S516RWP	Midland Red	S562RWP	Midland Red	S676SVU	Yorkshire	S820KPR	Southern National
S516UAK	Mainline	S563RWP	Midland Red	S677AAE	Bristol	S821AEH	PMT
S517RWP	Midland Red	S564RWP	Midland Red	S677SVU	Yorkshire	S821KPR	Southern National
S517UAK	Mainline	S565TPW	Eastern Counties	S678AAE	Bristol	S822KPR	Southern National
S518RWP	Midland Red	S566TPW	Eastern Counties	S679AAE	Bristol	S823KPR	Southern National
S518UAK	Mainline	S567TPW	Eastern Counties	S680AAE	Bristol	S823TCL	Eastern Counties
S519RWP	Midland Red	S568TPW	Eastern Counties	S681AAE	Bristol	S824TCL	Eastern Counties
S519UAK	Mainline	S569TPW	Eastern Counties	S682AAE	Bristol	S824WYD	Southern National
S520RWP	Midland Red	S570TPW	Eastern Counties	S683AAE	Bristol	S825TCL	Eastern Counties
S520UAK	Mainline	S571TPW	Eastern Counties	S684AAE	Bristol	S825WYD	Southern National
S520UMS	Midland/Lowland	S572TPW	Eastern Counties	S684BFS	Glasgow	S826TCL	Eastern Counties
S521RWP	Midland Red	S573TPW	Eastern Counties	S685AAE	Bristol	S827TCL	Eastern Counties
S521UAK	Mainline	S574TPW	Eastern Counties	S685BFS	Glasgow	S828TCL	Eastern Counties
S522RWP	Midland Red	S624KTP	Hampshire	S686AAE	Bristol	S829TCL	Eastern Counties
S522UAK	Mainline	S625KTP	Hampshire	S686BFS	Glasgow	S830TCL	Eastern Counties
S523RWP	Midland Red	S626KTP	Hampshire	S686BFS	Glasgow	S831TCL	Eastern Counties
S523UAK	Mainline	S627KTP	Hampshire	S687AAE	Bristol	S832TCL	Eastern Counties
S523UMS	Midland/Lowland	S628KTP	Hampshire	S687BFS	Glasgow	S838VAG	Capital
S524RWP	Midland Red	S629KTP	Hampshire	S688AAE	Bristol	S863LRU	Southern National
S524UAK	Mainline	S630KTP	Hampshire	S688BFS	Glasgow	S864LRU	Southern National
S525RWP	Midland Red	S631KTP	Hampshire	S689AAE	Bristol	S865NOD	Western National
S525UAK	Mainline	S632KTP	Hampshire	S689BFS	Glasgow	S866NOD	Western National
S525UMS	Midland/Lowland	S633KTP	Hampshire	S690AAE	Bristol	S867NOD	Western National
S526RWP	Midland Red	S634KTP	Hampshire	S690BFS	Glasgow	S868NOD	Western National
S526UAK	Mainline	S635XCR	Hampshire	S691AAE	Bristol	S869NOD	Western National
S526UMS	Midland/Lowland	S636XCR	Hampshire	S691BFS	Glasgow	S870NOD	Western National
S527RWP	Midland Red	S637XCR	Hampshire	S692BFS	Glasgow	S871NOD	Western National
S527UAK	Mainline	S638XCR	Hampshire	S693BFS	Glasgow	S872NOD	Western National
S528RWP	Midland Red	S639XCR	Hampshire	S694BFS	Glasgow	S924AKS	Midland/Lowland
S528UAK	Mainline	S640XCR	Hampshire	S697BFS	Glasgow	S925AKS	Midland/Lowland
S529RWP	Midland Red	S641XCR	Hampshire	S698BFS	Glasgow	S926AKS	Midland/Lowland
S529UAK	Mainline	S642XCR	Hampshire	S699BFS	Glasgow	S927AKS	Midland/Lowland
S530RWP	Midland Red	S644BSG	Yorkshire	S701BFS	Glasgow	S928AKS	Midland/Lowland
S530UAK	Mainline	S651RNA	Manchester	S720AFB	Bristol	S929AKS	Midland/Lowland
S531RWP	Midland Red	S652RNA	Manchester	S721AFB	Bristol	S930AKS	Midland/Lowland
S531UAK	Mainline	S653RNA	Manchester	S722AFB	Bristol	S931AKS	Midland/Lowland
S532RWP	Midland Red	S654FWY	Yorkshire	S723AFB	Bristol	S932AKS	Midland/Lowland
S532UAK	Mainline	S654NUG	Manchester	S724AFB	Bristol	S933AKS	Midland/Lowland
S533RWP	Midland Red	S654RNA	Manchester	S725AFB	Bristol	S934AKS	Midland/Lowland
S533UAK	Mainline	S655FWY	Yorkshire	S729TWC	Essex Buses	S935AKS	Midland/Lowland
S534RWP	Midland Red	S655NUG	Manchester	S730TWC	Essex Buses	S936AKS	Midland/Lowland
S534UAK	Mainline	S655RNA	Manchester	S731TWC	Essex Buses	S937AKS	Midland/Lowland
S535RWP	Midland Red	S656FWY	Yorkshire	S732TWC	Essex Buses	S938AKS	Midland/Lowland
S535UAK	Mainline	S656NUG	Manchester	S733TWC	Essex Buses	S955RWP	Midland Red
S536RWP	Midland Red	S656RNA	Manchester	S734TWC	Essex Buses	S979JLM	Eastern Counties
S536UAK	Mainline	S657FWY	Yorkshire	S735TWC	Essex Buses	S992UJA	Manchester
S537RWP	Midland Red	S657NUG	Manchester	S737TWC	Essex Buses	S993UJA	Manchester
S537UAK	Mainline	S657RNA	Manchester	S737TWC	Essex Buses	S994UJA	Manchester
S538RWP	Midland Red	S658FWY	Yorkshire	S738TWC	Essex Buses	S995UJA	Manchester
S538UAK	Mainline	S658NUG	Manchester	S781RNE	Midland/Lowland	SBK740S	Hampshire
S539RWP	Midland Red	S658RNA	Yorkshire	S791RWG	Mainline	SDT221Y	Mainline
S540RWP	Midland Red	S659FWY	Yorkshire	S792RWG	Mainline	SDT222Y	Mainline
S541RWP	Midland Red	S659NUG	Manchester	S793RWG	Mainline	SDT224Y	Mainline
S542RWP	Midland Red	S659RNA	Yorkshire	S794RWG	Mainline	SDT226Y	Mainline
S543RWP	Midland Red	S660NUG	Manchester	S795RWG	Mainline	SDT227Y	Mainline
S544RWP	Midland Red	S660RNA	Yorkshire	S796RWG	Mainline	SDT228Y	Mainline
S545RWP	Midland Red	S661NUG	Manchester	S797RWG	Mainline	SDT229Y	Mainline
S546RWP	Midland Red	S661RNA	Manchester	S798RWG	Mainline	SDT230Y	Mainline
S547RWP	Midland Red	S662NUG	Manchester	S799RWG	Mainline	SDT231Y	Mainline
S548RWP	Midland Red	S662RNA	Yorkshire	S801RWG	Mainline	SDT232Y	Mainline
S549RWP	Midland Red	S663NUG	Manchester	S802RWG	Mainline	SDT234Y	Mainline
S550JSE	Aberdeen	S663RNA	Yorkshire	S803RWG	Mainline	SDT235Y	Mainline
S550RWP	Midland Red	S664RNA	Yorkshire	S804RWG	Mainline	SDT236Y	Mainline
S551JSE	Aberdeen	S665AAE	Bristol	S805RWG	Mainline	SDT237Y	Mainline
S551RWP	Midland Red	S665RNA	Yorkshire	S806RWG	Mainline	SDT238Y	Mainline
S552JSE	Aberdeen	S667AAE	Bristol	S807RWG	Mainline	SDT239Y	Mainline
S552RWP	Midland Red	S667RNA	Yorkshire	S808RWG	Mainline	SDT240Y	Mainline
S553JSE	Aberdeen	S668AAE	Bristol	S809RWG	Mainline	SDT241Y	Mainline
S553RWP	Midland Red	S668RNA	Yorkshire	S810RWG	Mainline	SDT242Y	Mainline
S554JSE	Aberdeen	S669AAE	Bristol	S811RWG	Mainline	SDT243Y	Mainline
S554RWP	Midland Red	S669SVU	Manchester	S812RWG	Mainline	SDT244Y	Mainline
S555JSE	Aberdeen	S670AAE	Bristol	S813AEH	PMT	SDT245Y	Mainline
S556JSE	Aberdeen	S670SVU	Manchester	S813RWG	Mainline	SDT247Y	Mainline
S556RWP	Midland Red	S671AAE	Bristol	S814AEH	PMT	SDT248Y	Mainline
S557JSE	Aberdeen	S671SVU	Manchester	S814RWG	Mainline	SDT249Y	Mainline
S557RWP	Midland Red	S672AAE	Bristol	S815AEH	PMT	SDT250Y	Mainline
S558JSE	Aberdeen	S672SVU	Manchester	S816AEH	PMT	SDT251Y	Mainline
S558RWP	Midland Red	S673AAE	Bristol	S817AEH	PMT	SDT252Y	Mainline
S559JSE	Aberdeen	S673SVU	Manchester	S817KPR	Southern National	SDT253Y	Mainline
S559RWP	Midland Red	S674AAE	Bristol	S818AEH	PMT	SDT254Y	Mainline
S560JSE	Aberdeen	S674SVU	Yorkshire	S818KPR	Southern National	SDT255Y	Mainline

Reg	Fleet	Reg	Fleet	Reg	Fleet	Reg	Fleet
SDT256Y	Mainline	SND503X	Manchester	T258JLD	CentreWest	T471JCV	Western National
SDT257Y	Mainline	SND504X	Manchester	T259JLD	CentreWest	T506JNA	Manchester
SDT258Y	Mainline	SND507X	Manchester	T260JLD	CentreWest	T507JNA	Manchester
SDT259Y	Mainline	SND508X	Manchester	T261JLD	CentreWest	T508JNA	Manchester
SDT260Y	Mainline	SND509X	Manchester	T262JLD	CentreWest	T509JNA	Manchester
SDT261Y	Mainline	SND516X	Manchester	T263JLD	CentreWest	T510JNA	Manchester
SDT262Y	Mainline	SND517X	Manchester	T264JLD	CentreWest	T511JNA	Manchester
SDT263Y	Mainline	SND522X	Manchester	T265JLD	CentreWest	T512JNA	Manchester
SDT264Y	Mainline	SND523X	Manchester	T266JLD	CentreWest	T513JNA	Manchester
SDT266Y	Mainline	SND524X	Manchester	T267JLD	CentreWest	T514JNA	Manchester
SDT267Y	Mainline	SND529X	Manchester	T268JLD	CentreWest	T515JNA	Manchester
SDT268Y	Mainline	SNS827W	Hampshire	T269JLD	CentreWest	T575JNG	Eastern Counties
SDT270Y	Mainline	SOA658S	Midland Red	T270JLD	CentreWest	T576JNG	Eastern Counties
SDT272Y	Mainline	SPR40R	Hampshire	T271JLD	CentreWest	T577JNG	Eastern Counties
SDT273Y	Mainline	SPR41R	Hampshire	T272JLD	CentreWest	T578JNG	Eastern Counties
SDT274Y	Mainline	SRS56K	Aberdeen	T273JLD	CentreWest	T579JNG	Eastern Counties
SFJ100R	Western National	SSC108P	Midland/Lowland	T274JLD	CentreWest	T580JNG	Eastern Counties
SFJ101R	Hampshire	SSU437	Bristol	T275JLD	CentreWest	T622CEJ	Cymru
SFJ105R	Western National	SSU816	Midland/Lowland	T276JLD	CentreWest	T623CEJ	Cymru
SFJ106R	Western National	SSU821	Leicester	T277JLD	CentreWest	T624CEJ	Cymru
SFJ144R	Western National	SSU837	Midland/Lowland	T278JLD	CentreWest	T625CEJ	Cymru
SFX785R	Southern National	SSU857	Midland/Lowland	T279JLD	CentreWest	T626CEJ	Cymru
SHO628P	Cymru	SSU859	Midland/Lowland	T280JLD	CentreWest	T627CEJ	Cymru
SKF11T	Bristol	SSU897	Midland/Lowland	T281JLD	CentreWest	T628CEJ	Cymru
SMK664F	CentreWest	SSX602V	Midland/Lowland	T282JLD	CentreWest	T629CEJ	Cymru
SMK667F	CentreWest	SSX603V	Midland/Lowland	T283JLD	CentreWest	T630CEJ	Cymru
SMK672F	CentreWest	SSX607V	Midland/Lowland	T284JLD	CentreWest	T631CEJ	Cymru
SMK677F	CentreWest	STW19W	Yorkshire	T285JLD	CentreWest	T632CEJ	Cymru
SMK687F	CentreWest	STW21W	Essex Buses	T286JLD	CentreWest	T633CEJ	Cymru
SMK717F	CentreWest	STW22W	Essex Buses	T287JLD	CentreWest	T634CEJ	Cymru
SMK724F	CentreWest	STW23W	Essex Buses	T288JLD	CentreWest	T635CEJ	Cymru
SMK735F	CentreWest	STW27W	Essex Buses	T289JLD	CentreWest	T636CEJ	Cymru
SMK740F	CentreWest	STW28W	Essex Buses	T290JLD	CentreWest	T637CEJ	Cymru
SND101X	Manchester	STW33W	Bristol	T291JLD	CentreWest	T650SSF	Essex Buses
SND102X	Manchester	STW34W	Western National	T292JLD	CentreWest	T651SSF	Essex Buses
SND103X	Manchester	STW36W	Essex Buses	T293JLD	CentreWest	T652SSF	Essex Buses
SND104X	Manchester	STW37W	Essex Buses	T294JLD	CentreWest	T653SSF	Essex Buses
SND112X	Manchester	STW38W	Essex Buses	T295JLD	CentreWest	T654SSF	Essex Buses
SND114X	Manchester	SUA128R	Yorkshire	T296JLD	CentreWest	T660VWU	Yorkshire
SND115X	Manchester	SUA140R	Yorkshire	T297JLD	CentreWest	T661VWU	Yorkshire
SND122X	Manchester	SUA147R	Yorkshire	T298JLD	CentreWest	T662VWU	Yorkshire
SND126X	Manchester	SUM129W	Eastern Counties	T299JLD	CentreWest	T663VWU	Yorkshire
SND129X	Manchester	SWB287L	Mainline	T301JLD	CentreWest	T664VWU	Yorkshire
SND130X	Manchester	SWX533W	Yorkshire	T302JLD	CentreWest	T665VWU	Yorkshire
SND131X	Manchester	SWX534W	Hampshire	T303JLD	CentreWest	T701JLD	CentreWest
SND133X	Manchester	SWX537W	Yorkshire	T304JLD	CentreWest	T702JLD	CentreWest
SND135X	Cymru	SWX540W	Yorkshire	T305JLD	CentreWest	T703JLD	CentreWest
SND136X	Manchester	T59BUB	Yorkshire	T306JLD	CentreWest	T704JLD	CentreWest
SND137X	Manchester	T101VWU	Yorkshire	T307VYG	Yorkshire	T705JLD	CentreWest
SND138X	Manchester	T102VWU	Yorkshire	T308VYG	Yorkshire	T706JLD	CentreWest
SND139X	Manchester	T103VWU	Yorkshire	T309VYG	Yorkshire	T707JLD	CentreWest
SND140X	Manchester	T104VWU	Yorkshire	T310VYG	Yorkshire	T726REU	Bristol
SND147X	Manchester	T105AUA	Midland/Lowland	T311VYG	Yorkshire	T727REU	Bristol
SND148X	Manchester	T105VWU	Midland/Lowland	T312VYG	Yorkshire	T728REU	Bristol
SND149X	Manchester	T106AUA	Midland/Lowland	T313VYG	Yorkshire	T729REU	Bristol
SND150X	Manchester	T106VWU	Yorkshire	T314VYG	Yorkshire	T730REU	Bristol
SND415X	Yorkshire	T107VWU	Yorkshire	T315VYG	Yorkshire	T731REU	Bristol
SND416X	Manchester	T108VWU	Yorkshire	T316VYG	Yorkshire	T815NAK	Mainline
SND419X	Manchester	T109VWU	Yorkshire	T317VYG	Yorkshire	T816NAK	Mainline
SND424X	Yorkshire	T110VWU	Yorkshire	T318VYG	Yorkshire	T817NAK	Mainline
SND438X	Manchester	T112VWU	Yorkshire	T346EUB	Yorkshire	T818NAK	Mainline
SND441X	Manchester	T113VWU	Yorkshire	T347EUB	Yorkshire	T819NAK	Mainline
SND442X	Manchester	T114VWU	Yorkshire	T348EUB	Yorkshire	T820JBL	CentreWest
SND444X	Manchester	T131ARE	PMT	T349EUB	Yorkshire	T820NAK	Mainline
SND446X	Manchester	T132ARE	PMT	T350EUB	Yorkshire	T821JBL	CentreWest
SND447X	Manchester	T133ARE	PMT	T351EUB	Yorkshire	T821NAK	Mainline
SND448X	Manchester	T134ARE	PMT	T352EUB	Yorkshire	T822JBL	CentreWest
SND456X	Manchester	T135ARE	PMT	T353EUB	Yorkshire	T822NAK	Mainline
SND458X	Manchester	T136ARE	PMT	T354EUB	Yorkshire	T822SFS	Yorkshire
SND459X	Manchester	T157BBF	PMT	T356VWU	Yorkshire	T823JBL	CentreWest
SND460X	Manchester	T158BBF	PMT	T359VWU	Yorkshire	T823LLC	CentreWest
SND461X	Manchester	T159BBF	PMT	T430JLD	CentreWest	T823NAK	Mainline
SND464X	Manchester	T160BBF	PMT	T456JDT	Mainline	T823SFS	Yorkshire
SND469X	Manchester	T161BBF	PMT	T457JDT	Mainline	T824JBL	CentreWest
SND471X	Manchester	T162BBF	PMT	T458JDT	Mainline	T824LLC	CentreWest
SND474X	Manchester	T163BBF	PMT	T459JDT	Mainline	T824NAK	Mainline
SND475X	Manchester	T164BBF	PMT	T460JDT	Mainline	T824SFS	Yorkshire
SND486X	Manchester	T165BBF	PMT	T461JDT	Mainline	T825JBL	CentreWest
SND490X	Manchester	T166BBF	PMT	T462JDT	Mainline	T825LLC	CentreWest
SND491X	Manchester	T167BBF	PMT	T463JDT	Mainline	T825NAK	Mainline
SND497X	Manchester	T168BBF	PMT	T464JDT	Mainline	T825SFS	Mainline
SND498X	Manchester	T211VWU	Yorkshire	T465JDT	Mainline	T826AFX	Southern National
SND499X	Manchester	T257JLD	CentreWest	T469JCV	Western National	T826LLC	CentreWest
SND502X	Manchester			T470JCV	Western National	T826NAK	Mainline

T826SFS	Yorkshire	T877ODT	Mainline	TSJ74S	Southern National	URS318X	Aberdeen
T827AFX	Southern National	T878ODT	Mainline	TSU651	Aberdeen	URS319X	Aberdeen
T827LLC	CentreWest	T879ODT	Mainline	TSU682	Midland/Lowland	URS320X	Aberdeen
T827NAK	Mainline	T880ODT	Mainline	TSV612	Midland/Lowland	URS321X	Aberdeen
T827SFS	Yorkshire	T881ODT	Mainline	TTC537T	Bristol	URS322X	Aberdeen
T828AFX	Southern National	T882ODT	Mainline	TTC790T	Cymru	URS323X	Aberdeen
T828LLC	CentreWest	T883ODT	Mainline	TWH690T	Yorkshire	URS324X	Aberdeen
T828NAK	Mainline	T884ODT	Mainline	TWH691T	Yorkshire	URS325X	Aberdeen
T828SFS	Yorkshire	T889KLF	CentreWest	TWH692T	Yorkshire	URS326X	Aberdeen
T829AFX	Southern National	T890KLF	CentreWest	TWH693T	Yorkshire	URS327X	Aberdeen
T829LLC	CentreWest	T891KLF	CentreWest	TWN936S	Western National	URS328X	Aberdeen
T829NAK	Mainline	T892KLF	CentreWest	TWS915T	Western National	URS329X	Aberdeen
T829SFS	Yorkshire	T893KLF	CentreWest	TXI2426	Southern National	URS330X	Aberdeen
T830LLC	CentreWest	T894KLF	CentreWest	UAR586W	Western National	USV821	Southern National
T830NAK	Mainline	T895KLF	CentreWest	UAR587W	Cymru	USV823	Southern National
T831LLC	CentreWest	T896KLF	CentreWest	UAR588W	Cymru	UTO832S	Western National
T831NAK	Mainline	T897KLF	CentreWest	UAR589W	Western National	UTO836S	Hampshire
T832NAK	Mainline	T898KLF	CentreWest	UAR590W	Western National	UTU23V	Midland/Lowland
T833LLC	CentreWest	T899KLF	CentreWest	UAR591W	Essex Buses	UVF624X	Eastern Counties
T833NAK	Mainline	T901KLF	CentreWest	UAR593W	Essex Buses	UVF625X	Eastern Counties
T834LLC	CentreWest	T902KLF	CentreWest	UAR594W	Western National	UVF628X	Eastern Counties
T834NAK	Mainline	T903KLF	CentreWest	UAR595W	Western National	UWB183	Western National
T835LLC	CentreWest	T906KLF	CentreWest	UAR596W	Essex Buses	UWJ275Y	Mainline
T835NAK	Mainline	T907KLF	CentreWest	UAR597W	Western National	UWJ276Y	Mainline
T836LLC	CentreWest	T916SSF	Manchester	UAR598W	Cymru	UWJ277Y	Mainline
T836NAK	Mainline	T917SSF	Manchester	UAR599W	Essex Buses	UWJ278Y	Mainline
T837LLC	CentreWest	T918SSF	Manchester	UDM450V	PMT	UWJ279Y	Mainline
T837NAK	Mainline	T919SSF	Manchester	UFP233S	Leicester	UWJ280Y	Mainline
T838LLC	CentreWest	T988KLF	CentreWest	UFW40W	Northampton	UWJ281Y	Mainline
T838NAK	Mainline	T990KLF	CentreWest	UFW41W	Northampton	UWJ282Y	Mainline
T839LLC	CentreWest	TAH271W	Eastern Counties	UFX330	Southern National	UWJ283Y	Mainline
T839NAK	Mainline	TAH272W	Eastern Counties	UFX847S	Hampshire	UWJ284Y	Mainline
T840LLC	CentreWest	TAH273W	Eastern Counties	UFX848S	Hampshire	UWJ285Y	Mainline
T840NAK	Mainline	TAH275W	Eastern Counties	UFX860S	Bristol	UWJ286Y	Mainline
T841LLC	CentreWest	TAH276W	Eastern Counties	UFX940	Southern National	UWJ287Y	Mainline
T841NAK	Mainline	TBC42X	Leicester	UHW661	Western National	UWJ288Y	Mainline
T842LLC	CentreWest	TBC43X	Leicester	UKT552	Western National	UWJ289Y	Mainline
T842NAK	Mainline	TBC45X	Leicester	UKY901Y	Mainline	UWJ290Y	Mainline
T843LLC	CentreWest	TBC46X	Leicester	UKY902Y	Mainline	UWJ291Y	Mainline
T843NAK	Mainline	TBC49X	Leicester	UKY903Y	Mainline	UWJ292Y	Mainline
T844LLC	CentreWest	TBC50X	Leicester	UKY904Y	Mainline	UWJ293Y	Mainline
T844NAK	Mainline	TBC52X	Leicester	ULS101X	Midland/Lowland	UWW18X	Yorkshire
T845LLC	CentreWest	TDZ3265	Southern National	ULS103X	Midland/Lowland	UWW19X	Yorkshire
T845NAK	Mainline	TGG378W	Glasgow	ULS105X	Midland/Lowland	UWW20X	Yorkshire
T846LLC	CentreWest	TGG381W	Glasgow	ULS106X	Midland/Lowland	UWY66X	Hampshire
T846NAK	Mainline	TGG384W	Glasgow	ULS107X	Midland/Lowland	UWY68X	Yorkshire
T847LLC	CentreWest	TGG385W	Glasgow	ULS108X	Midland/Lowland	UWY69X	Yorkshire
T847NAK	Mainline	TGG386W	Glasgow	ULS109X	Midland/Lowland	UWY71X	Yorkshire
T848LLC	CentreWest	TGG739R	Cymru	ULS111X	Midland/Lowland	UWY72X	Yorkshire
T848NAK	Mainline	THX187S	Western National	ULS112X	Midland/Lowland	UWY74X	Yorkshire
T849LLC	CentreWest	THX220S	Western National	ULS113X	Midland/Lowland	UWY75X	Yorkshire
T849NAK	Mainline	TIB8511	Glasgow	ULS630X	Midland/Lowland	UWY90X	Yorkshire
T850LLC	CentreWest	TIB8512	Glasgow	ULS631X	Midland/Lowland	VAH277X	Eastern Counties
T850NAK	Mainline	TIB8513	Glasgow	ULS633X	Midland/Lowland	VAH281X	Eastern Counties
T851LLC	CentreWest	TJI3134	Southern National	ULS636X	Leicester	VAH282X	Eastern Counties
T851NAK	Mainline	TJI3135	Southern National	ULS637X	Northampton	VAY58X	Leicester
T852LLC	CentreWest	TJI3136	Southern National	ULS640X	Midland/Lowland	VBG114V	Southern National
T852NAK	Mainline	TJI3137	Southern National	ULS642X	Northampton	VBG115V	Western National
T853LLC	CentreWest	TJI3138	Southern National	ULS643X	Midland/Lowland	VBG118V	Western National
T853NAK	Mainline	TJI4681	Southern National	ULS714X	Midland/Lowland	VBG120V	Southern National
T854NAK	Mainline	TJI4682	Southern National	ULS716X	Midland/Lowland	VBG127V	Southern National
T855NAK	Mainline	TJI4683	Southern National	ULS717X	Midland/Lowland	VCA452W	PMT
T856NAK	Mainline	TJI4820	CentreWest	UOB366Y	Southern National	VCA464W	PMT
T857NAK	Mainline	TJI4822	CentreWest	UOI4323	Cymru	VCL461	Hampshire
T858NAK	Mainline	TJI4823	CentreWest	UPO232T	Hampshire	VDH244S	Cymru
T859NAK	Mainline	TJI4826	CentreWest	UPO233T	Hampshire	VDV108S	Western National
T860NAK	Mainline	TJI4828	PMT	UPO234T	Hampshire	VDV110S	Southern National
T861NAK	Mainline	TJI4829	CentreWest	UPO235T	Hampshire	VDV111S	Southern National
T862NAK	Mainline	TJI4830	CentreWest	UPO236T	Hampshire	VDV114S	Western National
T863NAK	Mainline	TJI4831	CentreWest	UPO237T	Hampshire	VDV116S	Western National
T864NAK	Mainline	TJI4832	CentreWest	UPO238T	Hampshire	VDV117S	Western National
T865ODT	Mainline	TJI4833	CentreWest	UPO239T	Hampshire	VDV118S	Western National
T866ODT	Mainline	TJI4834	CentreWest	UPO240T	Hampshire	VDV119S	Western National
T867ODT	Mainline	TJI4835	CentreWest	UPO242T	Hampshire	VDV120S	Western National
T868ODT	Mainline	TJI4836	CentreWest	UPO243T	Hampshire	VDV121S	Western National
T869ODT	Mainline	TJI4838	Western National	UPO244T	Hampshire	VDV134S	Southern National
T870ODT	Mainline	TJN502R	Essex Buses	UPO245T	Hampshire	VDV137S	Bristol
T871ODT	Mainline	TJY761	Western National	UPO246T	Hampshire	VDV141S	Western National
T872ODT	Mainline	TLJ372	Western National	UPO443T	Hampshire	VDV142S	Southern National
T873ODT	Mainline	TMS403X	Midland/Lowland	UPO444T	Hampshire	VDV143S	Bristol
T874ODT	Mainline	TND102X	Manchester	URF668S	Western National	VDV144S	Western National
T875ODT	Mainline	TPR34	Southern National	URL992S	Western National	VEX283X	Eastern Counties
T876ODT	Mainline	TPX41T	Hampshire	URS316X	Aberdeen	VEX284X	Eastern Counties
		TRS333	Aberdeen	URS317X	Aberdeen	VEX285X	Eastern Counties

The 1999 FirstGroup Bus Handbook

Reg	Operator	Reg	Operator	Reg	Operator	Reg	Operator
VEX286X	Eastern Counties	VWW361X	Yorkshire	WTU465W	PMT	XRF2X	PMT
VEX287X	Eastern Counties	VXI8734	Midland/Lowland	WTU472W	PMT	XRF2X	PMT
VEX288X	Eastern Counties	VXU444	Midland/Lowland	WTU483W	PMT	XSA219S	Midland/Lowland
VEX290X	Eastern Counties	WAG373X	Midland/Lowland	WVT900S	PMT	XSA220S	Midland/Lowland
VEX294X	Eastern Counties	WAS766V	Hampshire	WWL537T	Southern National	XSS331Y	Aberdeen
VEX297X	Eastern Counties	WBN955L	Manchester	WWY122S	Eastern Counties	XSS332Y	Aberdeen
VFX980S	Hampshire	WDR665M	Southern National	WWY123S	Eastern Counties	XSS333Y	Aberdeen
VIB9308	Essex Buses	WFS154W	Midland/Lowland	WYY752	Bristol	XSS334Y	Aberdeen
VJT738	Western National	WFX257S	Hampshire	XAN431T	Western National	XSS335Y	Aberdeen
VLT120	Capital	WJI5239	PMT	XAU700Y	Eastern Counties	XSS336Y	Aberdeen
VLT121	Capital	WLT357	Glasgow	XBU9S	Yorkshire	XSS337Y	Aberdeen
VOD125K	Western National	WLT408	Glasgow	XBU17S	Yorkshire	XSS338Y	Aberdeen
VOD372	Western National	WLT677	Glasgow	XDV601S	Western National	XSS339Y	Aberdeen
VOD594S	Southern National	WLT678	Glasgow	XDV603S	Western National	XSS340Y	Aberdeen
VOD615S	Southern National	WLT724	Midland/Lowland	XDV605S	Southern National	XSS341Y	Aberdeen
VOD616S	Western National	WLT741	Glasgow	XDV608S	Western National	XSS343Y	Aberdeen
VOD617S	Western National	WLT760	Glasgow	XDV609S	Western National	XSS344Y	Aberdeen
VOD618S	Western National	WLT770	Glasgow	XFF283	Western National	XSS345Y	Aberdeen
VPM642	Western National	WLT885	CentreWest	XFG26Y	Southern National	XTJ7W	Midland/Lowland
VTH941T	Essex Buses	WLT910	Glasgow	XFG27Y	Southern National	XWL539	Aberdeen
VTH942T	Western National	WLT976	Glasgow	XFG28Y	Western National	XYK761T	Essex Buses
VVV70S	Northampton	WNN734	Western National	XHK215X	Essex Buses	YBW489V	PMT
VWU331X	Yorkshire	WNO479	Essex Buses	XHK217X	Essex Buses	YDX100Y	Leicester
VWW327X	Yorkshire	WNO484	Cymru	XHK218X	Essex Buses	YEU6V	Southern National
VWW328X	Yorkshire	WNW156S	Yorkshire	XHK220X	Western National	YEV308S	Essex Buses
VWW329X	Yorkshire	WNW158S	Yorkshire	XHK221X	Bristol	YEV328S	Essex Buses
VWW330X	Yorkshire	WNW159S	Yorkshire	XHK223X	Western National	YFB969V	Bristol
VWW331X	Yorkshire	WNW163S	Yorkshire	XHK224X	Bristol	YFS306W	Hampshire
VWW332X	Yorkshire	WNW167S	Yorkshire	XHK225X	Western National	YJF16Y	Midland/Lowland
VWW333X	Yorkshire	WNW171S	Yorkshire	XHK228X	Western National	YKW655T	Southern National
VWW334X	Yorkshire	WNW174S	Yorkshire	XHK230X	Western National	YNF348T	Southern National
VWW335X	Yorkshire	WOC722T	Midland Red	XHK234X	Cymru	YPD116Y	Southern National
VWW336X	Yorkshire	WPW199S	Eastern Counties	XHK235X	Eastern Counties	YRV247V	Hampshire
VWW337X	Yorkshire	WSU428S	Midland Red	XHK236X	Eastern Counties	YRV248V	Hampshire
VWW338X	Yorkshire	WSU433S	Cymru	XHK237X	Eastern Counties	YRV249V	Hampshire
VWW339X	Yorkshire	WSU447	Aberdeen	XJF61Y	Leicester	YRV250V	Hampshire
VWW340X	Yorkshire	WSU460	Aberdeen	XJF62Y	Leicester	YRV251V	Hampshire
VWW341X	Yorkshire	WSU479	Midland/Lowland	XJF63Y	Leicester	YRV252V	Hampshire
VWW342X	Yorkshire	WSU480	Midland/Lowland	XJF64Y	Leicester	YRV253V	Hampshire
VWW343X	Yorkshire	WSU481	Northampton	XJF66Y	Leicester	YRV254V	Hampshire
VWW344X	Yorkshire	WSU487	Midland/Lowland	XJF67Y	Leicester	YRV255V	Hampshire
VWW345X	Yorkshire	WSU489	Midland/Lowland	XJF68Y	Leicester	YRV256V	Hampshire
VWW346X	Yorkshire	WSV135	Midland/Lowland	XJF69Y	Leicester	YRV257V	Hampshire
VWW347X	Yorkshire	WSV136	Midland/Lowland	XLV143W	Southern National	YRV258V	Hampshire
VWW348X	Yorkshire	WSV137	Midland/Lowland	XMS244R	Midland/Lowland	YRV259V	Hampshire
VWW349X	Yorkshire	WSV138	Midland/Lowland	XMS421Y	Midland/Lowland	YRV260V	Hampshire
VWW350X	Yorkshire	WSV140	Midland/Lowland	XNG207S	Eastern Counties	YRV261V	Hampshire
VWW351X	Yorkshire	WSV408	Western National	XOJ431T	Southern National	YSF85S	Southern National
VWW352X	Yorkshire	WSV409	Western National	XOJ432T	Southern National	YSF97S	Southern National
VWW353X	Yorkshire	WSV410	Cymru	XOV743T	Midland Red	YSF99S	Southern National
VWW354X	Yorkshire	WTH943T	Western National	XOV744T	Midland Red	YSO231T	Aberdeen
VWW355X	Yorkshire	WTH945T	Western National	XOV746T	Midland Red	YSO235T	Midland/Lowland
VWW356X	Yorkshire	WTH946T	Western National	XOV749T	Midland Red	YSV739	Southern National
VWW357X	Yorkshire	WTH949T	Essex Buses	XOV752T	Midland Red	YWX333X	Yorkshire
VWW358X	Yorkshire	WTH950T	Western National	XOV758T	Midland Red	YYL794T	Essex Buses
VWW359X	Yorkshire	WTH951T	Western National	XRF1X	PMT		
VWW360X	Yorkshire	WTH961T	Western National				

ISBN 1 897990 86 3

Published by *British Bus Publishing Ltd*, July 1999
The Vyne, 16 St Margaret's Drive, Wellington, Telford, TF1 3PH
Fax/ Answerphone and Evening orderline: 01952 255669
E-Mail - a2gwp@aol.com
Internet:- www.britishbuspublishing.co.uk